Isaiah's New
Exodus in Mark

Isaiah's New Exodus in Mark

Rikki E. Watts

Baker Academic
A Division of Baker Book House Co
Grand Rapids, Michigan 49516

Reprinted October 2000 by Baker Academic
a division of Baker Book House Company
P.O. Box 6287, Grand Rapids, MI 49516-6287
with permission of the copyright holder

This book first appeared in 1997 as *Isaiah's New Exodus and Mark,* volume 88 in Wissenschaftliche Untersuchungen zum Neuen Testament, 2d series, published by J. C. B. Mohr (Paul Siebeck), P.O. Box 2040, D-72010 Tübingen, Germany.

Printed in the United States of America

Library of Congress Cataloging-in-Publication Data

Watts, Rikki E.
  Isaiah's new Exodus in Mark / Rikki E. Watts.—[Rev., updated ed.].
      p.   cm. — (Biblical studies library)
  Includes bibliographical references and indexes.
  ISBN 0-8010-2251-7 (paper)
  1. Bible. N.T. Mark—Criticism, interpretation, etc. 2. Bible. N.T. Mark.—Relation to the Old Testament. 3. Bible. O.T.—Relation to Mark. 4. Bible. O.T. Isaiah—Relation to Mark. 5. Bible. N.T. Mark—Relation to Isaiah. 6. Bible. O.T.—Quotations in the New Testament. I. Title. II. Series.
  BS2585.2.W36   2000
  226.3'06—dc21   00-057924

For information about academic books, resources for Christian leaders, and all new releases available from Baker Book House, visit our web site:
                              http://www.bakerbooks.com

Preface

This book is a revised version of a doctoral thesis, outlined in papers read to the SNTS special study group on 'The Use of the OT in the NT' (UK) and to the Cambridge New Testament Seminar in Easter Term 1989, and submitted for the degree of Doctor of Philosophy while at Jesus College Cambridge in 1990. The revision consists primarily of some updating and, in taking advantage of the removal of the word limit, some structural rearrangement, extra detailing and reformulating of selected argumentation, and the addition of two new chapters.

The updating enabled me to interact with articles, monographs, and commentaries—notably R. H. Gundry's massive work on Mark—published since the original submission. One monograph in particular—*The Way of the Lord* by Joel Marcus of Glasgow University (1992)—has two chapters that gratifyingly offer independent support to elements of the thesis as originally proposed. The structural rearrangements amounted to laying out the material more in keeping with the literary structure of Mark as I understand it. This entailed breaking up and moving some of the original thesis chapters into different sequences. Some arguments, primarily those related to Jesus and the Isaianic 'servant' materials, have been rearranged and supported with further detail. Finally, the two new chapters cover materials not able to be treated in the original submission: Chapter 2, 'History as Hermeneutic: the Role of Ideology in Community Self-Understanding' which originally occupied three brief paragraphs in the thesis' Conclusion, and Chapter 9, 'Isaiah's Promise and Malachi's Threat: Part 2: Arrival in Jerusalem', which deals with the third and final section of Mark (i.e. chs. 11-16) .

I would also like gratefully to acknowledge all those who have contributed to attaining what at the outset seemed an impossible goal. It is easy to forget, in hindsight, what a quantum leap it is from merely longish essays, to a (hopefully) substantial book. My debt to many is great.

Without the substantial financial assistance of a Fellowship from the Church of the Pioneers (and Dr. Robert Cooley, President of Gordon Conwell Theological Seminary, who encouraged me to apply), an exceedingly munificent Tyndale House Research Grant over several years, an American Friends of Cambridge Scholarship, several allocations from Jesus College Bane Fund, generous help from the PCC of St. Barnabas, Cambridge, and our many friends in the United States, in particular Harold and Wendy Jacobi, and in Australia, including our community at Truth and Liberation Concern (Melbourne, Australia), Andy and Daphne Callow, and the Rev. Ross and Jenni Green, this thesis could not have been completed.   The Bible College of Victoria and Regent College, Vancouver, kindly allowed me to extend a visit to the latter so as to include several weeks at Tyndale House, Cambridge, in order to finish the last half of the final chapter during Michaelmas term, 1995.

I am especially grateful to my supervisor, Rev. Dr. Christopher Rowland, now the Dean Ireland's Professor of Holy Scripture in the University of Oxford, for his ready availability, thoughtful criticisms, and gracious good humour. An excellent supervisor, he allowed just the right balance between room to pursue whatever interests might arise and the need to keep the project within a reasonable timeframe. The Lady Margaret's Professor of Divinity in the University of Cambridge, Dr. Morna Hooker, also kindly supervised me for one term, and her many pertinent observations and clarity of writing have helped me greatly. Professor Hooker, correctly in my view, alerted scholarship to the many easy assumptions made about Jesus' relationship to the so-called Servant of Isaiah. Her work here was seminal and although I will on several occasions beg to differ it is only with the greatest respect.

Drs. Bill Lane, H. G. M. Williamson, Don Carson, Rev. R. T. France (who introduced me to Mark and in whose class this thesis began), and the members of the Cambridge New Testament Seminar and of the SNTS special study group on 'The Use of the OT in the NT' (UK) have all contributed through their kind encouragement, thoughtful comments, and gracious criticisms. Thanks are also due to my Professors at Gordon-Conwell Theological Seminary, Drs. Douglas Stuart, Gary Pratico, Christy Wilson, T. David Gordon, and particularly Drs. Meredith Kline, Gordon Hugenberger, and epecially Greg Beale for their inspiration and instruction on the use of the OT in the NT. Very special thanks are due to Dr. Gordon D. Fee and his wife Maudine. Gordon has proven a dear friend and honoured mentor, who introduced me to NT studies, in particular the practice of exegesis, and whose integration of a passion for Christ and a sharp mind have profoundly shaped by life.

I wish also to thank my former fellow students at Cambridge and the courteous secretarial and library staff at Tyndale House—a truly wonderful establishment—for their innumerable kindnesses and assistance during my time there, especially Dr. Steven Meyer, Dr. Peter Head, Rev. Dr. John Kleinig, Dr. Paul Wagner, Rev. Dr. Michael Thompson, Dr. Brent Kinman, Rev. Dr. Mark Dever, Dr. Steven Smith, Rev. Dr. Mark Labberton, Rev. David Deboys—who was an exceptionally helpful librarian—and last but not least the Warden, Rev. Dr. Bruce Winter. On my return to Australia Mrs. Ros Devenish and Mrs. Kathy Caddie, the librarians at the Bible College of Victoria, were ever helpful in facilitating inter-library loans during the antipodean summers of 1993-5, when much of this revision took place. Rev. Dr. Colin Kruse helped with some of the proof-reading. Ken Wade, a student assistant at B.C.V., kindly undertook the exceedingly onerous and thankless task of compiling the indices which he continued even after graduation. My BCV teaching assistants, Westan Johnson, and Ian Wragg have both been of considerable help. Scot Becker, my teaching assistant at Regent has also laboured hard and long in the final correlation and checking of the indices.

None of the above, of course, are in any way responsible for errors or deficiencies which may have remained. As this book was submitted in camera-ready copy, I have done my best to detect and eradicate errors—volunteer proof readers have helped in places—but I find proofing my own work most difficult. Consequently, I sincerely apologise to readers in advance for any mistakes that have slipped through.

I am delighted to express my appreciation to Prof. Dr. Martin Hengel and Prof. Dr. Otfried Hofius for accepting this book for publication in the WUNT 2 series. My genuine thanks, too, to the publisher and the editors for their considerable patience over the six years that have elapsed since the offer of publication was first made. My induction into the 'busyness' of a teaching post, the introduction of a new degree program by the Australian College of Theology, and then the recent move of our family to

Regent College, Vancouver, meant that the preparation of the text for publication has been considerably delayed.

Finally, I wish to dedicate this book to my parents, Pastor and Mrs. E. S. Watts, both now with the Lord, who trained me in the way that I should go, to my parents-in-law, Ian and Pauline Noble, who provided encouragement and much support, and especially to my lovely wife and true companion, Catherine, and our special children, Steven and Rebecca, for their unfailing confidence and loving support over the years.

Summer 1997   Rikk E. Watts
Regent College, Vancouver

Table of Contents

Abbreviations

Abbreviations of primary Greek and Jewish sources follow Loeb and *JBL* convention—in respect of the Qumran writings, I have elected to stay with the older abbreviations since they may help the reader more than a merely numerical designation—and those of series and journal titles as laid out in *JBL*, *NTA*, and *OTA*. These will not be repeated here. Standard reference works are cited either by author, for example, Schürer, 2.231, or by abbreviated author(s), for example, BDB, 123. References to multi-volume editions are indicated by volume and page number, separated by a period, for example, 1.115. In the case of works such as *TDNT*, articles are cited by author, volume, and page number, for example, Jeremias, *TDNT*, 5.701ff. These standard works are not itemised in the select bibliography. Footnotes in articles and books are signified by page number followed by n. or nn., for example, 101n35. Footnotes within this book are referred to as fn. or fnn., for example, fn. 104 when within the same Chapter, and p. 34, fn. 8, when not.

In the interests of space, bibliographic entries in the footnotes are cited by author, one significant word from the title, and page number, for example, Hahn, *Titles*, 345n42. Exceptions are the major commentaries on Isaiah and Mark, and the works listed below, which are referred to by author only, for example, Westermann, 203 (meaning his commentary on Isaiah), and Marcus, 57 (see the work referred to below). Occasionally in order to avoid confusion a key-word title is given, for example, Gundry, *Mark*, 341, which refers to the commentary. In the case of commentaries page numbers are commonly given only if considered necessary, otherwise the reference is to the discussion under the passage being considered.

Ambrozic, A. M.,   *The Hidden Kingdom: A Redaction-Critical Study of the References to the Kingdom of God in Mark's Gospel* CBQMS 2 (Washington, DC: Catholic Biblical Association of America, 1972).

Boucher, M.,   *The Mysterious Parable* CBQMS 6 (Washington: Catholic Biblical Commission, 1977).

Burkill, T. A.,   *Mysterious Revelation. An Examination of the Philosophy of St. Mark's Gospel* (Ithaca: Cornell University, 1963).

Dewey, J.,   *Markan Public Debate* SBLDS 48 (California: Scholars Press, 1977).

Grimm, W.,   *Die Verkündigung Jesu und Deuterojesaja* ANTI 1 (Frankfurt am Main, Bern: Peter Lang, 1981²).

Juel, D.,   *Messiah and Temple: The Trial of Jesus in the Gospel of Mark* SBLDS 31 (Missoula: Scholars Press, 1977).

Kelber, W. H.,   *The Kingdom in Mark* (Philadelphia: Fortress, 1974).

Kertelge, K.,   *Die Wunder Jesu im Markusevangelium: Eine redaktionsgeschichtliche Untersuchung* SANT 23 (Munich: Kösel, 1970).

Kingsbury, J. D.,   *The Christology of Mark's Gospel* (Philadelphia: Fortress, 1983).

van der Loos, H.,   *The Miracles of Jesus* NovTSupp 9 (Leiden: E.J. Brill, 1968).

Marcus, J.,   *The Way of the Lord: Christological Exegesis in the Old Testament in the Gospel of Mark* (Louisville, Kentucky: Westminster/John Knox, 1992).

Martin, R. P.,   *Mark: Evangelist and Theologian* (Grand Rapids: Zondervan, 1972).

Marxsen, W.,   *Mark the Evangelist: Studies on the Redaction History of the Gospel* trans J. Boyce *et al* (New York/Nashville: Abingdon, 1969).

Mauser, U.,   *Christ in the Wilderness: The Wilderness Theme in the Second Gospel and Its Basis in the Biblical Tradition* SBT 39 (Naperville, Ill.: Alec R. Allenson, 1963).

Pryke, E. J.,   *Redactional Style in the Markan Gospel* SNTSMS 33 (Cambridge: University, 1978).

Quesnell, Q.,   *The Mind of St. Mark: Interpretation and Method through the Exegesis of Mark 6.52* AnBib 38 (Rome: Pontifical Biblical Institute, 1969).

Richardson, A.,   *The Miracle Stories of the Gospels* (London: SCM, 1959).

Räisänen. H.,   *The 'Messianic Secret' in Mark's Gospel* trans. C. Tuckett, SNTW (Edinburgh: T&T Clarke, 1990).

Robinson, J. M.,   *The Problem of History in Mark* SBT 21 (London: SCM, 1957).

Schneck, R.,   *Isaiah in the Gospel of Mark, I-VIII* BDS 1 (Vallejo, CA: BIBAL, 1994).

Stonehouse, N. B.,   *The Witness of Matthew and Mark to Christ* (Philadelphia: Presbyterian Guardian, 1944).

Suhl, A.,   *Die Funktion der alttestamentlichen Zitate und Anspielungen im Markusevangelium* (Gütersloh: Gerd Mohn, 1965).

Trocmé, É.,   *The Formation of the Gospel According to Mark* trans. P. Gaughan (London: SPCK, 1975).

Weeden, T. J.,   *Mark—Traditions in Conflict* (Philadelphia: Fortress, 1971).

Introduction

In his 1978 survey of Markan scholarship, H. C. Kee observed:

> The history of recent research on the Gospel of Mark can be seen as the record of an attempt to discern the aim of the evangelist and so to discover the perspective which gives coherence to all the features of the Second Gospel.[1]

A decade later W. R. Telford noted that 'further investigation needs to be conducted into its (i.e. the Gospel's) place in the theological history of early Christianity'.[2] M. A. Tolbert's subsequent remark that 'no consistent interpretation of the Gospel in all its parts has yet been elicited'[3] suggests that Kee's observation still applies.[4] This book continues the line of inquiry.

Markan studies, recently reaching flood-like proportions and showing little sign of abating, have variously located Mark's main concerns in his portrayal of eschatological conflict,[5] use of the miracle traditions,[6] understanding of the Kingdom of God,[7] treatment of the disciples,[8] interest in instructing his community,[9] concept of discipleship,[10] Christology,[11] and more recently, in a straightforward apology for the Cross.[12] Given Mark's considerable interest in the OT, attempts have been made to postulate a Markan program either reflecting events in Israel's history,[13] in particular the Exodus,[14] or based on lectionaries[15] and calendars.[16]

---

[1] 'Recent', 353.

[2] 'Introduction', 22.

[3] *Sowing*, xi.

[4] See the surveys in Hurtado, 'Gospel'; Pokorny, 'Markusevangelium'; Lane, 'Present', and the comments of Gundry, 1022ff.

[5] Robinson.

[6] Kertelge; Koch, *Bedeutung*; Schenke, *Wundererzählungen*.

[7] Ambrozic; Kelber; cf. Marcus, *Mystery*.

[8] Weeden; Schmahl, *Zwölf*.

[9] Reploh, *Lehrer*; Schweizer, 'Leistung'; Beavis, *Audience*.

[10] Best, *Following*.

[11] Perrin, 'Christology'; Kingsbury.

[12] Gundry.

[13] Derrett, *Making*; Roth, *Hebrew*; also here Miller and Miller, *Midrash*.

[14] E.g. Farrer, *Study*; Hobbs, 'Exodus'; Swartley, 'Study'.

[15] Goulder, *Calendar*.

[16] Carrington, *Primitive*.

Various studies have examined the Gospel from the standpoints of narrative criticism,[17] rhetorical criticism,[18] and reader response,[19] while others sought the key to Mark's literary structure in ancient dramatic,[20] biographical,[21] rhetorical,[22] and reading[23] conventions. Still others offer sociological,[24] socio-political,[25] Marxist,[26] and structuralist analyses.[27] In spite of this plethora of approaches—or perhaps because of it—agreement as to that 'perspective which gives coherence' to Mark's theological emphases and literary structure has continued to elude scholars.

While this hiatus may indicate that no overarching unity exists, many of these studies have highlighted Mark's theological and literary sophistication—although this should not be overstated as has sometimes been the case.[28] It seems generally agreed that the Gospel is neither merely 'a passion narrative with an extended introduction' (Kähler) nor simply strung together 'like pearls on a string' (Schmidt). Consequently, to deny the existence of an overarching schema may well be premature.

This attempt to investigate Mark's organisational principles builds upon several lines of earlier endeavour. First, it assumes that the final form of Mark's Gospel is the best guide to what it was that the author wished to communicate.[29] It would seem that it is not merely Mark's own material or his adaptations of his sources, but also what he has taken up

---

[17] Williams, *Gospel*; Rhoads-Mitchie, *Story*; Kermode, *Genesis*; Best, *Gospel*.
[18] Dewey.
[19] Fowler, *Loaves*, and *Reader*; Tannehill, 'Disciples'.
[20] Bilezikian, *Liberated*; Standaert.
[21] Talbert, *Gospel*; Cancik, 'Gattung'; Hadas and Smith, *Heroes*.
[22] Robbins, *Teacher*; Tolbert, *Sowing*.
[23] Beavis, *Audience*.
[24] Kee, *Community*; Neyrey, 'Purity'; Watson, 'Social'; Mack, *Myth*.
[25] Myers, *Binding*; Waetjen, *Reordering*.
[26] Belo, *Reading*.
[27] Via, *Ethics*; Malbon, *Narrative*.
[28] As noted by e.g. Meagher, *Clumsy*, and Räisänen, 16ff. Nevertheless, one of the weaknesses of Räisänen's otherwise sage criticisms is his failure to appreciate the 'occasional' dimension of Mark's Gospel and therefore the possibility that Mark may have assumed some knowledge on the part of his readers. So e.g. Räisänen's observation that the episode of Jesus' temptation is 'strangely inconclusive' (16n64), tells us more about how the text strikes Räisänen than it does about how it might have appeared to Mark's intended audience. This is all the more likely if Mark's gospel is not a theological super-nova but instead represents traditions with which his 'community' was already well acquainted.
[29] See Lane's comments, 'Present', on the recent commentaries of Pesch and Schmithals; Gundry, 18ff; cf. Güttgemanns, *Candid*.

unaltered, both in terms of individual pericopae and their order, that together provide a reliable indication of his concerns.

I am also persuaded by those who have urged that the OT is foundational to Mark's thought world.[30] One also notes here C. H. Dodd's conviction that the NT and OT authors share the same *Weltanschauung*,[31] and that of Francis Foulkes, who saw the basis of this continuity to be in the belief that 'as God had acted in the past he would act in the future'.[32]

Two other factors contributed to the genesis of this book. As an Australian student studying in the United States I was fascinated by my lecturers' occasional references to 'four-score and seven years ago' and the uniformly 'knowing' response of my American fellow-students. Only on learning that the phrase was the first line of Abraham Lincoln's famous Gettysburg address did its significance became apparent. By evoking the Founding Fathers' ideology these few words functioned as a hermeneutical indicator, pointing not so much to the text of Lincoln's address *per se* (as in Dodd's 'text plot'), but to the larger interpretation of American history which Lincoln's speech assumed and with which it interacted. This raised the possibility, given Dodd's shared-*Weltanschauung* hypothesis, that Mark's use of OT citations might also function in a similar manner. Kee's recognition that OT citations appear at crucial junctures in Mark only served to strengthen this conjecture.[33]

The second contributing item, complementing and supporting the first, was the work of Jacques Ellul and Paul Ricoeur, both of whom stress the formative influence of a group's founding moment on its self-understanding.[34] This is especially so in times of uncertainty or internal conflict. These theories are significant on two counts.

First, Israel's founding moment was the Exodus. Not only did it shape the national identity and character but the prophets of the Babylonian exile

---

[30] In addition to those examined in Chapter 1: Fitzmyer, 'Judaic'; Best, *Story*, 140ff; and now Marcus, *Way*; cf. Kline, 'Origins'. On the citational conventions of the period, including the unique implications for the OT as authoritative literature, the degree of freedom to vary wording, and the constraints upon same, see the excellent work of Stanley, *Language*.

[31] *According*, 133. See Marshall's survey of recent discussion, 'Assessment'.

[32] *Acts*, 9.

[33] Kee, 'Function'. Following the completion of this thesis in its original form Joel Marcus, *Way*, has also argued strongly along these lines.

[34] Respectively, 'médiateur', and 'Function' and 'Science'; see Chapter 2.

used it as the paradigm for the deliverance they announced.[35] It is not surprising that several emergent groups within Judaism, including the movement known according to Acts as 'the Way', should also describe themselves in these terms.[36]

Second, the tensions between the 'Way' and the larger Jewish community, with the one claiming over against the other to be the legitimate heir of the norms and prophetic traditions of the past, only make it more likely that the former's *bona fides* should be couched in such historic terms.

There is, however, the danger of anachronism. Ellul and Ricoeur were discussing modern societies. Nevertheless, the basic model—the role of the founding moment in times of conflict—appears appropriate; at least on a surface reading of the NT materials. Given the difficulty of reconstructing the mental world of ancient societies, authors, and readers, the applicability of the model may finally have to be judged in terms of its ability to make more and better sense of the Markan data.[37]

These factors form the basis upon which the original contribution of this book is argued. Namely, as his opening editorial citation indicates, Mark's fundamental hermeneutic for interpreting and presenting Jesus derives from two sources: A) a positive schema whereby Jesus' identity and ministry is presented in terms of Isaiah's New Exodus (hereafter NE);[38] and B) a negative schema by which Jesus' rejection by the nation's leaders and his action in the Temple is cast in terms of the prophet Malachi's warning; a warning which itself concerned the delay of the Isaianic NE (hereafter INE). This dual perspective of salvation and judgement—both within the context of the INE—seems to provide the fundamental literary and theological structure of Mark's Gospel. This is not to deny the presence of other concerns (e.g. discipleship, Mark 13) or OT themes (e.g. Son of Man Christology), but instead suggests only that they presented within the larger literary and theological scheme proposed herein.

---

[35] See e.g. the survey in Fishbane, *Biblical*, 356-68, and earlier, 'Motif'.

[36] For further comment e.g. Horsley, 'Figures', 277-285.

[37] So also Tolbert, *Sowing*, 10-13. On a prodigious attempt to articulate a generalised first century Jewish world view, see now Wright, *People*.

[38] Other scholars have suggested to varying degrees and in varying guises such a motif, e.g. Swartley, Best, Lane, but have not sought to demonstrate this in a thorough-going manner concentrating primarily on Mark's prologue and his 'way' section. Subsequent to the completion of this thesis a more comprehensive approach along these lines has been argued strongly by Marcus, *Way*.

I. Outline

Chapter 1 surveys modern scholarship concentrating primarily on the OT and Mark's literary structure or his overall attitude to the OT. Other relevant works are discussed at appropriate junctures later in the book.

Chapter 2 concerns the social function of ideology—namely its schematisation of historical memory as the foundation of community identity—as a theoretical basis for what the rest of the book argues exegetically. The postulated constructs of social theory on the one hand, and the practical results of exegesis on the other, can stand alone and so confirm each other.

Chapter 3 argues that in line with ancient literary convention, Mark 1:1-3, Mark's only editorial OT citation and opening sentence, conveys the conceptual framework for his story. Isaiah 40:3 presages the inauguration of the long-awaited INE while the Malachi 3:1/Exodus 23:20 conflation ominously highlights the threat inherent in Yahweh's NE coming.

Chapter 4 submits that the INE also explains the prologue's integration of OT motifs. John is Malachi's Elijah who prepares the way for Yahweh's long-delayed INE coming. εὐαγγέλιον connotes the Isaianic conception of God's in-breaking reign, signalled by the rent heavens and the descent of the Spirit (Isa 63). The voice declares Jesus to be true 'servant'-Israel (son of God, Isa 42) who will deliver 'blind' Israel, the Davidic Messiah (also son of God, Ps 2), and perhaps the 'unique' Son of God (Gn 22).

Chapter 5 contends that Mark's three-fold structure comprising Jesus' powerful ministry in Galilee and beyond, his leading his 'blind' disciples along the 'Way', and arrival in Jerusalem echoes the INE schema where Yahweh as Warrior and Healer delivers his people from bondage, leads the 'blind' along the NE way of deliverance, and arrives at Jerusalem.

Chapter 6 proposes that Mark's asymmetric distribution of miracles is consistent with an INE hermeneutic. Jesus' exorcisms (Mark's first miracle) are linked to the Isaianic Yahweh-Warrior (3:22-30; Isa 49) and his healings (blind, deaf/ dumb, and lame,) and feedings are inaugural signs of the NE (Isa 35; 29). The section's final healing miracle (7:31ff; 8:22ff is transitional) summarises the people's amazed response, 'He has done all things well!'. At the same time several of Jesus' actions imply that his sonship goes beyond earlier categories: he is also the Son of God.

Chapter 7 argues that Jesus' outright rejection by Jerusalem's leaders at
the crucial Beelzebul controversy (Mk 3) echoes Israel's first Exodus
rebellion against Yahweh's Spirit (Isa 63) and results in the division and
judgement of Israel, now effected through the parables (Isa 6 in Mk 4). The
only other confrontation between leaders 'from Jerusalem' and Jesus prior
to his arrival in Jerusalem (Mk 7) is presented in similar terms (Isa 29).

Chapter 8 discusses the 'Way' section which is framed by the Gospel's
only 'sight' miracles. Picking up on Mark's interest in the disciples'
incomprehension ('blindness' and 'deafness'), it is argued that Jesus'
leading his 'blind' disciples in the 'Way' echoes wise Yahweh's leading the
'blind' along the 'unknown' NE way (Isa 42:16). The passion predictions
indicate that, in Yahweh's wisdom, the INE is to be effected by the
suffering and death of true messianic 'servant' Israel (Mk 10:45; Isa 53).

The two themes—Jesus as the one who fulfils the INE but who is
rejected by Israel's leaders—intersect in Mark's account of the events of
Jesus' arrival and death in Jerusalem.

Chapter 9 argues that, although Jesus' 'triumphal entry' is consonant
with Yahweh's arrival, his cursing of the fig tree and Temple cleansing
reflect the threat implied in the opening Malachi citation and Mark's
presentation of John as Elijah. At the same time, Jesus' rejection and
death echoes the career of the enigmatic Isaianic 'suffering servant'.

Chapter 10 draws on the Philosophy of Science, applying the theory
selection criteria of consilience, simplicity, and analogy to argue that an
INE hypothesis is the best explanation of the phenomena observed. The
concept of 'ideology' is reviewed to offer an explanation as to how the idea
of presenting Jesus in these terms could have arisen.

II. Limitations and Assumptions

1. 'Mark' is used to refer to the book's author, but implies nothing as to
his identity.

2. Without denying the importance of other influences, in keeping
with Mark's opening citation and the importance of the INE for Jewish
expectation, this book concentrates on Mark's use of Isaiah. Other
influences are discussed only as they relate to this central concern.

3. The NT makes little use of non-OT texts. While perhaps due to the unique authority granted the OT, it may be that many apocalyptic and pseudepigraphical texts were not widely known or accepted. There is also the problem of dating: to what extent do later texts (e.g. rabbinical materials, Targums) reflect earlier traditions? (And again how widely known and accepted were they?) By way of contrast, Synagogue worship and Temple instruction would have made the OT far more familiar. Consequently, while reference is frequently made to a range of ancient literature, it seems wise initially to grant priority to OT materials.

4. Anachronistic language such as 'Deutero-Isaiah' is avoided since Mark is hardly likely to have thought in these terms. Similarly, titles like Servant Songs and Suffering Servant are prefaced by 'so-called' or written in lower case and placed in inverted commas. This is not to exclude the possibility that some sort of integrated reading of these Isaianic texts, with a coalescing of the figure(s) described therein, might have been under way in the first century; only that it is not assumed.

5. 'Messiah', 'messianic', and related expressions do not imply the existence of a monolithic expectation within Judaism (even if, as I think, in an understandable reaction to past simplifications 'messianic' diversity is sometimes overplayed).[39] It is equally important to recognise that this does not mean that Mark (or his audience) shared a similarly diffused conception. Indeed, the opposite seems more likely in that the focussing of these ideas in the person of Jesus would have exercised a consolidating effect on what might have been, in other contexts, less consciously related concepts. In this respect, while recourse is often made to the ways in which various OT texts and expressions appear to have been understood within contemporaneous Jewish traditions, it must be borne in mind that

---

[39] See the discussions in e.g. Horbury, 'Messianic'; Charlesworth, 'Messianology' and *Messiah*; Neusner, *Judaisms*; Horsley and Hanson, *Bandits*; and Wright, *People*, 170-81, 307-20. Here as always caution should be exercised. Thus e.g. one implication of VanderKam, 'Enoch', and Kee, 'Christology', is that different titles do not necessarily imply different figures. Likewise, the scarcity of references to a Davidic messiah or his links with the 'kingdom of God' may no more suggest that these were not central ideas than a similar dearth of references to covenant indicate that this was not an important concept (on the latter, Wright, *People*, 260ff, citing Sanders, *Paul*, 420f). Given such texts as Jer 23:5ff; 30:9f; 33:14-26; Ezek 34:20-31; 37:15-28; etc. (and 2 Sam 7 is after all a covenant), it seems more likely that these associations were largely assumed—note the unaffected way in which Jesus' Davidic messiahship is mentioned—with exceptions being just that; cf. Horbury, 'Messianic'.

this book deals with their setting in Mark's Gospel, a Gospel which not only apparently post-dates the Pauline literature but also presupposes an emergent Christian perspective which may well have integrated not only these concepts but also 'other motifs and passages of the OT not previously regarded as "messianic"'.[40]

6. Methodologically, an allusion is considered more likely when:[41]

A) linguistic parallels and conceptual congruence are marked;

B) either the linguistic or conceptual parallels or both tend towards being unique to the proposed OT source passage;

C) themes evoked by the allusion not only cohere with but also clarify the meaning of the Markan passage under consideration;

D) the explanatory function of the allusion displays a high degree of congruence with broader Markan themes (this assumes a certain degree of thematic coherence in Mark's presentation of Jesus);

E) there is a similar application of the OT source passage elsewhere. This last criterion is not as weighty as the others listed. Although it may lend support to a similar use in Mark, neither the absence of such nor even the presence of a different application elsewhere can be taken to establish the negative. Mark must be allowed the creative possibility of seeing things in a new light. To this extent, the Markan context must always be given hermeneutical priority.

7. To maximise agreement on the data , if not its interpretation, I have by and large restricted myself to those texts which a substantial proportion of Markan commentators hold to reflect a specifically Isaianic influence.[42]

8. In keeping with my beliefs and without prejudice or polemical intent, BC and AD are used for dates, and the designations Old Testament and New Testament for the major divisions of the Christian Bible.

9. Finally, in keeping with first century Jewish and Christian practice, the deity is referred to in the generic masculine.

---

[40] Dunn, 'Messianic', 366, although his 'not previously regarded' ought to be qualified by 'in terms of the evidence we now have available'. See also Charlesworth's statement, 'Messianology', 10, that by at least ten years after the crucifixion 'Christ' became for Christians Jesus' proper name which may be taken to imply some degree of consolidation as to the meaning of the term; cf. Hengel, 'Between' and 'Paul'.

[41] The literature on this controversial matter is notoriously volumious, but see the nuanced discussion in Thompson, *Clothed*, 28-36, to whose work I am indebted, and also e.g. Hays, *Echoes*, and Stanley, *Language*.

[42] Including those where Isaianic citations/allusions are combined with other sources, e.g. Mal 3:1 and Ex 23:20 in 1:2f; Jer 7:11 in 11:17.

Chapter 1: Scholarship on the OT in Mark

I. Introduction

This chapter surveys seriatim rather than in narrative form only those works which either propose a thorough-going OT influence on Mark's literary/theological structure or discuss, as their main focus, Mark's overall attitude to the OT. Specialised studies such as those by U. Mauser, on the wilderness, L. Hartmann, on Mark 13, H.-J. Steichele, on the suffering Son of God motif, and more recently Joel Marcus, on Markan Christology, are not included here, being discussed along with other secondary literature if and when appropriate in the body of the book.

II. Survey

a) A. M. Farrer, A Study in Mark (1951), and, St. Matthew and St. Mark (1954)

A. M. Farrer's monographs are among the earliest in recent gospel studies to deal extensively with the OT's influence on Mark. Given Mark's frequent puns, Farrer feels that a sophisticated literary approach is justified and thus argues for a two-fold unifying literary-theological pattern.

First, Mark 'like all Christians sees our salvation through Jesus as a spiritual exodus and a conquest of the promised land' (pp. 55f).[1] Second, Mark developed this motif using a triple cycle of 'twelve-plus-one' callings (the twelve disciples plus Levi), healings, and loaves (the five and seven loaves plus the eucharist)[2] to indicate Jesus' institution of New Israel (pp. 69f. 'Thirteen' disciples is not problematic because, on the one hand, Israel was really composed of thirteen tribes, Ephraim and Manasseh replacing Joseph, and since, on the other, Levi had no tribal allotment and so is not included. Mark's awareness of this complexity is evident in Levi's individual treatment and absence from the list of twelve.

---

[1] This and other references refer to *Study* unless otherwise indicated.
[2] Added in his second study, *Matthew*.

Jesus' miracles provide further support. The legion exorcism is set by the sea and Jesus is accused of being an agent of Beelzebub, a play זבל, corresponding to Zebulun (cf. Gen 49:13), and Jairus is reminiscent of Jair the famous Manassehite judge (pp. 324ff). Of the thirteen healings, one involves a gentile which points to something greater for them (pp. 305f). The healings of the paralytic and of the shrivelled limb before a critical leadership correspond to Moses' miracles of the 'crawling' staff and leprosied hand when confronted with the Jewish leaders' unbelief (Ex 4:4ff). Jesus' retreat to the sea (3:7ff) and the drowning of the demonic swine (5:1-20) conform to Israel's escape and the destruction of Pharaoh (pp. 76ff). The Transfiguration is a new Sinai and the ensuing teaching 'across Jordan' prior to entering Jericho (Mk 9, 10) marks the beginning of a new conquest (pp. 110-3).

Although noting some helpful parallels, particularly with the Exodus, Farrer's intriguing theory is unconvincing. It is unclear why the callings and healings should be determinative—little in Mark suggests such—and he overlooks the 'fourteenth' loaf in the boat (8:14). Aside from the identification of healings with individual tribes, Farrer's structural patterning often seems contrived and inconsistent—frequent lapses are attributed to Mark's creative freedom—while in retrospect his divisions cut across Markan structural units, for example, one cycle breaks the series of conflict stories (2:12) and another the now widely-recognised 'Way' section (10:32).

b) P. Carrington, The Primitive Christian Calendar (1952), and, According to Mark (1961)

Appearing about the same time as Farrer's work, P. Carrington's proposal, elaborated in his later commentary, belongs to that stream of Anglo-Saxon scholarship which was particularly concerned with the influence of early Christian liturgy. Carrington argues that Mark's gospel was originally a distillation of lectionary readings in keeping with the Jewish calendar and later adapted to the Roman Julian year. The hermeneutical key is found in the Passover and Pentecost allusions in the feedings of the five and four thousands which, when recognised, enable the rest of Mark to be assigned to calendrical and hence liturgical schedules (although Mark 13 has to do double-duty and the passion narrative does not quite conform).

The chapter divisions of Vaticanus provide external verification,[3] while internal support is found in Mark's 'major triads', especially the three Markan mountains. These divide the Galilean Gospel (Mark 1-10) into four sections[4] which the agricultural pattern of the seed parables

---

[3] *Primitive*, xiii.
[4] *Ibid.*, 94ff.

relates to the rhythm and imagery of seed-time (the seed parables) and harvest (the Transfiguration), symbolising the growth of spiritual understanding. This goes back to Jesus' own utilisation of these festivals as occasions for his preaching, for example, the nuptial symbolism of Mark 2:18-22 which would be interpreted, via the Tammuz myth, as being connected with the restoration of the Temple. Indeed 'it might well be that Jesus would ... possibly play the part of the bridegroom' in local celebrations.[5]

The crowd's ordering in the feeding (read at Passover) recalls the Sinai host (Ex 19:21) and the 'sheep without a shepherd' recalls Moses' death (Nu 27:16f, pp. 12f). The feeding of the four thousand occurs at Pentecost because the presence of the crowds with Jesus reminded Mark of the first giving of the Law on the first Pentecost (Ex 19:11; p. 163). Mark 8:13-21, a key passage in view of Mark's concern with spiritual insight, is a midrash on Psalm 78, which describes Yahweh's guidance of, and provision for, his rebellious people during the Exodus. Moses' offer to die for Israel is reflected in 8:31ff while his ascent of Sinai is seen in the Transfiguration (Ex 19:9; pp. 192-6). These and other echoes demonstrate that 'the story of the gospel in Galilee, from the parables to the Transfiguration, is a new Exodus saga with a new Shepherd gathering a new people for God' (p. 170).

Although stimulating, Carrington's lectionary hypothesis has gained little acceptance. Apart from the lack of external evidence for the derivation of Christian lectionaries from the Jewish calendar (cf. Col 2:16), there is none that the Gospels functioned as proposed, or that, apart from the passion narrative, the chapter divisions of Vaticanus were related to liturgical use.[6] On internal grounds, the important mountain 'triad' has in fact no second mountain—it is 'imported' from John 6:3—while the frequent 'ironing out' of offending verses when they do not fit the theory tells against the proposal's plausibility.

c) O. Piper, 'Unchanging Promises: Exodus in the New Testament' (1957)
Otto Piper's more general article again suggests the importance of the Exodus event—from deliverance to conquest—noting its significance for the OT (especially Hosea and Isaiah) and the NT (p. 3). The conspicuous place of the wilderness in Mark (1:4, 12, 13, 35, 45) and its association with the kerygma is to be explained by the use of the 'Exodus as the model for the original Gospel story' (p. 17).

Malachi 3:1 and Exodus 23:20 together present the Baptist as the 'angel' who goes before the chosen people in the desert while Jesus' baptism is at

---

[5] *According*, 67ff, hereafter 'pp.'.
[6] See the critiques in Davies, 'Reflections'; Morris, 'Lectionaries', *Jewish*, 23-6, 29f; Talbert, *What?*, 14f.

once the escape through the Red Sea and the pre-conquest crossing of the Jordan (p. 18). The perplexing crisscrossing of Galilee and Jesus' journeys into Phoenicia and Caesarea Philippi (Mk 7-8) echo Israel's wanderings and 'the fact that of all Jesus' visits to Jerusalem only the last one is mentioned in Mark, and that it is described as the entry of a conqueror', shows that it is regarded as the goal of this New Exodus migration.

Jesus is the second Moses, 'not primarily as Lawgiver however, but as the leader of his people to the promised goal' (p. 18). Mark 10:45 reflects Moses' offer in Exodus 32:32, and the words of the Institution, 'chosen for their close resemblance with Exod. 24:8', present the new covenant in an Exodus setting (p. 19). Piper wisely recognises that not everything in Mark's gospel can be explained on the basis of Exodus. Instead, it provides the typological framework within which the material was arranged (p. 19).

Piper has surely noted a number of interesting parallels, although not all would accept his identifications. However, since so much of the Gospel's material and present order is unaccounted for, one wonders if he would be more justified in speaking of several Exodus cameos instead of an overarching framework.

d) E. C. Hobbs, 'The Gospel of Mark and the Exodus' (1958)
In a relatively unknown Ph.D. thesis from the University of Chicago, E. C. Hobbs takes up Farrer's spiritual Exodus model and posits an even more systematic Exodus influence on the progression of Mark's narrative (pp. 67f).

The escape through the Red Sea is echoed in Mark 3:6-19 where the leaders' hostility toward Jesus, Jesus' movement toward the sea and the mountain, and his miraculous signs correspond respectively to the hardness of Pharaoh's heart, Moses' withdrawal across the sea and the covenant at Sinai, and the signs which Moses performs. In the larger section of 4:35 - 5:20, the storm and the disciples' fear during the night, the opposition encountered on the other side, the drowning of the pigs, and the 'dread' that falls on the neighbouring countryside echo the fearful night attending the exodus crossing, Pharaoh's resistance to Israel's deliverance, the drowning of Pharaoh and his armies, and the fear that descends on the lands of Edom and Moab.

Israel's wilderness journey also provides the model for the extended midrash in Mark chapters 5-8 where, for example, the two healings of the daughters of Israel (5:21-43), the rejection of Jesus at Nazareth, and the sending out of the twelve disciples (6:1-29) correspond to the healing of Marah's bitter waters (Ex 15:22-26) and the twelve springs and seventy palms at Elim (15:27; pp. 40-2). The two feedings replicate the provision of manna, and the objections of the Pharisees (8:11-13) parallel Miriam and Aaron's opposition (Nu 12:1-15).

Numerous parallels exist between Sinai and the transfiguration—the six days, the three associates, the building of the tabernacles, God speaking from the cloud, the shining, and the failure of the disciples as the golden calf incident—while Mark 10:1 - 11:11 is a second giving of the law, again 'across Jordan', before arrival in Jericho (pp. 45-8). Finally, Jesus' passing through 'the waters of death' fulfils his creation of the new Israel (p. 68).

Hobbs takes up but modifies Farrer's 'twelve-plus-one' scheme where the call of Levi is proleptic of the Gentiles and thus parallels the Gentile healing (pp. 5ff. Mark's point in structuring his threefold 'twelve-plus-one' symbolism around these parallels is to indicate that just as Israel was called from bondage, saved through the sea from the threat of death and destruction, and sustained in her hunger, so too the church is called from bondage, is healed through baptism which cleanses and raises from death, and is fed on the eucharist (p. 55).

A number of Hobbs' suggestions are persuasive, for example, those linking the Transfiguration with Sinai. But, as he prudently recognises, a number of other Exodus connections are marginal, for example, Mark 5-6, and some perhaps incidental, so Mark 8:11-13. In terms of his general thesis, however, to the extent Hobbs follows Farrer the same criticisms apply. In terms of his own contribution, the three-fold interpretation of the church's Exodus is tenuous—not least considering Mark's apparent lack of interest in associating healings with baptism. A particular weakness of Hobbs (and Farrer before him) is his failure in varying degrees to integrate Mark's clearer OT citations and allusions with the overall Exodus schema of their proposals.

e) S. Schulz, 'Markus und das Alte Testament' (1961)
Influenced perhaps by more continental interests, S. Schulz locates his discussion of Mark's use of the OT within the milieu of emerging Gentile Christianity. Presupposing a distinction between the pre-Pauline Hellenistic *kurios*-kerygma and the diverse Palestinian Jesus-traditions, Schulz saw Mark as the first attempt to combine the two (p. 185).[7] The

---

[7] Schulz' initial distinction, apparently following Heitmüller, 'Problem', is questionable, not only because the terminology is vague, but also because a convincing historical reconstruction of the origins of a pre-Pauline Hellenistic Christianity has yet to be proposed. Hengel, 'Between', 27ff, argues that the translation into Greek of large parts of the synoptic tradition 'did not begin in Antioch, Ephesus or Rome but at a very early stage in Palestine itself' and was the work of the Greek-speaking Jews in Jerusalem in order that they might proclaim Jesus' sayings and activity to visiting members of the Diaspora, cf. Wenham, *Redating*. This tends to undermine Schulz' assertion, 184, that 'Paulus hat in der

influence of the former can be discerned in Mark's use of the Son of God title, in the 'sogenannte Messiasgeheimnis', in the discussions of Pharisaic piety and Mosaic Torah, and in Mark's emphasis on the passion—Schulz approvingly cites Kähler's aphoristic summary—which reflects the pre-Pauline Hellenistic kerygma's concern with Jesus' death (pp. 187f). Any interest Mark shows in the historical Jesus and the unity of his preaching and deeds is primarily an attempt to actualise Philippians 2:8, 'being found in fashion as a man' which resulted in the creation of the Gospel as a new genre (pp. 186f). Consequently,

> Markus kommt also nicht *evolutiv* von einzelnen alttestamentlichen Schriftstellen zu seiner Theologie, sondern umgekehrt: allein vom Kyrios-Kerygma und überhaupt der kerygmatischen Tradition des Heidenchristentums bekommt er die palästinischen Jesustraditionen und damit das Alte Testament in den Blickpunkt (p. 188).

Mark's view of the OT is, therefore, somewhat ambivalent. From the stand-point of Gentile Christianity, the Markan Jesus rejects Israel's *Heilsgeschichte* (Mk 12:1-12), the Law having no positive function as it did for Paul where Christ is its *telos*. The OT Torah and Pharisaic Mishnah stand in opposition to the Will of God as revealed in the obedience of Christ (pp. 193ff). On the contrary, this obedience is a matter of doing good and saving life (Mk 3:4), even on the Sabbath, even to the extent of saving Gentiles, and indeed even to the point of death. At this juncture, however, Mark is willing freely to draw on the whole of the OT for justification (cf. 3:4ff; 10:1ff; 11:15ff and 12:28ff). Mark's use of the OT, therefore, derives primarily from its capacity to justify his presentation of Jesus, viewed through the lens of his kerygmatic tradition:

> Die besondere theologische Leistung des Markus beruht nun aber darin, daß er dieses ὑπήκοος μέχρι θανάτου als Gehorsam gegenüber dem im Alten Testament manifest gewordenen, ursprünglichen Gotteswillen interpretiert hat (p. 196).

While it seems incontrovertible that some of Mark's concerns would have found special relevance in Gentile Christianity, as they would in any community facing the question of the relationship of Jews and Gentiles, it hardly follows that Philippians 2:8 provides the hermeneutical rubric for Mark. In addition, although the Markan Jesus is clearly concerned with the Law, Schulz' stress on the Gospel as an attempt to reinterpret it

---

von ihm übernommenen kerygmatischen Tradition des Heidenchristentums keinerlei Jesusüberlieferung - mit Ausnahme wenigen Spruchgutes im paränetischen Zusammenhang - urgemeindlichen Charakters übernommen' in that the Palestinian Jesus traditions may in fact be the presupposition of, and not a 'beziehungslos parallel' to, the so-called pre-Pauline Hellenistic *kyrios*-kerygma. Further, the assumption of Hellenistic syncretism as the grounds for the adoption of the title *Kyrios* is questionable (cf. Hengel's detailed argument 'Christology ', 33ff).

appears reductionistic, and his emphasis on the 'kyrios-kerygma' also seems at odds with Mark's interest in Jesus' pre-exaltation career.

Ultimately, the comprehensiveness of Schulz' theory is undermined by his terms of reference and his presuppositions concerning the origin of Mark's Gospel. While he correctly notes the role of the OT in Jesus' conflict with the Jewish leadership, he fails to consider seriously the significance of, for example, Mark's citation in 1:2f, the OT images in the prologue, or even the vineyard parable. In the case of the latter, it is the Jewish leaders' oversight of God's people that is revoked, not Israel's *Heilsgeschichte*.

f) J. Bowman, The Gospel of Mark and the New Christian Haggadah (1965)
Seeking to uncover 'how and why the Gospel as a literary form came about' (p. 311), John Bowman's monograph returns to a liturgical focus. Noting that the Exodus was the Jewish paradigm for deliverance and that the Passover meal became the focal memorial meal for Christians (p. 91), Bowman suggests that just as the Jewish meal was accompanied by an explanatory *haggadah*, so too the annual Christian equivalent was accompanied by Mark as its *haggadah*—the Passover being the one festival which clearly stands out in the Gospel (p. 158).

Such a usage explains why not only individual incidents in Jesus' life but the whole Gospel itself is a midrash on selected OT passages (p. xii). Thus Jesus' divine election, his being driven into the wilderness, and his forty day temptation is a midrash on Moses' call. The call of the first four disciples, the amazement of the crowds, and the opposition to Jesus, reflect the Exodus tradition of the response of the elders, the initial belief of the people, Pharaoh's response, and the slaves' anger with Moses (Ex 4:29ff; cf. 5:21ff; pp. 108-15). Mark's characteristic references to hardening (3:5; 6:52; 8:17; 10:5) are a deliberate point of contact with the Exodus—but ironically here of the redeemer's own people (pp. 121, 136, 180)—and the Transfiguration and the feedings reflect Sinai and the wilderness provision (pp. 157). Whereas the signs and wonders of the first Moses brought plagues, the miracles of the second removes them (pp. 159, 176).

The relative lack of 'testimonies' in Mark as compared to Matthew is not because Mark was written for Gentiles, after all they would not have had the necessary OT background. Instead, Mark presupposes the *testimonia* either because his Gospel represents a stage when the blatant scaffolding of 'that it might be fulfilled' is largely dismantled, or because its early Jewish hearers were so well versed in the fulfilment schema that they did not need them pointed out (pp. 19f).

Although several of Bowman's observations are helpful, others are less so. For example, seeing in the healing of the leper a *haggadah* on the healing of Moses' leprous hand, and in the cure of the issue of blood a 'direct counter' to Moses' plague of blood on Egypt (pp. 113, 147) seems rather too clever. Granted that there are occasions when Jesus could be understood in Mosaic terms (e.g. the feedings and transfiguration), it is not clear that all, or even most, of Jesus' actions are so cast. The fundamental weakness of Bowman's independent proposal, however, is that he does not establish any constitutive literary criteria for a Passover *haggadah*, nor does he explain why, for example, there are no Markan equivalents of the questions and answers. Last but not least, we have no evidence that Mark was ever used in a yearly celebration of a Christian Passover.

g) A. Suhl, Die Funktion der alttestamentlichen Zitate und Anspielungen im Markusevangelium (1965)

Published in the same year as Bowman's work, A. Suhl's volume marks a major shift in emphasis. Reflecting a redaction-critical approach, it is concerned primarily with Mark's more explicit use of the OT and still remains the only modern monograph to do so at length. Suhl proposes that Mark's OT citations are not a matter of '»Weissagung und Erfüllung«, *sondern um Auslegung des Jesusgeschehens mit Hilfe des AT*: Indem man das Neue in den »Farben« des Alten erzählte' (p. 47).[8] Mark merely wants to show that Jesus' history unfolds κατὰ τὰς γραφάς, as 'schriftgemäß' not 'Beweis' (pp. 157ff)—the emergence of the promise and fulfilment schema arising only with the delay of the parousia.

Suhl's thesis, stolidly following the view of his doctoral supervisor W. Marxsen, labours under two presuppositions. First, in view of the imminence of the parousia, Mark has abandoned all sense of history and has no room for *Heilsgeschichte* because all has been overtaken by the apocalyptic present. Second, Mark's gospel is 'Anrede' not 'Bericht' (pp. 9-25). Vital for Suhl's argument here is Paul's use of κατὰ τὰς γραφάς in 1 Corinthians 15:3f. He contends that Paul does not have salvation history in mind—κατὰ τὰς γραφάς is *Schriftgemäßheit* not *Schriftbeweis* (pp. 34ff)—and therefore, since it is a Gentile gospel, neither does Mark.

Apart from the weaknesses of Marxsen's existentialist thesis, questions are rightly raised when Suhl's easy acceptance of it leads him to dismiss what might otherwise be seen as the plain meaning of a text. *Contra* Suhl, Mark 14:49 does appear to address fulfilment (see also 7:6 and 14:21) and

---

8 As 'qualifizierte Sprache', 169, cf. 69; as material for the present preaching, 14; as illustration, 137.

his argument that the plural, γραφαί, reflects the Pauline plural, γραφάς, and thereby disallows any fulfilment motif, is hardly convincing. Suhl's treatment then does little to allay the suspicion that his presuppositions are skewing his exegesis.[9] Furthermore, it is not clear that 'Anrede' and 'Bericht' are mutually exclusive (cf. 1 Cor 15:1ff) and the typological character of Paul's comments elsewhere (1 Cor 10:1-11; 2 Cor 3:7-12; Rom 4; 5:12-21; and 9-11), despite Suhl's denials, suggests that Paul does have *Heilsgeschichte* in mind.

Matthew and Luke may well have a more pronounced use of the OT, but it is mistaken to judge Mark's 'introductory formula' by theirs. Granted, too, that not every OT citation or allusion in Mark necessarily invokes the *Schriftbeweis* schema, it is nevertheless difficult to imagine that a prophetic utterance like Isaiah 40:3, which held considerable significance for Israel's future (see Chapter 3), would not have implied a fulfilment motif. Indeed, why should Mark bother at all to present his account of Jesus as conforming to the OT in only the 'broadest sense'? When viewed against an implicit prophetic background, it is difficult to accept that Suhl has produced sufficient evidence to establish his case.

h) H. Anderson 'The Old Testament in Mark's Gospel' (1972)
Partly in response to Suhl, H. Anderson sets out to 'examine the main features of Mark's use of the Old Testament and to inquire to what extent, if any, this bears upon his aim and intention in his overall portrayal of Jesus Christ' (p. 218).

Recognising that Matthew and Luke subscribe to a promise-fulfilment formula, Anderson notes that there are few fulfilment phrases in Mark (1:15 and 14:49). However, given that beginnings and endings provide important clues to design and intent, it is significant that, although Mark's conclusion contains 'no express allusion to Scripture prophecy', his introduction contains the only occasion when Mark himself appeals to the OT (p. 281). Granted the questions surrounding Mark 1:1ff are complex, the unity of verses 1-13 suggests that Mark's linking of John and Jesus with the OT cannot easily be dismissed (*pace* Suhl; pp. 283-5). Instead, these verses are constitutive of Mark's overall interest in the OT, but, and herein lies Anderson's thesis, Mark's point is that the work of John and Jesus are in conformity, not with 'the letter of the Old Testament and its fulfilment', but with a more general expression of the divine will (p. 286).

Although the combination of Isaiah 56:7 and Jeremiah 7:11 in Mark 11:17, the use of δεῖ in Mark 8:31, and Psalm 118:22f in Mark 12:1-11 are

---

[9] See Grässer's review in *TLZ* 91 (1966) 667-9.

'eschatological',[10] that is, have an element of futurity (pp. 287, 293), they are not seeking to prove anything by matching a specific Scripture to an event. Mark wishes only to demonstrate Jesus' conformity to that 'set of Old Testament ideas concerning the persecution of God's true servants ... by his impenitent people...' (p. 299) '... under which the Christ goes forward through suffering and death to eventual vindication and victory' (p. 297).

All this is in keeping with Mark's prominent 'detainment' motif—as in the messianic secret, parable theory, and commands to silence. Just as Jesus' final vindication is 'held in suspension' so that the framework of suffering and passion must first be encountered, so too Mark's avoidance of the past fulfilment of the OT in Jesus' life enables him to focus his community's attention on its future in the light of the delay of the parousia. Likewise, the teaching of Mark's Jesus actually supersedes and transcends Scripture rather than making 'the Scripture point to himself as its fulfilment'—a fact which tells against Dodd's suggestion that it was Jesus himself who was behind the NT's creative use of the OT (p. 304).

It is also 'detainment', not a Gentile audience unfamiliar with the OT, nor a Jewish one so well-versed that it needed no help in recognising fulfilment, nor yet because the Gospel represents a stage when fulfilment formulae scaffolding had been dismantled, which explains Mark's 'comparative neglect of testimonies' (p. 305; *pace* Bowman). Compared then to Matthew and Luke, Mark stands 'at a rudimentary stage of the Christian community's apologetic endeavours to demonstrate from the Old Testament the relations between Jesus and that which is the messianic vocation' (p. 306).

Although rightly critical of Suhl, Anderson's proposal is also open to question. His 'detainment' motif hypothesis, namely that Mark is 'acutely conscious of having something new to say' which involves the '*as yet undisclosed* secret of who Jesus really is' (p. 305), seems unlikely. Aside from whether Mark is confronting the delay in the parousia, how realistic is the assumption that no-one in Mark's original audience would have been aware of who Jesus 'really is', particularly given the prologue? Further, if Anderson is correct, one would expect to see considerable use of testimonies after the passion narrative, but this is not the case. Nor need 'detainment' be the only explanation of what Anderson perceives as Jesus' reticence in applying Scripture to himself—assuming of course that

---

10 Following Fitzmyer's 'eschatological' and 'modernising' categorisation of OT usages in Qumran and the NT, 'Use', 316, where the former category expresses something that is yet to be accomplished, while the latter involves not only the taking over of an analogous situation in the OT and re-applying it to a new situation, but also the sense of completeness or fulfilment.

Anderson's perception is correct and not simply a failure to appreciate the highly allusive fashion in which Mark's Jesus uses the OT (e.g. Chapter 6 below). More problematic, however, is his distinction between fulfilment and a 'general expression of the divine will'. This sounds rather like Suhl's *Farbe*, and the same criticisms apply. Anderson's categorisation of Mark as representing a rudimentary stage reveals the fundamental issue: the common failing of using Matthew as a yardstick for Mark. Much to be preferred is an attempt to appreciate the OT texts as they were most likely understood among Mark's contemporaries, and when this is done, given the thorough-going Jewish character of the Jesus story, it is difficult to escape the impression that, for example, 1:2f would have had some kind of fulfilment connotation.

i) W. M. Swartley, 'A Study of Markan Structure' (1973); cf. 'The Structural
   Function of the Term 'Way' (Hodos) in Mark's Gospel' (1980)
Reflecting a shift back from redactional to more literary concerns, W. M. Swartley's little-known Princeton Ph.D. dissertation is a full-scale attempt to understand Mark entirely in terms of an Exodus paradigm. Observing that, although Farrer, Hobbs, Piper, and others had recognised a distinctive Markan use of the OT, little had been done to relate these insights to the Gospel's literary structure, Swartley sets out to rectify the situation.

Mark's introductory citation is programmatic for the themes of covenant, Temple, and cultic purity (Mal/Ex), and 'way' and 'desert' (Isaiah). These are variously picked up in Mark's 'Way' section, in the Temple cleansing, and Mark's transitional locations such as 'by the sea' (1:16-20), 'on the mountain' (3:13-35), and 'in the wilderness' (6:7-31). Deriving from events and places which structured Israel's Exodus memories, these motifs likewise provide the Gospel's six-fold literary framework.[11] That some of them are not immediately obvious complements the secretive nature of Mark's material (cf. 4:34 and 13:14).

The 'sea' motif (1:16; 3:7) delineates 1:21 - 3:6 as the place of deliverance for the new Israel (pp. 103-8). Opening with 'the mountain', 3:13 - 6:6 reflects the Sinai event with its election of a new community (3:13-19, 31-35) and God's self-disclosure (via parables and miracles, 4:1 - 5:43), while the Nazareth rejection echoes the golden calf incident (6:1-6; pp. 109-12). The 'wilderness' theme characterises 6:7 - 8:21(26) with God's provision (6:30-44 and 8:1-10), guidance and testing (cf. the disciples' incomprehension, 6:52), and the people's rebellion (cf. the Pharisees rejection of Jesus, 8:11f). The positive Gentile response (7:24-37) echoes those wilderness traditions

---

[11] 'Study', 36ff, hereafter 'pp.'; 1:14 - 3:6//3:13 - 6:6a//6:7 - 8:21//8:27 - 10:52; 11:1 - 13:37; 14:1 - 15:47; with 16:1-8 as epilogue.

which had connotations of hope (pp. 86ff), and the 'Way' section's presentation of Jesus' teaching on messiahship and discipleship reflects OT ethical and eschatological features (particularly Deutero-Isaianic, pp. 68-80). Finally, the 'Temple' theme (covering two panels, 11:1 - 16:8) represents Mark's use of the Temple's fate to symbolise the failure of the Jewish mission (e.g. 11:12-25) and the success of the Gentile one (e.g. 12:1-12, pp. 92-101). The emphasis on ἔρημος and ὁδός in Mark 1:2f speak of the isolated wilderness and so highlight the secrecy component (e.g. 6:31-35) which characterises the nature of Jesus' self-disclosure on the 'Way'.

Swartley develops this last idea in a later essay, arguing that the interleaving of typological exodus- and entrance- motifs (Mk 9 is a new Sinai) with discipleship themes reveals that Mark's 'Way' is 'The Way of Discipleship (Suffering and Cross) that Leads to the (Promised Land) Kingdom of God'.[12] Mark, finally, is a missionary document with an apologetic for the eclipse of Judaism expressed in the waning of Jerusalem and the increased prominence of Galilee (p. 226).

Swartley's attempt, first, to take seriously the formative nature of Israel's founding event, and second, to integrate possible echoes within one overarching literary structure, is to be applauded. It cannot, however, be deemed a success. Although the analyses of the 'Way' and 'Temple' panels have much to commend them, other characterisations fail to convince: the most significant sea story occurs not in the 'sea' section but in the 'mountain' section, and Mark 9 reflects more Sinai influence than the brief reference in 3:13ff. The treatment of Markan motifs is sometimes inconsistent: the Pharisees' hostility in 8:11f reflects the wilderness rebellion while their opposition in 2:1 - 3:6 is cast in other terms. Swartley's hypothesis rests on the integration of earlier transitionals with later panels, but can these brief and relatively obscure transitional comments bear the load placed on them, Mark's 'secrecy motif' notwithstanding? It is difficult to avoid the feeling that Swartley's structure is being read into rather than out of the text. Finally, apart from one or two exceptions (for example, 1:2f; 11:17), Swartley makes little attempt to correlate Mark's use of OT citations or more explicit allusions with his overall structure.

j) H. C. Kee, 'The Function of Scriptural Quotations and Allusions in Mark 11-16' (1975)

In this article just prior to his monograph on Mark, H. C. Kee seeks 'to determine which of the Scriptures are Mark's favorites (*sic*) and then to discover how he has interpreted and adapted Scripture in the service of

---

12 'Structural', 82. Swartley has recently restated his position in *Scripture*.

his own theological and literary aims' (p. 166). Although not covering the whole of the gospel—Kee deals primarily with the last third of the book but other sections are briefly mentioned—his focus on Mark's use of the OT, and the fact that it is here that Mark most frequently appeals to the OT, merits its inclusion in this survey.

Noting at least 57 quotations and 160 allusions to Scripture, Kee criticises Suhl's arbitrary decision to limit his investigation to explicit and extended quotations as inadequate 'for tracing the fuller hermeneutical picture'. He then observes that Mark not only 'clearly prefers prophetic and eschatologically interpreted passages of Scripture' but employs these quotations at the most crucial points in his developing argument (p. 173). Similarly striking is his 'synthesis' technique where, in close analogy with for instance the *Florilegium*, two apparently unconnected OT texts are brought together in order to make a new claim (so Mal 3:1 with possibly Ex 23:20 and Isa 40:3 in 1:2f; the voice in 1:11; Zech 9:9 and 10:10 with Ps 118:25-26 in Mk 11:1-11; pp. 175ff). Thus, fulfilment is not merely an apologetic device, nor is the appeal to Scripture merely to embellish or 'to give specific content to a simple kerygmatic formula' (p. 179). The Scriptures are instead Mark's 'indispensable presupposition', a 'necessary link with the biblical tradition that Mark sees redefined and comprehended through Jesus' (*ibid*).

Mark's 'Hegel-like' synthesis centres on three re-definitions. His re-definition of the covenant people invokes Isaiah and Zechariah, of the law almost exclusively appeals to Torah, and of the hope of redemption uses Daniel when dealing with the nature of the path to victory (that is, the necessity of suffering as a path to vindication), and both Isaiah and Daniel when re-defining the enemy. Christologically, Daniel influences the picture of Jesus as the prophet who unfolds the hidden meaning of Scripture whereas Isaiah modifies the traditional nationalistic treatment of the Son of David who becomes an eschatological agent through whom light comes to the blind. As with Qumran, there is no conflict between the concern for law (rules of admission and maintenance of fellowship) and for eschatology (pp. 177f).

In keeping with his interest in apocalyptic, Kee places considerable, but not exclusive, store on Daniel. But in view of the use of the blinding texts from the classical prophets (cf. Isa 6 in Mk 4 ; Isa 29 in Mk 7 and Jer 5:21/ Isa 6:9 in Mk 8:18), Kee's distinction between them and Daniel on the basis of hidden meaning seems unwarranted. Likewise, Kee's concentration on Daniel in dealing with the suffering motif is not in keeping with the evidence. On his own analysis of Mark 14-15, citations, allusions, and influences from the so-called Servant Songs considerably outweigh those from Daniel (pp. 170ff).[13] If, in addition, Mark 1-10 is regarded as the context for chapters 11-16, then the allusions to Isaiah 42:1 in Mark 1:11 (which Kee recognises) and 53:3 in 9:12 along with at least the influence of 53:10-12 in 10:45 further strengthen the case for some Isaianic component (cf. Isa 40:3 in Mk 1:2f). These criticisms aside, however, Kee's observations on Mark's 'synthetic' method, his preference for eschatological texts, and his placement of appeals to the OT at crucial junctures in his narrative, serve to highlight the importance of the OT for Mark.

k) M. D. Goulder, The Evangelist's Calendar (1978)
In yet another British revival of the liturgical approach, M. D. Goulder revamps the lectionary theory arguing that Mark is to be understood on the basis of reconstructions of the OT lections which would have accompanied the reading of the Gospel.

Aside from the considerable assumptions inherent in such a task, which it should be noted Goulder undertakes in painstaking fashion, the connections observed between the reconstructed readings and Mark vary greatly. It seems strange that Isaiah 34f is proposed as the OT lection for Mark 1:1-20, a selection which in any case runs right over a major Markan division, when Mark himself speaks of Isaiah 40 (p. 246). It becomes increasingly difficult to feel any certainty when, in dealing with other readings, Goulder has to refer to OT lections past or future in order to explicate the significance of the passage (pp. 249f). Other connections seem tenuous. For example, Goulder outlines a series of 'fulfilments' of Elijah-Elisha themes in Mark 5:35 - 8:1-10 based on the lections from 3 Kingdoms 1:7 - 4:42ff. Naboth is a type of John the Baptist and apostasy is the thematic link between Jesus at Nazareth and Elijah on Carmel. Nazareth, where Jesus could do no mighty work and is rejected, reflects Elijah's great miracle which causes the crowd's confessional response. Given the not-unlimited range of OT themes and the fact that the NT has its roots in the Old, one wonders if many of Goulder's points of contact are more co-incidental than intentional.

In terms of literary structure, a number of Goulder's divisions run right across recognised Markan intercalations: 3:21/22-30/31-35; 5:21-4/25-

---

[13] For Daniel, citations: Dn 7:13 in Mk 14:62; allusions: Dn 12:10 (LXX) in Mk 14:38. For Isaiah, citations: 50:6 in Mk 14:65 (ignoring 53:12 in 15:28); and allusions: possibly 53:12 in 14:21; *Tg. Isa* 53:5 in 14:58; possibly Isa 53:7 in 14:60; Isa 53:6 (LXX) in 15:15; Isa 50:2f in 15:33; Isa 53:9 in 15:43 and 46. Kee's 'lowest' category, 'influences', has Dn 7:21, 25 in 14:21; 10:16-19 in 14:34ff; and 7:25 in 14:35; while Isa 53:3-5 is seen in 14:65. Weighting this, for the sake of argument 3-2-1, gives Daniel '10' compared to the so-called Songs's '18'.

34/35-43; 6:7-13/14-29/30; and 11:12-14/15-19/20-35. It is hard to believe that this is Mark's intention.

Goulder provides interesting insights on the OT background of different events. However, in terms of his overall hypothesis, perhaps the most telling aspect is the considerable uncertainty and fluidity of the weekly readings which, when combined with the concerns above, tends to call the whole rather inflexible construction into question.[14]

l) W. S. Vorster, 'The Function of the Old Testament in Mark' (1981)
W. S. Vorster's article reflects the trend away from *Redaktions-geschichte* to narrative analysis. His contention is that Mark uses the OT as a 'literary' means to put across his narrative point of view. Reminiscent of Suhl, Vorster's Mark is likewise not interested in promise-fulfilment nor with the OT context (for example, 1:2f), but instead wants to establish 'perspectives through which the reader is presented with this story' (p. 62).

Although Mark eschews using the OT within the promise-fulfilment schema, his Gospel is structured according to prediction-fulfilment techniques.[15] Mark 14:27f contains combined predictive statements, verse 27 from Zechariah 13:7 and verse 28 from Jesus himself, which respectively find fulfilment in 14:49 and 16:7f. The significant point is that 'these quotations form part of the Markan narrative of Jesus and are fulfilled in that narrative' (p. 70). For Vorster, this 'embeddedness' in the narrative is further borne out by Pryke's observation that Mark sometimes suspends his quotation in the middle of a sentence,[16] so that 'they sound as if they are the words of the narrator or narrated figure although they stand in parenthesis' (*ibid.*). Similarly, Mark 1:2f does not present John's history as fulfilment but simply as part of the story of Jesus. The fact that the great majority of OT quotations are on the lips of Jesus is taken by Vorster as further support for his narrative theory.

While it is true that Mark's avoids Matthean fulfilment interjections, this hardly demonstrates that Mark is uninterested in fulfilment: the criticisms applied to Suhl's conception of OT prophetic literature also pertain here. Granted too Mark's general confinement of OT quotations and their 'fulfilments' to the narrative, this only tells us about his narrative style; it does not necessarily follow that he is thereby disinterested in OT *Heilsgeschichte*. Vorster's attempt to reconcile Mark's

---

[14] Cf. his admission in *Midrash*, 227n2.
[15] E.g. 1:2f as prediction, cf. 1:4ff as fulfilment; so 1:7 and 1:9ff; citing Petersen, *Literary*, 49ff.
[16] 1:1-4; 7:6-8; 10:5-8; 14:27f; Pryke, *Redactional*, 37.

lack of fulfilment formula vis-à-vis Matthew, with his apparent prediction/fulfilment structure is, therefore, ultimately unconvincing.

m) J. D. M. Derrett, The Making of Mark (1985)
J. D. M. Derrett's commentary constitutes another reading of Mark through the grid of the first 'trek' of Israel from Egypt to Canaan. Involving an exodus, an invasion, and a triumph, Jesus is presented as a second and greater Moses/Joshua. This Gospel 'of sermon outlines' is to be interpreted on the basis of precise passage by passage parallels to sections of the Hexateuch—namely the first half of Exodus, parts of Numbers, and nearly all of Joshua—although 1 Samuel, Lamentations, Canticles, Daniel, Isaiah 53, and Psalm 22 influence later chapters.

The complex citation at the outset (Mk 1:2f)—Mark's only explicit editorial use of the OT—merely serves to inform us that he intends to draw from all three sections of the Jewish Scripture. On the other hand, the single word ἀπέχει in the Gethsemane account recalls Yahweh's announcement in Deuteronomy 1:6 and 2:3 that the first trek is about to end. Likewise, passing over the question of the possible significance of the clear-cut OT quotation in the parables section, Derrett proceeds instead into a highly speculative *haggadah* on the manna traditions.

As this Chapter has suggested, the idea that Mark's gospel owes a great deal to Israel's history appears to have a solid basis. But Derrett's quixotic journey proceeds along such subtle paths that it becomes increasingly difficult to follow him, not least because his eclectic method and ingenious use of material appear to lack any consistent controls. Too much is built on the scantiest allusion and insufficient attention given to clear OT parallels for Derrett's undoubtedly innovative reading to carry conviction.

n) M. D. Hooker, 'Mark' (1988)
Although at first sight Mark appears to make little use of the OT, M. D. Hooker recognises that this is largely because of his distinctive approach. Not only is the opening quotation significant, 'his story is good news precisely because it is the fulfilment of Scripture', but 'Jesus' words and activities constantly echo OT scenes and language, until what is "written" of the Son of Man (9:12; 10:21) is finally fulfilled' (p. 220). Due to space limitations, Hooker's article focuses on Mark's use of the Pentateuch, and thereby his view of the law.

In the conflict over the Pharisees' and scribes' traditions, Mark 7:1-23 shows that while Jesus upholds the Law (vv. 1-13; cf. Nu 30:2; Dt 23:21-23) his authority is even greater than that of the Law (vv. 14-23). The same is borne out in examinations of 12:18ff and 28-34 (p. 224), and several Pentateuchal allusions (2:1-10; 2:23 - 3:6; cf. 1:44). Three other allusions recalling incidents in Moses' life serve likewise to demonstrate that Jesus is either Moses' successor (6:34, cf. Nu 27:17) or his superior (9:2-13; cf. Ex 24:15f; Dt 18:15), while 9:38-40 (cf. Nu 11:26-29) shows Jesus acting as did Moses.

Mark's presentation of Jesus' relationship to the Law is therefore somewhat ambiguous, and results at least once in Jesus abrogating one aspect of the Law (10:10ff; cf. also 7:19). Since such challenges occur in private, they reflect the fact that 'neither Jesus nor the earliest generation of Christians regarded the teaching of Moses abrogated ... but interpretation ... led inevitably to the point of rupture—a point which had not yet been reached when Mark wrote' (p. 228).

Hooker's observation that Mark's Jesus is faithful to the Law and yet above it, judges by the Law and yet decisively re-evaluates it when his own acts are called into question, is well put, and accurately reflects the tensions in a community coming to terms with past and present. On a smaller point, however, it is not entirely obvious that Jesus' abrogations are so private as to be left for a later generation to resolve, since the public statements and their clear implications can hardly be reconciled with Moses (7:14f and 10:5ff). Be this as it may, the 'tension' inherent in the response of Mark's Jesus to the Law is not dissimilar to Kee's account of Mark's larger scheme of 'redefinition'. Both phenomena suggest that an important Markan concern is the question of how past traditions and expectations are to be reconciled with what Mark is convinced is their present fulfilment.

o) W. Roth Hebrew Gospel: Cracking the Code of Mark (1988).
Inspired by several Markan features, namely, the expectation that 'Elijah must come first' (Mk 9:11-13), Mark's introduction (Ex 23:20 and Mal 3:1), and his portrayal of the Baptist, W. Roth's suggestion is that the Gospel's 'conceptual-narrative paradigm' follows 1 Kings 17 to 2 Kings 13 such that Jesus' Elisha plays successor to John's Elijah as they re-establish the Lord's reign. Accordingly, the Gospel is composed of four acts—Commissioning of the Kingdom's Bringer (1:1-13), his Authentication (1:14 - 7:37), Confrontation with Apostasy (8:1 - 15:39), and Vindication (15:40 - 16:8).

Evidence is found in Jesus' sixteen miracles up to 7:37 (equalling Elisha's miracles, cf. 'all' in 2 Kgs 8:4/Mk 7:37), and parallel feedings, Mk 6:32ff/2 Kgs 4:42f, and resuscitations, Mk 5:21ff/2 Kgs 4:18ff). Just as Elisha extends Elijah's miracles by eight, so too Jesus extends Elisha's (but not John's?) by eight (after 7:37 and including the rending of the Temple curtain). As Elisha traversed the land after the departure of his 'master', so also Jesus after John's egress. Further, Jesus' preaching of the 'good news' echoes the four lepers' announcement in 2 Kings 7:9, and 'repent and believe' represents 'the invitation to accept the scriptural paradigm of divine intervention that the gospel presents' (p. 11, presumably 1-2 Kgs). The seed parable's 'one hundred fold' recalls 2 Kings 1:9-12 (two fifties) and 18:13, and thus the three 'poor' soils echo the responses of Jezebel, Ahab, and Jehoram. Peter's threefold denial before the cock crows twice reflects Elijah's threefold refusal to leave Elisha and his two-fold endowment with his master's spirit. If this seems esoteric it is only because it is inherent in Mark's parabolic enterprise which is 'pointedly a journey of discovery by speaking the secret of the kingdom—without ever unveiling it' (p. 19).

Roth is correct in interpreting Jesus' miracles within the OT prophetic tradition rather than Hellenism, but even so, most of his parallels seem either forced, co-incidental (does Judas' kiss really echo the kissing of Baal in 1 Kgs 19:18?), or due to the broad intertextuality of biblical themes (cf. pp. 92ff). His paradigm fails to take seriously Mark's one clear editorial citation—Malachi's Elijah does not precede a new Elisha—and his outline cuts across otherwise clear indications of literary structure (e.g. the 'Way' section) or thematic markers (Jesus' only two confrontations with leaders from Jerusalem—both important and both outside Jerusalem—occur before Roth's 'Confrontation' section).

p) R. Schneck, Isaiah in the Gospel of Mark, I-VIII (1994).[17]
R. Schneck's thesis grows out of the contrasting claims of M. A. Beavis (Isaiah is Mark's favourite book) and A. C. Sundberg (Daniel is primary),[18] finding in favour of Beavis. Noting allusions to Isaiah in every chapter of Mark,[19] Schneck also finds extensive parallels between the themes of the original Isaianic context and the Markan setting. This indicates that Mark uses OT texts such that their original contexts inform his narrative (pp. 245f).[20] The same applies to combined citations. Mark does this not only because Jesus fulfils OT hopes (*pace* Suhl; p. 249) but also because he is following Jesus' own use of Scripture (with Dodd; p. 251).

Overarching OT models for Mark are rejected, however, since 'we can hardly expect to discover that any NT author would ever use the Isaian

---

[17] A revision of his 1992 thesis, Schneck's work came to my attention during the final stages of the preparation of this book. Consequently, I have been unable to interact extensively with Schneck in the body of my early Chapters, although comment may be found in the footnotes.

[18] Respectively, *Literary*, 110, and 'Testimonies', 274, cited on p. 1.

[19] Isaiah in parentheses: Mark 1:1a (40:9), 2-3 (40:3), 10 (63:19a), 11 (42:1); 2:7 (43:25-26), 16-20 (58:2-7), 20 (58:8); 3:27 (49:24-25); 4:12 (6:9-10), 24 (Tg. 27:8); 5:1-20 (65:1-7); 6:34-44 (55:1-3), 39-40 (25:6), 52 (6:9-10); 7:6-7 (29:13), 32 (35:5); 8:17b (6:9-10), and 25 (42:6-7).

[20] With Marcus but *pace* Juel, *Messianic*.

corpus as a model or paradigm ... in composing a new writing' (p. 3) because 'the prophetic material is quite diverse and the different pericopae do not appear to be organically constructed' (*ibid*). It is not clear, however, that a model or paradigm must necessarily be 'literary'—Isaiah 40-55 makes considerable use of the Exodus 'event'. Given, too, the prologue's function in antiquity,[21] that Mark's is replete with imagery from Isaiah 40-66 (pp. 40ff, 60ff) surely implies something about his overall agenda.

While not every identification is equally convincing (for example, Isa 53:2-7 in 2:16-17 and 53:8 in 2:20), Schneck marshals considerable support for his case—at least for Mark 1-8. This limitation is problematic since Schneck cites Kee's study on Mark 11-16 but fails to mention Kee's support for a primarily Daniellic influence; indeed, this alternative is not discussed. Nevertheless, Schneck's work is welcome since at the least he shows not only that Isaiah is of considerable importance for Mark, but also provides good evidence to suggest that Mark was aware of the OT context.

III. Analysis

Numerous studies on Mark's use of the OT have examined his technique (Suhl, Kee, Vorster, Schneck), his view of the Law (Schulz, Hooker), the impact of OT *Heilsgeschichte* (Farrer, Piper, Hobbs, Swartley, Derrett, Roth), the influence of Jewish/Christian religious observance (Carrington, Bowman, Goulder), and his attitude to fulfilment (Suhl, Anderson, Kee, Vorster, Schneck). Several features emerge.

In terms of technique, Mark tends to conflate OT references and to place them at critical points in his argument (Kee). He not only avoids editorial interjections, but has the great majority of OT quotations in the mouth of Jesus. Longer quotations are not infrequently suspended in mid-sentence (Vorster). Mark also prefers certain categories of texts for particular concerns: the Torah when he re-defines the Law (Kee, Hooker), Isaiah and Zechariah with regard to the re-definition of God's new people, and Daniel and Isaiah when re-defining redemption (Kee).

Mark's view of Jesus' relationship to the OT Law is not of major concern in this book, except to note that Mark's Jesus judges his critics by its standards, and yet decisively re-evaluates it in the light of his own person and mission (Hooker). It may not surprise us then if Mark's understanding of the OT reflects a similar approach.

---

[21] See Chapter 2, 54f.

A number of scholars observed the influence of Israel's *Heilsgeschichte* on Mark, notably the Exodus, suggesting that he intends to present the message and person of Jesus in such terms. In a number of cases there is good evidence that this is so. However, the scholars reviewed have been more successful in demonstrating this influence on individual sections than on the theology and literary structure of the Gospel as a whole. Further, there has often been little effort to integrate Mark's explicit uses of OT texts with the various structures proposed (Swartley is a part-exception). On balance, no suggestion along these lines has been satisfactory, lectionary and new *haggadah* hypotheses even less so.

In view of both the teleological aspect of the prophets and Mark's considerable interest in them (especially Isaiah) it is likely that he has fulfilment in mind (Kee, Hooker, Schneck; *pace* Suhl, Anderson, Vorster). Arguments to the contrary tend either to judge Mark in terms of Matthew or appear to suffer from a predisposed point of view. It seems Mark, at least in the case of Isaiah, uses OT texts to allude to their original contexts with the aim of illuminating his own narrative (Schneck).

Given the sometimes overly complex, contrived, and/or selective nature of the analyses surveyed, D. E. Nineham's early scepticism as to the existence of any 'single and entirely coherent masterplan' for Mark might appear justified.[22] Similar reservations are expressed by Martin who approvingly cites J. M. Robinson's critique of such approaches in that their 'argument is not built upon what Mark clearly and repeatedly has to say, but upon inferences as to the basis of the Marcan order, a subject upon which Mark is silent'.[23]

Robinson has put his finger on an important matter: does Mark really remain silent as to his order? It is generally agreed that certain sections of the Gospel betray conscious structuring, for example, the 'Way' section. But if here, why not elsewhere? And why, for instance, do nearly all the miracles occur only in the first eight chapters? The difficulty with the scepticism expressed by Nineham and others is that it is based on negative evidence. A critique of the models offered to date does not provide grounds for denying the possibility that Mark may have had an outline in mind. All that can be said is that these models do not adequately describe the data. Is there a way forward? This book suggests that there is. And it is to be found in terms of the relationship between a community's founding moment and ideology's role in maintaining social cohesion.

---

[22] *Mark*, 29; citing Cadbury, *Making*, 80, who asserts that there 'is scarcely any thorough-going theological theory that permeates the whole narrative'.

[23] *Evangelist*, 91; and *History*, 12.

Chapter 2: History as Hermeneutic: Ideology and Community Self-Understanding

Inherent in ideology's social function is the mediation of the ideals and energies of a group's founding moment. This provides an interpretative schema by which the group defines and understands itself. To the extent that various texts and motifs become associated with elements of this interpretative schema, their use in a given literary context serves to invoke elements of that schema and thereby provides an implicit hermeneutical framework. Mark's use of OT texts may function this way.

I. Introduction

In his ground-breaking book on Jesus' parables, Kenneth Bailey stresses the importance of common tacit knowledge in the interaction between Jesus and his audience. By way of illustration, he explains that when an Englishman relates the tale of King Arthur and Camelot to his countrymen, everyone knows exactly how the characters are expected to act. For example, knights obey the king, carry out daring quests, and rescue damsels in distress. Likewise, castles, dark forests, and so on, are never explained but are simply assumed as familiar images. This pool of shared expectations and stock figures constitutes the 'grand piano' upon which the English story teller deftly plays.

> Imagine then an Englishman telling the same story about Sir Lancelot to Alaskan Eskimos. Obviously the music of the "grand piano" will not be heard because the piano is in the minds of the English listeners who share a common culture and history with the story teller. In the case of the parables of Jesus, *we are the Eskimos.*[1]

Bailey's thesis is that in order to appreciate fully the point of Jesus' parables we too must enter into their world of shared expectations where everyone knows how a rich man ought to behave, how the Samaritans are beneath contempt, and how seasonal pressures weigh heavily upon a day labourer seeking work in an agrarian society. Only then will we be in a position to identify those 'points of reference'—usually stereotypical characters and situations—which aroused in the original hearers the particular

---

[1] *Through*, xiv.

expectations, generated and conditioned by the daily interplay of social roles and mores, upon which the point of the story turns. It is these unstated but universally known expectations, Bailey argues, that the parables presuppose and against which they are told such that their 'main points, climaxes, bits of humor (*sic*), and irony are all heightened by "variations on a theme," that is, by changing, reinforcing, rejecting, intensifying, etc., the known pattern of attitude and behaviour.'[2]

The aim of this Chapter is to suggest that a similar approach may explain aspects of Mark's use of OT texts and images. Perhaps they too function as keys on a larger 'grand piano' so that Mark's 'main points, climaxes ... and irony' are also 'heightened ... by changing, reinforcing, rejecting, intensifying, etc., the known pattern' not, however, of social 'attitude and behaviour', but of a similarly assumed pattern of OT interpretation and expectation.[3]

As briefly stated in the 'Introduction', it was while studying at a North American Seminary that I experienced how this might work. During a lecture one of my American professors underlined his point with a brief statement which included the phrase 'four score and seven years ago'. The class responded to this as one, whereas I failed to see the relevance of this additional and archaically phrased comment. Over morning coffee, I asked what had happened eighty-seven years ago, and was met with blank puzzlement. This surprised me. Further discussion was just as unhelpful until the phrase was retranslated back into the original. Immediately a

---

[2] *Ibid.* See also Baxandall, *Painting*, where he argues that the 15th C. Italian painters presupposed their contemporaries' sensitivity to the influence of significant social trends such as the moralism of religious preaching, the pageantry of social dancing, the shrewdness of commercial gauging, and the renewal of interest in the grandeur of Latin oratory that were characteristic of their time. Thus Baxandall sees in Giovanni Bellinni's work an example of the 'interaction between the painting and the visualising activity of the public mind—a public mind with different furniture and dispositions from ours', 48. It is this 'public mind' that provided the true medium for the painter, i.e. the capacity of the audience to see meaning in his work. On the congruence between literature and art in this respect see Ricoeur, 'Function'.

[3] In its concern with the way in which texts and images functioned in invoking elements of a generalised first century Jewish world-view, this study complements both Burridge's account of the Gospels, *What?*, as belonging to the Græco-Roman genre, βίοι, and the work of others who are concerned with the readers' (hearers') education and literary knowledge, cf. e.g. Bilezikian, *Liberated*; Beavis, *Audience*; and Tolbert, *Sowing*. For a more comprehensive delineation of the basic world-view in question also from within a narrative framework, see now Wright, *People*.

chorus of recognition informed me that this was the first line of Abraham Lincoln's Gettysburg address.

Speaking at the dedication of the national cemetery honouring the site of arguably the greatest battle in the American Civil War, Lincoln, in this time of great crisis, reminded his hearers of the ideals upon which the nation was founded. It was fidelity to these ideals, Lincoln suggested, that not only justified the North's commitment to its present course of action, and thereby sanctified the deaths of these thousands of her men, but also summoned her to even greater efforts. Only in so doing could the North lay true claim to the heritage of Washington, Jefferson, and others. Here then, in spite of employing a mere ten sentences scribbled out during the train ride to the site, Lincoln managed in a most extraordinary way to encompass the sweep of American self-understanding and to capture the nation's sense of destiny. This, I discovered, was what 'four score and seven ...' really meant in that lecture room setting.

Several points should be noted. Obviously the part-citation refers to the first line of a famous address. But it clearly does much more. The phrase is a pointer not merely to the text of Lincoln's speech but instead to the 'history' which that speech both assumes and interprets. And this 'history' is not merely the immediate event of Gettysburg or even the Civil War, but instead the setting of these events within the broader compass of U.S. 'history' as a whole. Furthermore, this broader setting is predicated on those founding events to which Lincoln himself alludes.

Even more importantly, this 'history' is not the 'objective', detailed, even quiescent version of the academic élite, but rather a popularist, highly processed and digested, yet pungent and persuasive 'history', cast in terms of the parameters set by the Founding Fathers mythology.[4] That is, although the text is a part-citation, its primary function is to allude to and therefore to invoke, a powerful hermeneutical framework originating with the Founding Fathers, namely, the ideologically shaped popular recounting of the 'essence' of U.S. history. In this sense the part-citation functions very much like the 'point of reference' in a parable.

---

[4] Throughout this Chapter 'myth' is used not to imply falsity or deception, but rather that which in attempting to draw out as fully as possible the significance of an event tends toward the heroic and poetic.

The procedure is almost unconscious. Again, as in the case of Bailey's account of the parables, it seemingly requires no great mental effort on the part of informed listeners to make the necessary connection—it simply strikes the right chord on the hearer's mental 'grand piano'. The point being, however, that the whole process presupposes a tutored audience whom it is simply assumed will make the right connections; the untutored (such as this Australian) occupying the place τοῦ ἰδιώτου.

Only the barest minimum of 'text' was supplied. The extent of the allusion/citation is determined primarily by the need to ensure that the correct connection is made—with perhaps some consideration for good style. Since in this case it is a part-citation, style is already fixed, but the archaic character of the expression naturally aids identification. In spite of its apparently fragmentary form, these few words are perfectly adequate to the task.

This particular instance serves to illustrate the way in which the true significance of a brief and even fragmentary citation may go far beyond what might otherwise appear to be the case. Although to the untutored the citation might seem of little importance, the fact remains that to trained hearers it has considerable allusive power and thereby serves to invoke a comprehensive hermeneutical framework.

The following analogy may help to explain the mechanics of the process. Suppose a given history is represented by a journey taken through an expanse of land. There are certain features: hills, valleys, grassy plains, unusual bluffs, small trees, large forests, rivers, mountains, deserts, and so on, which represent concrete events. Attempting to comprehend this history corresponds to mapping the journey, and just as all maps have to be selective as to which features are to be included, so too a given history must also make judgements as to which events are significant (crossing a lake) and which are not (stepping over a puddle). Completing the analogy, imagine a grid system overlayed on the map which enables easy reference to its various parts, and allow that this grid system represents various texts describing or interacting with those events.

Now neither the map nor the grid system are real in the sense that the events they 'map' are real. The grid reference ('four score and seven') is simply a shorthand way of using the grid system (here including Lincoln's address) to refer to the map (the schematised version of significant events) that is designed to make sense of the journey through the landscape (the course of the myriad events themselves). The point here is that neither the citations/allusions nor the texts they point to exist alone. They find their meaning within the larger interpretation of that on-going history which the texts themselves presuppose and with which they interact.

Returning to Mark, I suggest that his 'grand piano' is a schematised interpretive 'map' of Israel's 'history' and that his OT part-citations or allusions may function as 'grid references' to that map which gives expression and order to Israel's interpretation of her history, namely the OT. In other words, it may well be that Mark uses some of his OT texts in much the same way as Lincoln or my Professor used their 'points of reference'; that is, to indicate to his hearers/readers what particular aspect of their common tacit understanding he has in mind. This, of course, raises the same problem Bailey refers to: how are we, as 'Eskimos' listening to Mark's 'Camelot', to uncover the nature and content of this tacit knowledge? How might it be structured, and what is its basis?

The first question will be addressed throughout the following several Chapters as we seek to ascertain the significance of particular OT texts within Israel's larger historical self-understanding. The second question occupies the remainder of this Chapter, which is an attempt to lay out in a summary manner how social theory[5] may go some way toward providing a theoretical explanation of this process.[6] The first section (*The Social Function of Ideology*) outlines the way in which, according to Jacques Ellul and Paul Ricoeur, ideology facilitates social cohesion. This is effected particularly through ideology's *revivification* of the group's founding moment such that it becomes A) the shared and almost unconscious basis of the group's self-definition and B) its interpretative framework for understanding the world.[7] In order to do this, however, the group's ideology must be inculcated from birth. This requires that it be accessible

---

[5] For sage warnings on the dangers of positivism, reductionism, relativism, and determinism inherent in the uncritical use of social science models, see Herion's remarks in 'Reconstruction'.

[6] Dodd's discussion, *According*, refers to the shared *Weltanschauung* of OT and NT authors but does not go beyond a surface probing of the matter; see below.

[7] To speak blandly of a community's 'ideology', as if it were one homogenous and indivisible whole, clearly does not do justice to the more complex, variegated, and amorphous nature of the reality. Nevertheless, for the purposes of this exercise it seems justifiable to treat as a unit those major constructs about which the group would be in broad agreement.

to all members of the group. Consequently, ideology's re-telling must be *schematised* into digestible 'slogans'. The media of this schema are the *icon* and the *symbol* which, by means of *iconic augmentation*, serve as shorthand references to ideology's larger interpretive framework.

The second section (*Ideology and Crisis*) examines what transpires when a community's present experience contradicts the future projected by its ideology. Given the importance of maintaining the link with the founding moment, and therefore the community's heritage, one approach is to *re-present* the prevailing ideology whereby previously unconnected 'icons' are juxtaposed so as to explain the unexpected present. However, the new ways of seeing reality engendered by these juxtapositions may be rejected by members of the community if they exceed its *doxic threshold*. This may lead to a debate over who are the heirs of the community's traditions which is then carried out in terms of fidelity to the mores of the community's founding moment. The Chapter concludes with an outline of how this model might explain aspects of Mark's use of the OT.

II. The Social Function of Ideology

a) Ideology: A Provisional Definition

The issues involved in the continuing debate surrounding the definition of 'ideology'[8] and its relationship to 'myth' and 'utopian thought' are

---

[8] The term, generally believed to have been coined by Destutt de Tracy in 1796 to refer to a science of ideas that would allow the reconstruction of society on a rational basis, was soon used pejoratively to describe 'a naive logical construct, notable for its abstract neatness but lacking a genuine understanding of the complex givens of human nature and of historical reality', Bluhm, *Ideologies*, 2, before being denounced by Marx as a destructive falsehood. Some relevant areas of debate include: A) is ideology inherently negative as most assume or is there a positive or at least neutral role as per e.g. Geertz, 'Cultural'; Ellul, 'médiateur'; Ricoeur, 'Science'? B) does it properly beset only those classes wishing to legitimate their domination of others, e.g, Engels, *Anti-Dühring*; Arendt, *Origins*; or does it have wider application to any system of action oriented beliefs, e.g. Seliger, *Ideology*, or is it inseparable from all human consciousness e.g. Mannheim, *Ideology*; Geertz, 'Cultural'; Manning in O'Sullivan, *Structure*, ix? C) is the concept applicable only to post-Enlightenment societies, e.g. Habermas, *Towards*, 99; Mullins, 'Ideology'; or to pre-modern societies (including ancient Israel) as well, e.g. Meszaros, *Philosophy*, xi; to some extent Geertz, 'Cultural'; and note the ambiguity in Boudon, *Analysis*, 11, 33, 201; J. Thompson, *Surveys*; K. Thompson (ed.), *Beliefs*, 24; MacIntyre, *Against*, 5ff; Coole, 'Phenomenology', 136f? Interestingly, few biblical scholars who use the term seem aware of these aspects of the debate. It has also been suggested that due to these and other difficulties the substantive 'ideology' be abandoned and its critical component—namely the distorting or

complex, and as yet apparently unresolved.[9] Naturally, this introduces a degree of uncertainty into the discussion. However, while not ignoring the importance of accurate definitions, our particular concern is with the dynamics involved in ideology's shaping of community self-understanding; particularly as it is described by Ellul and Ricoeur. But before proceeding two preliminary comments ought to made.

First, the term 'ideology' has acquired negative connotations, due not only to its characterisation by Karl Marx as 'false consciousness' but also in more modern times to the American positivist school of social theory where it has come to be associated with the establishment and maintenance of totalitarian regimes. No such value judgement is presumed here. That ideology is often used to legitimate unjust distributions of power—usually to the degree that it is linked with authority—is indisputable, but whether this is essential or inherent in the unifying role of ideology is another matter.[10]

Second, it is well to offer at least a provisional definition of 'ideology'. Norman Gottwald in his materialist reconstruction of pre-monarchical Israel defines ideology as the:

> *consensual religious ideas which were structurally embedded in and functionally correlated to other social phenomena within the larger social system,* and which served, in a more or less comprehensive manner, *to provide explanations or interpretations of the distinctive social relations and historical experience of Israel* and also *to define and energize (sic) the Israelite social system oppositionally or polemically over against other social systems.*[11]

---

legitimating function to which ideas and myths are put—be retained by means of the adjective 'ideological', see Hanninen and Paldan, *Rethinking.*

[9] On the relationship between myth, utopia, and ideology, see especially Halpern, 'Myth', and Mullins, 'Ideology'. However, the fact that modern ideologies sometimes employ myths suggests that the dichotomy often posited between modern historical time and pre-modern mythical time is problematic. For a helpful discussion of the relationship between religion and ideology, see Grimes, 'Ideology'.

[10] On the relationship between ideology and authority, and the latter's catalytic influence on the emergence of the dissimulating and distorting potential of the former, see the discussion in Ricoeur, 'Science', 228.

[11] *Tribes*, 66; Gottwald's italics. Although having no 'principled objections' to terms like 'religious beliefs' or 'theology' which are often employed in describing Israel's constitutive concepts and attitudes, Gottwald prefers the term 'ideology' in that it takes account of the relationship between religion and social structures. This choice, however, should not be understood as presupposing either any assessment as to the truth or falsity of religious ideas or 'any particular view about the genetic or causal relationship between the religious ideas and the social relations of Israel', 66. In spite of the latter disclaimer it becomes increasingly evident that Gottwald's application of his models leaves him in a position where Israel's early religion is in fact a result of the 'economic and political

Couched in somewhat less technical terminology, but thereby perhaps more convenient, James Luther Adams regards ideology as:

> ... that composite myth by which a society or group identifies itself, not only for itself but also for other societies and groups. An ideology posits the group's goals and the justification of these goals in terms of which the group deals with other groups and with conflicts within the group; it defines and interprets the situation; ... it makes possible group action.
>
> An ideology articulates a myth of origin and a myth of mission ..., not merely in a general way ... but also in relation to the situation in which the group finds itself.[12]

The implications of the various details will be discussed as this Chapter progresses. But, in the meantime, we can perhaps express the salient components of these definitions in a more workable, although obviously provisional, definition where 'ideology' is *that all-pervasive interpretive framework by which a group not only understands itself, but also justifies and projects itself over against other groups.*[13]

b) Weber: Social Relation and Social Interaction

Ricoeur begins his discussion of the social function of ideology with Max Weber's analysis of social dynamics and its dual concepts of social action and social relation.[14] Social action occurs when individual agents perceive their behaviour as meaningful and when they mutually orient their behaviour toward the behaviour of others. The concepts of 'meaningfulness' and 'mutual orientation' imply the existence of a larger social framework. Here Weber introduces 'social relation' which emphasises those stable and predictable meaning systems which provide the common context within which social action occurs.[15] It is precisely at the nexus of social action and social relation that the phenomenon of ideology appears, in that ideology is intimately connected with the establishment and maintenance of stable and predictable meaning systems which themselves are integral to the fundamental need of a group to explain itself, 'to give an image of itself to itself, to represent and realise

---

interests' of the tribal confederacy which it then serves to legitimate. See the critique in Herion, 'Reconstruction', 15; also Gottwald, *Tribes*, 642-49, where his functionalist reconstruction grounds Yahwism in the social egalitarianism of pre-monarchical Israelite society.

[12] 'Faith', 466.

[13] Cf. Ball and Dagger, *Ideals*, 1-3, who suggest it is a generally systematic set of ideas which serves to explain, evaluate, orient, and motivate.

[14] 'Science', 222f.

[15] See Weber, *Theory*, 112-23.

itself'.[16]   In the sense that ideology is a function of the need of a group to provide a rationale for its existence, it is a 'natural ingredient of social life'.[17]

c) Ellul: The Founding Moment and the Mediatorial Role of Ideology

At this point Ricoeur, relying heavily on Ellul, draws attention to the formative influence of the community's founding moment upon its self-perception—its 'image of itself to itself'.   Not only true of more modern examples, as in the case of the American Founding Fathers mentioned above, the same can clearly be seen with regard to Israel where, as is widely recognised, her Exodus memory has not only imposed its categories on other events, for instance, conquest and Second Exodus, but has also profoundly shaped her social and legal structures.[18]

The way in which this past influence is effected in the present is through the action of ideology which serves to bridge the historical distance between the inaugural event and present social consciousness,[19] and thereby to foster social cohesion. (Indeed, it is doubtful if any such community could continue to exist if this indirect connection with its inaugural past were broken.[20]) This is done, first, by conveying the convictions of the founding fathers such that they become those of the community and, second, by propagating the energies of the founding moment beyond their first 'effervescence' into the future.[21]

The most striking example of this 'domestication by memory' is found in the ritual re-enactments, or revivifications, of the founding moment. Here the community's history is retold, the values, energies, and ideals enshrined in its founding moment inculcated, and the community re-constituted through succeeding generations. Israel's Passover *haggadah* is exemplary.[22]   This inculcation is not, however, restricted to ritual re-enactments.   Since life begins not as isolated individuals but within a

---

[16] 'Science', 225.

[17] Boudon, *Analysis*, 11.

[18] See e.g. Fishbane, *Interpretation*, 358-379; Loewenstamm, *Evolution*, espec. 23-68; Daube, *Pattern*; and Doron, 'Motif'. Van Seters, *Search*, argues that the biblical authors, in line with other early Greek historians, were particularly concerned with providing their readers with a sense of identity.

[19] 'médiateur', cited in Ricoeur, *ibid.*, 225f.

[20] *Ibid.*

[21] *Ibid.*

[22] See especially, Harris, *Exodus*.

social matrix, ideological consciousness is also formed, less overtly but perhaps more pervasively, at the level of everyday life. Here the social meanings of shared practices are signified and assimilated at a pre-conscious level and as contingent activities begin to resonate they result in the emergence of an historical *Gestalt*, an existential expression of ideology.[23] So, for example, those social mores and legal structures which David Daube noted had been profoundly shaped by the Exodus, by their very structuring of Israelite society, reflect back and confirm at an everyday existential level the values of that event.[24]

This leads to the further observation that just as motives in individual agents serve not only to justify but also to motivate, so too in societal terms 'ideology is always more than a reflection on the past', it is also *'justification and project'*.[25] That is, ideology's account of the founding moment furnishes categories not only for explaining and justifying the present but also for conceiving the future—which is not unexpected since the mind tends to apprehend the new in terms of the old[26]—and herein lies its dynamism and power. It is, therefore, not a dead thing of the past, but enlivens the present and activates toward the future. This is what Adams refers to when he defines ideology as positing a group's goals and its justification of those goals, linking an articulation of a myth of origin with the group's mission. Likewise Gottwald when he speaks of ideology serving not only 'to provide explanations ... of distinctive social relations' but also 'to energize (*sic*) the Israelite social system' (cited above).

Thus, Lincoln's appeal to the Founding Fathers not only justifies Gettysburg in the present but also undergirds and structures his vision of the future. Israel's prophets too, in addressing an Israel presently in exile, couch Yahweh's promise of a future deliverance in the language and imagery of the nation's founding moment, namely, the first Exodus/Conquest.[27] The same dependence upon the images of the

---

[23] Merleau-Ponty in Coole, 'Phenomenology', 136-7. What Merleau-Ponty is describing here is the pedagogical result of ideology being 'structurally embedded' (as per Gottwald, see above). Cf. Geertz, 'Cultural'.

[24] *Pattern; passim*; cf. Doron, 'Motif'.

[25] Ricoeur, *ibid.*, 226.

[26] Ricoeur, 'Function', 125. Cf. Heidegger's notion of the temporal projection of *Dasein* where understanding is tied to the ability to project possibilities, the shape of which are predicated upon the constructs of memory.

[27] Foulkes, *Acts*, in particular suggested that the reason for this phenomenon lay in Israel's belief in the consistency of Yahweh's acts—if he had done so once he would act thus

founding moment can be observed in several 'prophetic' movements in the NT era, where, for instance, Theudas promises that the Jordan will be divided once more, another prophet announces the repetition of the miracle of Jericho upon the walls of Jerusalem, and the weaver Jonathan foretells miracles in the wilderness.[28] Likewise, various rabbinic traditions regarded the Exodus as the model for the deliverance of the last days,[29] with an expectation in some circles that the Messiah would be revealed during the Passover.[30] Numerous studies on the NT literature similarly indicate that Exodus traditions are significant.[31]

It is in terms of this explanatory and justificatory capacity that two closely related characteristics of ideology become apparent. First, the convictions and energies of the founding moment become the 'overall' interpretative schema for the group not only for internal interaction but also for its understanding of history, and indeed the whole world.[32] Second, this interpretative schema is at the epistemological level of the Greek δοκεῖν or Freud's 'rationalisation' in that ideology's 'transformative power can be preserved only on condition that the ideas which it conveys become opinions'.[33] For ideology to be unifying and socially cohesive it must not only provide an overall interpretative schema but this schema must also become the atmosphere in which the group as a whole lives and thinks. Ideology, therefore, is not propositional but presuppositional and not just for some but for the whole group. It is, by its very nature,

---

again. If so, then this belief and the influence of ideology's categories would tend to reinforce one another.

[28] Respectively: Josephus: *Ant.* 20.97-9; 20.168-72 and *B.J.* 2.261-3; *Ant.* 20.168-72; cf. Mauser, 56ff; Theissen, *Sociology*, 60; Barnett, 'Prophets'; Hengel, *Zealots*; Mendels, 'Messianism'; Neusner, *Judaisms*; Horsley and Hanson, *Bandits*; and Wright, *People*, 170-81, 307-20.

[29] Cf. Davies, *Sermon*, 25-93, 111-21; Kittel, *TDNT*, 2.657ff; Jeremias, *TDNT*, 4.856-64, and the recent discussion in Bokser, 'Messianism'. Ben-Sira, in his one extended prayer for deliverance, prays for a repetition of 'signs and wonders' in a final redemption constructed on Exodus categories, Sir 33:6 LXX; cf. the *berakoth* of the *Tefillah* (7.10, 11, 14, 16).

[30] In analogy to the Exodus, the end-time glory would be revealed on the 14/15th of Nisan (*Mekhilta* on Ex 12:42, R. Joshua b. Hananiah, c.90; cf. *Tg. Yerus.* I Ex 21:42; *Tg. Yerus.* II Ex 15:18 cf. 12:42), and later, *Ex. Rab.* 18.12 on 12:24: 'Let this sign be in our hands: on the day when I wrought salvation for you, on that very night know that I will redeem you'; cf. *Ex. Rab.* 51:1 on Ex 12:2; Jeremias, *Eucharistic*, 207; Black, *Aramaic*, 173.

[31] E.g. Nixon, *Exodus*; Teeple, *Mosaic*; Chavasse, 'Jesus'; Goppelt, *Typos*, 67ff; Bruce, *Development*, 32-39; Dodd, *According*, 74-88; Manek, 'Exodus'; Piper, 'Origin'; 'Unchanging'; Smith, 'Typology'; Swartley, *Scripture*.

[32] Ricoeur, 'Science', 226. Gottwald and Adams note this explanatory dimension.

[33] *Ibid*.

uncritical about its own existence, being thought *from* instead of thought *through*.[34] Ideology is not so much what the group understands about the world, as it is the lens through which the world is understood. This is the sort of thing that Wolfhart Pannenberg describes when he says that the historical events of a given people ...

> ... have no meaning apart from the connection with the traditions and expectations in which men live. The events of history speak their own language, the language of facts; however, this language is understandable only in the context of the traditions and the expectations in which the given events occur.[35]

The presuppositional and ineluctable character of ideology can clearly be seen in that neither Lincoln nor Israel's prophets betray any urgency whatsoever to establish the normative character of their respective founding moments. This much is simply assumed. It is the stuff and substance of who they are. Again there is little question that the Exodus functioned in this way for Israel in the first century.

d) The Media of Ideology: Icon and Symbol
A corollary here is that ideology cannot then be a matter of complexes of difficult and/or detailed facts such as might suit a scholarly recital. If ideology's 'overall' interpretative schema is to become the opinion not just of some but of all then such intricacies must be pared down and moulded into a form sufficiently neat and manageable to be comprehended by the group at large; a process which necessarily involves idealisation if ideology is to maintain its justificatory and motivational character. Ideology's account of the founding moment is therefore 'simplifying and schematic'.[36] Further, given that ideology at this level is concerned with revivifying the founding moment and thus transforming an historical singularity into the typical and cyclical, it is not surprising that its account of the founding moment often takes on mythic qualities since myth stresses the latter over against the former.[37]

---

[34] *Ibid.*, 227.

[35] Thiselton, *Horizons*, 80, citing Pannenberg, *History*, 152-3.

[36] Ricoeur, *ibid.*, 226. Lash, 'Ideology', has pointed out how all recountings of history that seek to discern meaning require the use of analogy and metaphor since they are all not only from finite points of view but also constrained by the particularities of language.

[37] On the mythic quality of founding moments, see Mullins, 'Concept', 505. The mythic both expresses and is appropriated by the consensual side of ideology which is itself concerned with unifying 'around' rather than 'over against', i.e. with the group's internal social relations rather than the external, cf. Halpern, 'Myth', 137.

Since ideology constitutes the group's 'overall' interpretative framework, its schematising tendency inevitably impresses its categories on the community's understanding of its subsequent history which itself is also simplified and schematised. Israel's view of her history, at least as recorded in its Scriptures, seems then to be structured around several major events or periods: Creation, Patriarchs, Exodus-Conquest, Monarchy, Exile, Return, with the culmination to be found in some sort of expectation of a greater restoration.[38] Interestingly, in nearly every case these events are related to key personalities, for example, Adam, Abraham, Moses-Joshua, David-Solomon, various prophets, and apparently some sort of messianic figure. Furthermore, these events themselves tend to be described in ways which bring out their continuity with the concerns, themes, and trajectories of the founding moment.[39]

It is precisely at this point that the operation of symbols and images comes into play. Since ideology simplifies and schematises and therefore is 'readily expressed in maxims, in slogans, in lapidary formulas'[40] it is especially suited to the iconic and the symbolic. Because icons and symbols are not mere shadows or copies of reality but are creative images representing ways of perceiving the world, they have inherent in them 'the power to condense, spell out, and develop reality'; a concept which Dagognet terms *iconic augmentation*.[41] It is particularly this ability to abbreviate that enables them to function as compact and powerful conveyors of extensive webs of meaning and, when used in combination, to become powerful means of conveying and invoking matrices of ideology's opinions.[42]

Consequently, the symbolic revivifications of the past early become ritualised and stereotyped, have their own vocabulary, and are characterised by convention and idealisation[43]—once again Israel's Passover celebration is a case in point. Reinforced from youth, the icon

---

[38] See e.g. Daniels, *Hosea*, who argues that Hosea understood the history of Israel in terms of four main periods: Patriarchal, Exodus-Covenant-Wilderness, Canaanisation, and Renewal.

[39] In the cultic recital of Israel's origins even Abraham's call is subservient to the larger Exodus motif, Dt. 26:5ff.

[40] Ricoeur, *ibid.*, 226.

[41] Cited in Ricoeur, 'Function', 136.

[42] Cf. Ricoeur's discussion in 'Function'.

[43] Ricoeur, *ibid.*

and the symbol of, for example, the Passover meal enable whole tableaux
of ideology's interpretative schema to be invoked. Furthermore, this
iconic or symbolic function is not limited to images or objects. As the
Passover *haggadah* demonstrates, texts also function in this way. My
Professor's use of 'four score and seven' indicates that it was not merely an
allusion to a famous speech, but that it had become, due to its associations,
a 'textual' icon within an ideological schema. More germane perhaps to
the argument of this book is that a similar case can be made for Isaiah 40:3
in intertestamental and later Judaism.[44]

Given this close connection between the schematic and the iconic and
symbolic, it is not surprising that ideology's account of subsequent events
is couched in terms of those icons and symbols integral to its revivification
of the founding moment.[45] Thus the warrior motif associated with the
first Exodus becomes a prominent element in later deliverances.[46] There
is also a reflexive dimension present. Not only do the symbols and images
of the founding moment project forward into the accounts of subsequent
history, exercising a concomitant shaping of the portrayal of those events,
but their very use in that later history instils their use in earlier accounts
with additional significance, thereby exercising a cumulative effect on
their signification over time.[47]   So, for instance, the warrior motif no
longer speaks of only the Exodus moment but also entails associations
from its applications in later scenarios.

In this sense icon and symbol are to ideology what the stereotypical
figure and situation are to the social background of the parables. They
function as pointers to those larger frames of reference within which they
operate and, by invoking particular aspects of those frames, they signify
what particular hermeneutical templates their present settings presuppose.
This it seems is precisely how the phrase 'four score and seven years ago'
functions.   By way of its symbolic character it invokes that larger
ideologically shaped hermeneutical framework.

---

[44] See e.g. Snodgrass, 'Streams'; and Chapter 3, *infra*.

[45] This may well explain not only the phenomenon noted by Gunkel, *Schöpfung*,
wherein the future is indeed shaped by the past, but also the basis of those similarities on
which the whole enterprise of typology is based.

[46] See Cross, *Canaanite*, 91-111; and e.g. 1QM 12:10-14; 19:2-8; Wis 5:16-23; Sir 35:22-
36:17.

[47] See Castoriadis, *Imaginary*, 120ff, for further discussion on the constraints and
influences which earlier traditions of symbols impose on later usage.

One final comment. That ideology is schematic implies that it also tends toward the hierarchical. While certain events are more significant than others and so serve to provide the framework within which those others are understood, each of these larger elements themselves may encompass a series of events. So, Israel's retelling of its inaugural event—the Exodus/Conquest—includes reference to a schematised pattern of ideas and motifs, for example, the dividing and crossing of the sea, deliverance as the complement of the destruction of Pharaoh's armies, the presence of Yahweh represented by the cloud and the storm theophany at Sinai, desert wandering and miraculous provision, the giving of the Law, covenant, the occupation of the land, and the like, all of which stand together in a conceptual cluster as the predicate of the overarching subject: the founding event. Similarly, the New Exodus of Isaiah reflects the schema originating in the first Exodus, in that it too envisages several components—namely deliverance, journey, and arrival in Jerusalem—and these too are delineated further with their attendant motifs of, for example, Yahweh as warrior and shepherd (Isa 40:10f).[48]

---

[48] Although the paradigmatic influence of the Exodus on Isa 40-55 has been widely agreed to by scholars (see Chapter 3), some have tended to minimise its role. Spykerboer, *Structure*, 185-190, who sees 49:20f (*sic*, probably 48:20f); 52:11f; and 55:12f as later additions, denies that the NE provides a major theme. From the perspective of this book these texts are to be included. Herrmann's assertion, *Heilserwartungen*, 297ff, that the Exodus tradition has 'nur noch eine relative Bedeutung' and functions instead as reminiscence fails to appreciate the iconic quality and therefore evocative power of these images within the context of Israel's ideological self-conception. Kiesow, *Exodustexte*, denies any consistent perspective to the use of Exodus imagery, but fails to recognise that the Warrior and journey-to-shrine motifs are integral to the earliest accounts (cf. Ex 15, Ps 78), while Simon-Yofre's argument, 'Exodo', 530-53, that e.g. 48:20-1 and 51:9-11 derive from Ps 78 does not give due weight to the Exodus traditions behind that psalm. Haag, 'Weg', 39, argues that behind 'Die Kombination der beiden Begriffe ... «Wüste» .. und ... «Steppe»' lies the Hoseanic symbolism of judgement to which the Edenic 'redemption' materials are contrasted. However, in terms of the literary approach taken here, 'way' and 'highway' terminology have already been established in Isa 35 as Exodus journey imagery (albeit with wisdom connotations). Recently Barstad, *Way*, appears to deny that the physical return of the exiles was seen as a NE modelled on the flight from Egypt. Although he allows some influence of the earlier tradition he sees the language as metaphorical with the imagery deriving from a wide range of motifs, not just the Exodus, and asserts that 'passages dealing with the wilderness and desert ... should be regarded as poetical allusions to Yahweh's encroachment upon the course of history', 20. Granted that Barstad shows how various NE motifs could be interpreted as originating elsewhere, he fails to do justice to the paradigmatic nature of the Exodus as the model *par excellence* of Yahweh's 'encroachment upon the course of history' on Israel's behalf. From the perspective of social theory, in tending to treat all motifs in a monochromatic manner, Barstad, like Herrmann, has failed to appreciate the primacy of founding moment ideology and its influence on the hermeneutical framework of Israelite readers.

It naturally follows that ideology's icons and symbols, to the extent that they serve to invoke elements within its schema, will likewise assume a similar quasi-hierarchical structure consisting of central and peripheral elements.[49] Consequently, in ideology's schematic account of the Exodus, various constitutive elements such as the inaugural Passover meal, wandering in the desert, provision, guidance, protection, and so on, can be invoked through various icons or symbols such as the paschal lamb, 'forty years', manna, and fiery cloud respectively.

The salient point here is that it is this quasi-hierarchical relationship of ideology's iconic and symbolic shorthand that facilitates identification of precise areas of ideology's map. Certain icons or symbols, either singly or in combination, indicate which general event within the overall schema is in view, while others, once the general event has been identified, serve to focus attention more precisely on a particular aspect of that event. This process of demarcation is particularly important in that symbols, due to their abbreviated nature, tend to imprecision the more overarching they become. For example, in the Australian experience the term 'ANZAC' (Australia and New Zealand Army Corps) is something of an icon which evokes images associated with Australian involvement in World War I. However, the range of associated motifs is so extensive and diverse (for example, bronzed young men, bravery, naivete, camaraderie, the Australian relationship with Britain, etc.) that the term often requires further definition to indicate just what aspect is in view. However, when combined with another iconic term, namely, 'Gallipoli' (the scene of a costly but unsuccessful battle during that period) then particular sentiments such as the futility of war, inept leadership, national identity, and the like, tend to come to the fore. Even so, the use of language like 'such as' and 'tend to' indicates that more precise articulation may well be necessary, depending on what the speaker or author wishes to communicate.

By way of summary: in this section I have suggested that a group's self-perception and its understanding of the world is decisively shaped by its ideology which mediates the values and energies of the founding moment to the present. Integral to the process of understanding are appeals to

---

[49] Castoriadis, *Imaginary*, 127.

various components of ideology's schematic representation of the group's history. These are invoked in the minds of informed hearers or readers by means of icons and symbols whose quasi-hierarchical nature facilitates some degree of precision as to which particular aspect of ideology's schema is being considered.

III. *Ideology and Crisis*

Ideology continues to be mobilising only in so far as it continues to justify, for the generative power of ideology resides in its ability to demonstrate that the group who assents to it, is right to be what it is.[50] It is when the 'realities actually experienced by the group ... (are) unassimilable through the principal schema', when 'novelty seriously threatens the possibility for the group to recognise ... itself', that new interpretations or even formulations of the regnant ideology become imperative.[51] At this point ideology is no longer quiescent but its opinions, forced by events from the shadows into the foreground of more conscious thought, must in some way be defended if they are to continue as 'opinions'. A group's response to this crisis may vary depending on the degree of tension or social 'strain',[52] and on whether or not ideology's interpretative framework is able adequately to accommodate the new circumstances. Either there is a denial of the present and an affirmation of the past, or there is a repudiation of the past along with its interpretative ideology. Mediating between these two extremes is the attempt to re-configure or reinterpret the ideological schema in order to demonstrate that the group's ideology can account for the present.[53] This approach is obviously preferable if it is desirable to maintain continuity with the founding event.

---

[50] Ricoeur, 'Science', 225.

[51] *Ibid.*, 227; hence the inner antinomy of ideology as 'the interpretation of the real and yet the obturation of the possible'.

[52] See Geertz' discussion, 'Cultural', 218ff.

[53] This is somewhat akin to Fishbane's discussion, *Interpretation*, 443-503, of the mantalogical exegesis of prophetic texts that otherwise appear to be unfulfilled and is reflected in Qumran *pesher* technique. See also Rowland, *Open*, 145f, who in describing apocalyptic's considerable interest in and indebtedness to Israel's historical self-understanding points out how apocalyptic, appeals to divine revelation in order to explain events otherwise incompatible with Israelite traditions.

Since the media of ideology are the icon and symbol, one way of accomplishing this is by redefining and reinterpreting ideology's component icons and symbols or by bringing together previously unrelated symbols or icons so that new ways of seeing are opened up in order to explain the previously unexplainable present.[54] Ricoeur, in discussing the nature of metaphor, speaks of the 'increase in reality' which occurs when two previously remote semantic fields are brought together, engendering a semantic clash and shattering a prior categorisation.[55] This is precisely what transpires in Jesus' parables. Using known 'points of reference' to evoke particular social expectations, he then creates a reality which contradicts them or calls them into question, forcing his hearers to reassess their perspective. The perfect example here is the so-called 'Good Samaritan'—a clash of previously remote semantic fields to be sure. Or, on another tack, one may have as subject a Davidic concept of Messiah which has certain ideological predicates such as power, glory, military success, and so on. But when this subject is predicated with 'suffering' and 'lowly service'—and these two also have a place in Israel's ideological schema—then the sort of clash Ricoeur describes occurs, again with the possibility of opening up new ways of seeing. This, it seems, is precisely what Paul is doing in 1 Corinthians 1:18-25 when he draws attention to the bizarre notion of a 'crucified Messiah'.

Given the sorts of examples just noted, this naturally raises the possibility of alienating members of the group since it necessarily requires a realignment of older patterns of thinking which they for various reasons may not be willing to accept. The new perspective may appear either improbable or unpersuasive. In Ricoeur's words, based on the Greek δοκεῖν as noted above, it will exceed those members' *doxic threshold*.[56] Once this happens, debate may well follow as to who are the true heirs of the community's traditions, which is then carried out in terms of fidelity to the ideals and energies of the community's founding moment. So Jeroboam sets up his golden calves and declares, 'These are the gods who brought you out of Egypt', and Lincoln appeals to the Founding Fathers. If

---

[54] This is essentially the process Ricoeur describes in his treatment of metaphor, 'Function', 130.

[55] Ricoeur, *ibid.*, 130f.

[56] Based on his earlier discussion of the epistemological level at which ideology operates, see section (c), page 37, above.

a major issue in the NT is the question of who is the true Israel, then it is not surprising that NT writers should appeal to Israel's founding moment to make their case.

In concluding these two sections it must be stressed that, although I have tried to adduce appropriate examples, the preceding discussion of the social function of ideology is essentially theoretical. It is not reality, but rather an attempt to formulate a tool that can help in understanding a reality which undoubtedly is far more complex than any one approach (or mind?) can comprehend. The model propounded here is an attempt to analyse Mark's Gospel from one particular perspective, and only to the extent that the model provides a more satisfying explanation than has previously been offered should it warrant attention. The final section of this Chapter will seek to outline how the theory might suggest an approach to aspects of Mark's use of the OT with the aim of discovering that 'overall perspective' which gives coherence to his Gospel.

IV. Mark: OT and Ideology—History as Hermeneutic

The thorough-going Jewishness of Mark's Gospel seems undeniable. While much of this could be due to the cultural setting of Mark's story— Jesus was a Jew living in Palestine—that Mark never appeals, for instance, to non-Jewish literature to elucidate his account, suggests that more is involved. That he on occasion feels the need to explain Jewish customs also indicates that this is not because he is writing only to Jews who may not have been *au fait* with pagan literature, but suggests rather that the Markan Jesus can only properly be comprehended in terms of Jewish categories, and particularly those derived from the OT.

This being so, the next question is, what was the nature of these OT categories, how were they organised, and how did they operate? As such things tend to be the domain of tacit knowledge, attempts to answer these questions will necessarily involve some degree of speculation. But we are not without any evidence at all, for while Mark's Gospel may not explicitly answer such questions, it is nevertheless an artefact apparently wrought on the basis of some sort of understanding of the OT.

C. H. Dodd earlier suggested that the foundations of NT theology rested on the shared *Weltanschauung* of the NT and OT authors, an idea further developed by Francis Foulkes when he saw the acts of God as being paradigmatic for the Jews' subsequent comprehension of their history and structure of their future expectation.[57] This approach will be recognised as fully consistent with the preceding discussion of the mediatorial role of ideology and further suggests that Mark's categories for apprehending Jesus are to be located and understood within an ideologically schematised understanding of Israel's history. Ultimately grounded in the nation's founding moment and inculcated by means of the various Jewish festivals celebrated throughout the year, this self-understanding was by its very nature schematic and simplifying—it had to be if it was to carry out its unifying function. Within this framework various icons and symbols, including textual ones, served to evoke the various images and energies of that founding moment.

It is perhaps indicative of the basic validity of this model that, as the survey in the previous Chapter demonstrates, many students of Mark have intuitively recognised the importance of Israel's early history for the hermeneutic that his Gospel applies to Jesus. Numerous scholars focused in particular on Israel's founding moment and have seen in the various Markan motifs and narratives iconic or symbolic references to events within the larger Exodus framework. Naturally enough, the next step was to attempt to explain Mark on the basis of an overarching Exodus schema. So far, all of this is in keeping with what one might have expected on the basis of the social function of ideology.

A problem arises, however, in that these attempts have met with indifferent success. While there are isolated events and motifs which to varying degrees seem deliberately to echo Exodus categories, for instance, the feedings, the Mount of Transfiguration, the sea crossings, and perhaps the drowning of the swine, when taken as a literary unit Mark does not seem to adhere to an Exodus schema.

The explanation of this apparent contradiction, I would suggest, is two-fold. First, Israel's self-understanding not only derived from her ideologically shaped remembrance of her founding moment, but was also powerfully, if not decisively, influenced by her prophets who while

---

[57] *According* and *Acts* respectively.

working within the ambit of earlier traditions also transformed them.[58] All ideology necessarily has some forward-looking dimension, but Israel's distinctive prophetic tradition represents a specially potent impetus in this direction. Consequently, while many commentators have correctly noted the formative influence of the first Exodus, they have often failed to allow for the prophetic transformation of that founding moment into the future hope of a NE.[59] In other words, Israel's future lay in no mere repetition of her founding moment, but in the more glorious prophetic vision of a greater and more portentous NE. That Mark freely appeals to various icons or symbols evocative of the first Exodus within a NE schema is hardly surprising given the prototypical role of the former for the latter. This, I think, is the particular failing of the approach of scholars such as Suhl who, while rightly detecting that Mark's Gospel is cast in the colours of the OT, were unable to grasp the implications of this colouring.

A second weakness of previous approaches is their double failure, first to appreciate the necessarily schematic nature of ideology, and then to discern the priorities which give it its structure. There are two considerations here. First, perhaps because of our bookish training, scholars tend to seek explanations for the relationship between the OT and NT primarily in textual terms, often without giving due attention to the interaction between the text and what might have been in the minds of their authors and first readers, by which I mean, not only how various OT texts were interpreted but the role of ideology in giving shape to the significance of those texts. This is precisely Bailey's point in his treatment of the parables when he argues that their proper context is the matrix of first century Palestinian social mores and expectations. In terms of our discussion, Dodd, whose pointing to a common *Weltanschauung* showed the way forward, nevertheless seemed to miss the crucial point which is that the texts themselves presuppose mental maps as much as they seek to form and influence them. Now if Israel's founding moment is fundamentally a time when she is elected by Yahweh, then surely her relationship with Yahweh ought to be a key consideration in her history, as indeed the biblical text bears out. If so, then it may well be that Israel's

---

[58] See e.g. the work of Fishbane, *Interpretation*.
[59] Mauser, *Wilderness*, similarly tends to downplay the second Exodus in preference to the first. See now also Marcus, 23-26.

ideological construal of her history is ultimately cast in terms of the
initiative of Yahweh in his saving acts and of Israel's response (cf. e.g. Ps
78). The importance of Dodd's textplots then may lie not so much in the
surface of the OT textplot, that is, a place where textual 'gems' lying upon
the surface could be had for the picking, but in the underlying 'subtext' of
the relational dynamic between Yahweh and Israel.[60] In other words,
certain OT texts may be appealed to by Mark because they invoke, within
an ideologically schematised memory of Israel's history, some aspect of
Yahweh and Israel's historical relationship to which that text bears
witness. For example, if Isaiah 6 describes Yahweh's means of judgement
upon an already idolatrous Israel who has rejected his wisdom, then its
use in Mark may well presuppose that a similar impasse has been reached.

The second consideration is that these mental maps are necessarily
schematic and simplifying. A comparison of the first Exodus and its
derivative NE hope such as we have in the prophets suggests a common
underlying schema of deliverance, journey, and arrival at Yahweh's
dwelling (whether Sinai or Jerusalem/Zion).[61] If so, then it is this simple
pattern, rather than the more convoluted accounts that we find in the
Exodus narratives themselves—which texts I would argue presuppose
such a schema in any case—to which we should be looking. This is not to
say that such maps must therefore be simplistic and mono-dimensional.
As will become apparent throughout the book, even a basic schema allows
ample opportunity for development and complexity, but in an hierarchical
fashion which allows for accessibility in spite of the complexity.

Each new level of sophistication assumes a prior level of integration.
Once this prior level has invoked the required overarching schema, one
can focus more precisely on an aspect within that schema by using various
'icons' to invoke frameworks relevant to the particular aspect desired. For
instance, once Mark establishes that he is operating within a NE schema,
then an fitting textual 'icon', perhaps a text associated with the Yahweh-
Warrior, can indicate where in the NE schema one is operating, namely,

---

[60] Sundberg, 'Testimonies', is often cited as having discredited Dodd's 'textplot'
hypothesis, but when examined carefully Sundberg's arguments stand 'open to criticism at
every point', Marshall, 'Recent', 5ff.

[61] It appears that Isa 40-55 assumes such a schema; see Watts, 'Consolation'. Even the
Abrahamic story is one of departure, journey along an unknown way, and arrival in the
promised land. This itself may well originate in a reversal of the Fall: cast out from
Yahweh's bountiful garden/presence, wandering, city of Cain, cf. Gage, *Gospel*.

the deliverance section. Not only so, but that 'icon' also invokes a particular set of expectations on which basis Mark draws his picture of Jesus.

What we ought to have in mind, I suggest, is the ideologically shaped schema of Israel's history cast in terms of Yahweh's and Israel's relationship in which various texts act as hermeneutical pointers evoking sections of this schema. I am not proposing that every appeal to the OT necessarily functions in this way, only that it is not unlikely that a number of Mark's citations and allusions do, and if so may lead to the discovery of an overarching unity, assuming for the moment that such unity exists.

At this point we note some of the conclusions of Christopher Stanley's work.[62] Although appearing after the bulk of my own had been done, it articulates with precision what had at best been intuitive in the approach taken here. In order better to locate Paul's citational method in its first century context, Stanley surveyed citational techniques and tendencies in both Jewish and Græco-Roman authors and concluded that Paul generally adhered to the accepted practices of his day. First, the joining of two originally discrete verses or even commingling the language of such verses into a single 'quotation' to address a special literary or rhetorical concern is not uncommon.[63] Second, whether the author uses verbatim or adapted citations seems determined solely by 'how well the original wording coincided with the point that the later author wanted to make in adducing the passage'.[64] Third, it is common practice for an author either to omit various elements considered extraneous, to change the grammar, or even to replace a word or phrase with another in order to help the reader/hearer apprehend the point of the original text as the later author understood it.[65] Finally, 'the most noteworthy point about the adaptations ... is the sheer obviousness and even naivete with which many of them are carried out', which in the light of the ease with which various changes could be detected suggests the social acceptability of such practices.[66] After some brief comments on the way Græco-Roman hearers would have experienced the 'text', Stanley then proposes that '"interpretive renderings" are thus an integral part of every public presentation of a written

---

[62] *Language*.
[63] *Ibid.*, 342. On Mark's use of this technique see also Kee, 'Function', 175ff.
[64] *Ibid.*
[65] *Ibid.*, 343ff.
[66] *Ibid.*, 347f. See also the work of Fishbane, *Interpretation*, cited above.

text, a reality well understood and perhaps even anticipated by ancient audiences'.[67] This is even more so in the Jewish milieu where the reinterpretation of texts was inherent in their use of the Scriptures (e.g. Chronicles 'rewriting' of Kings, and the so-called 'rewritten Bible').[68]

On the basis of Stanley's findings, it seems highly likely that informed readers/hearers would not only have noted alterations but also have recognised that the altered form was of interpretative significance. It is not too big a step to suggest that they may also have been generally aware of the original context of a given passage and so have been equally alert to the implications of changes between the original context and the present setting. (Perhaps the Jewish leaders' response to what seems to be Jesus' retelling of Isa 5's vineyard parable in Mk 12:1ff is an example of this very process.) This 'sensitivity' parallels what Bailey proposed regarding the parables, and further undergirds what we have suggested with respect to a similarly assumed pattern of OT interpretation and expectation. Since there seems no reason to suggest that Mark operates any differently from Paul or his contemporaries, our reading of his use of OT citations and allusions will seek to take this awareness into account.

To return to the question of a Markan schema, in addition to the use of the Exodus model, many commentators have observed the influence of the book of Isaiah, particularly chapters 40-55, on Mark's Gospel and especially so in the prologue. This in itself already offers some encouragement that an NE schema, particularly that of Isaiah who is perhaps the greatest of all NE exponents, might be of importance for Mark. However, for whatever reason this observation has been confined to isolated sections of Mark and until recently very little has been done to develop it in terms of his overall outline and subsequent development.[69] It is with a view to further exploring this link that we now turn to examining Mark's opening sentences.

---

[67] *Ibid.*, 352; see also the discussion of a similar dynamic with regard to classical Greek drama in Watling's introduction to Sophocles' *Theban Plays*, 11-12.

[68] *Ibid.*, 350-53.

[69] Marcus, *Way*, has now recently emphasised the programmatic function of the 1:1-3 for the Gospel where Jesus is identified with 'Yahweh's triumphal march through the wilderness to Zion in an act of holy war on behalf of his people', 200.

Chapter 3: Mark's Introductory Citation

Mark's only editorial OT citation, occurring in his opening sentence, is programmatic for his Gospel. Perhaps reflecting his characteristic 'sandwich' structure, the Isaianic components invoke the prophecies of the NE as the conceptual framework of his work while the Exodus/Malachi component adds an ominous dimension by highlighting the threat inherent in Yahweh's coming.

I. Introduction

Although Mark's prologue is generally understood as setting the stage for his Gospel, there is considerable diversity of opinion as to what that 'stage' is. R. H. Lightfoot proposed that the introduction, by giving an insight into a Christology which remains secret throughout most of the Gospel, 'puts into the *readers'* hands ... the key which is designed to unlock the meaning of the contents of the book'[1] while Martin Dibelius regarded the baptism as the cue for a Gospel of secret epiphanies.[2] T. A. Burkill saw the Gospel turning on the struggle to understand the mystery of Jesus, already disclosed in the prologue as Messiah and unique Son of God.[3] Numerous commentators took a related approach, interpreting Mark's prologue, particularly the voice from heaven, as 'anticipating the crucial points in the history he relates', namely, the recognition that Jesus is the Messiah (8:29) and ultimately the Son of God (15:39).[4] J. M. Robinson and others understood Jesus' initial victory over Satan in the desert as setting the tone for the ensuing eschatological conflict with the demons, the cosmos, and human hardness of heart.[5] L. E. Keck, somewhat akin to E. Schweizer and

---

[1] *History*, 61ff.

[2] *Tradition*, 231f. Yates, 'Form', also began with Jesus' baptism which he suggested prefigured Israel's 'cleansing' as effected by Jesus in the remainder of the work.

[3] *Mysterious*, 5; cf. Matera, 'Prologue', 12-15.

[4] Lane, 45; cf. e.g. Hooker, *Message*, 5; Pesch, 1.97; Gnilka, 1.39f; Ernst, 31; Kingsbury, 60, 47-142.

[5] *Problem*, 141f and 32, respectively; earlier hinted at by Stonehouse, 21; cf. Burkill, 21ff; and the apocalyptic struggle envisaged by Kee, 75; Pesch, 1.98. Mauser, 93f, understood the differing responses—all come from Judea and Jerusalem (1:5), while only one

Ernest Best, sees the 'way of discipleship' as the primary concept with Mark introducing his gospel with 'the call to follow and the paradigm for doing so'.[6] Others are impressed by the presence of OT motifs, particularly in the opening citation, and either read Mark's Gospel in varying degrees as a repetition of the first Exodus,[7] or, observing along with R. Guelich that Mark casts his beginning 'in the light of Isaiah', stress this as setting the general 'eschatological tone' of what follows.[8] So, for example, Otto Betz, who discerns primarily Deutero-Isaianic but also Daniellic influences in Mark's prologue, sees the first half of the Gospel reflecting the Deutero-Isaianic Warrior who is also the Daniellic Son of Man, while in the second part this Son of Man is revealed as Isaiah 53's 'Gottesknecht'.[9]

Granted that Mark is probably not a first-rate literary genius, it seems untenable to attribute this lack of consensus to Markan ineptitude given the skill evident in, for example, his carefully constructed 'Way' section[10] and thoughtful placement and combination of OT texts.[11] Taken together with Mark's apparent awareness of contemporary literary techniques (e.g. his use of chiasm and hinge structures),[12] these factors suggest that he also understood the importance of his prologue. In literary antiquity the role of the prologue was, by convention, to provide 'an indication of what is to be said so that hearers can know beforehand what the work is about'.[13] In the first century AD, Quintillian speaks highly of Homer because 'his proems made his listeners attentive by his mention of the greatness of the theme and open to instruction by his swift sketch of the plot'.[14] One hundred years later, Lucian asserts that the good historian 'will make what

---

Galilean is mentioned (1:9)—as foreshadowing the on-going tension between Galilee and Jerusalem; cf. Lohmeyer, *Galiläa*; Marxsen, 54-116.

[6] 'Introduction', 370; cf. Schweizer, 'Contribution', 421ff, 431ff; Best, *Following*, 15ff.

[7] Swartley, 'Structural'; Hobbs, 'Exodus'; Farrer, *Study*; Piper, 'Unchanging'; Derrett, *Making*; cf. Mauser; Kelber, 67ff, 'Parousia', 109; Sahlin, 'Salvation', 83; Drury, 'Mark'.

[8] 'Beginning', 12, who notes a number of Isaianic influences in the prologue; also Lane, 43, and Steichele, *Sohn*, 52ff. Unfortunately, none of these authors develop this insight much beyond the prologue. But see now also Marcus who argues for the primary influence of Isaiah's message of salvation.

[9] 'Jesu', 72. Respectively: e.g. Isa 40:3, 42:1 in vv. 2f, 11; and 'der Stärkeren', cf. vv. 7, 12f; Dn 7:10-14.

[10] See Chapters 5 and 7.

[11] As noted by Kee, 'Function'; see also now Marcus, *passim*.

[12] Stock, 'Hinge'; van Iersel, 'betekenis', and 'Locality'.

[13] Aristotle, *Rhetoric*, 1414b. Cf. Bilezikian, *Liberated*, 52-58; Beavis, *Audience*, 32f.

[14] *Institutionis*, 10.1.48f, trans. Russell-Winterbottom, *Ancient*, 159, 387.

is to come easy to understand and quite clear, if he sets forth the causes and outlines the main events' noting that even if 'the subject matter requires no preliminary exposition ... he will use a virtual preface to clarify what he is going to say'.[15] So widespread was this convention that whether you were dealing with 'history, epideictic oratory, philosophical dialogue, political treatise or whatever, your first sentence had to announce what you were writing'.[16] The reasons for these rules were eminently practical, since:

> The technique of ancient book production, the physical nature of the volumen did not allow the reader easily to scan the body of the work to ascertain its subject. The first sentence and first paragraph performed much of the function of the title page and list of contents in a modern codex.[17]

Given this near universal agreement by ancient authorities on the purpose of the prologue, how is one to account for the wide variety of readings offered by modern interpreters? It is proposed here that the present hiatus is largely due to a failure to appreciate fully the 'iconic' function of Mark's opening mixed citation in establishing the interpretive framework for his Gospel. The rest of this Chapter will seek first to determine the length of the opening sentence and then to discern its hermeneutical implications.

II. Mark's Opening Sentence

Although 1:1 has commonly been regarded as a distinct unit, Guelich has recently urged that 'the use of καθὼς γέγραπται and the comparable function of ἀρχή in other »headings« make the reading of 1:1 with 1:2-3 imperative'.[18] Citing parallels in Qumran (with כאשר כתוב, e.g. 1QS 5:17; 8:14, where it also introduces Isa 40:3; CD 7:19; 4QFlor 1:12), in the LXX (e.g. 2 Kgs 14:6, cf. Dan 9:13 (θ)), and in the NT (e.g. Mk 7:6 (cf. 9:13; 14:21); Lk 2:23; Acts 7:42; 13:33; 1 Cor 1:31; 2:9 etc.), he points out that in the NT when καθὼς/ὡς γέγραπται is used as a technical formula to introduce an OT

---

[15] *Hist.*, 53.

[16] Earl, 'Prologue', 856; cf. Smith, 'Theory', who notes four categories.

[17] *Ibid.* My aim here is not to categorise Mark's prologue, but to stress its importance.

[18] 'Beginning', following Arnold, 'Mk 1,1'; cf. Kilpatrick, 'Punctuation'; Ambrozic, 18f. For a summary of earlier views, Wikgren, 'APXH'.

quotation,[19] it never begins a new thought,[20] but instead links the preceding with the following.[21] Verses 1 and 2f belong together. Mark's 'heading' reads:

> The beginning of the gospel of Jesus Messiah, [Son of God,] as is written in Isaiah the prophet, 'Behold I send my messenger before your face, who shall prepare your way; the voice of one crying in the wilderness: Prepare the Way of the Lord, make His paths straight'[22]

and should be construed as reflecting the concerns of the entire work.[23]

But G. Arnold has argued that in extra-biblical literature the anarthrous and verbless use of ἀρχή pertains either to the immediate introduction of a literary work or to the beginning of a main section as distinct from preceding preliminary comments.[24] As there are no preceding comments, verse 1 begins the immediate introduction and therefore verses 1ff relate only to the prologue.[25] However, even allowing the first sentence to introduce the prologue alone, the prologue itself, both in terms of literary convention and on empirical grounds (witness the opinions noted above), introduces the concerns and themes of the body of the work. It would be most unusual if the themes evoked in the opening sentence were fundamentally different from those dealt with in the body of the work.

Clearly then Mark's citation is crucial. As part of the heading it is programmatic for the prologue and therefore the whole Gospel, while ὡς γέγραπται also suggests that it is epexegetical of v. 1: the 'gospel' of Jesus Christ is that gospel about which Isaiah wrote. That this is Mark's only explicit editorial OT citation in the Gospel adds to its significance.

---

[19] Cf. Fitzmyer, 'Use', 7ff.

[20] *Pace* Taylor whose examples do not deal with the whole phrase.

[21] E.g. Lk 2:23; Acts 7:42; Rom 1:17; 2:24; 1 Cor 1:31; 2:9. Mark never begins a sentence with καθώς, Schweizer, 30.

[22] In spite of a verbless opening sentence; Guelich, 'Beginning', 14n26; cf. Stonehouse, 8f; Kilpatrick, 'Punctuation'; Ambrozic, 18; now Schneck, 29-31. *Contra* Lagrange's objection, 1, that this requires an article with Ἀρχή, the word never has one in Mark and further the absence can be explained by the fact that the verse is a heading, Gould, 2n1; Taylor, 152. Turner, 'Text', 150; Lagrange, 1f; and Lane, 42, take vv. 1-4 as comprising a single sentence with vv. 2f being parenthetical. See now also Gundry, 30f; Boring's survey in, 'Beginning'.

[23] E.g. Haenchen, 38n1; Marxsen, 138; Martin, 28; Pesch, 1.75; and more recently Marcus, 12-47.

[24] 'Mk 1,1'. Cf. on the one hand, Isocrates, *Phil.* 1; Philo, *de Sob.* 1§1; *Spec. Leg.* 1§1; Tacitus, *Hist.* 1.1.1; and on the other, Polybius, 1.5.1; Dion. Hal., *Ant. Rom.* 1.8.4; Jos., *B.J.* 1.30. Hos 1:2 is not applicable as it is not the heading of the book.

[25] So e.g. Arnold, 'Mk 1,1'; Cranfield, 34f; Lohmeyer, 9ff; Lane, 42; 'Meyer, 16; Guelich, 'Beginning'.

However, the well-known difficulty here is that Mark does not in fact quote Isaiah; at least not immediately.

III. The Citation

a) An Early Gloss?

One way of resolving this difficulty has been to argue that verse 2 is a very early gloss. The warrants normally advanced are: A) the incorrect ascription, B) the lack of agreement between σοῦ (v. 2c) and αὐτοῦ (v. 3c), C) the mixing of a merged Hebrew text with one that appears to derive from the LXX, D) Matthew and Luke cite Isaiah 40:3 and the combined Exodus/Malachi passages in different contexts, and E) verse 2b breaks the natural connection between the Isaiah reference and the Isaiah quotation.[26]

Although having some force these arguments are not necessarily compelling. The matter of the 'incorrect' ascription is susceptible to another explanation (see below). The lack of agreement presupposes that Mark would have felt constrained to assimilate, but this has to be demonstrated not assumed. Although this degree of merging of different text types is unusual in the NT, singularity is not in itself a sufficient ground for inauthenticity.[27] The later divergence of both Matthew and Luke (assuming Markan priority) may be explained by a preference for common 'Q' materials, but in any case it is not clear that they should be determinative for Mark.[28] Contrary to breaking the natural flow, Mark may have intentionally sandwiched the Exodus/Malachi text between the Isaiah ascription and quotation to ensure that it was understood within an Isaianic framework (see also below)—a technique which is not altogether unknown in his work. Finally, the lack of textual evidence and the coherence of these verses—including the Malachi/Exodus allusion as will

---

[26] E.g. Lagrange; Stendahl, *School*, 51; Best, *Temptation*, 114n1; Robinson, 'Elijah'. Lindars, *Apologetic*, 207, regards it as a serious possibility. Lachmann's conjecture, NA[26], that vv. 2-3 should be deleted has found few followers; see Wellhausen, 4, who mentions Ewald, and Hirsch (cf. Haenchen, 40).

[27] But cf. Mk 11:17, 13:24f; and Mt 2:6; 21:5 par. Jn 12:15; Stendahl, *School*, 99ff, 118ff; Gundry, *Use*, 91f; 120f.

[28] As Taylor admits.

Malachi/Exodus allusion as will be argued later—has convinced most recent commentators of their authenticity.

b) The Function of Mark 1:2f

Many have seen Mark's opening mixed citation as particularly important for his presentation, but in different ways. Most often Mark's selection of these particular texts has been explained on the basis of his concern to introduce John. Thus the phrase ἐν τῇ ἐρήμῳ carries with it 'the full weight of a great religious tradition embracing high hopes and promises as well as deep shadows of judgement'[29] and, as the setting for John's ministry, it bolsters the prophetic and eschatological significance of his activity.[30] Verses 4ff, it is suggested, may even comprise a verse-by-verse commentary on the OT citation where John who appears 'in the wilderness' proclaiming the 'stronger' 'coming one' echoes the 'messenger' who 'cries in the wilderness' and thus 'prepares the way'.[31] This line has been taken up recently by R. H. Gundry who argues with some vigour that 'vv 2b-3 ... covers only those verses whose subject matter corresponds to the OT quotations, i.e. vv 4-8'.[32]

While this view is not without merit in that John is clearly located at the beginning of Jesus' ministry (cf. Acts 1:21-22; 13:24-25 and the other Gospels), several factors indicate that this assessment may not go far enough. The unity of verses 1-3 suggests that 'the beginning' and the substance of what is actually beginning, τόν εὐαγγέλιον 'Ιησοῦ Χριστοῦ, ought not to be artificially separated. Given, too, the role of opening sentences in antiquity—for example, Gundry admits that on his view the placement of the quotations in the superscription rather than at the close of the narrative is 'unnatural'[33]—one would expect them to be descriptive of the whole work, not merely of Mark's brief account of John. Moreover, the emphasis on preparation (κατασκευάσει and ἑτοιμάσατε)[34] allows no

---

[29] On the significance of the desert motif, especially in Mk 1:3, 4, 13, Mauser; Talmon, '"Desert"'; Wright, 'Spirit'.

[30] Marxsen, 37; Robinson, 25.

[31] Lohmeyer, 9.

[32] *Mark*, 31. Later, however, Gundry seems to contradict himself when he argues that Mark's 'combinations of ... pronouns prepare for God's addressing Jesus in v. 11', 35.

[33] *Ibid.*, 34.

[34] Stendahl, *School*, 51; Longenecker, *Apostolic*, 138, see κατασκευάσει and ἑτοιμάσατε as uniting the two passages on the basis of a common expression—the phrase occurs elsewhere only in Isa 57:14 and 62:10, both of which deal with the return of the exiles. On this sort of combination as a rabbinic method see fn. 171, below.

mistaking John's subordinate role[35] and the three-fold repetition of 'way' terminology (ὁδός (*bis*), τρίβους) naturally raises the question as to whose 'way' is being prepared; the answer can hardly be the way of John. Along similar lines, the little that is said of John, namely, his call for repentance (v. 4; Mal 3:1, 23),[36] his unworthiness (v. 7), the anticipatory character of his baptism (v. 8),[37] and the inclusion of otherwise apparently insignificant details concerning his food and clothing,[38] is remarkably consistent with Malachi's Elijah whose primary role was that of forerunner (cf. 9:11-13). Finally, as noted earlier, several points of contact have been observed between the opening citation and Mark's account of Jesus in the body of the Gospel. There is thus a *prima facie* case that 1:2f, although naturally not excluding John in that he is clearly related to the 'beginning', actually imply a great deal about Jesus, who is, after all, the central focus of Mark's 'good news'.[39]

Other scholars, recognising that the Gospel as a whole is also in view, tend to offer only general and largely unexplored observations to the effect that these verses capture 'to a remarkable degree the essence of Mark's story',[40] or indicate that the Gospel concerns the fulfilment of the citation's promises.[41] For those who do attempt to go further, the appearance of ὁδός in both halves of the citation is often seen as proleptic of 8:27 - 10:52 such that 'Jesus is about to begin to go "on the way" which is prepared by

---

[35] Robinson, 24f; Ambrozic, 19f.
[36] Lane; cf. Bowman, 105f; Robinson, 24f. This is clearer in Luke, see Hooker, *Jesus*, 73n1.
[37] Wink, *John*, 4.
[38] Wink, *John*, 2f, 13f, 110; Hooker, *Message*, 8f; Hengel, *Charismatic*, 35ff; Kingsbury, 58f; *pace* Kraeling, *John*, 14ff. The desert played an important role in Jewish eschatological expectations and was in some traditions regarded as the habitation of the prophets (*Mart. Isa.* 2:8-11). Leather girdles are still worn today by some orthodox Jews and a mantle of animal skin may have been standard garb for the prophets (cf. Zech 13:4). Others, e.g. Böcher ,'Johannes', 75f; Guelich; and Gundry, translating בעל שער as 'hairy man' (LXX: ἀνὴρ δασύς, *Tg.*: נבר סערן), reject this identification seeing instead a general prophetic/desert-dwelling image (Zech 13:4; cf. Vielhauer, 'Tracht'). However, given that 2 Kgs 2:13f LXX translates 'mantle' with μηλωτή, 'sheep skin' or 'rough skin' (*Tg. Ps.-J.* to 2 Kgs 2:8 has שושפיה i.e. 'coarse cloak' (Jastrow)) and since בעל frequently means 'owner', Mark may be more precise, especially given 9:13. See also Chapter 4, p. 184, fn. 3.
[39] See now Burridge, *What*, 256, who concludes that the Gospels belong to the genre Βίος and, therefore, that the 'key to their interpretation must be the person of their subject, Jesus of Nazareth'.
[40] Kingsbury, 56f—an insight which unfortunately he neither substantiates nor develops; cf. Meyer, 16f; Bowman, 11; Schweizer; Lane; Pesch; Schweizer; Betz, 'Jesu', 72; Guelich, 'Beginning', 7.
[41] Grundmann, 26; Schweizer, 29ff; Wink, *John*, 2; Lane, 45; Ambrozic, 20; Ernst, 31; etc.

John the Baptiser and which ends in Jerusalem'.[42]   The most
comprehensive attempt to understand Mark's structure in terms of 1:2f is
that of Swartley who discerns (not without some effort) a recapitulation of
Israel's first Exodus way.[43]   A few draw attention to Mark's complex of
Jesus' cursing of the fig-tree and cleansing of the Temple (11:12-21)
suggesting that it may reflect the threat implied by Malachi 3:1.[44]   More
recently Beavis has noted the importance of Isaiah for Mark: he is quoted
as often as all the other OT prophets combined,[45] is the only one named
(*bis*: 1:2; 7:6) and shares many common motifs with Mark: a Spirit-filled
figure who brings a new message of deliverance to an Israel that suffers
from spiritual blindness and deafness.[46]   Finally, as noted earlier, Joel
Marcus has since argued for the programmatic nature of Mark's opening
citation in terms of the Isaianic New Exodus which he briefly develops,
particularly in terms of the Gospel's literary structure.[47]   Strangely,
however, apart from passing comments on a possible connection with
John the Baptist and the Temple and fig tree complex, no one seems to
grant much weight to the fact that Mark has also included the
Malachi/Exodus texts in his citation and that they too might be
programmatic.

Consequently, in order better to appreciate the hermeneutical function
of this composite quotation, it will be necessary to determine the OT
sources of Mark's opening citation and then to examine their OT contexts
and the way in which they may have been understood in Second-Temple
Judaism.

---

[42] Best, *Following*, 15; 'Discipleship'; e.g. also Luz, 'Geheimsmotiv', 25; Ambrozic, 19f;
Swartley, 'Study'; Kelber, 67; Malbon, *Narrative*, 68ff.

[43] See the review in Chapter 1, 19ff. Swartley is indebted both to Kelber, 'Kingdom',
and *Kingdom*, who sees the entry of Jesus into Jerusalem as echoing the Deuteronomic motif
of entry into the promised land, and to Windisch, 'Sprüche'.

[44] Dodd, *According*, 71; Swartley, 'Study', 145; Telford, *Barren*, 163.

[45] *Audience*, 110; 1:2; 4:12; 7:6; 11:17; 12:1ff, but see also 13:24, 25. Cf. Mal 3:1 in 1:2;
Zech 13:7 in 14:23; Dn 7:13 in 13:26 and 14:62; Jer 7:11 in 11:17.

[46] *Ibid.*

[47] *Way*, 12-47.

IV. OT Sources[48]

a) Texts

Mark 1:2f	Exodus 23:20		Malachi 3:1	
	LXX	MT	LXX	MT
Ἰδοὺ[T]	ἰδοὺ ἐγὼ	הנה אנכי	ἰδοὺ °ἐγὼ	הנני
ἀποστέλλω	ἀποστέλλω	שלח	ἐξαποστέλλω	שלח
τὸν ἄγγελόν μου	τὸν ἄγγελόν μου	מלאך	τὸν ἄγγελόν μου	מלאכי
πρὸ προσώπου σου	πρὸ προσώπου σου	לפניך		ופנה
ὃς κατασκευάσει	ἵνα φυλάξῃ σε	לשמרך	καὶ ἐπιβλέψεται	דרך
τὴν ὁδόν [T]σου	ἐν τῇ ὁδῷ	בדרך	ὁδὸν	לפני
			πρὸ προσώπου μου	

Isaiah 40:3

	LXX	MT
φωνὴ βοῶντος	φωνὴ βοῶντος	קול קורא
ἐν τῇ ἐρήμῳ	ἐν τῇ ἐρήμῳ	במדבר
ἑτοιμάσατε	Ἑτοιμάσατε	פנו
τὴν ὁδὸν κυρίου	τὴν ὁδὸν κυρίου	דרך יהוה
εὐθείας ποιεῖτε	εὐθείας ποιεῖτε	ישרו
τὰς τρίβους	τὰς τρίβους	בערבה מסלה
[⌐]αὐτοῦ	τοῦ θεοῦ ἡμῶν	לאלהינו

'In the prophets' (A W f[13] 𝔐) reflects the mixed character of the citation.

Mk 1:2:[T] ἐγώ in ℵ A L W f[1.13] 𝔐 vg[cl] sy[h] sa[ms] bo[ms]] text: B D Θ 28ᵛ 565 pc lat co; probably an assimilation to Ex and/or Mal (LXX) , or Ex (MT), or Mt 3:3.   [T] ἔμπροσθεν A f[1.13] 𝔐 f ff[2] l vg[cl] sy[h] sa[mss] bo[pt]] text: ℵ B D K L P W Θ 700ᵛ al lat sa[P] bo[pt], reflects Mt 11:10 which may echo Mal 3:1.   [⌐] τοῦ θεοῦ ἡμῶν D it] an assimilation to the LXX; Turner's suggestion ('Text', 150) that αὐτοῦ reflects Mt and Lk seems unwarranted.

Ex 23:20: MT [מלאך] כי 𝔐 𝕲 D. May be explained either by influence of MT v. 23, מלאכי, or by Mal 3:1 which appears to draw on this tradition (see below).

Mal 3:1 LXX: ° ἐγώ A Q W ℵ[c] Luc] omit: B ℵ* C. Perhaps an assimilation to Ex.

In spite of the Isaiah ascription, verses 2f appear to be a conflation of Exodus 23:20, Malachi 3:1, and Isaiah 40:3. In terms of the Malachi text both Mark's κατασκευάζω, which seems to render the MT's פנה as a piel whereas the LXX's ἐπιβλέπω suggests a Qal,[49] and his shift from first person

---

[48] See e.g. Gundry, Use, 9-12; Stendahl, School, 47-54; also Steichele, Sohn, 52-77. The fluidity and complexity of both the Hebrew and Greek OT textual traditions means that detailed analyses of this kind should be regarded as tentative and indicative rather than absolute or assured; see e.g. the discussion in Stanley, Language, 37-51.

[49] By the time of the NT ἐπιβλέπω means 'to look at, gaze at' (BAGD, LN, LSJM) or 'to appeal for help' (MM), while ἀποσκευάζω, the predominant choice in the versions for the piel of פנה in the context of 'preparing a דרך' (Aq., Sym., Theod. cf. Isa 40:3; 57:14; 62:10;

to second (τὴν ὁδόν σου), apparently in the interests of his Christology, suggest that the MT rather than the LXX is the source.

Due to the similarities between Exodus 23:20 and Malachi 3:1 there has been some question as to which is in view in verse 2. Earlier scholarship regarded the whole as deriving primarily from Malachi,[50] but some recent commentators, usually on the basis of ἀποστέλλω (v. 2b) and the phrase πρὸ προσώπου σου (v. 2c), consider it a direct quotation from Exodus 23:20 LXX partly enriched by Malachi 3:1 MT.[51] However, the latter option is not as certain as might initially appear.

In the first place any attempt to discern origins merely on the basis of form must reckon with the fact that Malachi 3:1 LXX already betrays the influence of Exodus 23:20 and *vice versa*.[52] Second, Malachi's (LXX) ἐξαποστέλλω, although known to the NT but used almost exclusively by Luke, is never used by Mark who instead prefers ἀποστέλλω (20 times).[53] Consequently, it is difficult to tell whether Mark's choice reflects a formal parallel with Exodus 23 or a stylistically influenced rendition of Malachi 3. Third, since Mark's rendering of פנה in verse 2e suggests the MT, his omission of the emphatic ἐγώ (v. 2a) and his τὸν ἄγγελόν μου (v. 2c, cf. Ex 23:20's מלאך) suggests the MT of Malachi. Fourth, although the position of the phrase πρὸ προσώπου σου (v. 2d) is consistent with Exodus 23, Mark's addition of σου (v. 2f) makes it ambivalent, in that in Exodus it is Israel in view whereas in Malachi 3 a similar expression refers to Yahweh—in Mark's version both apparently refer to Jesus. More importantly perhaps, Mark's apparent presentation of John as 'Elijah' suggests that he intended at least some allusion to Malachi.

The second half of the citation is almost verbatim Isaiah 40:3 LXX except that Mark substitutes αὐτοῦ for τοῦ θεοῦ ἡμῶν, again for apparently Christological reasons. It is commonly held that Mark uses Isaiah 40 to

---

piel of פנה in the context of 'preparing a דרך' (Aq., Sym., Theod. cf. Isa 40:3; 57:14; 62:10; Mal 3:1), is never used in this context in the LXX and does not appear in the NT. Cf. Hanhart, 'Bedeutung', where the controlling influence of the Hebrew form resulted in the diversity of NT's LXX readings; also Manson, 'Teaching', 315ff.

[50] E.g. Moule; Toy, *Quotations*, 31f; Turpie, *Old*, 59f; Dodd, *According*; Swete; and Alexander.

[51] E.g. Gundry, *Use*, sees a minimal influence of Mal 3.

[52] Pesch, 1.78; Guelich, 1.7f. The LXX reflects the interplay of the two Hebrew texts: Ex 23:30, מלאך, but LXX: τὸν ἄγγελόν μου, cf. Mal 3:1, מלאכי; and Mal 3:1, הנני, LXX: ἰδοὺ ἐγώ; cf. Ex 23:20, הנני אנכי.

[53] It also occurs in that ending of Mark contained in L Ψ 099, 0112, 274[mg], 579, etc.

explain the desert setting of John's ministry and that this depends on the LXX's syntactical rendering of ἐν τῇ ὁδῷ;[54] the implication being that it misrepresents the MT.[55] But Mark's use of the LXX may not be a matter of such transparent apologetics. There is evidence to suggest that the MT and LXX testify to competing renderings of a Hebrew *Vorlage*.[56] While the late Massoretic accentuation, perhaps reflecting a perceived parallelism between במדבר and בערבה, is supported by 1QS 8:14 and 9:19f, the LXX rendering is endorsed by the OT Peshitta, the Vulgate, and rabbinical exposition.[57] Although the Vulgate, and possibly the Peshitta, may reflect assimilation to the NT,[58] the rabbinic testimony from the Amoraic period[59] implies that the LXX reading remained a valid alternative. This, in addition to the matter of the imperfect parallelism—במדבר precedes פנה, whereas בערבה follows ישר—indicates some uncertainty about the original force of the Hebrew.[60]

V. OT Contexts

a) Exodus 23:20

The Exodus text belongs to the Book of the Covenant (20:22 - 23:33) which, set in the context of Israel's account of her founding moment, represents the ultimate constitutive document of the nation's identity and significantly exhibits several features amenable to covenant renewal (i.e. revivification) practices.[61] The preponderance of second person singular imperatives is suited to the Mosaic office of covenant mediator, and the

---

[54] E.g. Marxsen, 20ff; Edgar, 'Respect', 57; Nineham; Pesch; Fitzmyer, 'Use', 318.

[55] E.g. Stendahl, *School*, 48.

[56] For the following Bock, *Proclamation*, 95.

[57] Delitzsch, *Isaiah*; Edersheim, *Life*, 2.744; Michaelis, *Matthew*, 1.116. The Tg's pointing is disputed: Stenning follows the MT; whereas Gundry, *Use*, 10; and Edersheim, *ibid.*; the LXX. *Pace* Swartley, 'Study', 145, it is unclear how the deletion of במדבר de-eschatologizes Isa 40:3, especially when ἐρήμῳ remains.

[58] On the unresolved question of the Jewish or Christian origin of the Peshitta, Würthwein, *Text*, 80f.

[59] Str-B, 1.96f; 2.154; but cf. Braude, *Pesikta*, 587, on Piska 29/30b:6, which follow MT.

[60] Gundry, *Use*, 10, also notes that the syntax could connect פנו with קול קורא, and that בערבה could be a late insertion to match במדבר, there being no compelling reason for the LXX to delete it. The fact that the second half of the second line is not inverted argues against inverted parallelism.

[61] Childs, *Exodus*, 455f; Patrick, 'Covenant'; Chirichigno, 'Narrative', 473f; Steichele, *Sohn*, 64. I am indebted to Childs for this and much of the following.

introductory altar law (20:24ff) together with the concluding festival
calendar instructions (23:14ff) points to a cultic setting. The content is
permeated with covenant theology in that since God has revealed his
name he requires legitimate worship and therefore his name is not to be
reviled (22:28), sexual license and idolatry are prohibited (20:26; 22:19), the
weak are to be protected (22:21ff), and justice done (23:2, 8).[62] That these
commands are summarised in the motivation אַנְשֵׁי־קֹדֶשׁ תִּהְיוּן לִי (22:30,
MT)[63] highlights the centrality of Yahweh's and Israel's relationship in the
mores and energies of her founding moment.

The epilogue (23:20-33), from which Mark's text is taken, stands out
from the preceding material on several counts. Its style, with its series of
promises and warnings, differs strikingly from the preceding statutes.
Whereas the focus previously was on Yahweh's presence at Sinai, now it is
on the presence of the מַלְאָךְ and life in the land (last mentioned in 13:5).
Finally, its requirement of obedience is couched not in terms of the
immediately preceding laws as one might expect, but instead in terms of
Israel's relationship to the messenger 'in whom is my name'. The passage
may be outlined as follows:[64]

> 1. On the way (vv. 20-21)
>   a. The *'Messenger/Angel's'* task (v. 20)
>   b. *Israel's* responsibilities
>   i. Stipulations (v. 21a)
>   ii. Warnings (v. 21b)
>
> 2. In the Land (vv. 22-33)
>   a. *Yahweh's* action: destruction of the *nations* (vv. 22-23)
>   b. *Israel's* obligation:
>   i. Commands against idolatry (v. 24)
>   ii. **Blessings** for **obedience** (vv. 25-26)
>   a. *Yahweh's* action: destruction of the *nations* (vv. 27-31)
>   b. *Israel's* obligation:
>   i. Commands against idolatry (vv. 32-33a)
>   ii. **Warning** against **disobedience** (v. 33b, c)

Verses 20-21 introduce Yahweh's promised מַלְאָךְ,[65] defining his role
and outlining Israel's relationship to him. His task is to keep Israel ἐν τῇ
ὁδῷ (LXX) and to lead them into the promised land (cf. v. 23a). Israel, on

---

[62] On the social implications of the Exodus, Daube, *Exodus*; cf. 23:15 with 23:9.

[63] Cf. Paul, *Covenant*, 36ff; Greenberg, 'Postulates', 11f.

[64] Childs, *Exodus*, divides vv. 20-22, 23-26, and 27-32 on formal considerations, taking
vv. 23 and 27 as unconditional promises, but the logic of v. 22 suggests that the latter should
also be understood as conditional.

[65] LXX, Vulgate and ﬡ read מלאכי, cf. v. 23.

the other hand, is warned against disobedience[66] since he will not pardon their transgression כִּי שְׁמִי בְּקִרְבּוֹ—this latter phrase suggesting the virtual identity of Yahweh and the מַלְאָךְ.[67] This seemingly abrupt transition from the divine presence during the Covenant promulgation at Sinai (19:1ff) to the מַלְאָךְ-related stipulations and warnings emphasises the covenantal dimension of the מַלְאָךְ's role.[68] The conditional sentence (v. 22) which introduces the second half indicates that matters relating to the land presuppose a particular state of relationship: Israel must be obedient 'on the way'. The rest of the 'in the land' material comprises a pair of parallel sections, each of two parts, and again Israel's relationship to Yahweh is crucial. Each section outlines the responsibilities of both parties: Yahweh will prosecute Holy War against the nations (vv. 22-23, 27-31)[69] and Israel is to destroy the inhabitants' cults (vv. 24-26, 32-33).[70]

Several points should be noted. Although it is difficult to ascertain the relationship between the 'messenger' and Yahweh, the only apparent reason for the distinction made between them in verses 20-23 is that Yahweh is responsible for the nations' destruction while the מַלְאָךְ is related to the journey along the way. Second, the stipulations (vv. 25-26, 33b, c) and conditional promises of provision, health, fertility, and longevity depend on Israel's rejection of pagan influences and obedience to Yahweh, and imply that possession of the land is based on Israel's faithful maintenance of her covenantal relationship to Yahweh. The final commands are also identical to those at the beginning (20:23): Israel is to have no other gods which again stresses the relational dimension.

In conclusion, 23:20-33 constitutes a final warning prior to the sealing of the covenant (24:1-18) and its primary concern is that the 'integrity of Israel's relationship to Yahweh be guaranteed'.[71] This is entirely in keeping with the central theme of the book, namely, the covenantal coming of the delivering presence of Yahweh to his people. But this

---

[66] אַל־תַּמֵּר בּוֹ, lit. 'do not be bitter against him', LXX: μὴ ἀπείθει αὐτῷ.

[67] Gn 24:7, 27, 40, 48, 56; Nu 20:16 cf. 14:16; North, 'Separated', after an extensive survey, suggests that the basic sense of מַלְאָךְ is 'presence'; for a review of the five main theories, Ficker, *THAT*, 1.906ff.

[68] Knight, *Narration*, 152.

[69] Köhler, *Hebrew*, 98f.

[70] Covenant-making with foreign nations is proscribed since it constitutes an implicit recognition of the other party's deities, Hyatt, *Exodus*, 252.

[71] Durham, *Exodus*, 337.

coming of the presence is also a matter of holiness; sin will not be tolerated.[72] Consequently, obedience to the מַלְאָךְ is the presupposition of Yahweh's coming as Warrior on Israel's behalf, and Israel's continued blessing in the land depends on her keeping covenant faithfulness.

(i) Exodus 23:20 and the History of Tradition

Given the presence of the enigmatic messenger figure, it is not surprising that Exodus 23:20 figured prominently in speculation concerning a heavenly chief servant.[73] The *Apoc. Abr.* 10:1-14 refers to the angel Yahoel in whom God's name dwells (an allusion to Ex 23:20f). In Philo the angel of Exodus 23:20, who bears the name of God, is seemingly identified with the Logos (*Quaest. Exod.* 2:13 cf. *De Agr.* 51; *Migr. Abr.* 174) and the figure of Metatron/Enoch in *3 Enoch* appears to be influenced by Exodus 23:20 (cf. 12:5, 'my name is in him').[74] Exodus 23:20 is also appealed to in *b. Sanh.* 38b which tells of a debate between a rabbi and a 'heretic' over whether worship should be given to another other than God.

The importance of the themes of the delivering presence and Israel's disobedience were, however, brought out in less speculative literature. In the late *Exodus Rabbah* (although perhaps indicative of earlier traditions as reflected in the *haftarah* for Ex 23:20, see below) both themes, interestingly, are interwoven. First, there is the remembrance of Yahweh's presence at the founding moment to protect and deliver the fathers which becomes the basis and paradigm for the future expectation of protection and deliverance of the children (*Ex. Rab.* 32:6, 9; cf. *Midr. Ps* 90:9).[75] This future hope is expressed in 32:9: 'And it will be similar in the future, when he will reveal himself, and redemption will come for Israel, as it is said', citing Malachi 3:1, "Behold, I send my messenger, and he will clear a way before your face". But, second, there is a clear recognition that the sending of the angel was the direct result of Israel's faithlessness and idolatry (*Ex. Rab.* 32:1-3, 5, 7; cf. *Midr. Ps* 17:3)—this duality seems to have been an

---

[72] Also Durham, *Exodus*, xiff: 'the Book of Exodus may be seen as a series of interlocking concentric circles spreading outwards from the narratives of the coming of Yahweh'; Cassuto, *Exodus*, 483f.

[73] Hurtado, *One, passim.*

[74] Cf. Alexander, *OTP*, 1.243ff.

[75] 'He who guarded the patriarchs will also guard the children', citing also: Gn 24:7; 48:16; Ex 3:2; Ju 6:11-4; and Mal 3:1; see also Steichele, *Sohn*, 65.

important feature of Israel's recollection of her founding moment as in, for instance, Psalms 106:19-23, Nehemiah 9:9-25, and Isaiah 63:8-10.

To the extent that these passages reflect older traditions, they suggest that an appeal to Exodus 23:20 may well have evoked not only the memory of Yahweh's presence and redemption at the founding moment as the model for the future hope of presence and redemption, but also the poignant memory of Israel's faithless rebellion which occasioned the sending of the מַלְאָךְ. It might also serve this purpose in Mark.

b) Malachi 3:1

In spite of uncertainty over the date of composition, it is generally agreed that the historical setting of Malachi is one of disappointment and frustration in the light of the Return having failed to meet the expectations fuelled by the pictures of NE redemption offered in Isaiah 40-55/66 and the prophecies of Haggai and Zechariah.[76] Far from the nations flocking to Jerusalem, the returnees were still subject to Persian rule (1:8). The land had not become a paradise but instead locusts and drought ruined the crops (3:11). The righteous languished while the wicked prospered (2:17; 3:14f). Consequently, a crisis of faith had apparently arisen and doubts were being expressed concerning the utility of serving Yahweh (1:2, 13; 2:17; 3:14).

It is against this background of discontent that a brief introductory disputation reaffirms Yahweh's commitment to Israel (1:2-5).[77] Charges are then levelled against both the priesthood (1:6 - 2:9) and the people as a whole (2:10-16) claiming that it is they, and not Yahweh, who have been unfaithful. This establishes the perspective assumed by the disputations of the second half which focus on the prophet's central contention: Yahweh's coming has been delayed because of the nation's sin. The subsequent call for preparation reaffirms the certainty of Yahweh's coming (2:17 - 3:5)[78] and is followed by a reiteration of his desire for the nation's repentance (3:6-12)[79] and then a final warning concerning the fates of the wicked and

---

[76] See e.g. Verhoef, *Malachi*, 284, 294; Elliger, *Propheten*, 188; Glazier-McDonald, *Malachi*, 17; Ackroyd, *Exile*, 260f.

[77] On the linear and concentric pattern of the six major disputations see, Wendland, 'Linear'; cf. Pfeiffer, 'Disputationsworte'; Boecker, 'Bemerkungen'; Fischer, 'Notes'.

[78] Perhaps to establish a new covenant, von Hoonacker, *douze*, 731.

[79] Glazier-McDonald, *Malachi*, 175, 204; Wendland, 'Linear'.

the righteous (3:13-21MT).[80] The epilogue repeats the call to reformation, again in view of the coming day of Yahweh which is to be heralded by Elijah lest Yahweh find the people unprepared and curse the land (3:22-24).[81]

Mark's citation belongs to the fourth disputation (2:17 - 3:5).[82] The prophet's accusation that his hearers are wearying God with their words (v. 17a)[83] introduces the central concern: the question of Yahweh's justice in view of his failure to come to his people.[84] The addressees' identity is uncertain,[85] but considering the tendency to address the people as a whole (1:1; 2:11f; 3:5, 6-9f, 13f) and as the sins (v. 5) appear to constitute a representative list, it seems that the prophet has the nation in mind. However, the primacy of the priests' unfaithfulness in the disputations (1:6 - 2:16) and here (e.g. the threat to the Temple and priests precedes that directed at the people) should not be overlooked, especially as the maintenance of the covenant is contingent on the sincere observance of the cult and faithful instruction.[86] Both the people and their leaders are responsible, although the latter, because of their position, are clearly more so.

The addressees next demand proof (v. 17b). By way of response the prophet first cites their complaint against Yahweh: 'Everyone who does evil is good in the sight of the Lord and he delights in them. ... Where is the God of justice?' (2:17c, cf. 3:15),[87] which is tantamount to indicting Yahweh with covenant faithlessness.[88] He then declares Yahweh's intentions which, together with the prophet's outline of their complaint, appear to form a chiastic pattern centred on Yahweh's presence and justice:

A. (2:17c)   All who do evil are good in Yahweh's eyes   (**absence** of *justice*)
  B. (2:17d) Where is the God of justice?   (**absence** of Yahweh)
  B.' (3:1)   I am sending ...   (my presence is **coming**)
A.' (3:2f)   Who can stand?   (my *justice* is **coming**)

---

[80] 3:22ff MT being appendices.

[81] Wendland, 'Linear', 114, sees here a summary of the whole in a call for reformation, preparation, returning to Yahweh and the threat of punishment,

[82] Sellin, *Zwölfprophetenbuch*, 555; Verhoef, *Malachi*, 176; or *Diskussionswort*, Deissler, *Zwölfpropheten*, 330.

[83] The sinful nature of these words is suggested by Isa 43:22ff; Baldwin, *Haggai*, 242.

[84] Glazier-McDonald, *Malachi*, 124; Verhoef, *Malachi*, 283.

[85] Alternatives are: the whole community, an impious, pious, or in-between faction; see the discussion in Verhoef, *Malachi*, 283ff.

[86] Ahlström, *Joel*, 97; Glazier-McDonald, *Malachi*, 262f.

[87] Verhoef, *Malachi*.

[88] Smith, *Micah*, 327; Verhoef, *Malachi*, 176.

In this notorious crux, we are told that Yahweh is going to send מַלְאָכִי to prepare his way (3:1a, b), and then הָאָדוֹן will suddenly come to his temple (vv. 1c, d). However, this coming, in spite of the people's claim to 'delight' in מַלְאַךְ הַבְּרִית, will not be pleasant (vv. 2a, b).[89]

The major question here concerns the identity of these three figures and their relationship to one another.[90] For our purposes 3:23 (MT) identifies מַלְאָכִי as Elijah.[91] Although some have seen הָאָדוֹן as indicating a 'general recognition of superiority',[92] there are other considerations: A) it is Yahweh for whom the people wait (2:17), B) it is 'his' temple to which he comes, C) although not occurring alone like this as a reference to Yahweh אָדוֹן is used of him (cf. אֲדוֹן כָּל־הָאָרֶץ, Zech 4:14; 6:5),[93] and D) the coming which is to be prepared for is the יוֹם יהוה הַגָּדוֹל וְהַנּוֹרָא (cf. 3:23MT). Taken together these points suggest that הָאָדוֹן is none other than Yahweh himself.[94] This leaves the perplexing question of the identity of the figure in the parallel expression, מַלְאַךְ הַבְּרִית, a unique appellation in the OT.[95]

D. L. Peterson sees מַלְאָכִי and מַלְאַךְ הַבְּרִית as one and the same: a covenant enforcer upon whose success the coming of Yahweh depends (cf. v. 5).[96] Although the latter assertion is questionable—3:24b (MT) suggests otherwise[97]—arguments advanced in support of this identification include A) the common substantive מלאך naturally suggests that the two 'messengers' are identical, B) the third person reference (3:1b) indicates that the messenger is distinct from Yahweh, and C) the structure of the passage,

---

[89] Verhoef, *Malachi*, 176ff.

[90] See overviews in van der Woude, 'Engel', and Malchow, 'Messenger'. The latter argues that the מַלְאַךְ הַבְּרִית is proleptic of the idea of a priestly Messiah perhaps deriving from Zech 6:9-14.

[91] Most commentators regard vv. 23f MT as a secondary attempt to identify the figure in 3:1, cf. Malchow, 'Messenger '. For a defence of its originality see e.g. Glazier-McDonald, *Malachi*, 261-70.

[92] BDB, 11; e.g. Isbell, *Malachi*, 59; France, *Jesus*, 91n31, who sees one figure behind the three titles.

[93] See France, *Jesus*, 91n31.

[94] E.g. Smith, *Micah*, 328; Glazier-McDonald, *Malachi*, 130; Peterson, *Late*, 42f; Rudolph, *Haggai*, 278; Verhoef, *Malachi*, 288f; Cf. Köhler, *Theology*, 31; Eissfeldt, *TWAT*, 1.66.

[95] The exact sphere of this covenant is unclear: i.e. is it Sinaitic, Levitical (2:10; 3:3), or the new covenant of Jeremiah 31:31 which would fit well with the eschatological aspect of 3:1-3? McKenzie and Wallace, 'Covenant', 555, note that 3:7-12 exhibits strong parallels with the fertility concerns of Hos 2:16-24 (cf. Lev 26:16; Dt 1:13f; 28:11f, 18, 28) which suggests the Sinaitic.

[96] Peterson, *Late*, 42; see now also Webb, *John*, 250ff.

[97] Glazier-McDonald, *Malachi*, 131.

with the preparatory messenger and Yahweh being paired in verse 1a-d and then their respective roles explained (the messenger, vv. 1e-4, and the Lord, v. 5), is 'better understood' when the messengers are identical.[98]

However, these warrants are not without problems. Although the use of the third person (הִנֵּה־בָא) suggests a figure distinct from Yahweh, the Lord himself is so described (יָבוֹא) in which case אָמַר יהוה may simply mean 'utterance of Yahweh'. Likewise, verses 2-4 could also be a third person reflection on Yahweh's coming, but in any case hardly require the two messengers to be identical. Second, the severe purging (vv. 2-4, cf. Isa 65f; Zech. 13:9) seems more consonant with the events of verse 5 and of the יוֹם יהוה than the actions of a forerunner (cf. 3:23MT).[99] Third, the 'day of his coming' (v. 2a) more easily refers to the Lord who after all is the one whose coming is central (יָבוֹא, v. 1c). Fourth, the parallelism of the relative clauses, אֲשֶׁר־אַתֶּם מְבַקְשִׁים and אֲשֶׁר־אַתֶּם חֲפֵצִים, and the fact that they are the only figures who 'come' (יָבוֹא and הִנֵּה־בָא, v. 1c, f), suggest that הָאָדוֹן and מַלְאַךְ הַבְּרִית are closely related. Finally, given that the main concern throughout is with the long-delayed but greatly desired coming of Yahweh and that nowhere in the book is there any indication that the people 'delight' in a forerunner, it seems best to identify מַלְאַךְ הַבְּרִית with Yahweh himself. But how is this to be understood?

The unusual designation itself may provide the key since it echoes the enigmatic מַלְאַךְ יהוה whose identity, as seen earlier, appears to merge with that of Yahweh and whose name is 'a synonym of "the Lord" (אָדוֹן) ... i.e. Yahweh, not in Himself, however, but in a representative form'.[100] It

---

[98] See now especially Webb, *John*, 250ff.

[99] Glazier-McDonald, *ibid*. According to Ahlström, *Joel*, 66, 69, the expression 'messenger of the covenant' (3:1) is associated with the great and terrible 'day of Yahweh' (3:23 MT) in which Yahweh makes war upon his enemies, re-establishes his covenant with the faithful, and brings righteousness (צדקה) for those who remain.

[100] Driver, *Minor*, 318; and most others e.g. Marti, *Dodekapropheton*, 473; Smith, *Micah*, 328; Verhoef, *Malachi*, 289; von Hoonacker, *douze*, 730f; Chary, *prophétes*, 176ff; Rudolph, *Haggai*, 278; Lagrange, 'prophètes', 82; Deissler, *Zwölfpropheten*, 331; Glazier-McDonald, *Malachi*, 133; see fn. 67. Webb, *John*, 250f, rejects Glazier-McDonald's view that the 'messengers' are distinct *viz*. 3:1a describes a prophetic figure and the messenger of the covenant is the מלאך יהוה of Ex 23:20. His refutation of Glazier-MacDonald's appeal to Ex 23 is essentially that A) the order of appearance in Ex 23:20 supports his identification since in both cases the messenger precedes Yahweh, and B) the function of the מלאך יהוה in Ex 23 differs from מלאך הברית, cf. Mal 3:1e-f. The difficulties here are that A) the argument from order is ambiguous and still seems to hold because מלאכי proceeds Yahweh whether identical to מלאך הברית or not, and B) the contrast in action is in fact the ironic point of the message (see below).

seems then that the מַלְאַךְ הַבְּרִית is a reference to the מַלְאַךְ יהוה but, given the setting of the delayed NE and the question of Yahweh's absence/presence, couched in such a way so as not only to echo, ironically, the Exodus moment (see below) but also to stress the covenantal setting and thereby to heighten the gravity of Israel's disobedient condition.[101]

The central concern lies in the declaration that the Lord whom they seek, the messenger of the covenant, will come suddenly to his Temple. But, in view of the covenant unfaithfulness of the nation and particularly the priestly community—exemplified by the matters of blemished offerings, 1:6-14, false instruction which 'has caused many to stumble', 2:7ff, and apparently divorce, 2:10-16[102]—who can endure the day of his appearing (v. 2)? Indeed, Yahweh will come as a refiner to purge his people (3:3ff)[103] in order to restore right worship (cf. Isa 65f).[104] Consequently, lest his coming as מַלְאַךְ הַבְּרִית cause the land to be cursed, Yahweh will send Elijah to prepare his way (3:24MT).

On this reading, the essence of this section may be summarised as follows. In the larger context of the delay of Yahweh's NE coming, Israel accuses him of dereliction of duty since he has not dealt with evildoers. Yahweh's response is that, after sending a messenger to prepare his way, he will indeed come but his coming may not inaugurate the blessing his people expect since they themselves may well be the ones who are purged in the judgement.

(i) Malachi and Exodus

Of particular interest here, given that Malachi seems to have the NE in mind, are the verbal similarities between Malachi 3:1 and Exodus 23:20 which, according to Beth Glazier-McDonald, are too striking to be accidental and suggest that the former is a re-working of the latter:[105]

| Mal 3:1 | הנני שלח מלאכי | Ex 23:20 | הנה אנכי שלח מלאך לפניך |
| | פנה־דרך לפני | | לשמרך בדרך |

---

[101] Cf. Glazier-McDonald, 131. On covenant as a major theme in Malachi, espec. McKenzie and Wallace, 'Covenant'.

[102] On this very difficult passage, Smith, *Micah*; Verhoef, *Malachi*, and the literature cited therein.

[103] Cf. Amos 5:18-20, and בא in Mal 3:19 (bis), 23, 24MT, Verhoef, *Malachi*, 289.

[104] Dumbrell, 'Malachi', 49; McKenzie and Wallace, 'Covenant', 554f.

[105] *Malachi*, 130; apparently following Petersen, *Late*, 43f. Cf. Kittel, *TDNT*, 1.83n58; Schlatter, *Johannes*, 17; Pesch, 1.78.

There are also several contextual parallels. The sins listed in Malachi 3:5 are in breach either of the decalogue or the Exodus 23 covenant (see above).[106]   The conditions of failed crops (3:11f) and the famous 'intermarriage' crux (2:10ff) reflect the promises and commands of Exodus 23:24ff.[107] Similarly, the integrity of Israel's relationship with Yahweh which the covenant of Exodus 20ff was intended to preserve is the very thing that Israel's worship now lacks (which further supports the earlier suggestion that Malachi's construct form, מַלְאַךְ הַבְּרִית, may be intended to draw attention to this covenantal and relational dimension). In both cases there is the idea of preparation prior to Yahweh's coming.

It seems particularly *apropos* then, that Malachi, in explaining the delay of the NE, should appeal to a text not only taken from the NE's prototype, the first Exodus, but whose associations include both Yahweh's redemptive action and the sending of a מַלְאָךְ in view of Israel's faithless response. It may be objected, however, that the 'preparation' in Exodus 23:20 precedes Yahweh's action on Israel's behalf whereas in Malachi 3:1 it precedes Yahweh's action against Israel. On the contrary, this ironic contrast is the very point. In both cases the sending of the messenger prior to Yahweh's personal intervention is the consequence of Israel's faithlessness. In Exodus 23:20ff the threat of destruction inherent in Yahweh's coming is directed against the Canaanites who were to be dispossessed of their land because of their wickedness (Gn 15:16). In Malachi the tables are turned in that in Yahweh's coming it is the wicked in Israel who are now in danger of being removed (Mal 2:3).[108] In Exodus 23 the sending of the מַלְאָךְ preceded Yahweh's dispossession of Israel's enemies. In Malachi 3 the sending of the מַלְאָךְ might well precede Yahweh's dispossession of Israel.[109]

---

[106] Dt 5:1-21; Lev 19:13; Ex 22:18, 22-4; Smith, *Micah*, 330.

[107] Whether 2:10ff refers to intermarriage with pagan women or figuratively to idolatrous practices, both are in violation of Ex 23.

[108] McKenzie-Wallace, 'Covenant', 554; and Glazier-McDonald, *Malachi*, 130ff. Swartley, 'Study', 144, sees in Malachi's frequent use of 'Lord of Hosts' an intimation that a new conquest is to begin.

[109] Cf. Ginsberg, *Unknown*, 244, who notes a statement in the *Tanḥuma* (citation: end of *Mishpaṭim*, ed. Buber, 2.88) that in the end of days Elijah will destroy the Gentiles just as the angel in the first Exodus had done (Ex 23:23) citing Malachi 3:24 (MT).

(ii) Malachi and Isaiah

In addition to the Exodus parallels, many commentators have also noted
the striking similarity between Isaiah 40:3's פַּנּוּ דֶּרֶךְ and Malachi 3:1's
פִּנָּה־דֶרֶךְ—the expression is repeated in Isaiah 57:14 and 62:10 in what also
appears to be a post-exilic setting.[110] Given that the terminology is
characteristic of the NE motif in the book of Isaiah (see below), this
suggests that Malachi is referring in particular to the Isaianic expression of
the hope of Yahweh's NE coming.[111]

The post-exilic contexts of Isaiah 57:14 and 62:10 exhibit several parallels
with Malachi.[112] Isaiah 56-66 begins with a comparable warning
concerning Yahweh's imminent coming (56:1), and there is also an
element of threat levelled against false leaders (56:9ff; cf. ch. 65). There is a
similar longing for the fulfilment of the NE promises (64:1, 6f, 15) and the
delay is also explained in terms of covenant unfaithfulness (59:1f; chs. 58-
59; espec. 58:13f; 59:9ff).[113] Yahweh's destination is likewise Jerusalem, his
palace-Temple (e.g. 59:20; 62:11), and there is an equal concern for right
worship (56:1-7; 58:1-14; 66:3),[114] while 59:21 also suggests a new covenant
era (e.g. 61:6, 8).[115] Finally, as Mason notes, Malachi's opening charge of
'wearying' (יגע) Yahweh (2:17) is reminiscent of Isaiah 43:24.[116]

Admittedly, there is no unequivocal evidence indicating that Malachi
has Isaiah's NE in mind, but there is much to suggest that Isaiah's NE had
become a pervasive hope and if so then Malachi would not need to be
overly explicit. A single key word or phrase would suffice as a symbol or
icon to evoke that hope and in that case what better than פִּנָּה־דֶרֶךְ,

---

[110] Vuilleumier, 'Malachie', 243; Elliger, *Propheten*, 206; Glazier-McDonald,
Malachi, 136ff; Sellin, *Zwölfprophetenbuch*, 607; cf. Pesch, 1.78n16; Stendahl, *School*, 51;
and Abrahams, 'Rabbinic', 179. Verhoef, *Malachi*, 287, notes the verbal similarity but
argues for different contexts.

[111] Stendahl, *School*, 51, denies any influence on Mal 3:1 by these texts but without
explanation. On the contrary, as argued below, the return of Yahweh and the return of the
exiles are inextricably linked, cf. 62:10f, 40:10f. On the delay of the NE, see Churgin's
comment on the absence of any festival in the Bible to celebrate the Return in Smolar and
Auerbach, *Studies*, xxv; Wright, *People*, 215-338; the language in *berakoth* 2, 8, 10, and 14 of
the *Tefillah*, and the use of Isa 40 in second Temple Jewish literature (pp. 82ff below).

[112] Hanson's innovative reconstruction of this period, *Dawn*, (cf. Achtemeier,
Community) has recently been subject to some criticism, see e.g. Williamson, 'Concept'.

[113] I have argued elsewhere that within the context of the book as a whole Isa 40-55
has a similar role, cf. Watts, 'Consolation'.

[114] On this see below and especially Dumbrell, 'Purpose', and 'Worship', 6f.

[115] Cf. Fischer, *Yahwe*.

[116] *Preaching*, 249.

especially in a context where the point at issue is the promise of Yahweh's coming (cf. Isa 40:3b). Finally, as with his echoing of Exodus 23, there is an ironic reversal. While his audience may have conceived of the INE in terms of deliverance and exaltation, Malachi, as do the later chapters of Isaiah, reflects an awareness of the threat inherent in Yahweh's coming.[117]

(iii) Exodus or Isaiah?

Given the above, which of these settings does Malachi have in mind: Exodus 23 or Isaiah 40ff? The discussion above suggests that the larger issues of both are in view and that Malachi has used the one to interpret the other. This is not surprising since Isaiah's NE obviously presupposes the schema of the first Exodus (see below). On the one hand, he may well use Isaiah's 'preparing-the-way' motif because of the positive redemptive connotations of the INE. On the other, by combining this with the Exodus motifs of covenant/warning and messenger/preparation (i.e. מַלְאַךְ הַבְּרִית) he stresses that Israel's sin means that Yahweh's NE coming may not be the entirely unmitigated blessing otherwise expected, a concern similar to that found in the later chapters of Isaiah.

(iv) Malachi 3:1 and the History of Tradition

Given the discussion above it is not surprising that Exodus 23:20 and Malachi 3:1 were related in later Jewish traditions. J. Mann indicates that when Exodus 23:20 was read (*Seder* 61a) the *haftarah* included Malachi 3:1-8 and 23f.[118] As noted above, in *Ex. Rab.* 32:9 the two texts are seen as reflections on Yahweh's founding moment protection with the Exodus event providing the paradigm for the future hope expressed in Malachi.[119] While most of this evidence is late, it may well indicate earlier traditions; a possibility strengthened by the forms of both texts in the MT and the LXX which suggest that they were closely related at a very early stage.

Malachi 4:5's identification of the messenger as Elijah *redivivus* (LXX: τὸν Θεσβίτην 'the Tishbite'), gave rise to lively speculation in some eschatological traditions (e.g. Sir 48; *1 Enoch* 90:31; *Sop.* 19:9; *Tg. Ps.-J.* Dt 30:4;

---

[117] McKenzie and Wallace, 'Covenant', 554.

[118] *Bible*, 479.

[119] Michaelis, *TDNT*, 5.70n96; Robinson, 'Elijah'; reference is also made to Str-B, 1.597, but the evidence here is ambiguous. *Dt. Rab.* 11:9 is also commonly cited but seems less relevant in that the connecting theme is the term 'behold'.

Pesiq. R. 35.4; *Sipre Dt.* 41; *Pirqe R. El.* 43 [25a]; cf. Justin, *Dial.* 8, 4; cf. 49, 1).[120] The origins of the further association of this Elijah *redivivus* with the coming of 'the Messiah' (however conceived),[121] is a matter of considerable debate.[122] But in view of the belief apparently held by some that the Messiah's coming was in some way associated with the day of Yahweh,[123] the idea that Elijah would precede Messiah is understandable, although extra-New Testament evidence for such a belief in pre-Christian Judaism is thin.[124] It is important to note, however, that there is no

---

[120] Cf. the discussions in Jeremias, *TDNT*, 2.931ff; Friedrich, *TDNT*, 2.716; Moore, *Judaism*, 2.359f; Ginzberg, *Unknown*, 212, 243-55; Black, 'Witnesses', 227ff; Malchow, 'Messenger', 254; Böcher, 'Johannes', 75f; Steichele, *Sohn*, 67f; Str-B, 1.597; 3.9; 4/2.784-9.

[121] The literature on messianism is immense, Schürer 2.488-554; Klausner, *Messianic*, 246-531; Urbach, *Sages*, 649-92; Neusner, *Messiah*; Charlesworth, *Messiah*; and the works cited *infra* in regard to various specifics. On messianism comprising relatively stable and generally accepted beliefs, Horbury, 'Messianic', 38ff; on their diversity see Charlesworth, 'Concept', 'Messianology'. Charlesworth, 'Messianology', 35, asserts that the 'gospels and Paul must not be read as if they are reliable sources for pre-70 Jewish beliefs in the Messiah'. Given that C. is willing to marshal evidence from such a wide range of Jewish literature, it is difficult to understand why he should *a priori* exclude from his 'reliable sources' a body of literature written at least in part by Jews for Jews, inspired by a Jewish figure, and replete with both Jewish imagery and allusions to Jewish Scriptures.

[122] Especially Ginzberg, *Unknown*, 243ff; Faierstein, 'Why'; Allison, 'Elijah'; Fitzmyer, 'More'; Milikowsky, *'lyhw'*.

[123] Fitzmyer, 'More', disputes Allison's assertion, 'Elijah', that 'many first-century Jews' believed 'a Messiah would come on the day of the Lord'. At the outset this seems to me to be a reflection of the kind of scholarly atomism which Wright's, *People*, so effectively challenges (cf. also Chapter 1, p.7, fn.39). Nevertheless, *Pss. Sol.* 17:21-42 describes a messianic figure, the events surrounding whose advent (e.g. the destruction of unrighteous rulers and exposing corrupt officials, the purging of Jerusalem, God's gathering of a holy people) cohere with Malachi's 'day of Yahweh' (e.g. 3:2ff, 19-24 MT). 1QSa also details the preparation of the congregation of the last days (1:1f) for the coming of the two Messiahs (2:11ff), whose appearance inaugurates the climactic battle against evil (cf. also Josephus' accounts of numerous messianic movements leading up to the first revolt). The descriptions of this battle in 1QM and 4QM and 1QM 1:11's reference to this time as the הווה ליום i.e. on 'the day of Misfortune' (or 'the Day of Him who is' i.e. 'the Day of Yahweh', Dupont-Sommer, *Essene*, 171; or 'the day of calamity', Vermes, *DSSE*, 105), strongly suggest the possible connection, at least in some traditions, between the coming of a messianic figure and 'the day of Yahweh'; *pace* Fitzmyer, 296; cf. 1QS 9:11 (Dupont-Sommer, *Essene*, 94n3); 4Q174 1:10-13, 18f; *T. Levi* 18:1-9; *T. Judah* 24:1-6; Eversan, 'Days'; Brown, 'Messianism'; Beasley-Murray, 'Messiahs'; Vermes, *DSSE*, 52ff; Marcus, '"Written"', 47n2; Wright, *People*, 307-20.

[124] Faierstein, 'Why', 86, after examining the evidence commonly presented argues that there is almost no case for this concept being 'widely known or accepted in the first century C.E.' (cf. Fitzmyer, *Luke*, 671ff) although he does allow *b. 'Erub.* 43a-b as a possible, but flimsy, exception. Allison, 'Elijah', who challenged Faierstein has been criticised by Fitzmyer, 'More', because: A) Mark 9:9-12 makes no mention of a Messiah and the coming of Elijah 'first' could easily relate to the resurrection of the dead (cf. *m. Soṭa* 9:18, Allison, 257), and B) *b. 'Erub.* 43a-b cannot with certainty be attributed to first-century Palestinian Judaism (fn. 123). Faierstein's rejection of some of the evidence may be precipitate: A) the

specific mention of any messianic figure in Malachi.[125] The focus is instead on the threat inherent in Yahweh's coming, as per Sirach 48:10, where the task of Elijah is 'to calm the wrath of God before it breaks out in fury' by turning the heart of the father to the son and restoring the tribes of Jacob.[126]

c) Isaiah 40:3

The book of Isaiah is commonly recognised as falling into three major literary units. Chapters 1-39 deal primarily with the events prior to Judah's exile, chapters 40-55 cover events toward the end of that exile, and chapters 56-66 apparently concern some time after the return.[127] A second section is introduced by 40:1 while 40:12-31 constitutes a change to a polemical tone. This, along with internal considerations such as the linking phrases אֱלֹהֵיכֶם (vv. 1, 9) and אֱלֹהֵינוּ (vv. 3, 8), the key-word 'Jerusalem' in verses 1f and 9ff, the three הִנֵּה clauses in verses 9ff which balance the three causal clauses in verses 1f, and the imperative patterns in verses 1f and 9ff,[128] suggests that verses 1-11 should be treated as a unit with verses

---

papyrus fragment 4QarP (?) (Starcky, 'étapes', 497f), where the reading 'I shall send you Elijah befo[re] ...' is preceded by a reference to 'the eighth as an Elect One', itself perhaps a reference to David (1 Sam 16:10ff), may indicate the presence of this belief in Qumran (Fitzmyer's cautions notwithstanding, 'Aramaic', 355); B) Ginzberg's reference, *Unknown*, 250ff, to an early Palestinian, Pharisaic *berakhoth* associated with the *haftarah* clearly links the two figures (שמחנו ... באליהו הנביא עבדך ובמלכות בית דוד), even if not specifying the nature of the relationship (Faierstein, 85); C) Milikowsky, ''*lyhw'*, has recently argued that the presence of a two-appearance tradition—at the time of the Messiah and later at the time of war with Gog—in the relatively early *Seder 'Olam* (cf. Milikowsky, '*Sdr-'wlm'*) suggests that it is Jewish, not Christian, in origin. The cumulative effect of this evidence suggests that *b. 'Erub.* 43a-b, and consequently Justin's *Dial.*, 8, 4 (cf. 49, 1), should not be dismissed so easily.

[125] E.g. Robinson, 'Elijah', 263ff; Moule, *Phenomenon*, 71; France, *Jesus*, 92n31.

[126] Webb, *Baptizer*, 252, sees in *Liv. Proph.* 21:3 ('his word is judgement, and he will judge Israel' with most manuscripts adding that this judgement is 'with sword and fire') a reference to Elijah's *redivivus* ministry. It is perhaps better seen as referring to the two events subsequently related concerning the prophets of Baal (v. 10, killed by the sword) and Ahaziah's soldiers (v. 12, consumed by fire).

[127] Sweeney, *Isaiah*, 88, summarises the arguments for including chapter 55 with 56-66 although he acknowledges that it was first written as a conclusion to 40-54. At most he establishes that 55 serves as a bridge to 56-66. There are, however, literary-thematic structures that are best understood on the basis of the division 55/56: the structural role of the disputations within 40-55, Watts, 'Consolation', and the chiastic pattern in 56-66, Charpentier, *Jeunesse*, 79-80; Gottwald, *Hebrew*, 308; Polan, *Ways*, 14-5. Hessler, *Gott*, 98, 102, 253ff, sees 40:1-11 and 55:1-13 reflecting the structure of 40-55, their similarity indicating their function as prologue and epilogue.

[128] Dumbrell, 'Purpose', 123f.

1f and 9ff functioning as inclusios.[129] Whether or not some or all of these verses constitute a call narrative does not concern us here,[130] for it is the message not the messenger which is most important as is borne out by the veiled and ambiguous language surrounding his identity.[131]

The opening declaration in verses 1f, נַחֲמוּ נַחֲמוּ, sets the tone of the announcement and is most marked in the second half of the book which focuses on Jerusalem/Zion (49:13; 51:3, 12; 52:9).[132] This comfort is articulated in the parallel statements that Jerusalem's time of service is ended and her iniquity pardoned (v. 2). Using imagery that is commonly understood to reflect that of the ceremonial parades of Babylonian deities,[133] a call goes out for the preparation of the way for Yahweh's triumphant return to his people (vv. 3-5). The concluding phrase of this section, כִּי פִּי יהוה דִּבֵּר, introduces the theme of the third section (vv. 6-8): the eternal supremacy of Yahweh's word over the 'grass-like' intentions of men and by implication their idols.[134] Babylon's power was celebrated in the festivals marking the coming of their deities into the city, but now a far greater One was coming to his people and his coming would wither the pretensions of Babylon and its man-made gods. Similarly, just as many nations had witnessed Babylon's power, now כָּל־בָּשָׂר would see Yahweh's glory. On this basis the fourth and final section (vv. 9-11) commands Jerusalem to announce to the cities of Judah the news of Yahweh's return. On the one hand, he is depicted as the mighty warrior (v. 10; LXX: μετὰ ἰσχύρος) returning from pillaging his foes and bearing his people as his booty (שְׂכָרוֹ ...וּפְעֻלָתוֹ)[135] while on the other he is portrayed as a gentle shepherd bringing his 'flock' to Jerusalem (v. 11).

---

[129] The most comprehensive recent work is Kiesow, *Exodustexte,* 23-66, although his fragmentation of 6-8 and 9-11 is not convincing; also e.g. Hessler, *Gott;* Melugin, *Formation,* 82ff; Westermann; Schoors, *Saviour;* Spykerboer, *Structure,* 183f; Sweeney, *Isaiah,* 66f.

[130] E.g. Westermann, 31ff; Begrich, *Studien,* 61; Melugin, *Formation,* 83f.

[131] Westermann, 32, in view of the veiled terms and ambiguity of the speaker; Melugin, *Formation,* 84.

[132] On this contrast, particularly Mettinger, *Farewell,* 26; Hessler, *Gott,* 82ff; Melugin, *Formation,* 85; Kiesow, *Exodustexte,* 163; recently Wilcox and Paton-Williams, 'Servant', 82ff.

[133] Stummer, 'Einige', was one of the first to note this association.

[134] E.g. Westermann sees here a reflection of Israel's lament; while for Kiesow, *Exodustexte,* 37, it is 'sondern positiven Inhalt des Rufbefehls'.

[135] Elliger, *Deuterojesaja,* 37, prefers 'wages' as in the Jacob story (Gn 30:28-33; 31:8). However, Yahweh is scarcely a hireling. The military imagery is to be preferred, cf. Ezek 29:18ff with the parallel use of these terms and שלל and בז in the context of military campaign, cf. Begrich, *Studien,* 59.

It has been argued that these 'four sub-sections deal with major themes which are developed further in the book' (vv. 1f, 3-5, 6-8, 9-11).[136] Thus, the declaration of comfort sets the tone for the whole, the call to prepare the way alludes to the transformation of the desert (e.g. 41:17ff; 42:16f; 43:20 etc.), all flesh seeing Yahweh's glory is reflected in, for example, 52:10, the supremacy of Yahweh's word is echoed throughout (42:21; 44:26-28; 45:23; 46:10f; 48:14; 53:10; 55:10-14), and finally the introitus of Yahweh into Jerusalem is the central fact upon which all else hangs.[137]

From another perspective, verses 1-8 and 9-11 may constitute micro-cosms of chapters 40-48 and 49-55 respectively.[138] The image of the highway through the desert (vv. 3-5) recurs throughout chapters 40-48 (e.g. 41:17-20; 43:19-20), as do the motifs of the revelation of Yahweh's glory (v. 5; cf. 42:8ff; 43:7; 48:11; but see the epilogue 55:13b) and the reliability of Yahweh's word (but see also 55:10-11).[139] The feminine singular address in vv. 9ff anticipates the concern for Jerusalem/Zion in the last half (49:14-26; 51:9 - 52:12; ch. 54; 50:1-3), the messenger announcing Yahweh's return as king reappears in 52:7-10, and the victory of Yahweh's 'arm' in 51:5, 9; 52:10; 53:1.

Along similar lines, K. Kiesow notes that Jerusalem appears in the inclusio passages of verses 1-2 and 9-11.[140] He proposes that the three themes of the prologue are developed throughout chapters 40-55: consolation for Jerusalem (40:1-2, 9-11; 49:1 - 52:12), NE from Babylon (40:3-5; 40:12 - 48:22), and the power of the proclamation of the divine word to effect these transformations (40:6-8; 52:13 - 55:13). Although differing in their details these various approaches demonstrate the role of 40:1-11 as prologue in introducing the major themes developed throughout chapters 40-55.

---

[136] Spykerboer, *Structure*, 183f; also Hessler, *Gott, passim*; Melugin, *Formation*, 85; Bonnard, *Second*, 85; Kiesow, *Exodustexte*, 165.

[137] Spykerboer, *Structure*, 183.

[138] Melugin, *Formation*, 85f. Kiesow, *Exodustexte*, 165, followed by Dumbrell, 'Purpose', 124, sees vv. 6-8's reference to Yahweh's powerful word as foreshadowing 52:13-55:13. However, on the basis of the disputations in chs. 40-8 concerning Yahweh's ability and the reliability of his word, Melugin's proposal is preferable; cf. now Seitz, 'Divine'.

[139] Melugin, *ibid.*, also notes that the tense structure of vv. 1-2 'corresponds to the tense sequence of the salvation-assurance oracles' which, while pivotal to chapters 41-48, are relatively unimportant in chapters 49ff.

[140] *Exodustexte*, 23-66, cf. his diagram, 165.

(i) The Consolation: Announcement of the NE Deliverance

Although there has been some debate over the exact nature and form of the compositional unity of chapters 40-55, recent commentators have recognised their thematic unity.[141] The most universally recognised characteristic of these chapters is the great quantity of salvation words. The contrast to the preceding chapters is such that, 'When one turns from the thirty-ninth to the fortieth chapter it is as though he steps out of the darkness of judgement into the light of salvation.'[142]

Exodus typology, of some significance in chapters 1-39,[143] is central to this salvation theme.[144] Although other canonical writings appeal to the Exodus tradition,[145] here it is elevated to its most prominent status as a hermeneutic, and according to some commentators, shapes the heart of 40-

---

[141] The form critics Gressman, Köhler, Mowinckel, and Begrich viewed these chapters as independent oracles now artificially linked. Torrey and Muilenburg, in judging the forms of speech used by the prophet to be different in kind from his predecessors, saw instead a unified whole with a discernible literary progression. This debate has been mediated by Melugin, *Formation*, and Westermann, 'Sprache', *Isaiah*, who, although they tend to emphasise the contribution of one approach (Melugin smaller units, Westermann, longer), do not do so to the exclusion of the other. Schoors, *Saviour*, 296ff, and Elliger, *Deutero-jesaja*, deny an overall structure, but recognise a coherence to the prophet's thought. Bonnard, *Isaïe*, Lack, *Symbolique*, and Spykerboer, *Structure*, argue for a careful structure.

[142] Young, *Isaiah*, 17.

[143] Fishbane, 'Motif', 126ff. Exodus traditions can be seen in the דֶּרֶךְ through the desert motif (espec. ch. 35, Koch, *TWAT*, 2.301f), the return from exile (11:11f, 16; 19:23ff; 27:12f; see relevant sections in Wildberger; Kaiser), the theophany over restored Jerusalem (4:5f; cf. 25:4f, Kaiser, 2.57, also Ex 40:34; Num 9:15ff), and the combination of the mountain of the Lord and his glory before his elders (24:23 cf. Ex 24:9-11). The influence of Ex 15 on Isa 12 has long been noted, cf. Ackroyd, 'Presentation', 35ff, who describes ch. 12 as the climax and summary of chs. 1-11, highlighting three themes: the Exodus, Zion, and the exaltation of Yahweh (12:3 may refer to the water from the rock although it could be a reference to the water ritual of Tabernacles, cf. Mowinckel, *Psalmenstudien*, 2.100; and *Psalms*, 1.123n58; 131; 187). Perhaps also 27:1 (if the serpent refers to Egypt, cf. 30:7), 27:8 (the east wind, Ex 14:21), and 37:36 (the angel of the Lord, Ex 12:23); see Sweeney, *Isaiah*, 19.

[144] Clements, 'Unity', 121-5; Childs, *Introduction*, 328; Rendtorff, 'Komposition', 298, who notes the relationship between ch. 12 and ch. 40 (see fn. 143). See especially Anderson, 'Typology', 'Covenant', and Stuhlmueller, *Creative*, 59-98, who lists the following 'exodus' passages: 40:3-11; 41:17-20; 42:14-7; 43:1-7, 16-21; 44:1-5, 27; 48:20f; 49:8-12; 50:2; 51:9-10; 52:11f and 55:12f; also Stuhlmueller's table summarising commentators' opinions (note the lacuna on 48:20f), 272. Further Zillessen, 'Exodus'; Fischer, 'Problem'; Rose, 'Exodus'; Zimmerli, 'Verkündigung'; Beaudet, 'typologie'; Harvey, 'typologie'; Lubsczyk, *Auszug*; Blenkinsopp, 'Scope'; Fishbane, 'Motif', 132-8; Westermann, 22; Muilenburg, 399ff, 602; Dahl, *Volk*, 38-42; cf. van der Merwe, 'Echoes', 174, 244 (cited in Schoors, *Saviour*, 173); and Harner, 'Creation', 303. The same exodus imagery can also be found in several of the expanded readings in the *Tg. Isa* e.g. 43:2ff; 63:1ff; cf. Chilton, *Targum*, notes *passim*. See Chapter 2, p. 43, fn. 47, for a response to those critical of a pervasive NE schema.

[145] Hos 2:16-17 (MT); 11:1; 12:10-14 (MT); 13:4-5; Am 2:9f; 3:1f; 9:7; Mic 6:4; Jer 2:6f; 7:22, 25; 11:4, 7; 16:14f (=23:7f); 31:32; 32:20ff; 34:13f; Ezek 20:5-10; Anderson, 'Typology', 181.

55[146] even replacing the first Exodus as *the* saving event.[147] The allusions cover the whole Exodus experience, and their appearance in the prologue, the end of the first section (48:20ff), and the epilogue (55:12f) stress its significance. Of course, given the discussion of the preceding Chapter ('History as Hermeneutic'), none of this is unexpected. If Israel's founding moment was predicated on Yahweh's redemptive action in the Exodus from Egyptian bondage, then surely a second deliverance from exilic bondage, this time of Babylon, could scarcely be conceived of in other terms except those of the first Exodus?

The catalytic event is the summons to prepare a דֶּרֶךְ, (or מְסִלָּה) for Yahweh (40:3), and its prominence in the prologue (vv. 3, 5, 9, 10, 11) indicates that the emphasis of the NE lies on the return of Yahweh's actual presence. Without the coming of Yahweh there can be no salvation. Thus 40:9, in response to 35:4 (the most important NE chapter in 1-39), announces: behold your God (e.g. 52:6 etc).[148] It is, therefore, the advent of Yahweh as a mighty warrior that inaugurates the deliverance of his people from their bondage among the nations (40:10ff; 51:9ff; 52:10ff). As he had once led them through the sea (51:9ff), so Yahweh will accompany them through the waters and the fire (43:1-3), again leading the glorious procession (40:10-11; 42:16; 49:10), being both front and rear guard in the cloud and in the fire (52:12, cf. Ex 13:21f; 14:19f). Yahweh will shepherd them (40:11; cf. Ex 15:13; Pss 77:20; 78:52f) providing food and water (49:9f; cf. 48:21) in a miraculous transformation of the wilderness (43:19; 49:9ff; cf.

---

146 Espec. Sahlin, *Typologie*, 74-8; Holm-Nielsen, 'Exodus', 27; Begrich, *Studien*, 104.
147 von Waldow, 'Message', 276.
148 Westermann; Smart, *History*, 22; Fokkelman, 'Stylistic', 75f; Rendtorff, 'Komposition', 301f; Watts, *Isaiah*, 80f; as King, von Rad, *Theology*, 2.243. Preuß, *Deuterojesaja*, 45, believes that the 'Ziel des neuen Exodus ist nicht das Land allgemein, sondern ist der Zion, und es ist nicht primär das Volk, sondern Jahwe selber, der jetz dorthin, so daß von der Rückkehr des Volkes dann nur als der Folge und Begleiterscheinung der Rückkehr Jahwes', cf. Kilian, 'Strasse', 54. For Morgenstern, 'Terminology', 269-80, the expressions הִנְנִי/הִנֵּה and the אָנֹכִי/אֲנִי predications recall Yahweh's self-designation at the first exodus, Ex 3:13ff, which for Durham, *Exodus*, 36-41, indicate the redemptive presence of Yahweh among his people, cf. Stuhlmueller, '"First"', 189-205; Harner, *Grace*. On the other hand, Zimmerli, 'Ich', 32ff, notes in contrast to Hosea that there is no amplification which specifically links this self-designation to the Exodus. Instead, it is connected with Yahweh's activity as Creator—although Zimmerli recognises that when directed toward Israel the phrase is frequently related to the motif of 'Yahweh as Saviour' which suggests an Exodus background, itself a 'creation' moment.

Ex 17:2-7; Num 20:8),[149] and there will again be a revelation of his glory (40:5; cf. 52:10).[150]

As with the announcement of comfort, so too the goal of the NE is centred on the presence of Yahweh, that is, his enthronement in a restored Jerusalem.[151] Since Jerusalem is first and foremost Zion, the city of the great king, concern for the city is central and dominates both the prologue and the epilogue.[152] The word of comfort in 40:1ff culminates in a messenger announcing to Jerusalem the good news (40:9f) of her redemption and rebuilding (44:26; 45:13; 54:11f):[153] she will be re-established in righteousness, she will know divine protection and vindication, and all her accusers will be overthrown (54:14ff). Yahweh will pour his spirit upon Jacob's offspring (44:3-5) and they will glory in the Lord (45:24f), being both taught (54:13) and owned (44:5) by him.

On this reading, the prophet's message of deliverance presupposes both Israel's founding moment of redemption and an underlying three part Exodus schema: A) Yahweh's *deliverance* of his exiled people from the power of Babylon and her idols, B) a *journey* along the 'way' in which Yahweh leads his people from their exile to Jerusalem, and C) *arrival* in Jerusalem where Yahweh is enthroned in a gloriously restored Zion. In sum, the prophet presents the vision of 'Yahweh, (who) after smashing the powers of chaos and making a way in the wilderness, gently leads his flock home to Zion.'[154] This NE is ...

---

[149] Anderson, 'Typology', is probably incorrect in citing 41:17-20 in that this refers to the new creational restoration of the desolate land.

[150] Stuhlmueller, 'Creation', 459; *Creative*, 81ff, 94ff; perhaps here under the influence of Sinai traditions (Ex 16:7; cf. Isa 49:26b; Ex 9:16; 14:16ff; Anderson, 'Typology', 183). Elliger, *Deuterojesaja*, 20ff, relates this concern to כָּל־בָּשָׂר and its relevance to the nations. Eichrodt, *Theology*, 2.13, sees here the influence of Isa 6:3. Kilian, 'Strasse', 56, may posit a too-radical disjunction when on the basis of Ezek 10:18-22; 11:22-5; 43:1-11f; and Isa 60:4-5 he emphasises the differences between the return of Yahweh and the return of the people, arguing that 40:3 deals only with the return of Yahweh to Jerusalem, and hence that the manifestation of Yahweh's glory should not be amalgamated with the return of exiles.

[151] Schoors, *Saviour*, 243, 52:7; 41:21; 43:15; 44:6; cf. Ex 15:18; Spykerboer, *Structure*, 183; Rendtorff, 'Komposition', 306f; and Dumbrell, 'Purpose'; also Ezek 20:33 where Yahweh will reign as King in the NE.

[152] Rendtorff, 'Komposition', 307ff. Just as the deliverance of Israel reaches its climax at Sinai (Ex 3:12, cf. Durham, *Exodus*, xxiff), so here, when Sinai has been subsumed in mount Zion, the NE reaches its culmination in the arrival of Yahweh in Jerusalem. On Zion as Yahweh's throne city, see Ollenburger, *Zion*.

[153] Cf. Clements, 'Beyond', 108.

[154] Roberts, 'Isaiah', 140.

guaranteed by YHWH's creative power and decisive word which can overcome all obstacles to the performance of his will, making wonders in the desert, overthrowing rulers, raising up Cyrus as his instrument, frustrating all the devices of mankind and coming to the aid of his helpless people.[155]

However, as is indicated by the tensions present in Malachi and the later chapters of Isaiah, the hopes of the NE clearly did not fully eventuate. I have argued elsewhere that Isaiah 40-55 is in fact an apologetic for the failure of the return to realise it full glory; a failure resulting from Israel's refusal to accept Yahweh's methods and instruments (namely Cyrus, a pagan and an idolater).[156]   Consequently, the INE in its fullness was delayed until, according to one reading of the second half of the book of Isaiah, the enigmatic 'servant' would arise as Yahweh's agent of deliverance. In the meantime, however, the hopes of the INE continued to shape expectations of the future.

(ii) Isaiah 40:3 and the History of Tradition
Given the power of Isaiah's presentation, it is not difficult to see how 40:1-11 (and in particular 40:3) came to be understood as encapsulating the critical event upon which the whole of the NE depends: the call made by an unidentified 'messenger' to prepare the way in the desert for the coming of Yahweh whose advent as warrior and shepherd presages the redemption of his people. Not surprisingly, as with Malachi 3, this text was also used in eschatological contexts. The most celebrated examples are those at Qumran (1QS 8:12b-16a; 9:17b-20a) where Isaiah 40:3 functioned as a programmatic statement of the community's self-understanding in fulfilling the necessary preparations for the 'way' of God's return.[157] Similarly, in 4QTanh, immediately following a prayer (or prophecy) modelled on Psalm 79 where God acts to reverse the calamity of his people, there occurs a series of consolations from the book of Isaiah in

---

[155] Lindars, 'Tidings', 479.

[156] See Watts, 'Consolation'.

[157] Cross, *Ancient*, 78; Talmon, '"Desert"'; Bater, 'Church', 98ff; Swartley, 'Study', 148ff; Brooke, 'Isaiah'; cf. McCasland, '"Way"'; Fitzmyer, 'Christianity'; Steichele, *Sohn*, 56f. On the independence of NT and Qumran usage, Grindel, 'Origin'. Fabry, 'Wurzel', relates Qumran's use of שוב to Isa 40:3, cf. 56:1; Wolff, 'Thema'; Saner, 'Umkehrforderung'. Starkova, 'Ideas', highlights Isa 40-66's role in Qumran; Seitz, 'Praeparatio', notes themes common to Mark's prologue and 1QS: A) preparation in the wilderness; B) repentance: 5:1, 13f; C) confession of sin: 1:24f; D) baptism/washing: 3:4f; E) baptism/cleansing with the Holy Spirit: 3:6-9; F) conflict/struggle: 3:24; and G) the appointed time: 4:18f.

which 40:1-3 is given first place (40:1-3(5); 41:8-9; 49:7, 13-17; 43:1-2, 4-6; 51:22-23; 52:1-3; 54:4-10; 52:1-2).[158] Imagery from Isaiah 40:4ff also appears at the conclusion of *Baruch*'s Consolation Poem (5:5-7) where Jerusalem is summoned to stand on high (v. 5, cf. Isa 40:9; 49:18) to watch God bringing back the exiles (v. 6, cf. Isa 40:11; 60:4) as every high hill is cast down and valleys levelled (v. 7; cf. Isa 40:4; 49:22) so that 'Israel may go safely in the glory of God' (v. 7b, cf. Isa 40:5).[159] In Sirach 48:24f Isaiah's prophecies are described as providing comfort to the mourners of Zion (cf. Isa 40:1f; 49:8ff; 61:1-3)[160] while in *T. Moses* 10:1-5, the imagery of Isaiah 40:4 is used to portray the advent of Kingdom of God (cf. *1 Enoch* 1:6). Of particular interest is the way in which manifold allusions to Isaiah 35 and 40-55 form the basis of *Pss. Sol.* 11's midrashic anticipation of the eschatological return of the exiles and the restoration of Jerusalem. So pervasive are these allusions that J. Schüpphaus describes *Pss. Sol.* 11 as a 'pseudodtjes Rede' which stands 'in Nachahmung der auffordernd-ermunternden Redeweise Dtjes und unter Aufnahme der von Dtjes benutzen Bilder'.[161] The psalm opens with a signal trumpet ringing out good news and announcing God's mercy to Jerusalem as she is called to stand on a high place to observe the return of the exiles (vv. 1-2a; cf. Isa 40:1, 2, 9; 43:25; 44:23; 52:7) from the four corners of the earth (vv. 2b-3 ; cf. Isa 42:5; 43:5f; 49:18ff; 54:1f). The mountains are flattened and fragrant trees are caused to grow as the exiles proceed under the God's glory (vv. 4-6; cf. Isa 35:10; 40:2-4; 41:15; 42:15; 45:2; 49:7, 10f; 66:19f) and Jerusalem is summoned to prepare herself (vv. 7f; cf. Isa 52:1ff). Within the context of the Psalms as a whole, the agent of this deliverance (cf. Isa 49:6; 52:1 and 55:5 in *Pss. Sol.* 17:28; in vv. 27, 28 and 30; and in v. 30) is to be a Davidic scion who is described in terms of Psalm 2 (cf. Ps 2:9 in *Pss. Sol.* 17:23) and Isaiah 11 (*Pss. Sol.* 17:36, 37).

In later rabbinic literature, not only was Isaiah seen as the great prophet of salvation (Pisqa 29/30A.5; the descriptions in *Pesiqata* 32-37 of which 32, 33, 36 and 37 are reflections on Isa 54:11; 51:12; 60:1-2 and 61:10 respectively) but Isaiah 40:1-5 was apparently held to be a classic statement 'on the

---

[158] Allegro, *DJD*, 5.60ff. The order given by Allegro, which in view of the document's fragmentary nature is perhaps subjective, shows a 'random' selection around the theme of consolation, but see Stanley, 'Importance'; cf. Snodgrass, 'Streams', 30f.

[159] Burke, *Poetry*, 247-55; Pesch, 'Abhängigkeit', 261f.

[160] Skehan-Di Lella, *Wisdom*, 539.

[161] *Psalmen*, 56, cf. Ryle and James, *Psalms*; and Viteau, *Psaumes*.

comfort of God and as descriptive of God's activity at the end of the age', as is epitomised by the extended treatment in *Pesiq. R.* 29/30A, 29/30B, 30 and 33 (cf. *Tanḥ* on Dt 1:1.1 and later *Gen. Rab.* 100.9; *Lev. Rab.* 10.2, 21.7; *Lam. Rab.* 1.2.23, 1.22.57; *Midr. Ps.* 4.8; 22.27; 23.7; cf. *Lev. Rab.* 1.14; *Dt. Rab.* 4.11). Isaiah 40:3 was also the *haftarah* reading on the first Sabbath after the 9th of Av, a fast commemorating the destruction of the Temple, further demonstrating these verses' importance as a statement of God's comfort.[162] That *Tg. Isaiah* 40:3 speaks of the 'way' being prepared for the return of the exiles indicates the close link which was understood to exist between God's coming and the return of his people (cf. Isa 40:10f), while מלכותא דאלהכון in v. 9 stresses the kingly aspect of this activity.[163] In the NT, the other Synoptics use Isaiah 40:3 to relate John to Jesus, but again the central concern seems to be the coming reign of God (cf. Mt 3:3, 7-12; Lk 3:6-17).[164]

In summary, Isaiah 40:1-11 appears to have been regarded by various traditions within Judaism as a *locus classicus* for Isaianic salvation.[165] Of particular interest for Mark's use is the fact that, even more than Malachi 3, the emphasis seems not to have been on the figure of a forerunner but instead on the coming of the eschatological deliverance he heralds; namely, Yahweh's coming himself.[166]

---

[162] Snodgrass, 'Streams', 31f; cf. Str-B, 1.96; 2.154. Chilton, 'Commenting', 135, (citing Towner, *Rabbinic*, 166) notes in reference to the ten songs' midrash on Ex 15:1 in *Mek.* Shirata I that 'the passages are selected, and shaped into a chronological enumeration, framed by passages from Isaiah [30:29, 42:10], in which the victory of the Passover, as reflected in various other songs of victory, "instil(s) faith in future salvation and the world to come."'

[163] The latter is not anthropomorphic avoidance but an attempt 'to emphasise an aspect of God's activity', Chilton, *Targum*, xvi.

[164] Mt 3:3, par. Lk 3:4ff; Wink, *John*, 37f, 51f. Jn 1:23 more narrowly concerns the Baptist's identity but even here the pericope concludes by looking forward, vv. 26ff.

[165] Snodgrass, *ibid.*; Dodd, *According*, 84.

[166] De Jonge, '11Q', 307, notes that in Str-B's listing of texts in which eschatological salvation is announced, it is the salvation and not the messenger that is emphasised. Qumran writings can speak of God (1QS 8:12b-16a) and of a prophet, as well as two Messiahs (1QS 9:17b-20a); see bibliographies and discussion in Schürer, 2.488ff, 550ff; Charlesworth, 'Messiah', 190; and Fitzmyer, 'Aramaic', 349f.

VI. *The Origin and Function of the Citation*

a) *The Origin of the Citation*

As already noted, it appears that the Exodus and Malachi texts were not infrequently associated in some Jewish circles and Mark's merging of them likewise reflects a technique relatively common in some Jewish interpretative traditions.[167] Consequently, although the precise form of the first element of Mark's mixed citation is unknown outside the NT,[168] it would be unwise to rule out the possibility of a Jewish antecedent.

However, the addition of Isaiah 40:3, or perhaps more accurately, the insertion of the Malachi/Exodus combination between the Isaiah ascription and the Isaiah text as an interpretative 'gloss', appears unprecedented.[169] In view of Mark's characteristic 'synthesis' method,[170] and the existence of 'testimonia' at Qumran and collections of excerpts by Greek and Latin authors which may suggest the possibility of similar collections among first century Christians,[171] it is hard to tell if this particular amalgamation is his own or derives from an earlier source.[172]

---

[167] Kee, 'Function', 180ff.

[168] Cf. the near-identical 'Q' parallel in Mt 11:10 and Lk 7:27; Snodgrass, 'Streams'.

[169] See, however, *Dt. Rab.* 4.11 on Dt 12:20 which offers two alternative explanations on the meaning of the enlarging of Israel's borders, one of which centres around Isa 40:4 and the other around Mal 3:4, 23, and 1 (MT).

[170] Kee, 'Function', 176f; Bowman, 9. E.g. Mk 13:24f combines Isa 34:4; Joel 2:10, Isa 13:10 (= Ezek 32:7f), and Dn 7:13-14; Mk 11:17: Isa 56:7, Jer 7:11; Mk 14:62: Dn 7:13, Ps 110:1; Mk 1:11: Isa 42:1, Ps 2:7.

[171] E.g. 4QFlor (2 Sam 7:10-14; Ps 1:1; 2:1f); 4QTest (Dt 5:28f; 18:18f; Num 24:15-7; Dt 33:8-11; Josh 6:26; Lane, 'New', rejects this classification); 4QTanh (Isa 40:1-5; 41:8-9; 49:7, 13-17); 4QRP^a; 4QCatena^a; Rom 9:32f (Isa 28:16; 8:14); 1 Pet 2:6-8 (Isa 28:16; Ps 118:22; Isa 8:14; cf. *Barn.* 6:2-4; Cyp., *Test.* 2.16); and Iren., *Adv.Haer.*, 4.33.11 (Isa 35:6, 5; 26:19; 53:4). See further, Hunter, *Paul*, 58-64; Dodd, *According*, 126; Ellis, *Use*, 49f; Fitzmyer, 'Use'; Hartman, *Prophecy*, 102-41; Fishbane, 'Use', 351ff; and Stanley, *Language*, 74ff, who cites compilations of excerpts among Greek and Latin authors. Later collections in the fourth century may be indicated by Pap. Ryland Gk. 460 and Pap. Osloensis 11 (Roberts, 'Biblical'; cf. the Latin collection discussed in Dobschütz, 'Collection'). The method's origins are obscure, evidence for this approach being found among the rabbinic *midrashim* based either on key words (e.g. *Mek.* Ex 14:30; Abrahams, 'Rabbinic', 179; Daube, 'Rabbinic') or according to the method of חרז ('stringing pearls'; Michel, *Paulus*, 12f, 72, 83; Hommes, *Testimoniaboek*, 324-54; Stendahl, *School*, 216; cf. Stegner, 'Romans'), in the *haftaroth* (Stendahl, *School*, 96, 217) and in Qumran (Allegro, 'Further', 'Fragments'; Fitzmyer 'Testimonia', 'Use', 'Further'; Brooke, *Exegesis*; Fishbane, *ibid.*; Stanley, *ibid.*). Harris' testimony hypothesis (*Testimonies*, following Hatch, *Essays*, 203, 209-11) was an attempt to explain the appearance in different authors of similar: A) composite quotations, B) ascriptions to wrong authors, and C) readings which differ from known editions. Subsequent scholarship, among those favourable to the theory, tended not to speak of a single 'Book' in order to account for

Even so, on what basis might this conjunction have been made? There is evidence to suggest that Malachi had already related the concept of Yahweh's 'way' in Isaiah's NE to the motifs of Exodus 23:20ff so as to canvas the prospect that Yahweh's coming might entail judgement. Might it not be that the author of the complex in Mark 1:2f, in seeking to explain to his readers how Jesus could at once inaugurate the much looked-for Isaianic salvation and yet be rejected by Israel's leaders and thus announce a future judgement on the Temple (Mk 11:12-25; 13:1ff), owes the stimulus for his textual conflation to a considered reflection on the later prophet?

b) The Function of the Citation

In view of the above, what can be said of the function of this composite quotation? There is much to confirm earlier suggestions. The idea of a preparatory figure is certainly integral to the texts and this validates in the first instance their being used to introduce John the Baptist, most probably understood by Mark as Malachi's 'Elijah', whose activity rightly belongs to the beginning of the gospel. The widespread expectation of eschatological comfort associated with the Isaiah citation also supports those who have seen here a Markan evocation of an Isaianic framework in which Jesus' activities are to be understood.[173] In terms of the remainder of the Gospel, the ὁδός terminology and Malachi's interest in the Temple could well be programmatic, although this will need to be examined in detail later.

Nevertheless a number of re-considerations appear to be in order:

A) while on a purely syntactical and lexicographical basis Exodus 23:20 might be considered as the major influence on Mark 1:2b, our

---

those favourable to the theory, tended not to speak of a single 'Book' in order to account for the variations in order and text (Williams, *Adversus*, 7ff; Simon, *Versus*, 185ff; and Hunt, *Primitive*, 14; cf. Ungern-Sternberg, *Schriftbeweis*, 138f, who states 'dass bei einer beträchtlichen Stabilität des Inhaltes die Form flüssig, variabel wäre'). Stendahl, *School*, 210f, noted Harris' failure to consider the NT influence on post-Apostolic OT quotations. Dodd, *Apostolic*, and others subsequently put Harris' theory to rest—it may better describe the post-apostolic authors' use of the OT in the NT: 'The composition of "testimony-books" was the result, not the presupposition, of the work of early Christian biblical scholars', *ibid.*, 126; cf. Shigeo, 'Function'; Sundberg, 'Testimonies'; Koch, *Schrift*, 247-55.

[172] Marxsen, 37; Schreiber, *Theologie*, 193; Wink, *John*, 2n2; Swartley, 'Study', 155. Guelich, 'Beginning', 8n35, suggests, however, that the absence of any Elijah speculation behind vv. 4-8 supports a pre-Markan combination for these texts, which Mark then takes up although his main interest is in Isaiah.

[173] *Pace*, Fitzmyer, 'Use', 318, for whom 'the abrupt beginning of the Gospel of Mark makes it almost impossible to discern the motive in the use of the Isaian text'. See now also Marcus, 45ff; cf. Schneck, 42.

analysis of the histories of interpretation suggests instead Malachi. Not only did the Malachi passage have eschatological implications of a kind absent from Exodus 23—witness John as 'Elijah'—but Malachi apparently intends an ironic allusion to Exodus 23:20 as the basis of his warning to Israel. In any case, in both texts there is the dual motif not only of Yahweh's coming presence, but also of Israel's faithlessness.

B) given this faithlessness, it is not surprising that a fundamental concern of Malachi's is the threat associated with the coming of Yahweh's self-manifestation; hence the preparatory figure. Consequently, more emphasis should perhaps be placed on John's mission as implying a threat of judgement, especially against Israel's (religious?) leaders and the Temple.[174]

C) the brief observations of commentators who see Mark's use of Isaiah 40:3 as announcing the inauguration of Isaianic comfort are to be affirmed,[175] especially given the significance of 40:1ff as a *locus classicus* in materials concerned with Israel's eschatological hope. Mark is almost certainly announcing the beginning of the long-awaited INE.[176]

D) in the history of interpretation, and in the original contexts, the Malachi and Isaiah texts together focus on the event the messenger heralds—in contrast to the not uncommon opinion that Mark 1:2f applies primarily or even solely to John.

E) the application of these texts to Jesus suggests that he is to be identified in some way, not so much with 'the Messiah', but with none other than the הָאָדוֹן and מַלְאַךְ הַבְּרִית of Malachi and, in terms of Isaiah 40:3, the presence of Yahweh himself.[177]

From this perspective, while the appearance of John and Jesus properly belong to the beginning of the gospel, what Isaiah has written also

---

[174] Cf. Dodd, *According*, 70f; Swartley, 'Study', 144f; and espec. Chapter 9 below.

[175] I use 'Isaianic comfort' because from Mark's viewpoint the book would be a unity, and in the final form of the book NE imagery is not confined to any one of the three sections commonly accepted by modern critical scholarship.

[176] Bock, *Proclamation*, 97, has also seen this: 'It is within the larger context's inherent declaration of new and the *total* vindication of God's promise in salvation that Luke's and indeed the Synoptics' use of Isaiah 40 must be understood'; cf. Schweizer; Lane; Kingsbury; Mauser; Bowman, 8f. *Pace* Lindars, *Apologetic*; Hurtado; and Anderson, who see it serving only as identifying John; and also Suhl, 155ff, and Vorster, 'Function', who deny eschatological fulfilment connotations.

[177] Loisy, *Birth*, 64-7; Farmer, *IDB*, 2.956; Chamblin, 'John'; Knox, '"Prophet"', 23-4; Bretscher, '"Sandals"'; Hughes, 'John'; Stendahl, *School*, 48; and now espec. Marcus, 37-41.

concerns, fundamentally, the substance of that unfolding gospel subsequent to its immediate beginning. Consequently, Mark's use of Isaiah 40:3 concerns Yahweh's coming and the INE thereby inaugurated. However, the deliverance had been long-delayed and, as per Malachi, was to be preceded by the forerunner Elijah lest the nation be unprepared and Yahweh's sudden coming to his Temple result in his cursing the land. Hence Mark's interest in John; but that John is not his prime concern is clear from the minimal and brief attention accorded him.[178]

c) The Isaiah Ascription

What then are we to make of Mark's ascription of this composite citation to Isaiah? The most common responses are either that Mark has uncritically taken up a testimonium (whether formulated within the nascent church or e.g. by John's disciples) wrongly attributed to Isaiah,[179] or has made a simple mistake.[180] This apparent discrepancy has led several scholars to echo Jerome's assessment: 'O apostole Petre, Marcus filius tuus, filius non carne sed spiritu, instructus spiritalibus hoc ignorat'.[181] Three considerations militate against these hypotheses: A) there is no concrete evidence for Christian testimonia in this period, what we have being either inappropriate or too late,[182] B) Mark himself is not unfamiliar with the phenomenon of combined texts,[183] and C) as H. C. Kee has shown, Mark seems aware of the significance of such scriptural

---

[178] Cf. Pesch, 1.71, 78. This would be in accordance with Isa 40-55 where, as discussed above, the coming presence of Yahweh is the pivotal issue upon which the deliverance turns. John's importance depends not so much on what he says but who is, Wink, *John*, 4. Lohmeyer's understanding, 15, of the journey of the crowds to John as the Isaianic NE cannot, therefore, be accepted. John prepares for, but clearly does not himself represent, the NE coming of Yahweh; John makes no journey to Jerusalem, nor does he display any evidence of functioning as the Yahweh-Warrior in delivering the people.

[179] Swete, 2; Johnson, 33; Stendahl, *School*, 51; Fitzmyer, 'Use'. Anderson suggests that the 'error' may have originated among the Baptist's disciples from whom Mark took the complex.

[180] Weiss, *Markus*; Lagrange; Nineham; Hooker, *Message*, 4; Beavis, *Audience*, 40. Other examples of citing combinations of texts under the name of only one of the authors can be found in e.g. Irenaeus, *Adv. Haer.*, 3.20.4, where Micah 7:19 and Amos 1:2 are attributed to Amos alone and in Justin, *I Apol.*, c. 32, who attributes to Isaiah texts from Numbers and Isaiah, cf. Harris, *Testimonies*, 1.10f. Irenæus' attribution of a presumably spurious text first to Isaiah in 3.22.4 (it is not to be found in any of the ancient versions or Tgs) but then to Jeremiah in 4.22.1 further complicates the matter.

[181] C.C., 78.452.

[182] Fn. 171.

[183] Fn. 170.

citations, frequently placing them at crucial points in his narrative;[184] it appears unlikely that he has acted unthinkingly here.

Possibly Mark is following common Jewish practice in naming only one author with composite quotations.[185] But perhaps those who have seen the Exodus/Malachi text as an early insertion have unwittingly discerned a characteristically Markan technique, namely his 'sandwich' construction,[186] here applied to his opening and only editorial citation:[187]

A.   Καθὼς γέγραπται ἐν τῷ Ἡσαΐᾳ τῷ προφήτῃ,   (Isaiah)

   B.   Ἰδοὺ ἀποστέλλω τὸν ἄγγελόν μου πρὸ προσώπου
            σου, ὃς κατασκευάσει τὴν ὁδόν σου·   (Ex/Mal)

A.'   φωνὴ βοῶντος ἐν τῇ ἐρήμῳ,   (Isaiah)
            Ἑτοιμάσατε τὴν ὁδὸν κυρίου,
            εὐθείας ποιεῖτε τὰς τρίβους αὐτοῦ,

From this perspective, the Isaiah ascription together with the Isaiah 40:3 text provides the framework into which the Exodus/Malachi conflation is inserted. Two important considerations emerge:

A) taken on its own, Mark's 'blanket' ascription is suggestive of the larger framework of his thought[188] (as a number of commentators have realised).[189] This is more so if a type of 'sandwich' structure is intended.

---

[184] Kee, 'Function'; cf. Manek, 'Composite'; and Schneck, *Isaiah*.

[185] Gundry, *Use*, 125, and *Mark*, 42.

[186] Donahue, *Trial*, 58-63; Edwards, 'Sandwiches'. Manek, 'Composite', suggests that the combination of texts reflects the OT requirement for two or three witnesses, Dt 19:15.

[187] Cf. Mauser's comment, 81n1: 'If … an interpolation, it was done most ingeniously'.

[188] Moo, 'Tradition', suggests that an OT ascription may be intended to indicate a larger thematic context while the specific citation serves as a foil to an important subtheme. In examining Matthew 27:3-10, which essentially quotes Zech 11:13 but with the addition of several important elements which find no counterpart in Zechariah (e.g. εἰς τὸν ἀγρὸν τοῦ κεραμέως), Moo argued that the Jeremiah ascription is intended to draw attention to Jer 19 not only on the basis of the verbal links נקים דם (v. 4, LXX: αἱμάταων ἀθώων) and יוצר (vv. 1, 11, LXX: πεπλασμένον) but also because of the striking thematic parallels: a locality connected with potters (v. 1) will be renamed with a phrase connoting violence (v. 6) and used as a burial place (v. 11), as a sign of God's judgement upon Jerusalem (v. 1). Cf. Edersheim, *Life*, 2.596; Gundry, *Use*, 124f; Senior, *Passion*, 360.

[189] For Grundmann, 26, as Isaiah is the prophet *par excellence* of the messianic time; cf. Schmauch, *Orte*, 24-47. For Lane, 45, since it 'indicates that the proper context for understanding the gospel is the promise of future salvation found in the latter half of Isaiah' (he also surmises that the ascription is not intended to introduce the quotation at all but instead to locate the context in which John the Baptist understood himself to be functioning, 47n30). For Guelich, 'Beginning', 12, and *Mark*, 1.10, the Isaianic citation 'gives the reader the evangelist's perspective for interpreting the events as indicative of the eschatological moment promised by Isaiah'. Gnilka, 1.45, asserts 'daß jetzt nicht mehr auf dem Jesajazitat, sondern auf Vers 2 der Ton liegt', but fails to account for the Isaiah ascription.

B) in accordance with Markan, usage, the 'B' component may indicate a special stress on the threat element.[190] We shall see later that not only is this reading consistent with Mark's continued development of the threat/rejection motif, but as with his 'sandwich' citation he continues to link it with his overall Isaianic framework.

VII. Conclusion

In keeping with the role of the opening sentence in literary antiquity, Mark's sole explicit editorial citation of the OT should be expected to convey the main concerns of his prologue and, therefore, his Gospel. Mark's use of the Isaiah ascription and the 'iconic' function of the Isaiah 40:3 text within various Jewish traditions indicates that the overall conceptual framework for his Gospel is the Isaianic NE, the prophetic transformation of Israel's memory of her founding moment into a model for her future hope. This suggests that for Mark the long-awaited coming of Yahweh as King and Warrior has begun, and with it, the inauguration of Israel's eschatological comfort: her deliverance from the hands of the nations, the journey of her exiles to their home and their eventual arrival at Jerusalem, the place of Yahweh's presence.

At the same time, however, Mark's addition of Malachi 3:1 adds an ominous counterpoint. Thoroughly integrated within the Exodus/NE schema—on the one hand it looks back to the first Exodus in its ironic use of Exodus 23:20 and on the other it concerns the delay of the INE—it implies not only that Israel is not ready for Yahweh's coming, but also that a right response to John as Malachi's Elijah is imperative if the nation is to avoid the spectre of Yahweh's purging judgement which hangs over Jerusalem's *raison d'etre*, the Temple.

If and how Mark develops these two themes will be the subject of the rest of this study. We now turn to an examination of the remainder of his prologue where, if our proposal is correct, we should expect to find further evidence of these two concerns.

---

[190] Edwards, 'Sandwiches', 196, notes with regard to narrative that *'the middle story nearly always provides the key to the theological purpose* of the sandwich' (author's italics).

Chapter 4: The Markan Prologue

When read in the light of the NE Isaianic prophecies, the OT images and motifs in Mark's prologue form a coherent whole. The content of the εὐαγγέλιον is the drawing near of the reign of God which Isaiah prophesied, and the splitting of the heavens signals the inauguration of the long-awaited NE intervention of Yahweh on Israel's behalf. The descent of the Spirit and the voice declare Jesus to be Isaiah's Davidic-messianic-'Servant', who is at once new 'Servant' Israel and Israel's deliverer, and Son of God.

I. Introduction

In view of our assessment of Mark's opening sentence, it is significant that a number of commentators have argued for a pervasive Deutero-Isaianic influence on Mark's prologue.[1] However, although the presence of OT allusions is widely recognised, there is often little agreement as to their source and significance.[2] But, again, in view of the increasing recognition of Mark's literary skill, it seems highly improbable that he has intended such uncertainty. Consequently, after determining the extent of the prologue, we will seek to ascertain if the case for a INE framework can be sustained. Finally, we will argue that if such a framework is allowed, not only does it resolve many of the questions as to the origins of Mark's OT allusions in his prologue but it also accords his use of OT phrases and images a remarkable degree of coherence.

II. Extent of the Prologue

R. H. Lightfoot's critique of Hort and Wescott's earlier division (vv. 1-8) resulted in a new consensus which concluded the prologue with verse 13.[3]

---

[1] Especially Lührmann, 'Biographie', 27-30; Guelich, 'Beginning', 8-10, where 'For Mark, each event that forms this "beginning of the gospel" corresponds to Isaiah's promise for the eschaton'; Chilton, *God*, 78-95.

[2] Cf. surveys in Lentzen-Deis, *Taufe*, 127-93.

[3] *Message*, 15-20, noting also that vv. 13 and 14f are closely related while vv. 14f can be regarded as a summary of the early church's gospel. Cf. Kuthirakkattel, *Beginning*, 9-20.

The arguments advanced in support of this division are: A) the change of locality from the Wilderness to Galilee in verses 14ff,[4] B) the confinement of the key-words ἔρημος (vv. 3, 4, 12, 13) and πνεῦμα (vv. 8, 10, 12) to verses 1-13,[5] C) the difference between John's future-orientated preaching and Jesus' more immediate proclamation,[6] and D), from the perspective of a narrative reading, the information given in verses 1-13 is private while in verses 14ff it is public.[7]

Leander Keck challenged this consensus arguing that the prologue should include verses 14-15.[8] He regarded the presence of εὐαγγέλιον in verses 1 and 14f as an *inclusio*,[9] and saw John's παραδοθῆναι as of primarily theological interest and hence functioning as the climax to verses 1-15. Three further observations support Keck's view: A) the presence of the unifying *Stichworte*, for example, μετάνοια-μετανοέω (1:4, 15) and κηρύσσω (1:4, 7, 14), B) the parallel three-fold presentation of John (vv. 2-8) and Jesus (vv. 9-15) which suggests that they belong together in that both units begin with an 'identifying word from God' (vv. 2f, 11), both mention their respective subject's person and work (vv. 4-6, 12-3), and both culminate with a reference to preaching (vv. 7f, 14f), and finally, C), the account of Jesus (vv. 9-15) correlates with the Isaianic theme of verses 2f in that he is presented as the promised one and this is confirmed by the Isaianic allusion in the voice (v. 11; cf. Isa 42:1), the descent of the Spirit (cf. Isa 42:1; 61:1) and the 'splitting' of the heavens (v. 10; cf. Isa 63:19 MT).[10]

---

[4] Mauser, 79.

[5] Robinson, 28f, and Johnson, *Mark*, 35, note that πνεῦμα is the only theme that binds vv. 4-8, 9-11 and 12-13 together, cf. Lane, 48. 'Spirit' appears only three more times in Mark and only 3:29 relates directly to Jesus' work. On key-words as Markan linking devices, Sundwall, *Zusammensetzung*.

[6] Robinson, 24f. Schweizer's arguments for vv. 1-13 are based on his questionable theory of a threefold structure for the Gospel based on the theme of discipleship, see Keck, 'Introduction', 355f.

[7] 'Prologue', 5f.

[8] 'Introduction', 359-62. Earlier Wellhausen, *Marci*; Wendling, *Entstehung*, 3; Zahn, *Einleitung*, 220ff; and later Seitz, 'Praeparation'; and Kuby, 'Konzeption', had taken this position but Keck was among the first to defend it in detail.

[9] Note also the related κηρύσσω (cf. κηρύσσων καὶ εὐαγγελιζόμενος τὴν βασιλείαν τοῦ θεοῦ, Lk 8:1; 4:43 par. Mk 1:38) in vv. 1:4, 7, 14; Friedrich, *TDNT*, 2.718f.

[10] Pesch, 1.72f, 'Anfang'; Guelich, 'Beginning', 7-9; cf. Michaels' analysis, *Servant*, 44:

A:		The *gospel* of Jesus (v. 1);
	B:	John the Baptist *in the desert*, in fulfilment of Scripture (vv. 2-4);
		C: John *baptising in the Jordan* (vv. 5-8);
		C': Jesus *is baptised in the Jordan* (vv. 9-11);
	B':	Jesus *in the desert* (vv. 12-13);
A':		the *gospel* of God (vv. 14-15)

Norman Perrin takes a mediating position.[11] Apparently building on
the work of K. Schmidt,[12] he understands verses 14f as a transitional
passage serving both to conclude the prologue and to introduce the
Galilean ministry.[13] Although Perrin's overall thesis concerning the
Markan summaries has been challenged,[14] his assessment of verses 14f has
received additional support on the basis of the literary technique of
classical *rhetors*.[15] Following D. Müller[16] and H. Parunak,[17] A. Stock
discusses the technique of *concatenatio* (Müller) whereby a smooth
transition from one part of a narrative to another is effected.[18] Then,
picking up on the work of Bas van Iersel,[19] he suggests that Mark 1:14f is a
particular derivation of this approach known as an 'inverted hinge':
A/b/a/B. It consists of a transitional unit (b/a; vv. 14f), somewhat
independent from the larger blocks on either side (A/B; i.e. 1:1-13/1:16ff),
in which representative themes from the larger units are inverted (thus
b/a) to facilitate the flow of the narrative. Hence, 'Galilee' in verse 14
looks forward to Jesus' ministry, while verse 15, as fulfilment, looks back
to the promise of John's role in the wilderness verses 2ff. The strength of
Perrin's and Stock's approach lies in its appreciation of ancient literary

---

[11] 'Towards'; Perrin and Duling, *Introduction*, 239f.

[12] *Rahmen*, 320. 'Apparently' because Perrin has not published any independent
analysis of the summaries and his delineations follow Schmidt closely. See also Egger's
proposed modifications, *Frohbotschaft*, 44-69. Dodd, 'Framework', generally followed
Schmidt in his attempt to identify the traditional outline of Jesus' Galilean ministry; for a
criticism of Dodd see Trocmé, 28ff.

[13] Kee, 63f; Kingsbury, 50; Chilton, *God*, 53f; and Egger, *Frohbotschaft*. See also
Holtzmann's apparently inconsistent statements, *Synoptiker*, 11, 115, that v. 15 ends the
introduction and yet vv. 14f is *Überschrift* to the Galilean ministry, and Grant, *Gospels*, 87f,
180f, where 1:2-15 is the introduction and yet 1:14 - 9:50 is 'Jesus in Galilee'. Robinson, 22,
states that 'v. 14 provides a formal termination to John's ministry and a formal introduction
to Jesus' ministry'.

[14] Hedrick, 'Summary'.

[15] Stock, 'Hinge', mentions neither Perrin nor Hedrick. Hedrick's judgement,
'Summary', 294, that vv. 14f are not transitional is based on a too-restricted view of the
context (he ignores vv. 1-11) and an inconsistent analysis of 1:16 - 3:6 which it is said
'contains only one other reference to the preaching of Jesus', yet he later states that 1:21f,
27, 38f, 45, etc. describe Jesus' preaching or teaching.

[16] *Propheten*.

[17] 'Oral' and 'Transitional', 540ff.

[18] 'Hinge'. Lucian, *Hist.*, 55, states that when the historian 'has finished the first
topic he will introduce the second, fastened to it and linked with it like a chain, to avoid
breaks and a multiplicity of disjointed narratives'; 'always the first and second topics must
not merely be neighbours but have common matter and overlap'.

[19] 'betekenis' and 'Locality'.

method and its integration of the strengths of both Lightfoot's and Keck's positions.[20]

Recently, however, R. H. Gundry has vigorously revived the case for the prologue ending at verse 8 citing the following warrants: A) the OT quotations, since they speak only of preparation, are concerned solely with John, that is, verses 4-8, and so to go beyond verse 8 would 'violate the definition of the beginning by the καθώς-clause'; B) it would 'violate the use of ἀρχή ... for the first subject matter of the book'; and C) 'every phrase of v 9a' indicates the beginning of a new pericope.[21]

While it is true that the OT portions cited by Mark only specifically mention 'preparation', we have already seen that the immediate OT contexts and the understanding of these texts across a range of Jewish traditions have far more in view. They function almost as icons, evoking the larger schema of Israel's hopes for future salvation, namely, the coming of Yahweh to save his people. More telling, perhaps, is Gundry's assumption—and he is certainly not alone here—that Mark's audience would have been unaware of such implications. But how secure is such a position? Mark's frequent, if not ubiquitous, use of OT texts and motifs— particularly Isaianic ones and often, as Kee noted, at crucial points in the narrative[22]—is *prima facie* evidence of an intentionality which strongly suggests that at least some of his readership were reasonably familiar with parts of the OT. This is hardly surprising given that the OT constituted the Scriptures of the early church.[23] Indeed, it is highly likely that some awareness of the significance of these Scriptures would have been part of the catechism, if not the apologetic, of the earliest believers.[24] Furthermore, the longer Mark's 'community' had been in existence, the greater the likelihood of unlearned Gentiles having instruction in such matters. And all of this without taking into account the possibility that at least some of Mark's audience might have been Jewish Christians who presumably would have been more at home with OT allusions.

---

[20] Among the more recent commentators Feneburg, *Markusprolog*, argues for vv. 1-11, while Hort-Wescott have new champions in Scott, 'Chiastic', and now Gundry (see below).

[21] Gundry, 31ff.

[22] 'Function'; cf. Schneck, *passim*.

[23] See now, Ellis, *Early*.

[24] As long noted by e.g. Lindars, *Apologetic*. Of course the exact nature of the significance of OT texts for the early church is a matter of on-going debate.

Concerning Gundry's second point, it is not clear why the inclusion of verses 9-13 would 'violate the definition of the beginning' since Jesus' ministry proper does not begin until verse 14, nor is it clear why a 'new pericope' necessarily indicates the end of the prologue—must prologues have only one pericope? On the contrary, the preparation of Jesus, whose ministry is in fulfilment of the 'good news' of Yahweh's delivering action as implied, for example, by Isaiah 40:3, seems quite appropriate to the 'beginning ... (as indicated) ... by the καθώς-clause'. This is particularly so when seen over against verses 14-15ff which record the inauguration proper of that ministry. Indeed, one could argue that the parallel use of ἐγένετο in verse 9 (cf. v. 4), instead of indicating a primary break between verses 8 and 9, suggests the complimentary nature of verses 4-8 and 9-13 in that they serve to introduce the two protagonists and their related careers, namely, the preparatory figure John and the preparation of Jesus whose coming John announces. Gundry seems almost to admit as much when he says, first, that Mark takes 'care to note that Jesus did not start preaching good news till "after" (μετά) the end of John's ministry' and, second, that the beginning 'consists in John's preparing for and preaching about the stronger one before the stronger one begins his own preaching'.[25] These statements seem to imply that the key issue is the commencement of Jesus' preaching. Thus, on the one hand, the beginning ends with John's imprisonment while, on the other, Jesus' preaching marks the start of the body of Mark's account. Consequently, the end of the beginning continues to at least verse 13, in which case it seems that the approach of Perrin and Stock is still to be preferred.

Allowing then that the prologue hinges upon verses 14-15, and that verses 1-3 are its opening sentence, we will now examine the case for the presence of Isaianic NE imagery.

---

[25] Gundry, 31f.

III. Isaianic Materials in Mark's Prologue

a) The Gospel and the Kingdom of God

(i) *Mark 1:1, 15:* Ἀρχὴ τοῦ εὐαγγελίου ... κηρύσσων τὸ εὐαγγέλιον

Although clearly an important word for Mark,[26] his use of εὐαγγέλιον has engendered considerable discussion.[27] In the Hebrew Scriptures and the LXX, the theological use of the verbal form (בשׂר, εὐαγγελίζω) occurs almost twice as often in Isaianic NE contexts as in the rest of the OT.[28] Because the NT's use of the verb appears to be dependent on that of the OT,[29] a number of scholars hold that the Isaianic NE horizon is also determinative for the meaning of the substantive as it is utilized in the NT.[30]

A problem arises, however, in that בשׂורה/εὐαγγέλιον in the Hebrew and Greek Scriptures and in contemporary Jewish writings does not seem to share the religious/eschatological connotations of the corresponding verbal forms.[31] The occurrence of εὐαγγέλιον in the Pirene inscription has, therefore, led some scholars to suggest that the NT reflects a Pauline innovation deriving from imperial cult language.[32] Others, observing parallels between the Gospels and Hellenistic aretalogies, have proposed that these latter texts constitute the primary background for NT usage.[33] Peter Stuhlmacher, however, has recently challenged both of these latter positions, arguing that the Hellenistic use of εὐαγγέλ- in reference to divine men, popular philosophers, and the imperial cult, apart from the third century AD provenance of the first two groups, reflects the rhetorical

---

[26] 1:1, 14, 15; 8:35; 10:29; 13:10; 14:9 and (16:15), Marxsen, 117-50; Perrin, 'Literary', 4-7; Martin, 22ff; Keck, 'Introduction', 357f.

[27] Frankemölle, 'Evangelium'; Baarlink, *Anfängliches*.

[28] 40:9 (*bis*); 41:27 (MT); 52:7 (*bis*); 60:6; 61:1; cf. Hooker, *Jesus*, 66f; Friedrich, *TDNT*, 2.707-10; Stuhlmacher, *Evangelium*, 109-22; Seccombe, *Possessions*, 63ff.

[29] Stuhlmacher, *Evangelium*, 122; Strecker, *Evangelium*, 504.

[30] E.g. Schweizer; Cranfield; Guelich, '"Beginning"'; Hooker, *Jesus*, 66; Bruce, 'When', 325ff.

[31] The substantive occurs neither in Qumran nor in Philo and only occasionally in Josephus; Friedrich, *TDNT*, 2.721-6; Stuhlmacher, *Evangelium*, 112-3, 124.

[32] Strecker, *EWbNT*, 2.180; Harnack, *Reden*, 1.301-6; Deissmann, *Light*, 366; Schniewind, *Euangelion*, 1.78, 2.146f; Schneemelcher, *NTApoc*, 1.78ff; Bligh, 'Note'; cf. Friedrich, *TDNT*, 2.724-5; Stuhlmacher, *Evangelium*, 11-19.

[33] E.g. Bieler, ΘΕΙΟΣ; Hadas-Smith, *Heroes*; Petzke, *Tradition*; Smith, 'News'; Talbert, 'Biographies'; Cancik, 'Gattung'; cf. Tiede, 'Religious'.

and stylistic concerns of secular usage rather than having specifically religious interests.[34]

As neither contemporary Jewish nor Græco-Roman sources provide decisive evidence, Stuhlmacher argues that the NT usage of εὐαγγέλιον is a distinctive Christian innovation formulated specifically to relate Jesus Christ to OT promises. The evidence for a pre-Pauline gospel centred on Jesus' death, resurrection, and exaltation (1 Thess 1:9-10; Rom 1:2-4; 1 Cor 15:3-5) is supported by indications within the Palestinian church prior to the Gentile mission of a gospel dealing principally with the OT promises of the coming of the kingdom of God (citing Rev 14:6; 10:7; Mt 11:2-6 par. Lk 7:18-23; Lk 4:16-30; Mk 1:14f).[35]

The plausibility of a Palestinian provenance is strengthened in that the closest parallels to the NT diction are found in the *Tg. Nebarim*'s innovative rendering of the Hebrew שמועה with בסורה (e.g. Ob 1; Jer 49:14; Isa 53:1).[36] The use of this Aramaic term in, for instance, *Tg. Jeremiah* 4:15, *Tg. Ezekiel* 21:12, and *Tg. Isaiah* 53:1 has clear prophetic connotations, which are epitomised in the latter where בסורה refers to 'die Heil erschließende Offenbarungs-kunde'.[37] Consequently, although the extant Targumic evidence is late,[38] its fairly broad attestation of the prophetic use of בסורה and its shared cultural provenance with the Palestinian church suggests that the theological content of εὐαγγέλιον most plausibly finds its origins in the translational terminology for the prophet's message (שמועה and בסורה) and particularly for that message associated with Isaianic hope. (It is perhaps noteworthy then that Bruce Chilton has also argued that certain dominical sayings concerning the Kingdom of God appear

---

[34] *Evangelium*, 191-206; cf. Frankemölle, 'Gattung', 1672f; Tiede, 'Religious'. The exceptional religious connotations of εὐαγγέλιον in the Pirene inscription are mitigated since it uses the typically Hellenistic plural, εὐαγγελί[ων], suggesting a considerable distance between this inscription and the NT, Stuhlmacher, *ibid.*, 201. Noch, 'Apocryphal', 65, doubts if the common people would have been familiar with this use; but see Judge, 'Decrees'.

[35] *Ibid.*, 209-44; cf. Gillet, 'Evangelium', 175; Hahn, *Mission*, 40-41; Hengel, 'Between', 27ff; *pace* Strecker, 'Evangelium', 513-24.

[36] *Ibid.*, 131-33.

[37] *Ibid.*, 132; Burrows, 'Origin', 22, 32; Friedrich, *TDNT*, 3.706f. The Aramaic usage is borne out by the Syriac, Bowman, 'Term', 61ff; Chilton, *God*, 94n76.

[38] The dating of the various traditions within the *Tg. Isa* is notoriously difficult, cf. Chilton's redaction-critical approach, *Glory*, while on the date of compilation of the present written Targums, York, 'Dating'.

particularly to reflect the language of earlier Palestinian traditions which were later incorporated, again, into the *Tg. Isa*[39]).

Of further interest in this regard is again *Pss. Solomon* 11. Consisting of a collage of NE imagery drawn from Isaiah 40-66, it begins: κηρύξατε ἐν Ἰερουσαλὴμ θωνὴν εὐαγγελιζομένου. This juxtaposition of κῆρυξ- and εὐαγγελ- term-inology (the latter admittedly in verbal form) in the context of Isaianic hope is very similar to that in Mark 1:15's ἦλθεν ὁ Ἰησοῦς ... κηρύσσων τὸ εὐαγγέλιον τοῦ θεοῦ (cf. 13:10; 14:9).[40] The idea of an eschatological messenger (מבשר) who announces the time of Yahweh's intervention, again expressed in Isaianic terms, is also found both in Qumran (e.g. 1QH 18:14, which clearly echoes Isa 61,[41] and 11QMelch[42]) and in later rabbinic materials.[43]   From this perspective, Jesus' announcement of the nearness of the reign of God (Mk 1:15) seems to have been construed in the light of the מְבַשֵּׂר-tradition of Isaiah 52:7 and 61:1f (Mt 11:2-6 par.; Lk 4:16-30;[44] cf. Lk 9:6),[45] and, as Jesus' words and deeds became the content of the verb εὐαγγελίζω, the substantive appears to have become similarly understood (Mark 1:1).[46]

---

[39] Mk 1:15; Lk 4:18, 19, 21; Mt 8:11; Lk 16:16; Mk 9:1; Chilton, *God, passim; Rabbi*, 137-47.

[40] Martin, 23; Stuhlmacher, *Evangelium*, 146.

[41] '[that he might be], according to Thy truth, a messenger [in the season] of Thy goodness; that to the humble he might bring glad tidings of great mercy, [proclaiming salvation] from out of the fountain [of holiness to the contrite] of Spirit and everlasting joy to those who mourn'; trans. Vermes, *DSSE*, 206. Further, Stuhlmacher, *ibid.*, 142-46.

[42] While the identity of the משיח is uncertain (De Jonge, '11Q'; Fitzmyer, 'Further', 27-28), and granted the fluidity of the concept (de Jonge, 'Anointed'), the text does appear to indicate that the proclamation of good tidings was among the sphere of functions connoted by the designation 'Messiah', Aune, 'Jesus'. On the implications for the NT, De Jonge, '11Q', 309ff.

[43] In reference to Isa 52:7: *Pereq ha-Shalom* 13 (59b), attributed to R. Jose the Galilean (110), in the context of the Messiah's coming; *Tanḥ* במדבר Nu. 2:2; *Midr. Ps.* 147:1; further: Str-B, 3.9c, where Isa 52:7 and 60:3 are prominent. The 'messenger' may or may not be the Messiah, but in any case the point is the coming reign of God, Str-B, 3.9b, 10c. In connection with Isa 40:9; 41:27; 52:7; 61:1 and Nah 2:1, respectively: *Tanḥ* תולדות 16 and 135 (Schlatter, *Matthäus*, 122); *Pesiq.*, 28e; *Pesiq. R.* 36 (162a) and *Pesiq. R.* 35 (161a), *Tanḥ* במדבר on Nu 2:2; cf. Friedrich, *TDNT*, 2.714-7; Stuhlmacher, *Evangelium*, 135-53.

[44] Secommbe, *Possessions*, 44-69; Chilton, *God*, 123-77, see this text as influenced by the *Tg. Isa* 61:1f and 42:16.

[45] Stuhlmacher, *ibid.*, 142-151; 'Thema', 21; Chilton, *God*, 95; Schlatter, *Glaube*, 590; Betz, 'Evangelium', 70ff, for whom πιστεύετε is to be conceived in terms of Isa 53:1; Schnackenburg, 'Evangelium', 320f; Koch, 'Messias', 127.

[46] Stuhlmacher, 'Thema', 21ff.   The relationship between τὸ εὐαγγέλιον Ἰησοῦ Χριστοῦ and τὸ εὐαγγέλιον τοῦ θεοῦ, appears best understood as the logical consequence of the identification of the presence of the Kingdom of God as 'die Selbsterweisung Gottes' (i.e. God's powerful, saving, self-revelation) with the person of Jesus, his message and

In conclusion, although Stuhlmacher's position may 'textlich gesichert nicht realisiert werden',[47] that of Strecker *et al* seems to imply too radical a disjuncture between the act of proclamation indicated by εὐαγγελίζω and its content, εὐαγγέλιον, a disjuncture which is only heightened in view of the overall influence of OT hopes on the NT. Thus, εὐαγγέλιον appears dependent upon OT concepts[48] of which the *exemplarischen Belegen* are to be found in the prophecies of the book of Isaiah.[49] As such it connotes a renewed proclamation of the Isaianic NE coming of Yahweh's *Königsherrschaft*,[50] a connotation that is only reinforced given its close proximity to Mark's epexegetical OT citation. Mark's explicit identification of the Ἀρχὴ τοῦ εὐαγγελίου Ἰησοῦ Χριστοῦ with Isaiah's NE, 'connects the gospel to its OT Jewish roots'.[51]

(ii) Mark 1:15: ... ἤγγικεν ἡ βασιλεία τοῦ θεοῦ

Mark's introduction (vv. 1-3) is linked by the key-word εὐαγγέλιον to the transitional hinge of verses 14f which is widely recognised as Mark's programmatic beginning to Jesus' ministry proper.[52] The parallel construction of the two adverbial participles (κηρύσσων ... καὶ λέγων)

---

above all his ministry; cf. Weiss, *Predigt*, 16; Kuhn-Schmidt, *TDNT*, 1.571-4, 579-90; Chilton, *God*, 279, 283f; Guelich, 'Genre', 210f; Lemcio, 'Intention', 189f; but see Chilton's caveats in 'Introduction', 24. Such a self-demonstration is a primary concern of the NE announcement of Isaiah, cf. Watts, 'Consolation', 37-40.

[47] Frankemölle, 'Gattung', 1688, and, particularly with the Targums in view in, 'Jesus'.

[48] Stuhlmacher, *Evangelium*, 122ff; Baarlink, *Anfängliches*, 48-55.

[49] E.g. Stuhlmacher, *ibid*., 152, 109-22; 'Versöhnung', 44; cf. Schneemelcher, *Apocrypha*, 1.72, who argues for a Hellenistic origin but recognises the pervasive influence of Dt. Isa on the NT usage. See now also, Marcus, 18ff. Again, *pace* Gundry, 41, Mark's subsequent account of Jesus' actions suggest that connotations of victory and ensuing peace are to be seen here, see Chapter 6, also Friedrich, *TDNT*, 2.707-27; and again now Marcus, 26f.

[50] Fuller, *Mission*, 34ff; Bowman, 'Term', 55ff; Hooker, *Jesus*, 66f; Lane; Stuhlmacher, *Evangelium*, 'Thema'; Betz, 'Jesu'; etc. Gundry's demurral, 41, on the possibility of victory connotations fails to take into the account the battle imagery inherent in the whole NE tradition and Mark's emphasis on Jesus as the Yahweh-Warrior in e.g. 3:23-27, see further Chapter 6. It should be noted, however, that while Ἀρχὴ may relate only to the prologue's contents, the presence of εὐαγγέλιον in the title and in vv. 14-15 suggests that εὐαγγέλιον concerns the entire work, Hengel, 'Literary', 53n81. In other words, the gospel about Jesus is for Mark largely synonymous with Jesus' gospel of the Kingdom of God.

[51] Guelich, 'Genre'. Betz, 'Evangelium', 72ff, further suggests that Mk 14:9 (τὸ εὐαγγέλιον εἰς ὅλον τὸν κόσμον) reflects Isaiah 52:10, and, as the gospel particularly focuses on Jesus' death (note the pre-Pauline confession in 1 Cor 15:1-5), that Mark uses εὐαγγέλιον in 1:1 'weil es auch in (Tg) Jes 53,1 am Anfang des Berichtes über das Leiden des Gottesknecht steht', cf. לבסורתנא. Betz' connection, *ibid*., 59, of εὐαγγέλιον with the motif of the 'suffering servant' depends of course on the degree to which this motif can be demonstrated in Mark, see Chapter 8.

[52] Lightfoot, *Gospel*, 20; Ambrozic, 17; Robinson, 21; Marxsen, 66; Pesch, 1.100-7.

suggests that the second clause: Πεπλήρωται ὁ καιρὸς καὶ ἤγγικεν ἡ βασιλεία τοῦ θεοῦ, is epexegetical of the first: τὸ εὐαγγέλιον τοῦ θεου.[53] Given the perception of the Isaianic significance of εὐαγγέλιον, it is perhaps not surprising that several commentators regard the Synoptics' use of ἐγγίζω as also deriving from Isaiah 40-66.[54] And in fact, although ἐγγίζω occurs frequently in the LXX, it is indeed in Isaiah that it is primarily linked with the promise of the nearness of God's righteousness—understood as the just exercise of his kingly reign in bringing salvation to his people (46:13; 51:5; 56:1).[55]

---

[53] Black, 'Kingdom', 290, sees the parallel of πεπλήρωται (cf. Lam 4:18 [19]) as supporting the rendition of 'ἤγγικεν = *qérabhath (malkuth 'élaha)*', i.e. the Kingdom of God *has come*, cf. Ambrozic, 21f; Lohmeyer, 30. On the debate surrounding this verb: on the one hand, Dodd, *Parables*, 'Kingdom'; Hutton, 'Kingdom'; and, on the other, Campbell, 'Kingdom' and Clark, 'Realized' (*sic*); while mediated by Fuller, *Mission*; Robinson, 24; Kümmel, *Promise*; Black, 'Kingdom'; and Berkey, 'ΕΓΓΙΖΕΙΝ'.

[54] E.g. Preisker, *TDNT*, 2.331f; Fuller, *Mission*, 24; and Chilton, *God*, 58f, for whom this 'widely attested in the NT as an eschatological terminus technicus'.

[55] Ambrozic's discussion of the Kingdom of God in Mark, in spite of recognising the fulfilment aspect of Mk 1:2f, largely ignores the OT background. Of the other prophets, ἐγγίζω occurs most frequently in Ezekiel but concerns the destruction of Jerusalem, cf. 7:7; 9:1; 12:23; 22:4, 5. In Isaiah, Yahweh's announcement of the NE is a demonstration of his righteous commitment to מִשְׁפָּט (41:1f, 10; 42:1-7; 45:13; 51:4-7). צֶדֶק/צְדָקָה is primarily linked with salvation (יֵשַׁע: 45:8, 21; 46:13) and Yahweh's redemption of Israel; Rendtorff, 'Komposition', 313ff, Reiterer, *Gerechtigkeit*. Just as 12:1ff links the themes of comfort and the NE with יְשׁוּעָה, so too in 40-55. Yahweh is declared to be the only saviour of both Israel and the nations (45:15, 17, 21ff; 43:3, 11, 12; 49:25, 26); neither the idols (42:17; 45:16; 46:1-4) nor the various wise ones can deliver (47:13, 15). Salvation appears in parallel with צֶדֶק since it is Yahweh who creates both (45:8) and both will last forever (51:6, 8). Both terms dominate 40-55 as statements of God's imminent act (45:21, 25; 46:13; 54:14, 17). The relationship between these terms and מִשְׁפָּט as characteristics of Yahweh's righteous activity is exemplified in 51:4f where his coming intervention on Israel's behalf is a matter of צֶדֶק, מִשְׁפָּט, and יְשׁוּעָה; cf. Beuken, '*MIŠPĀṬ*'. This approach is further developed in the innovative use of the גאל language, Stuhlmueller, *Creative*, 99-123; Schoors, *Saviour*, 169, 172, 297. Yahweh's bond with Israel in her slavery (43:1-7) reflects the kinsman's obligation to rescue his brother from slavery. Israel is redeemed by her kinsman Yahweh who will give Egypt, Cush, and Sheba as her ransom (43:1-7; cf. 52:3). This concept also looks back to the deliverance from Egypt (51:10; cf. 48:20ff; 52:3, 10ff; Stuhlmueller, *Creative*, 59-98) and consequently Israel's NE redemption is linked with Warrior language (Lord of Hosts in 44:6; 47:4; cf. the frequent association of גאל with the title, קְדוֹשׁ יִשְׂרָאֵל: 41:14; 43:14; 47:4; 48:17; 49:7; 54:5ff) and is also a matter of judgement for Babylon as it was for Egypt (47:17). The Redeemer-Marriage motif is expanded in the theme of the childless and rejected bride, who is made miraculously fruitful by the restored marital love of Yahweh (54:1-10; 44:4; 49:19ff; 54:1-3; cf. 49:25), cf. Stuhlmueller, *Creative*, 103f, 115ff; and Krupp, *Verhältnis*, who discusses role of the marriage bond in covenantal perspective and sees it as the central point of reference for 40-55, and the highlight of Yahweh's return, such that ch. 54 forms the goal to which the whole moves.

This is supported by Chilton's proposal that *Tg. Isaiah* is the specific background to Mark 1:15.[56] When מלא/πληρόω is used in the MT and LXX to speak directly of God's act, it refers 'to the completion of a stated period or time or process'.[57] But Chilton argues that both verbs seem to lack independent eschatological reference, and, therefore, that neither the MT nor the LXX provide an explanation of 'how a phrase with πεπλήρωται and ὁ καιρός unmodified can have been used at Mk 1,15 with the apparent understanding that it would have been immediately understood'.[58] He then observes, however, that both terms reflect an eschatological purview within Aramaic and Syriac contexts, concluding that 'TIs is the single most important extant witness to the conceptions which are at the base of this announcement', with correspondences to 'three out of the four key terms in the saying (πληρόω, καιρός, βασιλεία), and language which is suggestive of ... the fourth (ἤγγικεν)'.[59]

These terms speak then of the time in which God acts (*Tg. Isa* 60:1, 22). The days of mourning are completed (*Tg. Isa* 60:20; cf. 57:18) as the reign of God breaks in (*Tg. Isa* 31:4; 52:7; in 40:9 it is the מלכותא דאלהכון which is revealed). All that remains is to announce the near coming in strength of God's presence (*Tg. Isa* 40:10; 56:1). On this basis, and in view of its connection with ἤγγικεν, Jesus' μετανοεῖτε is also to be understood in the light of OT prophetic usage, and again particularly of that in *Tg. Isaiah*.[60] Further, in view of the Isaianic background of εὐαγγέλιον (as per Stuhlmacher), Chilton finds that 'the appearance of a belief phrase with *bswrh* at Tg.Is. 53, 1 is a staggeringly close parallel to Mark 1, 15'.[61]

---

[56] *God*, 86-95.

[57] Moule, 'Fulfilment', 309; cf. Chilton, *God*, 78ff; Delling, *TDNT*, 4.287f.

[58] For this and the following, Chilton, *God*, 81ff. Pesch, 1.102, notes that they are especially characteristic of apocalyptic terminology for the establishment of the reign of God, *4 Ezra* 4:36f; *2 Bar.* 40:3. Pesch also lists Tob 14:5 but see Chilton, *op cit.*

[59] Chilton, *God*, 88f.

[60] Chilton, *God*, 90ff; *AB*, 11.xvi; cf. Trilling, 'Botschaft', 53; Kelber, 14; *pace* Wellhausen, 8; Lohmeyer, 30; Ambrozic, 5. The idea of repentance is consonant with the view that Isa 40-55 reveals a negative response, a failure to believe in Yahweh's announcement; Watts, 'Consolation'.

[61] Chilton, *God*, 95; *Tg. Isa* reads: מן הימין לבסורתנא, cf. *Tg. Isa* 40:9, 52:7.

This evidence suggests that Mark 1:14-15, while clearly not a citation, is probably best understood in the light of the traditions reflected in *Tg. Isaiah*. It appears most likely, therefore, that these verses constitute a proclamation of the inauguration of the NE deliverance and the breaking in, 'in strength', of Yahweh's reign. In this respect one might also note the suggestion that the κῆρυξ- verb also harks back to John's preaching of the coming 'stronger one'.[62] If so, then presenting Jesus in terms of the victorious Isaianic Yahweh-Warrior (see Chapter 6) would be consistent with an overall Isaianic NE motif.

Thus far, the results of the present study tend to confirm the proposal that Isaiah's NE is the consistent and dominant motif within the structurally significant opening (vv. 1-3) and transitional sections (vv. 14-15) of the prologue. The εὐαγγέλιον ᾿Ιησοῦ Χριστοῦ is, it seems, to be understood within the framework of the Isaianic expectation of the delivering self-revelation of Yahweh (εὐαγγέλιον τοῦ θεοῦ, ἤγγικεν ἡ βασιλεία τοῦ θεοῦ). At this point an intriguing ambiguity arises in that Yahweh's salvific self-revelation is not only proclaimed by Jesus (1:14-15) but is also apparently identified with him (1:1-3). Jesus not only proclaims but also effects the deliverance. In other words, or at least so it seems from Mark's point of view, the Isaianic herald is himself revealed to be the agent of Isaianic salvation (cf. Lk 4:16ff; we will see this sort of ambiguous dual identification again in Mark.) The next question then is whether or not there is any evidence that the accounts of Jesus' preparation (1:9-13) are also cast in terms of the Isaianic NE motif.

b) The Baptism

(i) Mark 1:10: ... εἶδεν σχιζομένους τοὺς οὐρανοὺς
καὶ τὸ πνεῦμα ... καταβαῖνον εἰς αὐτόν

The opening of the heavens is a familiar apocalyptic image.[63] Mark's account is distinctive, however, since there is no mention of further

---

[62] Ambrozic, 19; Guelich, 1.42 (see 22ff on possible identifications); and Gundry, on Mark's emphasis on the stronger one. Schneck, 38, discerns an allusion here to Isa 40:10. Note also the eschatological/messianic connotations of the ἦλθον sayings and John's preaching concerning the ὁ ἐρχόμενος, e.g. Arens, *HΛΘΟΝ*, 286-324, 348; Mußner, 'Gottes-herrschaft', 82; Schneider, *TDNT*, 2.668f; Webb, *John*, 261-306. From this perspective Marxsen's exegesis, 134, of 1:14f vis 'I am coming soon' misses the fulfilment motif.

[63] E.g. Ezek 1:1; Acts 7:56; Rev 19:11; 2 *Bar.* 22:1; *T. Levi* 2:6; 5:1; 18:6; *T. Jud.* 24:2 (the latter two may reflect Christian influence; De Jonge, *Testaments*; 'Influence'; Chevallier,

visionary revelation[64]—which suggests something other than an apocalyptic origin—but instead the Spirit descends,[65] thereby demonstrating
Jesus to be John's 'stronger one'.[66] This descent of the Spirit, in connection
with the strong language of 'rending', has among other things (e.g. 63:11,
14 LXX: κατέβη πνεῦμα παρὰ κυρίου) led several commentators to see
Isaiah 63:19 MT as the background to this passage (cf. Neh 9:20).[67]

Nevertheless, one of the most recent and thorough works on the
baptism of Jesus, that of F. Lentzen-Deis,[68] contests this view for the
following reasons: A) although Mark uses σχίζω instead of the more
common ἀνοίγω and thereby reflects the sudden irruption of Yahweh's
presence, the remainder of his account does not cohere with a 'theophanie'
Gattung, B) in contrast to Isaiah 64:1f, Mark does not describe God's descent
'zur Vernichtung der Feinde und damit zum Heil des Volkes' but instead
records the descent of the Spirit, and C) the judgement of the wicked 'ist
aber nicht ein möglicher Sinn für Mk 1:10'. Thus, while Lentzen-Deis
allows the possibility of an allusion to Isaiah 64:1, it cannot serve as
background to Mark 1:10 since the context of 64:1ff 'in ganz anderem Sinn
weiterentwickelt'.[69]

Lentzen-Deis' assessment, however, may be challenged on several
counts. Granted that ἀνοίγω is more common in this construction (e.g.
Gen 7:11; Ps 77:23 LXX; Isa 24:18; Ezek 1:1; Acts 7:56; 10:11 etc.), the LXX's use
of ἀνοίγω to render קרע in Isaiah 63:19 MT is anomalous. Mark's σχίζω,
therefore, appears not only more accurate, but may suggest a particular
interest in the MT's account with its more explicit statement of Yahweh's
coming.[70] Futhermore, not only is the Baptism the only place in the NT

L'Esprit, 125-30; Hultgard, 'Ideal'); cf. Acts 10:11; Rev 11:19. See also van Unnik, 'Himmel';
Lentzen-Deis, *Taufe*, 99ff; Taylor; Cranfield.

[64] Such disturbances may also be an indicator of eschatological judgement Job 14:12 LXX;
Ps 102:26; Hag 2:6, 21; *Sib. Or.* 3:82; 8:233, 431; Mt 24:29; 2 Pet 3:10; Rev 6:14, but as Gundry
notes, 50, neither 'by content nor by context can we say that Jesus' vision is apocalyptic'.

[65] Guelich, 1.33.

[66] Gundry, 49.

[67] See in particular, Buse, 'Markan', who notes a number of linguistic parallels, Gundry,
Use, 28f; Feuillet, 'bapteme', and now Marcus, 48ff; Gundry, 48, 51; Schneck, 44-47.

[68] *Taufe*, 99-127.

[69] *Taufe*, 101ff.

[70] Cf. Guelich, 1.32. The LXX does not reflect the MT's יָרַדְתָּ, although the Sinai
context implies Yahweh's presence. Mark's σχίζω may also reflect an ironic allusion to Mk
15:38, such that the rending of the heavens results in the rending of the veil, although in
the latter case σχίζω would be the expected verb, Maurer, *TDNT*, 7.959ff.

where the descent of the Spirit is described by καταβαίνω but only in Isaiah
63 LXX is this verb associated with both the Exodus—a theme central to
Mark's opening citation—and the descent of the Spirit.[71] Finally, it is also
noteworthy that both Mark and Isaiah link the 'descent'/'placement' (שׂים /
καταβαίνω) of the רוּחַ with 'coming up' out of water imagery.[72]

Second, the reliance on *Gattung* as a determinative criterion ('Dies ist
der wichtigeste Gegengrund') appears to be a methodological weakness.
Such categories may be helpful descriptive tools but Lentzen-Deis'
prescriptive application seems doubtful since it is not clear that Mark's
failure to conform strictly to *Gattung* necessarily entails a disregard for the
essential themes and motifs of the Isaianic context. Lentzen-Deis appears
to sense this when he goes on to add that the concerns of the two passages
are incompatible. It is at this point, however, that Lentzen-Deis' argument
seems most open to question, since an examination of the Isaianic context
reveals a number of motifs—in addition to the parallels noted above—
that are complementary to Mark.

It is generally recognised that Isaiah 56-66 reflects post-exilic
disappointment with the reality of the Return.[73] While there is the
reaffirmation of the hope of Yahweh's coming and the remaining exiles'
ingathering (56:8; 57:14ff; 60:4ff; 62:10ff; 66:20; cf. 58:8), there are also
indictments of (58:1-14; 56:9 - 57:13), and laments concerning (59:1-15a;
63:7 - 64:12), the wicked in the nation who are seen as impediments to the
promised eschatological salvation (59:1ff)[74] and hence attract severe
censure (65:11ff; 66:3ff, 14ff, 24). The whole intensifies until finally the
coming of Yahweh as Warrior (59:15bff; 63:1ff) sees the apostate Temple

---

[71] See Schneck, 45, citing Lohmeyer, *Evangelium*, 21. Schneck goes on to note that in
1 Cor 10:1-4 Paul compares Christian baptism to Israel's passing through the sea.

[72] These parallels raise the intriguing possibility that John's linkage of a water
baptism rite with his proclamation of a future bestowal of the Spirit may owe something to
Isaiah 63's unique account of Israel's Exodus experience. Perhaps John was symbolically
offering proleptic participation in a New Exodus—the re-enactment of passing up through
the water being a repudiation of Israel's past 'rebellion' (cf. Isa 63:11-13, 10)—in
anticipation of the 'coming one' whose 'baptism in the Spirit', i.e. at least the restoration of
Yahweh's life-giving presence, would consummate the renewal process (Isa 63:10-14).
Jordan-crossing/conquest models tend to focus on land possession and miss the Spirit
emphasis (as per Webb, *John*, 360ff). John is here much closer to Moses whose concern is
primarily with the presence of Yahweh (Ex 33:15f); as is Mark's opening citation.

[73] Rendtorff, *Alte*, 209; Fohrer, *Introduction*, 386; Gottwald, *Hebrew*, 507.

[74] Kraus, 'Endtheophanie', 322, where the promised theophanic deliverance has been
postponed because of the people's sin.

dignitaries cast out and replaced by the faithful servants of Yahweh whom they had excommunicated (65:13ff; 66:4-6, 14bff, 24). Jerusalem is then gloriously recreated amid new heavens and a new earth (chs. 60-3; 65:17-25; 66:7ff, 22f), her exiles return, and the survivors of the Gentiles proclaim the glory of Yahweh to the nations (66:19ff).[75]

The text under consideration belongs to the last great lament which, together with Yahweh's response, concludes the whole book (63:7 - 64:12ET; cf. Ps 77).[76] I. Fischer's suggestion that, within the context of the book as a whole, this distress represents the fulfilment (or a further one) of the threat in the *Berufungsvision* of Isaiah 6, if correct, makes the passage even more poignant.[77] The lament's main elements consist of an account of Yahweh's past acts of redemption (63:7-14), an appeal for help which includes references to the petitioners' desperate straits (63:15 - 64:4), a confession of sin (64:5f), and a final appeal which combines earlier themes (64:8-12).[78] Mark's possible allusion belongs to the central and most impassioned element, namely, 64:1-5a.[79] Couched in terms of the Exodus epiphany traditions of the ancient Divine-Warrior Hymns (64:1-3; cf. 59:15bff; 63:1ff), and, therefore, consistent with the preceding Exodus account (63:9ff cf. Ex 19:16ff; Ju 5:5), they form an appeal to Yahweh (אָבִינוּ, 63:16 (bis)) who is called upon to hear from heaven (LXX: οὐρανός, 63:15; 64:1) and to repeat the saving event of the nation's founding moment.[80]

From this perspective, if Mark is thinking in terms of the NE, then, *pace* Lentzen-Deis, his appeal to imagery from this text is eminently suitable. Not only is the passage itself part of the last great lament in Isaiah over the delay of the NE, but Mark's description of the baptism closely echoes that which the petitioners' long for: the descent of Yahweh through the rent heavens.

This brings us to Lentzen-Deis' second objection: in Mark it is the Spirit, not Yahweh, who descends. Here, I would suggest, he fails to

---

[75] On these themes, Achtemeier, *Community*; Hanson, *Dawn*; Pauritsch, *Gemeinde*; and their development in the structure of ch's 56-66, Charpentier, *Jeunesse*, 79f; Gottwald, *Hebrew*, 508.

[76] Hanson, *Dawn*; Westermann; Pauritsch, *Gemeinde*; Watts, *Isaiah*, sees a sermon-prayer, cf. von Rad, 'Levitical'.

[77] Wo, 289ff.

[78] Whybray; Westermann; Hanson, 79ff. The first unit is almost universally agreed, the others are debated.

[79] Westermann, 395; Whybray.

[80] Hanson, 87; Westermann; cf. Cross, *Canaanite*.

appreciate fully Isaiah 63's remarkable pneumatology. In addition to a unique emphasis on the רוּחַ קָדְשׁוֹ (63:10, 11, cf. 14) there is an unparalled association of רוּחַ הַקֹּדֶשׁ with the Exodus where the רוּחַ is presented as almost equivalent to Yahweh himself.[81] Further, the appeal to Yahweh 'to rend the heavens and come down' in 63:19 (MT) must surely be understood in the light of the immediately preceding context of the Exodus rememberance, which rememberance not only forms the very basis of that appeal but is, as already noted, replete with רוּחַ language. In other words, if the memory of Yahweh's great redemptive act, from Isaiah 63's point of view, is characterised by his 'placing' of his רוּחַ-presence in the midst of his people then it is hardly surprising if the long-awaited repetition of the saving event should also be so characterised.

Of some interest here, in light of our earlier treatment of the Malachi and Exodus texts, is the appearance of the enigmatic reference to מַלְאַךְ פָּנָיו (Isa 63:9).[82] Again there seems to be some degree of identity between the angel (or presence) and the רוּחַ in that the former saves the people (v. 9), and the latter dwells with them (v. 11) and leads them through the desert to the promised land (v. 14).[83] This is consonant both with the way the Spirit is presented in Isaiah 63[84] and with the fact that the מַלְאַךְ can function as a reference to Yahweh's self-manifestation. It is, perhaps, worth noting in passing that the implicit threat of the Malachi/Exodus texts are not far away. Here, too, there is the motif of Yahweh's presence (= 'angel' = 'Holy Spirit'?) becoming a threat due to Israel's disobedience, in that Israel's grieving רוּחַ קָדְשׁוֹ caused Yahweh to become their enemy (63:10; cf. Mark 3:29).

We turn finally to Lentzen-Deis' third objection: the destruction of adversaries (צָרֶיךָ) and the trembling of the nations (גוֹיִם, 64:1) are absent in

---

[81] On the one hand, there is a development toward the notion that all of God's acts can be attributed to his Spirit and, on the other, there is evidence of a trend toward a distinct hypostasis, Whybray; Westermann. This emphasis on the Spirit is in fact noted by Lentzen-Deis, *Taufe*, 102; cf. Gundry, *Use*, 30.

[82] Whybray follows the LXX and reads מלאך as absolute, adding the adversative ἀλλ' and reading פָּנָיו as αὐτός—'no messenger nor angel but his presence saved them'—partly because he considers the concept as it stands in the MT 'unique and improbable', cf. Westermann. In support of the MT (cf. DSS[Isa], θ ᴅ) there is much in the passage that appears unique and it may be that מַלְאַךְ פָּנָיו is an innovative reference to the מַלְאַךְ יהוה, with the genitive emphasising the desired aspect, i.e. presence, much the same as הַבְּרִית מַלְאַךְ in Mal 3:1. Cf. Delitzsch; Achtemeier, *Community*; Watts, *Isaiah*.

[83] Watts, *Isaiah*, 332.

[84] 'Yahweh's presence they uniquely interpreted as "his holy spirit"', Hanson, 90.

Mark. However, contrary to Lentzen-Deis, the judgement of Yahweh's enemies is perfectly compatible with Mark's account. The question turns on who is seen as the enemy. On the one hand, the Isaiah context envisages the destruction of the community's apostate leaders and Temple dignitaries at Yahweh's advent (65:1-15; 66:3-6, 14bff, 24).[85] This has strong affinities with the threat associated with Malachi 3:1 and Mark's portrayal of Israel's leaders (e.g. 11:12-25; 12:1-12; 13:1ff). On the other hand, several scholars have noted Mark's heavy emphasis on Jesus' eschatological conflict with Satan.[86] Although this will be developed more fully in Chapter 6, suffice it to say that for Mark the enemy is no longer the nations but the demons (thus in Mark's first miracle the unclean spirit not only designates Jesus as 'the holy one of God' but also perceives his mission, 1:24, cf. his plundering of Satan, 3:27, and the demise of 'Legion', 5:1ff).

Consequently, it appears that Mark's account of the descent through rent heavens of the Spirit upon Jesus is entirely in keeping with the last great lament of the Book of Isaiah. For Mark, Jesus is Yahweh's answer to that cry: he has indeed come, 'in strength', to announce and to effect Israel's long-awaited NE.

Several scholars have also drawn attention to the unusual Markan construction, εἰς αὐτόν (cf. ἐπ' αὐτόν in par.), seeing here an echo of Isaiah 63:11.[87] The OT text is difficult in that the MT's בְּקִרְבּוֹ appears on the surface to have one figure in view, but the singular pronoun's referent is not easy to discern, cf. the LXX's ἐν αὐτοῖς.[88] In any case, given that Mark could only reasonably have used the singular (εἰς αὐτόν), it seems unwarranted to press this into a presentation of Jesus as Israel's new shepherd, that is, a new Moses.[89] It is more likely, given it is Israel who comes up out of the water (cf. ἀναβαίνω in 63:10b (LXX) and Mk 1:10), that Jesus himself is apparently presented as being equivalent to, or representative of, Israel.[90] This identification finds further support not

---

[85] 56:9-12; 57:3-13a; ch. 59; Westermann, 301ff; Hanson, 134ff; Achtemeier, *Community*, 128f.

[86] E.g. Robinson, 28ff; Keck, 'Introduction', 362; Nineham, 63; Lane, 62; Pesch, 1.98; Gnilka, 1.59; cf. Kee, 119.

[87] Buse, 'Account'; Feuillet, 'bapteme'; Gundry, *Use*; now Schneck, 46.

[88] Is it the shepherd, i.e. Moses, or should 'shepherd' be read as plural, or is the singular used collectively of the people? See Whybray; Westermann.

[89] *Pace* Schneck, 46.

[90] See fn. 87.

only in Mark's recalling the more general staples of Israel's founding moment such as desert, water, and 'forty days', but also his emphasis on the baptism's correspondences with the distinctive features of the Isaianic account of that inaugural event (Isa 63:11ff; cf. 1 Cor 10:1ff).[91]

Such an identification raises a question: how can Mark portray Jesus as the one who both announces and inaugurates Israel's deliverance (as per the εὐαγγέλιον material above) and who at the same time re-enacts Israel's Exodus either as the 'true Israel' or her representative? Before dealing with this it is necessary to examine what is perhaps the most difficult section of Mark's prologue: the words spoken by the voice from heaven.

(ii) Mark 1:11: ... καὶ φωνὴ ἐγένετο ἐκ τῶν οὐρανῶν,
          Σὺ εἶ ὁ υἱός μου ὁ ἀγαπητός, ἐν σοὶ εὐδόκησα

The OT has generally been seen as the basis for interpreting 1:11. However, the voice's brief statement reveals no unequivocal OT allusion and the diversity of proposed origins, variously located in Psalm 2:7,[92] Isaiah 42:1,[93] Genesis 22:2, 12, 16,[94] Exodus 4:22f,[95] or combinations thereof,[96] makes precise identification difficult. Consequently, several scholars have taken the view that the allusions in the voice are so

---

[91] Buse, 'Account'; Lentzen-Deis, *Taufe*, 102; Bretscher, 'Exodus'; Hooker.

[92] Vielhauer, *Aufsätze*, 205f; Lindars, *Apologetic*, 140n2; cf. Justin, *Dial.*, 88, 103; Clem. Alex., *Paed.*, 1.6.25; *Ap. Con.* 2.32; *GEb.* frg 4; Meth., *Symp*, 8.9; *Did.*, 9; Lact., *Inst.*, 4.15.

[93] Following Bousset's original footnote, *Kyrios*, 57n2; Jeremias, *TDNT*, 5.701ff; *Theology*, 1.53ff; Cullmann, *Baptism*, 17f; *Christology*, 66; Maurer, 'Knecht', 31f; Fuller, *Mission*, 55; *Foundations*, 169; Gils, *Jésus*, 56ff. Pesch, 1.92, primarily Isa 42:1, but he rejects Jeremias' proposal for a υἱός/παῖς exchange.

[94] Turner, 'ΥΙΟΣ'; Gaboury, 'Deux'; Best, *Temptation*, 169-72; Vermes, *Scripture*, 222f; Daniélou, 'typologie'; Daly, 'Soteriological', 68ff; Wood, 'Isaac'; some noting the idea of Aqedah-typology, cf. *T. Levi* 18; *T. Judah* 24; Irenaeus, *Adv. Haer.*, 4.5.4; Athanasius, *Oratio*, IV; *Contra Arianos*, 24. Others who allow the possibility of Gen 22 as filial are less convinced about this aspect (fn. 96). While Aqedah-typology cannot immediately be discounted, e.g. παραδίδωμι in 1:14 sets 'the preaching and summons of Jesus into the divinely willed deathward work of John', Keck, 'Introduction', 360, the fact that Mark apparently does not develop the theme must tell against it, cf. Gaboury, 'Deux'; Pesch; Davies, *Matthew*; Guelich. That the NT knows little if anything of the Aqedah in comparison to later Christian writings also suggests that it is fundamentally a post-NT development, cf. Davies-Chilton, 'Aqedah' and literature cited therein. For more recent responses taking the opposite position: Hayward, 'Present'; O'Neill, 'Jesus'; Segal, 'He'.

[95] Bretscher, 'Exodus'; Feuillet, 'bapteme', 'personnalité'.

[96] Generally Ps 2 and Isa 42, although some allow Gn 22 as well: Marshall, 'Son'; Lührmann, 'Biographie', 27ff; Hahn, *Titles*, 339, 345n42; Moule; Taylor; Schweizer; Dodd, *According*, 31f, 89; Manson, *Jesus*, 110; Hunter, *Introducing*, 15; Mauser, 96; Lindars, *Apologetic*, 139f; Davies, *Setting*, 37; Lane; Gnilka; Hurtado; Matera, 'Prologue'; Derrett; Kee, 122ff; Kingsbury, 65; Lentzen-Deis, *Taufe*, 192; Schneck, 55-68.

fragmentary as to rule out any direct appeal to specific OT texts and thus regard Mark 1:11 as a more or less general statement of Jesus' filial relationship to the Father.[97] This seems something of a counsel of despair. In any case, the preceding analysis of Mark's use of OT imagery makes it unlikely that the pinnacle of his prologue,[98] fragmentary though its OT allusions might be, is offering only a 'general statement'. Fortunately, the task is simplified somewhat since our concern is only with possible points of contact with the Isaianic NE. The following table lists the most common proposals for OT sources:

Mark 1:11	*Psalm 2:7*		*Isaiah 42:1*	
	LXX	MT	LXX	MT
σὺ εἶ ὁ υἱός μου	υἱός μου εἶ σύ ἐγὼ σήμερον γεγέννηκά σε	בני אתה אני היום ילדתיך	(ὁ παῖς μου)	(עבדי)

	Gen 22:2, 12, 17			
	LXX	MT		
(ὁ υἱός μου) ὁ ἀγαπητός	τόν υἱόν σου τόν ἀγαπητόν	את־בניך את־יחידך		

			Ἰωκώβ ὁ παῖς μου	הן עבדי
			ἀντιλήψομαι αὐτοῦ	אתמך בו
			Ἰσραὴλ ὁ ἐκλεκτός μου	בחירי
ἐν σοὶ			προσεδέξατο αὐτὸν	רצתה
εὐδόκησα			ἡ ψυχή μου	נפשי
			ἔδωκα τό πνεῦμα μου	נתתי רוחי
			ἐπ᾽ αὐτόν	עליו

---

[97] Hooker, *Jesus*, 68ff; Suhl, 97ff; Carrington, 37; Ruckstuhl, 'Gottessohn', 208f.

[98] The Temptation appears to take a secondary role in terms of both information presented and a lessening of dramatic tension. In the baptism the movement of Jesus out of the water, the tearing of the heavens, the descent of the Spirit, and the intervention of the voice comprise a concentration of activity unmatched in the prologue; cf. Stonehouse, 16f; Kingsbury, 60.

(a)   **Σὺ εἶ ὁ υἱός μου** ὁ ἀγαπητός, ἐν σοὶ εὐδόκησα ...

Jeremias and others have argued that υἱός μου[99] is a secondary, Hellenistic interpretation of an earlier παῖς μου (cf. Isa 42:1 LXX) because the latter was felt to be offensive by Gentile Christianity.[100] Their arguments, however, are difficult to maintain.[101] Granted the possibility of such a shift,[102] there is no evidence of a more primitive παῖς Christology in a baptismal setting—although there are some signs of a later, patchy development along these lines[103]—and none of an earlier pre-Markan change. Further, that Jesus is designated παῖς in a Hellenistic work (Acts 3:13, 26; 4:27, 30) tends to undermine Jeremias' fundamental assumption.[104] Finally, textual support for a υἱός/παῖς exchange is totally lacking, while the presence of εἰ υἱὸς εἶ τοῦ θεοῦ in the Temptation narratives of Matthew and Luke suggests that υἱός μου is original to the voice.[105]

---

[99] In Inter-testamental material, the epithet 'son (of God)' is e.g. applied to:

A. the righteous: Sir 4:10; Wis 2:18;

B. OT figures: *T. Levi* 4:2 (Levi); *1 Enoch* 105:2 (Enoch?, cf. Black, *Enoch*, 99, 318f); Ez. *Trag.* 100 (Moses); *Pray. Jos.*, Frag. A., 7 (Jacob); Jos. *Ant.* 2.232 (Moses); *Jos. Asen.* 18:11; 21:4; 23:10 (Joseph);

C. holy men: *b. Ber.* 17b (Hanina ben Dosa); *b. Ta'an* 25a (Eleazer ben Pedath); *3 Enoch* 1:8 (Ishmael ben Elisha);

D. messianic figure/s:

1) 4Q246, although the identity of the individual is unclear, Fitzmyer, 'Contribution', 391ff; *Wandering*, 90-93; Ruckstuhl, 'Gottessohn', 203; Byrne, 'Sons', 61f; Hengel, *Son*, 45. Kim, *Son*, 22n33, citing Stuhlmacher and Betz, and Collins, 'Pre-Christian', (cf. Martínez, 'Nuevos'), are more certain.

2) 4QFlor 1:10f where the term 'son' is used but not the full title in a midrashic summary involving Ps 2 and 2 Sam 7:10ff.

3) 4 *Ezra* 7:28; 13:37; (possibly; Charlesworth, "Messiah", 202); Knibb, *Esdras*, 169; Box, *Ezra*, lvif, suggest chapter 13 is an eschatological commentary on Ps 2; Gero, 'Son', on the basis of the Georgian 'the elect, my anointed one' (ll.18, 20f; published in Blake, 'Georgian', 354) sees a genuinely ambiguous original ברי משיח in 7:28f and not merely a tendentious Christian rendering.

On this data the words υἱός μου are not sufficient in themselves to establish messianic or filial status, other contextual indicators being necessary. For further discussion: Byrne, 'Sons', 9-78; Lohse, *TDNT*, 8.340ff; Hengel, *Son*, 42-48; Dunn, *Christology*, 14ff; Delling, 'Bezeichnung'; Charlesworth, *Jesus*, 149-51.

[100] *TDNT*, 5.703; cf. Maurer, 'Knecht', 38; Hooker, *Jesus*, 109.

[101] Espec. Marshall, 'Son'. The readings ἐκλελεγμένος in Lk 9:35 and ἐκλεκτός in Jn 1:34 (textually uncertain, cf. 𝔓⁶⁶, 𝔓⁷⁵) are variants of ἀγαπητός and are not directly relevant to the question of παῖς replacement. At most they show that the 'servant' motif was associated with the voice, not that the 'son' motif was denied; *ibid.*, 328.

[102] Dalman, *Words*, 276f, where Wis 2:13ff and 12:19f reads παῖς as child yet uses language from Isa 40ff.

[103] *Mart. Poly.* 14.1; 20.2; *1 Clem.* 59:2-4.

[104] Cf. Lk 1:54, 69; Acts 4:25; Marshall, 'Son', 331f; Hooker, *Jesus*, 108; Guelich, 1.33.

[105] Cranfield, 'Study', 59ff; Schneck, 61f, sees echos of 'our father' in Isa 63:15f; 64:7ff.

Instead, many scholars see Mark's first line as alluding to Psalm 2:7, and that the psalm is often cited more fully in early references to the baptism lends support to this identification.[106] The change of word order, seen by some as militating against the allusion,[107] is readily explained by the customary form of emphatic first person address naturally consistent with the setting.[108] The 'omission' of a reference to Yahweh's having 'begotten' Jesus is only problematic if it is first established that it must be included in order for an allusion to be successful.[109] Furthermore, in the absence of chapter and verse divisions, part-citations were apparently used as short-hand references to larger contexts, and the same could reasonably be expected of allusions.[110] It may well be that Mark's interest in the matter of Jesus' relationship to David's son, frequently at important points in his narrative structure (10:47f; 11:10; 12:35ff; cf. 2:25),[111] reflects his understanding of this element of 'the voice', especially in view of the psalm's links with the coronation of a Davidic king.[112]

In Qumran, Psalm 2 was understood to refer to the time of eschatological conflict between the chosen and the sons of Beliar and a similar sentiment of dominion and victory over Israel's enemies is expressed in apocalyptic and rabbinic writings.[113] As Joel Marcus notes, 'Jewish sources from the biblical period on ... overwhelmingly interpret Psalm 2 as a reference to an eschatological victory by God, a victory sometimes won through the instrumentality of the Messiah'.[114] The elements of warfare and victory are key to the psalm's original setting, in that as a coronation psalm it 'marks the accession of a person to a position

---

[106] Lk 3:22 D; see fn. 92.

[107] Cranfield, 'Study'; Fuller, *Mission*, 86ff; Pesch; Gnilka; Vermes, *Scripture*, 222; Hooker, *Jesus*, 69; Ruckstuhl, 'Gottessohn', 202f; Chilton, *Galilean*, 128; Lentzen-Deis, *Taufe*, 185f.

[108] Cf. σὺ εἶ ... in 3:11; 8:29; 14:61; 15:2; par.; also Gundry, *Use*, 30n2; Marshall, 'Son', 332f; Lohmeyer, 23.

[109] E.g. Bretscher, 'Exodus', 302.

[110] Cranfield, 'Study', 59; Jeremias, *TDNT*, 5.701; cf. Dodd, *According*, 126f.

[111] On 2:25, Hurtado; see also Chapter 8.

[112] On parallels with 2 Sam 7:8-16, Rogerson-MacKay, *Psalms*, 19; Eaton, *Kingship*, 111. It ought to be noted, however, that although *Pss. Sol.* 17 makes considerable use of Psalm 2 and applies a range of titles to the Messiah it refrains from designating him as 'son of God', Marcus, 78.

[113] Lövestam, *Son*, 16-23.

[114] *Way*, 61; cf. 59ff, and in particular his discussion in 77-79; see also Bock, *Proclamation*, 100ff.

of power and authority' over the nations (vv. 7ff) at Yahweh's instigation (vv. 4ff).[115] All of this, of course, coheres with the hopes associated with the INE. Finally, not only is this theme congruent with the subjection of Israel's enemies as implied by Mark's use of Isaiah 63's 'rending of the heavens' and developed in his presentation of Jesus' eschatological conflict with Satan (Chapter 6), but again there is an element of threat in the call to do homage (vv. 10ff; cf. Mk 1:23f).

On the other hand, P. G. Bretscher and M. D. Hooker have pointed out that the designation 'my son/s' is not uncommonly used, by God, of Israel.[116] Further, the relatively rare singular ('son' rather than 'sons') designation is often found in contexts dealing with Exodus traditions (Ex 4:22f; Hos 11:1; cf. 'my firstborn son' in Ex 4:22; Jer 31:9; also Dt 1:31; Wis 18:13; and *Pss. Sol.* 17:27). Given that Mark surrounds Jesus' baptism with pervasive Exodus imagery and particularly that imagery associated with the account in Isaiah 63, it is difficult to avoid the impression that the 'son' designation carries 'Israel' connotations as well.

Once again we are confronted with ambiguity: is Jesus to be seen in terms of Psalm 2 and thus identified with the agent of Yahweh's eschatological victory—which seems to be what is in view with regard to the voice alone—or, is he to be understood in terms of the Exodus motif and thus be seen as the representative of (or ideal) Israel—which appears to be implied by the immediate context? And this in the light of the opening mixed citation which would lead one to expect the coming of Yahweh himself. At this point one begins to wonder if this duality is intentional; perhaps Mark has no desire to force a choice between the two options. Might it be that Mark's account is presenting Jesus as both Israel's 'royal' son of God and Yahweh's true son, 'Israel'? Once again, we need to hold in abeyance the question of how Mark could have come to such an understanding.

---

[115] Craigie, *Psalms*, 65f; Kraus, *Psalmen*, 145ff; Carlson, *David*, 97-128; Coppens, *Messianisme*, 37-63.

[116] 'Exodus' and *Mark* respectively; cf. also Fitzmyer, *Aramean*, 104ff.

(b)   Σὺ εἶ ὁ υἱός μου ὁ **ἀγαπητός**, ἐν σοὶ εὐδόκησα

Another possible INE link is the adjectival[117] ὁ ἀγαπητός.[118] The descent
of the Spirit in Mark 1:10 and the probable allusion to Isaiah 42:1 in the
second part of the verse (see below) have led some to see Isaiah 42:1 behind
this expression,[119] particularly as ἀγαπάω occurs in two closely-related
'servant'-contexts (41:8-9; 44:2).[120] It is argued that: A) Matthew 12:18
indicates ἀγαπητός to be an alternative translation of Isaiah 42:1's בָּחִיר,
B) Luke 9:35 replaces ἀγαπητός with the unusual ἐκλελεγμένος,[121] and
C) ἐκλεκτός is an alternative reading in John 1:34.[122]

However, ἀγαπητός never renders בָּחִיר in the LXX, and Matthew 12:18
is probably an assimilation to the baptismal account[123] either to establish
or to strengthen the link between the voice and Isaiah 42:1.   Luke omits
both ἀγαπητός and ἐν σοὶ εὐδόκησα, although it is possible that he
understood ἐκλελεγμένος as equivalent to the latter phrase,[124] while in
John υἱός is probably the original.[125]   The evidence, therefore, for
ἀγαπητός being a translational option for בָּחִיר in Isaiah 42:1 is not strong,
and the NT variations[126] are probably better understood as interpretive
developments indicating that an allusion to the Isaianic 'servant' was seen

---

117 Kilpatrick, 'Order', 112f; cf. 2 Pet 1:17.

118 Robinson, *Ephesians*, 231ff, argues on the basis of Mt 12:18 that Matthew must have
regarded ὁ ἀγαπητός as a (messianic) title, citing the majority of Old Syriac readings, *T.
Ben.* 11:2; *Mart. Isa.* 3:17, 18, etc. and its use as a title of Christ (Eph 1:6; *Bar.* 3:6; 4:3, 8;
Acta Thecla I; etc., cf. Bacon, 'Supplementary'; Davies, *Matthew*, 340). However, only *T.
Ben.* 11:2 offers the possibility of an independent witness as the relevant sections in *Mart.
Isa.* appear to be of Christian origin, Schürer, 3.336ff; Knibb, *OTP*, 2.147f. On ἀγαπητός as
an idiomatic equivalent to μονογενής, Turner, 'ΥΙΟΣ'; cf. Souter, 'ΑΓΑΠΗΤΟΣ'. See now
also the discussion in Marcus, 51f.

119 Jeremias, *TDNT*, 5.701ff; *Theology*, 1.53ff; Cullmann, *Baptism*, 17f; *Christology*, 66;
Maurer, 'Knecht', 31f; Fuller, *Mission*, 55; *Foundations*, 169; Gils, *Jésus*, 56ff; Feuillet,
'bapteme', 479; Gnilka, 1.50. Robinson, *Ephesians*, 232, suggests that 'the Beloved' and 'the
Elect' were interchangeable titles on the basis of Mt 12:18 and Lk 9:35.

120 Leenhardt, *bapteme*, 27n2; Gundry, *Use*, 30f; now Schneck, 53-55.

121 𝔓[45.75] ℵ B L Ξ 892. 1241 pcvg[st] sy[s.hmg co]; Metzger, *Textual*; Marshall, *Luke*;
Fitzmyer, *Luke*.

122 𝔓[5vid] ℵ* b e ff[2*] sy[s.c], electus filius a ff[2c].

123 Barth, 'Understanding', 126; Schweizer, *TDNT*, 8.368; Gundry, *Use*, 30, 112;
Marshall, 'Son', 333.

124 Zahn, *Lucas*, 386n99; Marshall, 'Son', 333; cf. Marshall, *Luke*; Fitzmyer, *Luke*.

125 Gundry, *Use*, 30; Brown, *John*; Metzger, *Textual*; but cf. Morris, *John*; Schnackenburg,
John.

126 John's account reflects his perspective of the Baptist's understanding, not necessarily a verbatim report.   Note: none of these major variations occurs in Mark and the
preponderance of textual evidence suggests that the Synopticists have not felt free to alter
the voice in the baptism account itself in this way.

in the second half of the voice.[127]   On the other hand, Matthew's and Luke's use of these terms suggests at least some degree of equivalence in certain contexts, for example, religious, such that being 'loved' may imply being 'elect' (cf. LXX Isa 41:8; 44:2; both in the context of παῖς terminology; cf. 43:4, 10).[128]   In any event, a strong case has been made that Mark's ἀγαπητός equates to μονογενής (cf. Mk 12:6):[129] Jesus is God's unique Son.

(c)   Σὺ εἶ ὁ υἱός μου ὁ ἀγαπητός, ἐν σοὶ εὐδόκησα

Of all the proposals concerning OT sources, the most widely accepted is that which sees in ἐν σοὶ εὐδόκησα an allusion to Isaiah 42:1.[130]   The fundamental argument against this view is that the language is not the same as the LXX (προσεδέξατο αὐτὸν ἡ ψυχή μου).[131]   Nevertheless, εὐδόκησα is the natural and most common rendering of ב רצה in the LXX[132] as is witnessed by the combined testimony in Isaiah 42:1 of Theodotion and the more idiomatically sensitive Symmachus[133] which versions may reasonably be understood as attempts to update the language in accordance with contemporary usage.[134] The motif of the coming of the Spirit upon Jesus further supports the allusion to Isaiah 42:1.

On this reading then, the attestation of Jesus in terms of an Isaianic 'servant' text further supports the general theme of the inauguration of

---

[127] Marshall, 'Son', 328; Davies, *Matthew*; Stendahl, *School*, 110; Gundry, *Use*, 112; (but see Barth, 'Understanding', 126); Fitzmyer, *Luke*; Bock, *Proclamation*, 115; Brown, *John*; Schnackenburg, *John*.

[128] Either on the basis of synonymy, or if not, of contiguity, cf. Robinson, *Ephesians*. On these terms, Silva, *Biblical*, 120ff. Thus, *pace* Marshall, it is not clear that ἀγαπητός 'avoids any suggestion of election', *Luke*, 156.

[129] Turner, 'ΥΙΟΣ', who also allows ἀγαπώμενος; Souter, 'ΑΓΑΠΗΤΟΣ'; Hooker, *Jesus*, 70f; Lövestam, *Son*, 96; Fuller, *Mission*, 87f; Lagrange; Taylor; Guelich. For the contrary view, e.g. Davies, *Matthew*, 340. Note, however, that 'beloved son' describes Jacob, *T. Isaac* 2:7, and Joseph, *T. Jacob* 1:13, neither of whom were 'only' sons, and the NT has other words to convey the idea of an only child (Turner, 'ΥΙΟΣ', 120) e.g. Rom 8:32 has ἴδιος not ἀγαπητός, while μονογενής is used of children: Lk 7:12; 8:42; 9:38; Heb 11:17; and of Christ: Jn 1:14, 18; 3:16, 18; 1 Jn 4:9. In post-LXX literature examples of ἀγαπητός as 'beloved' are found concerning Baruch (*Par. Jer.* (= 4 *Bar.*) 7:24), Israel (implied but never directly stated in the OT, *m.* '*Aboth* 3:15; cf. 2 *Bar.* 21:21; 4Q504 col. 3, line 6), Ezra (*Gk. Apoc. Ezra* 5:12; 7:13), the saints (*T. Isaac* 6:23), a righteous man (*Pss. Sol.* 13:9) and various other OT figures, cf. Davies, *Matthew*, *ad loc.*

[130] Fnn. 93, 96.

[131] Hooker, *Jesus*, 71f.

[132] Ps 44:3 (43:2); 149:4; 146 (147):11; Jer 14:10 (A); cf. Schlatter, *Matthäus*, 94; Stendahl, *School*, 108; Gundry, *Use*, 31; Lentzen-Deis, *Taufe*, 191f.

[133] Marshall, 'Son', 335; Moo, *Passion*, 114; Guelich, 1.34. I was unable to substantiate these authors' additional citation of Aquila in either Ziegler, 1st. or 2nd. ed.; or Field.

[134] On these versions, Jellicoe, *Septuagint*, 76-94; Würthwein, *Text*, 53f.

the Isaianic NE, especially in view of Isaiah 40-55's apparent presentation of a 'servant' figure as the agent of this NE.[135] Since we have discussed this in more detail elsewhere, suffice it to say that Isaiah 42:1ff presents an unidentified 'servant' as the agent who inaugurates Yahweh's sovereign universal rule over the nations and who, delivering the exiles from their prison, restores 'sight' to 'blind' Jacob-Israel.[136] The same understanding of this 'servant' as agent is present in a number of witnesses to *Tg. Isaiah* 42:1ff. In expansionist references to the return from the jail-like exile and opening of blind eyes (v. 7), the 'servant' is identified as the Spirit-anointed and victorious Messiah (cf. *Tg. Isa* 53)[137]—a not-insignificant association in view of the messianic connotations of the Psalm 2 allusion noted above in the first part of the voice.[138] Further, although the

---

[135] Watts, 'Consolation', 49-59. It is significant that the final summons to participate in the NE (Isa 52:1-12) and the concluding and most expansive song of restoration of Zion/ Jerusalem in 40-55 (54:17), perhaps seen as promise and fulfilment, are separated by the so-called fourth 'Servant Song', 52:13 - 53:12. Given that the final form of this material is the result of conscious editorial activity, and not merely haphazard compilation, the question must be asked as to why these materials are juxtaposed in this way? I suggest that they were perceived as being related, with the fourth song describing the way in which Yahweh's agent, the unknown עֶבֶד, will realise the NE, cf. 49:8-13; Sawyer, *Patmos*, 115; Dumbrell, 'Purpose', 126; Clifford, *Persuading*; 181; Ceresko, 'Rhetorical'; also cf. von Waldow, 'Message', 284f. This may also help explain why aspects of Isa 53 are attributed to the Messiah in *Tg. Isa* 53; Levey, *Messiah*, 63-67; Chilton, *Glory*, 86-96.

[136] Watts, 'Consolation', 50-52.

[137] Levey, *Messiah*, 102; Chilton, *Targum*, 105. The LXX, however, understands the 'servant' in 42:1 as Israel. The attribution of 'servant' characteristics to the SoM figure also in the Similitudes of *1 Enoch* suggests that *Tg. Isa*'s messianic interpretation may also be early, the Similitudes being generally dated pre-AD70, although the lacunae in Qumranic evidence suggests caution cf. Greenfield-Stone, 'Enochic'; Mearns, 'Dating'; Bamptfylde, 'Similitudes'; Schürer, 3.256-59; Charlesworth, 'Jesus', 39ff; but Knibb, 'Date', late first century. (It is not clear, therefore, that 'a date later than the time of Jesus has had to be conceded for the Similitudes', *pace* Lindars, *Son*, 5, let alone for the ideas themselves.) On the messianic interpretations of the 'servant' in *Tg. Isa*, Zimmerli-Jeremias, *Servant*, 59ff; Aytoun, 'Servant'. On messianism in the Targums generally, Humbert, 'Messie'; Seidelin, 'Ebed'; Brierre-Narbonne, *Exégèse*; Grelot, 'L'exégèse', 'L'interprétation'; Levey, *Messiah*; Chilton, *Glory*, 86ff, 112ff. On 'anointing' of the Messiah, Schürer, 2.503f, 517; Lentzen-Deis, *Taufe*, 140-70; De Jonge-van der Woude, *TDNT*, 9.509-27; De Jonge, '"Anointed"'; Charlesworth, 'Messiah'; Chevallier, *L'Esprit*. Cf. *Pss. Sol.* 17:37's allusion to Isa 11, 4QpIsa[a] as reconstructed in Allegro, *DJD*, 5.13f), and the readings of First and Second Rabbinic Bibles, Antwerp Polygot, Reuchlinianus, and Ms. Jews' College of *Tg. Isa* 42:1 and 11:2 (Stenning, *Isaiah*; Chilton, *Targum*, 80f, 28f) which suggest that anointing with the Holy Spirit (or Spirit of Yahweh) is in view.

[138] On the messianic uses of Ps 2:

A) in *Pss. Sol.* 17, Huntress, '"Son"', 120; Wright, *OTP*, 2.643f, 667f; Charlesworth, 'Messiah', 197f; Schüpphaus, *Psalmen*, 64ff, 124ff;

B) in Qumran: 4QFlor 1:10f, Flusser, 'Notes', 103; Betz, *What?*, 88ff; Gärtner, *Temple*, 30ff; espec. Brooke, *Exegesis*; 178ff, 185-219; 1QSa 2:11, יוליד is almost certainly

presence and import of 'servant' imagery in the remainder of the Gospel is a continuing source of contention into which I do not intend to enter at this point,[139] Kee's analysis of Mark 14-15 shows material from the 'Servant Songs' to be in some evidence.[140] Finally, the variations in the Gospels noted in the above discussion on ἀγαπητός, a term which it was noted has some importance in 'servant' passages, indicate an early interpretative tradition that understood an allusion to Isaiah 42:1 in the voice. (It should also be observed that although the descent of the Spirit is consonant with a presentation of Jesus as the Spirit-anointed messenger of Isaiah 61:1; cf. 52:7; Lk 4:18f,[141] the immediate context of Exodus imagery and the content of the voice together suggest that Isaiah 61:1 is not Mark's primary emphasis in the baptism account.)

The appeal to this 'servant' passage allows us now to address the question of Mark's previously noted ambiguity—is Jesus Israel's deliverer or Israel's representative? On the one hand, Hooker has argued that the three key-words in the voice, 'υἱός, ἀγαπητός and εὐδόκησα are all different from the normal translations of the verse(s) ... (and) together form a concept which in the Old Testament is applied only to Israel'.[142]

---

original, e.g. Barthélemy, *DJD*, 1.117; Cross, 'Qumran', 124n8; and makes good sense when it is recognised that the antecedent of אתם is השם אנשי, Gordis, '"Begotten"', 194.

C) in rabbinic literature, e.g. the *baraitha* in *b. Sukkah* 52a; *Midr. Ps.* 2:7 is illustrated with Ex 4:22; Isa 42:1; 52:13 and Ps 110:1, Manson, 'Teaching', 324; cf. Dalman, *Words*, 269ff; Lövestam, *Son*, 19ff; Str-B, 3.19; Lohse, *TDNT*, 8.361ff. See also: *Tg. Ket.* on Ps. 80:16, Huntress, '"Son"', 121; Byrne, *'Sons'*, 78f; Burger, *Davidssohn*, 16-24.

[139] See further below, e.g. Chapter 8, pp. 258-87, and Chapter 9, pp. 349-65.

[140] 'Function', 167ff. Isa 50:6 in Mk 14:65; and allusions, Isa 53:12 (?) in 14:21; *Tg. Isa* 53:5 in 14:58; 53:7 (?) in 14:60; 53:6 (LXX) in 15:15; 50:2f in 15:33; 53:9 in both 15:43 and 46. Note also the interpretive gloss of 53:12 in 15:28.

[141] Lührmann, 'Biographie', 27ff; Betz, 'Jesu', 70ff; Stuhlmacher, 'Thema', 21ff; Schlatter, *Glaube*, 590; Guelich, 'Genre', 206. With the dissection of chs. 40-66 the 'undoubted similarities' between the 'servant' and the 'messenger' were disregarded (*Tg. Isa*, however, interprets the latter as the prophet), cf. North, *Suffering*, 138f; Cannon, 'Isaiah'; Procksch, 'Jesus'; Koch, 'Gottesgeist'; Michel, 'Eigenart'; Zimmerli, '"Gnaden-jahr"', 'Sprache', 69ff (61:1ff is earliest interpretation of the 'Servant Songs'); Schreiner, 'Buch', 157; Smart, *History*; Delitzsch, *Jesaja*; Whybray; Achtemeier, *Community*, noting e.g. v. 1: 42:1, 7; 48:16; v. 2: 49:8, 13; v. 3: 42:3; 50:4; v. 4: 49:8; v. 5: 49:9. On the basis of a more holistic approach this separation seems indefensible, cf. Mettinger, *Farewell*, 10.

[142] *Jesus*, 72f. On Israel as son, Ex 4:22; Hos 11:1; Dt 1:31; cf. Byrne, *'Sons'*, 16f. The later application of sonship to the righteous (fn. 99) may reflect the division within Israel as implied by e.g. Isaiah 56-66, espec. 65; Westermann, 301ff, 402ff; Achtemeier, *Community*, 128ff; Hanson, 134ff; cf. Verseput, 'Role', 538. On εὐδόκησα: Ps 43:4 (44:3); 149:4; Isa 62:4; 2 Sam 22:20 etc.; cf. Robinson, *Ephesians*, 232. Bretscher, 'Exodus', also argues for this view but on the basis of an allusion to Ex 4:22f, with ἀγαπητός as equivalent to πρωτότοκος but without the latter's nationalistic overtones. However, ἀγαπητός never renders בכור in the

Although several detailed studies might raise some questions about the viability of arguments based on 'normal' translations,[143] the fact remains, in support of Hooker, that the prologue is replete with NE imagery. The matrix of the baptismal setting with the coming up out of the water, the descent of the Spirit, and the subsequent forty days in the wilderness, seems to be a conscious echo of Israel's Exodus experience.[144] Thus Jesus is apparently presented, if not explicitly then implicitly, as 'true Israel'— indeed for Hooker, only as 'true Israel'.[145] The difficulty here is not the identification, which has much in its favour, but its exclusivity. There is, after all, substantial evidence in the NT of Jesus being typologically understood in terms of several OT figures or entities and there is no good reason why several of them could not innovatively be brought together here.[146]

The עֶבֶד terminology associated with the Isaianic NE may well provide the key. One of the on-going debates over Isaiah 40-55's enigmatic 'servant' figure has been whether or not the 'servant' is an individual, Israel as a whole, or a remnant within Israel. I have argued elsewhere that the ambiguity of the 'servant' terminology is probably best understood in terms of the Book of Isaiah's remnant motif. On this reading, Jacob-Israel's failure to fulfil her 'servant' role appears to result in the reduction of 'true' Israel to a future and as-yet-unknown but faithful 'servant' Israel who will

---

LXX and Ex 4:22f does not appear to have played a major role in the NT or in early Christian literature—2 Pet 1:17 might be late, Heb 1:6ff (πρωτότοκος) does not include Ex. 4:22f in its list of texts, and the 'allusions' in Rom 8:32 and 1 Jn 4:9 are questionable. It is doubtful that only the *Gospel of the Nazarenes* contains the original tradition, and Bretscher's explanations for the early loss of the original meaning of the voice and for the origin of the 'well-pleased' phrase are unconvincing, cf. Moo, *Passion*, 112ff; Bock, *Proclamation*, 102. His case is further weakened in that the central argument turns on a reconstructed 'literal' translation of Ex 4:22f for which he provides no versional evidence and which itself depends on an original third person address at the baptism. Manson, 'Teaching', 324, cites *Midr. Ps.* 2:7 which refers to Ex 4:22.

[143] E.g. Stendahl, *School*; Gundry, *Use*; Manson, 'Teaching'; see 'OT Sources' above.

[144] See discussion of Isa 63:7ff above, and the 'father/son' terminology in Exodus/NE contexts: Ex 4:22f; Isa 43:6f; 63:36; Jer 31:9, 20; Hos 11:1); see also Mauser, 92ff; Lohmeyer, 25; Fuller, *Mission*, 85f; Feuillet, 'personnalité'; Bretscher, 'Exodus', 305; Lentzen-Deis, *Taufe*, 184. For hovering of the Spirit over true Israel see e.g. 4Q521 1 ii 6.

[145] Hooker, *Jesus*, 72f, although noting that sonship had been narrowed down to the righteous within Israel; cf. Mal 3:17; Eccl 4:10; *Pss. Sol.* 17:30; Wis 2:16, 18; also Byrne, 'Sons', 62f. See further Gerhardsson, *Testing*, 19ff; Hare, *Theme*, 7n2; France, *Jesus*, 50ff; LaRondelle, *Israel*, 64ff; Dodd, *According*, 126ff; Foulkes, *Acts*. Aside from the matter of distinguishing between the notion of 'true Israel' and that of identification with Israel, Marshall's objection to this view ('Son', 334)—that it is never explicitly stated in the NT— can probably be met in the same way he might defend the doctrine of the Trinity.

[146] France, *Jesus*, 43ff.

both deliver imprisoned Jacob-Israel from its blindness and deafness, and implement Yahweh's מִשְׁפָּט over the nations in accordance with the promises made to David.[147] (Note in this connection the presence of the Ps 2 allusion in the voice and *Tg. Isaiah*'s messianic interpretation of Isa 42:1ff.) If this assessment is correct then Mark's apparently dual presentation of Jesus, on the one hand, as the one whose baptism replicates Israel's Exodus experience and thus shows him to be 'true' Israel (cf. Mt. 1:15), and, on the other, as faithless (Jacob-) Israel's messianic 'servant' deliverer (note that both have Yahweh's Spirit put within or upon them, Isa 63:10ff, 42:1) seems best explained, again, in terms of an Isaianic NE background.

c) Other

(i) Mark 1:13 ... ἦν μετὰ τῶν θηρίων

One of the prologue's more difficult images, the peculiar reference in 1:13 to Jesus being with the beasts, may be an allusion to the motifs expressed in Isaiah 11:6-9; 34:14; 65:17-25; or perhaps to Isaiah 43:20.[148] In the first case, Jesus' (assumed) peaceful co-existence with the wild animals[149] is seen as signalling the dawn of new creation conditions associated with the Isaianic NE, while in the second, wild animals in the desert are also mentioned in the context God's provision in the NE. However, it should be noted that the idea of peaceful co-existence is not actually stated in the Mark, the desert does not 'bloom', nor are the animals portrayed as glorifying Yahweh (cf. Isa 43:20). While a categorical rejection might be precipitous, the possible parallels with Isaiah are simply too vague for any convincing case to be made.[150]

---

[147] Watts, 'Consolation', 54f.

[148] See discussion in Best, *Temptation*, xviff, 8f; Guelich, 1.39.

[149] Grundmann, *TDNT*, 7.797, and Guelich, 'Beginning', 8ff, also suggest that 1:13b, c reflects the new-Paradise hope of Jewish expectation (2 *Bar.* 73:6) where Jesus in overcoming Satan's temptation reverses Adam's fall, citing: *T. Naph.* 8; *As. Mos.* 10; *Adam and Eve*, 32-38; 2 *Bar.* 73:6; *b. Sanh.* 59b. This is 'commensurate with Isaiah's depiction of the age of salvation' (11:6-8; 65:25), Guelich, 'Genre', 206.

[150] See Gundry, 58ff.

IV. Isaianic New Exodus Themes in the Prologue

We are now in a position to summarise our findings:

A) Mark's use of εὐαγγέλιον (1:1, 14) appears best understood in terms of the Isaianic announcement of comfort (cf. Isa 40:9; 41:27; 52:7; 60:6; 61:1), namely, the proclamation of Yahweh's INE coming to his people. The thorough-going INE imagery throughout Mark's prologue lends further support to a Palestinian rather than Hellenistic provenance for the term. This is not to deny the possibility of a polemical edge in terms of εὐαγγέλιον's Hellenistic connotations, but only to argue that an exclusively or even primarily Hellenistic provenance seems improbable. From this perspective, Jesus in 1:14 stands in the 'messenger' tradition of Isaiah 61. Interestingly, however, Jesus seems not only to proclaim the immediacy of the INE but also to effect it.

B) the rending of the heavens and the descent of the Spirit (1:10) appears to echo the Isaianic lament over the delay of the INE (Is. 63:7 - 64:12) and, therefore, suggests that Yahweh's long-awaited 'in strength' intervention has come. In this case, Jesus seems to be portrayed either as Israel's representative or some conception of 'true' Israel in that his experience of passing through the water and the Spirit descending on him echoes Isaiah 63's account of Israel's Exodus experience.

C) the allusion to Isaiah 42:1 suggests that Jesus is that 'servant' (*Tg.*: Messiah) upon whom Yahweh has 'placed' his Spirit, who will deliver Israel's captives, and restore sight to 'the blind'. This is consistent with the Psalm 2 allusion which implies that he is also the messianic heir of David who will ultimately prevail in eschatological combat against the enemies of God's people.[151] However, Israel has also elsewhere been described using similar terms. The voice's language, in the context of the general Exodus imagery pervading the baptism and in addition to the particular parallels with Isaiah 63 (noted above), suggests that Jesus is also, in some sense, 'true' or representative Israel. Again it is the INE framework with its dual 'servant' motif that seems to provide the hermeneutic whereby

---

[151] Although 'son of God' may not yet be an exclusive technical title for the Messiah, it is not, thereby, an inappropriate description, cf. fn. 99 above. Later in Mark events occur which suggest that more is meant by this designation than meets the eye, see Chapters 6 and 8.

Jesus can fill the role of both 'true' ('servant') Israel and 'blind' Jacob-Israel's 'servant' (-Messiah) deliverer.

D) Jesus' preaching that the time is now fulfilled nevertheless entails a concomitant call to repentance (1:15). Here, too, and perhaps also to some extent integral to the Warrior-imagery noted above, the element of warning associated with Malachi's message may also be discerned.

IV. Conclusion

It was argued in the previous Chapter that Mark's introductory editorial citation of Isaiah 40 functions iconically, invoking the hermeneutical framework within which he wants his hearers/readers to understand his Gospel. They are to think primarily in terms of Isaiah's NE. Simultaneously there is a warning inherent in the Exodus/Malachi text. The leaders and the people must respond positively to the forerunner, otherwise Yahweh's INE coming will occasion a curse upon the land. The question was asked: is there any further evidence in the prologue to confirm that this is actually Mark's program? By way of response this Chapter has suggested that the prologue is indeed replete with textual icons derived from Israel's ideologically shaped recounting of her history. Set within the overarching schema of the INE, these 'subsidiary' icons form a coherent whole but also serve to emphasise particular elements crucial to Mark's account of the dénouement of Yahweh's intervention.

Mark's prologue begins with the problematic expression, Ἀρχη τοῦ εὐαγγελίου (1:1; cf. 1:14). It was argued that εὐαγγελ- language is particularly suited to the hope of the INE, being characteristic of its announcement. Further, according to Malachi (v. 2b, c), the long-delayed INE was to be announced by a forerunner whose task was the preparation of Yahweh's 'way'. Within this framework, the immediately following and highly selective sketch of John implies that he is indeed Malachi's preparatory Elijah (vv. 4-8). In this context, John's baptismal proclamation of 'the stronger one' is highly suggestive of Yahweh's INE coming, 'in strength', to deliver his people (1:7; 14f).

Having introduced the forerunner and thus preparing the 'way' for his chief protagonist, Mark's tapestry of motifs and images surrounding Jesus' preparation continues to weave together various 'iconic' strands associated with Israel's NE hopes. First, drawing on the last great lament of the book of Isaiah, the rending of the heavens and the descent of the Spirit at the baptism (v. 10) together signal the advent of Yahweh's personal and long-awaited intervention to restore Israel. Then, the divine attestation suggests that Jesus is both the Isaianic 'servant' who as Yahweh's agent of the NE is to deliver Jacob-Israel and to bring light to the nations, and simultaneously David's messianic son in whose reign the 'nations' will be brought under Yahweh's rule. At the same time, the 'servant' motif, the content of the voice, the Exodus imagery of the baptism (cf. Isa 63), and the forty-day wilderness sojourn also show Jesus to be 'true', 'servant' Israel. It was noted that this same ambiguity was characteristic of the way in which 'servant' terminology is used in Isaiah 40ff. Finally, in verses 14-15, Jesus' proclamation is uniquely appropriate to the announcement of the inauguration of Yahweh's INE coming 'in strength'. Furthermore, Jesus seems, at least secondarily, to be presented in terms of the 'messenger' tradition of Isaiah 61, such that he is not only the agent of Israel's deliverance but its herald as well.

Consequently, it appears to be the case that as far as his prologue is concerned Mark is operating out of a consistent INE hermeneutic. Given the role of prologues in literary antiquity, we should expect this then to establish the interpretive framework for the remainder of his work. In the next chapter, we will examine this hypothesis in terms of its implications for the structure of Mark's Gospel.

Chapter 5: The Significance of the Prologue for Mark's Literary Structure

Mark's Gospel exhibits a basic three-fold structure in which there is a progression from 'Galilee-and-beyond', along the 'Way', to 'Jerusalem'. Mark's over-riding NE interest in the prologue suggests that Isaiah's schematic of the NE from 'the nations', along the 'Way', to 'Jerusalem' provides the paradigm for his structure.

I. The Markan Structure

While it may be that Mark's general geographic movement from 'Galilee to Jerusalem' is nothing other than an attempt to provide the simplest possible structure to his Gospel, growing recognition of his literary sophistication suggests otherwise.[1] As noted in the 'Introduction', but while not wishing to overstate Mark's literary skill, few modern scholars would concur with earlier assessments that Mark is simply 'a passion narrative with an extended introduction' (Kähler) or merely put together 'like pearls on a string' (Schmidt).[2]

Although not exhaustive, the results of a representative survey of sixty one analyses of Markan structure revealed a considerable degree of uniformity in spite of the range of major structural units envisaged— ranging from two-fold, with three-fold being the most common, to eight and beyond.[3] While not attempting to offer individual critiques[4] it is clear that even in the face of differing organising rubrics there is substantial agreement as to the major Markan literary divisions.

---

[1] Initially Dibelius, *Tradition*, 219f; Güttgemanns, *Offene*, 74f; and cf. Kümmel, *Introduction*, 86.

[2] See Hooker's perceptive response that the analogy breaks down since pearls are hardly arranged haphazardly, *Message*, 3. More recently Gundry, 1045-49, seems to take this minimalist view.

[3] In addition to my own research, including material provided from Pesch, *Naherwartungen*, 50-53; Swartley, 'Study', 39-53; Baarlink, *Anfängliches*, 68-78; Lang, 'Kompositionsanalyse'; Koch, 'Gliederung'. See now further Boring, 'Beginning'.

[4] See the discussions in the authors listed in fn.3 above.

Of the proposals reviewed, whether presented in terms of geographical-chronological considerations, Christological/theological development centring on Peter's confession, or literary/dramatic conventions, by the far the most frequent divisions were those at 10:52/11:1 or 10:45/10:46 (50 x's), and 8:26/27 or 8:21/22 (45 x's, on three occasions 8:30/31).[5] The small amount of divergence can be explained in terms of these being 'transitional' or 'hinge' passages.[6] This suggests that Mark's basic outline consists of three major sections: 1:14/16 - 8:21/8:27; 8:21/8:27 - 10:45/11:1; and 10:45/11:1 - 16:8. But how are they to be understood?

II. Assessment

a) The 'Way': 8:22/27 - 10:45/11:1

As discussed in the preceding review of his work (Chapter 1) we noted that W. M. Swartley, in particular, emphasises the structural function of the term ὁδός in Mark's Gospel.[7] He begins by noting that several scholars have confirmed the literary integrity of Mark's 'Way'/'journey' section, namely 8:21/8:27 - 10:45/11:1, citing its three triads[8] consisting of passion predictions (8:31; 9:31; 10:32f),[9] the disciples' failure to understand (8:32-33; 9:32; 10:35-41), and subsequent teaching (8:34-38; 9:35-37; 10:42-45).[10] Other unifying themes are: an increasing focus on both Jesus' disciples and discipleship[11] and via the passion predictions on his messiahship, the Christological declarations in the bracketing 'healing of the blind' narratives (8:22-30 and 10:46-52), the recurring use of the SoM title, and the transfiguration scene.[12] Finally, there is Mark's redactional use of ὁδός.[13]

---

[5] Cf. Lang, 'Kompositionsanalyse', 1.

[6] See Trocmé, Perrin, Standaert, Van Iersel, 'beteknis', 'Locality'; Stock, 'Hinge'; and discussion in Chapter 4, p.93, above.

[7] 'Function', after e.g. Best, 'Discipleship'; Schenke, *Wündererzählungen*, 354ff; Malbon, *Narrative*, 68ff; see now also the discussion in Marcus, 31-37.

[8] Güttgemanns, *Candid*, 320ff; Perrin, '*Gattung*', and the comments of Stonehouse, 27, 34.

[9] Strecker, 'Passion'.

[10] Schweizer, 'Leistung'; Haenchen, 'Komposition'; Perrin, 'Towards'; Horstmann, *Studien, passim.*

[11] Weiss, 'Ekklesiologie'; Quesnell; Best, *Following*; Tannehill, 'Christology', 72ff.

[12] Perrin, 'Creative'; Vielhauer, 'Erwägungen'.

[13] 'Function', 77f; cf. Horstmann, *Studien*, 9; Hahn, *Titles*, 224; Minette de Tillesse, *secret*, 306f, and authors cited below. Granted we do not have Mark's sources, the presence of key-words and phrases are helpful indicators, Stein, 'Proper'; Best, *Temptation*, 9.

As Swartley notes, this term appears seven times in the 'Way' section, frequently in key contexts and in conjunction with imperfect verbs (8:27; 9:33, 34; 10:17, 32, 46, 52).[14] Markan redactional intent is suggested in that of these instances Matthew has only two parallels (both with aorists: 20:17b, roughly par. to Mk 10:32; 20:30 par. to Mk 10:46) and Luke merely one (18:35 par. Mk 10:46).[15] This is in stark contrast to the seven occurrences in Mark outside of this section (1:2f; 2:23; 4:4, 15; 6:8; 8:3; 11:8; 12:14) five of which are paralleled in both Matthew and Luke.[16]

Swartley then proceeds to argue that this ὁδός-terminology is strategically placed so as to elucidate both Mark's literary structure and important themes. The phrase ἐν τῇ ὁδῷ is found at the beginning and end of the 'Way' section where it is linked with the miracles of sight (8:27; 10:52), while in 9:33, 34 it locates the dispute over greatness as occurring 'on the way' (cf. 10:32). On the other hand, εἰς ὁδόν is the aborted form used of the rich man who comes into the way but does not follow ἐν τῇ ὁδῷ (10:17, cf. 10:52), while παρὰ τὴν ὁδόν is where the blind man sits (10:46c). The ἐν τῇ ὁδῷ in 8:27 is linked with the teaching on discipleship by the phrase ὀπίσω μου ἀκολουθεῖν in 8:34,[17] and in 9:33, 34 ἐν τῇ ὁδῷ again connects a passion prediction with teaching on discipleship. In 10:32 ἐν τῇ ὁδῷ introduces another passion statement, while in 8:27; 10:46 (παρὰ τὴν ὁδόν); and 10:52 it is connected with key Christological declarations in the crucial bracketing pericopae.

The import of Mark's use of ὁδός has been understood in various ways.[18] While some scholars see it as a mere linking phrase, an example of Mark's *Rahmen*,[19] others perceive a more significant role, for instance, in creating a sense of transition from Galilee to Jerusalem.[20] This sense of journey has been linked with the passion teaching and Jesus' increased concentration on the disciples such that the 'Way' is the way of suffering

---

[14] On the Imperfect as the foreground tense used for emphasis in past contexts where the Aorist is used as background tense, Porter, *Verbal*, 198ff.

[15] This is surprising in view of Luke's 'travel narrative' (9:51ff) and his use of ὁδός in Acts, cf. Repo, 'Weg'; Best, *Following*, 17n6.

[16] 'Function', 75ff.

[17] Perrin, 'Literary', 6.

[18] I am indebted to Swartley for the following survey.

[19] Schmidt, *Rahmen*, 216, 230; Bultmann, *History*, 257, 332; Rigaux, *Testimony*, 8f.

[20] Taylor, 374ff; Cranfield, 268, 335, 346; Michaelis, *TDNT*, 5.66ff.

discipleship reflecting Jesus' own 'way of the cross'.[21] This is then further understood by others as a hermeneutical tool contemporising Jesus' own history in the light of Mark's presently suffering community.[22] J. Schreiber's distinctive view is that Mark's use of ὁδός is redactional throughout and serves to unite the cross and exaltation by presenting Jesus' ministry as a journey leading to a royal enthronement in the Temple and crucifixion.[23] By interpreting Christ's life as an *anabasis* of the redeemer he seeks to explain why Jesus comes to Jerusalem only once.[24] Alternatively, W. H. Kelber argues that Mark combines his ὁδός-motif with another redactional theme, namely, 'entrance into the kingdom of God' (9:47; 10:15, 23, 24, 25 cf. 9:1, 43, 45; 10:15);[25] which terminology he argues derives from the Deuteronomic phrase of 'entering into the land' (LXX: Dt 1:8; 4:1; 6:18; 16:20).[26] On this basis, not only is the ὁδός theme in 8:27 - 10:52 modeled on the Exodus ὁδός-journey into the promised land, but Mark's use of ἐν τῇ ὁδῷ is intended to draw attention to the section as the explanation of the NE 'Way' spoken of in 1:2f with its citation of Exodus 23:20 and repetition of ὁδός-terminology.[27]

Swartley also affirms the programmatic function of Mark 1:2f and the Exodus-journey of the 'Way' section but notes further that the abundant use of ἐξέρχομαι and εἰσέρχομαι is suggestive of Israel's Exodus- and entrance-motifs. He observes in particular that the Exodus account and Mark's Transfiguration are both bracketed with 'entrance-formulas' (Ex 23:23-33; 33:1-3; Mk 9:1, 43-47), and finds an Exodus echo in Mark 9:1's statement that only some of the present generation would see the promised land (a somewhat intriguing example).[28] He favourably cites J. A. Ziesler[29] who in analysing the Transfiguration/Sinai motif observes

---

[21] E.g. Luz, 'Geheimnismotiv', 24f; Schweizer, 216, 221f, 385; Perrin, '*Gattung*', 6; Best, 'Discipleship', *Following; passim;* and Meye, *Twelve,* 73ff.

[22] Weiss , 'Ekklesiologie', 425; Reploh, *Lehrer,* 96, 107, 141, 222, 226.

[23] *Theologie,* 190ff, and Best's critique, *Discipleship,* 17. Gundry's rebuttal (based on ὁδός in 2:23), 442, of Schreiber's claim that Mark does not depict Jesus on a journey before 8:27 seems overdrawn in that it is the disciples who are specifically mentioned

[24] Schreiber, 'Christologie', 171.

[25] 'Parousia', 108ff; *Kingdom,* 67ff.

[26] After Windisch, 'Sprüche'.

[27] 'Parousia', 109; *Kingdom,* 67ff, following Ambrozic, 19f. Cf. Best, 'Discipleship', 326ff; *Following,* 15.

[28] 'Function', 80; following Kelber, 'Parousia', 140.

[29] 'Transfiguration', 265ff; but earlier, Hobbs, 'Gospel', 45ff; cf. Mauser, 111-18; Chilton, 'Transfiguration', 120ff; Lane, who also sees Mk 9:2-8 relating to Mk 14:1 - 16:8 as

the parallel themes of the mountain setting (Mk 9:2; Ex 24:12-15), the six days (Mk 9:2; Ex 24:16),[30] Moses and Jesus both taking three individuals along (Mk 9:2; Ex 24:1-9), a voice which comes from the overshadowing cloud (Mk 9:7; Ex 24:16), and (less convincingly) an ensuing discussion about σκηναί (Mk 9:5; Ex 34:29-35). Swartley adds the theme of the glistening countenances of both Jesus and Moses (Mk 9:7; Ex 34:29-35) and notes that in both accounts the voice comes from the cloud on the seventh day.[31] Jesus' encounter with the epileptic boy following the Transfiguration reflects Moses' confrontation with idolatrous Israel (Mk 9:19 γενεὰ ἄπιστος).[32] Others have suggested parallels between Moses' discourse on marriage (Dt 24), its location (Dt 1:1ff), and the divorce controversy which follows the Transfiguration (Mk 10:2-12, cf. 10:1, εἰς τὰ ὅρια τῆς 'Ιουδαίας [καὶ] πέραν τοῦ 'Ιορδάνου), and between Israel's final arrival at Jericho and Mark's distinctive statement that Jesus 'came into Jericho'.[33] Swartley, proposing that Exodus typology and discipleship materials alternate throughout 8:27 - 10:52,[34] concludes that 'Mark presents in this section of his Gospel "The Way of Discipleship (Suffering and

---

Isa 52:13-15 precedes Isa 53:1-12 (there is, however, little in the text to justify this supposition); Hurtardo; Hooker, 'What?'; also Pesch; Gnilka; Schweizer, who sees Exodus 24 as influential; *pace* Taylor, 386ff; and Cranfield, 293, who appears to regard historicity and symbolism as mutually exclusive. Kelber's attempt, 72-83, to set the Sinai story at odds with his Kingdom theology fails to realise that the first word of God to Moses when Israel arrives at Sinai concerns their being a kingdom of priests and a holy nation, Ex 19:6. The transfiguration has also been variously interpreted as: an anticipation of the parousia, (Lohmeyer, 172ff; Boobyer, *Transfiguration*; but see Riesenfeld's criticisms, *Transfiguré*, 293-98); as Jesus' eschatological enthronement as Messiah (Riesenfeld, *Transfiguré*; appealing to the Feast of Tabernacles and its supposed association with a postulated Enthronement Festival; cf. Smith, 'Tabernacles'; and Farrer, *Study*, 214, who does not however mention an enthronement); as prefiguring Jesus' glory at the Resurrection (Thrall, 'Transfiguration'); or a misplaced resurrection appearance (Bultmann, *History*, 259ff; Carlston, 'Transfiguration'; but see e.g. Boobyer, *Transfiguration*, 11-16; and Dodd, 'Appearances').

[30] Cf. McCurley, 'Six', although his thesis that the phrase is merely a literary device fails to account for the other Sinai allusions.

[31] 'Function', 80.

[32] Farrer, *Mark*, 110; Hobbs, 'Gospel', 45f.

[33] Farrer, *Mark*, 113f; Hobbs, 'Gospel', 47f.

[34] 'Function', 82:

Unit:	Exodus/Entrance Typology		Discipleship materials
1	8:27-30	Common introductory paragraph.	8:27-30
2			8:31-38
3	9:1-29		
4			9:30-41
5	9:43 - 10:31		
6			10:32-45
7	10:46-52	Common concluding paragraph.	10:46-52

Cross) that Leads to the (Promised Land) Kingdom of God"'.[35] Marcus, in his recent work on the subject, while affirming the popular understanding of Mark's redactional use of ὁδός in this section, also goes on to argue that it ought to be understood in terms of Deutero-Isaiah's presentation. Thus Mark's 'Way' section is not 'about the human way *to* the βασιλεία but rather about God's way, which *is* his βασιλεία, his own extension of kingly power'.[36]

Nevertheless, R. H. Gundry has recently launched a root and branch attack on the whole idea of there being a cohesive 'ὁδός' section.[37] With respect to the terminology he argues that a survey of Mark's use of ὁδός across the whole Gospel does not support the idea of a special theological sense in 8:27 - 10:52, nor is there is any link between the 'way' in 1:2f and 8:27 - 10:52 since the one concerns the way of repentance and the other the way of the cross. Neither is it Mark's 'device for moving Jesus from Galilee toward Jerusalem for the Crucifixion' since not only is Jesus initially heading north but Jerusalem is not mentioned as the goal until 10:1. Instead, ὁδός means 'simply the road on which an event takes place' irrespective of the 'direction or destination' of travel.[38] Furthermore, against this being a 'Way' of suffering discipleship in which the 'blind' disciples' eyes are 'opened' to the true nature of following Jesus, Gundry argues that A) the frequent presence of crowds undercuts any notion of a 'private ecclesiastical teaching' (e.g. 8:34 - 9:1; 9:14-27; 10:1-9, 13-16);[39] B) the commonly accepted prediction-incomprehension-instruction triads (8:31 - 9:1; 9:30-37; 10:32-45) constitute only one quarter of the total material which militates against them playing a determinative role and in any case portents of Jesus' death are found both before and after the so-called 'Way' section (e.g. 3:6, 21; 6:4, 17-29 and 14:8, 17-25, and 41-42), as are statements of the disciples' incomprehension (4:13, 40; 6:52; 7:18; 8:13-21);[40] C) the ἐν τῇ ὁδῷ language itself is not in fact associated with the standard three passion predictions: it occurs in 8:27 before 8:31ff, it does not occur in 9:9-13 which ought also to be considered a passion prediction (militating somewhat

---

[35] *Ibid*.

[36] *Way*, 33. Unlike Swartley, Marcus has given due weight to Mark's introductory citation.

[37] Especially, 440-42, 597, 1047.

[38] 442, 1047.

[39] 440.

[40] 440f

against Gundry's point (B)), in 9:33f it concerns the disciples' dispute not Jesus' passion, and in 10:32 it is linked with the crowd of pilgrims, not the disciples);[41] D) the 'healing of the blind' miracles cannot be seen as unique on the grounds of standing alone—if indeed they do (8:22-26 stands beside 7:24 - 8:21)—since the miracle in 9:14-29 is also similarly isolated, and neither do they symbolise the disciples' blindness since the only reference to such a blindness occurs in 8:18, which is outside the 'Way' section;[42] and finally, E) the continued incomprehension of the disciples not only while on the 'Way' (8:32-33; 9:6, 10-11, 18, 27, 32, 33-34, 38-45; 10:10, 13-14, 24-26, 35-38) but also after it—one betrays Jesus, and all but one of the others flee for their lives and he remains only to deny Jesus—flies in the face of any symbolic healing or 'way of discipleship' motif in which the disciples come to realise the true nature of Jesus' messiahship.[43]

What can be said in response to this impressive array? First, as is clear from the preceding discussion, the proponents of a 'Way' theology have always recognised that Mark uses ὁδός-terminology outside the so-called 'Way' section. Their argument, however, has been cast in terms of Mark's redactional interest, something to which Gundry does not really respond. Nevertheless, leaving aside the complex problem of discerning redaction in Mark and simply taking the text as it stands (which is, after all, what Mark's audience would have heard or read), the evidence is not as straightforward as Gundry suggests. Granted that various ὁδός constructions appear throughout Mark, the phrase ἐν τῇ ὁδῷ is in fact only used of Jesus when he and his disciples travel together in 8:27; 9:33f; 10:32, 34; and, depending on how one understands Bartimaeus, in 10:52. Even 11:8 may be included here since it concerns the conclusion of Jesus' journey proper as he arrives in Jerusalem. While this is hardly conclusive, it is still noteworthy that although Jesus and his disciples have been journeying together a great deal since the beginning of the Gospel, Mark nowhere uses this particular phraseology of those journeys, apparently reserving it for the materials associated with the 'Way' section.

Second, Gundry's proposed contradiction between the 'way of repentance' and the 'way of the cross' is problematic, not least because the

---

[41] 442, 1047.
[42] 597.
[43] 597, 442.

former is in fact the way of Yahweh's coming (one repents to prepare for
it). And the contrast between the two is indeed quite the point. Far from
dichotomising the two 'ways', Mark's wonderful irony, as his early
Christology and subsequent triadic passion predictions combine to show, is
that the 'way' of Yahweh's coming in triumphal deliverance of his people
turns out to be nothing other than the scandalous 'way' of Jesus to the
cross (see Chapter 8). Finally, Gundry's observation that Jerusalem is not
mentioned as the goal until well into the 'way' section is correct and ought
to be noted. But this is because the 'way' is not primarily the 'way' to
Jerusalem *per se* as it is a statement, from the perspective of this book, of
the true nature of Yahweh's INE way of restoring his people (again see
Chapter 8). Even allowing this, however, Gundry's rejection of Jerusalem
as goal seems too adamant. Given that Mark's Gospel is probably not a
theological supernova coming out of the blue to his community, it is not
too difficult to imagine that they know of his destination and would have
seen in Jesus' predictions of his passion and death the deepening shadow
cast by what they know awaits Jesus in Jerusalem. And of course, once
even the first-time reader reaches Jerusalem with Jesus, realisation soon
dawns as to where this journey has been heading all along. This is even
more likely given the framing effect of the only two 'healing of sight'
miracles, and Mark's particular use of ἐν τῇ ὁδῷ phraseology.

We may now consider Gundry's arguments directed specifically against
a 'way of discipleship' theology. A) Granted that the presence of the crowds
undercuts any claim that the 'Way' is exclusively concerned with the
private teaching of the disciples, the fact remains that the great bulk of the
material is concerned with their private instruction (8:27 - 9:13; 9:30-50;
10:23-45; even the public 9:14-17 is directed toward the disciples; the
presence of narrative seems a non-issue). This appears to constitute a
significant shift from the emphasis in earlier sections. B) *Pace* Gundry,
what gives the prediction-incomprehension-instruction triads their significance is not primarily their bulk, although it is not insignificant, but
rather their repetition, their obvious literary structure, and their
placement especially given the close conjunction of the first and third with
the framing 'healing of sight' miracles. Further, while Gundry is right in
noting portents of Jesus' death elsewhere, these are hardly comparable to
the extent of, and the compositional artistry evident in, the three

commonly accepted triads. (The incomprehension issue is taken up in (E) below). C) Granted ἐν τῇ ὁδῷ language, as far as it concerns Jesus and his disciples travelling together, may not occur precisely within the first two passion predictions *per se* (8:31-33; 9:30-32—it is in 10:32-34), nevertheless, they are very closely aligned with or integral to the passion prediction triads as wholes. Although Gundry states that 8:27 precedes a passion prediction, he later argues that verses 31ff are 'not ... a new pericope'[44] which tends to undercut his earlier point. The other occurrences, 9:33/34, are also integral to the second passion prediction, being found in the subsequent section which deals with the disciples' incomprehension. Finally, 10:32 is in fact speaking of the disciples and Jesus and not pilgrims generally since the implied pronoun (ἦσαν) is not only resumptive of verses 28-31 but leads naturally into the αὐτοῖς of verse 23b. D) Gundry is right in arguing that the uniqueness of the 'healing of the blind' miracles cannot be sustained on the grounds that they 'stand alone'. However, that they are the only two such miracles in the whole work and that they are so closely linked to the first and last of the passion prediction triads, suggests that they have a significant structural role in Mark's Gospel. This is even more so given the emphasis on Jesus' teaching of his disciples in this section—especially concerning his passion—and the metaphorical association of sight and wisdom and understanding (see Chapter 8). E) As to the disciples' continued incomprehension, Gundry is, in my view, correct. But this hardly excludes the idea of a 'way of suffering discipleship': after all the disciples do follow Jesus. More to the point is that the 'way' of the INE involves not only a confession that Jesus is at least the Christ, but also a recognition that he must suffer and die—which coheres exactly with Gundry's argument that Mark's purpose is to warn against being scandalised by the cross—something which the disciples have not yet grasped. The role of the inclusio 'healings of sight' is to highlight the need for this extra 'sight' (i.e. wisdom) that the disciples clearly have not yet attained and apparently do not at least until after the resurrection.

Finally then, whether or not all of the observations of those who see a 'Way' section are accepted, taken together they provide strong indications of a redactional unity in which the several concerns of wisdom/teaching

---

[44] 445.

and journey (quite possibly with Exodus/NE imagery) are combined. A natural consequence of this assessment is that Jerusalem and what happens there is the climax to which the 'journey' moves.[45]

b) Galilee and Jerusalem

The fairly obvious polarity between Galilee and Jerusalem led E. Lohmeyer and R. H. Lightfoot to posit their geographical theology.[46] Lightfoot notes that the technical term κηρύσσω, with its associations of the in-breaking Kingdom of God, does not appear in the Jerusalem section (apart from 13:10 and 14:9 where it concerns the future missionary activity of the disciples), and so he concludes that from Mark's point of view:

> The despised and more or less outlawed Galilee is shewn to have been chosen by God as the seat of the gospel and of the revelation of the Son of man, while the sacred city of Jerusalem, the home of Jewish piety and patriotism, has become the centre of relentless hostility and sin. Galilee is the sphere of revelation, Jerusalem is the scene only of rejection.[47]

Galilee is seen as the place of the mighty deeds, the home of Jesus' disciples, the place of his acceptance, where the resurrection appearances are to occur, while Jerusalem is the site of the rebellion against the SoM, it is where Jesus' enemies come from, and the place of the cross.[48]

It is doubtful, however, that the 'Galilee-Jerusalem' distinction is so clear-cut.[49] T. A. Burkill observes that revelation also takes place in the Judean desert near the Jordan, which is in fact the place where divine fulfilment begins (1:4f; cf. 1:11 and 9:7).[50] Granted the absence of κηρύσσω after 7:36, it is nevertheless questionable if much should be made of this since it is only used of Jesus' ministry in 1:14, 38f and 45. The two occurrences in 3:14 and 6:12 concerning the disciples may well have future missionary implications, and while it appears with some miracle stories (1:45; 5:20; 7:36) it is missing from the majority (1:31; 2:12; 3:6; 5:34; 7:30; 8:26; 9:29), which suggests that its absence from 10:52 is not of great

---

[45] Piper, 'Unchanging'; Kelber, *passim*, especially notes the sense of movement.

[46] The same duality informs Marxsen; Carrington, *Primitive*; Kelber, *Oral*; Boring, 'Beginning', 46; and to a lesser extent, Freyne, *Galilee*, 33-68, who, with more justification, contrasts the Galilean disciples with the Jerusalem scribes.

[47] Lightfoot, *Locality*, 124f; cf. Lohmeyer, *Galiläa*, 5ff.

[48] Mauser, 93f; Lohmeyer, *Galiläa*; Marxsen, 41.

[49] See especially Stemberger, 'Galilee'; also Faw, 'Outline'.

[50] 252ff. Note, too, that Mark does not explicitly say Jesus first began to preach in Galilee, only that Jesus came to Galilee after John's imprisonment.

significance.[51] On the other hand, διδάσκω which occurs in 4:1 also appears in the region of Judea (10:1) and Jerusalem (12:35; cf. 11:18), and the great crowds which are attracted by Jesus' mighty words and deeds include both Judeans and those from Jerusalem (3:7f).

Galilee is also the scene of considerable opposition. The controversy stories of 2:1 - 3:6 resemble those in 12:13-44.[52] Jesus is rejected in his *patriae* (6:1-6a) and an apparent parallel is drawn in 3:20-35 between the imperception of Jesus' family and that of the scribes (admittedly from Jerusalem) who, along with the Pharisees, again confront Jesus in 7:1-23 (cf. 8:11f). On the other hand, Jesus' triumphal entry into Jerusalem occasions a tumultuous welcome (11:8ff), his teaching appears both equally impressive and well-received (11:18, cf. 1:27; 2:12), such is Jesus' popularity that the hostile leadership are afraid to move against him (11:18; 12:12; 14:2), and the 'empty tomb' is situated in the environs of Jerusalem.[53] Admittedly, the crowd becomes antagonistic in 15:13f, but this is because of the action of the religious leaders (15:11). Burkill is, therefore, correct in recognising that Jerusalem is only associated with hostility to the extent that it is the seat of the religious authorities. Finally, it is true that Jesus does no major miracle in Jerusalem itself apart from cursing the fig tree, but in view of the foregoing discussion this will need to be explained in terms other than Lightfoot's revelation-rejection generalisation.

Even in geographical terms the designation 'Galilee' is not entirely accurate. Granted that most of Jesus' activity occurs within this region, nevertheless there are sojourns that include the Decapolis (7:31), Tyre and Sidon (7:24, 31), and in the Lohmeyer/Lightfoot structure, Judea and beyond Jordan (10:1).[54] These visits on their own would not perhaps be significant were it not for the striking saying to the Syrophoenician woman at the outset of these travels in 7:24-30. This must surely raise the question as to what Jesus is doing in these regions given that he is not concerned with reaching Gentiles *qua* Gentiles? Jesus' statement, together with L. E. Elliott-Binns' ample demonstration of the unshakeable

---

[51] *Pace* Lightfoot, *Locality*, 117f; see Stonehouse, 43ff.
[52] Burkill, 253ff; Dewey, 41ff, 163ff; Sergeant, *Lion*, 45.
[53] Stonehouse, 40-49.
[54] Stonehouse, 28f; Malbon, 'Galilee'; Stemberger, 'Galilee', 415-21.

Jewishness of the Galileans,[55] makes the theory that Galilee is primarily a symbol of the Gentile world equally untenable.[56]

Clearly, the simple designation 'Galilee' is inaccurate. But what then is the rubric under which the three-fold schema of movement from '"Galilee"', along the 'Way', to 'Jerusalem', is to be understood?

III. Mark's Isaianic NE

We have already noted the suggestion by several scholars that the use of όδός in Mark 1:2f has a programmatic role with regard to Mark's 'Way' section. This observation is further supported in that the Exodus 23:20-Malachi 3:1 complex (bearing in mind Mark's apparent presentation of John as Malachi's Elijah) is consistent with the concentration of Jesus' activity within the Temple and his purging it as his first major act on reaching the city. Further, just as the goal of Yahweh's 'Way' in Isaiah is Jerusalem—although combined with wisdom connotations (see Chapter 8)—and in Malachi the Temple, so too for Jesus in Mark. W. R. Telford proposes that Jesus' symbolic act of cursing the fig tree, bracketing as it does the cleansing of the Temple, is the fulfilment of the threat in Malachi 4:5f and suggests in passing its connection with Mark's introductory Malachi 3:1 quote.[57] Telford is, I think, correct here (see Chapter 9): Elijah has been sent and rejected (Mk 9:12), the outcome can only be purging judgement.

It may not be unimportant, therefore, that Mark's Jesus begins his ministry at the very moment of John's imprisonment, especially as the leaders' response to John is the central issue in the opening panel of the Jerusalem confrontations (11:27-33). Significantly, this confrontation is preceded by cursing/cleansing (11:12-25) and followed by the thinly veiled threat in the vineyard parable (12:1-12). The implication of Mark 1:2, that

---

[55] Elliott-Binns, *Galilee*, 13, 25; Mayer, 'Anfang'; Freyne, 'Galilean'.

[56] *Pace* Boobyer, 'Galilee'; Evans, 'Galilee'; Schreiber, *Theologie*, 170-80; Swartley, 'Study'. Appeals to Isa 8:23 would be more convincing if Mark gave some indication that he had it in mind. From this perspective, while 14:28 and 16:7 may reflect Jesus' response to his rejection in Jerusalem, I would suggest, given the associations 'Galilee' has within the NE schema, that it may also indicate that the resurrected Jesus as the Yahweh-Warrior is to continue the deliverance of the captives through the agency of his disciples, cf. Lightfoot, *Gospel*, 116; Carrington, *Primitive*, 88.

[57] *Barren*, 163. Dodd, *According*, 71, had earlier suggested that the purging of the Temple might be in mind in the use of Mal 3:1; cf. Lane, 405; Stock, *Call*, 33.

Jesus is to be identified in some way with the personal manifestation of Yahweh's judging presence, appears to be confirmed by his immediate action on reaching Jerusalem.[58] It might be objected that the threat of coming to the Temple is not explicitly stated in Mark 1:2.[59] But as a number of scholars have noted, the technique of quoting the first section of a verse while the latter unstated section is actually in mind is not uncommon in rabbinic writings.[60]

On the other hand, given what appears to be the programmatic function of the Malachi 3:1 allusion, it may be possible that Mark's emphasis on Isaiah's NE, not only in his introductory OT citation but throughout the prologue, might also be reflected in the broad structure of his Gospel. As we have argued, Isaiah's NE schema involves three stages:

A) Yahweh's deliverance of his exiled people from the power of the nations and their idols;

B) the journey along the 'Way' in which Yahweh leads his people from their captivity among the nations;

C) arrival in Jerusalem, the place of his presence, where Yahweh is enthroned in a gloriously restored Zion.

At first sight this appears to be reflected in the simplicity of Mark's basic literary outline which comprises 'Jesus' ministry in Galilee and Beyond' (1:16 - 8:21/26), the 'Way' (8:22/27 - 10:45/52), and 'Jerusalem' (10:46/11:1 - 16:8).[61] However, it is important to remember that this is not a matter of a straightforward national-geographical (i.e. Jew/Gentile) equivalence between Mark's so-called 'Galilee' section and Isaiah's 'nations'. Nor can it be a purely geographical opposition between receptive Galilee and resistant Jerusalem. Rather, Mark's point of contact lies in the *nature* of Jesus' actions *vis-à-vis* Yahweh's deliverance of his people from the powers of the nations and their idols.[62] The only geographical consideration is that this happens, as in the INE, outside of Jerusalem. That Jesus' delivering actions are not confined merely to Galilee is, therefore, exactly in keeping

---

[58] *Pace*, Kümmel, *Promise*, 118n53. Arens' argument, ΗΛΘΟΝ, that the ἦλθον sayings have messianic implications may well be justified; cf. Hughes, 'John'.

[59] Gould, *Mark*, 5, notes but does not develop the threat element.

[60] Cranfield, 'Study', 59; Jeremias, *TDNT*, 5.701; Marcus, 200; cf. Dodd, *According*, 126f.

[61] Koch, 'Gliederung', has already suggested the compatibility of Mark's geographical and thematic interests.

[62] I.e. the diaspora, but which now includes deliverance for *both* Jews and Gentiles, *pace* Boobyer, 'Galilee'; Evans, 'Galilee'; and Swartley who focus on Gentiles only.

with the idea of an Isaianic Yahweh-Warrior at work among a Jewish (cf. Mk 7:24-30) diaspora. Similarly, Mark's 'Way' section is, at least on the surface, compatible with the journey of Isaiah's NE 'Way', and in both cases Jerusalem is the goal.[63]

If Mark has been consciously following this pattern, we should expect to find parallels between the activities associated with a given section of the Isaianic NE schema and its equivalent in the Gospel. It is to a consideration of possible correlations that we now turn.

---

[63] See now also Marcus, 33-41.

Chapter 6: Jesus as Yahweh-Warrior and Israel's NE Healer and Provider in Mark 1:16 - 8:21/26

In keeping with the INE motif, Mark presents Jesus' deliverance of those in bondage to the demons as the equivalent of both the Yahweh-Warrior's and the enigmatic 'servant's' deliverance of the Isaian captive. Similarly, Jesus' healing of the blind, deaf/dumb and lame, his forgiveness of sins, and his feeding of the multitudes signals the inauguration of the Isaianic NE.

I. Introduction

In the previous Chapter, building on our estimation of the importance of the Isaianic NE prophecies for the Markan prologue, we suggested that the parallels between the NE schema and the structure of the Gospel are the result of Mark's conscious attempt to interpret Jesus within an Isaianic NE framework. The purpose of this Chapter is to test this hypothesis further by assessing to what degree, if any, correlations exist between the first component of the NE schema, that is, Yahweh's deliverance of his exiled people from the power of the nations and their idols, and Jesus' activities in the first major section of Mark.

Although I do not intend to undertake a detailed comparative study of the significance of miracles in Mark and other traditions of the NT period,[1] several points should be noted. In his analysis of the so-called pre-Markan miracle catenae, Paul Achtemeier states that 'any discussion of "signs and wonders" related to Jewish traditions must begin with the figure of Moses', and that 'the deliverance of the Exodus and of the messianic time is seen in typological relation with the desert wandering on occasion serving as a prototype of the messianic time'.[2]   Although

---

[1] See for example Kee, *Miracle, Medicine*; and Blackburn, *Theios*.

[2] 'Origin', 202; cf. Tiede, *Charismatic*, 178ff. The position taken here is that the OT provides the primary 'horizon' for understanding the Gospels' presentation of Jesus' miracles, cf. e.g. Meye, 'Horizon', 5f, and Blackburn, *Theios*, who notes how well many of Jesus' miracles correlate to activities otherwise the sole prerogative of Yahweh. Achtemeier builds on Meeks' argument in *Prophet-King* that Josephus, and especially

heading in the right direction given the priority of Israel's founding moment, attempts to fit Mark into a first Exodus model were not as we have seen convincing, and in any case fail to take sufficient account of the NE traditions in the prophets. Furthermore, apart from the fact that both Moses and Jesus worked wonders, even a cursory examination of the former's miracles, as recorded both in the OT and in the Moses literature of Hellenistic and Palestinian Judaism, reveals the degree of their dissimilarity—except perhaps for the feedings and, superficially, the sea crossings.[3]

Likewise, although the miracles of Elijah and Elisha apparently influenced the popular conception of the 'charismatic' rabbi,[4] similarities with any given miracle of Jesus are limited.[5] None of this is to deny the possible, perhaps probable, influence of Moses or Elijah/Elisha traditions on the accounts of some of Jesus' miracles. The point, however, is that several of Mark's more important categories of miracles do not appear to be susceptible of explanation on the basis of either of these traditions.

This Chapter will argue that Mark's presentation of Jesus' understanding of his exorcisms, his accounts of Jesus' healings of the blind, deaf-mute, and lame, of Jesus' pardoning sins, and of the miraculous feedings appear to be cast in an Isaianic NE perspective. It is interesting, therefore, that several scholars have regarded the miracles reported in, for example, 4:35 - 5:43, 6:34-44, 45-52; 7:32-37; and 8:1-10 as epiphanic.[6] Such powerful 'self-manifestations' are entirely in keeping with the proposal that Mark presents Jesus as the inaugurator of the

---

Philo, used the miraculous to authenticate Moses as a θεῖος ἀνήρ (but see Tiede's criticisms, *ibid.*, 237ff, and on the general problematic of θεῖος ἀνήρ most recently Blackburn, *passim*).

[3] Meeks, *Prophet-King*, in dealing with miracles in John mentions no Mosaic counterpart to Jesus' healing of e.g. the blind (9:1-12) or the lame (5:1-9). See further the examples cited in Tiede, *Charismatic*, 101-237, and the 'signs' promised by various 'prophets' in Josephus: *Ant.* 20.97f; 20.167ff; and *B.J.* 7.437ff; cf. Theissen, *Social*, 60; Tiede, *Charismatic*, 197ff; Smith, 'Occult', 251; espec. Betz, 'Miracles', 226-31, and *Studies*, 235f, where he proposes (unsuccessfully in my view, see fn. 127 below) that Jesus and the disciples crossing the lake reflects Moses' and Israel's journey through sea.

[4] E.g. Honi the Circle-Drawer (= Onias the Righteous) and Hanina ben Dosa; *b. Ber.* 34b (cf. 1 Kgs 17:91f; 18:42); *m. Ta'an.* 3:8; *b. Ta'an.* 19b (cf. 1 Kgs 18), 23a; *b. B. Meṣ.* 59b; see also Vermes, *Jesus*, 69-82; Betz, 'Miracles', 219f; Kolenkow, 'Miracles', 1484-86. On the sages' perception of miracles in this period, Urbach, *Sages*, 97-123.

[5] Cf. e.g. Heising, 'Exegese', 86f; Flammer, 'Syrophoenizerin', 470f; Kertelge, 116f, 152; Brown, 'Jesus'; Lindars, 'Elijah'; Achtemeier, 'Origin'. Roth's attempt, *Hebrew*, 8, to draw close parallels *en toto* between Jesus and Elisha must be deemed unsuccessful.

[6] E.g. Kertelge, *passim*; Achtemeier, 'Origin', 206; cf. Dibelius, *Tradition*, 91, 290.

Isaianic promises whereby Yahweh himself comes to deliver as he 'makes bare his arm' (cf. Isa 40:3, 10; 51:9; 52:10; 53:1; 59:16ff; 63:5).

II. The Distribution of Miracles

One of the arresting features of Mark's Gospel is the disproportionate distribution of Jesus' miracles.[7]   Although the inherent uncertainties in verse counting make it a rather blunt instrument, nevertheless, the importance of Jesus' miracles for Mark can be seen in that approximately 177 out of 666 verses, or 27% of Mark's Gospel deals with miracles (taking the shorter ending). If the passion narrative (ch. 11ff) is excluded, this rises to 40% (some 168 out of 425 verses).[8]   On the basis of the structure suggested earlier, if we concentrate on the first section alone (to 8:26) Jesus' miracles comprise an even higher 47% (approximately 145 out of 311 verses), while in the remaining two sections (8:27 - 16:8) miracles (an exorcism, a healing, a 'cursing', and the resurrection) represent only 11% (about 40 out of 355 verses). Furthermore, Mark's summaries, confined as they are to the first section, also reflect a similar interest in Jesus' healings and casting out of demons (1:32-34, 39; 3:10-12; 6:5, 53-56). Even allowing for some variation due to disagreement over what constitutes miracle material, this represents a rather lop-sided distribution.

It has been suggested that this apparent diminution of Jesus' miracle working is the result of increasing hostility and obduracy.[9] But this hardly accounts for the fact that a large number of miracles occur after the series of controversy stories. Nor, as we saw in the previous Chapter, can it be the result of a Galilee-Jerusalem antithesis.[10] On the other hand, this early concentration of miracles would in fact be consistent with an INE hermeneutic. Just as in the INE the deliverance and healing of Israel was the precursor to her return along the way to restored Zion-Jerusalem so

---

[7] Thus the transfiguration and resurrection are not included. If pericopae were to be counted as wholes—they have not been unless a concern for the miracle pervades the entire unit—then the proportion would be even higher and the distribution even more skewed.

[8] Cf. Richardson, 36f; Manson, *Jesus*, 34f. Many commentators recognise the structural function of the two sight miracles in 8:22-27 and 10:45 - 11:1, and Kolenkow, 'Beyond', 160, suggests that miracles serve a similar function in the controversy stories of 2:1 - 3:6.

[9] Sergeant, *Lion*, 45-62; cf. Tolbert, *Sowing*, 186.

[10] Chapter 5, pp. 132ff.

too Mark, prior to his 'Way' section, presents Jesus in terms of the Yahweh-Warrior who delivers the captives from demonic bondage, as Israel's healer, and as the one who forgives her sins.

III. *Jesus and the Isaianic Yahweh-Warrior*[11]

The pervasive Markan theme of Jesus' eschatological conflict with Satan has been widely recognised—even if there is some debate over its precise nature.[12]   What concerns us, however, is whether there is any evidence that Mark's presentation is influenced by Isaiah's account of the Yahweh-Warrior as the agent of the NE.[13]

a) *The Yahweh-Warrior in Isaiah*

The recognition of Yahweh-Warrior imagery in Isaiah is nowadays commonplace.[14] The programmatic prologue concludes with a portrayal of Yahweh coming בְּחָזָק ... זְרֹעוֹ מֹשְׁלָה לוֹ (40:10; LXX: μετὰ ἰσχύος) as he delivers his people—they become his booty (שְׂכָרוֹ ...וּפְעֻלָּתוֹ cf. 40:11)[15] —with an outstretched arm in the sight of all the nations (40:10; cf. 51:9; 52:10).[16] This introductory motif continues as Yahweh is presented as a

---

[11] On Yahweh as warrior: Fredriksson, *Jahwe*; von Rad, *Heilige*; Wright, *Theology*, 121-50; Stolz, *Jahwes*; Cross, *Canaanite*, 91-111; Weippert, 'Heiliger'; Miller, 'Divine'; *Divine*; Lind, *Yahweh*; Kang, *Divine*; Longman and Reid, *Warrior*.

[12] Weiss, *Predigt*, first drew attention to this aspect of Jesus' ministry (ET: *Proclamation*, 74ff); also e.g. Robinson; Barrett, *Spirit*, 55ff; Kümmel, *Promise*, 105ff. Kallas, *Significance*, 107, argues that 'eschatology cannot be understood apart from demonology'. Although Best, *Temptation*, 15, places the emphasis on an initial victory, he nevertheless appears to regard the exorcisms as part of the overall eschatological battle, even if only as mopping-up operations. Koch, *Bedeutung*, 172, denies, however, that the exorcisms function 'primär' in this way, but fails to take appropriate notice either of the Isaianic NE background in general, or of the structural and thematic importance of the Beelzebul controversy in particular (see below). On Qumran's Holy War motif and possible parallels with Jesus, see e.g. Betz, 'Heiliger', 'Sinai'; Perrin, *Kingdom*, 170f.

[13] Cf. Betz, 'Jesu', 72, cited on p. 54 above. Both Betz and Stevens, 'Mark', link the SoM with the ancient Divine-Warrior image, a possibility that lies outside the scope of this book. While it is readily accepted that many OT motifs are employed in Mark, the concern herein is to examine the influence of the INE.

[14] In addition to the standard commentaries see also Hanson, *Dawn*, *passim*.

[15] Elliger, *Deuterojesaja*, 37, prefers 'wages' as in the Jacob story (Gn 30:28-33; 31:8), but Yahweh is scarcely a hireling. The military imagery is to be preferred, cf. Ezek 29:18ff with the parallel use of these terms and שלל and בז, Begrich, *Studien*, 59.

[16] Ringgren, *TWAT*, 5, cols. 409f: 'Das Bild entstammt wahrscheinlich der Vorstellung von JHWH als Krieger'; see Ex 6:6; Dt 4:24; 7:19; 9:29; 11:2; and further Ex 7:5, 19; 8:1f, 13; 9:22; 10:12, 21f; etc.

mighty warrior and man of war (42:13-15; Ex 15:3) delivering the שְׁבִי גִּבּוֹר (49:24ff; 51:14) who have been plundered, despoiled, and hidden away in the darkness of prisons (42:22f; 49:9; 51:14; 52:2; cf. 35:3ff). Just as he had crushed the might of Pharaoh at the sea, so he will again deal with Jacob-Israel's oppressors (43:16f; 51:9f; Ex 14:25, 28; 15:10, 21; cf. 34:2ff).[17] Whereas in chapters 1-39, the title יהוה צְבָאוֹת[18] with its Warrior overtones primarily connoted judgement—as Yahweh had previously fought for Israel, now with 'outstretched arm' (5:25b; 9:11b, 16b, 20)[19] he would fight against her (1:7-9, 24f; 2:12; 3:1; 10:23 etc.)[20]—in chapters 40-55, יהוה צְבָאוֹת occurs primarily in salvation oracles which proclaim the NE (45:13; 47:4; 51:15; 54:5; cf. 13:1ff; 40:26).[21]

Although various nations are mentioned as the objects of Yahweh's judgements (primarily Babylon, but also others, 43:14; 47:1ff; 48:14; and 41:11ff; 49:26; 51:7f, 22f), his warrior activities are conceived fundamentally in terms of the nations' deities.[22] Hence the anti-idol polemics on the one hand (40:18-20; 41:9-20; 44:9-20; 46:5-7(8)), and the trial speeches on the other, are primarily directed against the gods who epitomise the wealth and power of Israel's oppressors (41:1-5, 21-29; 43:8-13; 44:6ff and 45:18-25).[23]

---

[17] Seidl, 'Yahwe'; Cross, *Canaanite*, 91ff. The term 'Jacob-Israel' is intended to reflect the Hebrew parallelism common in Isa 40-48 e.g. 44:1, 'But now listen, O Jacob, my servant, Israel, whom I have chosen' but which disappears in chs. 49-55, see Watts, 'Consolation', 49ff.

[18] Wildberger, 1.217; Miller, 'Divine', 102f, and *Divine*, 151ff; Cross, *Canaanite*, 91-99; Mettinger, 'YHWH.'

[19] Sheppard, 'Redaction', 126, sees this language adumbrating the judgements against the nations in Isa 13-23.

[20] See further, Isa 8:5-8, cf. Ps 69:3-24, Evans, 'Use', 95f; and also Isa 28:21, cf. Josh 10:6ff and 2 Sam 5:17ff, Kaiser, 2.255.

[21] Following Schoors, *Saviour*.

[22] Pharaoh was similarly regarded as a deity who, in imitation of Horus and Re, exercised absolute authority over all things; Beale, 'Exegetical', 149, citing Pritchard, 'Theology', 5f, and Ringgren, *Word*, 22.

[23] Clifford, 'Function'; Kim, 'Verhältnis'; Koole, 'beeldenstorm' (cited in Spykerboer, *Structure*, 29); Roth, 'Life'; Spykerboer; Westermann; Wink, *Naming*, 27. Kim, Koole, and Westermann add 42:17; 45:16f, 20b and 46:1f, and Koole alone, 48:5. Stuhlmueller, 'Transitions', 6, somewhat idiosyncratically sees 40:18ff; 41:6f; 41:21-29; 42:8f, 16f; 43:10; 44:6; 45:21; ch. 46; and 48:1-11 as warnings against idolatry. Bonnard, *Isaïe*, 23ff, has a prominent role for the polemics in his analysis of the structure of 40-48; cf. Spykerboer, 185ff. Clifford notes some of the themes: 44:6-22, a comparison between the nations *qua* idol-makers and Israel is central to this text, where Yahweh who fashioned Israel is contrasted to the nations who fashion their silent and dumb idols; 46:1-13, Yahweh is powerful, he consoles and bears his people, effortlessly delivering them. The nations' idols on the other hand are weak and need consoling, and even though much effort and wealth is expended upon them, they are carried by beasts of burden into captivity. The polemics are

The point being that Yahweh's redemptive exercise of his unilateral control of history will result in the total dethronement of the idols and therefore Israel's deliverance.[24]

At the same time, the role of Yahweh as Warrior does not preclude the complementary activity of his human agent: the conqueror Cyrus will be Yahweh's instrument (45:1-7; cf. 42:28; 45:13; 46:11; 48:14).[25] I have argued in more detail elsewhere, however, that for various reasons Israel rejects Yahweh's agent Cyrus and that this negative response apparently occasions the appointment of an 'unknown' and future 'servant' who will release the exiles (42:7; 49:9) and succeed in effecting Israel's NE (49:8-13).[26]

In the Isaianic accounts of the post-exilic hope (Isa 56-66), the Warrior imagery is also aligned with Exodus language (63:8-14, 19ff; cf. 57:14f; 58:8f; 60:4ff; 62:10f;[27] cf. 66:15f). Yahweh is described as a warrior who will bring avenging recompense on his enemies and deliverance to Zion (59:15b-20; 63:1-6),[28] and once again his coming is μετὰ ἰσχύος (LXX 63:5). The importance of this image is indicated by the fact that these extended Warrior accounts bracket the description of Jerusalem/Zion's restoration (60:1 - 62:12), which itself constitutes the heart of chapters 56-66.[29] The point is firmly made in both passages that, in the absence of anyone else to help, Yahweh's arm alone would bring salvation (63:5; 59:16). Such language is

---

situated as follows: 40:18-20 and 46:5-7(8), in disputations; 44:9f is contiguous with a trial speech involving Israel (Preuß, *Verspottung*, 208-15, sees this as applying both to Jews and Gentiles); 41:7 instead concerns the nations. Less generally accepted passages: 42:17 and 45:16, in proclamations of salvation; 48:5, in a disputation; 45:20 in a trial scene involving the nations and 46:1f specifically against Babylon.

[24] 'Das Endheil von Jahwe bringt notwendig auch die Entmachtung der Götzen mit sich,' Preuß, *Einführung*, 62. Cf. Clifford, 'Function', 459ff, who sees in 40:12-26 a succession of dethronements culminating in the power which brought the gods to their knees being given to Israel.

[25] On the importance of Cyrus, Watts, 'Consolation', 41-49; also: Barnes, 'Cyrus'; Simcox, 'Cyrus'; Jenni, 'Kyros'; Jones, 'Abraham'; Koch, 'Stellung'. As anti-type of Moses as deliverer, Ogden, 'Moses'. Schoors, *Saviour*; Westermann; Whybray; Clifford, *Persuading*; and Spykerboer, *Structure*, all grant a central role to Cyrus with Smart, *History*, being the lone dissenting voice.

[26] 'Consolation'.

[27] A catena of quotations from 40:1-11; 52:1-12; Muilenburg, 'Isaiah'; Westermann.

[28] Hanson, *Dawn*, 124ff, 203ff; Holmgren, 'Avenger'; Polan, 'Salvation'; Gross, 'Sion'.

[29] E.g. Dumbrell, 'Purpose', 112; Rendtorff, 'Komposition', 305; Gottwald, *Hebrew*, 508; and Clements, 'Unity', 128. This section draws more heavily from 40-55 than any other part of 56-66.

suggestive of the personal intervention of Yahweh himself which is of course consistent with the highly personal language of 40:1-11.[30]

In *Tg. Isaiah* there is a particular emphasis on the 'strength' of God in the expansionistic expression תקוף דרע גבורתיה (e.g. 40:10; 51:5 (*bis*); 53:1). At the same time, the activity of the enigmatic 'servant' figure is cast in messianic terms which stress his activity as liberator and 'warrior who despoils the enemies of his people and restores Jewish sovereignty'.[31] Again, although of uncertain date, *Tg. Isaiah* may well be suggestive of earlier traditions. In other Jewish literature more clearly from the NT period, Warrior imagery is used of Yahweh as he comes to deliver his people (e.g. 1QM 12:10-14; 19:2-8; cf. Isa 49:23 and 52:2; Wis 5:16-23; Sir 35:22 - 36:17; *As. Mos.* 10)[32] and sometimes of his word (Wis 18:15; cf. *Sib. Or.* 3:669-795). Similarly, military and/or Warrior language is used in some traditions of a messianic figure, who engages the ungodly powers and restores his people (e.g. *Pss. Sol.* 17:23-39;[33] *2 Bar.* 39-42, 72-74; *1 Enoch* 37-71;[34] *4 Ezra* 12:31-34; 13; Philo, *Prae.* 16 (91-97); cf. 1QSb 5:27; 1QSa 2:11f[35]; 4QpIsa[a]).[36]

---

[30] Whybray, 254; cf. Westermann, 382.

[31] Levey, *Messiah*, 102; Chilton, *Targum*, 105; thus 'to bring back their exiles, those who are like prisoners, from among the nations; and to deliver them from the bondage of empires', 42:7; 'then the glory of all the kingdoms will be for contempt and brought to an end; they will be weak and sickly', 53:3a; 'he will deliver over the mighty ones of the nations as lambs to the slaughter', 53:7b; also *Tg. Isa* 10:27 'and the nations shall be shattered before the Messiah', and 11:10; cf. *Yerus.* and *Neof. Tgs.* on Gn 49:11. The reference to the building of the Temple in 53:5, while helping to date that particular addition, should not be allowed to function as a *terminus a quo* for the rest of the passage, cf. Chilton, *Glory*, 93-96.

[32] This is particularly evident in Qumran, Ringgren, *Faith*, 152-66; Osten-Sacken, *Gott*, 34-41, 214-38. On the OT sources of this imagery throughout 1QM, Carmignac, 'citations'.

[33] Charlesworth, 'Messiah', 197f; and De Jonge, *TDNT*, 9.514, who may be justified in detecting an emphasis on the 'spiritual' dimension, seem to go too far when they then go on to exclude a national, political, military component. First, the expression 'sword of his mouth' is a metaphor which draws attention to the overwhelming authority of the ruler (Watts, 'Meaning') and does not at all exclude military means. Second, the language of 'not rely(ing) on horse and rider and bow' seems less a repudiation of military means *per se* as a reflection of the OT critique of the Israel's past self-reliance on her own military capability, which, after all seems to be the point of the final verse (cf. Ps 20).

[34] On the probability of there being a common referent for the four titles (Anointed One, Righteous One, Son of Man, and Chosen One) see VanderKam, 'Righteous'. Charlesworth's earlier compartmentalised account of the 'Anointed One' in these passages, 'Messiah', 206f, needs now to be read in the light of his recent endorsement of VanderKam's work, 'Messianology', 13.

[35] Which presuppose a holy war, so Vermes, *DSSE*, 100.

[36] On the various and widespread traditions concerning the Messiah's role in the end-time conflict and destruction of hostile powers, Schürer, 2.501-29 and the literature cited

b) Isaianic Yahweh-Warrior Imagery in Mark

In Chapter 4 we have already noted a number of elements in Mark's prologue which intimate the idea of divine conflict, whether implied in terms of Yahweh's coming 'in strength' (1:7, 14f) or suggested by the imagery of the rent heavens (1:10) with its connotations of divine intervention on exiled Israel's behalf. But does this motif come to prominence in the first section of Mark, as might be expected if an INE hermeneutic is operating? There are a number of indications which suggest that it does.

(i) The Beelzebul Controversy—Jesus, Demons and the Yahweh-Warrior

One possible case is the Beelzebul controversy in Mark 3:22-30. Here, in response to a charge laid by some leaders from Jerusalem, Jesus describes his exorcisms using the famous 'strong man' imagery: ἀλλ᾽ οὐ δύναται οὐδεὶς εἰς τὴν οἰκίαν τοῦ ἰσχυροῦ εἰσελθὼν τὰ σκεύη αὐτοῦ διαρπάσαι, ἐὰν μὴ πρῶτον τὸν ἰσχυρὸν δήσῃ, καὶ τότε τὴν οἰκίαν αὐτοῦ διαρπάσει.

---

therein; Leivestad, *Christ*, 3-8; Klausner, *Messianic*, 483-501; Charlesworth, 'Messiah', 'Messianology'; Levey, *Messiah, passim*; Kuhn, *Enderwartung*, 176-88; Betz, 'Heiliger'; Stevens, 'Jesus'. On the application of Isa 63:1-6 imagery to the Messiah, Grelot, 'L'exégèse'.

While recent discussions are to be applauded for their highlighting the diversity of messianic expectation, there are occasions when their only evidence is the silence of a given author. However, silence on an aspect of messianic expectation seems a dubious ground to argue that such an idea is not part of a given author's expectation, it being unreasonable to expect an author to say everything he believes about the Messiah in a given passage. Furthermore, some contrasts fail to carry conviction, e.g. Charlesworth, 'Messiah', makes some play of the fact that on occasions the Messiah is seen as acting while at other times God himself acts (even in one author, e.g. *2 Baruch*). But, given that throughout the OT a victory can be won by Yahweh's agent and yet Yahweh be proclaimed as the deliverer of his people, such a distinction may be too rigid.

In addition, many commentators often limit themselves to those passages in which a figure is explicitly described by 'Messiah/anointed' language, but as Dunn, 'Messianic', 366, and Charlesworth, 'Messianology', 10, note this almost certainly distorts the issue. The assumption that different titles necessarily indicate different eschatological figures and expectations also seems strange, not only in the light of the ease with which early Christians applied various titles to Jesus, but also given similar tendencies in *1 Enoch*, VanderKam, 'Righteous' (see fn. 34 above).

Finally, given that most of our sources are literary and that literary works tend not to be the products of the common people, there is a real danger that our reconstruction of messianic expectation might be predominantly that of the literary and wealthy classes and, therefore, tell us little of the perhaps less nuanced popular expectation/s of the vast bulk of the people who comprised Jesus' audience.

The pericope appears to reflect Mark's characteristic 'sandwich' technique in which the Beelzebul controversy (3:22-30) is inserted within the question about family[37] (3:20-21; 3:31-35).[38] J. Lambrecht proposes a threefold thematic chiasm:

a.		Jesus at home and the initiative of the relatives (3:20-21)
	b.	The scribes' accusation (3:22)
		c.	Jesus' apology (3:23b-29)
	b'.	scribes' accusation repeated (3:30)
a'.		Arrival of relatives and declaration of true kinship (3:31-35)[39]

While helpful, this analysis does not do justice to the role given to the crowds over against the negative response of Jesus' relatives in verses 22, 21 and 31, 32f—an important consideration because one of the issues of the passage concerns the nature of Jesus' true family.[40] Consequently, based on what appears to be Mark's interest in the response to Jesus of the three groups—crowds, family, scribes—the following 'broad-brush' analysis seems preferable:

a.		The crowds gather to Jesus (3:20)
	b.	Jesus' relatives' estimation: he his beside himself (3:21)
		c.	The scribes' accusation and Jesus' response (3:22-30)
	b'.	Jesus' relatives arrive 'outside' to take charge (3:31)
a'.		The crowds 'inside' and Jesus' true family (3:32-35)[41]

The linking of the scribes' blasphemous accusation, the misunderstanding of Jesus' relatives, and his description of his true family in terms of doing the will of God, highlights the importance of recognising aright who Jesus is—already the ground is being prepared for the warning in the following pericope to 'hear carefully' (4:9, 23-25). The significant point is the connecting of the issue of recognition with the charge of the scribes concerning the source of Jesus' authority. This charge, which constitutes the heart of the pericope, turns on Jesus' manifest authority over the demons.[42]

---

[37] οἱ παρ' αὐτοῦ is difficult. Although it may simply indicate 'friends', the 'sandwich' structure suggests 'family' (Best, 'Mark'; Hooker, 114; Guelich, 1.172), a fact which counts against Wansbrough, 'Mark', 234f; and Wenham, 'Meaning', 296f, who argue, respectively, that the crowd or the Twelve are in view.

[38] Cf. Hooker, 114; Guelich, 1.169. On the unity of this passage, Best, 'Mark'.

[39] 'Relatives', 252. See now especially, Shepherd, *Sandwich*, 111-38.

[40] Cf. Hooker, 114. Robbins, *Patterns*, 11 (in his original ms), sees the three charges: Jesus is beside himself (v. 21), he has Beelzebul (v. 22) and he casts out demons by the ruler of demons (v. 22).

[41] Cf. Gundry, 170, and the similar structure in 11:1 - 12:12; Chapter 9, p. 304, below.

[42] Jesus' authority is of primary importance in his first exorcism, Kertelge, 56f.

The central scene is set with the accusation that Jesus is possessed of 'Βεελζεβούλ'. The meaning of this title is unclear,[43] perhaps 'Lord of the Flies' (cf. Βάαλ μυῖαν θεόν, LXX 2 Kgs 1:3, 6; Jos. *Ant.* 9.19), although if זבול means 'dwelling' it may explain Jesus' use of the οἰκία-imagery—the house of the (strong) Lord of the House is being plundered by a Stronger One.[44] Whatever the case, the important point is that Mark's Jesus is here accused of being in league with the prince of demons (v. 22b; cf. 1QS 3:20-21; *T. Sol.* 2:9; 3:5; 6:1).[45]

Jesus' three-fold response demonstrates the fallaciousness of the charge (vv. 23-26). If it were true, not only would Satan be destroying himself, but he would already have met his end. Obviously this is not the case. The second part of Jesus' parable answer may then be intended to explain how Satan can be plundered if he is not destroyed, namely, that he is bound. The precise implications of verse 27 are difficult to disentangle: if Satan is already bound, when did this binding occur, and how then are individuals still within his power?[46] Are we to understand that now that Satan has been bound his demonic underlings are easy prey? Or, as Leivestad suggests, are we better not to search for a single decisive event but instead to regard each exorcism as an instance of binding and plundering?[47]

(a) The 'Strong Man' Saying

There is, however, a further and perhaps more important consideration: how does the 'strong man' saying relate to the fundamental issue, namely, the accusation that Jesus is in league with Beelzebul? W. Lane suggests that the term ἰσχυρός alludes to ὁ ἰσχυρότερος in the prologue where Jesus becomes the bearer of the Holy Spirit, and thereby refutes the charge that he is possessed by demons.[48] While an allusion to the prologue is likely (see below), it nevertheless seems a somewhat indirect way of making the point if that is all it is intended to do. Moreover, Lane's

---

[43] For a discussion and other alternatives see Langton, *Essentials*, 166f; Foerster, *TDNT*, 1.605f; MacLaurin, 'Beelzeboul'; Gaston, 'Beelzebul'.

[44] Hooker, *Message*, 37; cf. Gaston, 'Beelzebul', 247ff; Limbeck, 'Beelzebul', 39n1.

[45] Cf. Becker, *Heil*, 209f.

[46] There is some debate as to whether or not Mark understood this binding to have occurred in Jesus' wilderness temptation, cf. especially Robinson, 21-53; and Best, *Temptation*, 18ff; also Gundry, 56, 174.

[47] *Christ*, 46f.

[48] Lane, 143, where the 'strong man' saying answers the accusation of demon possession.

proposal requires the doubtful assumption that Jesus' accusers (not just Mark's audience) were aware, first, that he was so described by John and, second, that the description alluded to the empowering of the Holy Spirit.

On the other hand, the 'strong man' imagery may simply reflect a 'proverbial saying' about relative 'strengths' like that in *Pss. Sol.* 5:3, οὐ γὰρ λήμψεται σκῦλα παρὰ ἀνδρὸς δυνατοῦ—a passage which may well have shared a common source with, or arisen from, Isaiah 49:24f.[49] Given that Satan's house is not divided against itself and that Jesus is clearly 'plundering' it, Jesus can hardly be empowered by Satan (3:22b) since he is manifestly the 'stronger one'. But is there more going on? First, in view of the scribes' attribution of Jesus' authority to Satan, his initial denial (vv. 23-26) is quite natural. But, given the strong adversative ἀλλ' (v. 27), one might be excused for expecting here a positive indication as to the correct interpretation of Jesus' exorcisms. This would then lead more naturally into the following blasphemy warning (vv. 28-30) which already presumes a great deal about the true nature of Jesus' exorcisms (see below). Second, the language itself is not only unusual but is more expansive than its *Pss. Sol.* counterpart. In particular, why the connection between exorcisms and plundering, and why is it emphasised (διαρπάζω, v. 27 *bis*)?

Perhaps the key here lies in the fact that the imagery used in the 'strong man' saying is associated in some contemporary Jewish traditions with God's eschatological deliverance of his people. Both *T. Levi* 18:12 and *T. Zeb.* 9:8 (b, d, and g) characterise this intervention as a time when respectively 'Beliar shall be bound by him' (a priestly Messiah?) and 'the Lord himself ... will liberate all the prisoners of Beliar' (cf. *T. Sim.* 6:6; *T. Dan* 5:10-13).[50] Of particular interest is 11QMelch. Here the 'anointed' מבשר of Isaiah 52:7 (2:15-18)[51] announces the eschatological 'Jubilee' deliverance of the captives (השבויים, 2:4-6; cf. Isa 61:1; Lev 25:10; Lk 4:16-21) who are to be rescued from the hand of Belial and his spirits by the mysterious warrior figure,[52] Melchizedek, as he executes the judgements

---

[49] Ryle, *Psalms*, 54; Klostermann, 37; Bultmann, *History*, 98.

[50] Cf. Isa 24:22f; *Jub.* 10:8; *1 Enoch* 10:11f; 54:4f; *As. Mos.* 10:1; *Pesiq. R.* 36 (161a). De Jonge's theory, *Studies*, that the Testaments are largely of Christian origin has not been widely accepted; cf. Schürer, 3/2.767ff; Kee, *OTP*, 1.777f.

[51] On the text, Fitzmyer, 'Further'; De Jonge, '11Q'; Horton, *Melchizedek*, 73ff. The מבשר is probably distinct from Melchizedek, Horton, 78; De Jonge, *ibid.*, 306ff.

[52] De Jonge, *ibid.*, 306.

of God (cf. יום נקם לאלהינו).⁵³ Satan will be destroyed and the day of peace and salvation inaugurated in accordance with God's exercise of his kingship (2:16, 9; cf. Isa 52:7; 61:2-3).⁵⁴

Several elements appear regularly in these texts: A) the exiles or captives are portrayed as being under Satan's power, B) their deliverance is effected by a warrior figure, C) the whole is described in terms of God's reign and, D) is often expressed in ways reminiscent of the Isaianic day of salvation. Understood against this background, and especially if Mark understands Jesus' announcement of the Kingdom of God in Isaianic terms, it is significant that many commentators see here in Jesus' characterisation of his exorcisms the influence of Isaiah 49:24f⁵⁵ and also perhaps the spoils-of-victory imagery of Isaiah 53:12.⁵⁶

Taking Isaiah 49 first, although the absence of clear verbal parallels rules out any suggestion of a citation (but see ἰσχύω in 49:25, 26),⁵⁷ the conceptual parallels are so strong as to make it difficult to believe that no allusion is intended. In Isaiah these verses comprise the third and final

---

⁵³ Milik, 'Texte', 99, 106; cf. De Jonge, '11Q'; Fitzmyer, 'Further', 30.

⁵⁴ Lines 16, 19f; Milik, 'Texte', 99f, 108f.

⁵⁵ E.g. Cranfield; Lane; Nineham; Barrett, *Spirit*, 70ff; Gnilka; Hooker, *Servant*, 73; Dodd, *According*, 92; Pesch; Best, *Temptation*, 12f; Hurtardo; Schneck, 89ff. Luke 11:20ff makes the allusion more explicit.

⁵⁶ E.g. Grundmann, *TDNT*, 3.400f; Fuller, *Interpreting*, 72; Cranfield; Nineham; Legasse, „Homme". Gnilka also refers to Isa 65:1-7.

⁵⁷ Cf. Grimm, 88-92. The allusion is clearer in Lk 11:21-23. However, although the substantive form of γίγας is used to render גִּבּוֹר some sixteen times in the LXX, its synonym, ἰσχυρός, is twice as commonly used (thirty-two times, so HR). By the time of the NT, however, not only is γίγας absent from the NT and many contemporaneous writings (BAGD), but also in the one place where an OT text containing γίγας appears in the NT—the allusion to Ezek 39:20 LXX (ἐμπλησθήσεσθε ἐπὶ τῆς τραπέζης μου ἵππον καὶ ἀναβάτην, γίγαντα καὶ πάντα ἄνδρα πολεμιστήν) in Rev 19:18 (ἵνα φάγητε σάρκας βασιλέων καὶ σάρκας χιλιάρχων καὶ σάρκας ἰσχυρῶν καὶ σάρκας ἵππων καὶ τῶν καθημένων ἐπ' αὐτῶν) cf. Caird, *Revelation*, 247—γίγας is apparently rendered by ἰσχυρός (γίγας does, however, occur in the Patristic writings with the sense of giant or heretic, cf. Lampe). This suggests that in the NT semantic change resulted in the substantive form of ἰσχυρός displacing that of γίγας, in which case Mark's terminology may well constitute a parallel. Further, Isa 40:11 and 63:5 describe Yahweh coming as a mighty warrior (LXX: μετὰ ἰσχύος). The verb describing Jesus' plundering activity is also used in Isaiah LXX of the condition of the exiles: in 42:22 a blind and deaf Jacob-Israel (vv. 18-20) is described as διηρπασμένος, while v. 24 speaks of her as being given εἰς διαρπαγήν. It is perhaps possible that Jesus' use of the term implies an ironic reversal of sorts: the plunder is to be plundered, but this is uncertain. Betz, 'Sinai', 102, also suggests that σκεύη might be the result of a wordplay between נִכְנַס (εἰσῆλθεν) and נְכָסָיו (τὰ σκεύη αὐτοῦ) and Grimm, 91, thinks that οἰκία may have a geopolitical sense related to a rabbinic interpretation (not cited) where the 'house of the strong' is interpreted as the 'House of Esau'; cf. Chilton, *Targum*, 98, note on 49:24. See now also Schneck, 90.

part of an extended salvation oracle (49:14-26).[58] The whole section is important in that immediately following the installation of what appears to be a new 'servant' Israel,[59] it introduces the more positive themes of chapters 49-55.[60] This second half, in contrast to the polemical tone and immediacy of the first (chapters 40-48), consists almost entirely of future-oriented promises of the NE salvation as inaugurated by the new, unknown 'servant'.[61] Echoing the rhetorical question of verse 15, verse 24 asks 'Can the prey be taken from a strong man, or the captive of a terrifying adversary[62] be rescued?'. Of course the answer to both questions is 'no'. Nevertheless, Yahweh affirms that 'even the captive of the strong man will be taken, and the prey of the terrifying adversary will be rescued'.[63] In spite of the apparent hopelessness of Israel's position as a captive in exile to strong Babylon, her NE deliverance will be accomplished by the stronger warrior, Yahweh.

Given the foregoing, an appeal to Isaiah 49:25f imagery to explain the significance of Jesus' exorcisms would be particularly congruent with our contention that Mark understands Jesus' ministry within an INE hermeneutic.[64] Jesus is here presented as the stronger one[65] of the INE

---

[58] Westermann, 'Heilswort', 366-68; *Sprache*, 121, 132-33; Begrich, *Studien*, 14; cf. Schoors, *Saviour*, 106; Melugin, *Formation*, 148f.

[59] Melugin, *Formation*, 70f; Williamson, 'Concept'; Watts, 'Consolation', 54. Van der Merwe, *Pentateuch-tradisies*, (cited in Spykerboer, *Structure*, 52) further argues that (unnamed) Jacob-Israel as an historical identity is now distinguished from the chosen people of Yahweh, citing 48:1 where he sees the prophet denying the people the right to claim this title for themselves, cf. Day, 'DAʻAṬ', 101.

[60] Melugin, *Formation*, 151f.

[61] Watts, 'Consolation', 56f.

[62] The MT reads צָדִיק שְׁבִי 'a legitimate captivity', v. 24b. However, the LXX reading ἀδίκως 'unjustly' and ₵'s דשבו ושאין 'one which the righteous have captured' suggests some textual confusion. In view of the parallelism read עָרִיץ with 1QIsaᵃ, Vulgate, and Peshitta; so also BHS and many commentators.

[63] Much depends on the meaning of גַּם (v. 25b). If understood as a strong assertion, then the captive is Jacob-Israel in exile (e.g. Begrich, *Studien*, 21; Westermann, 'Heilswort', 367) but if as a concessive clause Yahweh is the strong man from whom it is impossible to take his prey, i.e. Jacob-Israel, e.g. Schoors, 'שבי'. However, the deciding factor is that v. 24 corresponds in literary function to v. 21 and is, therefore, to be understood as a complaint. Thus שְׁבִי and מַלְקוֹחַ appear to describe the exile; see the extended discussion in Schoors, *Saviour*, 114-17.

[64] An appeal to Yahweh's promise to overcome Babylon in Isaiah 49 would also be consistent with the use in the preceding verses of the military/political terms βασιλεία and οἰκία, cf. Oakman, 'Houses', 114. Schneck, 94ff, tries, not very convincingly, to establish further links between Isaiah 49 generally and other parts of Mark 3, e.g. Jesus' mother = estranged mother Zion, mission in 49:6 = the crowds, 49:5 = the Twelve as Israel led back, and 49:6 = salvation for the man with the paralysed hand. This seems to go beyond the

who, after binding Satan, the strong one, is spoiling his realm and loosing the captives.[66] Interestingly, the War Scroll at Qumran twice uses imagery drawn from this very passage in its paean to the mighty Yahweh-Warrior who comes to deliver his people (1QM 12:10-14 and 19:2-8; cf. Isa 49:23-24; cf. 52:1f; 54:11f). Again, given the emphatic personal language of Isaiah 49:25—'I myself will contend with those who contend with you'[67]—there is also the intimation that Jesus is in some way closely connected with the personal manifestation of Yahweh.

Second, to allow that this saying alludes to Yahweh's deliverance of his people would place it squarely within the expected flow of the argument:

    a. the scribes' accusation: Jesus casts out demons by the prince of demons (v. 22).
    b. Jesus' two-stage rebuttal:
        i. the implausibility of the accusation: Satan would not destroy, and has manifestly not destroyed, himself (vv. 23-26).
        ii. the alternative: on the contrary, Satan is bound and this binding is Yahweh's promised deliverance; thus the 'stronger man' saying (v. 27).
    c. therefore (as this is Yahweh's work): do not attribute the work of the Holy Spirit to Satan (vv. 28-30).

Third, that Yahweh's warrior activity in Isaiah is so that Zion and 'all flesh' may know that 'I am Yahweh your Saviour' (vv. 23-26),[68] is especially pertinent to the central issue here, namely coming to 'know' that Jesus' actions constitute Yahweh's salvation (1:14f).

Finally, as numerous commentators have observed, 'Satan', 'Spirit', and 'strong man' terminology occur together only here and in the prologue which conjunction suggests that the two are intended to be linked.[69] Seeing 3:27 as an allusion to Yahweh's warrior activity on behalf of Israel sheds light on why this may be so. Once again, if, as has been argued in Chapter 4, the descent of the Spirit on Jesus, ὁ ἰσχυρότερος, is to be understood as Yahweh's response to the prayer for deliverance in Isaiah

---

more evident intent of Mark's allusion to Isa 49:24f, namely, to explain the significance of Jesus' exorcisms.

[65] Meynet, 'Analuse', argues that the stronger one is the Holy Spirit, but this hardly fits Mark's presentation where John is clearly pointing to Jesus (1:7f).

[66] Note the double mention of διαρπαζέω. On the kingdom of Satan, Kruse, 'Reich'. Klostermann, argues that σκεύη must refer to the exorcised demons. However, on the basis of texts cited above, the 'booty' is more likely to consist of people. 1QM 12:10f speaks of Yahweh (עושי חיל, doer of mighty deeds) leading captives (שבה) and plundering (שלל) although here the objects are his enemies.

[67] The emphatic personal pronoun, אָנֹכִי, suggesting 'I *myself* ...'.

[68] Melugin, *Formation*, 152; Schoors, *Saviour*, 113ff.

[69] Espec. Mauser, 30; Otto, *Kingdom*, 100f; Robinson, 30ff; Best, *Temptation*, 10ff.

63:7 - 64:12, then an appeal to the Warrior imagery of Isaiah 49 to interpret Jesus' conflict with the demonic makes very good sense.

The linking of Isaiah 49 and Isaiah 63f also provides a coherent setting for the warning against blaspheming the Holy Spirit in the following verses. Barrett has observed that the closest parallel to this idea in the OT is Isaiah 63:10[70]—a passage which we have noted is not only central to Mark's prologue but also striking in its emphasis on the רוּחַ קָדְשׁוֹ. The writer humbly recalls how Israel, despite Yahweh's gracious Exodus deliverance on their behalf, had responded by grieving his Holy Spirit. Nevertheless the supplicant then goes on to ask that God in his mercy might act again on their behalf.[71] Barrett tentatively proposes that the long-anticipated intervention of Yahweh has happened in Jesus (as our reading would confirm), but that 'this new work of God was greeted in precisely the same way as the old'. Since 'this is God's final, eschatological, deed of salvation, those who utterly reject it can, in the nature of the case, find no salvation'.[72] This sits well with an INE framework. The long-awaited reign of Yahweh in the INE has begun, but, as in the first Exodus, there is the possibility of rebellion against Yahweh's Holy Spirit; a rebellion which will occasion the ultimate censure.[73] To reject Jesus is to reject the Kingdom (cf. 1:14f). At this point, Mark's introductory reminder of Malachi's threatened judgement is not far away.

In considering the second Isaianic allusion suggested, LXX 53:12 also exhibits something of a parallel in its portrayal of the 'servant' figure who

---

[70] *Spirit*, 104-5; Lövestam, *Spiritus*, 30-34, also cites Acts 7:39ff. The LXX's use of βλασφημ- does not suggest a regular Hebrew equivalent, Beyer, *TDNT*, 1.621, while παροξυν- (LXX Isa 63:10), which occurs frequently in the OT normally with reference to God, appears only twice in the NT and never of men's acts toward God: Acts 17:16; 1 Cor 13:5, cf. Seesemann, *TDNT*, 5.857. On the possible conceptual link between the two, in the sense of 'speaking a word against', cf. e.g. Num 14:2; Pss 78:19f; 106:25; *Sipre Num*. 112 on 14:30; CD 5:12; Tödt, *Son*, 316.

[71] Cf. the similar concerns of the post-exilic Ps 106; Allen, *Psalms*, 54f; Kraus, *Psalmen*, 2.906. On Israel's Exodus rebellions: Tunyogi, 'Rebellions'; Coats, *Rebellions*; Carroll, 'Rebellion'.

[72] *Spirit*, 105. Although conjecture, it is tempting to observe that the rebelliousness of Israel in the first Exodus reached its climax in the worship of a golden calf, i.e. in the attribution of Yahweh's delivering activities to an idol (cf. Acts 7:39-41 and e.g. Ps 106:19), which images the LXX and the NT later associate with demons. But cf. e.g. Oswalt, 'Concept', who sees in the bull an attempt to represent Yahweh.

[73] The idea of never being forgiven or of having committed an eternal sin, seems to be paralleled by e.g. 1 Sam 3:14 and Isa 22:14 and appears to carry with it the threat of being cut off.

divides the σκυλᾶ τῶν ἰσχυρῶν.[74] This would certainly be in keeping with a reading that sees the literary function of Isaiah 53 as indicating the way the NE is to be effected,[75] and which, according to *Tg. Isaiah*, involves a warrior-Messiah.[76] If *Tg. Isaiah* represents an earlier tradition, an appeal to the activities of the messianic-'servant' deliverer (cf. *Tg. Isa* 42:1ff) would be in keeping with the themes established by the voice in the prologue.   Admittedly, as Isaiah 53 implies that this plundering is subsequent to the suffering of the 'servant', the absence of any mention by Mark of Jesus' suffering suggests caution.[77] But an appeal to Isaiah 53:12 could signify that the deliverances adumbrate a greater victory to come—especially as Mark writes after the resurrection.[78] An allusion to Isaiah 53:12, although it cannot be established with certainty, would be congenial to the concerns of this particular passage and to what we have argued of Mark so far.[79] Furthermore, if this is the case, then the same ambiguity concerning Jesus' identity is observed here as in the prologue. On the one hand, Jesus is apparently described in terms used of Yahweh himself (Isa 49; cf. 1:2f) while on the other, the imagery is related to that of the messianic 'servant' (Isa 53; cf. 1:11).

(b) The Literary Function of the Controversy
It may be objected that this one example hardly suffices to establish that Mark presents Jesus as the Yahweh-Warrior.   But there are several grounds that tell against such an assessment.   First, the Beelzebul controversy is the only occasion in Mark where Jesus provides a rationale for his casting out of the demons and should, therefore, be accorded some attention[80]—perhaps even more so in view of Mark's interest in Jesus' silencing of the demons who apparently threatened to reveal information

---

[74] Especially for Luke, Legasse, „Homme".

[75] See Chapter 4, p. 115, fn. 135.

[76] On possible early messianic interpretations of Isa 53 in *T. Ben.* 3:8, the Similitudes of *1 Enoch*, the Peshitta (on the question of a Jewish Targumic or Christian origin, Würthwein, *Text*, 80f), the *Tg. Isa*, and the rabbis, see Zimmerli-Jeremias, *Servant*, 58ff; Aytoun, 'Servant'.

[77] Hooker, *Servant*, 74n1.

[78] Indirect evidence for this may be provided by the debate over the time, nature, and extent of Jesus' overcoming of Satan which suggests the fluidity of the motif, see especially the opposing views of Robinson, and Best, *Temptation*.

[79] *Pace* Hooker, *Servant*, 74n1.

[80] Cf. Hoskyns-Davey, 170f; Fuller, *Interpreting*, 39ff; Leivestad, *Christ*, 44; Kee, *Miracle*, 160-62.

along similar lines (1:34; 3:11f; cf. 1:24f). Given, too, that the middle
element in Mark's sandwich construction provides the theological key to
the whole,[81] and the strong possibility that Mark is operating with an INE
hermeneutic, the appearance of the INE Yahweh-Warrior motif in this
section is suggestive of its importance as an interpretive framework for
Jesus' ministry.

Second, in addition to the previously noted connection with the
prologue, other evidence suggests that the Beelzebul pericope plays a
crucial role within the literary structure of the opening chapters of the
Gospel. Although the series of five controversies in 2:1 - 3:6 is generally
separated from 3:20-35 by most commentators, the Beelzebul story
provides a natural climax not only to them, but also to the preceding
miracle accounts of 1:16-45.[82] The pericope serves to bring together both
the motif of Jesus' authority manifest in his miraculous activities and the
diverse responses of the disciples, the crowds, Jesus' family, and the hostile
leadership.[83] Mark not only draws attention to this conflict by means of
his distinctive 'sandwich' technique, this being the first such arrangement
in a narrative setting,[84] but his departure from the usual A-B-A' structure
to an A-B-C-B'-A' outline further emphasises its importance. In addition,
not only does the appearance of the scribes from Jerusalem raise the
tension to new level—this is no longer a local matter—but the clash is
proleptic of what Mark's readers presumably already know will happen
when Jesus reaches the capital: the scribes also attend Jesus' trial and the
discussion likewise concerns blasphemy, only this time they have the
satisfaction of having the upper hand (cf. 14:63f). Finally, as a climactic
summary dealing with Jesus' rejection by the leadership and the failure of
his family to understand,[85] it provides a transitional rationale for the
otherwise difficult appearance of the famous Parables Chapter and its
problematic use of Isaiah 6. It is in this final controversy of the section that
Mark, for the first time, overtly mentions parables, stating that Jesus spoke

---

[81] Edwards, 'Sandwiches', 196, cited in Chapter 3, p. 90, fn. 190.

[82] Cf. Smith, 'Opponents', 179f; and Hooker, 114, where 3:20ff moves 'back into the
atmosphere of conflict ... but [represents] another step forward in the development of this
theme'; see also Gundry, 109.

[83] Cf. Hurtado, 50; Guelich, 1.171f; and the discussion of characters in Rhoads-Michie,
Story, 101-36, although they fail to mention Jesus' family.

[84] Best, 'Mark', 314f; Edwards, 'Sandwiches'.

[85] See Stock, *Boten*, 68f; Mansfield, *Spirit*, 62.

to the leaders ἐν παραβολαῖς.[86] As will be argued in Chapter 7, Mark's presentation of Jesus' use of Isaiah 6 in explaining the purpose of the parables is exactly in keeping with the original Isaianic context of a Jerusalemite leadership that has finally decided to reject the wisdom of Yahweh in favour of its own idolatrous categories.

Third, there is evidence to suggest that for Mark Jesus' authority over the unclean spirits is the signal hallmark of his activity and one which Mark is concerned for his readers to note.[87] Ever since William Wrede scholars have been aware of the theological interests of Mark (something which had been granted much more readily to the Gospel of John). It is interesting to note, therefore, given that for many commentators John's presentation of Jesus' first miracle at Cana has considerable theological significance, that Mark's first miracle is the casting out of an unclean spirit (1:21-28). Might it not be that Mark's recording of this event as the first of Jesus' mighty acts is equally important, and is intended to alert the reader to a key feature of Jesus' ministry?[88] And even more so given Mark's sustained interest in Jesus' exorcisms?

The demon's opening question occurs frequently in the OT within the context of combat or judgement,[89] and H. C. Kee has further argued that Jesus' use of ἐπιτιμάω, when understood against the backgrounds of both the OT (e.g. גער in Pss 104:7; 18:16; 106:9 cf. Isa 17:13; 50:3) and later Jewish sectarian literature (e.g. 1QM 14:9f), is indicative of God's eschatological and new creational conflict with the hostile powers in which the latter are subjugated by means of a powerful word—Jesus later uses both ἐπιτιμάω and φιμόω when he rebukes the storm in 4:35ff.[90] From this perspective, the cry 'Have you come to destroy us?' (v. 24) becomes all the more momentous and suggests not only that the demon understood well the eschatological import of Jesus' activity—Satan's dominion was being overcome (cf. *T. Levi* 18:12 and the other texts cited above)—but that it

---

[86] Perhaps even 'began to speak', taking ἔλεγεν as an inceptive imperfect. Cf. Kelber, 25f; now Gundry, 181.

[87] Kertelge, 56-60, links the OT concept of Yahweh's authority with Jesus' 'eschatologischen Kampf'. Cf. Burkill, 'Notion', 44; Bultmann, *History*, 226; Gundry, 74.

[88] Admittedly Mark does not 'signpost' it as does John (2:11) but then Mark is recognised as 'mysterious' (Burkitt) and 'parabolic' (Donahue, 'Jesus'; Hamilton, 'Gospel'). See also Gundry, 74.

[89] E.g. Ju 11:12; 2 Sam 16:10; 1 Kgs 17:18; 2 Chron 35:21; etc. Cf. Lane, 73; Bauernfeind, *Worte*, 3-10; 14f, 28-31, 68f; and Bächli, 'Was?'.

[90] 'Terminology'.

speaks 'on behalf of all unclean spirits'.[91] Thus for Kee, the significance of
the story is not so much to glorify Jesus but to identify the exorcism 'as an
eschatological event which served to prepare God's creation for his coming
rule',[92] and as such it is 'paradigmatic for the gospel as a whole'.[93] (It is
also interesting to note, in view of the question of the source of Jesus'
authority in Mk 3, that it is his authority thus demonstrated in this first
miracle which impresses the crowd, 1:27).

P. Pimental's assessment of Mark's particular interest in 'unclean spirit'
terminology further supports this view.[94] When Mark describes
exorcisms he consistently establishes the spirit as 'unclean' (1:23; 5:2; 7:25;
9:25) and only then, having defined the issue as one of conflict between
purity and defilement, uses 'demon' as a synonym. Significantly, it is also
in the first exorcism that this interest is particularly evident. Not only is
there a concentration of 'unclean spirit' terminology which is unparalleled
in the rest of the Gospel, but only here is Jesus described as the 'Holy One
of God'. Similarly, in the Beelzebul controversy Mark is happy to speak of
demons until the warning about blasphemy against the Holy Spirit, at
which point he switches to 'unclean spirit'. If this is a Markan concern—
and Jesus' 'purifying' contact with the leper, the 'unclean' woman, and the
debate on purity (7:1-23) suggests that it may be—then Pimental could well
be correct in suggesting that this motif is to be understood in terms of
Qumranic and Pharisaic interest in purity such that Jesus' expulsion of
'unclean spirits' indicates that God's mercy is extending beyond the
community of faithful Israel to include those previously excluded. In
keeping with the eschatological conflict idea, the presentation of the Holy
One of God who drives out the 'unclean spirits' with a command is also
consistent with those traditions where the Messiah is seen as purifying the

---

[91] Gundry, 75.

[92] *Ibid.*, 243. Kallas, *Significance*, 64, suggests that Jesus' miraculous work on the
Sabbath indicated primarily the resumption of Yahweh's creative activities. On new
creation imagery in Isaiah, e.g. Habel, 'Yahweh'; Stuhlmueller, 'Theology', *Creation*;
Rendtorff, 'Stellung', and in Qumran, e.g. 1QS 4:25; Isa 43:19; 48:16 in 1QH 13:11f; further,
Sjöberg, 'Neuschöpfung', and 'Wiedergeburt'.

[93] *Miracle*, 161; Kertelge, 59f.

[94] '"Unclean"'. Compared to Mark's eleven occurrences, Matthew has two (10:1; 12:43)
and Luke five (4:36; 6:18; 8:29; 9:42; 11:24). Although not pursued in this study, the motif of
purity also has connections with the INE, cf. Isa 35:8 and Mal 3:1-5, 1QS 4:20ff.

land by the word of his mouth (e.g. *Pss. Sol.* 17:24, 36; 18:5; 1QSb 5:24; cf. Isa 11:4).[95]

Finally, Jesus' casting out of demons and unclean spirits is mentioned far more than any other single type of miracle or healing in individual accounts (cf. 1:21-28; 5:1-20; 7:24-30; 9:14-29).[96] The commissionings of the Twelve (3:15; 6:7-13) and the summary statements (1:34, 39; 3:10f) similarly reflect an emphasis on the exorcisms.[97] This emphasis is even more significant when considering the concerns of the Markan prologue, one of the implications of which is the inauguration of eschatological conflict between Yahweh and Jacob-Israel's oppressors (Chapters 3 and 4 above).

(c) Summary

It has been suggested that the Beelzebul controversy serves to focus the issues raised by the preceding material (1:16 - 3:19) as to the nature and identity of Jesus' authoritative ministry and in particular his exorcisms (cf. 1:32). The introduction of explicit parable terminology in the face of considered rejection sets the scene for the following section on the parables and their purpose. Given this pivotal setting, the allusion to Isaiah 49:24f takes on considerable significance. Jesus' authoritative ministry, characterised by his power over the demons and in Mark's literary arrangement confined (with one important exception) to the 'Galilee and Beyond' section, is not simply a matter of some general defeat of evil powers, but is to be understood more precisely within the horizons of the INE deliverance effected by the Yahweh-Warrior.[98]

---

[95] Theissen, *Miracle*, 255f. On the eschatological significance of purity in Qumran's messianism, Neusner, 'Geschichte', 121ff; Janowski, 'Endererwartung'. On this image as a metaphor for authority, Watts, 'Meaning'.

[96] Cf. healings of blindness twice (8:22-26; 10:46-52) and once each: a fever (1:29f, which may be demonic, van der Loos, 554), leprosy (1:40-45), paralysis (2:1-12), shrivelled hand (3:1-6), haemorrhage (5:25-34), and deafness/dumbness (7:32-37). Gundry, 74, who lumps all the healings together, nevertheless notes the importance of exorcisms for Mark. Kallas, *Significance*, 78f, argues that within the current cosmology fevers and 'plagues' (Mk 1:30; 5:29, 34) were ultimately the result of demonic oppression.

[97] Guelich, 1.173. For Kallas, *ibid.*, 86, exorcisms are at the centre of Jesus' message.

[98] The modern Western distinction between ontology and function should not be anachronistically applied to the NT. So e.g. in Jn 7:31 the performance of signs testifies to identity of the Christ. Similarly, how does one explain Mk 4:41 where, although the disciples have seen many powerful miracles, the calming of the storm strikes them with terror, unless this particular deed has implications for Jesus' identity that go far beyond his being a miracle worker or a prophet?

(ii) Isaiah's Nations and Mark's Demons

If Mark presents Jesus as the Isaianic Yahweh-Warrior, what, if any, is the connection between Isaiah's picture of Israel's bondage to the nations (and more importantly to the idols who epitomise those nations' power and wealth) and, for want of a better term, 'demon-possession' in Mark? One link, I suggest, lies in the growing association in the intertestamental period of demons with idols where the former are progressively understood as the reality behind the latter.[99]

While the Hebrew Scriptures make some allusion to this connection (cf. Dt 32:17; Ps 106:37), the relationship is made explicit in the LXX. Psalm 95:5, in announcing ($\epsilon\mathring{v}\alpha\gamma\gamma\epsilon\lambda\acute{\iota}\zeta\omega$) the coming salvation of God, reads 'all the gods of the nations are $\delta\alpha\iota\mu\acute{o}\nu\iota\alpha$' (אלילים). In Isaiah 65:3 and 11 the LXX specifically adds the mention of demons: 'they ... burn incense on bricks $\tau o\hat{\iota}\varsigma$ $\delta\alpha\iota\mu o\nu\acute{\iota}o\iota\varsigma$' and 'prepare a table $\tau\hat{\omega}$ $\delta\alpha\iota\mu o\nu\acute{\iota}\omega$' (cf. *Tg. Isa*). This tendency is continued in the Pseudepigrapha (e.g. *1 Enoch* 19:1; 80:7; 99:7; *Jub.* 1:11; 2:17; 11:4; 12:20; 22:17) and in Paul (1 Cor 10:20; cf. Rev 9:20).[100]

(a) Gerasene Demoniac—Demons, Tombs, and Pigs

But does Mark show any evidence of this understanding? F. Annen's detailed analysis of the Gerasene pericope (5:1-20) with its strange account of a tomb-dwelling demoniac and the destruction of the swine, suggests that he does.[101] A particular feature of this account is Mark's bracketing of the actual deliverance with two uncharacteristic departures from his usual formal style in which he stresses the tomb-dwelling (vv. 2-3) and the presence of swine (vv. 11ff).[102] Unusual enough motifs in their own right, this striking conjunction of the two has long led commentators to posit Isaiah 65:1-7 as the background to Mark's story, especially given the presence of demons in the LXX version, (on LXX Ps 67, see below).[103]

---

[99] Theissen, *Miracles*, 255f.

[100] Foerster, *TDNT*, 4.8-18; Annen, *Heil*, 181f; Böcher, *Dämonenfurcht*, 69, 139ff; Wink, *Naming*, 24f.

[101] *Heil*; cf. survey of literature in Cragan, 'Gerasene'. See now also Schneck, 137ff.

[102] Guelich, 1.277, 282; cf. Kertelge, 104. Given that the spirit is described first as $\mathring{\alpha}\kappa\acute{\alpha}\theta\alpha\rho\tau o\varsigma$ the unclean nature of both swine and tombs should be noted. On the latter cf. *b. Nidda* 17a; *j. Terum.* 40b, 23; Böcher, *Dämonenfurcht*, 65, 73, 117ff.

[103] E.g. Holtzmann, *Synoptiker*, 160ff; Cave, 'Obedience'; Sahlin, 'Pericope'; Pesch, 1.286; especially Craghan, 'Gerasene', 529f. The change from $\mu\nu\eta\mu\epsilon\acute{\iota}\omega\nu$ (v. 2) to $\mu\nu\acute{\eta}\mu\alpha\sigma\iota\nu$ (v. 3) may be due to the influence of LXX Isa 65:4; Grundmann, 142; Cave; Craghan; Pesch, *Besessene*, 30f.

Isaiah 65:1-7 (cf. 66:3, 17) constitutes a scathing indictment of apostate Israelites, probably in an early post-exilic *Sitz-im-Leben*, where tomb-dwelling (cf. LXX Ps 67:7) and the eating of swine's flesh are apparently some of the more repugnant *tupoi* of an idolatry behind which, according to the LXX, stand the demons.[104]

As Annen notes, in ancient times swine were linked with idol worship,[105] being offered to Zeus, Dionysus, Athena, and Nemesis[106] and also to the subterranean gods particularly in connection with fertility rites. The rite later became associated with the myth of Eubuleus, whose herd of swine had been swallowed up by the earth, and involved the throwing of piglets into a womb-like hole in the Temple of Demeter in Eleusis.[107] Similarly, there is evidence for the widespread sacrifice of pigs to Roman gods, especially to Mars but also with regard to fertility rites in connection with the gods below the earth.[108] Evidently, in the Roman world, pigs were favourite sacrificial animals, no Roman tomb was legally protected without a pig being sacrificed, and demons were understood to have a particular liking for them.[109]

Turning to the Near East it is suggested that the sacrificial use of pigs by the Canaanites partly lay behind the prohibitions in Leviticus 11:7-8 and Deuteronomy 14:8,[110] particularly as a number of archaeological finds in Syria and Palestine further suggest their cultic significance, for instance, a votive statue of a pig in Jericho (4th Millennium), pig-bones under a stone slab in a sanctuary in Gezer (3-2nd. Millennium), a libation container portraying a man carrying a pig (2nd. Millennium), an alabaster pig in a sanctuary at Ai (2nd. Millennium), and a cultic pillar with pig bones in a temple at Beth-Shean (mid 2nd Millenium).[111]

---

[104] Whybray, 266ff; Achtemeier, *Community,* 122ff; Westermann, 399ff; Watts, *Isaiah,* 2.343, 356; de Vaux, 'Sacrifices', 264; cf. Hanson, *Dawn,* 147.

[105] See his extensive discussion in *Heil,* 133-81, upon which I am dependent here; cf. de Vaux, 'Sacrifices'; Stendebach, 'Schweineopfer'; Derrett, 'Gerasene', 68f.

[106] Arbesmann, *Fasten,* 43; Deubner, *Attische,* 40-45; cited in Annen, 163.

[107] Annen, 164, citing Foucart, *d'Eleusis,* 65, 104f; Deubner, *Attische,* 40-51; Nilsson, *Greichische,* 313-22. He notes that this rite was also practiced at Potniai, Knidos, Delos, and Paros, while at Thesmorphia it entailed the casting of swine into the local chasm.

[108] Annen, *Heil,* 165, citing Krause, *PW Suppl,* 5.236-82; Orth., *PW Suppl,* 2/2.801-15.

[109] Derrett, 'Gerasene', 68f; cf. also the Babylonian incantation where a pig is offered as a residence in the place of the demoniac, Thompson, *Devils,* 2.3, 10-15.

[110] de Vaux, 'Sacrifices', 264.

[111] See further de Vaux, 'Sacrifices', 251-54; Annen, *Heil,* 166.

It is most probably this linking of idols, demons, and pigs in the ancient world that forms the backdrop of the Markan account and which, along with the tomb-dwelling, suggests that he uses Isaiah 65 as the horizon for his story thereby linking the powerful forces of 'Legion' with typical images of anti-idol polemic such that Jesus' victory over the demonic host corresponds to the end of the idols' power.[112]

(b) Military Imagery

Furthermore, the stress which Mark places on the strength of the demoniac,[113] and particularly the pericope's military terminology, not only highlights the conflict motif but, in view of its being linked with the storm-stilling, also provides important hermeneutical points of reference as to the significance of the double-event of storm-stilling and exorcism-drowning.

In the first instance, the statement in verse 4: οὐδεὶς ἴσχυεν αὐτὸν δαμάσαι appears to echo the ἰσχυρός terminology of the strong man passage in Mark 3, and also perhaps that of John's description of Jesus as the ἰσχυρότερος (1:7).[114] In the second, J. D. M. Derrett, noting the strange behaviour of the pigs, has observed the presence of military overtones in Mark's terminology. If we allow the clear military associations of λεγιών (v. 9)[115] to establish the semantic parameters of the account, ἀποστείλῃ (v. 10) then connotes a military command (i.e. to dispatch), 'ἀγέλη ('herd', vv. 11, 13), clearly inappropriate for pigs, indicates a band of military recruits, and ὥρμησεν (v. 13) describes troops rushing into battle.[116]

Given the military connotations, and the memory of the first Exodus where Israel witnessed the drowning of a large hostile force, Derrett suggests that the drowning of the demonised 'legion' of 'idolatrous' pigs is intended to recall the defeat of the Pharaoh-god during Israel's deliverance from bondage (cf. Ex 14:26 - 15:21).[117] Furthermore, the drowning of

---

[112] Annen, *Heil*, 185-86. Although allowing the possibility that Mark's language may reflect Isa 65, Gundry, 258, lists seven differences in detail between the accounts (not all are equally convincing) but thereby tends to miss the overall symbolism of the event.

[113] Guelich, 1.277, notes the presence of five *hapax legomena* here (κατοίκησις, ἅλυσις, πέδη, διασπᾶν, δαμάζειν) but this could be due to the unusual subject matter.

[114] Nineham, 120.

[115] Cf. Baird, 'Gadarene'; Preiker, *TDNT*, 4.68f.

[116] Derrett, 'Contribution', 5f, who cites contemporary usage in military contexts.

[117] *Ibid.*, 6f; cf. Trench, *Miracles*, 184; Hobbs, 'Gospel', 37-39; Betz, *Studies*, 238f; Cave, 'Obedience', 96, who notes that Luke's ἄβυσσον is found in Aq., Sym., and Th. of Ex 15:5.

Pharaoh's hosts in Israel's founding moment is appealed to on several occasions in Isaiah 40-55 where it not only provides evidence of the Yahweh-Warrior's ability to execute the NE—he caused them to 'lay down' in the sea 'never to rise again' (43:16f)—but also establishes the basis of the supplication for a similar intervention (51:9f, 13ff; cf. Ex 14:25, 28; 15:10, 21).[118]

Consequently, the strange conjunction of the OT images of anti-idol polemic, an oppressive demonic military host, and the drowning in the sea is entirely consonant with a portrayal of Jesus as Israel's INE deliverer. I would suggest that for Mark the pericope of the Gerasene demoniac shows Jesus to be the INE Yahweh-Warrior who defeats the hostile powers, now in their NT demonic manifestation as 'Legion', by drowning them in the sea, just as in the first Exodus.

(c) The Calming of the Storm

The rationale behind the linking of the drowning of the demonic legion with the storm-stilling seems likewise to derive from an INE motif.[119] Yahweh's victory over his enemies, expressed in creational 'chaos-defeating' language, is characteristic of the ancient Divine-Warrior Hymns of early Israel, of which Exodus 15 is perhaps the finest early example.[120] This influential motif comes to particular expression in the Psalms and Isaiah. In the Psalms, the creational content of Yahweh's 'rebuking' (גער / ἐπιτίμησις see above) of the watery chaos is frequently related to his division of the Red Sea in the Exodus (Pss 76:6f; 18:8-16; 104:7; cf. 89:9-15; 107:24-30).[121] In Isaiah 40-55, in his disputations with Israel, Yahweh argues that he is able to deliver by appealing to his power over the waters (44:27; 50:2)[122] and particularly the Red Sea. Thus Yahweh's defeat of

---

[118] Yahweh-Warrior language is found in 40:26; 42:13-15; 43:17; 44:27; 45:2; 49:24ff; 50:2 and 51:9f; cf. Miller, 'Council', 105ff, and Stuhlmueller, *Creative*, 86, for the links between the warrior language and *Chaoskampf* (see also below).

[119] The link between these two accounts has long been recognised: Bultmann, *History*, 210; Sundwall, *Zusammensetzung*, 30; Schmidt, *Rahmen*, 142. Goppelt, *Typos*, 84, suggests that the account is modelled on Jonah 1:1-16 but the differences are too great, so van der Loos, 464.

[120] See the extended discussions in Cross, *Canaanite*, 91-144; Hanson, *Dawn*, 299-316.

[121] Anderson, *IDB*, 4.806-10; Reymond, *L'eau*, 179-98; Cross, *Canaanite*, 112-44; Day, *Conflict*; Richardson, 90-93; now Gundry, 240, and relevant sections in literature cited in fn. 11. Hobbs, 'Gospel', 42, sees a parallel with Ps 77:19f.

[122] Watts, 'Consolation', 40. Cf. Miller, 'Council', 105ff; Stuhlmueller *Creative*, 86; Ollenburger, *Zion*, 73f; Kee, 'Terminology', 236; Anderson, *Creation*, 119ff.

the watery-chaos-monster Rahab at the Exodus[123] is recalled in Isaiah 51:9-11 while in 63:12ff the same combination forms the basis of an invocation for Yahweh again to make bare his holy arm (cf. Pss 114; 106:9).[124]

Mark's juxtaposition of the storm-stilling—where Jesus' use of ἐπιτιμάω and φιμόω appears to echo his programmatic conflict with the demonic (1:25, 4:39)[125]—with the deliverance of the Gerasene demoniac seems intended therefore to evoke the Divine-Warrior motif and particularly in an Exodus-like setting. In the first instance, Jesus appears as the Creator-Warrior of the first Exodus as he rebukes the chaos waters,[126] and, in the second, this same Creator-Warrior demonstrates his ability to deliver Israel from the oppressive legion of idol-demons by drowning them in the sea.[127]

A similar Warrior motif can perhaps also be discerned in Mark 6:45-52, particularly in the light of those OT texts where Yahweh tramples the waters, and thus serves to reinforce the Warrior connotations of Jesus' actions.[128] Of further interest in this second storm story is J. P. Heil's observation of a number of parallels between Jesus' 'ἐγώ εἰμι· μὴ φοβεῖσθε' and Isaiah 43:1-11 with its frequent 'I am/I will be' identifications/affirmations which are especially prominent in Isaiah 40-55,[129] its

---

[123] Westermann, 241, 'God's action as creator—pictured as a victory over the powers of chaos—is combined with the deliverance of Israel at the Red Sea in such a way that the transition from the one (v. 9b) to the other (v. 10) is barely noticeable'; cf. Jeremias, *Theophanie*, 96.

[124] Cross, *Canaanite*, 136f; cf. Stolz, *Jahwes*, 164f; Cross, *Canaanite*, 138f; Ollenburger, *Chaos*, 73.

[125] Cf. Kertelge, 96f, and Blackburn, *Theios*, 44f, 193ff. On the other hand see Gundry's cautions, 240, against the idea that ancients 'attributed storms to malevolent demons'.

[126] Cf. van der Loos, 646-48; Kertelge, 95; Stevens, 'Jesus', 328; Guelich; Grundmann; Moule; Hooker, *Message*, 43f; Hurtado; now also Blackburn, *Theios*, 142ff; and Marcus, 144; *pace*, Taylor. On new creation imagery in Isaiah, fn. 92 above.

[127] Cf. Stevens, 'Jesus', 328. Thus Theissen's suggestion, *Miracle*, 255, of an Elijah typology on the basis of τί ἐμοὶ καὶ σοί (cf. 1 Kgs 17:16 and Mk 6:14f) seems less likely. The suggestion of Betz, *Studies*, 235f, that Mark construes the sea crossing of the disciples under the guidance of Jesus in terms of Israel's crossing under Moses' leadership, while correctly noting the storm stilling's general iconographic significance, breaks down in that they are not escaping from enemies, nor can the other side of the lake be seen as the place of deliverance where Yahweh is to be worshipped.

[128] E.g. van der Loos, 665; Gnilka, 1.269; Achtemeier, 'Person'; Schenke, *Wundererzähl-ungen*, 246; Heil, *Walking*; and now especially the discussion in Blackburn, *Theios*, 145ff, where he argues for an OT rather than Hellenistic background.

[129] 41:4; 43:25; 44:6; 45:18; 46:4; 48:12; 51:12; 52:6. Morgenstern, 'Terminology', links the declaration אני הוא with the divine name and Ex 3:13ff, cf. Durham, *Exodus*, 36-41, which in both contexts (Isa and Ex) necessarily involves redemption, cf. Stuhlmueller, '"First"'.

commands (*bis*) not to fear, and its promise of Yahweh's presence 'when you pass through the waters'.[130]   These additional correspondences, testifying as they do to Yahweh's self-declaration, his delivering presence, and protection from the threat of the chaos waters offer further support for the presence of an INE hermeneutic: Jesus' delivering actions and control over the sea point to the breaking-in, in strength, of Yahweh's kingly reign as he inaugurates the long-awaited NE.

Finally, it is noteworthy that the Creator-Warrior motif is also prominent in Isaiah 63:12ff—not only has Mark earlier portrayed the cruical moment of the descent of the Spirit at Jesus' baptism in imagery derived from this very passage (i.e. 64:1, Chapter 4, pp. 102ff) but it also apparently underlies the warning against blasphemy in the similarly important Beelzebul controversy. There is an interesting connection here in that while Mark 1:10 indicates the beginning of the Yahweh-Warrior's intervention on Israel's behalf, the climactic Beelzebul controversy apparently interprets Jesus' exorcisms in precisely these terms with 3:29 warning against repeating the mistakes of the past by rejecting the Spirit's activity in this New Exodus.

It may, therefore, be significant that Mark 4:35 - 5:20 also exhibits several thematic parallels with this same text (63:7 - 65:7). Not only does Isaiah 63:19b - 64:2 reflect the ancient Divine-Warrior Exodus tradition,[131] but the response of the disciples suggests that the one 'who did awesome things that we did not expect' (Isa 64:2; Aq.: τὰ ἐπίφοβα ...; Sym., Th.: φοβερὰ ἃ οὐ προσεδοκῶμεν; cf. Mk 4:41, ἐφοβήθησαν φόβον μέγαν) has begun to execute a NE. Also, as we have seen, the imagery of the tombs and pigs appears to come from Isaiah 65:1-7—Yahweh's response to the preceding lament—where he claims that while he has allowed himself to be found, 'a stubborn and rebellious people' who 'sit among graves' and 'eat swine's flesh' did not seek him (65:1f; cf. Mk 5:7, 17).

It is possible then that Mark has been significantly influenced by this final Isaianic lament over the delay of the NE and Yahweh's response. He appeals to it in the prologue to describe the significance of Jesus' coming. He may well appeal to it in the Beelzebul controversy in his account of Jesus' warning against blasphemy of the Spirit. And Mark 4:35 - 5:20's

---

[130] *Walking*, 59f, although here with respect to Mt 14:22-33.
[131] Hanson, *Dawn*, 87-89; Cross, *Canaanite*, 170.

'parabolic' representation of deeds of the 'stronger one'[132] may also be a 'midrashic' reflection on this very passage.[133]

(d) The Ultimate Oppressors

Recently several scholars have commented on the political symbolism of this exorcism seeing Jesus' expulsion of 'Legion' as constituting a repudiation of Roman occupation.[134] The fact that Rome was later identified with swine, and that the Boar (although not a domesticated pig) was the emblem of the tenth legion, Fretensis, stationed in Palestine, lends tentative support to this interpretation.[135] The difficulty is that for these commentators demonisation is seen as both symptomatic and symbolic of political oppression and, therefore, tends to be subordinated to political realities. On the other hand, contemporary sources indicate that certain traditions within Judaism clearly understood that spiritual forces were aligned with and ultimately controlled Israel's enemies (e.g. *1 Enoch* 54:4-5; 1QS 4; 1QM, *passim*; 11QMelch 2:4-6; Jubilees 48; *T. Levi* 18:12; *T. Zeb.* 9:8; *T. Sim.* 6:6; *T. Dan* 5:10-13; cf. *Mek.* to Ex 15:1; *Ex. Rab.* 1:5).[136] Several New Testament writers also seem to share the view that the enemies of God's people are at bottom spiritual even though they make use of human agencies (Rev *passim*; Eph 6:12; cf. 1 Cor 15:50; Jn 18:36).[137] It seems more likely that Mark understands ultimate Israel's oppressors, not to be the Romans whom Jesus tends not to attack, but the demons[138]—the stark contrast between the relatively flimsy chains of human 'jailers' and the awesome might of the demons perhaps serving to underline this point.

---

[132] On miracles as parables: Fuller, *Mission*, 73, who sees 4:35 - 5:43, in relation to 4:1-34, as 'manifestations ... of the secret of the Kingdom'; Kertelge, 125f; Richardson, 48-49; Achtemeier, 'Catenae', 275; Hawkin, 'Symbolism'; Donahue, 'Parable'; Stock, *Call*, 77, 117-19; Hamilton, 'Parable'; Boucher, 79-83; Koch, *Bedeutung*, 193; Marshall, *Faith*, 60ff; Beavis, *Audience*, 157ff. On understanding of parable as a metaphorical event, see e.g. Dodd, *Parables*, 16; Funk, *Language*, 133-35; Keck, *Future*, 243ff.

[133] Cf. Sahlin, 'Pericope'.

[134] Mühlmann, *Chiliasmus*, 252; Theissen, *Miracle*, 255-59; Wink, *Unmasking*, 45-48; Myers, 190-94, 141-43. Cf. Hollenbach, 'Jesus', 253ff. Bowman's denial, 144, of the Roman military connotations is misplaced.

[135] Annen, *Heil*, 170f.

[136] Betz, 'Heiliger'; Stevens, 'Jesus', 328; Tiede, *Charismatic*, 188ff; Wink, *Naming*, 26-35.

[137] On the similar attitude of early Christians to exorcisms, Harnack, 'Conflict', 131f.

[138] Leivestad, *Christ*, 40; Betz, *Studies*, 238f; Perrin, *Kingdom*, 171. Cf. Bauernfeind, *Worte*, 54f, where the demon functions as the enemy of the Messiah. Given the link between idolatry and demons, it is the hostile Jewish leaders, if anyone, whose rejection of Yahweh's eschatological deliverer can be described as demonic (see further Chapter 7).

In view of the foregoing, I want to suggest that whereas in Isaiah it was the downfall of the nations' idols which would signal the coming of deliverance, in Mark it is the demise of the demons. In Isaianic terms, the 'occupying legions' keeping Israel in 'exile' from her God are demonic. And furthermore, it is Jesus who, as Yahweh the Creator-Warrior had done before him, delivers the prisoner while the oppressors are destroyed in the sea. It is, therefore, more than a little ironic that Jesus' first miracle is the casting out of an unclean spirit in a synagogue (sacred space), the home territory of those who were most concerned with ritual purity, and on the Sabbath (sacred time).[139]

(e) Jew or Gentile?

It is generally accepted that the demoniac is a Gentile because of the geography,[140] the presence of the pigs, the word of address,[141] the dwelling among the tombs, and fostered perhaps by a perception of Mark's interest in the Gentile mission.[142]   However, several lines of indirect evidence raise some questions about this assumption. It is not clear that ὁ θεός τοῦ ὑψίστου is especially indicative of a Gentile since it was also, apparently, a current Jewish expression.[143]   Similarly, although tomb-dwelling is not what one expects of a pious Jew, it does not establish the demoniac's nationality since it is presumably not incompatible with the demons who control him[144] and may simply testify to his desperate condition as does the Prodigal's tending of pigs (Lk 15:15). Furthermore, Isaiah 65:1-7, which many commentators see as the background to this imagery, is describing

---

[139] Myers, 141; Chilton, 'Repentance',15f. This irony is even more forceful if, as Chilton believes (*pace* Sanders, *Jesus, passim*), it was 'Jesus' habit of teaching an idiosyncratic understanding of purity and sacrifice' that occasioned his death, 'Repentance', 17.

[140] On the uncertainty surrounding both text and location, Annen, *Heil*, 201-9; Baarda, 'Gadarenes'; Guelich.

[141] Argued to be typical of non-Jews, e.g. Gn 14:18; Nu 24:16; Isa 14:14; by Schmid, *Evangelium*, 109; Swete, 94; Craghan, 'Gerasene', 532.

[142] E.g. Lightfoot, *History*, 89f; Nineham, 151; Sahlin, 'Pericope', 160; Craghan, 'Gerasene', 532; Kertelge, 107f; Pesch, 1.282; Gnilka, 1.207; Kelber, 51; Guelich, 1.283; but see Louw, 'bezetene'; Derrett, 'Contributions'; Schneck (apparently), 148; and Gundry, 257, who rejects Gentile symbolism, but nevertheless prefers to see a Gentile. See also the discussion in van der Loos, 386ff.

[143] Klostermann, *Markusevangelium*; espec. Dalman, *Words*, 198f, citing Pss 47:4; 57:3; 78:35; 9:3; Sir 46:5; 48:20 etc., cf. Lk 1:32, 35, 75; Acts 7:48, although vary rare among the rabbis.

[144] *b. Pes.* 3b; *b. Ber.* 3a, 62b; *b. Shabb.* 67a; *b. Git.* 70a; *b. Sanh.* 65b.

not Gentiles but Jews. Granted the presence of such a great number of pigs implies a Gentile region, there is, nevertheless, no necessary connection between their presence and the nationality of the man.[145] The primary warrant, therefore, is the Gentile region.[146] However, only on one occasion does Mark relate an encounter between Jesus and a clearly designated Gentile in a Gentile setting: the Syrophoenician woman whose daughter is also demonised.[147] But the pivotal feature is Jesus' initial reluctance to help (7:24-27; cf. Mt 15:24)[148]—a disinclination which appears to arise from the priority of the Jews and is reflected in other Gospel traditions as well as the behaviour of early Christian missionaries.[149] This raises a fundamental problem. If Jesus had already delivered a Gentile whom he had then sent out, presumably, among other Gentiles,[150] why here, in the first instance that unquestionably involves a Gentile, does

---

[145] The congruence between Isa 65's motifs and this pericope may imply that apostate Jews are in view, see Louw's suggestion, 'bezetene', that the demoniac's condition was the result of his keeping pigs; Farrer, *Matthew*, 23n1. Both Isa 65 and the parable of the Prodigal Son provide evidence that Jews, whether apostate or in dire straits, could involve themselves with pigs. In view of the little that is known about pre-AD70 religious observance especially in these regions, Goodman's discussion, *State*, 102-7, of the laxity of post-AD132 Galilean Jews is enlightening although his data is late, pertains to Galilee, and may reflect dislocations subsequent to the two revolts. Nevertheless, rabbinic Judaism was on the ascendancy and, if anything, applying pressure for greater conformity. On the other hand, the picture of Galileans in the NT suggests that this laxity was not new. Goodman states that in this period rabbinic authority was not all-pervasive with large numbers disregarding the purity laws and, to a lesser extent, Sabbath and tithing requirements. Of particular interest is his reference to *t. B. Meṣ.* 5:7 which indicates that a substantial trade of 'small cattle' went on even though keeping them was a serious enough sin, in R. Ishmael's opinion, as to contribute to the destruction of the village of Beth Aba (*t. B.K.* 8:14). It seems not impossible that some more-delinquent Jews in a Hellenistic environment could have gone further and been engaged in keeping swine for sale in the markets of the Decapolis. Jesus' involvement in the destruction of the pigs is understandable as an act of judgement on apostate/disobedient Jews, for which action we have some sort of parallel in the cursing of the fig tree symbolism. On the other hand, the act would be extraordinary if the pigs were owned by Gentiles. On the main conjectures, Ridderbos, *Coming*, 113-15; van der Loos, 386-93.

[146] Alt, *Where*, 26, suggests that this area would have been inhabited by Jewish peasants but does not deal with the difficult question of the presence of the pigs.

[147] This encounter is more obviously proleptic of the Gentile mission.

[148] Theissen, *Miracle*, 254, notes that in the non-Jewish petitioner accounts involving Gentiles (vis-a-vis Samaritans) the contrast/resistance motif is 'particularly prominent'.

[149] Mt 10:5f; 15:24; Acts 1:8; cf. Jervell, 'Lost'; Paul's attitude in Rom. 1:16, and missions in Acts. Gentiles on Jewish territory were not excluded but invite special comment (e.g. Mt. 8:10ff, par.; Jn 12:20ff), Jeremias, *Theology*, 133f.

[150] So Lohmeyer, 97; Taylor, 284; Pesch, 1.294; Guelich 1.289; but see Wrede, 140; Gnilka, 1.206; Theissen, *Miracle*, 146f.

Mark stress Jesus' hesitation to heal, and then attribute it specifically to the woman's non-Jewish status (7:26f)?[151]

On the other hand, we know that during the Maccabean expansion Alexander Janneus seized Gerasa *ca.* 82 B.C. (Jos. *Ant.* 13.391-4; *B.J.* 1.103-5) and that numbers of Jews remained in the region, at least to the time of the First Jewish Revolt (*B.J.* 2.477-80).[152] Not only would this reconcile the above-mentioned difficulty and the surprising lack of any comment that the man was a Gentile, but it coheres with Jesus' focus on his own people. If Jesus is being presented as the one who inaugurates the NE, then this account with its combined Exodus/Creation motifs (or, in terms of social theory, 'iconic' elements) would be entirely consistent with a journey into non-Jewish territory (or even once-Davidic lands) to effect the deliverance of a 'bound' Diaspora Israelite, even one who dwelt among tombs and did not seek him. However, because no direct textual evidence is available for either position and since the comparison with the Gentile woman is ultimately an argument from silence, dogmatism should be avoided.[153]

(iii) Mark's Literary Scheme

The observation that the destruction of the demons in Mark 5 reflects the fulfilment of the demon's question in 1:24[154] highlights the relationship between the three accounts we have analysed. It should be noted that these are the only detailed references to Jesus' encounters with the demonic in the first section (9:14ff appears to serve a different purpose, Chapter 8). Jesus' first authoritative confrontation presages the coming destruction of the demonic forces while the second explains both Jesus' actions and the source of his authority in terms of the Isaianic Yahweh-Warrior. The link between the second and third stories lies in the programmatic purpose of the former: while Jesus' use of a parable in response to his rejection by the Jewish leaders (3:23) provides the point of

---

[151] Guelich, 1.387; Jesus' secrecy (7:24) may simply reflect a desire for privacy, cf. *ibid.*, 385.

[152] Cf. Bietenhard, 'Dekapolis'; Schürer, 2.150; 3/1.13-17; Avi-Yonah, *Jews*, 16-19. The blanket assessment of this area as a pagan land (e.g. Sahlin, 'Perikope', 163) is, therefore, an oversimplification.

[153] Consequently, assertions such as Kelber's, 15, that the point of this 'massive miracle' pericope does not lie in the breaking of demonic power 'but in his breaking of the Gentile barrier', cf. Kertelge, 109, seem overstated.

[154] Hooker, *Message*, 39; cf. Burkill, 88f; Guelich, 1.279; Kelber, 51, who sees 5:1-20 as the Gentile counterpart of 1:21-28.

transition to the discussion on the purpose of parables in 4:1-34, the ensuing 'strong man' saying (3:27) comes to a fuller but equally 'parabolic' expression in 4:35 - 5:20.

Another feature of the conflict-with-demons motif is that all of the exorcisms are confined to the 'Galilee and Beyond' section (again 9:14-29 is the exception). This striking peculiarity contributed to E. Lohmeyer's and R. H. Lightfoot's 'geographical theology'.[155] But since their theory is untenable, how is this distribution to be explained? The Isaianic NE motif may help. Just as Yahweh's warrior activities are associated with deliverances out among the nations as a precursor to the restorational return to Jerusalem, so also Jesus' warrior activities against Israel's oppressors occur prior to the journey along the 'Way' to Jerusalem.[156]

(iↄ) Εὐαγγέλιον *and the Yahweh-Warrior*

With this overall scheme of Jesus as the Yahweh-Warrior in mind, and in view of the importance of εὐαγγέλιον in 1:1, it may not be insignificant that several of the religious uses of εὐαγγελίζω in the LXX involve this motif.[157] First, in Psalm 67:12 (LXX) εὐαγγελίζω pertains to the message which, in recalling the mighty acts of God at the Exodus (vv. 8f), describes the scattering of Yahweh's enemies (v. 2) as he mightily takes as prisoners those 'that act provokingly, even them that dwell in tombs' (v. 7; cf. Isa 65:3)[158] and then goes on to speak of the spoiling of the enemy (v. 13). The obvious parallels suggest that this version may also have exerted some influence on Mark 5.[159] Psalm 95:2 (LXX) concerns the declaration of Yahweh's mighty deeds in bringing about the return, and is one of the texts that describes the nations' gods as demons (δαιμόνια, v. 5). Finally, the third use, in Nahum 1:15 (LXX), concerns the proclamation of

---

[155] See Chapter 5, pp. 132ff, and the critique therein. Trocmé, *Formation*, 53n1, suggests that the thirteen to fifteen miracles which occur in Mark 1-9 may be explained on the basis of a 'lakeside collection'.

[156] *Pace* Burkill's suggestion, 255, that the demons provide supernatural testimony and are 'hardly required after Peter's confession' and 'the divine confirmation of it at the transfiguration'.

[157] Pss 39(40):9; 67(68):11, and 95(96):2; Nah 1:15.

[158] The LXX is quite different from the MT, introducing some ambiguity into the meaning of the phrase ἐξάγων πεπεδημένους: does it modify v. 7a and, therefore, describe the liberation of those who dwell alone, or, because of the LXX's ὁμοίως (v. 7c), does it describe the taking prisoner of idolators, cf. Isa 65:3? The context of this latter text makes it highly unlikely that Yahweh would be redeeming such wilful apostates.

[159] E.g. Nineham; Craghan, 'Gerasene'; Pesch, 'Markan', 361; Annen, *Heil*, 45, noting the *hapax* κατοίκησιν cf. LXX Ps 67:7.

salvation predicated on Yahweh's (the one who rules over many waters, v. 12) threefold announcement concerning the destruction of the idols and gods of Nineveh, the consequent burial of its King (v. 14), and the shattering of Judah's bonds (v. 13). Here again there is the conjunction of the motifs of Yahweh as Creator-Warrior victorious over both chaos and the nations' gods.[160] The Septuagint's use of the verb in these contexts appears not only to involve deliverance but associates the actions of the Yahweh-Warrior in overcoming the nations' demonic gods. This is entirely compatible with its use in Isaiah 40:9 (2); 52:7 and 61:1 where as we have seen εὐαγγελίζω connotes the idea of the deliverance of the captives by the Yahweh-Warrior.[161]

Finally, if, as is commonly held, Mark presents Jesus in eschatological conflict with Satan and his demons, and if εὐαγγέλιον, understood as the content of εὐαγγελίζω, relates to the promised deliverance of God's people, whence the antecedent? Surely the most obvious precursor is the general motif expressed throughout the OT of Yahweh's battles with the nations and their idols, particularly those in association with the great hope of the INE.[162]

c) Summary

The foregoing analysis suggests that Mark understands Jesus' exorcisms in terms of the Yahweh-Warrior's actions in inaugurating Isaiah's NE. But, whereas in Isaiah the captives were prisoners of the idols who were deemed responsible for Babylon's victory, in Mark it is the unclean

---

[160] Derrett, 'Legend', suggests Nah 1:4, 11-15 as background for Mark 5.

[161] Cf. 40:10; 52:1ff, 9f; 61:1. On the latter, note the literary structure involving the warrior in 59:15b-20 and 63:1-6.

[162] Longman 'Divine', addresses this connection but makes only passing reference to Jesus' conflict with the demons. Several writers, e.g. Bishop, 'Why'; more recently Fisher, 'Son'; Lövestam, 'Fils'; Berger, 'Messiastraditionen'; Duling, 'Solomon'; Brady, 'Role'; Chilton, 'Reflections'; note that the title 'Son of David' may have at a popular level referred to Solomon who was renowned as a formidable exorcist (Jos. *Ant.* 8.44-45; cf. Vermes, *Jesus*, 62-65) and suggest that Jesus may have been identified as a Solomonic Son of David. Duling, 252, asks that if Mark knew this material, why does it not appear in the first half, and why not in an exorcism (Bartimaeus, after all, is blind; cf. De Jonge, 'Son', 100f)? He suggests that Mark modifies a Solomonic 'Son of David' expectation as he does the 'royal' aspect, so the Bartimaeus miracle hardly fits with down-playing the idea. If this tradition was current, and more so if it had eschatological connotations (which does not appear so), then it may provide further insight into popular perceptions of Jesus' exorcisms (cf. Philo, *Lib. Bib. Ant.* 60.3), although our proposed interpretation of the Beelzebul controversy would suggest it plays a minor role, at least from Mark's perspective.

spirits/demons who are to be understood as the oppressors who hold God's people captive. Just as the prophecies of the NE had spoken of the dethronement and humiliation of Babylon's idols, who were seen as the source of her power, so in the fulfilment of Isaiah's prophecies Jesus defeats the demons who ultimately stand behind the idols and liberates their prisoners. Jesus' exorcisms, it appears, are the Markan equivalent of the release of the Isaian captive.[163] The NE motif may also explain the frequently noted phenomenon of Mark's near total confinement of Jesus' defeat of the demons to this first section of his Gospel in that Jesus' 'Warrior' activities likewise occur prior to the journey along the way to Jerusalem.[164]

IV. Jesus and the Isaianic Healings

Here, too, the concern is not to determine if Jesus' activities are to be understood in some general way as an expression of the breaking-in of the reign of God.[165] What is of interest is whether there is any evidence that Mark's presentation of Jesus' healing ministry has links with Isaiah's NE.

---

[163] This background, not disregarding Jesus' stated reason, 'because they knew him', may also shed some light on Jesus' commanding silence of the demons (1:25, 34; 3:12). Isa 52:15 describes how, as a result of their understanding the significance of Yahweh's actions, Israel's oppressors will be silent, a figure of speech indicating their imminent subjugation, cf. Job 5:16; Ps 107:42, Watts, 'Meaning'. *Tg. Isa* then develops this understanding by interpreting 53:7 such that it is the mighty ones who are silenced and hence 'none shall be before him who opens his mouth or speaks a word'. Perhaps the commands to silence reflect these ideas. First, as with the kings, the demons'/spirits' awareness of imminent subjugation is related to their recognition of who Jesus really is, as is indicated by their accurate testimony to Jesus' identity—and this, as in Isaiah, in contrast to Israel's failure to see and understand, Watts, 'Meaning'; 'Consolation'. Second, the commands to silence could reflect the fact of their subjugation as *Tg. Isa* emphasises, cf. Ebeling, *Messiasgeheimnis*, 114-218. This seems to be borne out by the fact that in Jesus' first miracle the command to silence is linked with that to come out (1:25b). The unclean spirit's obedience to both is what amazes the on-lookers (1:26).

[164] Schenke's attempt, *Wundererzählungen*, 396, to see all of Jesus miracles as 'auf dem Wege' citing e.g. Mk 1:21, 29, 35 etc. seems to ignore Mark's redactional use of 'way' terminology, cf. Swartley, 'Structural'.

[165] E.g. Loisy, *Evangels*, 160; Hoskyns-Davey, 167; Richardson, 43; and van der Loos, 236, who sees Jesus acting in a messianic capacity. Kallas, *Significance*, stresses the cosmic demonic dimensions, while Fuller, *Mission*, sees in the miracles the preliminary signs of the Kingdom, cf. Delling, 'Verständnis', 154; Schniewind, 85; Lohmeyer, 48. Kertelge, 170ff, understands the miracles as revealing Jesus' mission rather than directly Jesus' identity, although it is not clear if such a firm distinction between act and identity can be maintained in practice.

It should be noted that while it would be reductionistic to regard all of Jesus' miracles only as 'signs' or to deny that several motivations could be at work in the one miracle,[166] clearly aspects of some miracles function in the former way.[167]   The following material is concerned with those categories of healing miracles which, in the light of their treatment in the OT, could be interpreted as indicative of the NE.[168]

a) The Healing of Israel in Isaiah's NE

Although the OT has numerous references concerning Yahweh's desire to heal (רפא), whether individually (e.g. Pss 6:3; 41:5) or corporately of Israel (e.g. Jer 33:6; Pss 147:3; 60:4), statements concerning specific healings, for example, of the blind, deaf, dumb, lame, leprous, and of a shrivelled limb occur infrequently.[169]   The latter two cases are found only in historical narratives.[170]   The others, aside from a brief reference in the general thanksgiving hymn where Yahweh is described as the one who opens blind eyes (Psalm 146:8), are entirely confined to the prophetic utterances in Isaiah.[171]   From a literary perspective, the interest in the restoration of sight and hearing appears to originate in the pivotal Isaiah 6 which together with chapters 28-29 uses metaphorical blind and deaf terminology in the context of judgement.[172]   Similarly, the root רפא occurs first in 6:10 with reference to the healing that Israel, through blinding and hardening, is to be denied.   However, it is in the descriptions of Israel's restorational healing that this language is most frequently found.

---

[166] See the helpful discussion in van der Loos, 240-54.

[167] E.g. Richardson, 57; Menoud, 'signification', 185; Kertelge, 170ff.

[168] For Meye, 'Horizon', the miracles in 4:35 - 8:26 echo those in Ps 107. The parallels are clear enough, but their general nature and the lack of agreement in order, suggests that the similarities as due to common OT motifs, particularly those of the Exodus and Exile, cf. Kissane, *Psalms*; Kirkpatrick, *Psalms*; Snaith, *Five*, 17ff; Crüsemann, *Studien*, 73.

[169] The ὁ πυρετός mentioned in 1:31 is listed in LXX Dt 28:22 as one of the curses for covenant unfaithfulness, but Yahweh's healing of it is not mentioned, although perhaps implied in 1 Kgs 8:37f and par.

[170] Respectively: Moses (Ex 4), Miriam (Num 12) and Naaman (2 Kgs 5), and Jereboam (1 Kgs 13:4).

[171] Jeremiah 31:8, part of an oracle concerning the return of the exiles, briefly mentions the blind and lame as examples of the extent of Yahweh's compassion such that even they are included. There is no mention of healing. Ezek 3:26; 24:27; and 33:22 are concerned solely with the prophet's own experience. Goppelt, *Typos*, 70, notes that the healings of the blind, deaf, and lame (along with the exorcisms) have 'no parallel in the OT' among the 'men of God' but they are 'expected to occur in the new age'.

[172] Clements; Skinner, *Isaiah*; Kaiser; Oswalt, *Isaiah*; Beale, 'Retributive'.

In 29:18f the restoration of sight and hearing is one of the characteristics of Israel's redemption, while 32:1 speaks of the righteous king in whose reign the judgements of blinding and deafening will no longer occur and the tongue of the stammerer will speak clearly (vv. 3f; cf. chapters 6 and 28f). It is in chapter 35, however, that this restorational healing of Israel is set most firmly in the context of a NE.[173] Here 35:5 portrays this age as a time when the eyes of the blind will (literally?) be opened and the ears of the deaf unstopped.[174] This last example, which uses metaphors from the 'wisdom' genre (v. 8), may suggest the interplay between the literal and the metaphorical that characterises some of this language in Isaiah.[175] In terms of רפא, Isaiah 30:26, in keeping with the reversal of the judgement in 6:10, describes the day of redemption as a time when Yahweh will heal (יִרְפָּא) the bruise (מַכָּתוֹ) of his people and bind up the fracture he inflicted (cf. 1:6).[176] In the NE of chapters 40-66, one of the tasks of the enigmatic 'servant' figure is to open blind eyes and release the prisoners from their dungeon (42:7),[177] while in 42:16 Yahweh announces his intention to 'lead the blind along a way they do not know' (see Chapter 8). The general idea of healing (רפא) is also explicitly picked up on two occasions in these chapters: in 53:4f the suffering of the 'servant' figure is linked with Israel's healing, and in 57:18f (*bis*) it is applied to Yahweh's restoration of the nation.

In non-Biblical literature, although there are general references to healing or the banishing of illness in association with eschatological salvation (e.g. *Jub.* 23:29f; *T. Zeb.* 9:8; *2 Bar.* 73:2; *4 Ezra* 13:50), there is little evidence to suggest that a messianic figure was specifically connected with the healing of the blind, deaf, and lame during the NT period (but see now 4Q521).[178] We may conclude that in the OT specific references to Yahweh's

---

[173] E.g. Torrey, *Second*; Scott, 'Relation'; Olmstead, 'Isaiah'; Smart, *History*, 292-94; Brownlee, *Meaning*, 247-55; Clements, 275; Wildberger, 3.1358; Steck, *Bereitet*.

[174] Clements, 'Beyond', 125, cf. Wildberger, 3.1362.

[175] It is sometimes difficult to tell, however, whether this is metaphorical wisdom language or literal or perhaps even both, Gerleman, 'Bermerkungen'; von Soden-Wächter, *TWAT*, 5.190-93. On the wisdom connotations in Isaiah, see Chapter 8.

[176] Cf. Wildberger, 3.1205.

[177] Watts, 'Consolation', 51f. Paul, 'Cuneiform', 182, suggests, on the basis of royal cuneiform inscriptions, that 42:7a is 'a metaphor for the releasing of the imprisoned or "dwellers in darkness"'.

[178] Str-B, 1.593ff (Amoraic period or later); Vielhauer, 'Erwägungen', 159; Martyn, *History*, 84ff; Klausner, *Messianic*, 502-17; Volz, *Jüdische*, 173-86; Grundmann, *et al*, *TDNT*,

healing of the blind, deaf, and lame, understood variously in literal and metaphorical terms, are primarily characteristics of Isaiah's NE, especially as described in Isaiah 35 (and Isaiah 61).

b) Jesus and the Healing of Israel[179]

Unfortunately Mark offers no equivalent to the Beelzebul controversy to help us understand the significance of Jesus' healing miracles. However, both Matthew and Luke present an account of Jesus' response to John the Baptist's question, which response is near universally recognised as being couched in terms of Isaianic prophecies.[180]   Commentators are likewise largely agreed that the Markan healings of the paralytic (2:1-12),[181] of the deaf-mute (7:31-37, Mark's μογιλάλον, v. 32, appears to come directly from

---

9.505-27; Schürer, 2.497-554; Charlesworth, 'Messiah'. *Tg. Isa* takes blindness as referring to blindness to Torah (e.g. 35:5; 42:7; cf. 32:3f). However, 4Q521 seems to describe releasing captives, healing the sick, restoring sight, etc. (Isa 61:1ff) as messianic events (cf. Mk 10:46ff), although whether understood metaphorically or whether performed by Yahweh or his Messiah is difficult to tell, see Collins, 'Works'; Eisenman and Wise, *Uncovered*, 20ff. Importantly, the latter demarcation may well be inappropriate since in Isaiah there does not appear to be a firm distinction between Yahweh and his agent, Isa 35:5; 42:7, 16. John 7:31 (cf. 2:32; 6:14) may reflect an expected repetition of the miracles of Moses, Meeks, *Prophet*, 162-64, or of others, Martyn, *History*, 87f.   Solomon, a noted thaumaturge in folklore, does not appear to be an eschatological figure, although he *may* be in Bartimaeus' mind (Mk 10:46ff; see fn. 162 above).

[179] For a critique of Weeden's view of the negative function of miracles in Mark, *Traditions*, see Kolenkow, 'Beyond', and the excellent survey in Dowd, *Prayer*, 6-24.

[180] Mt 11:5 (par Lk 7:22; note especially the link with εὐαγγελίζω, Stuhlmacher, *Evangelium*, 218f) is widely understood as reflecting Isa 26:19; 29:18f; 35:5f; 42:17, 18; and 61:1; e.g. espec. Grimm, 124-30; but also Richardson, 43; Klostermann, *Matthäusevangelium*, 95; Held, 'Interpreter', 253ff; Brown, 'Miracles', 190; Schlatter, *Matthäus*; Fitzmyer, *Luke*; Marshall, *Luke*; cf. Irenæus, *Adv.*, 4. 55:2; Justin, *First Apology*, 48; Tertullian, *Adv. Marc.*, 4.8.   Achtemeier, 'Origin', 199n2, suggests that Justin's statement may indicate that 'such summaries (i.e. those found in the Fathers) may be … dependent on the idea of Christ fulfilling the prophecy of Is 35:6'.   Only the cleansing of the lepers is absent and while some (e.g. Marshall) see perhaps an Elisha typology (2 Kgs 5) it may be, as in the case of Mark's restoration of sight (see Chapter 8), that there is a symbolic reference to Israel's 'leprous' condition (cf. Isa 1:5ff; 53:1ff; Jeremias, *TDNT*, 5.690; Bowman, 65f).   Although speculation, it is also possible that the healing of the flow of blood in Mk 5:25ff (menorrhagia, Derrett, 'Technique', 476ff) is symbolic of Israel's cleansing, given that in Isa 64:5 (cf. Isa 30:22) this imagery is employed to stress the dire nature of Israel's defilement before Yahweh (cf. Lev 12 (espec. v. 7) with Mk 5:29, Guelich, 1.297; Pesch, 1.301; but cf. van der Loos, 509f); Lev 15:25-33; Hag 2:11-14; Whybray; Achtemeier, *Community*, 120.   That Jesus rebukes the fever of Peter's mother-in-law suggests that it may have been the work of a demon, cf. van der Loos, 552, who mentions the contemporary Palestinian belief in the demon Imm Maldam who caused fever.

[181] Pesch, 1.158, observes that Mark's παραλυτικός (not in LXX) differs from the LXX's χωλός (Isa 35:6). However, παραλυτικός is not listed in LSJM until NT and later and, therefore, only appears to have come into common use in the NT period, cf. BAGD, as a synonym for χωλός, cf. LN, 1.273.

LXX Isa 35:6,[182] but cf. 29:18f), and of the blind (8:22-26; cf. 10:46-52 which lies outside of the first section and along with 8:22ff serves a dual function, see Chapter 8) primarily reflect Isaiah 35:5f (cf. 29:18; 32:3f).[183] It hardly needs to be added that this is exactly what might be expected if Mark, in keeping with the orientation of his introductory sentence and prologue, is presenting Jesus as the one who inaugurates the Isaianic NE.[184]

Other considerations offer further support for an INE hermeneutic. A parallel has been suggested in Mark 2:1-12 between Jesus' offer to forgive the paralytic's sins and the scribes' indignant response, and Yahweh's declaration—also in the midst of a confrontation—to Israel in Isaiah 43:25 (cf. 40:1-3; 44:22).[185] One of the major themes in the Isaiah passage concerns a theology of past and future in which Jacob-Israel's remembering and Yahweh's remembering are treated in parallel.[186] Jacob-Israel makes accusation that Yahweh has been unfaithful which he refutes by pointing to their corrupt worship (vv. 23f). Echoing the language of the prologue's programmatic announcement of Yahweh's coming (40:2), one of the central concerns of this polemical confrontation (43:22-28) lies in the call to forget the past and to look instead to the future (43:18) just as Yahweh himself is doing in forgiving Jacob-Israel's transgressions and acting to effect their deliverance (43:25; cf. 44:22).[187] From this perspective, if Mark is presenting Jesus as the one who inaugurates the INE then the offer of forgiveness is strikingly consistent with Yahweh's pardoning of sin as a 'sign' of the INE (cf. Ex 34:6f).[188] Furthermore, as B. Blackburn notes, this

---

[182] Hoskyns, 'Jesus', 72ff. Hawkin's suggestion, 'Symbolism', 105, that Isa 6:6-9 is in view appears unlikely, but at least recognises the origins of much of the 'blind/deaf' language in Isaiah; see Watts, 'Consolation'.

[183] Espec. Kee, *Community*, 125f, who sees strong Isaianic links, Hoskyns-Davey, 167ff; Lohmeyer, 151; Richardson, 81-89; Fuller, *Interpreting*, 60f; Hawkin, 'Symbolism', 102f; Evans, *Beginning*, 29; Nineham; Goulder, *Calender*, 246; Barrett, *Spirit*, 70ff; Achtemeier, 'Catenae', 289; Hooker, *Message*, 42ff; Lane; Gnilka; Pesch; Broadhead, *Teaching*, 133.

[184] Sanders, *Jesus*, 161ff, argues against Isa 35:5f as background on the grounds that healings of the blind, dumb, and lame were common, and that Jesus also performed other miracles which are not mentioned in Isa 35. This seems to me to fail to give full weight to the fulfilment aspect of John the Baptist's question of Jesus, but more importantly ignores, at least in Mark's case, the role of the prologue in literary antiquity.

[185] E.g. Grimm, 135-37; cf. Gnilka, 1.100; Guelich, 1.87; margin NA[26]. See now also Schneck, 70ff.

[186] Melugin, *Formation*, 116f.

[187] *Ibid*; Westermann, 133; Schoors, *Saviour*, 190ff.

[188] Grimm, 135-37; cf. Lane; Pesch; Ernst; Gnilka; Guelich; Klauck, 'Sündenvergebung', 236f. On Israel's critical response to the message of Isa 40-55, see Watts, 'Consolation'.

text 'constitutes a very significant assimilation of Jesus to God';[189] an 'assimilation' that would hardly be out of place given that Mark has already intimated earlier on that Jesus is somehow to be identified with the personal presence of Yahweh (1:2f).

A unique feature of this healing, however, is that it is the only occasion in Mark when Jesus offers forgiveness of sins. Furthermore as Chris Marshall notes, the link between forgiveness and healing is not merely incidental but demonstrates the 'inseparable connection that exists between healing and forgiveness within the activity of Jesus'.[190] The question is, however, why is it mentioned here and nowhere else, and what, if any, is the significance of the individual being a paralytic?

It is noteworthy that this constitutes the first occurrence of the πίστις- πιστεύω word group since Jesus' programmatic announcement of the coming of the kingdom 'μετανοεῖτε καὶ πιστεύετε' (1:14f). In addition, 2:1-12 is the first in Mark's series of controversy stories which will eventually conclude with the climactic Beelzebul confrontation. Interestingly, these two accounts are the only ones involving charges of blasphemy prior to Jesus' trial (where the final charge of blasphemy appears), both concern matters of Jesus' authority, and both involve scribes (although the second group comes from Jerusalem). In 2:1-12, the γραμματεῖς reject Jesus' statements as blasphemous, while in the Beelzebul incident the sandal is on the other foot: it is the scribes' assessment of his exorcisms that Jesus regards as blasphemous. This pericope may, therefore, be seen as somewhat pivotal.

But why the link between sins and the paralytic? Isaiah 33:23f may provide a clue. The restoration of Israel's fortunes under Yahweh as rightful king is described in terms of the forgiveness of sins which is specifically linked with the absence of sickness (cf. Ps 103:3). This new wholeness is such that even the lame would participate in the spoils of Yahweh's victory (Isa 33:23). If this background is in mind, then Jesus' granting of forgiveness (see Isa 33:24; 43:25 cf. 40:2; 44:22f) in association with the healing of the lame man (33:23; cf. 35:6) may be intended to testify to the breaking-in of Yahweh's reign expressed in INE terms (33:22; 52:7; cf. Mark 1:15, *Tg. Isa* 40:9). Furthermore, although there is evidence of a

---

[189] *Theios*, 139.
[190] Marshall, *Faith*, 89.

general expectation of an eschatological removal of sin and purification of the land and the people,[191] there are no clear grounds to suggest that forgiveness of sin is pronounced by any other than Yahweh.[192] That Jesus forgives sins further reinforces the idea—articulated by the watching scribes, implied by Mark 1:2-3, and reinforced by the storm-stillings—that he is, in some way, to be associated with the personal manifestation of Yahweh (cf. Ex 23:21).[193]

In the case of the deaf mute (7:31-37), in spite of several Jewish features in the narrative—Jesus addresses him in Aramaic (v. 34),[194] the crowd's response recalls LXX Genesis 1:31,[195] and Mark's μογιλάλον (v. 32, see above)—the recipient is generally seen, at least in terms of Mark's retelling, as a Gentile and this again purely on the basis of the geographical setting.[196] The story occurs after Jesus' last confrontation with those from Jerusalem before he reaches the capital (7:1-23). He then moves into what are customarily understood as Gentile regions, finally arriving at the Sea of Galilee. Here he effects a healing of a kind promised in the INE (i.e. Isa 35:5f), but on this occasion receives a positive response (7:37; cf. 6:56 and 7:1ff; and Isa 63:7?). Once again, as with the Gerasene demoniac, it is difficult to tell whether Mark is working with a clear-cut Gentile versus Jew motif such that Jesus' healing of a Gentile indicates that the future of Christian mission lies in the Gentile world of the Diaspora, or in view of the clearly Jewish features, is depicting a Diaspora Jew. The problem with the former view is Jesus' professed reluctance to extend his mission to the Gentiles; there is nothing in the text that indicates that Mark's Jesus has changed his mind.[197] On the other hand, the account may be analogous to that of the Gerasene demoniac, in that Jesus effects the signs of the INE out among the 'exiles' of Israel.

Compared to the clear Isaianic associations of the healings of the lame, the deaf mute, and the blind, interpreting Jesus' raising of the dead girl is

---

[191] E.g. 11QMelch 2:6ff; *1 Enoch* 10:20-22; *Pss. Sol.* 17; *T. Levi* 18:9; *Tg. Isa* 53:4, 6; cf. *4 Ezra* 6:27f; *2 Bar.* 73:4; *Jub.* 4:26.

[192] Lane, 95; Gnilka, 1.100; Hofius, 'Vergegungszuspruch'; Maisch, *Heilung*, 89f; Gundry, 113, 117-23; *pace* Vermes, *Jesus*, 67ff. Koch's attempt, 'Messias', to see evidence of messianic forgiveness in *Tg. Isa* 53 is not convincing, Klauck, 'Sündenvergebung', 238f.

[193] Blackburn, *Theios*, 137ff.

[194] Martin, 211.

[195] Richardson, 54n, who sees an allusion to Christ's work as a new creation.

[196] Martin, *Evangelist*, 211.

[197] See also Jeremias, *Promise*, 33.

rather more complex. The resuscitation of the Shunammite's son and the revival of the man whose body touched Elisha's bones are the sole OT narrative accounts,[198] while only Daniel 12:1-2 is generally accepted by modern scholarship as an unambiguous reference to any future or eschatological event. A number of scholars have noted the parallels with Elijah.[199] Others have seen a possible allusion to Isaiah 29:18 in Jesus' response to the Baptist's messengers[200] which suggests that the one resuscitation in Mark could be understood, along with the other miracles listed there, as integral to the Isaianic prophecies of deliverance.[201] It may be the case that there is an integration of several traditions concerning Israel's eschatological hope (cf. the promise concerning infants in Isa 65:19f),[202] but the evidence is far from conclusive and the origin and nature of any deeper significance must remain uncertain.[203]

---

[198] 1 Kgs 17:17ff; 2 Kgs 4:18ff; 13:20f.

[199] E.g. Goppelt, *Typos*, 70f; Lindars, 'Elijah'.

[200] Fn. 180. Jeremias, *Theology*, 104, cites a tannaitic list where being lame, blind, a leper, or childless is considered as being as good as dead.

[201] On the diverse Jewish views of a general resurrection, Schürer, 2.539ff.

[202] Along the lines suggested by Heising, 'Exegese'.

[203] Why does Mark, or whoever redacted the "miracle catenae" (see Fowler, *Loaves*, 24-31, for a critique of Achtemeier), follow up the storm-stilling and deliverance of the demoniac with the intercalated accounts of the raising of the dead girl and the healing of the flow of blood (on the unity of 4:1 - 5:43, Tolbert, *Sowing*, 148f)? It has already been proposed that Mk 4:35 - 5:20 could be a reflection on Isa 63:7 - 65:7 where Jesus, already identified with Yahweh's intervention by the prologue's allusion to the same passage (63:19; Mk 1:10), is presented as the Divine-Warrior. In addition, in fn. 180 I suggested that the healing of the flow of blood might be symbolic or 'parabolic' of Israel's cleansing— Mark appears to use miracles (particularly Isaianic ones) in this way, see fn. 132. Interestingly, this unusual imagery is found in Isaiah 63:7 - 64:11 MT where it graphically describes the hopelessness of Israel's attempts at righteousness (64:5). More striking, however, is Yahweh's reply (Isa 65:1-25) which speaks of the longed-for, new-creational restoration as a time when weeping will cease, 'the infant will not die', and all will live out their allotted days (65:19f; cf. *Jub.* 23:27-30). In Mark, Jesus queries the need for weeping (5:38f) and reverses the untimely death of a young girl by restoring her to life (5:41f), and in each of the four miracles the response is one of fear or awe (4:41; 5:15, 33, 42; cf. Isa 64:2 MT). Could it be that this whole section, 4:35 - 5:43, is redacted around the final lament of the people in the book of Isaiah, as they await the NE, and Yahweh's response? If so, then in 4:35 - 5:20 Jesus is presented as the Divine-Warrior who commands the sea and delivers the oppressed, even those who dwell among the tombs and who do not seek him, while in 5:21-43 he symbolically demonstrates that he is the one who heals Israel of her uncleanness and, by restoring the child to life, signals the inauguration of the promises of Yahweh's new creational restoration of Israel. In other words, these miracles bear all the hallmarks of indicating that, in response to the lament and promise which concludes the book of Isaiah, Yahweh has indeed 'split the heavens' (Mk 1:10; Isa 63:19), sent his Holy Spirit among his people (Mk 1:10; 3:22-30; cf. Isa 63:10-14), and come down in Jesus, as the mighty Warrior (Mk 3:27), to inaugurate the NE.

c) Summary

Jesus' healings of the blind, deaf/dumb, and lame (the resuscitation may reflect Isa 65:20) display substantial and unique parallels with those prophesied in the book of Isaiah as being characteristic of the INE. This coheres with the overall framework suggested by his opening sentence and prologue. Consequently, Mark's presentation of Jesus' healing ministry can be understood as evidence, not of some generalised 'messianic time',[204] but particularly as 'iconic' indicators associated with the inauguration of the Isaianic NE.[205]

V. Jesus and the Isaianic NE Provision for Israel

Finally, there is the matter of the miracles of provision in 6:34-44 and 8:1-10. Although scholars regularly note parallels with the Exodus event (see below), it is hardly surprising, given the paradigmatic nature of Israel's founding moment, that echoes of the past should also be integral to her prophetic hope of deliverance and indeed the INE contains numerous promises concerning Yahweh's future provision for his people as he comes 'like a shepherd' gently leading and providing for his flock.

a) The Provision for Israel in Isaiah's NE

Drawing perhaps on the traditions of provision in the first Exodus, the prophet concludes his opening declaration of salvation (40:1-11) by likening Yahweh to a shepherd who tends his sheep, gathers his lambs in his arms, and gently leads the nursing ewes home to Zion (40:11; cf. 63:11; Ex 15:13; Pss 77:21; 78:52f). Given the prologue's programmatic character,[206] it is not surprising that similar imagery reappears throughout subsequent chapters. The newly released and returning prisoners, whose bread Yahweh promised would not be lacking (51:14), are described as pasturing on the heights (49:9) as their compassionate God (רחם, 49:10, 13;

---

[204] E.g. Richardson, 43, who sees here messianic miracles but 'of Isaianic prediction'.

[205] E.g. Fuller, *Mission*, 36. Along the lines of e.g. Kallas, *Significance*; (although he emphasises the Daniellic influence), and Kertelge, 201, if Mark is operating with a INE hermeneutic and as this is a matter of the reign of Yahweh, (cf. Chapter 3, p. 81, fn. 151), it is difficult to see how these particular miracles could not be signs of the inbreaking Kingdom, *pace* Koch, *Bedeutung*, 173ff; Best, 'Miracles', 539. In the latter's case it is not clear how a pastoral purpose excludes e.g. a concern for Christology or eschatology.

[206] See Chapter 3, p. 78.

cf. 40:17; 54:7, 10) provides food for the hungry and water for the thirsty (49:10f; 48:20f; cf. 35:7; Ex 17:2-7; and Num 20:8), and miraculously transforms the wilderness (35:6f; 43:19f; 41:17-20 (?);[207] 49:9ff).[208]

b) INE Feedings in Mark

Many have observed Moses traditions in the feeding of the 5000 (Mk 6:34-44), primarily because of the miraculous provision (cf. Neh 9:15; Pss 78:17-32; 105:40), the location in the desert (ἔρημος τόπος, vv. 31, 32, 35 cf. LXX Ex 16:1, 3, 10 etc.), the references to the sheep without a shepherd (Nu 27:16ff),[209] the division into hundreds and fifties (Ex 18:21), and perhaps in the question about provision (cf. Nu 11:21f; Ps 78:19f).[210] Derrett, followed by Schneck, sees an allusion to the 'wisdom' invitation of Isaiah 55:1ff.[211] But the parallels are superficial, being based on common terminology—for instance, Isaiah contains a summons to 'buy bread without money', the disciples in Mark have no money to buy bread—without any substantive connection between the respective concerns of each passage.[212] Lane suggests Isaiah 25:6-9, reading it in terms of a messianic feast. But to equate the rather spartan loaves and fish with 'aged wine ... the choicest of meats and the superior wines' seems somewhat generous.[213] Others see the influence of the Elisha feeding story (2 Kgs 4:42ff; cf. 1 Kgs 17:8-16; 2 Kgs 4:1-7)[214] where there is a similar command to provide food (1 Kgs 4:42b; Mk 6:37a) as well as a super-abundant provision (1 Kgs 4:43b, 44b; Mk 6:42-3). Although a combination of both could be in view, particularly if the Elisha

---

[207] The imagery in 41:18 (cf 43:20) suggests that 41:17-20 could pertain to the NE.

[208] Anderson, 'Typology'; cf. Stuhlmueller, *Creative*, 272.

[209] E.g. Mauser, 50n1, 92, 104f, 135; Hooker, 'Mark', 226. On the imagery of Yahweh and Messiah as shepherd, Jeremias, *TDNT*, 6.488-89.

[210] E.g. Richardson, 94-99; Ziener, 'Brotwunder'; Hobbs, 'Gospel', 40-42; McCasland, 'Signs'; Friedrich, 'Erzählungen', 18ff; Goppelt, *Typos*, 71f; van der Loos, 631-37; Kertelge, 133f; Bowman; Nineham; Cranfield; Achtemeier, 'Origin', 202f; Hurtado; Guelich. See, however, van Iersel's objections, 'Speisung', 188, who suggests the influence of Ps 23; cf. Heising, 'Exegese'; Pesch. There is no reason why Ps 23 could not also be included.

[211] Respectively, *Making*, 1.122, and *Isaiah*, 153. Begrich, *Studien*, 59-61; Melugin, *Formation*, 25; and Clifford, *Persuading*, 190ff; see here an imitation of Wisdom Genre; cf. the summons to life: Prov 3:13-18; 4:22; 8:35; 9:6ff; Sir 4:12; to eat and drink: Prov. 9:2, 5; Sir 1:17; 15:3; 24:19, 21.

[212] Schneck, 155, himself admits that the major parallel between the two—'eating bread'—occurs throughout the OT and then turns to 2 Kgs 4:42ff.

[213] *Mark*, 232.

[214] E.g. Bowman; Cranfield; Nineham; LaVerdiere, 'Feed'; Pesch; Ernst; Guelich; Schneck, 155.

stories themselves were influenced by the Exodus narrative,[215] the number of Exodus parallels suggests that it is predominant.

However, the importance of Isaianic imagery for Mark thus far, and the fact that there is little correlation between the miracles of Exodus 13-17 and those in the first section of Mark,[216] suggests the possibility of reading the feeding accounts in the light of Yahweh's provision for his people in the INE. As noted above, the sheep/shepherd imagery is highly developed in the Isaianic NE (cf. also 'scattered sheep' in Ezek 34:5, 26-29) as is the motif of Yahweh's compassion (cf. Mk 6:34; 8:2) and his provision for his people. Some have proposed that the 'green grass' is indicative of the new creational restoration of the wilderness (Isa 35:1f, 6f; 43:20; cf. 41:19) although this is far from certain.[217] Further, the Qumran community, which defined itself in terms of Isaiah 40:3, used similar groupings of fifties and hundreds when describing the gathering of true Israel in the desert in the last days (e.g. CD 13:1; 1QS 2:21-22; 1QM 4:1-5; cf. 4Q521 1 ii 13b). Taken together, these factors suggest that the feeding of the 5000 should be seen in terms of Yahweh's NE provision for his people.[218] Since Mark's presentation of the second feeding seems deliberately to parallel the first, it is highly likely that it should be similarly understood.[219]

VI. *Conclusion*

At the outset of this Chapter we posed the question as to whether there was any evidence in this first section that Mark, in keeping with the apparent thrust of his opening sentence, prologue, and literary structure,

---

[215] Heising, 'Exegese'; *Botschaft*, 38; Achtemeier, 'Origin', 204; cf. e.g. Masuda, 'Bread'; Cranfield; Bowman; Nineham.

[216] Mauser, 136, noting Ezek 34:26ff; Achtemeier, 'Origin', 203n32; Marcus, 24, cites Isa 51:3.

[217] Friedrich, 'Erzählungen', 18ff; Mauser, 136f; but cf. e.g. Pesch, 1.350n11, who sees instead Ps 23:2.

[218] This is not to exclude any possibility of a Eucharistic element, an examination of which lies outside the immediate interests of this section. For a discussion of other alternatives, including Schweitzer's 'anticipation of the eschatological banquet', *Mystery*, 186-74; see Boucher, 70ff; Quesnell, 5-28.

[219] On why the feedings precede Mark's 'Way' section—one might have expected them within it—and why one exorcism and one healing of the blind occur outside of Mark's first section, see the excursus, pp. 292ff, below.

was operating with some expression of a consistent INE hermeneutic. In the light of the foregoing we can now make the following observations.

Mark's first section seems to serve several purposes. First, the presentation of Jesus' deliverance of his people from the oppression of demons and his healing of the blind, deaf, and lame is consistent with the prologue's apparent designation of Jesus as the one who inaugurates the Isaianic NE. Mark's recounting of these INE 'icons' testifies to the in-breaking reign of God. At the same time, the juxtaposed 'iconographic' accounts of Jesus' storm-stilling and the drowning of the demonic legion echo the Isaianic linkage of the destruction of Pharaoh and creator Yahweh's victory in the *Chaoskampf*. Given that in Isaiah this linkage is intimately connected with the hope of a NE, Mark's account serves to underline the INE motif. Furthermore, the Beelzebul controversy, the storm-stilling, and water-walking all seem to suggest that Mark's Jesus is very closely identified with the personal presence of Yahweh.

Second, related to the Isaianic Yahweh-Warrior imagery is the question of the identity of the forces who hold Yahweh's people captive. The account of the Gerasene demoniac in particular, but also the Beelzebul controversy, and Mark's considerable interest in demons and unclean spirits in general, strongly suggest that for him the ultimate oppressors are not the Romans *per se*, but rather the demons.[220] Third, just as a large number of Jesus' healing miracles cohere with the expectations of the INE, his forgiveness of sins—particularly given its connection with the healing of the lame—echoes Yahweh's self-declaration as the one 'who blots out your transgressions' which accompanies the announcement of the INE (Isa 43:25). Fourth, at the climax of Isaiah 40-55's prologue, Yahweh is not only presented as a warrior come to deliver his people, but as a shepherd who would provide for his people-flock. Mark's presentation of Jesus' feeding miracles also coheres with this motif.

Consequently, it appears that Mark's presentation of Jesus is aimed at emphasising several points of contact between Jesus' ministry and the

---

[220] Wrede, *Messianic*, 45, dismissed outright any idea of a tension between a political and spiritual concept of messiahship. Nevertheless, allowing for the anachronism inherent in contrasting these terms so starkly, Mark's Gospel suggests that some shift in emphasis along these lines may not be so improbable in that Mark's Jesus may well be wishing to make the point that Israel's problem is not so much the external conditions imposed by the Romans as much as the idolatrous state of their 'hearts'; see Chapter 7 on Isa 6 in Mk 4.

events of the INE: A) Jesus' exorcisms and storm-stillings recall the INE presentation, and linkage, of Yahweh as Creator and Yahweh as delivering Warrior, B) many of Jesus' healings resemble those associated with the INE, C) Jesus' forgiveness of sins echoes Yahweh's self-designatory offer in the INE, and D) Jesus' feeding of the crowds, who are like sheep without a shepherd, answers to the flip-side of the Yahweh-Warrior, namely that of Yahweh as tender shepherd of his people.[221] Given an overarching INE perspective, it should be noted, however, that the miracles of Jesus are not only evidence pointing to Yahweh's coming as a mighty Warrior waging war against his people's oppressors but are also genuine expressions of his compassion as shepherd of his people (1:41; 6:34; 8:2; cf. Isa 40:1, 10f; 49:10, 13, 15; 51:3; 54:7f).[222]

The difficulty in identifying those involved in several key miracles, namely the Gerasene demoniac, the deaf-mute, and the crowd in the second feeding, is a constant frustration to all attempts to cast these miracles in terms of a simple nationalistic/geographical frame (i.e. Jew/ Gentile or Galilean/Judean). If, on the one hand, the Gerasene demoniac and the others are in fact Gentiles, then this suggests that for Mark this NE transcends traditional categories. Jesus comes to deliver all people whether Jew or Gentile, whether inhabitant of Judea, Galilee or elsewhere. Membership in the new people of God is open to those from all nations, but now understood in terms of the intensely personal and individual nature of Jesus' liberating activities—in other words it is as individuals, not as collectives, national, ethnic, or otherwise, that deliverance is experienced.[223]

On the other hand, if these events, although located in predominantly Gentile regions, are nevertheless primarily concerned with 'exiled' Israelites (and Mark's account of Jesus' extremely reticent response to the one clearly identified Gentile—the Syrophoenician woman—lends considerable weight to this latter alternative), then Jesus can be seen acting in harmony with a stricter INE agenda. So why then Mark's ambiguity? It

---

[221] This is the strength of Richardson's position over against Kallas, in that the latter does not sufficiently allow for the symbolic dimension of the miracles.

[222] Cf. Meye, 'Horizon', 8, who notes the dimension of compassion in Jesus' miracles.

[223] Cf. Perrin, *Kingdom*, 171, 199. This may reflect the tension already evident in Isaiah 56-66 between a national and individual perspective, Westermann, 302f, 403ff; Hanson, *Dawn*, 134ff; Achtemeier, *Community*, 128ff.

may be that his Gospel represents a combination of both agendas: Mark's Jesus restricts his activity to Israel, but Mark, by means of his indeterminate identifications, foreshadows that Jesus' ministry will ultimately result in 'light to the Gentiles'.

Granted the foregoing, the next question is whether or not Mark's 'Way' section also betrays signs of an INE hermeneutic. However, before addressing that issue, it is important to face another theme which is foreshadowed in Mark's opening sentence, becomes increasing evident throughout the series of controversy stories, and finally culminates in the Beelzebul confrontation: namely the possibility that Israel, as Malachi suggested, might not be ready for Yahweh's INE coming.

Chapter 7: Isaiah's Promise ...
and Malachi's Threat: Part 1
Judicial Blinding

In contrast to his opening portrayal of Jesus' powerful words and deeds, Mark soon shifts his focus to the growing tensions between Jesus and the Jewish leadership. In keeping with the warning implicit in Malachi and employing the Isaianic motif of Yahweh's hardening of the nation's self-reliant 'wise' ones, Mark shows how the present leadership's rejection of God's INE reign in Jesus results, by means of the parables, in a similar judicial blinding.

I. Introduction

In the preceding Chapter it was argued that Mark construes Jesus' miracles, not merely in terms of some general in-breaking of God's rule, but particularly within the horizon of the INE expectations. The exorcisms, storm-stillings, healings of the lame, the blind, and the deaf and dumb, forgiving of sins, and mass feedings are all iconic testimonies to the inauguration through Jesus of Yahweh's INE coming as warrior and shepherd on behalf of his people. But this, unfortunately, is not the whole story. Jesus is ultimately rejected and crucified by the very heirs of the INE promises. How is this astonishing outcome to be understood, especially given that the nation's leadership, who above all ought to have discerned Yahweh's purposes, are central to this rejection? Once again Mark's explanation is couched in terms of OT motifs.

First, as discussed earlier, Mark's appeal to Malachi in his opening sentence (Mal 3:1 in Mk 1:2) sounds a note of warning. Far from being anomalous, the failure of a significant proportion of Israel through unpreparedness to participate in Yahweh's saving INE activity had always been a possibility. Then, on the only two occasions in his first major section where Jesus is challenged by religious authorities from Jerusalem, Mark's account contains appeals to two related judicial blinding and hardening texts from Isaiah: Isaiah 6:9f in Mark 4:12, and Isaiah 29:13 in Mark 7:6f. Entirely congruent with Malachi's warnings, these appeals to the OT further develop the theme of the unpreparedness of Israel's leadership by reminding Mark's audience of the existence of a profoundly disturbing precedent. Not only is this not the first time that Israel's leadership have relied upon their own wisdom and thereby refused Yahweh's offer of deliverance, but it was this very attitude that led to the nation's exile in the first place. It would hardly be surprising if it should do so again.

II. Isaiah 6:9f in Mark 4:12[1]

a) The Markan Setting: Tension Between Jesus and Israel's Leadership

At the very beginning of his Gospel Mark implicitly warned his readers, or reminded them as the case may be, that the good news of the inauguration of Yahweh's reign in the INE might not be an occasion of unalloyed joy. On the contrary, the Malachi/Exodus component of his introductory citation, although quite properly belonging within the sphere of the INE hope, sounds a note of foreboding.[2] For Malachi, the INE had already been delayed because of the unpreparedness of Israel and, in particular, her religious leaders.   The prophet warned that in order to be ready for Yahweh's coming they must respond appropriately to his messenger, identified at the conclusion of the book as 'Elijah'.

In Mark's eyes, as is generally agreed, this forerunner appears to be none other than John the Baptist (1:6; 9:13).[3] However, in spite of the initially promising signs—'all of Judea and Jerusalem' came out to hear him (1:5)—John is imprisoned.   That Mark apparently regards this

---

[1] The literature here is immense, see the recent discussions in Quesnell, 72ff; Marcus, *Mystery*, 1-6, 73-121; Evans, *See*, 91-106; Beavis, *Audience*, 69-86, 131-155; and Lambrecht, *Astonished*, 107ff. Tuckett, 'Concerns', offers one of the more nuanced analyses.

[2] See Chapter 3, pp. 67ff, above.

[3] See now Trumbower, 'John'; Webb, *John*, 51-55, and literature cited therein; Camery-Hoggath, *Irony*, 95f; also Chapter 3, p. 59, fn. 38, above. The ambiguity of 1:4ff has led several recent commentators to reject this identification, but, given the attestation in 9:13, the importance of John for all four Gospels, and the likelihood that the basic content of Mark's Gospel is largely common knowledge among his audience, it seems highly likely that John, even in 1:4ff, would have been understood to be Malachi's Elijah.   On 9:13, for example, see Marcus, 94-100, whose treatment is to be preferred to that of Gundry, 464. The latter, although correctly noting the emphasis on ἀποκαθιστάνει (v. 12a), appears not to recognise that the issue is not whether Elijah has yet restored all things, but rather to question the scribes' supposition that restoration of all things by Elijah was guaranteed, as Jesus' next statement suggests (cf. Mal 3:1, and כן in 3:24b).

moment as the catalyst for Jesus' commencement of his own ministry hardly augurs well (1:14a; cf. especially 3:7f with 1:5). The ominous nexus between John and Jesus is further strengthened by A) the detailed account of John's subsequent death at the hands of Herod in 6:14-29, B) the link between Jesus' death and the rejection of Elijah 'who has come' (9:9-13), and C) Jesus' appeal to John in justifying his Temple action (11:27-33; see Chapter 9). If the national leadership had failed to respond appropriately to John, how much the less for the more public and provocative Jesus?

The implications of this unpreparedness of Israel's leadership soon becomes a major focus of Mark. Having established Jesus' identity and significance by means a series of 'breathless' (cf. εὐθύς) and almost terse accounts of his authoritative words and powerful deeds—a διδαχὴ καινὴ κατ᾽ ἐξουσίαν—Mark quickly turns to the increasingly hostile response which Jesus attracts.[4] In a prolonged series of controversy stories we meet the criticism, antagonism, and finally outright rejection which eventually leads to Jesus' death (2:1 - 3:6).[5] As noted earlier, these controversies culminate in what amounts to a crucial turning point in the gospel: the Beelzebul debate wherein Israel's chief religious authorities—for the first time scribes from Jerusalem—announce their considered response to this Galilean exorcist: he himself is possessed by the chief demon, Beelzebul.

However, to censure Jesus and to attribute his exorcisms to the only realistic alternative, Beelzebul, is to blaspheme the Holy Spirit and thereby to repeat the rebellion of the first Exodus (cf. Isa 63:10). In this context, Mark's 'bracketing' the controversy with teaching about Jesus' true family (3:21, 31-35) highlights the significance of the various responses to his ministry. A clear division is now appearing within Israel (cf. John's

---

[4] Mark's frequent and somewhat idiosyncratic use of καὶ εὐθύς lends an urgency to his account that is strangely reminiscent of the style of Isa 40-55. See in particular Snaith's detailed comments, 'Study', 149-53, on the vigour and urgency of the prophet whose style is 'one of hurrying, of rushing tumultuously on', where it is a case of 'immediately if not sooner'. Stuhlmueller, *Creative*, 140f, similarly notes that the 'new thing' Yahweh promises will happen *'suddenly and surprisingly'* (his italics), cf. Spykerboer, *Structure*, 152.

[5] On the unity of these passages and the increasingly adversarial stance of Jesus' opponents, see especially Dewey; Kiilunen, *Vollmacht*; Tannehill, 'Narrative', 68; Kingsbury, *Conflict*, 67ff. Gundry, 108f, sees these more as stories concerning Jesus' authority, but even so he notes the progression from silent accusation (2:6f) through to questioning (2:16, 18, 24), to attempted entrapment (3:2), and finally to plotting Jesus' demise (3:6). This, in combination with Malina's observations on the honour/shame axis in social conflict, *Insights*, 25-49, suggests that 'controversy' is not an inappropriate term.

warning, Mt 3:12; Lk 3:17; and the appointment of the Twelve, Mk 3:13-19). No longer it is a matter of bloodline but rather adherence to Jesus' teaching, himself the 'S/son of God' (1:11), that determines whether or not one is a member of his true family, that is, also a 'son of God'.[6] Already the threat implicit in Malachi is coming to pass (cf. Mal 3:2-5, 18). The crucial point here, however, is that this decisive confrontation—couched explicitly in terms of the first overt mention of Jesus' teaching in parables (3:23)—leads immediately into Mark's extended account of the purpose of parables. This suggests that the former occasions the latter[7] and that the parables themselves not only function in some way as a response to those who have rejected Jesus but that they do so in terms of the judicial blinding and hardening expressed in the notorious crux, Isaiah 6:9-10.

b) Textual Matters[8]

Mark 4:12		Isaiah 6:9f	
	LXX	MT	Targum
ἵνα βλέποντες βλέπωσιν	Ἀκοῇ ἀκούσετε	שמעו שמוע	הדין דשמעין משמע
καὶ μὴ ἴδωσιν,	καὶ οὐ μὴ συνῆτε	ואל תבינו	ולא מסתכלין
καὶ ἀκούοντες ἀκούωσιν	καὶ βλέποντες βλέψετε	וראו ראו	וחזן מחזא
καὶ μὴ συνιῶσιν,	καί οὐ μὴ ἴδητε	ואל תדעו	ולא ידעין
μήποτε	... μήποτε	פן ...	... דלמא
	ἴδωσιν τοῖς ὀφθαλμοῖς	יראה בעיניו	יחזון בעיניהין
	καὶ τοῖς ὠσὶν	ובאזניו	ובאודנחון
	ἀκούσωσιν	ישמע	ישמעון
	καὶ τῇ καρδίᾳ συνῶσιν	ולבבו יבין	וליבכהון יסתכלון
ἐπιστρέψωσιν	καί ἐπιστρέψωσιν	ושב	ויתובון
καὶ ἀφεθῇ αὐτοῖς	καί ἰάσομαι αὐτούς	ורפא לו	וישתביק להון

Mark's citation is clearly paraphrastic. The seeing and hearing clauses of Isaiah 6:9bc MT, LXX, and *Tg. Isaiah* are reversed, perhaps due to Mark's interest in 'sight' as reflected in his two restoration-of-sight miracles which bracket his 'Way' section.[9] The second person forms of 6:9bc MT and LXX—the latter uses emphatic denials as opposed to the MT's imperatives

---

6 See now Shepherd, *Sandwich*, 136. On 'son (of God)', see Chapter 4, pp. 110ff above.

7 Gundry, 186, notices this relationship but primarily on the basis of the common 'parable' terminology.

8 See Gnilka, *Verstockung*, 13ff; Gundry, *Use*, 33f; Stendahl, *School*, 129ff; Evans, *See*, 17-80; and now Schneck, 102ff.

9 See Chapter 8.

while *Tg. Isaiah* treats then as relative clauses describing the present condition of the people—are altered to third person in keeping with the narrative setting and so may not necessarily reflect Targumic dependence.[10] Mark's ἀφεθῇ, as with *Tg. Isaiah's* שבק, explicates the significance of 'healing' (cf. Isa 33:24) but more importantly echoes the threat of 3:29.[11] Most of Isaiah 6:10 has also been omitted, probably to capture the co-ordination of the ἵνα and μήποτε clauses.[12] Although it is often claimed that the Markan diction is closest to that of *Tg. Isaiah*, Mark's divergences suggest that an assumption of Targumic dependence should be treated with caution.[13]

c) The ἵνα Clause

Many commentators have found the telic force of 4:12 unacceptably harsh and/or difficult to reconcile with the apparent emphasis of the preceding parable (vv. 3-8) and with the injunctions concerning careful hearing (cf. vv. 3, 9, 23, 24).[14] Numerous attempts have been made along grammatical and linguistic lines to resolve these apparent difficulties, suggesting that Mark's ἵνα is either: shorthand for ἵνα πληρωθῇ,[15] a mistranslation of the Aramaic relative ד,[16] causal with μήποτε as 'perhaps',[17] consecutive with

---

[10] *Pace* Manson, *Teaching*, 76ff; Chilton, *Galilean*, 91; Schneck, 104. Now also Goulder, 'Outside', 296.

[11] Coutts, '"Outside"'; see fn. 65 below.

[12] Black, *Aramaic*, 214.

[13] See Wenham's criticisms, 'Synoptic', 25n59, of Jeremias, *Parables*, 15, and now also Goulder, 'Outside', 296f.

[14] See the surveys in Ambrozic, 67f; Räisänen, *Parabeltheorie*, 11-20; Klauck, *Allegorie*, 245-55; Evans, *See*, 92ff; Beavis, *Audience*, 69ff; and Schneck, 105-13.

[15] Lagrange, 99; Siegman, 'Teaching'; Schelke, 'Zweck'; Jeremias, *Parables*, 17. It is not clear, however, that fulfilment avoids the issue since it too has a telic force, Evans, *See*, 94, citing Metzger, 'Formulas'.

[16] Manson, *Teaching*, 76f; with μήποτε either as conditional or 'perhaps', cf. Ar. דלמא. A mistranslation, while possible, is highly unlikely 'since whoever rendered the Aramaic saying ... certainly had more difficult constructions to contend with, and could never have succeeded if this particle ... proved too difficult for him correctly to understand', Chilton, *Rabbi*, 93; cf. Black, *Aramaic*, 212ff; Burkill, 114ff.

[17] Burkill, 112ff; Windisch, 'Verstockungsidee'; cf. Lampe, 'Deutung'; Moule, 'More'; Holzmeister, 'Verstockungszweck'.

μήποτε as 'unless',[18] imperatival,[19] or telic but ironic.[20] The absence of the fattening of the heart clause (Isa 6:10), seen by some as 'the very basis' of the hardening theory, is also taken as mitigating the purposive force.[21] Alternatively, a substantial number of more recent commentators have upheld the 'purposive' intention.[22] How is one to decide among this plethora of alternatives? Given the overall approach suggested in the preceding Chapters of this book it may well be that Mark expects his readers to have something of the Isaianic context in view.

d) Isaiah 6 in Context

(i) Rebellion as the Precursor to Isaiah 6

It is generally agreed that Isaiah 1 constitutes the introduction both to the whole work and specifically to chapters 1-12.[23] From the outset judgement is foreshadowed as Yahweh institutes legal proceedings against his faithless people (Isa 1:2ff).[24] The case begins with a two-fold thematic statement concerning the nation's faithlessness and culpable, even wilful, ignorance.[25] On the one hand, there is Yahweh's complaint, as father, against his rebellious 'sons' (בָּנִים ... פָּשְׁעוּ בִי, 1:2b) and, on the other, there is a wisdom parable citing Israel's failure to understand (לֹא יָדַע ... לֹא הִתְבּוֹנָן, 1:3).[26] The impressive catalogue of charges which follows essentially details these twin failings.

---

[18] Peisker, 'Konsekutiv'; Suhl, 149; Anderson, 131; Chilton, *Rabbi*, 91-98, on the basis of the apparent contradiction between 4:11 and 4:33f (cf. Jeremias, *Parables*, 17f); and rabbinic exegesis, so Str-B, 1.662f.

[19] Cadoux, 'Imperatival', 173.

[20] Moore, 'Micaiah'; cf. Hurtardo, 59f; Davis, 'Literary', 346-50. Romaniuk, 'Exégèse', 196ff, suggests the verse should be a question.

[21] Kelber, 35; Moule, 'More', 100; following Manson, *Teaching*, 78.

[22] Especially: Marcus, *Mystery*, 119-21; 'Epistemology'; Beavis, *Audience*, 78ff; Evans, *See*, 95-106; Räisänen, 83; Gundry, 202; cf. e.g. Boucher, 44f; Gnilka, *Verstockung*, 45-50; Black, *Aramaic*, 213ff; Ambrozic, 'Concept'; Kee, 58; Pesch, 1.237; Schneck, 128.

[23] E.g. Wildberger, 1.9ff; Clements, 28f; Sweeney, *Isaiah*, 21ff; Watts, 1.10. On the question of whether or not 2:1-4/5 ought to be included along with chapter 1 in the prologue, see Sweeney, *Isaiah*, 30ff; Ackroyd, 'Note'; Tomasino, 'Isaiah'; and the appropriate material in Clements and Wildberger.

[24] E.g. Nielsen, 'Gerichts', 27-29; Wildberger, 1.9ff, 74; Wright, 'Lawsuit'; Sweeney, *Isaiah*, 120-23; Watts, 'Formation'; Niditch, 'Composition'. Clements, accepting the legal dimension, denies that it is covenantal in orientation.

[25] Vriezen, 'Essentials'; Hamborg, 'Reasons', 157. Oswalt, *Isaiah*, 66, sees unfaithfulness to Yahweh as the natural consequence of pride. See Kaiser, 2.95, 'without faith Israel does not exist'; and Hamborg, 'Reasons', 157, for whom the most prominent reason for judgement of both Israel and the nations, although reasons for the latter are not always given, is pride, characterised by essentially religious terms: revolt, rebellion, or contempt

The opening woe formula of verse 4 reiterates the nation's abandonment of Yahweh while the collection of oracles in verses 5-20 emphasise the people's, and especially the rulers' (v. 10), failure to understand (vv. 5-9). Their intensified religious observance (vv. 10-15), apparently to be interpreted as misguided attempts at remedying their present distress, is futile since what Yahweh requires is justice (vv. 16f).[27] He then invites them to 'reason together' with him (vv. 18-20), offering salvation—'you will eat the best of the land' (v. 19b)—if they repent, but annihilation—'you will be eaten by the sword' (v. 20, cf. v. 9)—if they refuse and continue to disobey.

The offer, however, seems to fall on deaf ears. In verses 21-23 Yahweh laments the faithlessness of Jerusalem and the rebellion of its rulers, concluding in verses 24-31 with an avowal to purge the city. Although Yahweh proclaims that he will 'separate between the righteous and the wicked', redeeming the one and judging the other,[28] by far the greater emphasis lies on the utter destruction of sinners and rebels with the final threat being cast in images associated with the decadent cult's terebinth worship (vv. 29-31). Such worship, Yahweh declares, will turn into sparks that, flaring up, will consume both the idolators and their works together.[29]

Following on from this introduction, chapters 2-5 reflect similar concerns. Although expressing some prospect of hope (2:1-4/5; 4:2-6)[30] they overwhelmingly constitute a sustained determination of impending doom. Two themes are noteworthy. First, consistent with the introduction's conclusion (1:29-31) there is considerable emphasis on idolatry and witchcraft (2:6-8, 18-20; 3:3b; cf. 6:12-13). R. E. Clements comments that the 'most striking feature' of such passages 'is their emphasis ... upon the faithlessness and idolatry' and 'upon the worship of images and the resort

---

for Yahweh; cf. Roberts, 'Divine'; Love, 'Call'; and Vriezen, 'Essentials', 134f, who cites as expressions of this: contempt (3:8f; 2:4f, 24; cf. 8:6; 28:12; 29:15f; 30:9-13, 15) and derision (5:18f) for Yahweh, rebellion (1:5, 23; cf. 30:1; 31:6), neglect of Yahweh (17:10; 22:11), pride or boasting (2:7ff; 3:16ff; cf. 19:8ff; 10:5ff; 22:15; 28:1ff, 14ff), not having faith (7:9; 22:11; 31:1), and being disobedient (1:19f; cf. 28:12; 30:9, 15).

[26] Sweeney, *Isaiah*, 102ff; Wildberger, 1.12ff.

[27] Cf. Gitay, *Audience*, 31f.

[28] Sweeney, *Isaiah*, 122.

[29] Wildberger, 1.72f.

[30] On the delimitation of these particular units, see especially the relevant discussions in Wildberger, and Sweeney, *Isaiah*.

to illicit forms of cultus' which is understood to have occasioned Jerusalem's destruction.[31]   Hence, although it is certainly true that one of the major lines of Yahweh's indictment of Judah is her injustice, idolatry or at the very least an idolatrous attitude (which arguably leads to injustice) appears to be the major concern.[32]

Second, the primary responsibility for the present state of affairs rests squarely with the leaders of Jerusalem (1:10, 23-26; 3:12ff; 5:18-24).[33]   The vineyard song (5:1-7) presages the desolation of the nation, and introduces a series of woes aimed primarily at Jerusalem's leadership.   The scathing indictment, in verse 24b, of the leaders' repudiation of Yahweh's instruction suggests that 'a complete break with Yahweh' has now occurred (cf. 10:1-4).[34]   It is hardly surprising, then, that the final woe (vv. 25-30) is cast in terms of a war oracle which describes 'impressively and graphically an invading enemy who functions as God's punishment'.[35]   The verdict has already been given.   Purging judgement is unavoidable.   The only question now concerns its implementation and this it seems is the point of the following 'call narrative' of chapter 6.

(ii) Isaiah 6: Ironic Judgement on Idolatrous Wisdom

Given the great difficulty had by many concerning particularly Isaiah 6:10b, several points should be observed.   Within the present literary structure of the book, the mandate in Isaiah 6:9ff presupposes a rebellious, idolatrous, and culpably uncomprehending nation.   The point of the extensive preceding material is to show that all of Yahweh's attempts at reconciliation have consistently been refused and that Judah's severe judgement is, therefore, justified.[36]   Thus, when Yahweh appears in his

---

[31] 'Prophecies', 425-428ff, which passages are perceived by Clements to be later glosses.   The Targum repeatedly clarifies the idolatrous character of certain actions described in the Hebrew text, e.g. *Tg. Isa* 1:29; 2:6; 8:19 (2); 17:11; 28:10, 21; cf. 57:5, 8; 65:3, 11; cf. Smolar-Auerbach, *Studies*, 150ff.

[32] Whatever the intricacies of the historical situation—see e.g. Jensen's criticisms, *Use*, 47f, 53f, 123, of Whedbee, *Isaiah*—in terms of a first century perspective, idolatry was almost certainly seen as the primary issue, see fn. 31 above.   In any case, the use of such imagery could well be part of a particularly sharp polemic against the wise whose dismissal of Yahweh's word through the prophet for their own learned opinions is regarded, by the prophet, as tantamount to idolatry.

[33] 2:6 - 6:1 is especially directed against arrogant leaders, Schreiner, 'Buch', 149; cf. Jensen, *Use*, 65-104; Clements; Sweeny, *Isaiah*, 38f.

[34] Wildberger, 1.213 (here ET).

[35] Gitay, *Audience*, 116.

[36] Räisänen, *Hardening*, 59, 62; Nielsen, 'Dramatic', 14; Evans, *See*, 42.

Temple to commission Isaiah it is first and foremost as Zion's great king
(6:1-5)[37] but now in his capacity as holy judge to implement the sentence
already passed on his apostate people.[38] Isaiah's preaching, then, is merely
to effect the verdict of the divine King by confirming his hearers in their
persistent and wilful ignorance and, thereby, ushering them towards the
consequences of their rebellion.

Second, in the light of the pre-eminence of idolatry, it is not
insignificant that the sentence is couched in terms of blindness, deafness,
and lack of understanding. Psalms 115:4-8 and 135:15-18 reflect a tradition
that associates the onset of these conditions with the practice of idolatry:
'those who trust in idols will become like them, they have ears but they
cannot hear, eyes but cannot see'.[39] In the two psalms, only 'seeing' (ראה,
LXX 113:13b; 134:16b, ὁράω) and 'hearing' (שׁמע, LXX 113:14a, ἀκούω; 134:17a,
ἐνωτίζομαι) are in view, but the metaphor is clearly understood later on in
Isaiah 44:17f where blindness and hardness of heart are equated with lack
of understanding (LXX, v. 18, γιγνώσκω, φρονέω) and comprehension
(νοέω).[40]

Yahweh's people, and above all their leadership, have chosen to reject
him for idols. In response, he suits the punishment to the crime: they are
to be as blind, as deaf, and as incapable of understanding as are their idols.
Having rejected Yahweh their maker, he will now confirm them in their
decision by recreating them, as it were, in the image of the gods they have
chosen. Consequently, Isaiah is commanded to declare to the people,

---

[37] On the kingship of Yahweh in Isaiah, Eissfeldt, 'Jahwe'; Maag, *Malkût* , 129ff;
Gray, 'Kingship'; Liebreich, 'Position'; Mettinger, 'YHWH'; Roberts, 'Divine'; and
Dumbrell, 'Worship'; cf. the broader theological motif in Ollenburger, *Zion*.

[38] Knierim, 'Vocation', 55ff; Gray, 1.109; cf. Rendtorff, 'Komposition', 312. In his
section on the original context of Isa 6:9f, Schneck, 114-23, devotes most of his study to the
meaning of 6:13 in which he detects an indirect reference to the Davidic kingship (= 'seed';
cf. seed in Mk 4) but pays almost no attention to the setting which Isa 1-5 provides for ch. 6.
Later, however, he notes the prominence of the preceding confrontations.

[39] Dr. G. Beale, Gordon-Conwell Theological Seminary lectures 'OT in the NT', Fall
1985; see now Beale, 'Taunt'. Opinions on the dating of Ps 115 are divided: Mowinckel,
Psalmenstudien, and Weiser, *Psalms*, suggest late pre-exilic or early post-exilic, while
Preuß, *Verspottung*; and Kraus, *Psalmen*, on account of these very verses see it later than the
anti-idol polemics of Isa 40-55. Ps 135 is generally regarded as late (except Weiser who sees
it as pre-exilic) on the basis of linguistic features and what appears to be extensive
borrowing from other literature.

[40] Cf. Botterweck, *TWAT*, 3.487, 491f. Watts, 1.liif, notes that groupings of at least
three of the words 'know, understand, hear, see, and turn' occur in 5:20f (?), 6:9f, are most
frequent in chapters 28-30, and appear in chapters 37-39.

'Listen but do not perceive, look but do not understand'. His preaching is to 'make the heart of this people fat, their ears heavy, and their eyes dim, lest they see with their eyes, hear with their ears, and turn and be healed' (6:9f). That this blinding and deafening is an ironic judgement upon the nation's idolatrous condition appears confirmed when her salvation, characterised by restoration of sight, hearing, and understanding (e.g. 29:18f; 32:1; 35:5), involves a concurrent rejection of idols (2:20; 17:7f; 27:9; 30:22; 31:7).[41]

Third, not only does the language of seeing and hearing in association with heart, understanding, and comprehension terminology have links with anti-idol polemics but such expressions are also the *tupoi* of ANE wisdom traditions (note the appearance of a wisdom parable at the outset of the lawsuit, 1:3). The relationship between hearing, understanding, and the heart can be found, as M. Lichteim noted, as far back as the Old Kingdom of ancient Egypt, where for example one finds 'He who hears is beloved of god, he whom god hates does not hear. The heart makes of its owner a hearer or non-hearer'.[42]

The wisdom connotations of this language are particularly appropriate given the central role of Jerusalem's leadership.[43] Set in the context of Jerusalem's crisis in the face of foreign invasion, the picture is of the Judah's 'wise' ones who refuse to accept Yahweh's instruction or teaching (תּוֹרָה 1:10; 5:24b; cf. 30:9),[44] who scoff at the prophet's warnings (5:19; cf. 28:9-14, 22), and instead increasingly rely on the nations and their idols as

---

[41] Beale, 'Taunt'.

[42] *Ancient*, 74; also Brunner, *Altägyptische*, on the heart, 110f, on hearing, 131ff. If an understanding heart is the gift of the god one worships then it may follow that idolators receive a heart commensurate with that of their god. On the connection between Egyptian and Israelite wisdom, Whybray, *Wisdom*. Evans, *See*, 24-52, has an extended survey on obduracy texts in Isaiah and the OT, but fails to note the connection with either wisdom or idolatry.

[43] On wisdom in Isaiah 1-39: Fichtner, 'Jesaja', 75-80; Lindblom, 'Wisdom', 192-204; Martin-Achard, 'Sagesse', 137-44; Blanchette, 'Wisdom'; McKane, *Prophets*; Wildberger, 1.188f; espec. Whedbee, *Isaiah*; and Jensen, *Use*.

[44] The term should not perhaps be restricted solely to a regulative code. Jensen, *Use*, 135, sees תורה as referring generally to the wisdom of Yahweh (cf. parallel with דבר־יהוה (2:3) and אור יהוה (2:5)) and not a particular body of law, although such a monochromatic approach may not be justified if some form of covenantal relationship to Yahweh is presumed by the prophet; see now Kitchen, 'Fall'. The crucial distinctive is the divine authority that attaches to תורה, whether formulated as law, taught by priest, or announced by prophet; cf. Gutbrod, *TDNT*, 4.1044ff; Scharbert, *LTK*, 4.816; also 1:10; 5:24b; 30:9; also 9:7-12; 22:12ff (cf. vv. 15-25); 28:1ff (cf. 29:15ff).

they formulate foreign policy (7:9-13; cf. 2:22; 28:15; 30:1-5 (6f); 31:1-3).[45] Nevertheless, Yahweh's purposes will be accomplished (10:12-19; 19:3-11; עֵצָה: 5:19; cf. 19:17; 25:1; and יעץ: 14:24, 26f; 19:12; 23:9) and the leaders' rejection of his wisdom brings their ruin upon them (7:12-20; 10:5ff; cf. 14:24ff; 30:1ff; 31:1ff). They are condemned to be incompetent, that is, blind and deaf (6:9ff, cf. 28:9-14; 29:9-21), and hence to pursue policies that will result in the devastation of the land and exile (1:3; 5:13a; chs. 7-8; cf. 29:15ff; 30:1-5, 12-17; 31:1-3).

The conjunction of judicial blindness and deafness, anti-idol polemics, and wisdom language is, therefore, closely bound up with the people's idolatrous stance over against the prophet's revelation of Yahweh's wisdom. More specifically, the issue turns on their leaders' reliance on a counsel for the future preservation of Jerusalem which is, at heart, dependent on the idolatrous outlook of the surrounding nations.[46] Such a course can only lead to disaster.

(iii) The Judgement Effected: The Encounter with Ahaz
It is hardly co-incidental that Yahweh's commissioning of Isaiah to implement the divine verdict is immediately followed by an encounter with the nation's ultimate leader, Ahaz (7:1ff). Ahaz's 'pious' rejection of Yahweh's word is not only paradigmatic, but also provides the archetypal illustration of how the prophet's message confirms the nation's unbelieving and idolatrous authorities in their blindness.[47]

The form of Yahweh's word to Ahaz is also significant. It is expressed primarily through the parabolic names of the prophet's 'sign-children'

---

[45] For Kaiser, 'Verkündigung', consultation with foreign powers and their deities is a refuge of falsehoods, cf. 28:14-18.

[46] Whedbee, *Isaiah*, 144f, sees the debate over whether Yahweh's counsel is in fact wise, whereas for Jensen, *Use*, 53f, cf. 122ff, it is whether or not the prophet had a special insight into Yahweh's plan which the wise themselves did not have. Thus for Jensen, 57, the 'signs' of chs. 7-8 are intended to counter the rational arguments of the wise, and consequently it is because the counsellors recognised that if Yahweh's עֵצָה could be known they would have to yield, that their fault of voluntary blindness to the light already offered is so culpable. From the literary perspective taken here, arguments as to the secondary nature of contrary texts (e.g. 31:2, Jensen, *Use*, 52n31) are not applicable. In any case it may well be that both matters were at issue, as Jensen seems almost to admit, 55. Cf. also Martin-Achard, 'Sagesse'.

[47] Liebreich, 'Position', in particular sees Isa 6:9f implemented in Ahaz' blind self-reliance and his consequent judgement; cf. Schreiner, 'Buch', 148; Jensen, *Use*, 57; Nielsen, 'Dramatic', 7, 9ff; Steck, 'Bermerkungen', 198ff; 'Beitrage', 161; Wildberger, 3.1646f.

(8:18)[48] which function as proleptic testimonies to the nature and certainty of Yahweh's future intervention (7:11, 14; 7:3, and 8:3). However, the crucial element is that Yahweh's word be heard with faith. It is the hearer's response that alone determines whether Immanuel means blessing or curse.[49] The preceding chapters indicate, however, that Ahaz, along with his officials and the bulk of the nation, have consistently rejected the word of Yahweh. Their continued—but in the light of their previous responses hardly unexpected—rejection of the offer of salvation ensures that the proffered salvation of 'God-with-us' becomes a word of devastating judgement (7:17ff).[50]

(iv) Summary

Isaiah 6:9f introduces one of the more significant motifs of chapters 1-39: 'the enigma of obduracy to Yahweh's offer (which) runs through the whole of Isaiah's activity'.[51] Presupposing a recalcitrant nation, Yahweh's judicial blinding of the leadership as projected in 6:9ff is to be understood in terms of an ironic judgement upon the self-reliant wisdom of those who have rejected his word. The blatant refusal of the nation's wise ones to attend to Yahweh's instruction precedes and occasions Isaiah's mandate. This mandate, effected by means of parabolic 'child-signs', then serves to confirm them, archetypically so in Ahaz, in their rejection of Yahweh's word. Trapped in their own wisdom, the leaders will remain 'blind' and 'deaf', which condition will ultimately lead to their destruction.[52]

e) Mark's Beelzebul Controversy and the Parables Chapter

(i) Isaiah and the Beelzebul Controversy

It is readily apparent that Mark's account of Israel's religious authorities and their response to Jesus exhibits close parallels to the situation in Isaiah. As we have argued in the previous Chapter, the Beelzebul altercation in Mark 3 constitutes the literary climax of the preceding

---

[48] Nielsen, 'Dramatic', 12ff; Jensen, *Use*, 109f; cf. parallel use of אוֹת and מְשָׁלִים in Ezek 14:8.

[49] Hasel, *Remnant*, 285-87; Evans, 'Context', 142.

[50] Steck, 'Bermerkungen', 199f; Clements, 89.

[51] von Rad, *Theology*, 2.154f.

[52] Thus both the 'because' and the 'purpose' senses are valid since they are two sides of the one coin. Seen from this perspective, *Tg. Isa*'s relative clause merely recognises that this condition already prevails among the people. Rabbinic interpretations of Isa 6:9f are mainly concerned with mitigating the text's severity, Evans, *See*, 137-45.

confrontations by bringing to a head the question of Jesus' identity and the diverse responses of various groups, particularly, the hostility of the scribes from Jerusalem.[53] The latter's repudiation of Jesus, it was suggested, recalls Isaiah 63's recounting of the rebellion of Israel in the first Exodus with the implication that Yahweh now becomes their enemy (Mk 3:29, cf. Isa 63:10). It was also proposed that Mark's 'Parables Chapter' is intended to explain the significance of Jesus' parabolic response.[54] This section will argue that the appeal to Isaiah 6 in Mark 4, given the Isaianic context noted above, not only provides the interpretative link between these two Markan passages but, in light of Malachi's warning, articulates a prior OT hermeneutic for the response of Israel's leaders to Jesus.[55]

To begin, certain features in Mark 3:20-35 are noteworthy. As already observed on several occasions, the controversy comes as the capstone, not only to a series of Jesus' 'mighty words and deeds', but also to a consistent pattern of questioning and rejection by various leadership groups. Second, although in 3:6 the Pharisees and the Herodians plot Jesus' death,[56] this is the first time open rejection surfaces (3:22). Third, it is also the first time that the officials are described as coming 'from Jerusalem', thereby implicating the national centre. Finally, this climactic controversy gives rise to Mark's first explicit statement that Jesus spoke ἐν παραβολαῖς.[57]

---

[53] See Keegan, 'Leaders', for a survey of views on Mark's presentation of the geographical relationship between the scribes and the Pharisees.

[54] Isa 63, after recalling Israel's grieving of God's Holy Spirit at the Exodus, goes on in v. 17 to lament God's present hardening of their heart (cf. Isa 6:10). Given that God's hardening judgement comes on his people when they become his enemies (cf. Isa 1:24 and 6:10; Ps 95:8ff), it may well be that the same motif pertains here. In the Beelzebul controversy, the leaders who have seen Yahweh's work, nevertheless, reject it and so grieve his Holy Spirit (3:29a). Yahweh then becomes their enemy (3:29b) which leads to the motifs of blinding, hardening of the heart, etc. (4:12).

[55] Although it cannot be entered into here, it seems to me that the whole question of whether or not the fulfilment of a particular OT text is 'understood' by the NT authors often founders on a confusion over what 'fulfilment' means. If anything, the use of e.g. Hos 11:1 in Mt 2:15 or the way in Jesus is seen as 'fulfilling' the Law (Mt 5:17; cf. Rom 10:4) ought to suggest that the NT authors are operating with a conception of fulfilment which assumes the paradigmatic or typological significance of the OT—as Yahweh had done he would do again; as per e.g. Foulkes, *Acts*; Dodd, *According*, 127ff—rather than the more commonly assumed literal prediction.

[56] This may be the impetus for the implied election of a new leadership in 3:13-19; e.g. Cranfield, 127; Rengstorf, *TDNT*, 2.326; Schweizer; Lane; Guelich. Pesch, 1.204n4, draws attention to LXX Isa 43:1 and 44:2 etc. where concerning Israel it reads: ὁ θεὸς ὁ ποιήσας σε, cf. Lk 22:30; Jervell, 'Twelve'. On new creation in Isaiah, see Chapter 6, p. 155, fn. 92.

[57] Also now Gundry, 181. Jesus may use parables earlier, e.g. 2:21f, but 3:20ff marks a turning point in their function, see below. On the breadth of the parable *genre* and the

The parallels with the Isaiah context are significant. First, given the nature of the wisdom debates in Isaiah, it is noteworthy that the most prominent opponents of Jesus are the scribes, who are mentioned alone (1:22; 2:6; 3:22; 9:11, 14; 12:28, 38), with the Pharisees (2:16; 7:15), the chief priests (10:33; 11:18; 14:1; 15:31), and the elders and chief priests (8:31; 11:27; 14:43, 53; 15:1).[58] They were professionally concerned with the Law and had at least three duties: A) to interpret and elaborate the Law appropriate to the times; B) to instruct students, and C) to participate in judicial activities.[59] Thus, they had a significant role as the nation's advisers, analogous to the 'wise' in Isaiah's day.

Second, just as Isaiah's polemics were directed primarily against the counsellors and the leaders of Jerusalem, so too Mark notes that these scribes are 'from Jerusalem'. Third, in Isaiah the confrontation between Yahweh and the leaders is set within the context of his divine kingship. In Mark the overall context is the proclamation of Yahweh's reign in terms of the advent of the Kingdom of God as Yahweh comes 'in strength', the parables concern the kingdom, and the Beelzebul debate itself is cast in terms which imply kingdoms (Mk 1:14f; 4:11, 26, 30; cf. 3:24).[60] Fourth, in the book of Isaiah the leaders' hostility toward, and rejection of, Yahweh's instruction was the presupposition of the judicial blinding of Isaiah 6. Similarly in Mark, the opposition to Jesus and the criticism of his teachings and deeds, which had been building for some time but are now out in the open, provide the immediate context of Jesus' use of the judicial blinding motif of Isaiah 6.[61] Fifth, and finally, in both cases this considered rejection of Yahweh's word, whether spoken by the prophet or revealed by Jesus, is explicitly met with parabolic forms of communication (Isaiah 7:1ff; Mark 3:23).

---

consequent difficulty of definition see Bowker, 'Mystery'; Boobyer, 'Redaction', 64ff; Minette-Tillesse, *Secret*, 201-16; Boucher, 17ff; Drury, 'Sower', 375ff, and *Parables*, 7-38, and *passim*.

[58] Osten-Sacken, 'Streitgespräch', 376-81; Kingsbury, 'Religious', 46; Smith, 'Opponents', 167. On scribes and esoteric wisdom, Jeremias, *Jerusalem*, 237-43. Note also the presence of 'two pairs of parallel wisdom sayings' in 4:21-22, 24-25, Boucher, 53.

[59] Gnilka, 1.79; Saldarini, 'Pharisees', 10, cited in Malbon, 'Leaders', 265. Gundry, 357, observes that 'the wisdom of Jerusalemites was well known', cf. *Lam. Rab.* 1.1 § 4.

[60] Cf. Schneck, 123.

[61] So also Gnilka, *Verstochung*, 205; Mann, 264; and now Schneck, 127.

(ii) Israel's Leaders and Blinding Judgement

Given these parallels, it is worth noting that there are also several striking similarities between Mark 3:20-35 and 4:1-34:[62]

A) both passages contrast those who are 'outside' with those who are 'around' Jesus (3:21, 31ff; 4:10f),[63]

B) both passages concern kingdoms, in that 3:24 implies Satan's kingdom while 4:11 speaks of the kingdom of God,

C) both the Scribes from Jerusalem in 3:23a and the outsiders in 4:11 are addressed in parables,

D) both passages have warnings concerning non-forgiveness (3:29; 4:12c),[64]

Given the literary proximity of the two passages, these similarities strongly suggest that Mark's account of the teaching on the purpose of the parables flows directly out of Jesus' parabolic response to the open repudiation of his exorcisms by the Jerusalem Scribes.

In the light of the parallels between the Isaianic[65] and Markan contexts,[66] the appeal to Isaiah 6:9f suggests that the judicial blinding effected by Jesus' parables (whether understood narrowly as his words or inclusive of his actions, cf. τὰ πάντα v. 11b[67]) concerns those who have

---

[62] On the structure of 4:1-34 see e.g. Standaert, 201-18; Dewey, 147-52; Lambrecht, *Astonished*, 86ff; Marcus, *Mystery*, 221 (who follows Dupont, 'Transmission'); Beavis, *Audience*, 133ff; Fay, 'Introduction'.

[63] Cf. now Gundry, 196.

[64] Ambrozic, 53f; Coutts, '"Outside"' (who as noted above sees 4:12's ἀφεθῇ reflecting 3:29); Cerfaux, 'connaissance'; Farrer, *Study*, 240; Fusco, *Parola*, 247.

[65] Two other Isaianic influences on Mk 4:1-34 have been suggested. Evans, 'Isaianic', suggests that the idea of the remnant in 6:13 and the metaphor of word as seed in 55:10-11 'provide the basis for a skillfully (*sic*) developed midrash' which 'against the background of Mark's theology of the cross' expresses the Isaianic theology: 'out of judgement comes salvation', 466f. Apart from questions as to the interpretation of Isa 6:13, one is hard-pressed to find the concept of remnant in 4:1ff while the theology of salvation out of judgement is hardly unique to Isaiah. Williams, *Gospel*, 46, also picks up on the idea of Jesus' death pointing to Isa 53:10 ('he shall see his seed') suggesting that the seed that is sown is the Son of Man. Given that the only substantive link is the word 'seed' and even then it is used in different senses—agricultural versus genealogical—Williams' suggestion is tenuous.

[66] Gundry, 198, states that 'Mark does not inform his audience that the OT language of God is being used (contrast 1:2-3; 7:6-7; 14:27); so the emphasis rests solely on the obscurative purpose as such'. Apart from it being unclear whether Gundry's conclusion necessarily follows, the fact remains that untold numbers of readers have seen here a very close rendering of the OT passage, and it is therefore strange to suggest that none of Mark's readers would have made the same connection.

[67] Boobyer, 'Redaction', 61ff; Boucher, 85f; Marcus, *Mystery*, 56, 109-11; and the literature cited in Chapter 6, p. 163, fn. 132. Gundry, 200, argues that τὰ πάντα refers only

steadfastly rejected Yahweh's delivering activity manifest in Jesus.[68] If so, then the judgement in 4:11f is directed against those religious authorities, particularly the ones 'from Jerusalem' but also presumably the others who have plotted his death in Mk 3:6 (v. 5: 'hardness of heart'), who categorically opposed themselves to Jesus in 3:20-35[69] and who have become his most implacable enemies.[70] Just as in the past Yahweh had refused to countenance forgiveness (Isa 2:9b; 6:10; cf. e.g. 1:24f, 28, 31; etc.), so also having come under the ultimate sanction for attributing the activity of the Holy Spirit to Beelzebul (Mk 3:29)[71] these leaders are now the 'outsiders'[72] for whom the parables function as judgement (Mk 4:12c; cf. 12:9).[73] Here too, Immanuel—this time expressed in terms of Yahweh's INE presence— becomes a word of judgement when not met with repentance and faith.

On this line of thinking, the ἵνα clause is clearly purposive. As Judah's rebellious rulers had been confirmed in the consequences of their unwavering refusal to accept Yahweh's plan, so too in Mark. The nation's present leaders, who in the 'blindness' of their 'idolatrous wisdom'[74] have

---

to Mk 4's kingdom parables and nothing else. However, as is evident in our discussion of the significance of Jesus' miracles and in particular his exorcisms which are, after all, the catalyst for Mark's 'parables chapter', these actions clearly have a parabolic dimension.

[68] See also Chapter 6, pp. 152ff. Cf. Coutts, '"Outside"'; Boobyer, 'Redaction'; France, *Jesus*, 68; also Hubaut, 'paraboles'; Myers, *Binding*, 173. This also explains Matthew 13:13's ὅτι. *Pace* Manson, 'Mark', 133f, Jesus' use of parables in this sense more imitates than transcends the prophet's earlier 'failure'—where much depends on what one regards as failure. Evans, who has done the most work on the Isaianic context, fails to consider the preceding Beelzebul pericope in his discussion of the general context of Mk 4, *See*, 101-3.

[69] Others have already plotted against Jesus in 3:6 but the key issue here is that Jesus' rejection is now officially in the open and, more importantly given the city's theological significance, it carries the imprimatur of Jerusalem.

[70] Kingsbury, 'Religious'; Malbon, 'Leaders', 270f; Ambrozic, 56-62; but cf. Burkill, *Light*, 216ff, on the Pharisees.

[71] *Pace* Guelich, 1.180, who sees Jesus' stopping short of such judgement.

[72] Other suggestions have been: non-disciples (Behm, *TDNT*, 2.576; Meye, 'Those'); non-Christians (Nineham, 237f); non-initiates (Smith, *Secret*, 236); old Israel (Gnilka, *Verstockung*, 85); see further the discussion in Beavis, *Audience*, 70-75.

[73] Evans, 'Note', in particular observes that both Isaiah and Jesus speak a word of obduracy in the context of Israel's judgement; cf. Guelich, 1.208; Farrer, *Study*, 240ff; Coutts, '"Outside"'; Cerfaux, 'connaissance'; Trocmé, 'Parables', 462f; Boobyer, 'Redaction', 68f; Fusco, *Parola*, 228; Marcus, *Mystery*, 89-95; Klauck, *Allegorie*, 248; Trocmé, 'Parables', 460. Boucher, 82, is correct to see the 'outsiders' in 4:11f as representing Judaism only in the limited sense implied by 12:1ff which depicts the removal of Israel's present leadership. *Pace* Chilton, *Galilean*, 97f, 4:11f is not merely a 'temperamental irascibility ... directed against outsiders and insiders alike' which seeks 'to shame them into a more positive appreciation of his message'.

[74] On this metaphorical use of 'idolatry', see Chapter 8. *Pace* Johnson, 'Theme', 230, Mark's application of blindness is consistent with OT and NT practice. In view of the link

spurned God's wisdom for their own reasonings (cf. διαλογίζεσθαι in 2:6ff, 11:31) and rejected the inbreaking INE reign of Yahweh in Jesus (1:14f), are confirmed in their 'blindness' and thereby given over to their ruin.[75] That this is so seems supported, for example, not only by the use of the censure of Isaiah 29:13 in Mark 7 but also by Mark 12:12 (cf. Isa 5:1ff!). The 'understanding' of the chief priests, scribes, and elders (11:27), who perceive that the vineyard parable is 'told against them', actually sets their self-destruction in train since what matters is not mere perception but a perception that leads to the repentance and faith called for by Jesus' programmatic announcement in Mark 1:15: μετανοεῖτε καὶ πιστεύετε.[76] They now face a new and perhaps final eschatological exile (see Chapter 9 on the use of Isa 5:1ff imagery in Mk 12:1ff; cf. Mk 13).

(iii) The Crowds, Outsiders, and Insiders
However, this 'purposive' sense raises difficulties largely due to the uncertain status of the crowd in 4:1 and of the 'them' in 4:33f. The 'insider-outsider' terminology (3:31ff) and the distinction implied in 4:10f and 4:33f together suggest that the groups in 4:1 and 4:33f are outsiders.[77] But how is this to be reconciled with Mark's more positive treatment of the crowds elsewhere in the gospel (e.g. 3:32ff; 6:34; 7:14), let alone the injunctions to hear (4:3, 9, cf. vv. 23f)?[78] This long-recognised problem derives primarily

---

between idols and demons (Chapter 6, p. 157), the attribution of blindness to Israel's hostile leadership may support Robinson's suggestion, 35-42, that these leaders are the human counterpart of the demonic (cf. Rev 2:9 and LXX Num 16:3; Caird; Sweet, 28f; Beasley-Murray); see further Ambrozic, 56f; Danker, 'Demonic', 56ff, 65f; *pace* Best, *Temptation*, 21.

[75] So also especially Marcus, *Mystery*, 111-17; cf. Beavis, *Audience*, 102f. Kirkland, 'Earliest', 15, whose observation that the parables 'confound what the dullard may *think* he already knows' is correct except that it is the wise who are confounded by their knowledge. Whether those on the outside are irrevocably so probably depends on whether they continue in their self-reliant wisdom, cf. Moule, 'More', 99. Kelber's statement, 25f, that 'from now on speaking "in parables" becomes Jesus' habitual mode of speech reserved for the opposition', is close to the mark, if overstated. On parables and concealment in apocalyptic settings: Harvey, 'Mystery'; Siegman, 'Teaching'; Patten, 'Form'; Minette-Tillesse, *Secret*, 194ff; and Marcus, 'Epistemology', although it should be evident that this conception is entirely at home in the traditions of Israel's classical prophets.

[76] Cf. e.g. Boucher, 81, who is followed by Kingsbury, 17; *pace*, Räisänen, *Parabel-theorie*, 27-33; Lambrecht, *Astonished*, 139-43; and Gundry, 198, who holds the 'riddling parables' to be 'meaningless to outsiders'; see further Chapter 9.

[77] E.g. Räisänen, *Parabeltheorie*, 7; cf. Ambrozic, 55.

[78] Ambrozic, 55-70; Jeremias, *Parables*, 18; Räisänen, *Parabeltheorie*, 27-47, and 'Messianic', 92ff; Moule, 'More'; Guelich, 1.201. On the crowd in Mark: Citron, 'Multitudes'; Mosley, 'Audiences'; Tagawa, *Miracles*, 57-63; Trocmé, 'public'; Minear, 'Audience'; Best, 'Role', 390-93; Malbon, 'Disciples'. For summaries of other apparent inconsistencies in Mk 4, Räisänen, 76ff, Goulder, 'Outside', 289ff.

from an assumption that there are only two categories in Mark, 'insiders' and 'outsiders'.[79]   But is this stark dichotomy valid?

To begin, it seems unlikely that the crowd in 3:32, 34 is to be identified with ὁ ὄχλος πλεῖστος in 4:1.[80]   Not only do the 'very many and contrasting roles ... show that the crowd possesses no unitary role in the gospel',[81] but the fact that Mark can speak variously of either a crowd *simpliciter*, or an ὄχλος πολύς, or an ὄχλος πλεῖστος indicates that for him 'crowd' is merely a way of referring to an indefinite group.   Further, the distinctive characteristic of the first 'crowd' is that they are περὶ αὐτόν (3:32, 34), the same identifying characteristic of those 'with the twelve' in 4:10 who, according to 4:11, are distinguished from the multitude in 4:1.[82]

Second, granted that 4:10 sets the Twelve and those around Jesus apart from the ὄχλος πλεῖστος, 4:11 applies the negative function of the parables only to οἱ ἔξω (cf. 3:20ff).[83]   Although this may be read to imply that those outside and the great crowd are one and the same,[84] the different designations suggest caution.[85]   And again, what then would be the point of the warnings and injunctions if the 'great crowd' of 4:1 is already 'outside'?   Third, 4:33f introduces yet another designation, a vague 'them', who are contrasted to the disciples who receive explanations.

In terms of the concerns of this analysis there are, therefore, five different designations of groups in these contiguous accounts:

A) an ὄχλος who sits περὶ αὐτόν (Jesus) and who receives his commendation (3:32, 34),

B) ὄχλος πλεῖστος (cf. ὄχλος in 4:2) who, unlike the first crowd, are not described as being περὶ αὐτὸν and who are enjoined to hear carefully (4:1, 3, 9),

---

[79] E.g. Quesnell, 85f; Marcus, *Mystery*, 106f; 'Epistemology'; Lane, 157; Boucher, 43; Räisänen, 78f; and Guelich, 1.203ff, who seems uncertain as to where the crowds belong.

[80] As does Minear, 'Audience', 82f, although he recognises the possibility that they are distinct.   It is difficult to tell if the crowd in 3:20 is to be identified with those in 3:32ff, or whether the latter is a subset of the former.

[81] Best, 'Role', 392.

[82] Lambrecht, 'Redaction', 279.

[83] Minear, 'Audience', 83; cf. Gundry, 196ff.

[84] As 'the reader must assume', according to Räisänen, 78; cf. Boucher, 43.

[85] Cf. Guelich, 1.208; and now also Tolbert, *Sowing*, 160, who recognises that the disciples/crowd polarity is not to be equated with the outsider/insider category.

C) οἱ περὶ αὐτὸν σὺν τοῖς δώδεκα, who are 'insiders' and apparently regarded as disciples (4:10, 34),[86]

D) οἱ ἔξω for whom the parables function as judgement (4:11),

E) the enigmatic 'them' (αὐτοῖς, 4:34) who (i) are not περὶ αὐτὸν, (ii) may be identical to group (B), (iii) only receive parables καθὼς ἠδύναντο ἀκούειν (4:33), (iv) are contrasted with Jesus' disciples, and (v) do not, therefore, receive further private explanation (v. 34).

How are these groups related?

Since the preceding account concerning the Beelzebul controversy and the nature of Jesus' true family provides the immediate context for the ensuing material on parables it may offer some help.[87] The controversy itself, as we have seen, strongly suggests that the scribes from Jerusalem are on the 'outside', but what of the members of Jesus' very own bloodline who are twice described as being 'outside' (ἔξω στήκοντες in 3:31, and ἔξω in v. 32)? Although Mark aligns Jesus' family with the scribes in that both groups misunderstand him,[88] nevertheless some distinction seems in order since they neither explicitly repudiate Jesus' activity by attributing it to Beelzebul, nor are they, consequently, addressed in Jesus' rebuke.[89] What then is Mark driving at? Given that Jesus' family is obviously 'outside' in the spatial sense, the metaphorical use of ἔξω in 4:11 nevertheless suggests that Mark is already looking forward to the parables material.[90] And indeed, the spatial 'outside-inside' distinction (vv. 31-32) is quickly transposed into the matter of membership of Jesus' true family

---

[86] Marcus, *Mystery*, 89. Κατὰ μόνας emphasises the distinction between his followers and others. The latter group comprises not just outsiders (*pace* Gundry, 196) but also the undecided crowds (see below).

[87] Both Wendling, *Entstehung*, 31ff, and Goulder, 'Outside', 298, regard the appearance of ἔξω in 3:31f and 4:11 as the key lexical link in their interpretations. The οἱ παρ' αὐτοῦ κ.τ.λ. in 3:21 also serves to link the Beelzebul controversy with Jesus' statements about his true family in 3:31ff; Best, 'Mark'; Guelich, 1.168-72, 208; see Chapter 6, p. 145 above.

[88] E.g. Crossan, 'Relatives', 113; Lane, 147; Guelich, 1.186; Hooker, 114. Goulder, 'Outside', 298, who aligns Jesus' family with the scribes and then, in a way reminiscent of Weeden, Tyson, and Crossan, ingeniously casts all this in terms of Mark's re-writing the past in the context of a present conflict between Mark's pro-Paul community and a Pharisaic Jerusalem church ruled by Jesus' family. On the contrary, Mark's anti-Jerusalem polemic (if it can indeed be so called) equally reflects a thorough-going OT prophetic critique of the failure of Israel's leadership.

[89] Also Gundry, 180, 199, cf. Lambrecht, 'Relatives', 245f; *pace* Edwards, 'Sandwiches', 209f. However, as Hooker, 115, observes 'madness was often regarded as due to possession by a demon'.

[90] E.g. Marcus, *Mystery*, 89; now also Goulder, 'Outside', 291.

(vv. 33-34); a designation which is reserved for those who do the will of the father, which in the context translates into being περὶ αὐτὸν (Jesus) and hearing his teaching.[91]

Although Mark does not elucidate further, it may well be his purpose, having already shown that outright rejection of Jesus excludes one from God's kingdom, to indicate that even the closest kinship ties are not sufficient grounds to assume inclusion either. And if insufficient for Jesus' own kith and kin, how much less for the average Israelite? In this sense Jesus radically alters both national and familial obligations: he alone must be the locus of their loyalties.[92]

If this reading is correct, then Mark in 3:20-35 is concerned to establish two key parameters.[93] First, to reject Jesus (as have the representatives of the national leadership) is to invite the severest judgement, and, second, even that most sacrosanct of all ancient inter-personal obligations, that of bloodline, is insufficient to gain access to the Kingdom. It appears that with his account of the Jerusalem scribes' pivotal rejection of Jesus and his explanation of the parables, Mark exposes an emerging division, a sifting of Israel into 'insiders' and 'outsiders'[94] and within this context affirms the absolute priority of the need to respond in repentance and faith to Jesus, irrespective of religious-cultural and familial loyalties. In the light of the immediately preceding appointment of the Twelve, the implication for Mark seems to be that only as one identifies with the 'S/son of God' can one become a true 'son of God', a true Israelite.[95] Otherwise, one becomes

---

[91] Cf. Guelich, 1.208; Goulder, 'Outside', 295.

[92] On family obligations and loyalties see Malina, *World*, 94ff; Pilch and Malina, *Social*, 70ff. According to Josephus, the Law ranks honouring parents 'second only to honour to God', *Ap.* 2.27; cf. *Ant.* 4.260-5; Philo, *De Spec. Leg.* 2.225, 226; Lev 20:9; and Dt 21:18-21.

[93] See the structural outline in Chapter 6, p. 145 above.

[94] A division entirely consistent with the concerns of Malachi (as already noted) and Isa 56-66, in particular 65:8-16 and 66:5; see e.g. Hanson, *Dawn*; Westermann, *Isaiah*, 302ff; Williamson, 'Concept'; Achtemeier, *Community*, 17ff.

[95] See Chapter 4, p. 112, on the title 'my son' as a designation for Israel. From this perspective the appointment of the Twelve in 3:13ff may prefigure the establishment of a renewed Israel under a new leadership, with loyalty to Jesus as its central characteristic (12:9, see also fn. 56 above). Given the Isaianic 'servant' imagery earlier in Mark, it is interesting to note how the faithful action of the 'servant' in Isa 53 seems to be the catalyst for the appearance of other 'servants' in Isa 54; see Watts 'Consolation', 55. Thus Gnilka, 1.153, 'Diese jüdische empfundene Maxime (vgl. Röm 2,17f) erfährt im Wort Jesu einen neuen Orientierungspunkt'.

an 'outsider' which, given its usage elsewhere, could well imply no longer being an Israelite.[96]

It is intriguing that the same conclusion seems to be reached at the climax of a series of increasingly acrimonious polemics between Yahweh and Jacob-Israel in Isaiah 40-55.[97] And this too in the context of Yahweh's announcement of salvation (40:1ff). Having already had to remind the exiles of his supremacy over the idols, and that it was their faithlessness, not his, that caused their present distress, Yahweh's anger finally boils over at their questioning his wisdom in using Cyrus as his agent. Jacob-Israel might swear 'by the name of the Lord' and 'confess the God of Israel' but it is 'not in truth or right' (Isa 48:1). They are Israel in name only. Immediately after this Isaiah 49 announces the election of a new servant. It seems that a similar pattern is being repeated here.

Cast in such terms, it is plain that groups (A) and (C) are 'insiders' to whom the mystery of the kingdom of God[98] has been given.[99] Group (D), the outsiders, consists for the present of those religious authorities in 3:20-35 for whom the parables now function as judgement on their own wisdom. This, of course, leaves groups (B) and (E) which, in the presence of the injunctions to hear and the statement about Jesus' teaching 'them' in so far as they are able to hear, do not happily fit either category.[100]

One solution is to assume that Mark is either not particularly competent or simply not concerned to smooth over every discrepancy,

---

[96] Thus, although Goulder, 'Outside', 291, in noting the use of the language to refer to non-Jews (Str-B, 2.7) rejects the notion that 'outsiders' can mean those outside Israel, it may well be that this is precisely what Mark has in mind, in that to refuse to identify with 'the' Son is to exclude oneself from faithful Israel (cf. Sir, *Prol.*, 1 Cor 5:12f; Col 4:5; 1 Thess 4:12; Swete, 76; Lagrange, 'but', 26; and Siegman, 'Teaching', 173, where 'outsiders' became 'a standard rabbinic term for Gentiles or for Jews less instructed than the Pharisees', cited in Boucher, 43n4).

[97] See the argumentation and literature cited in Watts, 'Consolation', 35-49.

[98] Of primarily Semitic background of 'mystery', Brown, *Semitic*; Bornkamm, *TDNT*, 4.820f; Bowker, 'Mystery'; Marcus, *Mystery*; Beasley-Murray, *Kingdom*; Bockmuehl, *Mystery*; but cf. Harvey, 'Mystery'; and Beavis, *Audience*, 143ff. On its significance in Mark, especially Boucher, 80ff; Tuckett, 'Concerns', 16f; Dahl, *Memory*, 141-66.

[99] Lane, 156; Minear, 'Audience', 82; Marcus, *Mystery*, 89f. On the confining of explanations to the inner group throughout the gospel, Baird, 'Pragmatic'.

[100] So also Goulder, 'Outside', 290, who notes 'apparently the crowd *is able* to hear the word in part—a distinction is made between "them" and "his own disciples", who receive a full explanation privately'. Drury, *Parables*, 60, resolves the tension by taking 'as they were able' to mean 'without comprehension', cf. 4:11f; but this seems to fly in the face of the injunctions to hear carefully.

even rather blatant ones.[101] On the other hand, a more nuanced approach is possible. In the buildup to this section, various crowds have been present at the beginning, during, and after the end of the five controversy stories (2:4, 13, 3:9). Furthermore, not only does the climactic Beelzebul/ family controversy take place in the context of a gathering crowd (3:20) but the parables material likewise begins with a similar reference (4:1). All this suggests that in addition to those who are committed to Jesus and those who reject him, Mark is also concerned with the various crowds who follow Jesus and particularly so given the increasing polarisation which Jesus occasions.

Consequently, while it is true that for Mark there are, in the end, only two fundamental categories, namely, insiders and outsiders (cf. 3:33f), nevertheless, the existence of groups (B) and (E) indicate that it is not yet the case, as is often assumed, that everyone must necessarily be, immediately, either inside or outside.[102] On the contrary, the point seems to be that, in the face of the increasing criticism and now open rejection of Jesus, the moment of decision has crystallised. While some have taken sides, there are the large numbers of uncommitted folk who are as yet neither 'outsiders' (as are the hostile religious authorities) nor 'insiders' (those περὶ αὐτὸν) but who are now confronted with the need to decide where they will stand.

Such ones—co-extensive with the ὄχλος πλεῖστος and the 'them' if Mark excludes both the religious authorities and Jesus' followers from the two groups,[103] or, if Mark is deemed to include 'outsiders' and 'insiders' within these groups then comprising only part of the ὄχλος πλεῖστος and

---

[101] Cf. Meagher, *Clumsy*; Chilton, *Galilean*, 94ff; Räisänen, 33, 'If however one stops expecting anything like full consistency, a portrait might emerge of Mark as ... a relatively skilful writer'. Along similar lines many commentators are exercised by the various shifts in scene and audience, e.g. how can Jesus who is alone and seated in a boat (4:1-2) be approached (v. 10), so e.g. Guelich, 1.203f; Gnilka, 1.164? While it might be that Mark was unaware of such dilemmas it is also possible that he expects a modicum of readerly expertise, akin perhaps to the modern film-goer who copes rather well with such things as 'unannounced' scene changes and flashbacks. The fact that commentators notice such 'discrepancies' suggests that Mark has indeed signalled his scene and audience changes. Furthermore, the composite nature of the account simply serves to indicate that Mark's real interest lies in the dynamic way in which the various juxtaposed scenes interact rather than a plodding blow-by-blow account (cf. Ball, *Seven*, 55-103).

[102] As e.g. Quesnell, 85f; Marcus, *Mystery*, 106f; Lane, 157; Boucher, 43; Räisänen, 78f; cf. Guelich, 1.208, who recognises that the crowds are not 'outsiders' but then not being sure what to do with them takes refuge in a convoluted redactional history; 1.258f.

[103] With most commentators who see the crowds as distinct from 'insiders'.

the 'them'[104]—are, therefore, spoken to καθὼς ἠδύναντο ἀκούειν and exhorted 'to hear' carefully.[105] This is, after all, precisely the point of the parable of the soils: the word is being proclaimed and hearers must be careful how they respond (4:9).[106] If they hear and repent and believe then to the little they have, more will be added.[107] The mystery of the kingdom will be accessible to them. If they reject Jesus' teaching and refuse to be περὶ αὐτὸν, then, having chosen not to do God's will (cf. 3:35), the parables will effect judicial blinding so that as with the religious authorities even the little they have will be taken away (4:24f; cf. 12:9; 13:2).[108]

(iv) The Disciples

Although more fully discussed in Chapter 8, some comment on the matter of the disciples' lack of understanding (4:13; 7:17f; 8:14-21; 10:10-12) is appropriate since it is also frequently cited as evidence of inherent contradictions in Mark. Such a view correctly observes that the 'wisdom' terminology in Mark 4 (blindness, deafness, lack of understanding, etc.) constitutes the datum for its use in the rest of the gospel.[109] The fact that such language is indicative of an irrevocable bifurcation in Israel only adds to its significance.

However, although the disciples' incomprehension may at first blush appear to characterise them as 'outsiders', in fact neither 'blindness' nor 'lack of understanding', whether in terms of Mark or of a broader INE perspective,[110] can be construed as sure signs of being either under

---

[104] As Gundry, 190, 234.

[105] Thus e.g. 7:14 is not the contradiction Räisänen, 90, imagines. Vv. 33f do not involve hardening and offer little support for Marcus' two-stage hardening theory, *Mystery*, 107f.

[106] Boucher, 43ff, 82ff; Kingsbury, 17; and Tolbert, *Sowing*, 150f, who notes 'the vital role of hearing for the whole process is stressed by the constant repetition', citing thirteen occurrences of ἀκούειν including at the beginning (4:3) and end (4:33); cf. Gundry, 204.

[107] On various backgrounds to this wisdom proverb, Gerhardsson, 'Parable', 180f, citing 2 *Esd.* 9:29-33; Boucher, 43; Quesnell, 81-85; Guelich, 1.197; and Marcus, *Mystery*, 154f, who notes Qumran and rabbinic parallels (the latter from Lindeskog, 'Logia-Studien', 148ff).

[108] Cf. Gundry, 203, where the parables presuppose, instead of cause, division; although it is not clear that Jesus thereby successfully predetermines his death. Marcus' apocalyptic 'secret' model, 'Epistemology', misses the point because he reads Mark through the lens of Qumran materials. Furthermore, granted the predestinarian nature of e.g. 1QH 1:19f; other texts e.g. 1QS 4:11; 8:11f; 9:17ff; CD 8:32ff; can also describe God's response to those who have already rejected his word, cf. 1QH 2:9-19; 1QS 5:11f. Whatever the underlying theological implications of 'he who has ears to hear', Mark seems not to make predestinarian hay from them. Rather, Mark's concern is the response of faith to Yahweh's revelational INE coming in Jesus, as Marcus almost seems to admit, 562n20.

[109] Especially Beavis, *Audience*, 87-130.

[110] See further, Chapter 8.

judgement or an 'outsider'.[111]   Instead, the central issue is not whether one sees for in one sense all the human observers involved are blind and labouring under misconceptions of some sort. Instead, it is whether or not one is willing to let go of conventional wisdom, to follow and 'be around' Jesus, and so participate in the revelation of the mystery of the Kingdom. Jesus' question in 4:13, although probably expressing frustration, is from this perspective more ironic than extirpative: if you disciples cannot grasp this parable about the need to understand properly (vv. 3-9), how will you ever understand any of the parables?[112]   Nevertheless, since they have been given the mystery of the kingdom,[113] Jesus offers instruction.[114] That he will continue to lead these 'blind' disciples (Mk 8:17) along a path they do not know is the very point of Mark's increasing tendency to focus on the disciples' incomprehension which, beginning with Mark 4, prepares for his 'Way' section.[115]

f) 'The Parable Theory'

Finally, some observations on the implications of the above for the so-called *Parabeltheorie* are almost *de rigeur*. In its common form the theory posits A) a sharp division between Jesus' disciples and others, and B) that the parables are predestinarian in intent, essentially incomprehensible,

---

[111] Myers, *Binding*, 172, notes a similar tension in Daniel and Ezekiel, where e.g. the wise understand but the wicked do not, and yet the seer confesses his own failure to understand (Dn 12:8, 10b, LXX). Perhaps the further instruction of the disciples indicates that the time of the 'sealing up' of the words concerning the end of days is at an end (cf. Rev 22:10). On Daniel in Mark, Sundberg, 'Testimonies', 274; and Kee, 'Function'.

[112] *Pace* Boobyer, 'Redaction', who argues that 'this parable' is vv. 11f. First, he fails to appreciate this broader sense of 'hearing aright', cf. Wenham, 'Synoptic', 18n24; Quesnell, 79-81; and second, his solution fails his own test for it is not clear how merely understanding that one has been given the mystery will 'make the disciples men with understanding "to know all the parables"', 67, cf. Tuckett, 'Concerns', 17.

[113] Marcus, *Mystery*, 98, sees the parables as the channel of the divine gift, but in v. 11 the disciples' epistemological status is no different from the crowds to whom the mystery has not been given. A similar criticism may be levelled against Brown, 'Secret'. The condition of having been given the mystery is to be distinguished from understanding it, cf. Tuckett, 'Concerns', 16.

[114] Following van Iersel, 'System', 91f, who indicates mysteries are normally 'revealed' not 'given' (citing e.g. ἀποκαλύπτω LXX: Sir 3:18; 27:16, 17, 21; Theod.: Dan 2:19, 28, 29, 30, 47, 49; and ἀνακαλύπτω in LXX: Dn 2:28, 29; Theod.: Dn 2:29; and other verbs), Gundry, 197, draws a helpful distinction between 'mystery' and the 'kingdom' where the 'kingdom' having been given—as opposed to having been 'revealed'—does not contradict the need for the 'mysterious' content of the parables to be explained.

[115] Cf. Petersen, 'Composition', 205ff, who sees the disciples' incomprehension, not Wrede's messianic secret, 87-117, as the main theme of 4:1 - 8:26.

and designed to harden.[116]   While it is true that the crisis precipitated by
Jesus' ministry initiates a fundamental and ultimately final separation
between 'insiders' and 'outsiders', Mark's so-called 'contradictions', I
submit, are instead the result of the ambiguity which necessarily arises out
of the fact that the sifting of Israel is still in process. Some have made up
their minds for or against Jesus, but the vast majority have not. These
latter constitute a third category (viz. the 'crowds') who are taught καθὼς
ἠδύναντο ἀκούειν and are regularly exhorted to listen carefully;
presumably, that they might enter into the mystery of the kingdom and
avoid coming under the judgement now initiated upon the hostile
'outsiders'.   Again Mark's opening evocation of Isaiah's promise of
salvation (40:1ff) and Malachi's warning to the unprepared is not far away.

Second, the parables may be held to be incomprehensible—but only in
the terms that Mark himself sets up for us. As many commentators have
noted, it is clear that the parables are neither utterly indecipherable code
nor gibberish, even to outsiders (e.g. 12:1ff).[117]   It is possible that Mark may
have been so dull as to have missed this apparent 'contradiction'. But it
seems more likely that his concern is with a genuine comprehension that
leads to repentance and faith in Jesus as the inaugurator of the INE
Kingdom of God. This is entirely in keeping with Jesus' programmatic
announcement (cf. 1:1, 14f).[118]   Once again, as noted in the case of the
disciples, the issue is not a matter of whether or not one fully understands
but instead whether one repents, has faith, and follows Jesus. It is this that
ultimately distinguishes the disciples, and even the undecided crowds,
from the Jerusalem scribes. The latter alone have firmly shut the door on
Jesus and his message.[119]

H. Räisänen, in particular, has challenged this kind of approach largely
because it denies, he claims, the patently obvious predestinarian character
of 4:11-12.[120]   The difficulty here is that, if the Isaianic sense and the larger

---

[116] See discussions in e.g. Marcus, *Mystery*, 73f; Beavis, *Audience*, 78ff; Räisänen, 76ff.

[117] E.g. Räisänen, 87ff; Boucher, 83ff. Gundry, 200, who recognises this fact, skirts the
difficulty by reducing the referent of 'parables' in 4:11f to include only those in Mk 4 which
deal with the kingdom. The difficulty here is that Mark does not seem to make this
distinction himself, cf. vv. 33f.

[118] Cf. Gnilka, 1.172; Marshall, *Faith*, 72ff; Boucher, 82ff; Marcus, *Mystery*, 103-6.

[119] Cf. Guelich, 1.208, 211.

[120] "*Messianic*", 88, who also warmly commends Meagher, *Clumsy*, 120-22, for taking
'seriously the sternly predestinarian character of 4.11f (in conjunction with 4.34)', 29.
Räisänen's assertion seems to rest on the correctly noted 'purposive' sense of the ἵνα and

Markan context are any guide, the reason for the parables (4:11f) cannot, *simpliciter*, be deemed predestinarian in the usual sense.[121] As we have seen earlier, Isaiah 6:9-10 comes as Yahweh's judicial *response* to a people and a leadership who have already repeatedly refused his overtures. The same considered refusal is manifest in Mark's account—although it should be noted that in Mark only the leadership have made this break and hence the greater possible 'openness' of the parables to the people at large (4:33f). This is precisely the point of the series of controversies, culminating as they do in Jesus' rejection by the leadership, namely scribes from Jerusalem. From this perspective, T. W. Manson's comment that Mark 4:12f is a 'definition of the sort of character which prevents a man from becoming one of those to whom the secret ... is given'[122] is true, but only in terms of the considered recalcitrance described above.[123]

Mark's account of Jesus' use of Isaiah 6:9-10 is, then, not so much a matter of predestination as a judicial response to those who have already refused his message, that is the 'outsiders', which both confirms them in their logic and consigns them to the consequences of their choices.[124] This is still the case when considering Jesus' implicit use of parables prior to Mark's explicit reference in the Beelzebul controversy[125] since the leadership had even then rejected Malachi's preparatory Elijah, John the Baptist (cf. Mk 1:14; 6:17ff; 11:27-33). Thus, allowing first that the word

---

μήποτε clauses, 82f. However, it is not clear how having a purpose makes something predestinarian.

[121] Of the recent major monographs it is surprising that only Evans, *See*, 17-52, examines the Isaianic context in depth. Both Räisänen and those with who he disagrees (e.g. Boucher, Kingsbury, and even Beavis who is more aware than most of the Isaianic background) fail to give more than a cursory examination of the Isaianic setting. While many commentators note the extent to which 4:11f coheres or contrasts with what follows, e.g. Marcus, *Mystery*, 228ff, very little attention is given to the preceding Markan context.

[122] Manson, *Teaching*, 80, cited in Moule, 'More', 99 (cf. 101); see also Gerhardsson, 'Parable', 180f; Cranfield, 'Mark', 61; Kirkland, 'Understanding', 13; Guelich, 1.213.

[123] Although the text does not overtly state the importance of the hearers' reaction, in Mark as in Isaiah, the context presupposes it, *pace* Räisänen, *Parabeltheorie*, 8.

[124] On the other hand, the true significance of the parables seems not always to be immediately apparent—they appear to require further explanation by Jesus—which suggests that there could well be a certain 'hiddenness' to the parables. If so, then there may be some grounds for seeing a divine veiling at work. Cf. Marshall, *Faith*, 73, who recognises that hiddenness 'is the very strategy of revelation' but does not appear to see hiddenness as an impediment to understanding and so places all his emphasis on human responsibility. To argue from the soils being only what they are to some sort of determinism, Marcus, *Mystery*, 225, again ignores Jesus' exhortation to hear carefully.

[125] If taking, e.g. the line of Boobyer, 'Redaction', who argues that the earlier parables are also in view here.

'hardening' is not used,[126] it is only in this specific sense that the parables can be considered as 'hardening': they harden those who have already hardened their hearts, just as in Isaiah's day.[127]

g) Conclusion

Mark's 'Parables Chapter' is his programmatic response to the climactic Beelzebul controversy.[128] This is evident not only in the way one leads directly into the other, thereby providing its immediate context, but also in their significant similarities. In keeping with Malachi's warning, and as revealed by the Beelzebul/family controversy, a widening split is now occurring within Israel.

Whereas Jesus' announcement of Yahweh's INE coming 'in strength' signals the restoration of sight to the blind,[129] the national leaders' categorical rejection of his ministry means that the parables confirm them in their 'blindness'. Such people have in fact rejected the Kingdom (cf. 1:14f) and what little they have will be taken away. As 'outsiders', Yahweh's manifest presence ('Immanuel') means only judgement (12:1ff).

---

[126] Although the terminology does not explicitly occur here, the concept is integral to the discussion as is apparent in Isaiah and Mark, as Beavis, *Audience*, 89ff, notes. Cf. Boucher, 84, who although recognising the ambiguity of the concept, nevertheless correctly observes that in this sense 'the parables are the means both by which God judges the hearers, and by which the hearers bring judgement on themselves'.

[127] Space precludes a detailed proposal on the coherence of 4:1-34 but the following suggestion is offered: in view of the fact that a division is under way within Israel (3:13-19) the crowds who have been following Jesus are confronted with a choice, inside or outside (3:20-35), and this turns on how they 'hear' (4:1-9). Why does Jesus' speak in parables (v. 10)? Because, on the basis of Isa 6, it is part of Yahweh's plan to confound the wisdom of the wise who reject his purposes (vv. 11f, cf. 3:20ff). Jesus then ironically comments on the disciples' inability to hear properly (v. 13) and goes on (vv. 21ff) to explain that his speaking in parables is not intended to conceal the truth but to manifest it (in accordance with God's prior objective, cf. Quesnell, 81-83), although again stressing that the central issue is how one hears. Vv. 14-20 explain the parable, noting how the nature of the soil is revealed in response to the sowing of the seed. Using the imagery of the light of the lamp, vv. 21-25 picture the revelatory impact of the parables, and again warns about hearing aright: the little wisdom that the scribes have will be taken away but to those who have ears to hear, 'it' (the explanation of the mystery of the kingdom) will be given (vv. 23ff). The reason for careful hearing is then presented: the kingdom is not coming as the wise expect it (vv. 26-32) and the whole concludes with a statement re-affirming Jesus' desire to reveal the truth, but on his terms (vv. 33f).

[128] Cf. e.g. Weiss, *Evangelium*, 57f, who sees the 'parable theory' as the basis of the messianic secret rather than the other way about; Boobyer, 'Secrecy', for whom 4:11f represents the 'truly definitive account of the evangelist's point of view' (both cited in Marcus, *Mystery*, 111n133); and now particularly Beavis, *Audience*, 87-130, 157ff.

[129] See pp. 170ff above. Anderson, *Understanding*, 447, sees Isa 40:1f as reversing the judgement of Isa 6:9ff; Melugin, *Formation*, 83f, compares 1:4 with 40:1; Rendtorff, 'Komposition', 298ff; Ackroyd, 'Presentation', 45f; Evans, 'Unity', 137.

On the other hand, those who hear and respond in humble faith—even if they barely understand—find that they have been given the mystery of the kingdom and receive further instruction (4:24f; cf. 1QH 4:32f; 1QS 5:11f).[130] But for the undecided who are, as it were, in the middle, the parables are in a very real sense open-ended. They may lead to life, or death, and hence the urgent exhortation to 'hear carefully'. Everything depends on it. The parable of the sower, with its exhortations to careful hearing, sounds a warning against 'hearing' like the now 'outside' leaders whose increasingly critical stance toward Jesus has culminated in their attributing to Satan that which derives from the Holy Spirit.

On this basis, the primary point of Isaiah 6 in Mark 4 does not appear to be concerned with accounting for the blindness of the Jewish people *en toto*—although the use of this hardening motif in John 12:37ff and Acts 28:26ff suggests that it may well foreshadow it.[131] In Mark's story, the crowds *per se* are not yet presumed subject to the negative effect of parables. The building conflict cycle and its climactic culmination which precede Mark 4 are focussed on Israel's leadership, and especially those from Jerusalem. It seems, therefore, that the primary interest of the Beelzebul-Parables complex in its immediate context is to explain how the leadership's rejection of Jesus only leads to their judicial blinding. Nevertheless, there is surely another concern, namely, to warn others of the need for an appropriate response.

III. Isaiah 29:13 in Mark 7:6f

a) The Markan Setting: Tension Over Purity

It is noteworthy that on the only other occasion prior to Jesus' arrival in Jerusalem when he is challenged by authorities *from Jerusalem* his response is again couched in terms of an Isaianic judgement text.[132] The confrontation in Mark 7 arises out of the disciples' failure to purify their

---

[130] Marcus, *Mystery*, respectively, 105f, and 90f.

[131] *Pace* Lindars, *Apologetic*, 159f, who separates Mk 4:11f from the issue of parables, seeing here an explanation for Jewish unbelief. In this sense Mack, *Myth*, 155, is correct. Mk 4 is about the fate of Israel, and I might add, just as was Isa 6 before it.

[132] Cf. Grundmann,146; Schmid, 198; Malbon, 'Leaders', 264f. There are further confrontations in 8:11-13; 9:14; and 10:2-12 but these do not involve leaders explicitly from Jerusalem.

hands (κοιναῖς χερσίν) after visiting the marketplace (vv. 1-5; cf. v. 4).[133] Coming to his disciples' defence, Jesus rebukes the critics, denouncing them in terms of a citation from Isaiah 29:13 LXX (vv. 6f). Then, citing their practice of Corban, he exposes the hypocrisy of their demanding strict adherence to the traditions of men while permitting the circumvention of the commands of God (vv. 8-13). This leads to a 'parable' addressed to the crowds (cf. v. 16) where the nature of true purity and defilement is explained (vv. 14-23): it is a matter of the heart, not the hands.

Before going on, however, several points should be noted. Although 7:1-23 is generally regarded as breaking with the preceding narrative,[134] Mark's summary account of Jesus' ministry in 6:53-56 appears to set the scene for chapter 7, not only because the controversy immediately follows, but also because of its reference to the sick who are being brought ἐν ταῖς ἀγοραῖς. This is the first time ἀγορά occurs in the gospel.[135] It only appears once more before Jesus arrives in Jerusalem[136] and that is a few verses later in an editorial insertion where Mark explains the Pharisaic practice of not eating without washing if they have come ἀπ᾽ ἀγορᾶς (v. 4; cf. vv. 2, 5).[137] While possibly a co-incidence, the fact that both occurrences are in editorial comments strongly suggests otherwise.

Mark seems to intend that 7:1ff be read in the light of the general ministry summary of 6:53ff. If so, then Mark presents a situation similar to that which obtained in Mark 3:20 - 4:34. There, Jesus' deliverance of demonised Israelites had been met, not with thanksgiving, but censure. Here, Jesus' healing the sick is met, not with joyful praise (cf. 7:37), but with renewed criticism, this time for transgressing what is presented as a tradition of the elders. Furthermore, both instances exhibit a number of parallels.[138] First, there is the same overall literary structure. Mark begins

---

[133] The problems with Mark's description are well known. Neusner, *Pharisees*, 230ff, denies that the Pharisees possessed such traditions, but see the extended discussion for the contrary in Gundry, 358ff. In our context we are concerned only with Mark's presentation.

[134] See e.g. Lane, 244; Gundry; Hooker; Gnilka.

[135] Myers, *Binding*, 218, notes Mark's mention of the marketplace but sees it only in terms of economic oppression, suggesting that the disciples' contamination results from previous contact with the Gentiles.

[136] 12:38 is the only other instance.

[137] The text is ambiguous because of an ellipsis. Pesch, Taylor, and Guelich supply a plural impersonal pronoun so that 'things' from the market place are washed, citing the lack of evidence for individuals washing themselves in this manner. On the other hand, Cranfield, Gnilka, and Lane stay with the natural sense of the middle.

[138] Cf. Ambrozic, 70f, 101; Heil, *Walking*, 135f; Beavis, *Audience*, 92ff; cf. Gundry, 187.

with a controversy which is followed by a parabolic response both in word and in deed.[139]

Controversy (3:20-35)	**Controversy** (7:1-13; cf. 6:53-56)
- who is at work, *Beelzebul* or *Yahweh*?	- who is *clean* or *unclean*?
- scribes from Jerusalem and Jesus' family misunderstand	- Pharisees, and scribes from Jerusalem as hypocrites,
	- **Isa 29:13**, hearts far from God
Parables as Response:	**Parables** as Response:
in **Word** (3:23-27; 4:1-34)	in **Word** (7:14-23; cf. v. 17)
- **Isa 6:9-10**: see but not perceive, hear but not understand, (v. 12)	
- Disciples do not understand (οἴδατε, v. 13, γνώσεσθε, v. 13b)	- Disciples without understanding (ἀσύνετοί ἐστε; ου νοεῖτε, v. 18)
in **Deed** (4:35 - 5:43): *Jesus as the INE Yahweh-Warrior*	in **Deed** (7:24-37): *purity and the Gentile regions*
- storm (disciples' do not understand (v. 41))/demoniac;	- Syrophoenician woman
- unclean woman/Jairus' daughter	- deaf and dumb man

Parallels also exist in the details of the accounts. After the confrontation, Jesus addresses τὸν ὄχλον (v. 14a; cf. 4:1) and in language reminiscent of the parables material he exhorts them to hear and to understand a parable (v. 14b; cf. 4:3, 9). After a change of scene (v. 17; cf. 4:10), the disciples again ask for an explanation (v. 17; cf. 4:10)[140] and yet again are rebuked (v. 18; cf. 4:13). Mark 3:20 - 4:34 was in the context of Jesus' exorcisms, here the confrontation is set in the context of Jesus' healings, both activities being key indicators of the INE.[141] Just as Jesus responded to the first controversy by continuing his parabolic Yahweh-Warrior activities (4:35ff) so here he responds to this confrontation in a similar fashion and again in apparently Gentile regions.[142] These similarities strongly suggest that Mark intends 6:53 - 7:13ff to be read in terms of the issues raised in 3:20 - 4:34. What is of further interest is that Isaiah 6 and Isaiah 29, as we shall

---

[139] In particular, Lane, 244. Tolbert, *Sowing*, 148f, 164f, highlights the relationship between 4:1-34 and 4:35 - 5:43; now also Malbon, 'Echoes', 218f, and particularly 224f, where 4:1-34 precedes a series of parabolic δυνάμεις.

[140] Note also the scribal addition of v. 16, εἴ τις ἔχει ὦτα ἀκούειν ἀκουέτω, cf. 4:9, 23.

[141] In comparing the summary statements in 3:7-12 and 6:53-56 the former has a greater emphasis on Jesus' power over unclean spirits while the latter on his healing.

[142] Lane, 259; Schmid, 198; Pesch, 1.384; Grundmann,146; Ambrozic, 224.

see, are also closely related in that the latter appears to describe the implementation of the former.

b) Textual Matters

Mark 7:6f	Isaiah 29:13	
	LXX^{NAQ}	MT

Mark 7:6f	LXX^{ℵAQ}	MT
	ἐγγίζει μοι	נגש
Οὗτος ὁ λαὸς	ὁ λαὸς οὗτος	העם הזה
	ᵀ	בפיו
τοῖς χείλεσίν	τοῖς χείλεσιν αὐτῶν	ובשפתיו
με ⸀τιμᾷ,	τιμῶσίν με	כבדוני
ἡ δὲ καρδία αὐτῶν	ἡ δὲ καρδία αὐτῶν	ולבו
πόρρω ἀπέχει ἀπ' ἐμοῦ·	πόρρω ἀπέχει ἀπ' ἐμοῦ·	רחק ממני
μάτην δὲ σέβονταί με	μάτην δὲ σέβονταί με	ותהי יראתם אתי
διδάσκοντες διδασκαλίας	διδάσκοντες ἐντάλματα	אנשים מלמדה
ἐντάλματα ἀνθρώπων.	ἀνθρώπων καὶ διδασκαλίας	מצות

Mk 7:6: ⸀ ἀγαπᾷ in D W it^{a, b, c}

Isa 29:13 LXX: ᵀ ἐν (om Luc) τῷ στόματι αὐτοῦ, καί ἐν in LXX^B 𝔏 D Luc

The manifold variants in the last part of the Isaiah 29:13 suggest that the Hebrew text is corrupt,[143] but for our purposes the significant variations are few. Mark's text may represent a very slight abbreviation of the already shortened LXX^{ℵAQ}, although if the omission of ἐν τῷ στόματι κ.τ.λ. parallels the tendency seen in Mark 4:12 to omit repetitive ideas, then his source may be LXX^B. In any case, the MT's meaning is not significantly altered. The same applies to the change to τιμᾷ to accommodate the omission of the possessive plural. The major issues concern Mark's dependence on the LXX which apparently read וְתֹהוּ over against the MT's וַתְּהִי, and a Piel masc. pl. (מְלַמְּדִים, so also the Tg.) instead of the MT's Pual fem. sg. (מְלֻמָּדָה) thereby suggesting a causal clause. Comment on this will be left until after the following discussion.

c) Isaiah 29 in Context

Isaiah 29 belongs to that series of utterances in chapters 28-31 which, building on the earlier polemics against idolatrous wisdom in the earlier chapters, constitute the book's most sustained attack on the nation's

---

[143] See Watts, 1.384; Stendahl, *School*, 56ff; and Gundry, *Use*, 14; and *Mark*, 350.

leaders.[144] The historical setting is Judah's abortive participation in a rebel coalition against Assyria, and, although chapter 28 announces the coming of judgement upon the proud crown of the drunken and corrupt leaders of Ephraim (vv. 1-4), by verse 14 it is clear that the prophet is warning the rulers of Jerusalem who have rejected his message.[145] The issues are precisely the same as those addressed earlier in the book.[146] Set in the context of Jerusalem's crisis, the 'wise' (included in the 'obstinate children' in 30:1, 9; cf. 1:2) reject Yahweh's instruction or teaching (30:9-11), and increasingly resort to the nations and their idols as they plan their foreign policy (28:15; 30:1-5 (6f); 31:1-3). Nevertheless, Yahweh will accomplish his purpose (28:2f, 18-22): condemned to be blind and deaf (28:9-14; 29:9-21) the nation's 'wise ones' will pursue policies that will result in the devastation of the land and ultimately exile (30:1-5, 12-17; 31:1-3).

In the light of this background, Isaiah 29 opens with a woe oracle against the capital which declares that Yahweh himself will lay siege to the city (vv. 1-8; cf. Mk 13).[147] Verses 9-14, a chiastic formulation in which each stanza is a variation on the theme of incomprehensibility,[148] launch into a derisive indictment of Jerusalem's blind and deaf leaders. Once again, although verse 13 reads הָעָם הַזֶּה, it is clear that the leaders are again the primary targets (vv. 10, 14).[149]

The passage from which Mark's Jesus cites begins with a difficult verse. The point, however, seems clear enough in that it taunts those who ought to have known Yahweh's will but because of their wilful rejection of his word are likened to staggering drunkards (v. 9; cf. 28:7):

> ... blind yourselves and be blind, be drunk but not with wine, stagger but not because of strong drink, for the Lord has poured upon you a spirit of deep sleep. He has shut your eyes, prophets, and your heads, seers, he has covered (Isa 29:10).

---

[144] Sweeney, *Isaiah*, 56-58; Vriezen, 'Essentials', 134n9.

[145] Exum, 'Literary', 124; Wildberger, 3.1044; cf. Clements, 229.

[146] See pp. 188ff above; cf. Jensen, *Use*, 115ff.

[147] Vv. 5-8 are difficult because of the apparent sudden reversal of Yahweh's attitude. Clements regards them as a later redaction while Wildberger has Isaiah changing his stance. For Exum, 'Broken', 345, the point is that even though Assyria is Yahweh's tool she will eventually be punished for her arrogance.

[148] Exum, 'Broken', 347.

[149] McKane, *Prophet*, 70f; Jensen, *Use*, 51, 55f, 67f; Clements, 236; Evans, *See*, 43.

This insensible condition is Yahweh's doing (v. 10) and the unique expression הִשְׁתַּעַשְׁעוּ וָשֹׁעוּ in verse 9[150] strongly suggests that it is in fulfilment of the prophet's earlier commission where he was instructed הָשַׁע וְעֵינָיו (6:10, cf. 32:3).[151] If this is so, then we have here a picture of the nation's head and eyes—its prophets and seers—who are now so incapable of comprehending Yahweh's plan (i.e. vision[152]) that it is as impenetrable as a sealed book to an illiterate (v. 12). Nevertheless, leaders and people together apparently persist in earnest prayers and performance of religious duties, even though they pursue strategies directly at odds with Yahweh's will[153]—a situation not dissimilar to that which we have already described in Isaiah 1:10-15. Consequently, Yahweh indignantly rejects their honour of him as mere lip service and empty adherence to cultic regulations:[154]

> Because this people draw near with their words and honour me with their speech but remove their hearts from me, I will again once again deal wondrously with this people ... and the wisdom of their wise men shall perish, and the discernment of their discerning men shall be concealed (Isa 29:13f).

Using language otherwise associated with his past saving acts, Yahweh ironically announces that he will 'wondrously' (cf. Jos 3:1; Ps 78:12; 98:1 etc.) subvert the wisdom of the wise such that their plans will lead instead to utter devastation, a theme that quite pervades these chapters (vv. 14, 29; cf. 28:1ff, 13-22; 29:1-4, 19; 30:1-5, 12-15).[155]

Isaiah 29:13f thus presents a picture of a national leadership and a people, already under the effects of the judicial blinding pronounced in Isaiah 6, who are further given over to their own wisdom and, consequently, destruction. Yet at the same time as they secretly pursue their own rebellious plans, they continue to profess their loyalty to

---

[150] Schmidt, 'Gedanken', followed by Watts, reads הִשְׁתְּעוּ and שְׁעוּ for שֹׁעוּ: 'delight yourselves and gaze intently'. We follow Wildberger in that the omission in the LXX and the differing renderings of the versions are not sufficient reasons to emend the text; cf. *BDB*, 1044.

[151] Watts, 1.385; cf. Clements, Delitzsch. The unifying principle is 'the focus of each poem on vision', Exum, 'Broken', 351. Although the LXX omits the MT's 'blinding' phrase in 29:9a, its καμμύειν in v. 10 picks up Isa 6:10.

[152] Or 'revelation', see Exum, *ibid.*, 348f; Kaiser, 2.269. Exum takes it to refer to the contents of the poem while Wildberger, 3.1115f, sees the entire message of God to the people.

[153] Clements, 238f; Dietrich, *Politik*, 173ff; Wildberger, 3.1120.

[154] On מִצְוַת אֲנָשִׁים as cultic regulations, Wildberger, 3.1121f. Jensen, *Use*, 67, however suggests that it is a reference to the teachings of the wisdom tradition.

[155] Cf. Clements, 239; Exum, 'Broken', 348; McKane, *Prophets*, 70f.

Yahweh who disdainfully rejects such hypocritical worship as merely adhering to rules taught by men.

d) Isaiah 29 in Mark 7

It has been contended that the point of the argument in Mark 7:1-13 depends on the LXX because it supports an attack on the teachings of men whereas the MT and *Tg. Isaiah* are rather concerned with a deficient worship of God 'commanded by men and learned by rote'.[156] Two comments can be made. First, there is in fact little substantive difference between the senses of either the LXX or the MT. Since in both cases Yahweh is clearly displeased with a worship that fails to reflect his priorities and concerns[157]—and in any case the major change in the LXX, 'in vain', is not explicitly taken up by Mark.[158]

Second, to focus on the 'traditions of men' seems to miss the larger point which is evident in both the MT and the LXX. The concern in Isaiah is not merely a matter of rote recitation versus sincere religious practice, although this may be part of the problem. The matter of worship as mere adherence to religious rules 'taught by men' arises only in the larger context of the more fundamental issue, namely, rebellion against Yahweh's purposes.[159] This is precisely the situation in Mark, and I suggest, the reason for the similarities noted earlier between the two controversies in 3:20 - 4:34 and 7:1-23.[160] The religious authorities from Jerusalem have already rejected Yahweh's INE reign begun in Jesus by attributing his exorcisms to Beelzebul. They have set their faces against

---

[156] Booth, *Purity*, 91f; cf. Schweizer, 145; Nineham, 194f; Lindars, *Apologetic*, 165; Stendahl, *School*, 58; Gould, 128.

[157] The LXX's 'in vain' makes explicit what is already implicit in the MT and the LXX's epexegetical participle, διδάσκοντες, reflects the MT's adjectival phrase; cf. Lane, 248; Guelich, 1.367. Against Crossan's hypothesis that Mark used *Egerton Papyrus 2*, see Gundry, 362; and Schneck, 173-82.

[158] France, *Jesus*, 150.

[159] Cf. Suhl, 81, 'Die Haltung der Gegner läßt sich sehr gut mit den Worten Jesajas umschreiben. Sie sind damit als solche qualifiziert, die schon immer die Feinde Gottes waren'. Booth, *Purity*, 92, takes a somewhat idiosyncratic position (he cites no other authorities) in arguing that Isa 29 constitutes an attack against the obstructionist teaching of the wise which prevents people from true learning. This misses the point both of the larger Isaianic context and the meaning of 'hypocrite'; see fn. 166 below.

[160] Gundry's observation, 349, that 3:22 'has prepared the ground for an accusatory question' is, therefore, heading in the right direction.

Yahweh's plan, grieved his Holy Spirit, and so he has become their enemy.[161] Consequently, Jesus' parabolic teaching, and in all likelihood his miracles as well, merely serve to confirm them in their blindness (Mk 4). Not unexpectedly then, when in Mark's account the leaders are confronted with Jesus' healings (6:53-56, cf. ἀγορά in v. 56, and 7:4), they again respond with criticism, this time of the disciples' failure to conform to their traditions (7:1-5). Jesus' response is exactly in keeping with the Isaiah 29's denunciation: although the religious authorities appear to serve Yahweh their 'worship' is nothing but ἐντάλματα ἀνθρώπων since the truth of the matter is that they are at bottom opposed to God's purposes.[162]

The accusation regarding the practice of Corban serves to illustrate this.[163] Commanding others to keep τὴν παράδοσιν τῶν ἀνθρώπων while in the name of piety ἀφέντες τὴν ἐντολὴν τοῦ θεοῦ may be manifestly 'hypocritical' to a twentieth century reader, but more to the point it demonstrates a consistently ungodly proclivity to 'set aside' what God wants for the sake of their own traditions.[164] Again, this is exactly the larger issue at stake throughout Mark. What God wants is that they should 'repent and believe' (1:14f). But, as Mark has demonstrated earlier throughout his extended series of controversies (2:1 - 3:6), the religious authorities have constantly preferred their own traditions (2:7f, 16, 18, 24; 3:4f)[165] and thus they have continued to reject Yahweh's purposes.[166] With some considerable justification, καλῶς Jesus may add that παρόμοια τοιαῦτα πολλὰ ποιεῖτε. How can the authorities be expected to respond

---

[161] The response of Jesus' family in 3:20ff may be echoed in Jesus' rejection at Nazareth, 6:1ff, which suggests the following chiastic structure:

[3:7-12 Summary statement echoing John's success (prior to his rejection) in 1:5 which concludes first section of Jesus' mighty words and deeds and series of five subsequent confrontations.]
3:13-19　　　Twelve chosen (word and deed)
　3:20-36　　　　Rejection of Jesus by the scribes and his family
　　4:1-34　　　　　Parables as response: in word (Isa 6)
　　4:35 - 5:43　　　Parables as response: in deed
　6:1-6　　　　Rejection at Nazareth in his *patria*
6:7-13　　　Twelve sent (word and deed)

Cf. Fisher and von Wahlde, 'Miracles', with 'preaching' and 'exorcism' instead of 'word' and 'deed' (but 4:35 - 5:43?) and different verse selection (e.g. sending the Twelve: 6:7-33).

[162] Gundry's comment, 351, that Mark limits Isaiah's 'this people' to the religious leaders, fails to take into account that the leaders are in fact the focus in Isaiah (as above).

[163] On Corban, see e.g. Derrett, *Studies*, 1.112-17; Wilcox, *ANRW*, 2.25:2; Gundry, 363.

[164] Cf. Gnilka, 1.282, and Wilkens, *TDNT*, 8.564.

[165] Thus whereas Lane, 248, speaks of the Pharisees living 'a lie because they had not surrendered themselves to God', for Mark this means believing and following Jesus.

[166] Wilkens, *TDNT*, 8.564, where 'hypocrite' 'always denotes the wicked man who has alienated himself from God by his acts'. Gundry's attempt, 361, to infer 'hypocrisy', understood in the more modern sense of dissembling, is therefore unnecessary.

appropriately to the new thing God is doing in Jesus when, in the name of 'piety', they have all along been avoiding what God's law requires?

This implicit threat also suggests that there is more to the singling out of the practice of Corban than meets the eye. Honouring parents is, according to Ephesians 6:2, the first commandment with promise—that you may live long in the land (cf. LXX Ex 20:12 and Dt 5:16).[167] It is possible that Mark's Jesus is raising the spectre of covenant sanction, namely, destruction and exile from the land (cf. Ex 21:15, 17; Lev 20:9; Dt 21:18-21; 27:16). Again, this is not only in keeping with the thrust of Isaiah 29, but also with Mark 12:1ff and Mark 13.[168]

e) Conclusion

Just as Isaiah 6:9ff announced the sentence of judicial hardening and 29:9-14 describes its implementation, so too the effects of Mark 4:11f are being worked out in 7:6f. The authorities in Isaiah 28f, in spite of their continuing religious profession, had in fact rejected Yahweh's plan and were consequently under judicial hardening and consigned to pursue a course of action that would ultimately destroy them and their city. The same situation holds in Mark with regard to the religious authorities from Jerusalem. Having already rejected Jesus' exorcisms, they are now subject to Yahweh's judicial blinding. When faced with Jesus' 'parabolic' healings, the true nature of their loyalty to Yahweh is revealed, and their blindness is further confirmed. The threat of judgement looms. This, of course, is the point of both the parable of the tenants in Mark 12:1ff and the predicted destruction of the Temple in Mark 13. Indeed, if Yahweh had met such hard heartedness with destruction in the past, it would hardly be surprising if he should do so again.[169]

IV. Conclusion

Mark's opening composite citation not only evoked the expectation of the INE but also the warning inherent in Malachi that Israel, and particularly

---

[167] On filial responsibility in the OT, Phillips, *Ancient*, 80ff, and various rabbinical traditions, e.g. *b. Qidd.* 31b; *Mek. R. Ish.* Baqodesh 8:14ff; Blidstein, *Honor.*

[168] See e.g. Gaston, *Stone*, 478f; Marshall, *Faith*, 145f.

[169] Given this Isaianic background, it may well be that Mark 13 owes more to the stimulus of the classical prophets than to any particularly apocalyptic mode of thinking.

the religious authorities, must be prepared for Yahweh's coming. Unfortunately, they were not. John, Yahweh's forerunner, is rejected and imprisoned (11:27-33; cf. 1:14; 6:14-29; 9:11-13) and Jesus himself is denounced.

Following his initial presentation of Jesus as the inaugurator Yahweh's INE reign, Mark quickly turns to an extended series of debates culminating in the pivotal Beelzebul controversy where Jesus' exorcisms, for the first time, are publicly repudiated by the Jerusalem authorities. Jesus' response, also for the first time, is explicitly described as being 'in parables' and concerns the 'strong man'. This gives rise to two developments. First, the incipient mention of parables and its particular occasion leads directly into the explanation of their purpose. In terms of the Isaiah 6 citation, the parables effect judicial blindness on the religious authorities who, in rejecting Yahweh's INE deliverance, have grieved the Holy Spirit and have placed themselves on the 'outside'. Having refused Yahweh's purposes and rejected the call to repent and believe, he now becomes their enemy. From this point on a fundamental and increasingly open division within Israel is under way, with the 'crowds' being put on notice that they too must choose.

Second, the 'first' parable concerns the 'strong man'. Immediately following the explanatory parables in word (4:1-34), Mark returns to this motif in the paired miracles of the storm stilling and the drowning of the demonic legion (4:35 - 5:20) which at the least echo Israel's Exodus founding moment. Jesus is further shown to be the one who inaugurates Israel's NE. If one also includes the intercalated healing of the woman and the raising of the young girl (5:21-43), then perhaps the four miracles together constitute a pastiche reflecting Isaiah 63:7 - 65:25.[170]

Mark 7, however, continues the Malachi 'trajectory' by invoking the futile situation of Isaiah 29 where the nation's leadership, already under the influence of judicial blinding, continues to resist Yahweh's purposes while at the same time earnestly adhering to strict religious practice. In both Isaiah 6 and 29 judgement is the unavoidable outcome. With this background it is, therefore, not surprising that on reaching Jerusalem much of Jesus' activity involves the announcement of the same.

---

[170] See Chapter 6, p. 176, fn. 203, above.

On the other hand, returning to Isaiah's hope of a NE, there are the 'insiders' who have chosen to follow Jesus. Often described in terms more appropriate to 'outsiders', these 'blind' and dull-witted disciples are, nevertheless, those to whom the mystery of the kingdom has been given. What is one to make of this incongruity? Given the proposal offered here—that Mark is to some extent operating with an INE model—it is intriguing that his next major section is not only bounded by his only two 'healing-of-the-blind' miracles, but also tends to concentrate on Jesus' leading these 'blind' followers 'along a way they do not know' (Isa 42:16).

Chapter 8: The Way of the New Exodus: Mark 8:21/26 - 10:45/11:1

Mark's interest in the disciples' incomprehension prepares for his 'Way' section. In Isaiah, Yahweh's healing of 'blind' Israel and his leading them along the 'way' was indicative of Israel's need to accept his wisdom as part of their deliverance. So also Mark's 'restoration of sight' miracles on the 'Way' illustrate the 'blind' disciples' need to understand that the INE would be accomplished through a suffering Messiah.

I. The Disciples' Incomprehension

a) Introduction

One of the most well-recognised and perplexing motifs that unfolds throughout the last half of the first section of Mark's gospel is the disciples' incomprehension (4:13, 41; 6:52; 7:18f; and 8:17ff).[1] It is one thing for Mark's Jesus to apply Isaiah's ancient metaphors of judicial blindness and deafness to the hostile religious authorities. It is quite another when he so describes his disciples. How is it that 'insiders', to whom the mystery of the kingdom of God has been given, can be so devoid of understanding, so blind, and so deaf? What is it that they do not understand? And how is it that they are not also subject to judgement?

---

[1] See e.g. Wrede, 231ff; Tyson, 'Blindness'; Weeden; Focant, 'L'incompréhension'; Hawkin, 'Incomprehension'; Quesnell; Reploh, *Lehrer*; Tannehill, 'Narrative', 69ff; Stock, *Call*, 103-17; Wright, *Search*; Maloney, 'Vocation'; Malbon, 'Fallible'; 'Disciples' (but see now 'Echoes'); Klauck, 'Rolle'; Matera, 'Incomprehension'; Räisänen, 195-222. But, taking the gospel as it now stands (as opposed to the redaction critical approach of e.g. Best, 'Role', 'Discipleship'; see Black's critique , *Disciples*, of this method particularly in regard to the disciples in Mark), who does Mark mean by 'disciples': the 'twelve' or the 'twelve' plus other followers? Black, *Disciples*, 273n5, suggests they ought not be distinguished since, A) the Twelve are sometimes merged with a larger group; B) often they are not 'rigorously' differentiated from the 'disciples'; and C) behaviour associated with the Twelve or the disciples is frequently attributed to others. But perhaps it is wisest to avoid categorical exclusion since: A) at times Mark does distinguish between the Twelve and the larger group (4:10; 10:32); B) it may sometimes (but not always) suit Mark to talk about both groups under one head or he expects the context to show that the smaller group is in view; and C) it is not behaviour *per se* but instead following Jesus that distinguishes a disciple from others (e.g. 5:20; 7:17; 9:38).

This paradoxical presentation has led to polarisation.[2] Some stress the disciples' merits, emphasising their role as guarantors of the tradition.[3] For others, the failings of the disciples are far more important and they become proxies for Mark's opponents and as such are little better than heretical reprobates.[4] A third group, seeking to mediate between these two extremes, gives due weight to both realities such that the disciples in both their successes and their failures serve to encourage Mark's audience.[5] What is clear is that, although the disciples are surely 'insiders', as the narrative progresses they are increasingly described in terms applicable to the 'outsiders', climaxing in the sharp reprimand in 8:17ff. How is this tension to be resolved? Given, too, our hypothesis of an INE framework, to what extent does Mark's 'Way' section cohere with the Isaianic descriptions of Yahweh leading Israel along the 'way' to Jerusalem? And how, if at all, are these two matters related?

This Chapter proposes that Mark's presentation of Jesus' disciples exhibits significant parallels with Isaiah 40-55's description of exiled Israel awaiting deliverance.[6] 'Blind' and 'deaf', the nation continued to misunderstand Yahweh's purposes and constantly queried the wisdom of his actions. Even so, Yahweh declares that he 'will lead the blind by a way they do not know, along paths they do not know I will guide them. I will turn the darkness into light before them' (Isa 42:16a). Similarly, at the end of Mark's first section Jesus' uncomprehending disciples are also described as 'blind' and 'deaf'. Nevertheless, Jesus leads them along the 'Way' to Jerusalem which, significantly, begins and ends with Mark's only healing-of-sight miracles. On this 'Way' the disciples are likewise confronted with Yahweh's unconventional wisdom: the revelation that the ultimate expression of his INE coming and Israel's deliverance is nothing other than the scandalous way of Jesus to the cross. Just as the mysterious career of Isaiah 53's 'suffering servant' was integral to the INE, so Mark's NE

---

[2] See the helpful summary of the Markan data in Black, *Disciples*, 41-46, and his subsequent discussion.

[3] In particular, Meye, *Jesus*, but see also e.g. Kertelge, 'Funktion'; Budesheim, 'Jesus'; Schmahl, *Zwölf*; Stock, *Boten*.

[4] Notably, Tyson, 'Blindness'; Weeden, 'Heresy'; *Conflict*; but also earlier Kuby, 'Konzeption'; and then Kelber, *Story*, 'Apostolic'; Selvidge, 'Feared', *Woman*, 39f.

[5] Reploh, *Lehrer*; Focant, 'L'incompréhension'; Hawkin, 'Incomprehension'; Best, 'Twelve', *Following*; Malbon, 'Fallible', 'Disciples', and her critique of Kelber in 'Text'.

[6] See now also Marcus, 31ff.

'Way' reveals the enigma of the messianic S/son of God who is also the suffering Son of Man (8:31-33; 9:30-32; 10:32-34; cf. 8:29 and 10:45).

This suggests that Mark's primary concern is not so much to describe the path of suffering discipleship—although it is surely important—nor to recount the disciples' attaining full cognition, for clearly they do not. On the contrary, Mark's point appears to be that participation in the INE 'way' inevitably involves the recognition and affirmation of two critical data. First, that the Markan Jesus is not only Israel's Messiah, the royal son of God, but in a unique and extraordinary sense the divine Son of God.[7] And second, as the three-fold passion predictions indicate, that in Yahweh's wisdom Israel's NE redemption is predicated on the death—and resurrection—of 'true Israel', namely the Son of Man.

b) Themes and Emphases

The outline of 3:7 - 8:21 overleaf is not yet another attempt at the structure of this notoriously difficult section,[8] but instead seeks to highlight those themes that might have some bearing on the 'incomprehension' motif. The larger division into two sections, Mark 3:7 - 6:52 and 6:53 - 8:21, has been made simply to emphasise similarities in the way Mark handles certain incidents and the manner in which he connects them.[9]

In terms of the materials leading up to the 'Way' section, a number of observations can be made. First, as previously noted, the two 'Controversy and Response-through-Parables' stories (3:20 - 5:43; 7:1-37) exhibit a number of parallels. They begin with a controversy involving religious authorities from Jerusalem to which Jesus responds with parables of word

---

[7] Cf. Israel as 'son' and Jesus as 'Son', see Chapter 6, p. 186, and Chapter 4, pp. 110ff.

[8] For a survey of earlier alternatives, Quesnell, 28-36. Also more recently, Petersen, 'Composition', who gives a primary structural role to the boat scenes, 195f; as does now Malbon, 'Echoes'; and Fowler, *Loaves*, 113, who observes a series of interlocking doublets centred on the two feeding accounts, 113.

[9] Given the chiasm suggested above (Chapter 7, p. 217, fn. 161), perhaps also:

6:14-29	Herod, Jesus, and John's death: Herod does not understand Jesus' signs
6:30-44	Feeding of the 5000
6:45-56	Miracles: storm stilling and healing the sick
7:1-23	Authorities from Jerusalem: Isa 29 and the traditions of the elders
7:24-37	Miracles: the demonised daughter and the deaf-mute
8:1-10	Feeding of the 4000
8:11-13	The Pharisees seek a sign
[8:14-21	Conclusion: warning of the leaven of the Pharisees and Herod]

The warning concerning the leaven of the Pharisees and Herod (8:14-21) functions as the conclusion to the section by bringing together Herod (6:14ff), the Pharisees (8:11ff), the feedings (6:30ff; 8:1ff), and the disciples' lack of understanding; all of which prepare for Mark's 'Way' section.

and then of deed. But the disciples themselves 'understand' neither the spoken parable nor the true significance of the deeds.[10]

Outline of 3:7 - 8:21: Parallel Literary Structures

Mark 3:7 - 6:52	Mark 6:53 - 8:21
Summary (3:7-12)	Summary (6:53-56)
Choosing the Twelve (3:13-19)	

Controversy (3:20-35)
- who is at work, *Beelzebul or Yahweh*?
- scribes from Jerusalem and Jesus' family misunderstand

Controversy (7:1-13; cf. 6:53-56)
- who is *clean or unclean*?
- Pharisees, and scribes from Jerusalem as hypocrites,
- **Isa 29:13,** hearts far from God

Parables as Response:

in **Word** (3:23-27; 4:1-34)
- **Isa 6:9-10**: see but not perceive, hear but not understand, (v. 12)
- Disciples do not understand (οἴδατε, v.13, γνώσεσθε, v. 13b)

Parables as Response:

in **Word** (7:14-23; cf. v. 17)

- Disciples without understanding (ἀσύνετοί ἐστε; οὐ νοεῖτε, v. 18)

in **Deed** (4:35 - 5:43): *Jesus as the INE Yahweh-Warrior*
- storm (disciples' do not understand (v. 41))/demoniac;
- unclean woman/Jairus' daughter

in **Deed** (7:24-37): *purity and the Gentile regions*
- Syrophoenician woman

- deaf and dumb man

Rejection at Nazareth (6:1-6a)
Sending the Twelve (6:6b-13)
Herod and John Baptist (6:14-29)
     - misunderstands the miracles (v. 14)

Feeding of 5000, and *loaves* (6:30-44)

Feeding of 4000 and *loaves* (8:1-10)

Pharisees seek a sign, refused (8:11-13)

Boat in the storm/water walking (6:45-52)
- disciples astounded (v. 51)

- disciples do not understand (συνῆκαν) about the *loaves* (v. 52a)

- hearts are hard (v. 52b)

Bread in the **Boat** (8:14-21)
- beware the leaven of *Herod* and the *Pharisees* (v. 15)

- disciples do not understand (οὔπω νοεῖτε οὐδὲ συνίετε) about the *loaves* and *broken pieces* (v. 17)

- 'are your hearts hard?', cf. **Jer 5:21, Ezk 12:2; Isa 6:9;** blind eyes, deaf ears, etc. (vv. 18f).
- 'do you not yet understand (συνίετε)?' (v. 21)

---

[10] On confrontation-parable-miracle as a Markan pattern see also, Keller, 'Jesus', 36f, although his subsequent analysis is open to question.

Second, in 6:30 - 8:21 there are two boat scenes which also feature the disciples' incomprehension: fear at Jesus' walking on the water in 6:45-52 and misconstrual of the leaven warning in 8:14-21. In both cases this incomprehension is linked to the preceding feeding accounts (6:30-44; 8:1-10) by means of statements about loaves (6:52; 8:17-21).[11] Third, the feeding stories themselves (6:30-44; 8:1-10) are bracketed with accounts that also concern 'understanding' (see the outline below). Both Herod and the Pharisees are interested in signs, and particularly ones that will establish Jesus' identity (6:14-29; 8:11-13).

Herod mistakes Jesus for a resurrected John Baptist	(6:14-29)
Feeding of 5000, and *loaves*	(6:30-44)
... *intervening material* ...	(6:45 - 7:37)
Feeding of 4000 and *loaves*	(8:1-10)
Pharisees seek a sign from Jesus and are refused	(8:11-13)
Leaven and loaves: summary warning about Pharisees and Herod	(8:14-21)

Further, both of these accounts are alluded to in the leaven warning ('Ορᾶτε, βλέπετε ἀπὸ τῆς ζύμης τῶν Φαρισαίων καὶ τῆς ζύμης Ἡρῴδου) which then forms the basis of the concluding pericope 8:14-21 (taking vv. 22ff as transitional to the 'Way' section). Fourth, this concluding pericope (8:14-21) seems to function as something of a summary since it brings together a number of the concerns, themes, and motifs from the preceding material:[12] the reference to Herod and the Pharisees (6:14ff; 8:11ff; cf. 3:5f), the disciples' failure to understand (combining terms used in 6:52 and 7:18), mention of the 'loaves', the disciples' hard-heartedness (6:52), and the superabundance of the feedings It is also the last time Mark records Jesus questioning the disciples' incomprehension.[13] That this series of questions is the most extensive to date (8:17-21) only heightens the sense of crisis. But what is it that the disciples do not understand, and why is their incomprehension particularly connected with the loaves?[14]

---

[11] E.g. Fuller, *Mission*, 74; Keck, 'Christology', 356n96; Glasswell, 'Miracles', 158f; Hawkin, 'Symbolism'; Quesnell, *passim*; Fowler, *Loaves*, 109-14; Meye, 'Horizon', 4; Schweizer, 126; Pesch, 1.385; Guelich, 1.316f; Malbon, 'Echoes'.

[12] Cf. Hawkin, 'Incomprehension', 495; Quesnell, 125, 176; Heil, *Walking*, 131-44; Guelich, 1.419.

[13] The closest he comes after this is 9:19 but this is specifically about unbelief, not lack of perception, although the two are probably related.

[14] The literature here is considerable, for surveys: Quesnell, 1-28; Boucher, 69-80; Gibson, 'Rebuke'.

c) Mark 8:14-21 and Mark 4:1-34: the Feedings as Parables
The summary character of 8:14-21 suggests that it must, in some way, be pivotal to the incomprehension problem.[15] The reference to the disciples forgetting to bring bread (v. 14) might recall the preceding feedings, but in terms of the narrative setting is more likely intended to provide, by means of word association, the occasion for Jesus' warning about the leaven (v. 15)—much as the word 'salt' functions as a key-word link between the 'salt-sayings' of 9:49f.[16] In the context of the Pharisees' demand for a sign (v. 11) and Herod's confusing Jesus with John (6:14-16), the 'leaven' metaphor seems most naturally to refer to that which blinds both Herod and the Pharisees to the true significance of Jesus' parable-deeds.[17] The fact that the disciples quite misunderstand the 'leaven' warning, thinking it to be a veiled rebuke at their forgetting to bring sufficient bread (v. 16), demonstrates its timeliness and occasions Jesus' reprimand (vv. 17-18). The lack of bread is simply not the issue. Jesus could easily have provided more, as his questions indicate (vv. 19a, 20a) and as the disciples' answers reveal they well know (vv. 19b, 20b).[18]

What *is* of concern is the disciples' failure to understand the point of the 'leaven' metaphor.[19] This failure to perceive is characteristic of a thoroughgoing condition which has been evident since the first mention of their incomprehension (4:13) where they failed to understand the parable of the soils and seed. Hence the final question, 'Do you still not understand?' (8:21). Just as Jesus had earlier lamented the disciples'

---

[15] E.g. Perrin, *Introduction*, 246ff; Beck, 'Reclaiming', 49f; Guelich, 1.426f; cf. Klauck, 'Rolle', 13.

[16] It is not clear that the exception clause, v. 14b, is as enigmatic as is often supposed, cf. 6:8.

[17] Quesnell, 232-57; Pesch, 1.413; cf. Boucher, 77f; and on the symbolism of leaven, Windisch, *TDNT*, 2.902-6; Str-B, 1.278f.

[18] Gibson, 'Rebuke', 31. On the argument (as e.g. Gundry) that the disciples do not recognise Jesus' ability to provide, see fn. 24 below.

[19] Gundry, 408f, arguing that Mark emphasises not the disciples' dullness but rather the superabundance of the feedings (vv. 19-20), sees the emphasis on 'Jesus' miraculous power' and his ability to meet 'the present need'. There are several problems here. On this reading it is difficult to see why Mark should include vv. 15-16 at all since the point would be well made without them. Gundry also seems to misread the exchange in that Jesus' questions are aimed at disabusing the disciples of the idea that he is concerned about bread (v. 16). The 'leaven' warning itself can hardly be about failure to appreciate the fact of a miracle since even Herod and the Pharisees recognise that Jesus performs such. What matters is the significance of the miracles as is borne out by the use of blind, deaf, lack of understanding, etc. terminology as discussed in the previous Chapter.

inability to grasp the parable about the importance of genuine understanding (4:13), so here he is amazed at their inability to understand his warning about the dangers of misunderstanding. Two complementary warnings—about understanding and misunderstanding—thus seem to bracket the material which continues directly from the Beelzebul controversy up to the beginning of the 'Way' section.

The connection between 8:14-21 and 4:1ff becomes more obvious when it is recognised that the language of Jesus' rebuke (8:17f) follows closely that used in the parables material: συνίημι (4:9, 12; cf. 7:18), βλέπω (4:12; cf. 4:24), ἀκούω generally (4:3, 12, 15, 16, 18, 20, 24; cf. 4:33), and in particular in the question ὦτα ἔχοντες οὐκ ἀκούετε; (4:9, 23).[20] M. A. Beavis has noted that 4:1-20; 7:14-23; and 8:1-20 all reflect a similar structure. They each begin with a parable or parable-event in a public setting (4:1-9; 7:14-15; 8:1-10), and then are followed by a private expression of the disciples' incomprehension (4:10; 7:17; 8:16), a rebuke by Jesus in the language of Isaiah 6:9f (4:11-13; 7:18; 8:17f, 21), and conclude with an explanation of the parable (4:14-20; 7:19-23; 8:19-20).[21] Finally, the language of hardening, which is integral to Isaiah 6:9f, is explicitly mentioned in 6:52 and in 8:17. Although most recent commentators hold the language in 8:18 to be primarily a combination of Jeremiah 5:21 and Ezekiel 12:2[22] with echoes of Isaiah 6:9f, Beavis has argued that 8:18 is '*a deliberate allusion*' to the unquoted part of Isaiah 6:9f in Mark 4 since neither the cognitive language (συνίημι, νοέω) nor the hard-heartedness (ἐπαχύνθη, Isa 6:10; πεπωρωμένη, Mk 8:18) is found in Jeremiah 5 or Ezekiel 12.[23] While not denying that the latter two texts are in view, given the importance of Mark 4 it seems

---

[20] The programmatic nature of Mark 4 has been discussed previously in Chapter 7, see especially pp. 208ff.

[21] *Audience*, 158. 8:19-20 comprises rhetorical questions which function negatively by showing that the leaven parable cannot refer to the lack of bread, *ibid.*, 111. Lemcio, 'Structure', also proposes a common structure between 4:1-20; 7:14-23; and 8:14-21. Whatever the merits or otherwise of the proposed units—ambiguity, incomprehension, surprise and/or rejoinder, and explanation—it surely discerns that there is at least some relationship between the three.

[22] It appears closer to Jer 5:21 and less so to Ezek 12:2, but as a question it is closer in context to Isa 42:18-20; cf. v. 16. With less likelihood Derrett, *Making*, sees Ex 14:17a and Josh 11:20 while Myers, *Binding*, argues for Dt 29:2-4. See now also the extended discussion in Schneck, 204-20.

[23] *Audience*, 114, see also 90f; cf. Suhl, 152; Pryke, 55. On this technique in the rabbis, see again Cranfield, 'Study', 59; Jeremias, *TDNT*, 5.701; Marcus, 200; cf. Dodd, *According*, 126f.

that they are to be understood within the Isaiah 6 framework already established.

This linking of the disciples' incomprehension of the feedings with the parables material suggests that Mark intends the former to 'be understood in some way similar to the parables'.[24] But what is it that the parable-feedings are intended to reveal and that the disciples in 8:14-21 do not understand? If the feedings themselves are parables, then perhaps the best place to begin is Mark's 'Parables Chapter'.

d) The Parable-Feedings and Jesus' Identity

In view of the importance of Mark's 'Parables Chapter' for both the intervening material on the disciples' 'leaven-like' incomprehension (cf. e.g. 6:52; 7:18) and the concluding pericope (8:14-21), it is probably of some significance that 4:1-34 (and 4:35 - 5:43) is itself closely related to the larger question of Jesus' identity and the significance of his actions.[25]

Although an issue earlier (e.g. 1:11, 24, 27; 3:11), the matter of Jesus' identity becomes decisive in the climactic Beelzebul controversy (3:20ff) which, we have already argued, is the catalyst for the following exposition on the significance of the parables. From this perspective the mystery of the kingdom (4:11) concerns not only the mystery which is the kingdom, but also the mysterious way in which the kingdom is expressed and revealed in Jesus' mighty deeds, in his powerful words, and ultimately, linked to his identity.[26] And all this within the parameters of Israel's hopes and expectations concerning the inauguration of God's INE reign.

---

[24] Boucher, 69; cf. Blomberg, 'Miracles'; Beavis, *Audience*, 103-14; Heil, *Walking*, 136-40. Given the disciples' response to the spoken parables (4:13; 7:18) it is not surprising that they fail to understand about the 'loaves'. Gundry, 133f, interprets 6:52 to mean that the disciples did not understand the feeding of the 5000 to be a miracle (e.g. Mark makes no mention of amazement on behalf of the crowd or the disciples—an argument from silence) asserting that if the disciples had realised that it was they would not have been surprised at the walking on the water. It is not clear that Gundry's latter point stands, since although miraculous feedings involving human beings (namely, prophets) have OT precedents (e.g. Moses, Elisha; see Chapter 6, pp. 178f), walking on the stormy sea, itself an 'advance' on the storm-stilling in 4:35-41, does not. Furthermore, the use of πωρόω and συνίημι elsewhere in Mark suggests that it is not the fact of the feeding miracle but its significance that is not understood.

[25] See also Heil, *Walking*, 125ff. Integral to the question of Jesus' identity are his unacceptable *modi operandi* which are the central issues in the five controversy stories, 2:1 - 3:6.

[26] Cf. e.g. Marcus, *Mystery*, 51ff, 56; Beavis, *Audience*, 146. For this reason, Gundry's distinction, 201, between the kingdom and the person of Jesus seems insufficiently nuanced.

For the disciples, Mark's increasingly important question concerning Jesus' identity finds its initial expression on the other side of the 'parables of word' material (4:1-34), where, in the first of the boat scenes, they ask 'Who then is this?' (4:41).[27] Interestingly, the paired motifs of a parable-δύναμις and the disciples' incomprehension are also found in both the intervening and final boat scenes (6:45-52; 8:14-21).

On this basis it would seem that the first boat scene (4:35-41) is programmatic for the other two, which suggests that the fundamental question for all three concerns Jesus' identity and significance.[28] If so, then Mark's recording in the final boat pericope (8:14-21)—which also concludes his first section—of Jesus' vigorous warning about the 'leaven' of Herod and the 'sign-seeking' Pharisees simply underlines the point. Herod hears of Jesus' δυνάμεις but confuses him with a resurrected John, while the Pharisees, who are already somewhat hostile to Jesus, continue to find his signs ambiguous (6:14; 8:11-13; cf. 3:5-6).[29] Accordingly, Jesus cautions his disciples against the 'leaven' of both since it leads to a misconstrual of his actions and a concomitant failure to recognise who he really is.

That the question of Jesus' identity and significance is the primary emphasis of the material up to this juncture is further supported by what Mark does next. Immediately after Jesus' warning comes Mark's first of only two accounts of the healing of the blind. It is generally agreed that he is intending 8:14-21 to be interpreted in the light of the transitional story of the 'laborious' healing of the blind man (8:22-26) and of Jesus' increasingly pointed questions concerning his identity which then lead directly to Peter's confession (8:27-30; espec. v. 28; cf. 6:14-16).[30] Not only so, but

---

[27] Cf. Malbon, 'Echoes', 219ff, 224f, for whom the parables material concerns the question: 'to what shall we liken the kingdom of God?', whereas 4:35 - 8:21 concerns Jesus' identity. But this is already at issue, or so it seems to me, certainly in 3:20ff and even earlier.

[28] Cf. Hawkin, 'Incomprehension', 496, who sees the fundamental question posed by the first section as 'Who is this?'; also Kuby, 'Konzeption'; Malbon, 'Echoes', 224; and Kingsbury, 80ff.

[29] Hawkin, 'Incomprehension', 495; Petersen, 'Composition', 210f; Guelich, 1.423. Although the evidence is late (e.g. *Mek.* on Ex. 16:25 (c. 110); *2 Bar.* 29:8; *Qoh. Rab.* on 1:9; cf. Volz, *Eschatologie*, 388f; Behm, *TDNT*, 1.477; Heising, *Botschaft*, 46; van Cangh, *multiplication*, 119, 50-53), something like an expectation of the repetition of the Manna miracle might be what the Pharisees have in mind, especially as Mark has their request immediately following the second feeding.

[30] Lightfoot, *History*, 90f; Richardson, 86; Best, 'Discipleship', 325ff; Hawkin, 'symbolism', 104f, 'Incomprehension', 499f; Focant, 'L'incompréhension', 170; Heil, *Walking*, 138; Guelich, 1.420, 426. Lane, 269, observing structural similarities between the

Peter's 'trees-as-men-walking' declaration suggests that this incomprehension is remedied, but only partially, by his pronouncement that Jesus is ὁ Χριστός.[31]

From this perspective, the disciples' question in Mark 4:41, 'Who then is this?', signals this section's recurring interest in their incomprehension. It resurfaces in the second boat story, 'For they did not understand about the loaves, because their heart was hardened' (6:52), is picked up by Jesus, 'Do you still not understand?' (8:21), alluded to in his question 'what do you see?' (8:23), then sharpened at Caesarea Philippi when Jesus asks the disciples 'Who do people say that I am?' (8:27) and again more pointedly in his 'But who do you say that I am?' (8:29a), and is finally answered in part by Peter's response, 'Σὺ εἶ ὁ Χριστός' (8:29b).

Consequently, the connection between the three boat stories bears further investigation. In the first instance, the parable-sign of the storm-stilling is met with terror and lack of understanding (4:41). In the second, the water-walking evokes a similar response but the disciples' incomprehension is related not, as might be expected, to the preceding and somewhat parallel storm-stilling but instead to the interposed first feeding (6:50, 52). Then, in a clearly ordered progression, the third boat scene concentrates solely on the feedings (8:14-21).

Several questions arise: why is the all-important question of Jesus' identity ultimately connected, through the boat scenes, with the feedings? And why does Mark first focus on Jesus' authority over the sea but then

---

two feedings (6:31-44; 8:1-9), crossings (6:45-56; 8:10), conflict scenes (7:1-23; 8:11-13), bread sayings (7:24-30; 8:14-21), healings (7:31-36; 8:22-26), and confessions (7:37; 8:27-30), suggests that the healing miracles symbolically refer to the opening of the disciples' ears and eyes. Matera, 'Incomprehension', 167ff, sees 6:45 - 8:26 as centred around a journey to Bethsaida which, interrupted by the storm of the disciples' incomprehension in 6:45 - 8:21, is finally completed in 8:22ff where the blind man is healed. He also notes, 171, structural parallels between: A) Bethsaida and villages of Caesarea Philippi, B) 'Do you see anything' and 'Who do men say that I am?', C) the man sees clearly and Peter correctly identifies Jesus, and D) the man is forbidden to enter the village and the disciples are commanded to tell no one.

[31] Matera, 'Incomprehension', 169. The proposal that Jesus rejects Peter's confession, often argued on the basis of redactional theories (e.g. Petersen, *Literary*, 61ff; Weeden, 64ff; Kelber, 82f; Perrin, 'Christology'; Charlesworth, 'Messianology', 12, citing Fuller, *Foundation*, 109) seems to be made on other grounds, and in our case where we are concerned with Mark as it now stands, is hardly to be accepted, Hooker, *Message*, 52f; Kingsbury, 91ff; Gundry, 445. What precisely Peter had in view (for Mark) is difficult to tell, although whatever else it seemed not to include the ideas of 'suffering', 'failure', or 'rejection'. That Peter makes the confession hardly rules out the possibility that God has revealed it to him, cf. Charlesworth, 'Messianology', 12n25.

apparently abandon this to concentrate on the miraculous provision of food? I suggest that they represent Mark's account of the failure of the disciples to discern the significance of Jesus' parable-actions: first in the storm-stilling/sea-walking, and then in the feedings.

Most probably the reason why the disciples fail to apprehend the significance of the storm-stilling and sea-walking is because they imply considerably more about Jesus' identity than anyone might have reason-ably expected.[32] As regards the storm stilling, the disciples who were earlier apparently terrified by the storm itself are now even more terrified by the profound implications of Jesus' authoritative rebuke (ἐφοβήθησαν φόβον μέγαν, 4:41). This is no ordinary prophet; if indeed merely a prophet at all.[33] The same point is made even more forcibly in the later sea-walking. In addition to the Divine Warrior materials cited earlier in conjunction with 4:35-41,[34] the expression παρελθεῖν αὐτούς (6:48b cf. Ex 33:19-23; 34:6; 1 Kgs 19:11)[35] and Jesus' ἐγώ εἰμι (6:50 cf. Ex 3:14; Isa 41:4; 43:10-11)[36] suggest that the disciples are witnessing an epiphany of the 'One who Walks over the Water' (e.g. Job 9:8, espec. LXX; Ps 77:20 MT, *Tg.*).[37] If anything, this goes beyond their earlier traumatic experience: whereas Jesus had previously commanded the sea now he walks upon it!

The implications of both deeds are far-reaching, although quite in keeping with Mark's opening composite citation (1:2f)[38] and his account of the rent heavens (1:10).[39] Jesus, the one who both announces the εὐαγγελίον of the INE and as Messiah inaugurates it, is also, it seems, to be closely identified with the actual presence of Yahweh himself. For Mark, Jesus appears not only to be both Messiah and the true son of God (i.e. true Israel) but also the Son of God (cf. 1:1,[40] 24; 3:11; 5:7; 15:39; Mt 14:33).[41] Yahweh has, in a unique way, 'come down' among his people to save

---

[32] On possible antecedents, Blackburn, *Theios*, 152-82.

[33] On the possible Isa 63-64 horizon for this account and the following miracle collection, see Chapter 6, p. 176, fn. 203.

[34] See Chapter 6, pp. 160ff, above.

[35] Lohmeyer; Kremer, 'Jesu', 226-28.

[36] Heil, *Walking*, 69f; Guelich, 1.351.

[37] Heil, *Walking*, 17-30, 37-56; and especially now Blackburn, *Theios*, 145-52; Marcus, 144f. Stegner, 'Walking', has suggested that this event is also modelled on Israel's deliverance during the Exodus, in particular the account in Ex 14.

[38] See Chapter 3, p. 87, point (D).

[39] See Chapter 4, pp. 102-7, above.

[40] On the textual problem, Head, 'Study'.

[41] Boucher, 71f; Heil, *Walking*, 56; Pesch, 1.361; Guelich, 1.350; cf. Kingsbury, 140ff.

them (Mk 1:10, cf. Isa 59:15b-20; 63:1-5, 19). But all this is too much for the disciples to grasp and results in fear and amazement rather than the recognition that constitutes faith.[42]

With the feedings, however, things are less problematic. While it is certainly true that they have prophetic counterparts[43] it is also the case that they constitute the one category of miracle which has as its clearest antecedent the provision of manna in Israel's founding moment Exodus experience, a provision that in some Jewish traditions was expected to be repeated in the age to come.[44]

Thus, in regard to our first question—why is the all-important matter of Jesus' identity ultimately connected with the feedings?—Madeleine Boucher is, I think, correct. It appears, for Mark, that of all the 'signs' which Jesus performs the miraculous provision in the wilderness should have been the clearest indication that the NE was beginning, with Jesus being at least Israel's shepherd-Messiah.[45] Although the specific healings of the blind, the deaf, etc., are in their individual particularity signs of the INE and recognisably so once one allows an INE framework, in terms of general categories they, along with the exorcisms and resuscitations, are not *sui generis*. The prophets and others (cf. Lk 11:19) have performed similar miracles.[46] Hence it is not surprising that Mark can record that many regarded Jesus as a prophet (6:15; 8:28).

Mark's linking of the feedings with Peter's confession, Σὺ εἶ ὁ Χριστός, coheres with the circle of ideas found in some traditions where the Messiah (Anointed One) was associated explicitly with the repetition of the provision of manna (2 *Bar.* 29:3, 8; cf. John 6:5-15) and/or more generally

---

[42] See Marshall, *Faith*, 216ff.

[43] Particularly Elisha see e.g. van der Loos, 624ff; Blackburn, *Theios*, 195f, and the materials cited in Chapter 6, pp. 178f, above.

[44] See Boucher, 74, who cites 2 *Bar.* 29:8; *Sib. Or.* frag. 3:46-49; *Midr. Qoh. Rab.* on Eccl 1:9; *Midr. Tan. bᵉsullah* 21; *Mek* on Ex 16:25 etc., and Blackburn, *Theios*, 195f.

[45] Boucher, 74. Cf. Stock, *Discipleship*, 123f; Matera, 'Incomprehension', 164; Pesch 1.350; van Cangh, 'multiplication', 344; Tooley, 'Shepherd'. *Pace* Fowler, *Loaves*, 130, who sees the 'controversy between Jesus and the disciples' as the 'central focus' of the feedings. Koch, *Bedeutungen*, 112, who correctly observes the link between the nature miracles and the disciples' incomprehension, is nevertheless mistaken when he states 'Markus will ... die Möglichkeit ausschließen, die ‚Natur' wunder als unzweideutige Epiphanien Jesu ... zu verstehen.' The severity of Jesus' rebuke over the feedings suggests otherwise.

[46] Van der Loos, 237-39; Theissen, *Miracle*, 265-76; Blackburn, *Theios, passim*; and the brief discussion in Chapter 6, pp. 137ff, above. Cf. Dunn's critique, 'Messianic', 94, of Wrede where he argues that the miracles are not unambiguously messianic.

with Moses and/or a New Exodus (e.g. *Frg. Tg.* Ex 12:42; *Ex. Rab.* 18:12; *Qoh. Rab.* 1:28; *Tg. Ket.* Cant 4:5; 7:4 and Lam 2:22).[47] (An intriguing conjunction of 'anointed' terminology and New Exodus imagery is found in Isaiah 45:1. Here Cyrus, as Yahweh's agent of Israel's NE deliverance from Babylon, is described as 'his anointed'—the only place where מְשִׁיחַ occurs in chapters 40-55.[48]) Along similar lines, the groups described in Mark 6 are not unlike those envisaged by the Qumran Covenanters as they waited for and anticipated eating with the Messiah of Israel (1QS 2:11-22).[49] Consequently, as most commentators agree, Mark's Jesus is revealed by the feedings as Israel's messianic Shepherd (cf. Ezek 34:23; *Pss. Sol.* 17:40; Jn 6:15).[50] If so, then it appears that for Mark the feedings were the clearest signs that Jesus is at least the Messiah and as such he is inaugurating Israel's long-awaited NE.[51]

Returning to the second question—why does Mark first focus on Jesus' authority over the sea but then apparently abandon this to concentrate on the miraculous provision of food?—the interpretation just offered might help us understand Mark's purpose in relating the boat scenes as he does. Echoing the thematic statement on Jesus' identity as 'S/son' in 1:11,[52] the

---

[47] See also the numerous materials cited in Jeremias, *TDNT*, 4.859-63. Again, due caution should be exercised in light of the difficulty of dating. On the Targums see Levey, *Messiah, ad loc.*

[48] Cf. some readings of *Tg. Isa* 42:1 and LXX where the 'servant' (in this text, without necessarily implying the same for the other 'songs') is identified as the Messiah (cited above in Chapter 4, p. 115, fn. 137); also Jer 23:5ff; 30:9f; Ezek 34:20-31; 37:15-28 which discuss a Davidic scion as the shepherd of Yahweh's people in the context of their NE restoration. It is noteworthy, however, that this Davidic figure presides over the restored nation rather than effects its deliverance. See also Hanson, 'Messiahs', 71f.

[49] See Talmon, 'Concepts', 108-13, and the materials cited above in Chapter 6, p. 179.

[50] As discussed earlier in Chapter 6, pp. 177ff. *Pace* Gundry, 328, that the crowd is likened to 'sheep without a shepherd' almost requires that Jesus in his compassion be seen as their shepherd, and this regardless of whether or not the disciples eat of the loaves Jesus provides now, or later in 7:2. Similarly, it would appear to be a methodological error to argue that the absence of identical terminology (e.g. ἔρημος τόπος) excludes conceptual congruence with the wilderness of the Exodus.

[51] While this interpretation does not necessarily utterly exclude the possibility that Mark's community also understood the remaining loaves, or the one loaf in the boat, as alluding to the Jewish/Gentile composition of the church (see e.g. Boobyer, 'Miracles'; Hawkin, 'Incomprehension', 495; Kelber, 58; Beck, 'Reclaiming'; Gibson, 'Rebuke'; cf. Sundwall, *Zusammunsetzung*; but see Hooker's cautions, *Message*, 46ff) it does urge that such is not the primary point. Peter does not confess, 'Thou art the One bread who feeds both Jew and Gentile', and there is no indication that by failing to include something to this effect he misunderstood the real point of the loaves. Humphrey, 'Wisdom', suggests that the feedings reveal Jesus as the personification of Wisdom.

[52] Kingsbury, 60-71.

summary in 3:11 (cf. 5:7) records the exorcised demons' confession of Jesus as the ὁ υἱὸς τοῦ θεοῦ. But given the diverse usage of this sort of terminology[53] what does it mean when applied to Jesus?

The crucial 'Beelzebul controversy' is not only the one place where Mark's Jesus gives any indication of his understanding of his exorcisms, but in keeping with Mark's opening citation and 1:10 also seems to indicate that they are to be construed in terms of the Isaianic Yahweh-Warrior. While 4:1-34 then picks up and develops the implications of the 'controversy' element (i.e. Jesus' response to his rejection), the following (and first) boat scene involving the disciples (4:35ff) returns again to the 'Warrior' motif. Invoking themes associated with the first Exodus through the storm-stilling and the drowning of legion, Mark's account further develops the link between Jesus and the Yahweh-Warrior with Jesus exercising authority traditionally associated only with Yahweh himself: he directs the sea and effects the watery demise of the demonic enemy, Legion.

However, coming to terms with the implications of such extraordinary actions appears beyond the disciples. Their fear suggests that they have at least some intimation of what all this means but are simply unable to accept the conclusion to which the evidence points. If this is too much, then the feedings—when interpreted as parable-signs which, given the language used in 6:52 and 8:14ff, is apparently how Mark's Jesus understands them—provide a more accessible starting point since they do not entail the staggering implications of the sea miracles. At least, then, Jesus is the messianic Shepherd-king who inaugurates the NE (although for those with eyes to see, his actions might even more closely resemble those of the 'Yahweh-Shepherd' of Isaiah 40-55).[54]

From this perspective, part of Mark's rationale in interleaving the three boat scenes with the feeding accounts appears to be the detailing of the development, or rather lack thereof, of the disciples' appreciation of Jesus' identity. Mark's point at the conclusion of the second boat scene (6:52)

---

[53] See again Chapter 4, p. 110, fn. 99, above.

[54] See Chapter 6, pp. 177f, above. Boucher, 74, also notes the presence throughout this section of Isaianic motifs such as wilderness (40:3; 43:19-20), divine power over the waters (43:2, 16), the shepherd feeding his flock (40:11), deafness and blindness (42:16, 18, 20; 43:8), 'I am he' (41:4; 43:10, 13, 25), and 'fear not' (35:4; 41:10). The exception to Yahweh as shepherd in Isa 40-55 is found in 44:28 where the MT, along with several MSS, Syr, and Vg,, has Cyrus as 'my shepherd' although perhaps 1QIsa[a] reads 'my friend'.

seems to be that it is hardly to be wondered that the disciples were unable to grasp the meaning of Jesus' walking on the water since not only had they failed to understand the significance of the storm-stilling, but they had trouble enough with the considerably less problematic implications of the feedings.[55] As J. P. Heil remarks, this is probably why the Markan Jesus reverts to focussing on the loaves until Peter finally perceives Jesus to be the Messiah (8:14-30).[56]

This being so, two further questions arise. Why Mark's interest in the disciples' inability to comprehend that Jesus is at least the Messiah, if not the Son of God, who inaugurates the INE? And why is Peter's confession used to introduce the 'Way' section? William Wrede suggested that the disciples' incomprehension formed part of the 'Messianic Secret',[57] but as J. Tyson and T. J. Weeden recognised it is not so much that the disciples knew of Jesus' messiahship and were forbidden to reveal it; they fundamentally misunderstood its nature. For Tyson and Weeden[58] the disciples are better understood as representatives of a viewpoint that Mark needed to refute. Although the disciples have recently fared better being seen as fallible models exhibiting both positive and negative characteristics,[59] the

---

[55] Boucher, 73; Lane, 238; Guelich, 1.352.

[56] *Walking*, 142.

[57] *Messiasgeheimnis*. The literature here is immense and the issue exceedingly complex (see e.g. the surveys of the debate in Blevins, *Research*, and Tuckett, *Secret*), not least because of difficulties in defining what is to be considered part of the secret and what is not, and whether or not there is even an overarching Markan 'secrecy' motif, see e.g. Luz, 'Geheimnismotiv' and Räisänen, '*Messianic*'. Without going into detail, our assessment of Mark 4 suggests that it is not so much part of a Markan 'secrecy' project as an act of judgement akin to that experienced earlier in Israel's history. Similarly, Mark's framework for understanding the incomprehension of Jesus' disciples might owe more to OT categories, particularly Isaianic ones (see below), than an overarching Markan 'secrecy' schematic. In respect of this latter point, i.e. the general atmosphere of incomprehension, Robinson's suggestion, 'Gnosticism', 142, that Mark is seeking to 'push back the hermeneutical turning point' might be helpful—even if his anti-Gnostic polemic theory is less so. It could be that Mark is seeking to show that, although even Jesus' disciples did not fully appreciate who he was, nevertheless, evidence supporting Christian claims about Jesus was in fact implicit in Jesus' words and actions. It took the radical paradigm shift inherent in the resurrection to enable his followers to make the 'leap' from struggling with the 'impossible' implications of e.g. Jesus' forgiveness of sins and sea-miracles, to finally affirming them not merely as the possible but the factual.

[58] 'Blindness', 'Heresy'; cf. Kelber, *Kingdom*; *Oral*.

[59] Albeit in varying degrees: Quesnell; Peacock, 'Discipleship'; Reploh, *Lehrer*; Best, 'Peter'; 'Twelve', *Following*; Focant, 'L'incompréhension'; Tannehill, 'Disciples'; Freyne, 'Disciples'; Klauck, 'Rolle'; Malbon, 'Disciples', 'Fallible'. Schmahl, *Zwölf*, and Stock, *Boten*, stress their unique historical role. Meye, *Jesus*, takes the most positive position.

distinction between the disciples' acknowledgment of the fact of Jesus' messiahship and their understanding its nature remains valid.[60]

e) Jesus' Identity, Peter's Confession, and the 'Way'

At the level of the narrator, then, Mark's first section employs a number of Israel's ancient icons to present Jesus not merely as Messiah who inaugurates the INE, but also as the true S/son of God.[61] Within the narrative, however, things are not so obvious. In contrast to the demons, the human participants, including the disciples, have considerable difficulty in apprehending the full significance of Jesus' words and deeds. Thus, although Peter's declaration represents something of a climax, Jesus was clearly much more; provided one had eyes to see. Nevertheless, one must be thankful for small mercies, and if 'Messiah' represented the extent of the disciples' perception then so be it. Consequently, it is Mark's account of Peter's 'trees as men walking' confession of Jesus as Messiah that serves to introduce the 'Way' section where the unexpected destiny of this Messiah is revealed: he must give his life a ransom for many (10:45).

As others have noted, it is almost a truism that these two major sections are related by means of a thematic progression whereby 'the unveiling of the secret of Jesus' identity'—or at least partial unveiling— 'leads the way for the unveiling of the mystery of his destiny'.[62] The one caveat would be that, at least for this section of Mark, the limiting factor is not so much Jesus' hesitancy to reveal his identity (although this might well be a contributing factor, cf. 3:12; 9:9) as it is the disciples' inability to grasp the full implications of Jesus' words and deeds.

What is striking in this regard is that Mark's presentation of Jesus as the Yahweh-Warrior who inaugurates the INE is orientated not, as might traditionally be expected, toward the political subjugation of Israel's perceived human enemies (in this case the Romans), but instead the true source of evil, that is, the demonic hordes and their prince Beelzebul. It might well be that it is this perspective, given the intertestamental

---

[60] Focant, 'L'incompréhension', 185; cf. Hawkin, 'Incomprehension', 493.

[61] Kingsbury, *Christology*, is correct in emphasising the importance of 'Son of God' terminology, although the stress appears not so much on 'royal' connotations but instead on the divine; cf. now also Blackburn, *Theios*.

[62] Hawkin, 'Incomprehension', 500; cf. e.g. Kuby, 'Konzeption', 58; Luz, 'Geheimnis-motive', 23; Best, 'Discipleship', 325; Quesnell, 161f. On Strecker's criticism of this distinction, fn. 114.

conjunction of idolatry and the demonic, that both confuses the disciples and ensures that those who set themselves over against Jesus—in particular the Jerusalem scribes—are regarded as the descendants of Israel's idolatrous rulers of old and so incur a similar judgement (as argued Chapter 7 and further in Chapter 9).

What, then, is the rationale behind Mark's stress on the disciples' incomprehension as a precursor to the 'Way' section?[63]   Several observations may be made. First, I suggest, he wants to show that participation in the parable-$\nu\nu\alpha\mu\epsilon\iota\varsigma$ does not necessarily entail comprehension (even though failure to understand is culpable, 8:14-21).[64] Consequently, Mark pointedly relates the disciples' incomprehension in the context of the most perspicacious of the miracles: the feedings. Even Jesus' closest followers can participate in the miraculous signs which attend, or better perhaps announce, the inaugurated INE. But when it comes to perceiving Jesus' identity, they are like those with hardened hearts in that they too do not understand the true significance of the events in which they are caught up. This not only draws attention to the pervasive 'blindness' of the human participants,[65] but also distinguishes participation in the signs from true participation in the actual event itself. This is perhaps why Mark does not locate the feedings in his 'Way' section as might be expected on the basis of an INE hermeneutic. While the feedings advertise the inauguration of the INE, genuine participation depends on much more, not least the acceptance of the suffering and scandalous 'way' of the cross (cf. 8:34 - 9:1).[66]

---

[63] Cf. Fuller, *Mission*, 74; Glasswell, 'Miracles', 158f; Hawkin, 'Symbolism'; Quesnell, *passim*; Fowler, *Loaves*, 109-14; Petersen, 'Composition'; Pesch, 1.385; Guelich, 1.316f; Matera, 'Incomprehension'; Best, 'Twelve', 31.

[64] Petersen, 'Composition', 215; cf. Hooker, *Message*, 54, who observes this dynamic in the teaching parables.

[65] While it is true that various individuals come to Jesus in healing faith, I would argue that in none of the cases does this necessarily constitute an affirmation of and personal commitment to Jesus' messiahship.

[66] Although we feel no urgency to force everything onto a Procrustean INE bed—the feeding accounts can happily be understood independently of a NE schema without negating the overall thesis—Mark's editorial skill and evident interest in linking the feedings with the incomprehension motif suggest that he has something in mind. From a literary stand-point, having assumed an INE hermeneutic the reader might expect to find the feedings in the 'Way' section. By misplacing them, and thereby contradicting the reader's expectation, Mark draws attention both to the feedings and, perhaps more importantly, to the incomprehension motif, thus underlining the fact that participation in the signs is not to be

Second, even if one partially perceives Jesus' identity, this too is not enough and hence Mark's integration of Peter's confession with the account of the two-stage healing.[67] For Mark, such confession amounts to a precondition of embarking on the INE 'way' in that it is only when Peter confesses at least that Jesus is the Messiah—with, most likely, the concomitant expectations of some sort of national salvation[68]—that the disciples can then begin to be taught the more difficult but essential lesson that the ultimate means of the INE salvation is for Jesus to give his life a ransom for many (10:45).[69] This, it seems to me, is precisely the point of Mark's 'Way' section with its emphasis on the private instruction of the disciples concerning the true nature of Jesus' messiahship. Only when it is accepted that God's wisdom[70] means that the realisation of Israel's NE and the nations' salvation (cf. Isa 56:7 in Mk 11:17) is predicated on the scandal of Χριστὸς ἐσταυρωμένος (1 Cor 1:23) can one begin to participate truly in the INE.[71] Of course, in keeping with the earlier Markan themes, this must be accompanied by an affirmation of Jesus' divine Sonship.

Finally, in terms of Mark's overall agenda, it appears that he is concerned to show that no one really understood the full significance of Jesus' words and deeds, not even those on the 'inside'. If Jesus' disciples made such a meal of it, then it is hardly to be wondered that the bulk of

---

equated with entry into the INE 'Way'. (This is not, however, to suggest that Mark seeks to denigrate Jesus' miracles; see the literature cited above in Chapter 5, p. 172, fn. 166.)

[67] Best, *Following*, 135; Kingsbury, 95; cf. Derrett's suggestion, 'Trees', 36, that the second healing is related to perception.

[68] *Pace* Pesch, 'Messiasbekenntnis', 25, and Charlesworth, 'Messianology', 12n25, the messianic/Son of David elements in this section combined with the assumptions underlying Mark 10:32-45 (see below) suggest that for Mark Peter's conception had at least some nationalistic overtones. See e.g. *Pss. Sol.* 17:21ff; concerning Qumran, Loader, 'New'; and in general Mendels, 'Pseudo', and the literature cited therein.

[69] The point is twofold. First, the disciples are now taught that the Messiah must die *simpliciter* and then after three days be raised. Although Wrede argued that this is inconsistent since Jesus' passion is already evident in 2:19, Mark's overall picture of the disciples provides little grounds for supposing that they fully understood its implications. Second, there is the matter of the purpose of Jesus' death. One aspect lost in the discussion is how alien this must have sounded to those who did not have centuries of Christian belief behind them.

[70] Although Mark does not specifically mention 'wisdom', such Markan terminology as e.g. βλέπω, ὁράω, ἀκούω, συνίημι, and γινώσκω is characteristic of Israel's wisdom tradition.

[71] Cf. Hengel, *Atonement*, 43f: 'Although countless Jews were crucified under the Seleucids, the Hasmoneans and above all the Romans, and although there were so many crucified pious men and teachers, as far as I can see we find only one reference to a crucified martyr in rabbinic sources ... Deuteronomy 21.23 evidently made it difficult to turn a crucified man into a religious figure or a hero'.

the Messiah's own people likewise misunderstood, and even continued to misunderstand. And this without the additional and almost insuperable impediment of a Messiah who is crucified. In this respect, Mark might well be addressing the same sort of issue faced by Paul in Romans 9-11: how is it that God's own people could miss, to borrow N. T. Wright's phrase, the climax of the covenant? Mark's response, once again, is couched in terms of the nation's past as expressed in her Scriptures. There had been on many occasions a hard-heartedness in Israel and her leadership that led them to prefer their own wisdom to that of Yahweh. For Mark, this tendency recurred in Jesus' day, blinding the nation's religious authorities and even Jesus' own disciples. The great difference being that the latter, although 'blind' (10:32), nevertheless followed.[72]

Granted the above, what about the overall proposal of an INE hermeneutic for Mark? If Mark's Jesus is at one and the same time, Israel's Messiah and 'true servant Israel' (Mk 1:11), the true son of God, who is also uniquely identified with the Yahweh-Warrior (thus Son of God) and whose words and deeds reflect the icons of Israel's 'Exodus' deliverances and as such announce the inauguration of the INE, what are we to make of Mark's 'Way' section? Are there, as we have suggested earlier, correlations between the INE 'way' and Mark's 'Way' section? We will now turn first to a discussion of the 'way' image in the Isaianic NE, and then see if a case can be made for its influence on the manner in which Mark develops his 'Way'.

II. Blindness and Understanding: Mark's 'Way' Section

a) Introduction

As noted earlier scholarly opinion is largely agreed on several features of Mark's 'Way' section (see Chapter 5). By way of recapitulation, Mark's

---

[72] The question as to why Yahweh chose to effect his deliverance in this unexpected way lies beyond the scope of this thesis, although a similar dynamic can be seen in Isaiah 40-55 where the enigmatic 'suffering servant' (and indeed Cyrus) seems to stand in marked contrast to more conventional hopes of perhaps a new David (given the language of Isa 9 and 11) or a new Moses (given the Exodus imagery). It might be that Yahweh's strategy in operating in this unexpected manner was to subvert human reliance on its own wisdom (cf. Watts, 'Consolation', 41-49), an issue apparently central to the account of creation and the expulsion in Gen 3 and perhaps echoed in Isaiah's account of the wisdom debate as central to the reason for Israel's exile.

central journey section focuses not only on the issues of discipleship, but fundamentally on Jesus' relatively private teaching of his disciples about his future suffering. The healing-of-the-blind miracles which introduce and conclude this segment further symbolise the disciples' need to understand. Mark's redactional use of ὁδός emphasises the sense of journey (in geographical-theological terms, toward Jerusalem, the place of Yahweh's presence) and is associated not only with each of the three passion predictions but also with both the rich man who rejects Jesus' call to follow and Bartimaeus who does follow. The appearance of ὁδός in Mark's opening citation is also in all likelihood programmatic, pointing forward to the 'Way' prepared for by John[73] that Jesus as the suffering Messiah must take to Jerusalem and wherein the disciples must follow.[74]

The question that concerns us is to what extent, if any, does Mark's linking of the motifs of sight/understanding and 'Way' reflect the Isaianic NE? The next section of this chapter will examine the role of the motifs of sight, understanding, and 'way' in Isaiah's NE. We will argue that the INE 'way' in chapters 40-55 (cf. ch. 35) involves the reversal of Israel's idolatrous rejection of Yahweh's wisdom and her subsequent judicial 'blinding and deafening'. Thus the metaphorical aspect of her healing indicates her acceptance of Yahweh's wisdom, in particular his plan for national salvation, and the rejection of her idols.

b) Isaiah and the NE 'Way' as the 'Way' of Yahweh's Wisdom

(i) Idolatry, Blindness, and the Rejection of Yahweh's Wisdom
In the previous Chapter we saw that throughout Isaiah 1-39 the thematic contrast is between judgement and redemption, promise and threat, with the emphasis increasingly falling on the negative.[75] Yahweh's people are accused of being impious, evil-doers, speakers of folly (9:15), godless (10:6),

---

[73] As noted briefly in Chapter 7, pp. 184f, above.

[74] Best, *Following*, 15f. Cf. e.g. Burkill, 'Strain', 32; Kertelge, 181; Kelber, 95. Lane, on the basis of parallels between 6:31 - 7:37 and 8:1-30 (fn. 30), excludes 10:46-52 from the disciples' lack of understanding motif, seeing 8:22-26 as concluding the previous section, e.g. Klöstermann, 77; Koch, *Wundererzählung*, 71f; Pesch, 1.421; Guelich, 1.430. Others see it as introducing what follows, e.g. Lightfoot, *History*, 90f; Best, *Disciples*, 3; Johnson, 'Bethsaida'; Gnilka, 1.315. However, there is no reason why 8:22-26 cannot function as a 'hinge' transition, Best, 'Discipleship', 325; Robbins, 'Bartimaeus', 236ff.

[75] See pp. 188-94 and pp. 213-16 above. Chs. 1-12 are ordered around ch. 6 with chs. 1 and 12 as book-ends: the former primarily of judgement and the latter of hope; Ackroyd, 'Presentation', *passim* and 45f; Rendtorff, 'Komposition'.

unjust, corrupt, greedy, intemperate, and violent (e.g. 1:15ff; 5:7-12). Far from being 'holy,' the nation is characterised by sin (e.g. 1:4; 33:14), iniquity (e.g. 1:4; 28:9), evil (e.g. 3:9; 32:7), and transgression (1:2, 28; etc.).

The root of these social and moral evils lies in the fact that the people are inflated with pride and boastful arrogance (2:7f; 3:16ff; 5:21; 9:7ff; 28:1). Yahweh is not only neglected but derided, his purposes and counsel despised, and his law rejected (1:4b; 3:8f; 5:12, 18f, 24b; 8:6; 17:10; 22:11; 28:12; 29:15f; 30:9-13, 15). Having forgotten the God of her salvation (17:10), which ignorance is from the outset coupled with her rebellion (1:2b, 4, 5; cf. 30:1, 13), the nation demonstrates that she neither knows nor understands (1:3, LXX: γιγνώσκω, συνίημι; 5:13a, LXX: εἶδαν), and consequently her religion is effectively mere pretence (1:11-15; 29:13ff).

More importantly we noted that the quintessence of the nation's sin—revolt against Yahweh (1:2; 30:1, 9) and a wilful refusal to recognise, believe, or to have obedient faith (7:9)—was the practice of idolatry (1:29f; 2:6, 8 (cf. vv. 18, 20); 10:10f; cf. 17:8; 27:9b; 30:22; 31:7; cf. witchcraft, 3:3b; 8:19; 17:8, 10; cf. 2:6). This comes fully into focus in Ahaz' persistent refusal to accept Yahweh's offer of salvation, preferring instead his own political machinations (chs. 7-8; cf. chs. 28-33). We then argued that the blinding and deafening announced in Isaiah 6 and described in Isaiah 29 and elsewhere was to be understood as Yahweh's ironic judgement on Israel for relying on its own idolatrous wisdom. The people and in particular their leaders were, metaphorically, to be 'recreated' in the image of the lifeless and uncomprehending idols they worshipped. Consequently, Jerusalem's self-reliant wise men would inevitably lead the country toward that very destruction which they so ardently sought to avoid.

(ii) Restoration of Sight: Being Taught by Yahweh
Understood against this background, Isaiah's redemptive promises of restorational seeing and hearing take on greater significance. Irrespective of any physical referent, they too function as metaphors describing the reversal of Yahweh's judicial application of the 'idolators curse', and often do so in the context of the purified remnant returning on the 'way' of Yahweh's wisdom to Jerusalem.[76] In other words, Israel's restoration is described by means of wisdom terminology based on 'seeing' and 'hearing'

---

[76] Cf. e.g. 10:20, and Gerleman, 'Bermerkungen'; von Soden-Wächter, *TWAT*, 5.1190-93. On the remnant motif, Hasel, *Remnant*.

metaphors interweaved with the spatial language of exodus journeying along the 'way' to Zion.

The following examples should suffice. In 30:21f Yahweh is presented as Israel's 'teacher' who will no longer hide himself from his people. Their eyes will see him, they will hear a voice directing them in הַדֶּרֶךְ they should go, and they will cast away their idols.[77] That 29:18's depiction of the restoration of sight and hearing should also be understood along these lines is suggested by verse 24 which promises that those who err in mind will know the truth and those who criticise will accept instruction (cf. 29:9-16; 28:9-14).[78] A similar conjunction also occurs in 32:3 where the cessation of judicial blinding is paralleled by a description of its consequences such that the hasty will discern truth. This is then followed by a homily on the contrast between the fool and the noble man (vv. 4-8; cf. *Tg. Isa ad loc*). Chapter 35, Isaiah 1-39's most expansive account of a New Exodus reversal of Isaiah's judgement commissioning, links restoration of sight to the blind and hearing to the deaf with a description of the holy way (vv. 8-10; cf. 6:3)[79] upon which neither the unclean nor fools will walk (v. 6) and which leads to Zion.[80]

From this it is evident that 'way' terminology has both spatial and sapiential connotations (cf. also *Tg. Isa* 35:1-10). This dual emphasis might be the point of the author's using both דֶּרֶךְ and מַסְלוּל in 35:8 where the latter seems specifically to refer to a prepared highway perhaps leading to the locus of Yahweh's presence, namely the Temple,[81] while the former is elsewhere used in sapiential contexts, for example, 8:11; 30:11, 21.[82] The sapiential dimension of the nation's restoration can also be seen in the emphasis on Yahweh's counsel and wisdom in the depictions of the future

---

[77] Kaiser; Clements and Wildberger render מוֹרֶיךָ in the singular. On the wisdom associations, espec. Jensen, *Use*, 131ff; Watts, *Isaiah*, 1.398f.

[78] Clements, 'Beyond', 104, notes the connection of gloom and darkness with 8:23, 'thereby linking this imagery with that of blindness'; light/darkness is widely used for prosperity/disaster, Hempel, 'Licht'. On the wisdom influence in 29:16ff, Whedbee, *Isaiah*, 73-75, 130-31.

[79] Kaiser, 2.365, sees the way as leading to the Temple; Roberts, 'Isaiah', 312ff, regards Yahweh's holiness as the locus of his dealings with his people, cf. 4:3; 6:13; 29:23.

[80] On a sapiential understanding, Kaiser, 1.364; Wildberger, 2.1362. Clements, 125, sees the imagery of deafness and blindness here in a literal and not metaphorical sense, but seems to equivocate in 'Unity'.

[81] Bergmann, Haldar, Ringgren, Koch, *TDOT*, 3.278.

[82] On the difficulties in distinguishing the various semantic fields of 'way' terminology, Bergmann, *et al*, *ibid.*, 271f, 276f; Michaelis, *TDNT*, 5.49ff.

idealised Davidic prince. In contrast to the nation's present corrupt rulers, רוּחַ יהוה will rest upon him granting wisdom, knowledge, counsel, strength, knowledge, and the fear of Yahweh (11:2ff).[83] Likewise, accounts of restored Zion in which Yahweh's presence dwells present Yahweh residing there as teacher of Israel and the nations (2:3f; cf. 33:6).

From this perspective, the 'way' of the NE is not only the 'way' of the returning exiles to Jerusalem but is also a matter of rejecting the idolatrous wisdom of the past and embracing Yahweh's teaching. Similarly, whether understood in physical terms or not, the blind 'seeing', the deaf 'hearing', and the 'lame' walking upon the 'way' of holiness which leads to the place of Yahweh's presence, Zion, should also at least be seen as metaphors for the attaining of that wisdom which signals fidelity to Yahweh and therefore the return to his presence.[84]

(iii) Leading the Blind in the INE

Moving into Isaiah 40-55, it is noteworthy that blindness and deafness terminology reappears throughout[85] in descriptions of captive Jacob-Israel.[86] Not only is the language associated with anti-idol polemics (espec.

---

[83] Cf. Whedbee, *Isaiah*, 145; Jensen, *Use*, 124-30; Koch, 'Gottesgeist', 250ff; Roberts, 'Divine'.

[84] Put in these terms, it may be that the Exodus pattern derives in part from a perception that it represents a reversal of the paradigmatic expulsion from Eden (it is noteworthy that Isaiah 40-55 regards the NE as a new creation, see Chapter 6, p. 155, fn. 92 above). Just as rejection of Yahweh as the wise King results in being driven away from the presence, so now acquiescence to his wisdom characterises the return.

[85] On the influence of wisdom terminology in chapters 40-55, e.g. von Waldow, *Hintergrund*, 47ff; 'Message', 270, where the prophet functions 'like a wisdom teacher'; McKane, *Prophets*, 81-85, 94-97; Melugin, *Formation*, 31ff, who discusses the disputations in terms of Wisdom genre; Whybray, *Counsellor*; Ward, 'Knowledge'; and Terrien, 'Quelques', who argues that it was the wisdom poem Job that 'introduced the motif of creation into the very heart of the existential struggle. Deutero-Isaiah took this theme and applied it to his interpretation of Israel's mission in history' (310).

[86] Watts, 'Consolation', 41-49. The term 'Jacob-Israel' reflects the Jacob-Israel parallelism frequently found in Isaiah 40-55 (e.g. 40:27; 41:8; 41:14f, 20f; 42:24; 43:1, etc.) and is here used to distinguish between Israel *per se* and the 'servant' figure portrayed in the so-called 'Servant Songs', see 'Consolation', 35. While e.g. Juel, *Messianic*, 125, rightly rejects the idea that contemporary Jewish exegesis presupposed a unified approach to the 'Songs', he notes that this does not rule out the possibility that early Christians linked elements of the 'servant' texts—just as some editions of *Tg. Isa* identified the 'servant' in Isa 42 and parts of Isa 53 with the Messiah (Chapter 3, p. 115, fn. 127)—but on the basis of a different messianic conception, *ibid.*, 131. Thus e.g. Luke applies elements from the various 'songs' to Jesus, i.e. Isa 42:1; 49:6; and 53:12; Bock, *Proclamation*, 85f, 104, 137-39. But if others could make the connection—and note here later Jewish notions of vicarious messianic suffering, possibly on the basis of the career of Simon bar Kokhba, cf. Vermes, *Jesus*, 139, *b. Sukk.* 52a; Segal, *Children*, 64-67, 86; cited in *ibid.*, 127—why not Jesus, especially if he saw himself

44:9-20),[87] but it is linked with Yahweh's complaints concerning Jacob-Israel's consistent lack of understanding and unwillingness either to obey his תּוֹרָה or to walk בִּדְרָכָיו (e.g. 42:18-25, note v. 17!; 43:8; 48:8, 18-20).[88]

Perhaps even more striking, given the usually positive construction given to these chapters, is the stridently polemical use of blind and deaf metaphors in the disputations. Comprising the nexus of Yahweh's altercation with his people, these centre on their refusal to accept Yahweh's 'anointed' deliverer, namely Cyrus.[89] Once again the matter at issue is Israel's criticism of Yahweh's wisdom as it relates to his means of effecting salvation and deliverance for his people (cf. Isa 7-8, 30f).

As I have suggested elsewhere, this implies that the prophet regards the exile, by and large, as having changed nothing.[90] The people are as blind and deaf as before. They continue to insist on dictating to Yahweh how and when he ought to save them. This it would appear explains why the post-exilic community is still described as those who 'grope for a wall like the blind, like those who have no eyes' (59:9-10). That this last expression is also to be understood within the same 'wisdom' framework is evident

in messianic terms and, in the light of the implied suffering of Dn 7's SoM, integrated the 'servant's' suffering into his messianic self-understanding? Much depends, therefore, on the validity of e.g. Hooker's arguments, *Servant*, that Jesus did not appeal to Isa 53 when describing his sufferings—but on this see below—although Dodd's suggestion, *According*, 109f, that the seminal impetus lies with the individual genius of Jesus seems to me to make better historical sense. Similarly, if certain Isaianic 'servant' activities could be attributed to a single figure (e.g. the Messiah in *Tg. Isa* and *1 Enoch*, see VanderKam, 'Righteous') then it is not a large step to reflect on the 'servant' as a unified figure in his own right. On the other hand, the ambiguity of his identification might have created difficulties, no less then as today. In arguing his case Juel also presumes that the early Christians necessarily engaged in what is held to be the characteristically atomistic exegesis of first century Judaism. However, this commonly held estimation of first century exegetical technique has been questioned, both with regard to the rabbis (see Instone-Brewer, *Techniques*) and the NT (see the various essays in Beale, ed., *Doctrine*).

[87] On these passages, Watts, 'Consolation', 36, 38. Merrill, 'Language', has cited examples of elaborate Babylonian rites in which the eyes and ears etc. of the idols are opened by their worshippers. In a conversation he pointed out the irony of idolators 'opening' the eyes of their gods' representative forms while Yahweh has to open the eyes of his representatives, Israel, cf. Isa 42:18-20; 43:8-13.

[88] 'Ways' meaning a broader conception of תורה, cf. 42:21, 24c; Chapter 7, p. 192, fn. 44.

[89] Watts, 'Consolation', 41-49. For Clements, 'Unity,' 125, blindness, deafness, and lack of understanding are allusions to Isa 6:9f's prophetic commission, where the 'entire period of Israel's subjugation to the Mesopotamian powers (is viewed) as a one of national blindness and deafness' and 'the theme of Israel's blindness and deafness ... appeared ... as a very striking feature of the prophetic explanation for the catastrophes which had overtaken Israel'. In 'Beyond', 102, he states: 'the theme of Israel's blindness and deafness, understood in a metaphorical sense, is clearly of central importance to Is. 40-55'.

[90] Watts, 'Consolation', 47-49; cf. Ward, 'Knowledge', 127f.

in the final lament where, in language reminiscent of 6:9f, 63:17 asks 'why do you cause us to wander from your ways and harden our hearts so that we do not fear you?' The appearance, therefore, of 'blindness' and 'sight' terminology in conjunction with the NE דֶּרֶךְ in 40-55 also implies, as in 1-39, a sapiential aspect to the deliverance.[91]

Given the overarching theme of the wisdom debate with its 'way' of wisdom motif, Isaiah 42:16 is of particular interest. Here Yahweh announces that he will, nevertheless, lead the blind בְּדֶרֶךְ לֹא יָדָעוּ (cf. 50:10f which contrasts those who hear the word of Yahweh's servant and yet are in darkness with those who seek independently to establish their own 'light' by which to walk[92]). The passage is a proclamation of salvation which in responding to a communal lament declares that although Yahweh had been silent he is now going to act on behalf of his people.[93]

However, there is some debate over the significance of the blindness imagery which has been variously interpreted as referring to the exile,[94] to travellers who cannot see the path,[95] to hopelessness,[96] or to the lack of perception of Yahweh's plans.[97] Those who reject the fourth alternative usually do so on the basis of there being no mention of unbelief, but several lines of evidence suggest that it is to be preferred.

First, as we have seen, 'blindness' and 'deafness' language consistently bears sapiential/religious connotations throughout Isaiah and is one of the unifying themes of chapters 1-39 and 40-55. Second, the form and content of the summary statement (42:16c-17) derive from wisdom literature which implies that a sapiential context is intended.[98] Third, there is the otherwise unexpected censure of those who trust in idols (v. 17) which, considering 1-39 and the anti-idol polemics throughout 40-48, suggests that the 'unknown way' of Yahweh is to be contrasted to the 'known way' of

---

[91] Cf. Stuhlmueller, *Creative*, 67, 'In Dt-Is' understanding of *derek* ... past and present overlap, morality and geography commingle'. Again דֶּרֶךְ is used as idiom: in parallel to אֹרַח for understanding in 40:14; of the way of Yahweh's תּוֹרָה (42:24; 48:17; 55:8f); and of the lifestyle of sinners who reject that תּוֹרָה (53:6; 55:7, 8f). Also Muilenburg, 495.

[92] See e.g. Westermann, but with v. 11 being understood as a picture of those who seek to overcome the darkness by dint of their own effort, the LXX's τῷ φωτὶ being a paraphrastic rendering.

[93] Melugin, *Formation*, 102f; Westermann; Schoors, *Saviour*, 90f.

[94] Fischer; Whybray; Schoors, *Saviour*, 92; Elliger.

[95] Skinner; Kissane.

[96] Calvin; Cheyne; McKenzie; Westermann.

[97] Delitzsch; Leupold; North; Smart; Young; cf. Muilenburg.

[98] Melugin, *ibid.*; cf. Childs, *Assyrian*, 128-36; Whedbee, *Isaiah*, 75-79; North.

the idols.[99]   Fourth, in the immediately succeeding verses Jacob-Israel's captivity is attributed to a blindness that is unequivocally related to a refusal to walk in the ways/תּוֹרָה of the Lord (42:18-25). Finally, the Hiphil of דרך (cf. אַדְרִיכֵם in v. 16b) occurs only in one other place in 40-55 and there it describes Yahweh's role as teacher (48:17).[100]

Taken together, these themes are consistent with those found in the wisdom debates of chapters 1-39. Consequently, when placed in the context of chapters 40-55, the phrases בְּדֶרֶךְ לֹא יָדָעוּ and בִּנְתִיבוֹת לֹא־יָדְעוּ (42:16) seem best interpreted as the unexpected means by which Yahweh in his wise counsels has determined for the NE to be accomplished, namely, his scandalous election of a pagan, Cyrus, to be Israel's deliverer. Israel is 'blind' and does not 'know' this 'way' because by and large she refuses to accept Yahweh's wisdom as expressed in his choice of Cyrus.[101]

This sapiential concern is further stressed in the purpose of the NE which is so that Yahweh's people יִרְאוּ וְיֵדְעוּ וְיָשִׂימוּ וְיַשְׂכִּילוּ that it is he alone, not the idols, who delivers (41:20; cf. 43:10; 49:23; Ex 6:5-7).[102] Likewise, the restoration is characterised as a time when Jerusalem's numerous children will be taught by the Lord (54:3, 13; cf. 48:17-19). The continuation of the wisdom theme might also be the point of the chapter 55 which bears remarkable similarities to the speech of Dame Wisdom in Proverbs.[103] Here at the conclusion of 40-55 an invitation is made to enter into life by accepting instruction in accordance with Yahweh's wisdom.

Once again a similar understanding is evident in some of the interpretive traditions contained in *Tg. Isaiah* where, for example, in 42:18 those who are deaf and blind are explicitly described as being רשיעיא (wicked) and חייביא (ungodly/sinners) with either judgement or potential blessings being couched in terms of either rejecting or observing the law (vv. 14, 21, and 24). Likewise, 'deafness' in 48:8 means rejecting the instruction of the law, while 55:1ff is couched in terms of learning and

---

[99] Westermann's contention, 109, that blindness is not a sin, fails to take into account both the origins of this condition and the severity of Yahweh's response to it, cf. 48:1-8. On anti-idol polemics: Chapter 6, p. 141, fnn. 23, 24, above; Watts, 'Consolation', 36-38, 44.

[100] Elliger.

[101] Watts, 'Consolation', 41ff; cf. the literature cited in fn. 97.

[102] That Israel might 'know Yahweh' is one of the major themes of Exodus: Ex 6:6f; 10:2; 16:12 (cf. v. 6); 29:46; 31:13.

[103] Begrich, *Studien*, 59-61; Melugin, *Formation*, 25; and Clifford, *Persuading*, 190ff, see here an imitation of Wisdom Genre cf. the summons to life: Prov 3:13-18; 4:22; 8:35; 9:6ff; Sir 4:12; to eat and drink: Prov 9:2, 5; Sir 1:17; 15:3; 24:19, 21).

attending diligently to Yahweh's *Memra*. The same perspective is also evident in the Qumran community's self-defining document, 1QS, where to prepare Isaiah 40:3's 'way of the Lord' (1QS 8:12b-16a; 9:17b-20a) means to study Torah (8:15; 9:9bf) and to 'walk' תמים בכול דרכיו (2:2; see also 1:12f; 3:9bff; 5:7b-11; 9:17f; and the 'way' language *infra*).[104] According to CD 1:9ff, the members of the community were כעורים וכימגששים דרך (cf. Isa 59:10; see also 2:2-6, 14-16; etc.) but now they are exhorted to 'hear' that their eyes might be 'opened' so that they might 'see' and 'know' the works of God and as a result be able להתהלך תמים בכל דרכיו (CD 2:14ff; cf. the use of the language of healing over against blindness in 1QS 4:6b-11a; cf. 4QpHos[a] 1:8; CD 16:1ff). Here, too, the prophetically reconstituted icons of Israel's founding moment are integral to the self-understanding of a Jewish eschatological community.

(iv) Conclusion

The wisdom connotations of 'sight', 'hearing', and 'understanding' suggest that the NE 'way' has more than a merely spatial focus. The language originates in Isaiah's commissioning and reflects Yahweh's judgement on Israel's adherence to idols in preference to his 'wisdom': the idolators will become as blind, deaf, etc., as their inanimate idols. The NE 'way' is thus also a holy 'way', a sapiential 'way' of Yahweh's wisdom wherein the restoration of sight and the rejection of idols signifies the rejection of human wisdom and the acceptance of and reliance upon Yahweh's peculiar counsels in bringing about his NE purposes for Israel. They are two sides of the one coin: true holiness entails true wisdom and *vice versa*.

c) The 'Way' in Mark

Given these themes within the setting of the INE, the next question is whether or not a similar theological construct is evident in Mark. We have already argued for the theological significance of Mark's 'Way' section particularly with regard to the motifs of 'journey', discipleship, and the 'restoration of sight'. But what about the 'wisdom debate' over Yahweh's methods of delivering his people, and Yahweh's frustration with the persistent 'blindness' of those whom he has come to deliver? Is there any evidence of Markan counterparts? In a word, yes.

---

[104] See e.g. Leaney, *Rule*, 222f.

(i) 'Blindness' and the Disciples

First, there is clearly a general similarity between Mark and Isaiah (LXX) both in vocabulary (βλέπω, ὁράω, ἀκούω) and in the diversity of terms related to 'understanding' (γιγνώσκω, συνίημι, εἶδον, νοέω). Second, just as Isaiah 6:9 is the *Grundlage* for the imagery of blindness and deafness etc. in Isaiah, so also in Mark the interpretive context for this cluster of terms is his appeal to Isaiah 6:9 in 4:12f where for the first time, βλέπω, ὁράω, ἀκούω, συνίημι, εἶδον, and γινώσκω are found together.[105] This fits well with the suggestion made earlier that the circumstances surrounding Jesus' appeal to Isaiah 6 are consistent with an Isaianic polemic against Jerusalem's wise ones who reject Yahweh's plan for their deliverance. Further support is found in Mark 7, where again in response to the only other challenge by authorities from Jerusalem outside of Mark 11ff Jesus quotes Isaiah 29:13, which as we have seen is particularly important in linking the judicial blindness of Israel's leaders with sapiential concerns.[106] I suggest that the conflict between Jesus and Israel's leaders, given the firm continuity between Isaiah 6 (Mk 4) and the themes of blindness, etc. in Isaiah 40-55, reflects the more extreme response in the Isaianic wisdom debate. The Jersualem authorities have rejected Jesus outright. These 'blind and deaf' leaders, by and large, amply fill the role of those who are unremittingly critical of Yahweh's plan, and especially his choice of agent (cf. Jacob-Israel's response to Cyrus, see above), as he effects the NE.

But what then are we to make of the application of this language to the disciples? Does Mark intend that they, like Israel in the Isaiah (and, presumably, apostate Jews from the more contemporary perspective of Qumran), are idolatrous and under judgement?[107] This might appear so except that this terminology as we have seen is applied not only to Israel under sentence of judgement but also to Israel in exile to whom deliverance has been announced. The fact that Mark's portrayal of the disciples combines not just Isaianic 'wisdom' imagery (Mk 4 etc. in his first section and the two sight miracles), but also 'way' imagery (both in his

---

[105] Lemcio, 'Structure'; Petersen, 'Composition'; Johnson, 'Theme', 227; Beavis, *Audience*, 157ff.

[106] Lemcio, 'Structure', 337f, noting the obduracy motif, suggests the structure of 4:1-20; 7:14-23; and 8:14-21 reflects 'the sort of didactic interchange' experienced by the prophets.

[107] Johnson, 'Blindness', 37, 227, recognises the importance of 4:10ff for the disciples' incomprehension motif but provides no discussion of the Isaianic significance of these terms.

introduction and throughout the second main section), indicates that his focus is on Israel's deliverance. Several data confirm this.[108]

First, just as Israel in Isaiah 42 is rebuked for having seen many things but failing to understand, so too the disciples (Mk 8:14-21; cf. 4:13; 6:52; 7:18). Given our interpretation of the relationship between the demons and the nations' idols, and especially in the light of the latter's role in Isaiah's wisdom debates, Jesus' rebuke of Peter—"Υπαγε ὀπίσω μου, Σατανᾶ—may in one sense be seen as analogous to Yahweh's rebuke of exiled Israel's adherence to idolatrous wisdom.[109] Second, Israel's rebuke is yet on the threshold of Yahweh's proffered deliverance; salvation is still available for those who would follow. Likewise, Mark places Jesus' rebuke immediately preceding his 'Way' section.[110] Third, a characteristic of the INE is that Yahweh will lead the blind along a path they do not know (provided, of course, they are willing)—which imagery we have argued refers to the unexpected nature of Yahweh's plan for deliverance. And,

---

[108] See now also Marcus, 34f.

[109] Cf. Danker, 'Demonic', 63. Osborne, 'Stumbling-Block', notes Qumran's belief that thoughts opposed to God's 'way' were understood as coming from Satan. In what sense, however, is it appropriate to speak of an 'idolatrous way of thinking' and is there any evidence for such a metaphorical usage? In e.g. 1QS 4:11; 1QH 4:19; CD 2:14f; CD 16:2f; CD 2:16f the language of stubbornness of heart, blindness, deafness, and going astray, is contrasted with that of seeing, understanding, and walking in the 'way'. Of particular interest is the expression בשרירות לב which appears in the curse pronounced over the false member of the community who blesses himself while he continues to walk in the stubbornness of his heart, 1QS 2:14, cf. Dt 29:19. This duplicity is attributed to his having entered the community along with 'the idols of his heart' (בגלולי לבו, 1.11), the idols being those things which cause him to fall into iniquity, cf. CD 20:9; and especially Ezek 14:3-7, Davies, *Damascus*, 184. גלולים, which appears 39 times in Ezekiel (out of 48 in OT), refers to cult objects but with a strong sense of uncleanness (e.g. 16:36, Zimmerli, *Ezekiel*, cf. CD 3:17), itself a major concern at Qumran (e.g. Huppenbauer, 'Sektenregel'). Eichrodt, *Ezekiel*, 180, understands a secret syncretism which, while not countenancing public apostasy from Yahweh, nevertheless adopted 'the prevailing pagan attitude of mind' combining 'a recognition of Yahweh's lordship with recourse to subordinate powers'; cf. Schoneveld, 'Ezekiel', who sees the wearing of amulets. However, Greenberg, *Ezekiel*, rejects syncretism as he can find no reason for the prophet's silence until this point, noting instead that the elders apparently esteem themselves worthy of Yahweh's attention. Greenberg suggests that the real sin is their assumption that all is well between themselves and Yahweh without having resolved those issues that caused the exile in the first place: 'The "idols" in the people's thoughts ... must be a rubric for an unregenerate state of mind', 253. In any case it is inconceivable that members of the monastic brotherhood (the provenance of 1QS if not CD) could have secretly worn amulets or practiced syncretism. What appears to be indicated is an idolatrous attitude also described as stubbornness of heart which along with blindness and deafness are characteristics of those who reject the 'Way'.

[110] Cf. Ambrozic's criticism, 69, of Jeremias, *Parables*, 15, noting that the damning conclusion of 4:12 is missing from 8:18; cf. Marcus, *Mystery*, 101; Burkill, 'Blasphemy', 65.

just as Yahweh takes the initiative by leading the blind in Isaiah, so also in Mark the initiative lies with Jesus in his call to follow.[111]

It seems significant, then, that Mark places his only two 'sight' miracles at the beginning and end of his 'Way' section, along which 'Way' Jesus will lead his disciples.[112] As several scholars have argued, the sight miracles seem to highlight the sapiential (Best: 'spiritual') aspects of the journey. In Mark's case, the major 'wisdom' issue, judging by the carefully structured placement of the three passion predictions, is the extraordinary lesson that Israel's Messiah (and S/son of God) must suffer.[113] That this is Mark's central concern is supported by his placement of the first passion prediction, and Peter's rejection of the same, immediately following his confession at the opening of the 'Way' section while the last immediately precedes Bartimaeus' confession at its conclusion.[114]

(ii) Healing of Sight and the Way of the Cross

Given the foregoing, it appears that Mark intends the sapiential-spatial journey of the INE to be the hermeneutical horizon for his 'Way'. What Yahweh had promised to do for 'blind' and 'deaf' Israel, leading them along a path they did not know, Jesus does for his disciples. They are his true family (and faithful Israel, 3:13-19, 21, 31-35). But even though given the mystery of the kingdom (4:11) they fail to understand the nature of the 'path' that Yahweh's wisdom has planned (as is evident in their responses to the passion predictions, 8:32-33; 9:32; 10:35-41). Nevertheless, Jesus leads them along the INE 'way' which they too 'do not know'. And again, the central point for Mark is that the 'way' of the INE, the 'way' of Yahweh's wise deliverance, revolves around the death of his messianic S/son.[115]

---

[111] Best, 'Discipleship', 327; Focant, 'L'incompréhension', 185; Maloney, 'Vocation'; cf. Schweizer, 'Portrayal'; Hawkin, 'Incomprehension', 493. For a helpful discussion on the reconciliation of the disciples' continued failure to see after 20:45, Best, *Following*, 136f.

[112] On the literary and thematic integrity of this section, see Chapter 4, pp. 124-32.

[113] E.g. Strecker, 'Passion'; Best, 'Discipleship', 325ff; Perrin, '*Gattung*'; Reedy, 'Ending'; Kingsbury, 89f.

[114] Strecker's criticism, 'Passion', 438n49, of Lightfoot, *History*, 90f, and Burkill, 150, that 8:27ff cannot anticipate Peter's confession because 'one does not hear about the elimination of the "blindness" of the disciples' is only partially correct. To see Jesus as Messiah constitutes a partial healing, but the disciples are still blind as to Yahweh's plan for the NE. In denying a distinction between the disciples' misunderstanding before and after 8:27ff, Strecker, 439n50, as does Johnson, 'Bethsaida', 382, fails to appreciate the significance of the loaves.

[115] Cf. the 'suffering' of Isa 53 as the means by which the INE is effected; see below, and the literature cited earlier in Chapter 4, p. 115, fn. 135.

In view of the above, one final comment is warranted on the relationship between the two sight miracles and Mark's 'Way' section. A number of commentators recognise that the two-stage healing which begins the section indicates that Peter's confession needs the additional insight that the Messiah must die. This raises the question of the significance of Bartimaeus' healing. For Ernest Best, 'after full instruction, we have' in Bartimaeus 'the healing of a blind man who immediately follows Jesus "on the way", i.e. he is regarded as a true disciple'.[116] However, Best is aware that the disciples themselves fail to act as 'true disciples', even after instruction while on the 'Way', and therefore appears to suggest that Bartimaeus symbolises what ought to happen.[117]

But how so? Not only does Bartimaeus promptly disappear from the story, but it is not obvious that his following 'on the way' implies that he understands or even knows of Jesus' death—the disciples who most of all follow 'on the way' clearly do not and there is nothing in the narrative that suggests Bartimaeus is any different.[118] On the contrary, he only recognises Jesus as the 'Son of David' and, as Best admits, his confession comes 'while he is blind, just as Peter used "Christ" at the time when he could not see properly'.[119] Bartimaeus is no more a 'true disciple' than Peter: both 'blind' men have made imperfect confessions and even though both follow in the 'way' there is nothing in the text to suggest that either have grasped the truth that the Messiah must die or its significance.

The key, therefore, seems not to lie in the role of Bartimaeus as a model disciple but instead in Mark's editorial purposes in linking the healings of sight with the INE 'way' as the 'Way' of the suffering Messiah. Given Mark's apparent evocation of the Isaianic way/wisdom framework and his emphasis on the disciples' blindness, etc., it would appear that the two sight miracles are there to inform the reader of the true significance of his 'Way' section: it is all about understanding the 'way' of Yahweh's INE wisdom. Consequently, as many have recognised, the first, 'two-stage'

---

[116] *Following*, 136; cf. Robbins, 'Bartimaeus', 226. As the 'healing' is Aorist and the 'following' Imperfect, it might be that the emphasis lies on the act of 'following', although the difference in tenses might simply reflect the comparative temporality of the actions.

[117] *Ibid.*, 136; cf. Johnson, 'Bartimaeus', 198. Gundry, 442, 597, places considerable emphasis on the disciples' failure.

[118] Cf. Lane, 389; Kingsbury, 104f. *Pace*, Schenke, *Wundererzählungen*, 368, although he correctly interprets the Markan symbolism.

[119] *Ibid.*, 140.

healing signifies the incompleteness of Peter's confession; the deficiency of which is indicated both by Peter's refusal to accept that the Messiah must die and Jesus' pungent response. What follows is a carefully constructed account wherein the subsequent passion predictions reiterate that Jesus the Messiah—now, however, identified in each case as ὁ υἱὸς τοῦ ἀνθρώπου— must die. Only after this has been driven home, do we then find another 'messianic' confession linked with sight. This time, however, sight is restored by one simple command (Mk 10:46ff). Mark's literary point seems clear: the only messianic confession that coincides with Yahweh's wisdom is one predicated on the teaching that the messianic 'Son of Man' must die as a ransom for many. Genuine restoration of sight, and therefore the genuine 'understanding' which is the *sine qua non* of truly journeying on the INE 'way', can only come by accepting that the INE 'way' of Yahweh's redemptive wisdom is expressed in Christ crucified (cf. 1 Cor 1:18-25).[120] Only when understood from this perspective can we then agree with Best 'that Mark views true discipleship with real understanding as a possibility after 10:45'.[121]

d) Jesus and the Isaianic 'Servant'-Teacher

It was argued in Chapter 6 that Jesus' healing and delivering activities are portrayed by Mark in terms applicable not only to the Yahweh-Warrior but also to the Isaianic 'servant'-deliverer who also plays a major role in the NE.[122] In the light of both this and the preceding discussion on the sapiential significance of 'blind-and-deaf' terminology and of Mark's sight miracles for his 'Way' section the possibility of correspondences between Jesus as teacher and the apparent teaching role of the Isaianic 'servant' warrant brief examination.

The enigmatic 'servant' figure in Isaiah 40-55 is not only instrumental in delivering Jacob-Israel from bondage (e.g. 42:1ff; see Chapter 6) but also opens the eyes of the blind (42:7; 49:6; cf. also 61:1f).[123] In contrast to the 'deafness' of Jacob-Israel (ἠνοιγμένα τὰ ὦτα, καὶ οὐκ ἠκούσατε, 42:20 LXX; cf. 48:6-8 LXX), the 'servant' is described in 50:4 as having ὠτίον ἀκούειν. In

---

[120] Cf. Johnson, 'Bartimaeus', 197. Perhaps Jesus' question in 10:18 is to show the inadequacy of the διδάσκαλε ἀγαθέ confession as a prerequisite to discipleship (10:17-22).

[121] *Ibid.*, 136.

[122] Cf. Chapter 6, pp. 142-43; and also Chapter 4, pp. 114-18, on Isa 42:1 in Mark's prologue.

[123] Watts, 'Consolation', 50-56.

view of the sapiential connotations of both 'sight' and 'hearing' imagery throughout, we may be justified in seeing here a teaching or instructional role for the 'servant' (50:4f, 10; cf. 30:21; 32:3; 33:5).[124]

Although a notoriously problematic text, Isaiah 53:11 might also refer to the 'salvific' knowledge of the 'servant'.[125] A. Gelston has recently argued that בדעתו cannot mean 'knowledge' primarily on the grounds that it does not fit the immediate context.[126] On the other hand, the united testimony of the LXX and the later Greek versions, the Peshitta, and *Tg. Isaiah*, all of which understand something along the lines of 'knowledge,' suggests that this option ought not be dismissed too quickly. Given that the suffix is almost certainly subjective then we have something like 'his knowledge', but does it go with what precedes or what follows? Since we are dealing with poetry it is perhaps not surprising that there is some ambiguity, and perhaps even intentionally so.

Taking בדעתו with what precedes, one could translate 'he will be satisfied with/by/in his knowledge'. Contextually, granted there is no immediate indication of the nature of this knowledge, it is not impossible that the most recent speech of the 'servant' which concerns his teaching role (50:4-9) is in view. If so, then the idea might well be that the 'servant' will be satisfied (יִשְׂבָּע) 'in' his knowledge of Yahweh's promised vindication (cf. 50:7-9; and Ps 16:7-11).[127] This coheres well with 'he will see light' (53:11a; following 1QIs[a], 1QIs[b], and LXX),[128] not least in view of the salvific and sapiential connotations of the imagery (cf. 50:10-11). In other words, the 'servant' has earlier castigated those who seek to provide their own light, warning them of their impending 'discontent' (מַעֲצֵבָה;

---

[124] E.g. Westermann, 228f, 234f. As noted earlier, an invitation to hear is found in what appears to be a 'Dame Wisdom' speech which concludes 40-55, i.e. 55:1-3; see further the literature cited in fn. 103 above.

[125] In part the issue in 53:11 turns around A) the meaning of בדעתו (which can no longer be understood as 'humiliation'; cf. Johnstone, '*YD*''), B) whether it is to be taken with what precedes or what follows, and C) whether the suffix is objective or subjective. See the discussion and literature cited in Gelston, 'Knowledge'.

[126] 'Knowledge', 134f.

[127] Psalm 16:7-11 expresses a similar conjunction of trusting in Yahweh's word of instruction and a confidence in the face of threatening death which leads to שֹׂבַע שְׂמָחוֹת. See Kraus, *Psalms 1-59, ad loc*; Craigie, *Psalms 1-50, ad loc*.

[128] The MT also makes sense on this basis. Whereas he earlier walked in darkness and had no light (50:10b), now, as a result of his obedience, 'his soul will see' (53:11: נַפְשׁוֹ יִרְאֶה; note the use of the verb without direct object in 6:10; 29:18; cf. 30:10; 49:7; 60:5).

50:11). He, however, 'knows' (cf. v. 7; אָדַע) that although he walks in darkness, he will yet, as one who trusts in Yahweh, see light (50:10).

The expression in 53:11b seems to describe, in contrast to the disconsolate reprobates of 50:11c, the full vindication ('satisfaction') of the 'servant' in his reliance on, and adherence to, Yahweh's wisdom.[129] This is perhaps why the 'fourth' song opens with sapiential and reversal themes (52:15b; 53:1: those who thought they understood, do not, etc.). Not only are they entirely congruent with Isaiah's 'wisdom debate' as a whole, but also with the distillation of this issue as reflected in the life of the 'servant'.

On the other hand, if בדעתו is taken with what follows, then we have something like 'by his knowledge my (righteous?) servant shall justify many'. Chapters 40-48 earlier focussed on the debate over Yahweh's ability to save Israel, his concern for them, and the wisdom of his choices. If this context is borne in mind, then, in contrast to the failure of servant Jacob-Israel, the faithful 'servant' through his obedience to and proclamation of Yahweh's instruction becomes Yahweh's ultimate agent of deliverance, not only for Jacob-Israel but also for the nations (49:6).[130]

In sum, whereas the first alternative focuses on the impact of Yahweh's wisdom on the 'servant' himself, namely his vindication, the second deals with the consequences of his faithful adherence to Yahweh's word for Jacob-Israel and the nations, that is, they will be 'justified'. Either approach makes good sense, and it is not unlikely given the poetic nature of the material that the reader is invited to see both meanings here.[131]

This conception of the 'servant' as a teacher is supported by the expansionistic renderings of *Tg. Isaiah* where in 42:7 it understands 'blindness' as blindness to the law (כסמן מן אוריתא), while the deafness in v. 20 is a refusal to hear instruction, קבילתון אלפן (cf. v. 24). Furthermore, 50:4 is interpreted as referring to the ability to teach wisdom to the righteous and to open sinners' ears to instruction. Similarly, in 53:11 it is through his wisdom that the 'servant' justifies 'the just so that many might be subject

---

[129] On this theme in the 'songs' see Beuken, 'MIŠPĀṬ'; Ward, 'Knowledge'.

[130] Although Cyrus initiates the process the full promises of the return are now predicated on the action of the 'servant', Watts, 'Consolation', 54-57.

[131] See e.g. the helpful comments in Ward, 'Knowledge', 131. One might note that this sort of ambiguity is not only one of the hallmarks of the lyrics of modern poets but adds to their appeal, e.g. the work of T. S. Eliot and more recently Bob Dylan.

to Torah'. Likewise, Qumran's programmatic and self-definitional statements in 1QS 8:13-16 and 9:16-21 also interpret 'making straight the way' of
Isaiah 40:3 as fulfilled in their study of Torah (8:15; 9:17) in the desert.
Here, too, there is a confluence of the spatial and the sapiential. It is
intriguing, given the Isaianic colouring of the community's self-understanding,[132] that this teaching is largely under the guidance of their
esteemed 'Teacher of Righteousness' who is recorded as describing himself
in terms reminiscent of, among other OT figures, the 'servant' of Isaiah (in
addition to the frequent use of 'servant', see especially 1QH 15:10; 16:36; [cf.
Isa 50:4]; 17:29-31; [cf. Isa 49:1]; and also 23:14f; [cf. Isa 61:1f]).[133]

Given this 'wisdom' dimension, Mark's interest in Jesus as teacher
might take on greater significance.[134] We have already seen that not only
are promises of instruction characteristic of the NE but in Isaiah 42:1-9, a
passage already of importance for Mark in identifying Jesus (1:11), it is the
task of the Spirit-endowed 'servant' figure to bring liberation *and* sight,
that is, understanding of Yahweh's wisdom.[135] With this in mind, several
points can be noted. First, a similar dual delivering-teaching role is
highlighted by R. T. France when he comments on 'the striking and
emphatic use of διδαχή in Mark 1:22, 27 in the context of an exorcism'—an
exorcism which he too has seen as 'programmatic for Jesus' ministry'—
and then concludes that, for Mark, Jesus' teaching and action contribute
'together to the fulfilment of his messianic role'.[136] Second, in Mark 4, a
chapter which we have already argued is heavily indebted to Isaianic
'wisdom' language, Jesus' repeated summons—῟Ος ἔχει ὦτα ἀκούειν
ἀκουέτω (vv. 9, 23; cf. v. 24)—and the preponderance of 'hearing' terminology (4:3, 12, 15, 16, 18, 20, 33) coheres perfectly with an Isaianic 'servant'
paradigm (espec. e.g. Isa 50:4). Third, not only does Mark 4 provide the

---

[132] Starkova, 'Importance', and literature cited previously in Chapter 3, p. 82, fn. 157.

[133] See further, Dupont-Sommer, *Writings*, 358-67; Kittel, *Hymns*, 130, 136; Ringgren,
Faith, 196ff.

[134] Evans, *Beginning*, 43-61; Martin, 113; France, 'Teaching'; cf. Riesner, *Lehrer*;
Robbins, *Teacher*; Baarlink, *Anfängliches*, 148-74; Achtemeier, 'Reflections'; Hooker,
'Mark'; Piper, 'Unchanging', 19.

[135] On the expectation of the Messiah as teacher, particularly in Isaianic terms,
Riesner, *Lehrer*, 304-44 (although he does not appear to deal with the wisdom connotations
of 'blindness' and 'sight' terminology); on Isa 11 Jensen, *Use*, 124ff. On the wisdom element
in Jesus' message, Hengel, *Charismatic*, 45ff.

[136] 'Teaching', 107, 110f; cf. Kee, *Miracle*, 161; Koch, *Bedeutung*, 42-45; Egger,
Frohbotschaft, 165ff; and Chapter 6, pp. 154ff, above.

basis for Jesus' subsequent use of sapiential language but it also follows hard on the heels of Jesus' redefinition both of his true family and, since he is S/son of God, also of Israel (3:20-35).

In the light of Mark's prologue and especially Jesus' programmatic announcement of Yahweh's INE coming (1:14f), these data suggest that reconstituted Israel's participation in the INE is dependent on hearing Jesus' teaching (4:9, 23; and 3:34f). It is possible, then, that we have here an echo of the 'servant' inviting 'deaf' Jacob-Israel to hear and respond (cf. Isa 42:20). It is noteworthy that in both Qumran and *Tg. Isaiah* the focus of the INE instruction was Torah. In Mark, however, the focus is on Jesus' teaching which implies that, for Mark, it now 'replaces' Torah on centre stage.[137]

The presentation of Jesus as 'deliverer-teacher' is, therefore, particularly apposite if Mark is operating with an INE hermeneutic. This is especially so given the previously discussed motif of the uncomprehending 'blind' disciples and the widespread recognition that in the 'Way' section Jesus narrows his teaching from the crowds at large to focus on his disciples (including the Twelve) who arguably represent the New/Reconstituted Israel (cf. Mk 3:13-19, 31-35).[138] If so, then Mark's 'Way' section would be consistent with an understanding of Jesus as the Isaianic 'servant-deliverer-teacher' who, as Yahweh's agent, leads blind Israel in a NE along a way they do not know.

e) Conclusion

There has been considerable debate over what Mark intends to be understood by his use of ὁδός terminology, usually with emphasis being placed on one or another of several alternatives.[139] From the perspective taken here, Mark's purpose is perhaps best understood as multifaceted. Based on the Isaiah 40:3 imagery to which Mark's opening citation appeals,

---

[137] Cf. Hooker, 'Mark', who addresses this tension between Jesus' teaching and Torah.

[138] See briefly Chapter 4 , pp. 128ff, and Chapter 7, p. 195, fn. 56, above.

[139] See Marcus' analysis, 29-45, of the meaning of Mark's 'Way' sets out the differences in perspective between Snodgrass, 'Streams'; Swartley, 'Function'; and Kelber, 'Kingdom'; on the one side, and that of Lohmeyer, *Markus*, on the other. He agrees with Lohmeyer that the main emphasis is on Yahweh's saving action and only secondarily on human response. While not denying for Mark the ontologically prior status of Yahweh's action, there seems no reason why this should necessarily relegate the need for human response to secondary importance. That is, since Yahweh has acted through the INE 'Way' of the cross, it is now incumbent on all to accept his wisdom and in so doing themselves participate in its fulfilment.

his 'Way' seems clearly to be the 'way' of Yahweh's INE coming. In addition, however, the sapiential connotations of Mark's language suggest that his 'Way' serves to show that true participation in the INE entails acceptance of Yahweh's wisdom, namely, that the Messiah, S/son of God, must go the 'way' of the cross. Furthermore, given the prominence of Isaianic wisdom language in Mark, it is hardly surprising that his INE 'way' of Jesus is likewise a journey of instruction.

More generally, the above assessment suggests that Mark's 'Way-journey' motif coincides with (and might thus inform) that early and particularised conception of the Christian life which described itself as 'The Way' (e.g. Acts 9:2; 19:23; cf. *Bar.* 18-20; *Did.* 1-5; also περιπατέω in e.g. Gal 5:16; Rom 6:4; and Eph 5:15). It thus shares a similar cultural milieu not only with Qumran's Isaianic 'spatial-sapiential' self-conception in particular (e.g. 1QS 8:13-16; 9:16-21) but also more broadly with the absolute use of 'way' terminology in Judaism at large (e.g. 1QS 3:9 - 4:26; *Jub.* 23:20f) through which it traces its roots to the OT.[140]

III. Jesus: 'Suffering Servant' and Son of David?

a) Introduction

In the discussion of the prologue we argued that the voice from heaven contained allusions to Psalm 2 and Isaiah 42 which indicated that for Mark Jesus was to be understood in terms of the Isaianic 'servant' and David's messianic son. Similarly, Mark's editorial use of Isaiah 40:3—given its larger ideological and intertextual connotations—might also be seen to have similar implications. In view of the prologue's introductory function, we would expect these identifications to be echoed throughout Mark's Gospel, and we have argued at numerous points that this is indeed so. In the context of Mark's 'Way' section, this raises two questions: does Mark in 10:45 also understand Jesus in terms of the suffering of the 'servant' figure of Isaiah 53, and does he, as some claim, present Jesus as repudiating Davidic messiahship (10:46-52)?

---

[140] Cf. Bergmann, Haldar, Ringgren, Koch, *TDOT*, 3.291-93; Michaelis, *TDNT*, 5.48-96; Nötscher, *Gotteswege*, 76-96, 100f; Repo, *Weg*; McCasland, '"Way"'; Fitzmyer, 'Christianity'; Swartley, 'Study', 163-90.

b) Jesus and Isaiah's 'Suffering Servant': the INE and Mark 10:45

Several observations have been made throughout on the similarities between Jesus' delivering, healing, and teaching activities and those ascribed to Isaiah's enigmatic 'servant'. It has also been suggested that Isaiah 53, within the literary context of the book's final form, indicates the way in which the NE promises were finally to be realised.[141] Likewise, Jesus' concentration on reorienting his disciples' conception of messiahship appears to parallel Israel's need, in the light of the debate over Yahweh's wisdom, to reconsider her expectations of how her redemption is to occur. Given, then, that many scholars have seen in Mark 10:45—the conclusion of the third and final passion prediction collection (10:32-45)[142] and itself at the climax of the 'Way' section—an allusion to Isaiah 53:10-12,[143] a foray into this well-known minefield seems unavoidable.

In the light of the unified Isaianic presentation which this book is proposing, an allusion to Isaiah 53 would not be surprising. But this is hardly a forgone conclusion and several weighty arguments have been mounted against it.[144] On the other hand, most scholars although recognising the existence of conceptual similarities—how else would the debate have arisen?—tend to approach the question by means of detailed linguistic studies and seem ultimately to base their decision on the existence or otherwise of exact and one-for-one correspondences between words in Mark and words in Isaiah.[145] Granted the validity of this method, some caveats are in order, not least because of Mark's *modus operandi* elsewhere.

---

[141] Again see Chapter 4, p. 115, fn. 135, above.

[142] A prediction (vv. 33-34), misunderstanding (vv. 35-41), and teaching (vv. 42-45); Perrin, 'Gattung', 6.

[143] The literature is immense. However, in addition to the works cited *infra* see e.g. Pesch 2.163f; Trocmé, 157; Taylor, 445f; Cranfield, 342; Tödt, *Son*, 200ff; Haenchen, 369; Schweizer, 219; Lane, 383f; Kee, 135; Gnilka, 1.104; Ernst, 310; Lindars, *Son*, 78; also Grimm, 231-77; Stuhlmacher, 'Vicariously'. Moulder, 'Background', adds Dn 12:3. Dissenters include Best, *Temptation*, 140-44, and Anderson, 257, while Hurtardo, 159f, ignores the issue.

[144] Notably the seminal contributions of Barrett, 'Background', and Hooker, *Jesus*. The latter is concerned with Jesus' self-understanding, not Mark's presentation. However, since Hooker's work predates the rise of redactional analyses of Mark her treatment is applicable to the present discussion which concentrates on the final form of the text. Kee, 'Function', 183, concludes, 'There are no sure references to Isa 53.'

[145] To varying degrees in e.g. Hooker, *Servant*; Barrett, 'Background'; Higgins, *Jesus*; Moulder, 'Background'.

In the only other place where Mark records Jesus offering some sort of explanation of a significant aspect of his activity, namely his exorcisms (Mark 3:23-29), the conceptual parallels are such that he is generally understood by the majority of commentators to be alluding to Isaiah 49. And this in spite of the absence of unambiguous lexical parallels. We have also argued that a similar relationship obtains between the immediately following 'blasphemy' saying and Isaiah 63. Given these precedents, not only would it not be surprising if Mark's account of another of Jesus' explanations is similarly 'allusive' but it might even be expected. In addition, given not only Mark's 'mixed' OT citations and allusions elsewhere but also similar practices evident in contemporary Jewish literature,[146] an assumption of a single exclusive influence behind the saying might well be reductionistic.

Second, most of the earlier linguistic approaches tended to focus, naturally enough, on Mark 10:45 itself.[147] In practice this took place to a greater or lesser extent in isolation from the rest of Mark. But since Jesus' predictions of his passion, references to his future suffering, and Mark 10:45, relate to the same event, surely some consideration ought to be given not only to the question of their overall coherence but also to the fact that the former materials constitute the immediate interpretive context for the latter. Along similar lines, assuming an overarching unity to Mark's gospel some weight should also be given to its larger conceptual framework as proposed herein, namely, the INE.

Finally, it is important to remember that while the use or non-use of like material in contemporary sources might provide background to Mark's account of Jesus' understanding, it cannot be determinative. It is always possible that a creative mind with a different 'horizon' may validly—provided the wording of the text is not violated—see new things in the text that others because of their particular presuppositions have not.

(i) OT Setting of Jesus' Suffering: Mark 9:12

Granted the foregoing, it is well to ask if Mark's Jesus himself gives any indication of the background from which his understanding of his

---

[146] See Chapter 3, p. 85, fn. 170; in terms of the latter, e.g. VanderKam, 'Righteous', and Stanley, *Authority*.

[147] Later works such as Caragounis, *Son*; and Kim, '"Son"', give greater attention to the overall coherence of Jesus' statements on these matters.

suffering derives. In fact, he does. No matter how prevalent the ideas of giving one's life for another might have been among Mark's contemporaries (perhaps under the influence e.g. of the Maccabean martyrs),[148] it seems quite clear that in 9:12b the Markan Jesus links his understanding of his suffering specifically to the OT (καὶ πῶς γέγραπται; cf. δεῖ in Mk 8:31).[149] But if the source of his understanding is derived from the OT, and if as may at least initially be assumed its content is reflected in Jesus' words, what passage or passages lie behind Jesus' language of πολλὰ πάθῃ καὶ ἐξουδενηθῇ?

Although M. D. Hooker notes there is no direct OT prophecy of a suffering SoM,[150] she nevertheless sees in ἐξουδενηθῇ a pointer to Daniel 7 (citing ἐξουδένημα in Ps 21:7 LXX, see below).[151] There is possibly an implication in Daniel 7 of the SoM identifying with, if not sharing in, the suffering of the saints.[152] The problem is that, conceptually, it is only an

---

[148] See e.g. Barrett, 'Background', 12f; Hooker, *Servant*, 158f; Hengel, *Atonement*, 6-28; and Gundry who appeals to δοῦναι τὴν ψυχὴν in Græco-Roman literature, citing Büschel, *TDNT*, 2.166; but cf. the comments of Best, *Temptation*, 143f.

[149] So e.g. Lindars, *Apologetic*, 81; France, *Jesus*, 123f; Moo, *Passion*, 87; Gundry (but of different interpretation), 465; Marcus, 94-110; cf. Hooker, *Mark*, 220; Ernst, 263; Gnilka, 41ff; although the expression is used elsewhere to introduce exegetical conclusions derived from the OT, Marcus, '"Written"', 44f. Aside from our passage (par. 14:21), Mark's Jesus uses γέγραπται only with reference to the OT (7:6; 11:17; 14:27; cf. 1:2). Against the possibility that γέγραπται refers to Apocryphal writings, see Ellis, *Canon*, 3-50; Beckwith, *Canon*, *infra*. Also, ἐξουδεν- and its variant spellings only occur in 1 Macc 3:14 and 2 Macc 1:27 and in neither of these cases do the contexts fit Jesus' saying in Mark 9:12. Taken together this evidence suggests that Mark intends us to see in 9:12b an allusion to the OT. In spite of some commentators' concerns, the reference to Elijah in v. 13 probably means no more than just as the OT prophet had been rejected by Israel's idolatrous leadership so too had John. This much is at least implied by the warning in Mal 3:24b MT. To read 9:13 as though it suggests a violent fate for the eschatological Elijah figure not only goes beyond the text, but fails to take seriously the determinative status that Mark's Jesus implicitly gives the OT allusion. Marcus, '"Written"', denies this possibility on the grounds that there is no explicit mention of typology. But to assume that NT authors must always explicitly indicate typological correspondences in the way that Marcus suggests fails to appreciate typology's metaphorical nature. On the Jewish idea of eschatological tribulation, Allison, *End*, 5-25.

[150] *Mark*, 220. This, of course, assumes that SoM is a title with OT roots, and not a term of general reference. The debate continues, see e.g. Moule, 'Facts'; Casey, 'Idiom'; Slater, 'One'.

[151] *Ibid.*

[152] See e.g. Moule, *Phenomenon*, 83; Hooker, *Son*, 27ff; Barrett, 'Background', 13f; and the literature cited in Moo, *Passion*, 101n3. Casey, *Son*, 24-27, 39ff, vigorously denies this arguing that A) the author's emphasis in Dn 7:13, 14 is on the ultimate victory of Israel as symbolised by the SoM and thus excludes any notion of suffering for the latter; B) if the author does not explicitly attribute 'suffering' to the SoM, then it must be excluded; C) the notion of a suffering SoM is found nowhere among ancient exegetes. While Casey's point about the emphasis is valid, his second does not necessarily follow—not least because it

implication and, linguistically, none of Mark's suffering language (or synonyms thereof) is found in either the LXX or later Greek versions of Daniel 7, either with regard to the saints or the SoM.[153] Further, the notion or description of a suffering Son of Man figure is unknown in contemporary Jewish literature. At best it seems that the explicit descriptions of suffering are derived primarily from elsewhere in the OT and then used to explicate the implied suffering of Daniel 7's Son of Man.

Turning to other possibilities, a more likely candidate perhaps is Psalm 21:7 (LXX) which is later cited on two occasions in the passion narrative in Mark 15:24 and 34 (appealing to LXX Ps 21, verses 19 and 2 respectively). The petitioner's description of himself as one scorned by the people is certainly appropriate to Jesus; although Mark uses a verbal form whereas the LXX uses ἐξουδένημα. Similarly, given Mark's use of Psalm 117:22 (LXX) elsewhere (12:10, cf. 8:31), some have also suggested its influence here.[154] Since it is a hymn of thanksgiving for deliverance, an appeal to this psalm might not be inappropriate. Even so, it is not clear why Mark should use ἐξουδενέω here when elsewhere he retains the LXX's ἀποδοκιμάζω (in 12:10; cf. 8:31).[155] Psalm 118 (LXX), which is not usually mentioned in this regard, might also be a possibility. Dealing in places

---

allows no room for the subtlety of the *implicite*. Since the first four symbols in Dn 7 relate to *both* the success and the downfall of their referents, it might be that the reader is being encouraged to bring the same 'reversal' paradigm to the fifth, i.e. the SoM, even if the emphasis lies on the SoM's exaltation. The thorough-going motif of vindication after suffering in Dn 2, 3, 5, and 6 (bearing in mind their chiastic literary structure, Lenglet, 'structure'; cf. also ch. 12), likewise encourages readers to see the SoM's 'coming on the clouds' to be one, not of descent, but of ascent, i.e. of exaltation and vindication. And if vindication, then this implies suffering which coheres naturally with the larger themes of the book and also with the experience of 'the people of the Saints' in Dn 7 whom the SoM clearly represents. Similarly, ancient exegetical tradition can hardly be taken as normative since it could equally be the result of presuppositions which might have *a priori* excluded the possiblity of suffering for such an exalted figure (cf. the messianic interpretation of *Tg. Isa* 53). A change of horizon might enable readers to see in Dn 7 motifs that their former worldview caused them to miss. Consequently, not only does Dn 7 not exclude the suffering of the SoM/Israel prior to vindication, but on the contrary might imply it.

[153] Again, although the SoM self-designation might be understood as alluding to Dn 7 in general, given the 'mixing' of texts in Mark and the intertestamental integration of concepts from different passages (see fn. 146 above), it seems unwarranted to assume that all of Mark's SoM predications must be found in Dn 7.

[154] E.g. Gundry, 485.

[155] Gundry, 485; cf. Steichele, *Sohn*, 93n203, whose appeal to Luke's use of ἐξουδενέω in Acts 4:11 falters when he cites Mark 8:31 as an allusion—Mark here uses ἀποδοκιμάζω just as he does in his citation in 12:10 (cf. 1 Pet 2:7). Appeals to Paul's stylistic preference are likewise unconvincing and Gundry fails to respond to France's criticism, *Jesus*, 123f, that the contexts are too dissimilar.

with a righteous sufferer, verse 22 records the psalmist petitioning Yahweh to deliver him from ἐξουδένωσιν, and in verse 141 he describes himself as faithful and yet ἐξουδενωμένος.[156]

Finally, when Symmachus, Aquilla, and Theodotion translate Isaiah 53:3, they display an unusual degree of unanimity in rejecting the LXX's somewhat idiosyncratic choice and uniformly adopting ἐξουδενώμενος[157] —the standard rendering elsewhere in the LXX.[158] (Where בָּזָה occurs elsewhere in Isaiah, 37:22 and 49:7 (!), the translator/s have also gone against the norm in using φαυλίζω.) We have already seen that although Mark apparently uses the LXX, he is clearly not bound by it, and will go his own way when it suits.[159] Mark's term here might well reflect what he considers the more appropriate 'standard' or common translation.

Bearing in mind that we are speaking of only one word, it is hardly surprising that the evidence is ambiguous. One, or some combination, of the three psalms might be in view. On the other hand, it is possible that ἐξουδενηθῇ represents a more common rendering of בָּזָה in Isaiah 53.

But there is also the first part of the phrase: πολλὰ πάθη. At a conceptual level, Psalm 21 (LXX) and Isaiah 53 have extensive descriptions of the sufferings undergone by their respective subjects. Psalms 117 (LXX) and 118 (LXX) mention suffering in places but to a lesser degree, while Daniel 7 at least enters the lists in that it mentions the suffering of the saints (v. 25), and might thereby imply that of the SoM.

From the perspective of linguistic parallels, in marked contrast to its frequent use in the NT πάσχω is found relatively rarely and late in the LXX (including the Apocrypha) with only a few of these occurrences

---

[156] Moo, *Passion*, 90, cites Ps 88:39 (LXX) as using ἐξουδένωσας to speak expressly 'of the rejection by Israel of its Messiah'; however, it is actually Yahweh who is accused of covenant unfaithfulness. Ruppert, *Gerechte*, posits an influential role for the Psalms' 'righteous sufferer', but barely considers the OT origins of Mark's material, while Steichele, *Sohn*, 100ff, gets somewhat sidetracked by the Elijah reference (cf. fn. 149 above). See Best, *Temptation*, xlviiff, for a critique of the 'righteous sufferer' position.

[157] France, *Jesus*, 123f, cf. Cranfield, 298. Gundry, 485, argues against the applicability of these versions since they are not pre-Christian. But given that Mark freely modifies the LXX when it suits, as Gundry himself implies when he argues that Mark's ἐξουδενηθῇ 'is a non-Septuagintal alternative to ἀποδοκιμασθῆναι' (cf. also pp. 61f, 130, and 186 above for examples of this practice) at least the later versions provide some indication of translational alternatives. The LXX is also considerably earlier than the NT and allowance ought to be made for the semantic shifts of the kind discussed earlier; see especially Chapter 6, p. 148, fn. 57, above.

[158] Cf. Santos, *Expanded*, 23; Hooker, *Servant*, 94.

[159] See e.g. the discussions in Chapter 3, pp. 61ff, and Chapter 7, pp. 186ff, above.

having Hebrew counterparts in the MT. (Is this yet another case of diachronic semantic variation?) In Amos 6:6 it renders the Niphal of חָלָה, 'to be weak, sick' and thus 'to be in pain, to suffer', and in Esther 9:26 it translates מָה־רָאוּ (what they 'saw', i.e. experienced). Both Zechariah 11:5 and Ezekiel 16:5 have it for Qal forms of חָמַל, 'to have compassion', while Daniel 11:17 seems to have mistakenly used it for וְלֹא תַעֲמֹד (cf. Theodotion's καὶ οὐ μὴ παραμείνῃ).[160]

Of the above examples, while Esther reflects more the original meaning of 'experience something', only the Septuagintal use of πάσχω in Amos 6:6 corresponds to the sense found in the Markan passage. The fact is that the LXX uses a wide range of words, and some in greater numbers than πάσχω, to render the considerable semantic range of חָלָה. They are, in order of frequency: ἀρρωστέω, πονέω, ἀσθενέω, μαλακίζομαι, ἐνοχλέω, μετριάζω, and φλεγμαίνω.[161] What is striking, however, is that although various nominal forms of these verbs are found throughout the NT, the primary verbal forms used by NT authors are ἀσθενέω and ἐνοχλέω,[162] and these two convey the more narrowly defined expressions of unpleasant experience, respectively, 'to be weak, to be sick' and 'to cause trouble, to annoy'.

Given this data, it seems a reasonable conjecture that the remaining, 'missing' verbs—where they have not coalesced into other terms (e.g. ἀρρωστέω might well have been absorbed into ἀσθενέω)—were largely replaced by πάσχω, which, although originally meaning 'to experience' either good or ill, has in the NT clearly come to mean 'to suffer, to endure'.[163] If so, then we may be justified in seeing in πάσχω a contemporary Greek counterpart of חָלָה in its specific sense of 'to suffer or endure'.

Returning to possible OT backgrounds of πολλὰ πάθῃ, we find that none of the relevant verbal or substantival forms of חָלָה or its Septuagintal counterparts are found in either the Hebrew, the LXX, or, as far as could be discovered, the later Greek versions of any of the candidate

---

[160] Cf. Michaelis, *TDNT*, 5.907f.

[161] Seybold, *TDOT*, 4.402, who also notes the derived nouns ἀρρωστία, μαλακία, νόσος, πόνος, ἁμαρτία, and τραῦμα.

[162] However, ἀρρωστέω does occur in a variant reading to Mt 14:14 in D, and several occur in Philo, Josephus, and early Christian literature; see the relevant listings in BAGD.

[163] Cf. BAGD, 633f. See further the discussion in Michaelis, *TDNT*, 5.907ff.

psalms or Daniel 7. On the other hand, Isaiah 53 has two substantives and a Hiphil form of חָלָה: חֳלִי (in v. 3), חֳלָיֵנוּ (v. 4, rendered τὰς ἁμαρτίας ἡμῶν), and הֶחֱלִי (v. 10), while the LXX has μεμαλάκισται (v. 5) and μαλακίαν (v. 3; cf. πόνος, v. 4). The versional evidence includes Aquilla reading ἀρρωστία, Symmachus ἐπίπονος and νόσος, and Theodotion μαλακία in 53:3, Symmachus νόσος in 53:4, and Aquilla (Eus.) ἀρρωστία in 53:10. One can only conclude that if the words πολλὰ πάθη are intended to evoke a passage in the OT, Isaiah 53 would seem to be the primary candidate.[164]

To summarise our findings so far, in terms of conceptual parallels the prime OT candidates are Psalm 21 (LXX) and Isaiah 53; although some suffering on the part of 'one like a human being' is probably implied in Daniel 7. From the point of view of linguistic parallels ἐξουδενηθῇ on its own is ambiguous since it could point either to one or more of several psalms and/or to a more customary rendering of Isaiah 53:3. The absence of any linguistic parallels disqualifies Daniel 7. However, the phrase with which Mark's Jesus begins his statement, πολλὰ πάθη, suggests only one of the candidate passages: Isaiah 53.

Consequently, while it must be recognised that we are dealing with an allusive saying rather than a direct citation, and that we have only a short phrase, nevertheless, the unavoidable conclusion to which all three lines of evidence—OT origins, conceptual and linguistic parallels—run seems to be that if any OT text lies behind Mark 9:12b's πολλὰ πάθη καὶ ἐξουδενηθῇ it is Isaiah 53. Again, engendering a semantic clash by conjoining subjects (SoM) with largely unexpected or even dissonant predicates (Isaiah 53) is somewhat characteristic of Mark, and as H. C. Kee observed, not least when he is citing or alluding to Scripture.[165]

---

[164] Cf. Moo, *Passion*, 91. However, in arguing for the primacy of Isa 53 I would not exclude other influences. Gundry, 485, denies the possibility of an allusion to Isa 53:3 on the grounds that there is no hint of atonement here, and that Mark nowhere else appeals to Isa 53:3. The former is simply an argument from silence and is especially dubious given that there is no suggestion at all of purpose in either this saying or the three passion predictions proper which means nothing more than Mark's Jesus has nothing to say on purpose at this point—although Mark 10:45 suggests that Jesus had one in mind. Gundry's second argument has weight only if one assumes that Mark must always allude to OT texts at least twice in order to show that he is aware of them. Furthermore, Gundry's discussion of πολλὰ πάθη, 446 (on 8:31), seems not to treat adequately the OT origins that 9:12 suggests.

[165] 'The process in all of this is the interpretation of Scripture by Scripture, but with an eschatological aim that sees in Jesus the fulfillment (*sic*) of what can be discerned only when the synthesis of unrelated passages has been achieved', 'Function', 177.

If we take this data and its context seriously, that is A) Jesus declares that his suffering is in accordance with 'what is written' and B) he then describes his suffering in language alluding primarily, but not exclusively, to Isaiah 53, then it seems a reasonable initial assumption that the content of his other 'suffering' sayings should at least be consonant with this text. If not, then the net might need to be cast further afield. However, if it could be shown that Mark's passion predictions consistently betray clear resonances either linguistically and/or conceptually with a given text(s) then very good cause would have to be given as to why that text(s) should not be taken as determinative for the background of the sayings as a whole.

(ii) OT Setting of Jesus' Suffering: The Passion Predictions
The three passion predictions in Mark are generally taken to be 8:31; 9:31; and 10:33-34. Each one speaks of Jesus' death (cf. Mk 10:45, δοῦναι τὴν ψυχὴν αὐτοῦ). The characteristic actions described are, respectively, πάσχω πολλά, ἀποδοκιμάζω, ἀποκτείνω, and ἀνίστημι μετὰ τρεῖς ἡμέρας (8:31); παραδίδωμι, ἀποκτείνω, and μετὰ τρεῖς ἡμέρας ἀνίστημι (9:31); and παραδίδωμι, κατακρίνω θανάτῳ, ἐμπαίζω, ἐμπτύω, and μαστιγόω (10:33-34). Since the Markan Jesus is undoubtedly speaking of the one event, we are justified in treating all three groups together. A survey of the appearance of the same or similar language in the LXX reveals some interesting data.

We have already seen that πάσχω πολλά in Mark 9:12, if referring to the OT at all, is most likely alluding to Isaiah 53. There is nothing to suggest that the same source is not in view in Mark 8:31. Occurring only in the saying in Mark 8:31, ἀποδοκιμάζω is also found in the citation of Psalm 117:22 (LXX) in Mark 12:10 and might well be an allusion to that psalm.[166] This does not, however, undermine the general influence of Isaiah 53 but merely serves to confirm what we know of the Markan Jesus' use of the OT elsewhere: he is not averse to combining various texts to make his point. The similarities between Isaiah 53 and the thanksgiving psalm genre, to which Psalm 117 (LXX) belongs, only enhances the likelihood of such combination.[167]

Although frequent in the LXX, ἀποκτείνω (8:31 and 9:31) does not appear in any of the texts suggested as backgrounds for Mark 9:12b.

---

[166] Black, 'Passion'; Gundry, 429, 446.
[167] See e.g. Whybray, *Thanksgiving*, 132ff, who categorises Isa 53 as a third person, individual, thanksgiving Psalm.

However, the third passion prediction, Mark 10:33, reiterates the thought but reads κατακρινοῦσιν αὐτὸν θανάτῳ. Psalm 21:16 (LXX) has εἰς χοῦν θανάτου κατήγαγές με and Psalm 117:18, τῷ θανάτῳ οὐ παρέδωκέν με. But again it is apparent that Isaiah 53, even if one insists that the language is metaphorical, has a far greater emphasis on the 'death' of the 'individual' involved (cf. θάνατος in vv. 8, 9, 12; LXX). Further, the idea that this 'death' is due to 'judgement'[168] (cf. κατακρινοῦσιν in Mk 10:33) occurs explicitly only in Isaiah 53:8 (מֵעֹצֶר וּמִמִּשְׁפָּט, cf. the LXX, κρίσις).[169]

'Being handed over' to one's opponents (παραδίδωμι in 9:31 and 10:33f) continues the judgement theme[170] and is found in Psalm 118:121 (LXX) where the psalmist prays that he might not be 'handed over' to those who oppress him. Jesus' prediction, however, seems to be heading in the opposite direction. J. Schaberg has proposed that 9:31's παραδίδοται εἰς χεῖρας and μετὰ τρεῖς ἡμέρας ἀναστήσεται echoes Daniel 7:25, where the latter's ἕως καιροῦ καὶ καιρῶν καὶ ἕως ἡμίσους καιροῦ can mean a half 'week' (cf. Dn 9:27)—hence Mark's μετὰ τρεῖς ἡμέρας—with the resurrection element being drawn from Daniel 12:2;[171] a passage which according to some scholars has strong affinities with Isaiah 53.[172]

Schaberg's proposal is not unattractive—there is evidence to suggest that Mark also understands Jesus as 'true Israel'—and has an inherent plausibility as a general paradigm. In addition, Daniel 3 and 6 seem designed to function as personal 'resurrections' which adumbrate the national vindication of Israel writ large in the symbolism of the SoM in Daniel 7 (cf. the resurrection metaphor used in Ezek 37).[173] On this reading, and taking the overarching theme of Daniel into account, Mark's Jesus sees himself as the SoM who lives out the experience of the saints, that is, Israel, who themselves suffer עַד־עִדָּן וְעִדָּנִין וּפְלַג עִדָּן and are then vindicated. It has been objected that Daniel is concerned with duration

---

[168] Cf. e.g. Whybray, *ibid.*, 99f, who, although disputing whether or not literal death is involved, nevertheless recognises the language of trial and imprisonment.

[169] This is so even given the diverse approaches taken by e.g. North, *Suffering*, 149f; Westermann, 264; Clines, *Literary*, 17f; Whybray, *Thanksgiving*, 99f; cf. Watts, *Isaiah*, 2:220ff.

[170] See the discussion in Moo, *Passion*, 92ff.

[171] 'Passion', 209ff; cf. Caragounis, *Son*, 199.

[172] E.g. Ginsberg, 'Oldest'; Nickelsburg, *Resurrection*, 24ff; Collins, *Daniel*, 385, 393.

[173] Cf. Collins, *Daniel*, 273.

whereas Mark focuses on a point after the period of suffering.[174] This is somewhat pedantic since both Daniel and Mark are ultimately interested in the final vindication of those who suffer. That the 'after three days' apparently contradicts what Mark says elsewhere[175]—allowing that he knows the content of his own passion narrative (and may therefore see no contradiction)—could be taken to indicate that he intends a Daniellic allusion over against, for example, Hosea 6:2 (see below). This might perhaps be supported by the presence εἰς χεῖρας, but since it is only found in Mark 9:31 some caution might be in order.

At the same time, παραδίδωμι occurs twice in Isaiah 53 (vv. 6 and 12, LXX) to describe the 'servant' who is 'handed over'.[176] The text does not mention to whom,[177] although this is hardly a problem since the natural assumption is that they are opponents of the 'servant', whether the nations or Israel or both.[178] Mark's three different groups therefore constitute no difficulty. Questions about who it is that 'hands over'— whether Judas, Yahweh as the one who stands behind Scripture (cf. καὶ πῶς γέγραπται in Mk 9:12 and δεῖ in Mk 8:31; cf. Rom 8:32), or Pilate (why not all three?)—are ultimately unhelpful since the text does not say and it would be unwise to invoke a given subject as a reason for or against an

---

[174] Gundry, 506, who adds that Mark's 'men' into whose hands Jesus is given do not correspond to the 'king' in Dn 7. However, given the Dn 7 allusion (see also here Allison, *End*, 128-40), Jesus' mention of the elders, chief priests, and scribes suggests that they are to be indentified with the 'beast'. Thus, the stunningly ironic implication of Jesus' response in Mk 14:62 (cf. 10:33)—if he is the 'cloud riding' SoM, what does that make the High Priest?

[175] Schaberg, *ibid.*, 211, here cites Strecker, 'Passion', 429, who notes 14:58; 15:29; and the implication of Mark's passion account when the method of Greek counting is considered.

[176] See Moo, *Passion*, 92-96; cf. Caragounis, *Son*, 197, who although he is intent on establishing a Dn 7 background recognises here the influence of Isa 53. Hooker, *Son*, 94, arguing that this is merely 'the natural word to use in the context' (which might also be why it was used in Isa 53), questions any attempt to use it to establish allusions. Granted. But, on the other hand, if an allusion was intended what other word would one use?

[177] Gundry's contention, 506, that the omission of 'into hands of ...' disqualifies this parallel (cf. Caragounis, *Son*, 199), very much depends on where one puts the emphasis. That Mark's Jesus himself uses different modifiers—εἰς χεῖρας ἀνθρώπων (9:31) but τοῖς ἀρχιερεῦσιν καὶ τοῖς γραμματεῦσιν (10:33)—suggests that not much store should be placed on the precise identification of the recipients, which imprecision is, by the way, not all that different from Isa 53.

[178] At least Israel, Watts, 'Consolation', 53n93 (cf. Miller, 'Prophetic', 79ff; Begrich, *Studien*, 153; Beuken, '*MISPĀT*'; Orlinsky, 'So-Called', 53f) but in view of their surprise (Isa 52:13ff) perhaps also the nations. Whybray, *Thanksgiving*, 119, understands Babylonian authorities.

allusion here.[179]   What is abundantly clear is that the 'servant' is also
'handed over' to face 'death': something that is not immediately evident in
Daniel 7 (but then see Dn 3 and 6).[180]   Again, the best option is apparently
Isaiah 53, but this ought not be allowed to rule out a Daniellic influence as
well—after all Jesus' self-designation is 'Son of Man'.

Mark 10:33-34, the third and final prediction, expands on the suffering
more than any of the others, adding that the SoM will be mocked, spat
upon, and scourged.   While none of these terms is found in any of the OT
texts presently under consideration, it is noteworthy that the last two occur
in another 'servant' song, Isaiah 50:6, where they describe the affliction of
the 'servant' (cf. μάστιγας and ἐμπτυσμάτων).[181]   Finally, the μετὰ τρεῖς
ἡμέρας ἀνίστημι is not explicitly found in any of our proposed OT sources
and is often seen as a reference to Hosea 6:2.   On the other hand, there is
Schaberg's proposal as discussed above, and both Psalm 21 (LXX) and Isaiah
53 indicate an expectation of deliverance from death, irrespective of
whether the latter is interpreted as impending, actual, or metaphorical.[182]

In summary, several points can be made.   First, it is apparent that any
attempt to isolate one and only one influence on Jesus' predictions of his
passion is mistaken.   A substantial case can be made for varying degrees of
influence from several passages.   Second, while it is possible that Mark's
Jesus is one of the first to see and so develop from Daniel 7 the idea of a
suffering SoM, the conceptual and linguistic data suggest that he derived
the descriptive details of this suffering from other sources.   Third, if one is
to accept some degree of congruence between the OT background of Mark

---

[179] Gundry, 506, rejects the notion of God 'handing over' (and thus Isa 53) since he only
does so 'out of anger or animosity' and there is nothing like that here. While often true, Isa
53:6 (LXX; cf. 53:10 MT, see e.g. Moo, *Passion*, 94f) does not, however, mention Yahweh's
anger. In terms of Gundry's argument, the distinctive character of Mark's 'handing over'
(i.e. without anger or malice) seems only to strengthen the case for an Isaianic allusion.

[180] The nature of the fourth beast, the literary proximity of Dn 6, and the apparent
chiastic parallel between Dn 3 and 6 (Lenglet, 'structure') might well suggest that 'being
handed over' implies 'to death'.

[181] See Moo, *Passion*, 88f; and on Ps 22 in Mark 15, Marcus, *Way*, 174ff. Gundry, 576,
suggests that the reversed order of the words and the 'remarkable' omission—since it
appears in Mk 14:65—of the middle term, ῥαπίσματα, are grounds against an Isa 50:6 (LXX)
allusion. *Au contraire*, given that Jesus has already indicated his suffering is in keeping
with the Scriptures, the omission of the middle term might simply be a case of expecting an
informed listener/reader to supply what is missing.

[182] This is so even for Whybray, *Thanksgiving*, 79ff, 120. Note also here, Snaith's
comment, 'Study', 207, that although the 'servant' suffers the ultimate thrust of the songs is
his vindication and triumph.

9:12 and the passion predictions—and there is no obvious reason not to do so—and if the data is considered as a whole, rather than piecemeal, it is difficult to see how Isaiah 53 (cf. also, however, Isa 50:6 LXX) should not be regarded as the most influential background. In other words, even if Jesus is elucidating the implied suffering of the SoM in Daniel 7, Isaiah 53 apparently provides the basic quarry for details of the suffering motif which is then filled out and developed by allusions to other texts concerning suffering and vindication.[183]

(iii) The Passion Predictions and Mark 10:45

Granted this case for the centrality of Isaiah 53 as background for Jesus' predictions of the *details* of his future suffering—nothing has yet been said of its *purpose*—we are now in a position to review some of the arguments for and against Isaiah 53's influence on the text to which they lead, Mark 10:45. Before doing so, however, it is well to say something on the relationship between these findings and the overall Markan context.

We have already suggested that Mark's 'Way' section, carefully bracketed by his only two 'healing of sight' miracles, is built around the theme of the blindness of Jesus' disciples to the means by which Yahweh has chosen to fulfil his Isaianic promises of a NE: namely the suffering of his Messiah. The three passion predictions and the disciples' uncomprehending responses serve to illustrate and underline the point: Yahweh must lead the blind along a path they do not know. Given this carefully constructed literary pattern, it is significant that although Mark's Jesus three times predicts the *fact* of his suffering, it is only at the conclusion of his 'Way' section and immediately preceding the final bracketing healing-of-sight miracle that we find any indication of the *purpose* of the 'coming' of the SoM; namely, Mark 10:45b. That 10:45b ought not be segregated from the prediction of 10:32-34 is indicated by the otherwise consistent tripartite structure of A) prediction (8:31; 9:31; 10:32f), B) failure to understand (8:32-33; 9:32; 10:35-41), and C) subsequent teaching (8:34-38;

---

[183] On this approach, in particular, Hartmann, *Prophecy*. Hooker, *Son*, 95, recognises that '… the predictions do correspond broadly with the picture of Isa. 53'. Interestingly, the primary 'servant' passages alluded to in Mark are Isa 42 and Isa 53—precisely those which *Tg. Isa* identifies with the Messiah. In view of the Targum's attempt to isolate the Messiah from any of Isa 53's suffering, it might be that the initial identification of Jesus with Isa 42 is intended to sharpen, on one level, the later allusions to Isa 53 in the Markan Jesus' predictions of his messianic sufferings.

9:35-37; 10:42-45).[184] In terms of Markan literary technique, this pattern of progression culminating in an explanation is not dissimilar to the build-up to the Beelzebul controversy and the explanation contained therein.

Consequently, while verse 45a, οὐκ ἦλθεν διακονηθῆναι ἀλλὰ διακονῆσαι, is obviously of a piece with the immediately foregoing material, verse 45b, δοῦναι τὴν ψυχὴν αὐτοῦ λύτρον ἀντὶ πολλῶν, clearly goes beyond the concerns of the present context.[185] Not only is Jesus' point well made without it but it constitutes a shift in horizon. So what is it doing here? I suggest, first, that verse 45b, by neatly summarising the thrust of the preceding passion predictions, serves to refocus the discussion back on the over-riding concern of the 'Way' section: the SoM has come δοῦναι τὴν ψυχὴν αὐτοῦ. Second, and more importantly, at the climax of the whole section—it is immediately followed by the concluding granting-of-sight miracle—verse 45b introduces at last the reason for the passion: ... λύτρον ἀντὶ πολλῶν. From this perspective, Mark 10:45b functions as the final explanatory capstone to Mark's 'Way' section.[186] This, it might be noted, is entirely congruent with the literary function of Isaiah 53 within Isaiah 40-55 which, as has already been suggested, indicates the way in which Israel's INE is to be accomplished.[187]

(iv) Mark 10:45 and Isaiah 53

In the light of the above, one might be forgiven for expecting to find in Mark 10:45 an allusion to Isaiah 53 since the latter not only links suffering with redemption of others[188] but apparently indicates the way in which the hopes of the INE are fully to be realised. However, as observed earlier, a number of scholars have demonstrated that an Isaiah 53 allusion is not as straightforward as might be supposed.[189] Although this ground has been well worked over, in the light of the above it seems worthwhile to

---

[184] See Chapter 5, p. 124, above.

[185] *Pace* e.g. Hooker, *Jesus*, 75, who correctly stresses the need for context but then restricts it merely to the immediate pericope, vv. 42ff. It is also, therefore, more than a 'topical illustration', *pace*, France, *Jesus*, 117.

[186] This understanding appears to underlie the use of δεῖ in Mk 8:31 (cf. 9:12; 14:21, 49; also Bayer, *Predictions*, 201ff)—in literary terms 8:31 and 10:45 respectively introduce and conclude the 'passion/suffering' motif in the 'Way' section and may therefore be understood as interpreting each other.

[187] Again see the literature cited previously in Chapter 4, p. 115, fn. 135.

[188] See the discussion on the relevant sections of Isa 53 below.

[189] Typically Barrett, 'Background'; Hooker, *Jesus*, 74ff; Grimm, 235-46.

reassess the arguments. Since most commentators tend to break the verse into two units[190] we will tackle it accordingly.

With regard to verse 45a, ὁ υἱὸς τοῦ ἀνθρώπου οὐκ ἦλθεν διακονηθῆναι ἀλλὰ διακονῆσαι, it was formerly held that the service envisaged alluded to that of the 'servant'. However, it has since been argued that although the root עבד is rendered in the LXX by a great variety of Greek words—particularly δοῦλος and δουλεύω in Isaiah 40-55, while παῖς is preferred of the 'servant'—διακονέω is not among them. In fact, διακονέω is unknown in the LXX and although used in the NT it is urged that it there concerns domestic service.[191] Further, Peter Stuhlmacher has argued that rather than emanating from the 'servant' passages, διακονέω derives entirely from an earlier wordplay on the roots שׁרשׁ/שׁרת[192] and this in 'unmistakable contrast' to the 'ruling SoM' tradition in Daniel 7 and *1 Enoch*.[193] And in any case, as Hooker has pointed out, in Isaiah the 'servant's' service is directed toward God whereas in Mark others are in view.[194]

Clearly, the syntax of the sentence itself is *prima facie* evidence that the service motif stands in contrast to expectations of a ruling SoM—although it should be noted that Daniel 7:13-14 reads λατρεύω (Theod.) or δουλεύω (Orig.).[195] But this raises the more fundamental question: how is one to explain the predication of 'ministering' to an otherwise exalted and ruling SoM? While there is an implication of suffering in Daniel 7, the idea of self-giving service is not present. C. K. Barrett argued that the οὐ-ἀλλά contrast in 10:45 arises out of the 'circumstances of the ministry of Jesus' who as the SoM nevertheless comes in 'humility to serve'.[196] But this view fails to take seriously the thorough-going OT background to Mark's gospel (notably 1:2f) and particularly Mark's account of Jesus' self-understanding in 9:12 which together suggest that the dual concept of suffering-service is derived from the OT. Perhaps aware of this, Barrett

---

[190] See the literature in fn. 143.

[191] Hooker, *Servant*, 74; cf. Barrett, 'Background', 4.

[192] Proposed by Delitzsch, *HebNT*, and Dalman, *Jesus-Jeshua*, 118, respectively; cf. Emerton, 'Aramaic'.

[193] 'Vicariously', 21; cf. Dn 7:10; *1 Enoch* 45:3-4; 61:8-9; 62:2. Citing Theisohn, *Richter*, 15ff, on the dependence of *1 Enoch* 46:1f on Dn 7:9-10, 13-14.

[194] Hooker, *Servant*, 74f, 185n6; followed, apparently, by Gundry, 591.

[195] Stuhlmacher's other references, *1 Enoch* 45:3-4; 61:8-9; and 62:2 ('Vicariously', 21) are, as far as I am aware, not extant in Greek.

[196] 'Background', 9, apparently responding to the 'literary influence' (i.e. Isa 53) theory of Jackson and Lake, *Beginnings*, 1.1, 381-92.

also notes that the concept of 'service' is found in many other places in the OT and lists numerous OT characters as examples. However, these figures are all historical (i.e. non-eschatological) and they are 'all described as *God's* servants' (my emphasis).[197] In other words, his examples do not belong to the schema of Israel's future hopes, nor do they exemplify service of the kind mentioned here: a 'suffering' service directed toward 'the many' (i.e. not God) and, anticipating verse 45b, characterised by dying.

Moreover, Mark has clearly established a context in which his story of Jesus and particularly his 'Way' section is to be understood. The preceding Chapters of this book have sought to show that this context, not surprisingly in view of the role of ideology in shaping community self-understanding, is the Isaianic hope of a New Exodus. In addition, the INE rubric affords a considerable degree of consanguinity within Mark. Consequently, if we are to take Mark's context seriously, then in relation to Mark 10:45 we need to ask if there are any OT figures who are associated with the biblical expectation of a NE deliverance and who could be described as willingly assuming the position of suffering 'service' toward others? (We already know the 'service' includes suffering and even death because of Mark 9:12 and the three passion predictions.) Everything so far points primarily to the Isaianic 'servant' of chapter 53 (and chapter 50).[198] But Hooker and Barrett deny an Isaiah 53 background because the terminology and the recipients of the service differ: Isaiah 53 has the δουλ- stem, but Mark διακονέω, and in Isaiah 53 the 'servant' serves God but in Mark the service is directed towards others. The two objections are related.

First, the categorical distinction between types of service is more apparent than real. The LXX states that the 'servant' also serves the 'many' (53:11: εὖ δουλεύοντα πολλοῖς), while in Mark Jesus' death is also in obedience to God (14:36).[199] The 'servant' in Isaiah is primarily described in terms of his relationship to Yahweh because that is the very matter at issue with Jacob-Israel. The nation ought to be Yahweh's servant but has failed miserably and hence the need for a faithful 'servant' of Yahweh. But this, as Isaiah 53:11 (LXX) indicates, is scarcely intended to imply that the

---

[197] *Ibid.*

[198] Cf. Wolff, *Jesaja*, 65. On the question of integrating various themes from the different 'Songs', and on aspects of the various 'servant' passages being seen by some Jewish traditions as eschatological and messianic, see fn. 86.

[199] Cf. France, 'Servant', 34n40.

'servant' offers no service to others. After all, this 'servant' is commissioned not only to restore Jacob-Israel but also to be a light to the nations (e.g. Isa 42:1b-4, 6bf; 49:6, 8b, 9a; 53:12).[200] The two types of service are simply different facets of the one reality: to be Yahweh's 'servant' means 'to serve the many'.

This leads to the matter of terminology. In the NT διακονέω is not in fact restricted solely to strictly domestic service (cf. Matt 25:42ff) and even here in Mark 10 the context concerns political domination (vv. 37, 42) with Jesus having more in mind than merely serving at table (v. 45b).[201] More to the point, as Barrett rightly notes, διακονέω and its cognates appear either not at all or only rarely (and late?) in the LXX (e.g. 1 Macc 11:58; 4 Macc 9:17).[202] But then how does one explain the term's relatively 'sudden' and widespread use in the NT? It appears that either the δουλ- or διακον- stem, or both, had by NT times undergone a semantic shift with διακον- taking over some of the former's functions. This evidence raises the possibility that by NT times διακονέω was a viable, and in some cases perhaps even a preferable, rendering of the LXX's δουλεύω.[203]

Returning to Mark 10:45, the Semitic parallelism between Mark 10:43 and 44 merely tells us what we have already suspected: διάκονος and δοῦλος are closely related and might in some cases be regarded as synonyms.[204] But why then διακονέω in verse 45? Higgins suggested that it was influenced by verse 43 such that διακονῆσαι echoes the primary strophe of verse 43.[205] If so, then the choice could have been determined by some sort of 'sandwich' motif (διάκονος - δοῦλος - διακονέω) and, what-

---

[200] Watts, 'Consolation', 50-56, and the literature cited therein. In regard to the texts cited, it needs to be remembered that first century readers would not be engaged in a critical reconstruction of the text, as is the case in, e.g., North, *Suffering*.

[201] See Beyer, *TDNT*, 2.82ff, 88-89.

[202] 'Background', 4; cf. Hooker, *Servant*, 74. His case would be stronger if the διακον-stem had been widely used in the LXX but not in the so-called Servant Songs. Mark's choice could then with more warrant be read as a move away from the Isaianic 'servant'.

[203] That Symmachus takes neither option but uses λατρεύω in Isa 53:11 only underlines the fact that semantic fields were indeed shifting (cf. Jer 8:2 in Acts 7:42). The reason/s for this is/are difficult to discern. In addition to diachronic factors, there might also have been synchronic concerns, such as cultural issues. E.g. the LXX was primarily for Jews for whom the idea of subjugation in δοῦλος might have been acceptable (in religious settings), whereas for Gentiles either such connotations might have been less acceptable or, perhaps more likely, διάκονος offered a more nuanced sense of personal service, cf. Beyer, *TDNT*, 2.81, followed by Weiser, *EDNT*, 1.302:2.

[204] France, 'Servant', 34. On synonyms see, Silva, *Biblical*, 120-29.

[205] *Son*, 42.

ever the literary purpose, Mark's διακονέω would be of less significance in disallowing an Isaiah 53 allusion. While possible, this proposal is not certain. Another reason might arise from the balanced active-passive syntax of the sentence which in the case of the passive element naturally excludes the use of δουλεύω since it does not form the passive.[206] If so, the argument from different terminology again falls to the ground.

However, there is one further consideration. Although διακονέω and δουλεύω (and their substantives) are near synonyms (or at least contiguous),[207] there appears to be a tendency in the NT to use one or the other to emphasise different aspects of the same individual's service. For example, Paul largely uses the διακον- stem when he is emphasising his 'service' in Christ oriented towards others, but uses δουλ- when discussing his 'service' oriented toward Christ.[208] Granted this is a trend and not a fixed rule, it nevertheless suggests that different terms can be used of the same service depending on what facet of that service is in view. Mark 10:45's διακονέω might reflect this tendency and thus constitute a more nuanced allusion to the 'servant' which emphasises that aspect of his general 'service' toward God that results specifically in service toward others as per Isaiah 53:11.

In turning to the second section, verse 45b, καὶ δοῦναι τὴν ψυχὴν αὐτοῦ λύτρον ἀντὶ πολλῶν, the question of linguistic parallels must again be preceded by that of the origin of the central idea. Once more Mark 9:12 forces us back, not to the Maccabean martyrs or to Græco-Roman or rabbinical backgrounds but to the OT. Where in the OT is there any such general concept of a 'serving' figure, in an eschatological context, who gives his life for 'the many'? It is immediately obvious that the notion of suffering, even to the point of death, because of (or for) others' sins and specifically as a means to their restoration, is not a common one in the OT.

---

[206] Higgins, *Son*, 42n1; BAGD, 205.

[207] See on this terminology, again, Silva, *Biblical*, 120-29.

[208] Respectively e.g. Rom 13:4; 15:8; 2 Cor 3:6; 5:18 (cf. 1 Tim 4:6), and Rom 14:18; 16:18; and 1 Thess 1:9 (cf. Paul's self-designations in Rom 1:1; Phil 1:1; etc.). See further Gal 4:8; Mt 6:24 (par.); Acts 20:19. The only possible exceptions might be 2 Cor 11:23 and 2 Cor 4:5 (but even here this is 'for Jesus' sake'; cf. 1 Cor 9:19) but the latter is clearly rhetorical (cf. Gal 1:10), while the former seems best understood as comparing hardships endured in order to minister to the Corinthians; cf. BAGD, *ad loc*. Of Stuhlmacher's references in Josephus, *Ant*. 18.280 represents a pagan's view of Jewish service to the Law; in 10.72 'service' is noted as directed toward the people; in 5.344 Samuel's 'service of God' is ambiguous; and 8.354 describes the service of Elisha to Elijah. However, it must be noted that e.g. John 12:26 could suggest that the trend is not uniform, and there are times when because of the nature of the genitive (e.g. objective or subjective) it is difficult to tell.

In fact, Isaiah 53, granted that certain elements of its interpretation are problematic, is the foremost contender.[209] The INE context of Mark and the strong likelihood of an Isaiah 53 background to both Mark 9:12 and the passion predictions make an allusion to it here even more likely.

As Barrett recognises, it is absurd to deny a measure of parallelism between δοῦναι τὴν ψυχὴν αὐτοῦ and Isaiah 53:12. But he immediately qualifies this by noting that הֶעֱרָה לַמָּוֶת נַפְשׁוֹ is unique in the OT and that

---

[209] Whybray, *Thanksgiving*, has argued at length and with some vigour that vicarious suffering is not in view in Isa 53, cf. Orlinsky, 'So-Called'; Williams, *Death*, 107-11. His case—and many of his points are well made—is too detailed to discuss at length here. Nevertheless, some points may be noted. A) W. places considerable weight on the supposition that the exiles are presently suffering for their sins, and so the 'servant' cannot be said to suffer in their place (e.g. 30, 58, 61, etc.). This assumes that the 'servant's' suffering is related to Israel's pre-exilic iniquities. But if Isa 40:1-2 announces Yahweh's forgiveness of the past, then as I have argued (Watts, 'Consolation') the fundamental problem facing Israel now is her present obduracy (e.g. Isa 42:18ff; 48:1-16) which has not only caused her to reject Yahweh's announcement of salvation but also prolongs her suffering (e.g. Isa 56-66). It is on account of this present transgression that the 'servant' suffers; cf. Beuken, '*MISPAT*', 27. B) as all agree, in addition to our imperfect understanding of Hebrew tenses, particularly as regards poetry, many of the expressions in this chapter are unique and quite difficult, not least the all-important 53:10a. This suggests that the writer, even if using older terminology, might be seeking to give expression to new ideas—something that W. refuses to countenance. E.g. on the basis of 59:16 and 1 Sam 17, W. rejects the idea that יפגיע in 53:12c could mean to intervene by dying or being humiliated, since it 'would not convey to those who heard it the idea of a man who obtained deliverance for his people not by victory over the enemy but by being himself defeated and wounded or killed', 73. But this is precisely the point. The response of the speakers is exactly such that their salvation has been achieved in an utterly unexpected way, i.e. the suffering and 'death' of the 'servant'. Furthermore, his 'death' is not the end, he is 'resurrected'—just as Israel will be if she adheres to Yahweh's word (cf. Ezek 37). What if Yahweh's method of achieving his victory in 59:16 entails his using the 'death' of his 'servant'? After all, the ideas of sacrifice and Yahweh's victory were already integral to Israel's deliverance in the Exodus on which pattern Isaiah 40-55 is predicated, cf. Ex 32:30. C) this leads to W.'s rejection of the notion that the admittedly difficult use of אָשָׁם in Isa 53:10a could be vicarious because the Jews found the idea of 'human sacrifice' unthinkable, and that the efficacy of an אָשָׁם was in any case quite limited and certainly not applicable to the sins that led to the exile (65). But is Isa 53 speaking about human sacrifice any more than, say, 2 Macc 7:37f; 4 Macc 6:27ff, 17:22; 18:4 (indeed, one might well ask where the ideas expressed in Maccabees originated; cf. e.g. Fishbane, *Biblical*, 493, on the probable influence of Isa 53 on Dn); *m. Sanh.* 6:2; *Lev. Rab.* 20:7; or *Sipre Dt.* 333? Or is it simply suggesting that the 'servant's' innocent suffering was accepted by Yahweh as (i.e. in the place of) an אָשָׁם'? With regard to the appropriateness of an אָשָׁם, again it is not evident that 'high handed' pre-exilic sins are in view and in any case a human אָשָׁם goes far beyond anything previously known.

One point is agreed: the 'servant' is suffering not for his own sins, but because of those of others. But is this in any way related to Jacob-Israel's salvation? W., 126, observes that the 'speakers in Isa. 53:4-6 thus acknowledge that they themselves have been restored to a full state of well-being in consequence of the experiences undergone by the Servant'. The 'servant's' sufferings and deliverance are instrumental in the speakers' salvation and restoration. Again such a view is consonant with that mentioned earlier where Isa 53 describes the way in which Jacob-Israel is to experience her 'resurrection'.

לָמֶוֶת 'is generally excised by editors on metrical grounds'.[210] However, Barrett's caveats are hardly telling. Whatever the preferences of modern editors, there is no textual evidence for an alternative reading and it is clear that the Greek versions and *Tg. Isaiah* reflect the MT. It is, therefore, exceedingly doubtful if Mark or his audience would have been meditating on an excised text. As for uniqueness, this in itself is of no consequence— what else does one call singularly new ideas, and how does understanding grow without new ideas?—except perhaps to make the idea even more striking and therefore allusions to it more readily recognised. Further, δοῦναι τὴν ψυχὴν αὐτοῦ constitutes a close parallel to another unique Isaianic expression תָּשִׂים ... נַפְשׁוֹ (53:10).[211] More importantly, this phrase does not occur alone. It is not the giving of a life, but rather giving one's life as a λύτρον ἀντὶ πολλῶν that Jesus has in view.

Barrett has argued that not only is λύτρον never found in the LXX as a sacrificial term, being instead concerned with compensation, but there is no evidence that λύτρον and אָשָׁם were ever connected.[212] Barrett proposes that the idea of the Hebrew root כפר lies behind Jesus' use of λύτρον.[213] He cites rabbinic examples (*b. Qidd.* 31b; *m. Sanh.* 2.1; *Est. Rab.* 13a; *m. Neg.* 2.1) and suggests that behind these conventional expressions of piety lies the example of the martyrs (2 Macc. 7:37f; 4 Macc 6:27ff; 17:22; 18:4),[214] and earlier still the offer of Moses (Ex 32:30) which in later rabbinic tradition concerning Moses' subsequent death (Dt 34:5-8) is seen as an atonement for the sin of the golden calf or that at Peor (cf. *b. Sota* 14a).[215] It is this concept of devotion which informs Mark 10:45.[216]

But, again, the difficulty with the Maccabean martyrs is that they lie outside Mark's OT. The case of Moses is more interesting. Here is an

---

[210] 'Background', 5. For Hooker, 248, 'these words mean little more than ... "he gave up the ghost"'. True, but the significance of this observation is unclear, since what matters is correspondence between clusters of semantemes, not the meaning of single elements.

[211] France, 'Servant', 34, citing the Vulgate's even closer rendering; Moo, *Passion*, 122ff. Barrett, 'Background', does not discuss this possibility.

[212] 'Background', 5f.

[213] Cf. Mk 10:45 in Delitzsch, *HebNT*.

[214] 'Background', 12f; cf. Lohse, *Märtyrer*, 38-112.

[215] 'Ransom', 22f; see Jeremias, *TDNT*, 4.854; cf. Piper, 'Unchanging', 19.

[216] Barrett, 'Ransom'; cf. Lohse, *Märtyrer*, 113-203, according to whom the application of Isa 53 to Christ's death was mediated through Jewish martyrology; see Hengel, *Atonement*, 60ff, but also his cautions regarding the righteous sufferer and martyr-prophet motifs.

Exodus setting where salvation is jeopardised by the people's rebellion and Moses, to rectify the situation, offers to make 'atonement' for them.[217]

Given Barrett's rejection of Isaiah 53, largely because of the absence of sufficiently close linguistic parallels, his suggestion is surprising since aside from the verb—Mark has the noun—there are no linguistic points of contact with Exodus 32. Even this connection is problematic, however, since although the substantive כֹּפֶר is rendered in the LXX by λύτρον, it appears that the verb כָּפַר was not translated by λυτρόω.[218] Further, it is not clear that Moses offers his life to facilitate idolatrous Israel's continued Exodus journey. There is an element of bargaining—if you will not forgive then blot me out of your book—but this could easily be identification instead of substitution. Exodus 32:30ff hardly explains the explicit thrust of Mark 9:12 and 10:45. On the other hand, the story might have inspired a trajectory of reflection for another prophet who was likewise struggling with the problem of an idolatrous Jacob-Israel on the threshold of a later Exodus.[219] The strong Isaianic colouring of the passion predictions and Mark 9:12 point us again to this very situation.

Unlike Barrett, Hooker is aware of the significant place of λυτρόω in Isaiah. Although it generally renders גָּאַל (a similar relationship obtains between λύτρον / λύτρωσις and גְּאֻלָה) it is primarily related to the original Exodus (Ex 6:6; 15:16; Deut 7:8; 9:26; Isa 43:1; Mic 6:4), to the long-awaited return from Exile (Isa 52:3; 62:12; Mic 4:10; Jer 15:21; 38(31):11), and is especially used for the NE activity of Yahweh in Isaiah (35:9; 41:14; 43:1, 14; 44:22-24; 52:3; 62:12; 63:9; cf. פָּדָה in 51:11).[220] But, although granting the existence of 'considerable evidence to justify the linking of λύτρον with ... the expected redemption of Israel by Yahweh', this cannot be extended to

---

[217] See further, Childs, *Exodus*, 571; Durham, *Exodus*, 432f.

[218] I could discover no instance in Hatch and Redpath, 2.890.

[219] On Moses and the 'servant', cf. Bentzen, *Messias*, 64ff, cited in Davies, *Sermon*, 117f; von Waldow, 'Message', 284; Woods, 'Jesus', 22f, 48, citing Lampe, 'Holy'; and now especially the detailed analysis of Hugenberger, 'Servant', 129ff. There is also the strong OT tradition ascribing the title 'servant of God' to Moses (e.g. Ex 14:31; Nu 12:7f; in Jeremias, *TDNT*, 5.663, cf. 681). Concerning the later rabbinic materials cited above on Dt 34:5-8, it is difficult to tell whether this theologising on Moses' death is a response either to Christianity or the demise of the Temple (i.e. analogous to the rise of Aqedah theology, Davies and Chilton, 'Aqedah') or are an independent reflection on Ex 32. Whatever the case, the biblical materials nowhere suggest that Moses' death is so understood.

[220] *Son*, 144; also Ringgren, *TDOT*, 2.354f.

the 'servant' of whom גאל and פדה are not used.[221]   Hooker, therefore, denies any connection in either thought or language between Isaiah 53 and Mark 10:45, except perhaps for πολύς.   But even this is dubious since it is very probably an Aramaism reflecting more a general Isaianic universalism than Isaiah 53 in particular.[222]   Likewise for Barrett, not only is the concept common in the OT but Isaiah 53:11f is at most 'only one example, though an outstanding example' of the pervasive OT theme of the One for the Many.[223]

Hooker is correct in noting that גאל and פדה are not used of the 'servant', but is this really a problem?   While Yahweh is almost invariably the subject of the verb—he will redeem his people[224]—the question is 'how?'.   As we have already mentioned on several occasions, the literary structure of Isaiah 52-54 strongly suggests that Yahweh's INE redemption of Israel is intimately related to the 'death' of his 'servant' 'for the many'.[225]   In Isaiah 52:1-10 Zion is instructed to bestir and prepare herself, and in 52:11-12, using language reminiscent of the first Exodus, the captives are exhorted to depart.[226]   Then in chapter 54 there is the dual picture of Yahweh's reconciled wife and an enlarged and dazzling Zion rejoicing over the return of her children.[227]   Thus the content of the proclamations move from deliverance out of bondage to the promise of tranquillity in restored Zion.   The question is, what is it that facilitates the shift from one scene to the other?   That Isaiah 53 sits between the two suggests that the suffering of the 'servant' is integral to this transition.

In spite of the well-attested Exodus imagery pervading Isaiah 40-55, Ceresko observes that little work had been done on its influence in the 'Servant Songs'.[228]   He then demonstrates that the description of the 'servant's' suffering in Isaiah 52:13 - 53:12 is not only heavily indebted to the stories of Israel's pre-Exodus affliction before deliverance, but also to

---

[221] *Servant*, 76ff; cf. Procksch, Büschel, *TDNT*, 4.328-56; Hill, *Greek*, 58-80. *Pace* Barrett, 'Background', 7, the theme of the eschatological ransom of Israel is not so widespread as to preclude an Isaianic background (see Chapter 4, p. 100, fn. 55, above).

[222] Hooker, *Servant*, 78f.

[223] Barrett, 'Background', 7; Suhl, 119.

[224] In only two out of seventeen occurrences of גאל in Isa 40-55 is the subject not clearly Yahweh. פדה occurs only once but here too Yahweh appears to be the subject.

[225] Once more, Chapter 4, p. 115, fn. 135, above.

[226] Westermann, *Isaiah*, 248; Melugin, *Formation*, 164-67; Ceresko, 'Rhetorical', 48.

[227] Sawyer, *Isaiah*, 150ff; Westermann, *Isaiah*, *ad loc*.

[228] *Ibid.* But see now Hugenberger, 'Servant'.

the language of Deuteronomy 28's covenant curse. In fact, the former is the basis of the latter such that Israel's unfaithfulness will cause her to be afflicted with the plagues of Egypt. 'Infidelity involves a reversal of the exodus and of the Abrahamic promise'.[229]

As we have seen, Jacob-Israel in Isaiah 40-55 is indeed rebellious (e.g. 45:9-13; 48:1-22)[230] and it is not difficult to see the exile as a reversal of the Exodus (cf. 52:4). In this setting, Ceresko concludes that the 'Song ... describes the Servant bearing in his own person the effect of these [i.e. Deuteronomy's] curses' and 'he thus effects the "healing" his people require (53:5d)'.[231] Consequently, because of the servant's bearing of the Israel's guilt, 'the whole people is now free to enjoy the great gift—the land'.[232] How then does Yahweh redeem Israel, effecting the move from Isaiah 52 to 54? By causing his 'servant' to bear the covenant curse 'for many'. It is immediately following this section that we also find the first mention of plural 'servants' (Isa 54:17);[233] apparently anticipating the success of his mission (cf. Isa 49:6). Here then is a picture of Jerusalem and her people restored.[234]

From this perspective Hooker is correct to relate λύτρον to Yahweh's redemptive activity on Israel's behalf. But in the light of the above this hardly excludes Isaiah 53 in Mark 10:45. On the contrary, since Isaiah 53 apparently relates how Yahweh will effect his redemption of Israel, it makes perfect sense for Mark's Jesus to describe his death as a λύτρον when speaking of its purpose if he believes that Yahweh has purposed his death as the means of redemption for 'the many'. Consequently, Mark's ἀντὶ πολλῶν, although clearly not a citation, is not inappropriate as an allusion

---

[229] Blenkinsopp, 'Deuteronomy', 106, cited in *ibid.*, 50.

[230] See pp. 241-47 above.

[231] *Ibid.*, 50 and 53; cf. now Hugenberger, 'Servant', 136-38.

[232] Clifford, 'Isaiah', 573, cited in Ceresko, 'Rhetorical', 54. *Tg. Isa's* messianic interpretation of Isa 53 further supports this causal link; cf. Chilton's notes, ArB, 11:103ff.

[233] Watts, 'Consolation', 55.

[234] Dumbrell, 'Purpose', 111; cf. Clifford, *Persuading*, 181; and Melugin, *Formation*, 169, for whom '52, 13 - 53, 12 is an important bridge to the conclusion of the collection in chapters 54 and 55'. Sweeney, *Isaiah*, 85-87, notes the relationship between Isa 52, 53, and 54, but reads Yahweh's announcement to Jerusalem in Isa 52 as a *fait accompli* whereas the promised restoration is not actually described until Isa 54, see Melugin, *Formation*, 164. *Tg. Isa* also seems to understand Isa 52-54 in this way when it presents the Messiah in 52:13ff as the one who realises Yahweh's promises of 52:1-12 resulting in the situation in 54:1ff; cf. 52:12 with 52:13; 53:8, 10. See further the discussion on Jerusalem's restoration in Chapter 9.

to Isaiah 53:11f and given the contextual markers there seems little justification to look elsewhere.[235]

Werner Grimm, however, has recently argued along somewhat similar lines but sees Isaiah 43 as the primary background.[236] Isaiah 53 could not be the primary background since neither לרבים nor ברבים is equivalent to ἀντὶ πολλῶν and in any case 'λύτρον ist mit dem hebr. כפר identisch', a root not found in Isaiah 53.[237] Isaiah 53:12 LXX 'fehlt hier das "Lösegeld" und heißt es nicht δοῦναι sondern παρεδόθη, so daß man wegen des ἀντὶ πολλῶν allein keinen Einfluß ... wird annehmen können'.[238]

Since δοῦναι τὴν ψυχήν is best rendered by נתן נפשו and λύτρον ἀντί by כפר תחת, Grimm argues that the closest parallels are in Isaiah 43:3f where Yahweh announces to Israel, 'I give (נָתַתִּי) Egypt as your ransom (כָּפְרְךָ), Ethiopia and Sheba in exchange for you (תַּחְתֶּיךָ), ... people in return for you (תַּחְתֶּיךָ) and nations for your life (תַּחַת נַפְשֶׁךָ)'.[239] Isaiah 43:3f is appealed to in, for example, *Mek.* 21:30; *Ex. Rab.* 11:2; and *Sipre Dt.* 333 on 32:43, which portray the nations being cast into Gehenna in Israel's place.[240] The SoM could either correspond to or derive from אָדָם (43:4c), while the antithesis perhaps reflects Yahweh's rebuke in 43:23ff.[241] Grimm posits, therefore, that Isaiah 43:3f is the primary influence on Mark 10:45, although he affirms an Isaiah 53 allusion in Mark's πολλῶν.[242] Thus, Jesus takes the nations' place as Yahweh's 'ransom' for Israel, while the Isaiah 53 allusion indicates that the nations are also included in this redemption.

Although one might query his linking the SoM with אָדָם, Grimm's work is certainly insightful. Mark's δοῦναι τὴν ψυχὴν αὐτοῦ λύτρον at first glance constitutes a remarkable echo of תַּחַת נַפְשֶׁךָ (v. 4d), particularly in the context of נָתַתִּי כָפְרְךָ (v. 3c) and תַּחְתֶּיךָ ... אֶתֵּן (v. 4c) and given the language of Exodus 21:23 and 30:12 (MT and LXX).[243] Grimm also cites *b. Berakoth*

---

[235] Cf. Stuhlmacher, 'Vicariously', 24, further argues that Jesus is presented as the Son of Man who instead of being served by the nations (Dn 7) gives his life in their place for the redemption of Israel.

[236] 231-77; cited approvingly by Stuhlmacher, 'Vicariously', 23, although he grants a greater influence to Isa 53 than Grimm.

[237] 235.

[238] 236.

[239] Reading אֶתֵּן אָדָם, cf. 1QIsa[a]; 1QIsa[b] *pace* Westermann, 114.

[240] 245f.

[241] 253, 302.

[242] 236f. Again, see also Stuhlmacher, 'Vicariously', 24.

[243] Respectively, נֶפֶשׁ תַּחַת נָפֶשׁ נָתַתָּה and נָתְנוּ אִישׁ כֹּפֶר נַפְשׁוֹ; and δώσει ψυχὴν ἀντὶ ψυχῆς and δώσει λύτρα τῆς ψυχῆς αὐτοῦ.

62b and *Tg. Isaiah* 43:2 which further suggest that תַּחַת נַפְשֶׁךָ implies death for the substitute.[244] His position, however, requires important caveats.

First, while it is true that λύτρον is an acceptable rendering of the root כפר, it is not the only alternative. In Isaiah, the root כפר occurs six times, two of these in chapters 40-55: כָּפְרֵךְ in 43:3 (the only nominal form) and כַּפְּרָה in 47:11. However, on not one of these six occasions does either the LXX or the later Greek versions use λύτρον or λυτρόω. Instead, λυτρόω most commonly translates גָּאַל (seven occasions in Isa 40-55) while the only occurrence of λύτρον in these chapters is for מְחִיר (45:13). In terms of the Isaianic context, the connection between λύτρον and כֹּפֶר is somewhat tenuous, let alone as strong as Grimm suggests. Second, in Isaiah 43 it is Yahweh who 'gives', whereas in Mark 10:45 the SoM gives himself. It might be this shift of subject rather than an allusion to Isaiah 43 that explains the change from παρεδόθη to δοῦναι. Third, Grimm argues that in the context of a 'Heilstod eines messianischen Menschen', πολλῶν alone is sufficient to indicate an Isaiah 53 allusion. But as Kim notes, if the threefold repetition of רבים in Isaiah 53:11f serves to locate Mark's πολλῶν given the 'Heilstod' context,[245] then surely the same applies to the threefold occurrence of נפשו in verses 10-12—the same three as πολλῶν— and Mark's τὴν ψυχὴν αὐτοῦ?[246] Fourth, the idea of giving one's life, δοῦναι τὴν ψυχήν, is still clearer in Isaiah 53 which stresses the 'death' for 'the many' of the one who 'serves' (53:11 and θάνατος in vv. 8, 9, 12; LXX).

Then there is the issue of the preceding Markan context. The passion predictions and 9:12 are heavily dependent on Isaiah 53 (and 50). It would be more than passing strange if Mark 10:45, which we have argued belongs to the climax of the 'Way' section, should suddenly initiate a complete shift away from what has otherwise provided an important interpretative horizon. At the same time, given the congruence between the passion predictions and Mark 10:45, the concept of an 'individual' who 'suffers' is much more developed in Isaiah 53—in Isaiah 43 the nations (pl.) are given and there is no explicit mention of the nations' suffering or dying.[247]

---

[244] *Ibid.*, 248.

[245] Grimm, 236f; cf. Jeremias, *TDNT*, 4.540-46; North, *Suffering*, 127; Lindars, *Son*, 81; Dalman, *Studies*, 171f; France, 'Servant', 36.

[246] '"Son"', 53f. As we have suggested earlier, Kim also notes that in Isa 43 Yahweh is the one who gives, whereas in Mark 10:45 the SoM gives himself.

[247] *Ber.* 5:5 notwithstanding, Kim, '"Son"', 54; *pace*, Grimm, 253.

Finally, although much has been made of the distinction between compensation (λύτρον) and penitential offering (אָשָׁם), it is noteworthy that the literalistic Aquilla uses λύτρωσις to translate אָשָׁם in Leviticus 5:18 and 25 (cf. 7:1). While this ought not be overplayed, it is indicative of at least one later translational tradition that did not recognise a major difference between the two words. Given what we have already seen in terms of diachronic semantic shifts, this data should at least encourage some tempering of otherwise absolute claims.[248]

So then, while Grimm correctly notes the relevance of Isaiah 43:3f, the factors above strongly counter his arguments for an almost exclusive reference in 10:45. If there is a link between Isaiah 53 and 43 it is more probable that Mark's Jesus sees the former as a fuller development of the ideas suggested in the latter (cf. 'service', 'death', 'for many') but this time perhaps with a more positive outlook for the nations whom Jesus might have included in the ambiguous 'many'.[249] (Both the literary structure and extent of the material suggests that Isaiah 53 is more significant than Isaiah 43.) The nexus between the two texts is thus captured by λύτρον such that Jesus, who as SoM might have been expected to judge the nations, instead has come to serve not only Israel but also them. He does so by taking their place through his obedient suffering and death at the hands of both and so effects Yahweh's NE redemption of both.[250] That the nations should be prominent here is understandable, not only given the immediate context in which the rulers of these nations are being discussed (Mark 10:42f) but also perhaps in the light of Isaiah 56:7 in Mark 11:17.

Finally, this integration of SoM and 'servant' motifs has been criticised for being too 'elaborate' and inappropriately joining 'the title of an

---

[248] See also Kellerman, *TDOT*, 1.433f, on Lev 5. This might offer slight support to those scholars such as Jeremias, *Servant*, 100; Higgins, *Son*, 45f; France, 'Servant', 35; BDB, 79f; de Vaux, 2.418-21; Moo, *Passion*, 125; for whom Mark's λύτρον ἀντί should not be construed as fundamentally distinct from Isaiah 53:10b.

[249] Grimm, *ibid.*, 254; Kim, '"Son"', 56-58; Schede, 'Fragen'; but on the latter see, Werner, 'Frage'. On the nations in Isaiah, van Winkle, 'Relationship'. Isa 53 might reflect a more nuanced view of the nations in the light of Isa 49:6 and perhaps 45:22; cf. Isa 52:14f.

[250] Kim, '"Son"', 55-57, suggests that Grimm's contribution in pointing out Isaiah 43:3f was to draw attention to this very link, which, for Kim, is based on the 'material correspondence' of כפר and אָשָׁם (Kim's proposal may offer some confirmation for the view expressed here which was formed before being aware of his position); cf. Stuhlmacher, 'Righteousness', 40-43; Beale, 'Reconciliation', 556.

apocalyptic figure ... to the sufferings of a prophetic one'.[251] Although such a distinction between 'apocalyptic' and 'prophetic' appears something of an anachronism, it does, however, raise the question of the fusing of ideas and for completeness should be addressed.

Apart from the questions canvassed above concerning the sufficiency of Daniel 7 alone as background to Mark 10:45, it may be asked if this merging is so improbable, especially in view of evidence suggesting the contemporary integration of the SoM motif with several aspects of the Isaianic 'servant'. 11QMelch 2:18 describes the bearer of good tidings (Isa 52:7) as 'the Anointed One' (cf. Isa 61:1; 42:1)[252] 'of whom Daniel said ...', at which point the text breaks off. Although J. Milik and Geza Vermes propose a reference to Daniel 9:25,[253] William Horbury suggests that Daniel 2:34f or 7:13 would be appropriate.[254] Considering the importance of the Similitudes of *1 Enoch* in the discussion,[255] the pervasive influence of 'servant' imagery on its description of the SoM is significant.[256] Thus, 'the term "the Elect One" points ... unequivocally to the elect Servant of Second Isaiah' (e.g. 48:4-6 cf. Isa 42:6; 49:2-7; 60:10; 61:1f; and *1 En* 62:1; cf. 49:1ff).[257] The constant humiliation of the kings and the mighty (46:4; 62:3; 62:1-9; cf. 46:6; 48:6) is also reminiscent of Isaiah 49:7 and 52:14f.[258] Not only will he slay the wicked with the sword of his mouth (62:2; cf. Isa 49:2; 51:16), but he will be the light of the Gentiles (48:4 cf. Isa 42:6; 49:6; also Mk 13:10).[259] Along similar lines, but less direct, is the later discussion concerning the time of Messiah's return in *b. Sanhedrin* 98a where for

---

[251] Hooker, *Servant*, 96, in relation to the other passion predictions, e.g. 8:31; 9:12, 31 10:33. But the argument applies here. Although Hooker's concern is with whether Jesus would have made the connection, one may ask why not Jesus if Mark does so (see below)? It is generally agreed that in the final form of the gospels SoM has both Daniel 7 and messianic connotations, e.g. Perrin, 'Creative'; Walker, 'Question'; Müller, *Ausdruck*. On the possibility of pre-Christian messianic connotations for the SoM motif, see Horbury, 'Messianic'. On the use of the SoM idea in Mark, see e.g. Hooker, *Son*; Tödt, *Son*, 279f; Perrin, 'Creative'; Seitz, 'Future'; Coppens, 'Logia'; Lindars, *Son*, 60-84, 101-14; and for surveys of the larger debate, Walker, 'Recent'; Donahue, 'Recent'.

[252] Fitzmyer, 'Further', 40.

[253] '*Milkî*', 97ff, 108 and *DSSE*, 301 respectively.

[254] 'Messianic', 42.

[255] On the question of date, Chapter 4, p. 115, fn. 137, above.

[256] Jeremias, *Servant*, 58ff; Coppens, *Fils*, 134f; Theisohn, *Richter*, 114-25; Black, *Enoch*, 181-252. Hooker, *Son*, 33-48, omits any mention of these parallels.

[257] Black, *Enoch*, 189.

[258] Cf. Watts, 'Meaning'.

[259] On this fusing, see again Chapter 3, p. 85, fn. 170, above.

example Isaiah 59:20; 59:16; 48:11 and 60:22 are cited alongside Daniel 7:13 as pertinent to the issue. Later still, Isaiah 52:13; 42:1, together with Daniel 7:13f, are applied to a messianic figure in *Midr. Psalms* 2:9.

Moreover, as noted earlier, Hooker readily affirms that the background to Jesus' ministry is 'Deutero-Isaianic'[260]—it is the identification of Jesus with the 'servant' that she rejects—and therefore, given the SoM self-designation, there is already a fusion of an Isaianic (i.e. prophetic) conception of Jesus' ministry in general and the SoM figure (i.e. apocalyptic) in particular. If Mark presents Jesus using a combination of various images and actions appropriate to the Yahweh-Creator-Warrior, the Isaianic 'servant-deliverer', and the SoM (not to mention the influence of several other OT figures),[261] is it so elaborate that the suffering element, instead of deriving from Daniel 7, should also come from one or two of Isaiah's 'servant' texts where it is far more prominent?[262]

(v) Concluding Considerations

It would appear, then, that those who reject an Isaiah 53 influence on Mark 10:45 tend to do so on the basis of assessing isolated words or phrases.[263] When taken in isolation, it is true, none of the elements point unquestionably to Isaiah 53. But Mark has not given us individual words without a context. We have consistently argued for a constant, under-girding INE motif for Mark. And, without wishing to overstate the case, Mark's 'Way' section with its three-fold passion predictions shows clear signs of intentional structure. When the whole is taken as Mark put it together, it is difficult to see how one could deny that there are more

---

[260] *Servant*, 66, 67f, 73, cf. 95; *Mark*, 249; cf. Grimm, *passim*; Schürmann, *Reich*, 240.

[261] See especially, France, *Jesus*, 43-50, 103-10.

[262] 'Wenn man aber im Zentrum der Verkündigung Jesus Abhängigkeit von DtJes nach-weisen kann, warum dann nicht auch in den Gottesknechtsliedern?', Schürmann, *Reich*, 240, with cautions, 241-3; cf. Lindars, *Son*, 82. Horbury, 'Messianic', 42-47, argues that messianic exegesis characteristically integrated various texts in creative ways; on the possibility of Jesus himself being the originator, cf. Dodd, *According*, 109f; Hengel, *Atonement*, 59.

[263] As does Hooker's argument, cf. Jeremias, '*Jesus*', 142f; France, 'Servant', 36f. Casey's dismissal, *Son*, 206, of an Isa 53 allusion on the basis of its dissimilarity to 'contemporary Jewish exegesis' seem to presume that neither Jesus nor the early Christians were capable of independent thought; a rather surprising assumption for a movement confessing a crucified Messiah, cf. Grimm, 65. On a *possible* eschatological interpretation of Isa 53 involving a saviour-figure who 'achieves atonement for all the sons of his race', who 'teaches the will of God', whose word 'works to the ends of the earth', and who also apparently both suffers at the hands of his enemies and is involved in 'sorrows' (...ל. ומכאבין and ... נגדי מכאביכה; cf. Isa 53:4), see Starcky, 'étapes', 492; Hengel, *Atonement*, 58.

explicit parallels, conceptually and verbally, with the 'servant' figure of Isaiah 53 than with any similar grouping of characteristics ascribed to any other OT figure in a given passage.[264] This is surely the case with the SoM in Daniel 7 whose only explicit connection with Mark 10:45 appears to be in the title; the ideas of bringing Israel's deliverance through his suffering for the many having to be more or less implied or imported as both Barrett's and Hooker's constructions illustrate.[265] And as we have seen, even those who are least warm to the 'servant' idea nevertheless admit that Jesus' predictions of his passion 'correspond broadly' to Isaiah 53.[266]

On the other hand, the argument for the primary influence of Isaiah 53 on Jesus' predictions of his suffering and death ought not be taken as excluding a role for Daniel 7 or other passages. As already suggested several times earlier in this book, there is a strong case for Jesus being presented as 'true Israel'. This being so, Hooker's suggestion that the term SoM serves to identify Jesus as 'the one true Israelite who is able to accept the mission and destiny of his people' is to be affirmed.[267] My concern is that this identification should not exclude other OT patterns.

In the end, Mark's account of Jesus' interpretation of his suffering appears to reflect an integration of Isaiah 40-55's prophecies of how Israel's salvation was to be effected. Yahweh's redemptive INE (cf. λυτρωθήσεσθε in Isa 52:3 LXX) seems to be accomplished by the 'servant's' suffering and death which is accepted not only as a reparation and 'guilt offering' for 'diseased' Israel (אָשָׁם; Isa 53),[268] but also as a substitute for the nations who were to be Israel's 'Lösegeld' (Isa 43).[269] Interestingly, such an innovative

---

[264] Cf. e.g. Kümmel, *Promise*, 73, who rejects any idea of 'servant' consciousness in Jesus.

[265] 'Background', 9-15; and *Son*, 27-30, 140-47, respectively; but see the criticisms of France, 'Servant', 47ff; Higgins, *Son*, 41-50; Casey, *Son*, 205f.

[266] Hooker, *Servant*, 95, cf. 74f.

[267] *Son*, 193.

[268] Is there a connection between the priestly requirement for lepers in Lev 14:25 and Israel's 'leprous' wounds in Isa 1:5f, with the latter being borne by the 'servant' in 53:4-6? Jeremias *Servant*, 62f, discusses Aquilla's translation of נגע by ἀφημένον (so Jerome), cf. Vulgate: *quasi leprosum* and *b. Sanh.* 98b where the wounds are those of a leper. The whole issue of sacrifice is very complex, see Milgrom, *Cult*, and *Leviticus*; and Kiuchi, *Offering*.

[269] Cf. Lindars, *Son*, 78, who regards λύτρον as 'interpretative' in that 'the ransom idea is a legitimate way of interpreting the prophecy as a whole'. Tit 2:14 relates Christ's death to both redemption and cleansing (ἔδωκεν ἑαυτὸν ἵνα λυτρώσηται ... καὶ καθαρίσῃ) in the context of his having a λαὸν περιούσιον; the latter phrase being used in Ex 19:5 LXX of God's intention for his people in the first Exodus, cf. Dt 14:2; 7:6; Ex 23:22. Further, this understanding would be consistent with my proposal in 'Consolation' in that although

and creative hermeneutic is not dissimilar to that in Mark 3:27 where Mark's Jesus interprets his exorcisms in terms of the Yahweh-Warrior's activities on Israel's behalf (Isa 49:24ff). It is worth noting the substantial similarities between these two passages.

Both statements play a major role in Mark's account of Jesus' self-understanding and both occur at the climactic moments in their respective sections.[270] In both cases this self-understanding is crucial to interpreting central features of those sections: Jesus' exorcisms and his passion. Both statements appear on Jesus' lips, and both exhibit the same allusive character.[271] And as noted, both provide evidence of a similar, innovative hermeneutic. Hooker's observation on Mark 3:27 is, therefore, apposite:

> Although there is no verbal correspondence between the Greek text and the LXX version of Isaiah 49. 24f., the similarity in meaning is so great that there is little doubt that Jesus had this passage in mind when he spoke these words; nor is there any comparable picture elsewhere in the Old Testament.[272]

I submit that the application of these criteria to Mark 10:45 should result in a similar verdict concerning the influence of Isaiah 53. The pervasive impress of that text on Mark 9:12 and the passion predictions only serves to reinforce the suggestion.

Returning to Mark 10:45 in its immediate context, while the disciples are arguing about status and power, Jesus explains that this is not what his present capacity as SoM entails. This is not to deny a 'cloud-riding' role to the SoM but for Mark's Jesus this is future (13:26; 14:62). His present 'coming' (note the ἦλθεν) is, instead, διακονῆσαι. So while Stuhlmacher is right in insisting that the immediate contrast is with the SoM's expected role,[273] I would urge that the underlying and ultimately crucial presuppositional shift that facilitates the contrast finds its impetus in the linking of the concerns of Daniel 7 and Isaiah 53 and 43 with Israel's deliverance. Daniel 7, with its SoM symbolism, only deals with the fact of suffering Israel's vindication and exaltation—that is, her return from Exile. It does

---

Yahweh offers to give the nations on Israel's behalf, her rebellious response indicates that not merely redemption but expiation of guilt is required; the 'servant' accomplishes both.

[270] See Chapter 5, and in addition to the arguments above, Hengel, *Atonement*, 42.

[271] France, 'Servant', 29, following Taylor, 'Origin', 163, regards the allusive character of Mark 10:45 as evidence of its authenticity; cf. Lindars, *Apologetic*, 77-79.

[272] *Servant*, 73.

[273] Barrett's comment, 'Background', 8, that if the saying derives from Isa 53 then to say he comes to serve would be 'a little precious' is peculiar. After all the 'service' in Mark is not being predicated of the 'servant' but of the SoM.

not explain how this will come about. Isaiah 40-55, which also deals with the return from Exile, provides the explanatory 'how' in Isaiah 53 and 43. Suffering Israel's salvation and vindication, as 'one like a son of man', is to be brought about by the redemptive suffering service of the true 'servant' Israel of Isaiah. But this is not just for Israel; the nations will also benefit.

For Mark, true Israel, and therefore the one truly like a SoM, is none other than Jesus. At the same time, Jesus' unconventional messianic self-understanding—that he is to die as a ransom for many—is consistent with the misunderstood career of the 'servant' of Isaiah 53 whose rejection, suffering, and death 'for' the sin of 'many' becomes Yahweh's equally unexpected means of effecting Israel's NE.[274]

c) Jesus and the Son of David

Given the theme of messiahship throughout the 'Way', some comment should be made on Mark's attitude to Jesus as 'Son of David'. In Mark 10:46-52 it has been observed that although Jesus does not overtly reject Bartimaeus' confession he does not explicitly affirm it. This has led some commentators to see in Jesus' lack of affirmation his tacit rejection of Davidic messiahship.[275] However, since this argument is only by implication all are agreed that it is necessary to go elsewhere for firmer evidence, and proponents of this view go to Mk 12:35-37 which, according to Paul Achtemeier, clearly shows that the Christ, that is Jesus, is not of Davidic descent.[276]

Several points can be made in response. First, it is not clear that this reading of Mark 12 is self-evident. As an interrogative of manner, πόθεν does not necessarily imply a negative answer,[277] while πῶς may seek an

---

[274] The death of Christ in the NT is related to reconciliation and the opening of the way of entering into God's presence, themselves key components of the NE, Eph 2:13-19; Heb 4:16; 1 Pet 3:18; cf. Beale, 'Reconciliation', espec. 578ff; Hengel, *Atonement*, 52; Stuhlmacher, '"Peace"', 187ff.

[275] Kelber, 96; Achtemeier, 'Discipleship'; surveys in Schneider, 'Davidssohnfrage'; Burger, *Davidssohn*, 52-59; and the discussion in Matera, *Kingship*, 84-89.

[276] Achtemeier, 'Discipleship', 130; cf. Bultmann, *History*, 136f; Lohmeyer, 262; van Iersel, 'Fils', 121f; Kelber, 96. Chilton, 'Reflections', 101, has Jesus presuppose son of David identification but 'denies this is a messianic claim'; cf. Suhl, 93f; Fitzmyer, 'Tradition'; Lövestam, 'Fils'. Achtemeier sees 10:46-51 as a discipleship story and not an introduction to the entry. But why cannot both interests be in view? See also Matera, *ibid.*, 68, and 87f, where the larger context indicates the issue is corrected not rejected messiahship.

[277] There might be a sense of incredulity in Mk 8:4, but in Mk 6:2; Mt 13:27, 54; 21:25; Lk 1:43 it is used of an unsettling or surprising fact that requires explanation. Cf. LN, 2.789: 89.86; BAGD, 732.

explanation.[278] Jesus could simply be discomforting the scribes by posing them an apparent contradiction—hence, presumably, the crowd's glee.[279] Given the widespread expectation of a Davidic Messiah, if Jesus *was* denying that the Christ was David's Son the crowd's response would be difficult to explain. On the contrary, then, there is no denial that the Christ is the Son of David, only that he cannot merely be 'son';[280] an assertion that is particularly appropriate considering the pericope's placement at the conclusion of Jesus' Jerusalem controversies and as an introduction to his denunciation of the scribes.

Second, the Caesarea Philippi confession, linked as it is with the preceding healing, is rightly understood as parallel to this pericope, and there Jesus accepts Peter's messianic confession.[281] Assuming that Mark 12:35 suggests that for Peter and Bartimaeus υἱὸς Δαυίδ and Χριστός were synonymous,[282] the 'Way' begins with a second-best recognition of messiahship and similarly ends with a confession of 'Son of David'[283] and the crowd's messianic acclaim (11:1ff), but in the meantime establishes that the Messiah must die. Therefore, although Mark's Jesus does not use these titles of himself, and although they might not be Mark's most important Christological designations, he no more has Jesus rejecting 'Son of David' than he does 'Messiah'.

---

[278] Cf. Mt 12:29 where the exception clause states the conditions under which the otherwise unexpected can take place; also e.g. Mt 21:20; 22:12, 43; Jn 4:9; 9:10; etc., BAGD, 732. In Mk 12 the question is left unanswered but this is a long way from a denial. It is the context, not the particle, that is determinative.

[279] Fitzmyer, 'Tradition', 123f; Lane, 436n62; and Kingsbury, 109, correctly note the haggadic character of Jesus' question. Achtemeier, 'Discipleship', 141n39 cites *Barn.* 12:10-11 as a similar 'denial', but this deals with the charge that if Jesus is the Christ then he cannot be Son of God since the Christ is the Son of David. The response is that even David calls his son, 'Lord', hence Jesus is both Son of David and Son of God.

[280] E.g. Lane, 437; Burger, *Davidssohn*, 64ff; Robbins, 'Bartimaeus', 242; Hurtardo, 192; cf. Pesch, 2.251; Gnilka, 2.171f; Daube, 'Earliest', 182. Kelber, 95n24, cites an impressive array of scholars who see Jesus rejecting Davidic sonship in favour of sonship of God.

[281] Robbins, 'Bartimaeus', 227; cf. Hooker, *Message*, 63; Best, *Following*, 140. Achtemeier, 'Discipleship', 131, although citing Robbins, ignores this important element of the context.

[282] Cf. also *Pss. Sol.* 17:23; and the rabbis in *b. Sanh.* 98a (AD 110); *y. Ta 'anith* 4.8, 68d (AD 130); *b. Sanh.* 97a (AD 150); also Burger, *Davidssohn*, 16-24; Lohse, *TDNT*, 8.484-86; Fitzmyer, 'Tradition', 115ff.

[283] Cf. Hooker, *Mark*, 253. Chilton, 'Reflections', 101, sees Jesus' healing affirming 'Son of David' in the Solomonic sense (cf. Chapter 6, p. 168, fn. 162); but see Marcus, 151f.

Third, appeals to missed opportunities to stress Jesus' Davidic heritage (2:23-27; 6:1-3) amount to second-guessing Mark,[284] and arguments that a positive interpretation requires drawing on other NT evidence (e.g. Mt 22:42-45; Rom 1:3f) cuts both ways.[285] It could equally be that Mark is not more explicit because he never expected any of his readers to doubt for a moment that Jesus is the Davidic Messiah. But then, having disallowed the importing of other NT evidence, Achtemeier's assessment of the 'unusual ambiguity' of 11:9-10 itself depends primarily on a comparison with Matthew.[286] But Matthew is frequently more explicit than Mark (witness his fulfilment formulae), and hence when Achtemeier asserts that Mark 'would surely have followed the procedure of Matthew'—one is tempted to ask who is writing Mark's gospel, Mark or Matthew?

On the other hand, the point of the crowd's unusual expression, 'the kingdom of our father David' seems precisely to show that they, like Peter earlier, are thinking in terms of traditional military-political categories. Achtemeier also misconstrues $\dot{\rho}\alpha\beta\beta\text{ou}\nu\acute{\iota}$[287] which is instead to be understood within the context of the 'wisdom' imagery and Jesus' teaching which has dominated the 'Way' section: Jesus, messianic 'servant' and Son of David, on the way to his death as a ransom for many, is the wise Teacher who gives 'sight'. Further, if our understanding of the messianic confession being a prerequisite to true NE 'sight' is correct, then the two healing miracles not only set the scene for Jesus' Son of David debate and his rejection in Jerusalem, but also poignantly reveal the inadequacy of the 'blind' crowd's confession who see Jesus solely in terms of the 'ἡ ἐρχομένη βασιλεία τοῦ πατρὸς ἡμῶν Δαυίδ' (11:10) and do not follow 'in the way'.[288]

Finally, there is the matter of Mark's opening OT citation and of the imagery associated with the rending of the heavens and the voice, with the Beelzebul controversy, and with the sea-walkings. The implication in these cases tending toward identifying Jesus as the Son of God. This, I suggest, is what Mark 12:35-37 is driving at. Jesus is not *simpliciter* the

---

[284] Achtemeier, 'Discipleship', 130.
[285] Achtemeier, *ibid.*; cf. Kelber, 96.
[286] *Ibid.*, 130.
[287] *Ibid.*, 131; Suhl, 93.
[288] Robbins, 'Bartimaeus', 227, 240.

messianic Son of David whom the scribes, and no doubt many others, are expecting. He is also David's Lord.[289]

IV. Conclusion

Although the voice from heaven reveals Jesus' identity and the unclean spirits recognise him, for his people Israel things are less clear. Jesus is variously regarded as an extraordinarily authoritative teacher, a wonder-worker, a prophet, a family member who is beside himself, or an exorcist who is in league with Beelzebul. The question insistently pushes itself forward: who is this? This, too, is the matter which the disciples must resolve. Peter's confession that Jesus is the Christ might well be imperfect, but it provides, for Mark, the basis upon which Jesus' death can be portrayed as the effective means of the INE.

This is not to deny that Mark's 'Way' section has a paradigmatic function in instructing the church on the life of discipleship. Nevertheless, the INE motif seems predominant. On this interpretation, Mark has placed the great majority of his miracles within the first section to demonstrate that the INE is being inaugurated in Jesus. However, he also appears to be interested in showing that participation in the miracles of the messianic-'servant'-Deliverer *cum* Yahweh-Warrior does not necessarily imply participation in the INE. What matters is understanding, and here even the disciples are blind, failing to discern the significance of what transpires (8:14-21). Peter's confession surely marks a turning-point. But it is only a 'men-as-trees-walking' confession. The one thing that sets the disciples apart is not that they immediately understand, but instead when called they follow, even though hardly comprehending.

Accordingly, just as Isaiah's 'servant' teacher would through his ministry effect Israel's NE, so too in Mark. Jesus the teacher opens the eyes of the 'blind' by instructing them in the 'Way' of Yahweh's wisdom, even though they like Israel of old are slow to see. In Isaiah the climax lies in the unexpected suffering of the 'servant'. In Mark, everything hinges on a SoM-Messiah who is, against all expectation, to be rejected and crucified.

---

[289] Cf. Burger, *Davidssohn*, 64ff; Kingsbury, 112. See now also Gundry's response, 721ff, and the more nuanced approach of Marcus, 142-45 and 151-52.

In this Isaianic NE, as Joel Marcus correctly observes, Jesus goes to Jerusalem not to launch a war of conquest by killing his enemies but by being killed.[290] Not by taking others' lives, but by giving his. This is not a denial of the prophesied coming of the Yahweh-Warrior, only a radical inversion of it. It might well be that this, ultimately, is the content of the 'secret' which is spoken of in the Parables Chapter; and is perhaps the Markan equivalent of Paul's μυστήριον τοῦ θεοῦ (1 Cor 2:1; cf. 1 Cor 1:18-25).

In Isaiah the NE 'way' leads to a new enthronement of Yahweh as King in gloriously restored Jerusalem which then becomes the centre of the nations' pilgrimage for teaching and worship in his presence. We might have expected something similar except that Mark has already sounded several notes of caution: Malachi's warning is cited in the opening sentence, John as Elijah *redivivus* is rejected, imprisoned, and executed, and Jesus himself has met with hostility and censure. As we shall see in Chapter 9, matters turn out rather differently from Israel's expectation.

Excursus: Misplaced Miracles?

It has often been remarked that the healing of the possessed boy and of blind Bartimaeus are the only two healing stories that occur outside the first section.[291] Given Mark's interest in miracles and his obvious redactional activity, any treatment seeking to explain the significance of miracles for Mark must account for this particular phenomenon. I have already suggested that the 'disproportionate' distribution of miracles is integral to Mark's INE hermeneutic. His first section corresponds to Yahweh's delivering of his people from bondage and appropriately contains the vast majority of Jesus' miracles. But how are these apparent departures from his NE framework to be explained?

The answers will again depend on the degree of skill one attributes to Mark. Either Mark was unconcerned with consistency, in which case the NE schema still remains largely intact, or, as a number of scholars have argued, Mark although not to be overdrawn as a literary giant did intend

---

[290] *Way*, 36.
[291] E.g. Brown, 'Miracles', 168; Best, 'Miracles', 542; Robbins, 'Bartimaeus', 225; and as noted in Chapter 6, above.

to communicate something by his placement of these miracles. It is to the various proposals along the latter line that we now turn.

The most influential explanation, at least in the case of the demonised boy, is that of a polemic against a 'divine man' Christology, illustrated by the disciples' failure to accomplish a miracle.[292] Alternatively, Best implies that the two miracles concern Mark's growing focus on discipleship,[293] while others have seen evidence of an increasingly difficult battle against the demonic.[294] Of these suggestions, the first and last do not explain Bartimaeus whereas Best at least provides a rationale for both. He does not explain, however, why Mark includes only these two miracles. Does an INE model provide a more satisfactory account?

In the light of the preceding discussion, Mark's inclusion of only two healings of the blind, and these two in particular, are explained as integral to the wisdom themes of his 'Way' section (cf. Isa 42:16). As in the case of the feedings, although Mark generally adheres to the INE schema he is willing to adapt the pattern in order to make a more important point. But what about the boy?

This story has posed severe difficulties for commentators with no generally agreed solution yet proposed. What we have in general terms is a moment of glory on the mountain, an interlude during the descent concerning Jesus and Elijah, and finally the failure of the 'faithless' disciples to deal with the demonic. What makes this particularly interesting is that 9:14-29 is A) the only encounter with the demonic outside of the first section (intriguingly an ἄλαλον καὶ κωφὸν πνεῦμα, cf. Ps 115:5f MT), B) the only instance in the gospel where the disciples are directly involved in a specific healing, and, C) they fail (cf. 6:7-13). Why then has Mark included it, and what is his point, especially given the disciples' earlier success (Mk 6:7-13; cf. ἐκβάλλω in 6:13 and 9:18)?

As noted previously a number of commentators are convinced that Mark's transfiguration account has Moses' experience on Sinai in view (Ex 24:16).[295] Consequently, in terms of the following confrontation scene,

---

[292] See e.g. Koester, 'Jesus'; Keck, 'Christology'; Achtemeier, 'Origin'; Kelber; Donahue, *Trial*; etc. Some scholars, however, never accepted this view, e.g. Schulz, *Stunde*; Burkill, 'Dualism'; see further, Dowd, *Prayer*, 15ff.

[293] 'Miracles', 544f.

[294] E.g. Sergeant, *Lion*, 57f.

[295] See the previous discussion in Chapter 5, pp. 126f.

several scholars see a reflection of the descent of Moses from Sinai and his subsequent confrontation with idolatrous Israel (Ex 32).[296] Others have detected in γενεὰ ἄπιστος the influence of God's *Klage* against his people (especially Dt 32:20 LXX, cf. Mt 17:17; Lk 9:41).[297] Not surprisingly another suggestion reads the incident in terms of the continued and exasperating failure of disciples to 'understand'.[298] Finally, some see in Jesus' use of ἀνέχομαι an allusion to Yahweh's 'bearing' his idolatrous people in Isaiah 46:4 (cf. Isa 40:11).[299]

Under an INE rubric all of these observations prove constructive. First, in the paradigmatic first Exodus, Moses' experience on Sinai (Ex 24) is intimately linked with his descent to encounter a faithless people (Ex 32). Here in Mark, Jesus' transfiguration on the mountain is likewise followed by a confrontation with his faithless disciples who are then rebuked for being a γενεὰ ἄπιστος. In terms of the second and third proposals, this designation is linked with Israel's idolatry (cf. LXX Dt 32:20 and 32:16f, 21, probably with the golden calf incident of Ex 32 in mind) and, given the continuity between in Mark between idolatry (and its demonic expression) and failure to understand, the rebuke sits well with the motif of demonisation and Jesus' frustrated questions of his uncomprehending disciples in Mark 8:17f (cf. Dt 32:6, 28).[300] And turning to the fourth suggestion, similar themes recur in the disputation introduced by Isaiah 46:4 (ἀνέχομαι, LXX). There, in the setting of the announcement of a second Exodus, Yahweh restates his superiority over the idols (vv. 5-6), expresses his frustration with the nation's faithless inability to learn from their past experiences (vv. 8, 12), and yet affirms his commitment to effect the NE salvation in spite of the nation's obduracy (vv. 10f, 13).[301] Finally, in the light of the above discussion on the possible influence of Exodus 32

---

[296] Vv. 9-13 notwithstanding, *pace* Best, 'Miracles', 544. It might be that Mark's subsequent placement of an extended teaching section (Best, *Following*, 75-133), while still integrated with his account of Jesus' journey and the passion predictions, is also part of a New Sinai pattern: Jesus as the greater-than-Moses gives instructions for the New Israel. Recognising first Exodus parallels does not damage the thesis since Isaiah's NE derives from Israel's founding moment and there is no reason why Mark could not integrate themes from both to make his point, especially if there is a Moses-'servant' connection.

[297] Gnilka, 1.47; Pesch, 1.90; Hooker, 223.

[298] Lane, 329, citing Ebling, *Messiasgeheimnis*, 172-78; Schenke, *Wundererzählungen*, 324f, 345; Best, *Following*, 66, sees instead a failure to act.

[299] Martin, 109, following Tödt, *Son*, 179.

[300] Therefore, *pace* Best, *Following*, 67, the rebuke might not be 'pointless'.

[301] Schoors, *Saviour*, 273ff, 150ff; Melugin, *Formation*, 131ff.

on Isaiah 53, an Exodus 32 motif here in Mark's 'Way' section would not be out of place: in the first Exodus an idolatrous and uncomprehending Israel needed someone to intercede, so too here in the second.

All four suggestions can, therefore, be integrated if Mark 9:14-29 is understood as a continuing portrayal of Jesus' faithfulness when confronted with the disciples' incomprehension and failure—even when on the INE 'Way'—a faithfulness modelled on Yahweh's faithfulness in the face of Israel's failure in both the first Exodus and its Isaianic counterpart.

If this analysis of the two sight miracles and the exorcism of the deaf and dumb spirit is correct, then in accordance with the NE schema, Mark places all of Jesus' healing miracles and exorcisms in the first section, but he makes exceptions of these, and only these, because of their didactic contribution to the overall purpose of his 'Way' section.[302]

---

[302] The 'cursing of the fig tree' will be addressed in Chapter 9.

Chapter 9: Isaiah's Promise ...
and Malachi's Threat: Part 2
Arrival in Jerusalem

*Jesus' arrival in Jerusalem bears little resemblance to the expectations of
the Isaianic NE in that the initial popular euphoria is quickly
overshadowed by official hostility. In this final section of his Gospel,
Mark brings together the logical outcome of Malachi's threat and Isaiah's
theme of judicial blinding—the Temple and its hierarchs are 'cursed'. On
the other hand, the Isaianic NE is ultimately effected through Jesus'
'servant' death.*

I. Introduction

Although the Isaianic NE reaches its culmination in the joyful reception
and enthronement of Yahweh in a gloriously restored Jerusalem, Mark's
story concludes somewhat differently. Jesus' cursory visit to the Temple
and his refusal to stay in the city overnight is unsettling enough, but the
next day sees the tension which has been building throughout the
previous sections finally erupt as, in his first major action on reaching the
city, Jesus 'cleanses' the Temple (11:15-19). This act, accompanied by the
disturbing cursing of the fig-tree (11:12-14), his probing question about
John (11:20-33), and the provocative parable of the tenants (12:1-12), sets
the tone for an increasingly acrimonious and ultimately deadly conflict
with the Jewish authorities. After emerging victorious from a series of
confrontations (12:13-40 [41-44]), Jesus announces the Temple's destruction
(13:1-37), interprets his death as initiating a covenant (14:24), and is tried,
sentenced, and executed (15:1-47). Finally, in a remarkably brief passage,
Mark subsequently informs us that Jesus was raised from the dead,
apparently concluding with the unusual statement that the first witnesses
told nobody for they were seized with fear and amazement (16:8).[1]

---

[1] On the thematic unity of this material, see e.g. the overview in Hooker, 'Traditions',
8-11; cf. also Donahue, *Trial*, 115ff.

The aim of this Chapter is to investigate how much of Mark's carefully crafted final section is consistent with an INE paradigm. After dealing with Jesus' entry, we will examine the imagery of the cursing of the fig-tree, the use of Isaiah 56:7 and Jeremiah 7:11 in Mark 11:17, and the allusion to Isaiah 5:1ff in Mark 12:1-9 within the context of Jesus and the Temple. Given the argument of the previous Chapter on the influence of Isaiah 53 on the passion predictions and Mark 10:45, we will weigh the case for echoes of Isaiah 53 in the words of institution, and Jesus' subsequent passion. Finally, we will offer one or two very brief comments as to how the end of Mark's Gospel might also relate to the INE.

It will be argued, in general terms, that the promise and the warning inherent in Mark's opening citation and which have been present throughout the narrative are finally brought to their respective climaxes. More particularly, Mark's recounting of Jesus' 'triumphal' and 'messianic' entry, his declaration of what the Temple ought to have become (Isa 56:7), and his explanation of his death (Isa 53) are all at home within the framework of the INE fulfilment. On the other hand, Malachi's threatened 'cursing of the land' comes to the fore in the judgement of the fig-tree and the recitation of Jeremiah's famous utterance on the Temple.

II. The 'Triumphal' Entry

a) The INE Expectation of Yahweh's Return

The hope of the Isaianic NE culminates in the glorious return of Yahweh to a restored Jerusalem. Just as worshipping Yahweh at Sinai was the guarantee and sign of the prototypal first Exodus (Ex 3:12), the goal of the INE is the enthronement of Yahweh in a restored Zion-Jerusalem.[2] Hence

---

[2] Schoors, *Saviour*, 243; cf. Durham, *Exodus*, xxiff. Sinai is subsumed in Mount Zion, and the New Exodus reaches its culmination in the arrival of Yahweh's presence in Jerusalem. Muilenburg, 'Isaiah', entitles Isa 40-48, 'The imminent coming of God', cf. also Spykerboer, *Structure*, 183; Rendtorff, 'Komposition', 306f; and Dumbrell, 'Purpose'. As noted earlier, Preuß, *Deuterojesaja*, 45, makes the point emphatically (as does Kilian, 'Strasse') when he says that the 'Ziel des neuen Exodus ist nicht das Land allgemein, sondern ist der Zion, und es ist nicht primär das Volk, sondern Jahwe selber, der jetz dorthin, so daß von der Rückkehr des Volkes dann nur als der Folge und Begleiterscheinung der Rückkehr Jahwes'.

the declaration: 'your God reigns!' (52:7; cf. 41:21; 43:15; 44:6; and Ex 15:18).[3] Consequently, concern for Jerusalem, the Zion of Yahweh, appears immediately in the prologue (40:1-11) where as noted earlier the city appears in the inclusio passages of verses 1-2 and 9-11.[4]

Previously, in Isaiah 6, the prophet had seen Yahweh as the Lord enthroned in his Temple-palace in Jerusalem. Ominously set in the time of King Uzziah's death, this portent prepares us for the outcome of the imminent clash of two imperiums (7:1ff): the heavenly King, now awesome judge, and the corrupt Davidic monarchy.[5] Confronted with pious unbelief, Yahweh's promised coming—Immanuel (7:14)—can only mean devastating judgement (7:17) and this, as we have also seen, is particularly focussed on Jerusalem (3:1, 26; cf. 6:11-13).[6]

But as in judgement, so in redemption. Jerusalem-Zion, as the urban symbol for Israel, is again central. In the prologue the word of comfort in 40:1ff culminates with what seems to be a messenger announcing good news to Jerusalem (40:9f, LXX; $\epsilon\grave{v}\alpha\gamma\gamma\epsilon\lambda\iota\zeta\acute{o}\mu\epsilon\nu o\varsigma$ (*bis*)),[7] and then throughout Isaiah 40-55 and up to the closing scenes of chapters 65-66 there is a tendency to focus on Jerusalem-Zion's restoration. The city is clearly pivotal in Yahweh's plans (cf. 2:1ff).[8]

Thus, although Cyrus and Yahweh's 'blind and deaf' 'servant' Jacob-Israel are the focus of the polemical chapters 40-48 (but see 44:26; 45:13), in the largely proclamation-of-salvation section (49-55) the restoration of Jerusalem—and the role of the enigmatic 'servant'—is clearly to the fore.[9] Zion's waste places will become like Eden as Yahweh effects a new creation (51:3, cf. 41:17-20[10]).[11] Chapter 54 comprises something of a climax with its

---

[3] Cf. Ezek 20:33 where Yahweh will reign as King in the New Exodus.

[4] Kiesow, *Exodustexte*, 23-66, see Chapter 3, p. 78, above.

[5] Dumbrell, 'Worship', 2; and Liebreich, 'Position', where Isa 6 contrasts King Yahweh with the kings of Isa 7-8.

[6] See e.g. the discussion in Chapter 7, pp. 189-90, and Chapter 8, pp. 213ff, above.

[7] The meaning of the phrase מְבַשֶּׂרֶת יְרוּשָׁלַם is unclear. The LXX takes it as 'messenger to Jerusalem', cf. *Tg. Isa*; see Watts, *Isaiah*, 2.82.

[8] Dumbrell, 'Purpose'; Rendtorff, 'Komposition', 305ff; and Clements, 'Unity', 128.

[9] On this Watts, 'Consolation', 49, 56f, citing Mettinger, *Farewell*, 26; Hessler, *Gott*, 82ff; Melugin, *Formation*, 85, who sees this prefigured in Isa 40:1-11; Kiesow, *Exodustexte*, 163; and Wilcox and Paton-Williams, 'Servant', 82ff.

[10] Isa 41:17ff refers to the land not the desert crossing, as per van der Merwe, *Pentateuchtradisies*, 51-57, cited in Beuken, '*MISPAT* ', 20.

[11] Schoors, *Saviour*, 300, sees only a vague implication of redemption as new creation, following Rendtorff's observation ('Stellung') that the creation terminology is primarily confined to disputations or salvation oracles where it serves other purposes. However,

picture of glorious Zion (52:7-9; 54:11f), now re-established in righteousness, knowing divine protection and vindication, and whose accusers will
all be overthrown (54:14ff),[12] while 55:1-5 concludes with what Spykerboer
suggests is an invitation to return to the New Jerusalem.[13] The summons
in Isaiah 52 to the exiles to prepare to depart also recalls Isaiah 35 where
the redeemed, walking along the 'way of holiness', enter Zion 'with
singing' and, crowned with שִׂמְחַת עוֹלָם, are overtaken by שָׂשׂוֹן וְשִׂמְחָה (v. 10).

In facing the delay of the NE (Isa 56-66), the restoration of Jerusalem-
Zion is even more clearly the focal point.[14] In 60:1 (presumably prostrate
daughter) Zion is summoned to arise[15] for the glory of Yahweh is about to
dawn upon her (cf. 4:5). Explaining what this entails involves a series of
salvation proclamations (60-62),[16] arguably the pinnacle of the book.[17]
From the first, the imagery of light (60:1, 3, 19; 62:2) stands in stark contrast
to the present gloom and darkness (59:9ff; cf. 9:1ff). The description of the
city's splendour (60:17f; cf. 54:11f) is only outshone by her spiritual glory
with its emphasis on 'peace, righteousness, salvation, and climactically,
praise' (60:17ff)—again in stark contrast to the present (59:9, 11, 16f).[18] A
new development here is the attribution of characteristics of Yahweh—
light and righteousness—to Israel and Jerusalem (58:8; 60:17, 21; 61:10;
62:2).[19] Once destroyed by foreigners, Jerusalem will now be rebuilt by
them (60:10). No longer forsaken she will not only enjoy the fruits of her
labour (62:8; 65:21ff) but she will be nourished by the wealth of the nations
(60:15ff). So comprehensive is this transformation of the desolation (e.g.
64:10f) that the whole is crowned in an edenic description of the new
creation (65:17f). Not only is marvellous longevity seen as the norm for
her inhabitants, but, as in 40-55, there will be a miraculous increase in the

---

when considered in combination with the Chaoskampf/warrior imagery and the interpretation of the first Exodus as a creation event, and given that both are in proclamations,
Stuhlmeuller's assessment, *Creative*, is to be preferred; also von Waldow, 'Message', 277.

[12] Clements, 'Beyond', 108.

[13] 'Invitation'. Often seen as a wisdom invitation, the two may not be mutually exclusive, given the link between accepting Yahweh's wisdom and the restoration of Jerusalem.

[14] See fn. 8.

[15] Muilenburg; cf. 50:1; 51:17ff; 52:1f etc.

[16] See Westermann, 352f.

[17] Charpentier, *Jeunesse*, 79-80; Westermann, 296-308; Gottwald, *Hebrew*, 308; Polan,
Ways, 14-15.

[18] Muilenburg, *ad loc*; cf. Bonnard, *ad loc*.

[19] Rendtorff, 'Komposition', 313.

numbers and strength of her people (60:22; cf. 54:1ff). Not surprisingly, this creation of a new Jerusalem is greeted by great joy (65:18).[20]

As the final lament reveals, all this is predicated on Yahweh's presence (63:7 - 64:11).[21] Jerusalem's restoration is primarily a matter of the return of Yahweh's glorious presence which is both the goal of the NE and the hallmark of the restoration; hence the same kind of self-designation which in 40:9f and 35:4 characterised the coming of Yahweh appears in 62:11.[22] Whereas in the earlier chapters of Isaiah Yahweh's glory was the stimulus for Jerusalem's judgement, here it becomes the chief attribute of redeemed Zion and her inhabitants (cf. 60:7, 9, 13, 19; 61:3) and so much so that the entire city seems to become one all-encompassing Temple to Yahweh (60:1-3; cf. 2:2ff; 4:5f). Although the sun and moon apparently remain, Yahweh himself will be the city's light (60:19f). It is this to which the nations are drawn (62:2; cf. 2:1-5) and which causes righteousness and praise to spring up among them (61:11; 62:1f, 7): praise and joy again being the major characteristic of the peoples' response to Yahweh's saving intervention (56:7; 60:5, 6, 20; 61:2f, 7, 10, 11; 66:18ff).

Given the preceding discussion of Isaiah 53 and Mark 10:45, one also notes the centrality of the λύτρον-λυτρόω word group. The most prominent motif in this respect is that of the 'redeemer'-(גֹּאֵל) marriage where Jerusalem, the once childless and rejected bride, is now miraculously fruitful due to the restored marital love of Yahweh (54:1-10).[23] Although Jerusalem had played the harlot (cf. 12:21), her husband Yahweh's judgement of her was a matter of discipline not divorce (54:4f;[24] cf. 50:1-3).[25] So although forsaken for a time, she will be saved by Yahweh, her loving kinsman spouse, and once-barren Jerusalem is portrayed as rejoicing over her myriad descendants (44:4; 49:19ff; 54:1-3; cf. 49:25; alluding perhaps to the patriarchal promises). And this in contrast to

---

[20] See Ollenburger, *Zion*, 48; and Rendtorff, 'Komposition', 299.

[21] So Fischer on 63:7 - 64:11, 'Das Problem der Klagenden ist die gebrochenen Beziehung zu JHWH', *Wo?*, 254. Cf. Ex 33:15ff.

[22] Rendtorff, 'Komposition', 301; see Chapter 3, p. 80, fn. 148, above.

[23] Stuhlmueller, *Creative*, 103f, 115ff. Krupp, *Verhältnis*, who discusses role of the marriage bond in covenantal understanding, sees it as both the central point of reference for chs. 40-55, and the highlight of the coming of Yahweh, such that ch. 54 forms the goal to which the whole moves.

[24] van der Merwe, 'Echoes'; cf. Hos 1-3; Jer 2-3.

[25] Melugin, *Formation*, 156; although divorce is not an uncommon metaphor of punishment for idolatry, Jer 3:8; Hos 2:4.

proud 'daughter Babylon' who will be childless and widowed (47:8f). It is not surprising, then, that גאל-language also appears in connection with the momentous chapters 60-62, both in terms of Yahweh's advent as Warrior (59:20; 63:4) and in the crowning designation of Yahweh's people (62:12).

Given, too, the role of the 'servant' in effecting Jacob-Israel's redemption, some comment on his relationship to Jerusalem is appropriate.[26] The idea of 'comfort' for Jerusalem is key to the opening proclamation of 40:1 and recurs in 51:3, 12; 52:9; and 54:11, all in 49-55 and thus probably related to the action of the 'servant'. Indeed, in 49:13 the installation[27] of the 'servant' is seen as Yahweh comforting his people and his suffering in 53 apparently effects Jerusalem's restoration. That 'comfort' is picked up again in 57:18 in conjunction with NE imagery (cf. 57:14f)[28] and reiterated in 66:13 where Yahweh comforts his people in restored Jerusalem underlines its importance.[29] Since in 56-66, the announcement (and inauguration?) of comfort, release, sight (LXX), etc. is the task of the individual in 61:1-3, it is worth examining his relationship with the earlier 'servant'.

The similarities between this figure and the preceding 'servant' poems have long been noted: the same monologue style, similar language, the anointing with the Spirit of Yahweh (cf. 42:1), the proclamation of liberty to the captives (cf. 49:6),[30] and (perhaps) the proclamation of the day of vengeance (cf. 49:8).[31] On the other hand, there are differences: there

---

[26] On the complexities of this issue, see now Steck, *Gottesknecht*, especially his last chapter, 173-207.

[27] Williamson, 'Concept', 146f; cf. Melugin, *Formation*, 70f; van der Merwe, *Pentateuch-tradisies* (cited in Spykerboer, *Structure*, 52).

[28] Westermann, 327, citing Zimmerli suggests that the 'way' language here takes on a more paraenetical sense.

[29] Rendtorff, 'Komposition', 299.

[30] Westermann's proposal that this refers not to the captives but to imprisoned debtors (58:6) has some merit. But in view of the postponed NE background, of 59:9ff, the imagery in 40-55, and the nature of 'deliverance' throughout, there may also be a wider referent.

[31] Cannon, 'Isaiah', sees it of a piece with them, cf. Hanson, *Dawn*, 65ff; Koch, 'Gottesgeist'; Michel, 'Eigenart'; Zimmerli, '"Gnadenjahr"' (the latter suggests that 61:1ff represents the earliest interpretation of the 'servant' songs, 'Sprache', 69ff; Schreiner, 'Buch', 157); cf. Cheyne; Driver; Mettinger, *Farewell*, 10; and Smart. Delitzsch, 620, notes the following similarities: endowment with the Spirit of Yahweh (42:1), Yahweh has sent him and with him his Spirit (48:16?), he comforts the weary (50:4; cf. 42:3), and the deliverance mentioned here does not seem a mere prophetic announcement but an announcement that necessarily initiates, and is integral to, liberation (vv. 3, 4f; cf. 42:7; 49:9). Whybray, 239f, also notes the correspondence between v. 2 and 49:6. Achtemeier, *Community*, notes the following correspondences: v. 1, 42:1, 7; v. 2, 49:8, 13; v. 3, 42:13; v. 4, 49:8; v. 5, 49:9; and v. 11 (?) with 49:18; although she sees the 'servant' as the community.

appears to be no specific connection with the nations, there is no hint of suffering or rejection, and the phraseology מָשַׁח יהוה אֹתִי (61:1) is unparalleled.[32] Who, then, are we intended to see as the speaker?

For many commentators it is the author of this section, whoever he is understood to be, while others see an individualisation of the faithful community (interestingly, both options are also proposed for the earlier servant songs).[33] On the literary reading taken here, several of the older commentators' observations are worthy of attention. This kind of self-disclosure characterised earlier 'servant' passages[34]—that the 'servant' title does not appear is not overly problematic as it is also absent from 50:4-9. In addition, if chapters 56-66 represent the reconfiguration of the NE hope and given that the picture of restored Zion in chapters 60-62 is its heart, it would be fitting that the final announcement has a 'servant' figure at its centre, especially given what appears to be the function of the other 'servant' passages in regard to the INE.[35] This would support the natural reading of בַּשֵׂר (61:1) as reflecting the concerns of 40:9 and 52:7.[36] While a 'mission' to the nations is not apparent—neither is it mentioned in two of the earlier 'songs' (Isa 50 and 53)—it is not entirely absent here. From a literary perspective, if the restoration of Jerusalem forms the centre, then the coming of the nations comprise the bookends (56:3-8; 66:18ff). This structure suggests that Jersualem's restoration inaugurates, or is at least integral to, the movement of those from the outer regions toward the centre.[37] The reference in the two Warrior passages to Yahweh's astonishment (שמם) that אֵין מַפְגִּיעַ (59:16) or וְאֵין סוֹמֵךְ ... אֵין עֹזֵר (63:5), stresses both his intimate connection with the figure of 61:1ff and Israel's total incapacity. Much as in the case of the 'servant' poems of 40-55, there is the same marked contrast between the parlous condition of Israel

---

North's final reason, *Suffering*, 138f, for excluding 61:1ff—chs. 60-62 are not an integral part of Deutero-Isaiah—is, in view of his admission of the 'undoubted similarities', tacit support for its inclusion on the basis of the literary approach taken here.

[32] Whybray, *Isaiah, ad loc.*

[33] Hanson, *Dawn*, 66; Smart, 259; Achtemeier sees a 'Levitical-prophetic Servant community'.

[34] Delitzsch; cf. Muilenburg, who sees the prophet here nevertheless notes, 'it is surely a profound and impressive mission that is given to him: he is the eschatological prophet in a superlative degree.' Whybray notes the tension between such a lofty self-designation and yet restricted function when compared to the earlier prophets.

[35] Cf. Achtemeier, 89ff; and Beuken, 'Servant'.

[36] *Pace* Westermann, 365f.

[37] *Pace* Bonnard, *Isaïe*, 416n2; cf. Achtemeier, 147f.

throughout 56-66 and the figure in 61:1-3. And just as the 'servant's' role in 52-54 is linked to the democratisation of the promises to David (55:3), introducing the first reference to plural 'servants' in 40-55, so also here.[38]

Admittedly the issue is difficult but the similarities with the preceding songs (cf. 42:1; 49:9) can hardly have been accidental. Within the confines of the book it seems most natural to take the speaker as the same kind of figure envisaged in the earlier 'songs' but with the prophetic dimension emphasised (*Tg. Isa* 61:1 reads 'the prophet'; cf. 1 Kgs 19:16; Ps 105:15).[39] On balance, 61:1ff appears to describe a 'servant' figure who is intimately related to the INE restoration, certainly by way of its proclamation and most probably also its inauguration. At the same time, in the two Warrior passages of 59:15-21 and 63:1-6 there is considerable emphasis on Yahweh seeing that there is none to help, taking the initiative and himself coming to Jerusalem's aid.

From this perspective then, the restoration of Jerusalem is a matter of Yahweh coming as Warrior, but also involving a human agent (usually understood by later interpreters as a messianic figure; so *Tg. Isaiah*[40], and cf. e.g. *Pss of Sol*, given its INE imagery[41]).

Finally, there is one critical distinguishing characteristic of the salvation described in these later chapters. It is no longer assumed to include Israel as a whole. Just prior to the conclusion of the book, we have Yahweh's response to the preceding laments (65:1ff): he has allowed himself to be found by those who were not seeking him—the phrase הִנֵּנִי הִנֵּנִי as we have seen has strong connections with the NE of 40-55[42]—but they did not respond (65:2ff).[43] So, in contrast to 40-55 where salvation was offered to the whole community, the threat implicit in, for example, chapter 48 has developed into a definite cleavage between the faithful and the wicked.[44] Yahweh now also has an ironic word of 'comfort' for his enemies (57:6; 66:5; cf. 1:24). Isaiah 65:13-16 is exemplary of this decisive rift

---

[38] Beuken, 'Main', 81-85, noting that עבד in 56-66 is always plural, (see further below).

[39] Cf. Emmerson, *Isaiah*, 42.

[40] See again the role of the Messiah in several editions of *Tg. Isa* 42:1ff; 52:13f; and 53:10ff; also Chapter 4, p. 115, fn. 137.

[41] E.g. *Pss. Sol.* 17:21, 32. In the light of *Pss. Sol.* 17:21, cf. Isa 42:1ff; 49:1ff, etc.; *Pss. Sol.* 17:31; cf. Isa 55:5; *Pss. Sol.* 17:24; cf. Isa 49:2; 27b; *Pss. Sol.* 17:27; cf. Isa 54:13; *Pss. Sol.* 17:30; cf. Isa 45:14; 49:22. See also Schüpphaus, *Psalmen*, 124ff and 115.

[42] Also Rendtorff, 'Komposition', 301.

[43] On the literary unity of this section, Webster, 'Rhetoric'.

[44] Westermann, 301f, 330f, 399f.

with its fivefold comparison between עֲבָדַי and the idolatrous.[45] Even the mention of the voice of Yahweh's retribution in the הֵיכָל in Isaiah 66:6 suggests the judgement motif that was earlier associated with the temple in Isaiah 6, and again the recipients appear to be faithless Israelites.[46] Several observations are in order.

First, in view of the interest in the early chapters on idolatry, it is significant that not only do the words of judgement in 56-66 consistently follow accounts of idolatry (57:13, cf. vv. 1-12; 65:6f, cf. vv. 1-5; 65:12a, 13-15, cf. v. 11f; 66:4, cf. vv. 3, 17), but idolatry is almost exclusively given as the reason for judgement. The relationship between blindness/deafness and idolatry is implicit in the fact that it is in precisely these contexts that the language of deafness occurs (65:12; 66:4).[47]

Second, the term עֲבָדַי highlights an interesting development. In chapters 40-55 the application of the 'servant' designation was apparently reduced to an individual, the 'servant' *par excellence*. However, after the completion of his activity, the plural reappears and seems to be related to those who are the beneficiaries of his activity (עַבְדֵי יהוה, once only, 54:17).[48] In chapters 56-66 this trend continues.[49] While the term 'servants' in 63:17 may recall Israel's earlier election, it could also look forward to those who will be redeemed in the now-deferred New Exodus and indeed 'servants' is used thereafter solely in this latter sense (65:8, 9, 13-15 (5 x's); 66:14). What is particularly noteworthy, if I am correct in reading the עֶבֶד terminology in this way, is that, for the first time in the entire book, indeed in the introduction of 56-66, foreigners are described as ministering to Yahweh as his עֲבָדִים (56:6; cf. v. 8; see below).[50]

In conclusion then, the INE restoration of Jerusalem is closely linked with the return of Yahweh himself and the career of an enigmatic 'servant', who in later interpretation is sometimes and only in part understood in messianic terms. At the same time, there is an bifurcation in national Israel with Yahweh distinguishing between his 'servants', who

---

[45] See Beuken, 'Main', 78f; Achtemeier, 122ff.
[46] *Pace* Westermann; cf. Whybray.
[47] Perhaps also cf. 56:12 and 65:11.
[48] So e.g. North, cf. Westermann.
[49] So now also Beuken, 'Main'.
[50] See also Westermann, 312; Achtemeier, 35f.

now apparently include foreigners, and those who although natural born have apostatised.

b) Jesus' Entry into Jerusalem

The healing of blind Bartimaeus, replete with the messianic connotations of his plea for help, is intended by Mark not only to conclude his 'Way' section by recalling Peter's 'trees-as-men-walking' confession but also to set the scene for Jesus' carefully orchestrated entry into Jerusalem.[51] In this respect David Catchpole notes the repetition of ὁδός terminology (Mk 10:46, 52; 11:8), of the Davidic acclamation (10:47f; 11:10), of the reference to ἱμάρτιον (10:50; 11:7f), of the prominence of the salvation theme (10:52; 11:9), and of the linking of acclamation with the act of following (10:52; 11:9).[52] That Mark devotes as much space as he does to a detailed chronicle of what at first seems immaterial detail ought to alert us to its significance. At the same time this section is part of a larger, double intercalation:[53]

Jesus' identity and authority: 'triumphal' entry (Ps 118:25f)	(11:1-11)
Cursing of the fig-tree	(11:12-14)
Incident ('cleansing'?) in the Temple (Isa 56:7/Jer 7:11)	(11:15-19)
Withered fig-tree, and mountain-moving	(11: 20-25)
Jesus' identity and authority: authority questioned, response	
in the vineyard parable and stone saying (Ps 118:22f)	(11:26 - 12:12)

Similarly, F. J. Matera had earlier suggested that Mark frames this material in three ways: the Son of David issue (11:10, [cf. 10:47f]; 12:35f), the double quotation of Psalm 118 (11:9f; 12:10f), and references to the Mount of Olives (11:1; 13:3).[54] Mark, therefore, seems to regard this section as forming a unified whole which deals in some way with the relationship between the coming of Jesus and the Temple and, once again, the key issues are his identity and authority (11:28; cf. the programmatic response to the first miracle: τί ἐστιν τοῦτο; διδαχὴ καινὴ κατ᾽ ἐξουσίαν, 1:27).[55]

---

[51] Catchpole, 'Entry', 321ff. Gundry, 634f, who allows no special relationship between the two but sees 10:46-52 only as being integral to Jesus' preceding ministry, regards 11:11ff 'as an uneventful entry by a private pilgrim', 635. This hardly seems the plain meaning of 11:8-10.

[52] 'Entry', 319. While not wishing to overstate the connections, Gundry's dismissal of them, 634, seems hasty.

[53] Cf. Hooker, 261, but with 12:1-12 added.

[54] *Kingship*, 68f.

[55] See Chapter 4, pp. 227ff, above.

In terms of general background, Catchpole and Brent Kinman have both drawn attention to the importance of the entries of visiting dignitaries in the ancient world.[56] Catchpole notes the basic features of such entries wherein Jerusalem was involved: they are often the consequence of having won a great victory and having already achieved considerable status, involve a 'formal and ceremonial entry', entail greetings, acclamations, and invocations of God, peak in a visit to the Temple, and embrace some sort of cultic activity. Jesus' entry clearly shares a number of these standard traits.[57]

In addition, granted Mark's interest in the OT as *Rahmen* for his gospel and the thorough-going OT language of the acclamation (11:9f), we should perhaps also look for possible OT antecedents; but as Kinman points out celebratory entrances into Jerusalem are not commonly detailed in the OT.[58] Nevertheless, without minimising the substantial agreement with features of contemporary entries, the OT parallels suggests that Mark also intends Jesus' entry to be understood particularly in the light of 'royal' (to use Kinman's terminology, 1 Kgs 1; cf. Zech 9:9-10), and possibly 'coming of the ark' (2 Sam 6), arrivals.

First, in terms of the 'royal' category, the accent on 'Son of David' in the preceding Bartimaeus pericope and the kingdom language (cf. ἡ ἐρχομένη βασιλεία τοῦ πατρὸς ἡμῶν Δαυίδ, Mk 11:10) stress its 'regal' nature.[59] Jesus also rides upon a animal rather than walks (cf. 1 Kgs 1:33, 38; Zech 9:9),[60] he is hailed as king (Mk 11:10; 1 Kgs 1:34, 39; Zech 9:9), the attendant chorus

---

[56] Kinman, *Entry*, 25-65, from whose work—although it is concerned primarily with Luke—a number of the following points are drawn. See also the briefer summaries in Catchpole's earlier article, 'Entry', 319-21, where he notes various parallels with the arrivals of Alexander in Jos. *Ant.* 11.325-39, 342-45; Apollonius in 2 Macc 4:21f; Judas Maccabaeus, 1 Macc 4:19-25; 5:45-54; Jos. *Ant.* 12.312, 348f; Jonathan Maccabaeus, 1 Macc 10:86; Simon Maccabaeus, 1 Macc 13:43-48, 49-51; Antigonus, *B.J.* 1.73f; *Ant.* 13.304-6; etc., and now Duff, 'March', 59ff; Coakley, 'Messianic', 470ff, citing also Peterson, 'Einholung'.

[57] Catchpole, *ibid.*, 321; cf. Kinman, *Entry*, 91-122; and Duff, 'March'.

[58] Kinman, *Entry*, 48-65.

[59] See also Matera, *Kingship*, 70-74. Gundry's claim, 626, that Mark is uninterested in Jesus' kingship since he fails to quote Zech 9:9 (Mt does) and because of the ambiguity of πῶλος, is difficult to reconcile with his statement that Jesus is acting 'messianically by carrying out Zech 9:9', 633. While Mark may not wish to emphasise the fact, the parallels here offered suggest that a kingship motif is not far away. Rather than repudiate the idea of Jesus as Israel's king, Markan Christology recasts Israel's ideal of kingship.

[60] Mark's πῶλος, while perhaps indicating 'horse' to a Roman audience (so Gundry, 626), is a not uncommon Palestinian term for a donkey colt and Mark's audience could have been familiar enough with the story to recognise what animal was in view, Michel, 'Frage'.

from those who participate[61] has messianic overtones (Mk 11:9f; cf. Ps 118:26),[62] and the covering of the path with garments recalls Jehu's acclamation (cf. 2 Kgs 9:12-13).[63]   The detailed account of Jesus' preparations, in particular the thorough instructions, and the subsequent recital of their fulfilment not only suggests their import but thereby invites comparison with the pattern of David's preparations for Solomon (1 Kgs 1:33, 38).   Of course, Mark has twice informed us that Jesus has accepted the designation 'Son of David'.   And as, for example, *Psalms of Solomon* 17:21-22, 30-33 makes clear—granted this is a royal task in the OT (e.g. 2 Kgs 12; 23)[64]—the coming of the Davidic King sits alongside an expectation of the purging of Jerusalem which is in effect what Jesus signals in the outer court of the Temple (see below).[65]   In addition, there are such features as the ἀγγαρεία conventions[66] and, depending on the extent to which the later written sources reflect earlier traditions, similarities with the 'colt' of the messianically interpreted oracle of Genesis 49:10-12[67] which further heighten the royal and messianic character of the event.[68]   Taken together this data suggests that Mark intentionally presents Jesus' coming in 'royal', and almost certainly, 'messianic' terms which are then picked up in Jesus'

---

[61] It is important not to overestimate the size of the crowd involved. Mark uses the terms πολλοί and ἄλλοι, but does not use ὄχλος πλεῖστος, as he does in e.g. Mk 4:1. On the comparative size of Jesus' entry versus that of Pilate, see Kinman, *Entry*, 159-72.

[62] Werner, '"Hosanna"', citing e.g. *b. Pesah* 117b; *y. Meg.* 2.1; Lohse, *TDNT*, 9.682-84, citing *Midr. Ps.* 118:22; Schneider, *TDNT*, 2.667-71; Jeremias, *Eucharistic*, 257ff; Str-B, 1.845-50. Although much of the evidence is quite late, see Burger, *Jesus*, 48, it is widespread which suggests an early origin, Coakley, 'Messianic', 473ff, citing also *Tg. Pss* 118. On the probable meaning of 'Hosanna', see Fitzmyer, 'Interpretation'.

[63] Coakley, 'Messianic', 472f, in citing the case of the younger Cato (Plutarch, *Cato Minor* xii. I) who 'was accorded similar treatment ... by his troops' suggests that the military overtones would suit a messianic leader. Burkill, 'Strain', 34, and Kinman, *Entry*, 95, also suggest the 'Mount of Olives' setting (Zech 14:1-5; cf. 2 Sam 15:30); but see Gundry's criticisms, 633.

[64] Jeremias, *Jesus*, 41-44.

[65] Marcus, 138; Davenport, '"Anointed"', 68; Hamilton, 'Temple', 370ff; also Kee, *Community*, 126, where he cites the use of the cleansing motif in Isa 56 in connection with a Davidic king at Qumran in 4QFlor and 4QPBless, but I have not been able to substantiate his claims; see Seeley, 'Act', 277.

[66] Impressment, while permitted for others, was very much a 'royal prerogative', Stauffer, 'Messias', 85; Derrett, 'Palm'. The ὁ κύριος probably means no more than one who is a 'legitimate claimant', Judge, *NDIEC*, 1.43.

[67] On the messianic interpretation of Gen 49:10ff (e.g. *Tg. Onq.*; *Tg. Ps.-J.*; *Tg. Neof.*; cf. 4QPBless) and its connection with Zech 9:9, Blenkinsopp, 'Oracle'; Matera, *Kingship*, 71ff; cf. Pesch, 2.179.

[68] *Pace* Kelber, '*Kingdom*, 94ff, who has Mark rejecting the acclamation; see the discussions in e.g. Catchpole, 'Entry', 326; and Telford, *Barren*, 251-69.

anointing (14:3), the repeated statements during the trial (15:2, 9, 12), Pilate's epigraphy on the cross (15:26), and the mockery of the Jews (15:32).[69] That Mark records that 'those going before and after' offered a messianic acclamation hardly means he rejects the notion of Jesus as Messiah. Aside from indicating how Jesus should have been received, it is also an ironic indication that the crowd, who has not been privy to Jesus' passion predictions or ensuing teaching, is no further advanced in its perception of what this entails than was Peter when he offered his confession at the beginning of the 'Way'.

But what of the idea of Yahweh's coming himself which is so crucial to the INE? Kinman has suggested some parallels with the 'coming of the ark' model which has both 'royal'—'the Lord is King' (cf. Ps 24:8; Isa 43:15; Zeph 3:15)—and 'military' associations, but is first and foremost representative of Yahweh's kingly presence.[70] He points out that Mark's interest in Jesus' preparation for his entry is not only reminiscent of those for Solomon but also for the coming of the ark to Jerusalem in 2 Samuel 6—'each being a royal welcome of a sort'.[71] In this case 'the concern for the transport of Jesus, the king, could be seen as analogous to the preparations made for the coming of Yahweh, the king, symbolically in the ark'.[72] In this respect, Kinman notes the 'newness' of the wagon (2 Sam 6:3), suggesting it is set aside for sacred purposes, comparing it with the 'unused' colt. Granted that when comparted to Luke's treatment of this connection, Mark's presentation is not quite as obvious.[73] Still, given Mark's account of Jesus to date, the expression 'in the name of the Lord' almost certainly means 'with authority to act on behalf of the Lord' and therefore Jesus is at the very least Yahweh's representative.[74]

Can we say more? We have already suggested that Mark's introductory sentence and Jesus-as-Yahweh-Warrior motif imply that Jesus is in some

---

[69] On the kingship of Jesus in the passion narrative, see especially Matera, *Kingship*.

[70] See his discussion of the OT pattern, *ibid.*, 58-60.

[71] *Ibid.*, 91.

[72] *Ibid.*, 92.

[73] *Ibid.*, 101f. However, in the light of Jesus' judgement on Jerusalem, it is interesting that according to the LXX of 1 Sam 6:19 the sons of Jechoniah die because they do not rejoice at the return of the ark, cf. Ps 68:1ff.

[74] Gundry, 631. Duff, 'March', 59f, observes that on occasion Græco-Roman entries were described in epiphanic terms taking on the aspect of the entrance of a deity. Given the OT echoes, however, it is doubtful if Mark intended his account to be read primarily in this light.

way uniquely to be identified with the very presence of Yahweh, that is, he is the Son of God. The motifs in Mark 11:1ff would certainly not be antithetical to the OT idea of a 'divine' entry.[75] Further, as Catchpole pointed out, these entries often came as a celebratory consequence of a victory already achieved. Is this the case for Mark? Catchpole, in rejecting Reimarus' opinion that Jesus has in mind a 'secular kingdom', points to 'the presupposed victory that is clearly gained by healings, of which Mark 10:46-52 is intended as a typical example'.[76] Assuming an INE paradigm, this is certainly the case in that Jesus' healings testify to Yahweh's coming 'in strength' on behalf of his people.[77] It is even more so, however, if one reads the entry in the light of Mark's constant and emphatic portrayal of Jesus as the one who has defeated the demonic (3:22-27; cf. 1:21-8; 5:1-20; 7:24-30; 9:14-29; also 3:15; 6:7-13; and 1:34, 39; 3:10f).[78] This connection would only be reinforced if the 'entry' genre led one to expect the possibility of an earlier victory.

Along similar lines, Paul Duff has recently argued on the basis of a putative Zechariah 14 background to Mark 11:1-23 and again understood within the Græco-Roman genre of 'entries' that Mark presents Jesus as the Divine Warrior (of Zechariah) who comes to Jerusalem and purges the Temple, among other things, of its traders.[79] Granted that the idea of the Yahweh-Warrior motif is pivotal, apart from the conceptual idea of expelling the traders which may reflect Zechariah 14:21b[80]—although Mark's Jesus ejects not just the sellers but also the buyers—there is in fact very little else of Zechariah 14 echoed here.[81] Starting out at the Mount of Olives (Mk 11:1) may just possibly be an allusion to Zechariah 14:4, but then, Mark 11:23 notwithstanding, there is nothing that corresponds to the predicted cataclysmic results (Zech 4:4b, 6-8). That all the cooking pots in Jerusalem will be holy (Zech 14:21) differs from Jesus' interdicting those

---

[75] See Kinman, *Entry*, 59f, citing LXX Pss 23:7-10; 46:6ff; 67:24ff; 131:7f.

[76] 'Entry', 322ff.

[77] See Chapter 6, pp. 170ff, above.

[78] See again Chapter 6, pp. 152-60, 163-64, 166-69.

[79] 'March', 65nn42 and 44, citing in support of a Zech 14 horizon, Evans, 'Galilee'; Roth, 'Cleansing'; Schweizer, *Mark*, 231; Hiers, 'Purification'; Malbon, *Narrative*, 121-24; and Catchpole, 'Entry'.

[80] Recently, Tilly, 'Kanaanäner', in examining the Targums has shown that כנעני can also refer to 'betrügerischen' and 'sozial disqualifizierte Händler', 35f. But whether this is what Jesus implies by ληστaί is another matter (see below).

[81] See Duff, 'March', 66.

carrying a vessel (Mk 11:16),[82] and although Zechariah 14:5b might be a reference to Yahweh's procession to Jerusalem it is not in fact unambiguously so. Nevertheless, given Mark's earlier presentation of Jesus, it would appear that we have here the entry of the victorious 'Divine Warrior' into Jerusalem.[83] In the same vein, the exultant praise of the 'many' is entirely in keeping with the joy and praise which accompany Yahweh's restorational coming to Zion in the INE.

Given the foregoing and our argument for the correlation of Mark's 'Way' with the INE, it is possible that there are also echoes of the joyous procession of Yahweh and his people to Zion in Isaiah 35. Although displaying but few direct linguistic parallels (e.g. 'blind', 'way'), there are a number of interesting conceptual correspondences: A) the coming of Yahweh's presence in Jesus, the Son of God and Yahweh-Warrior with vengeance 'to save' (11:9f; Isa 35:4), B) the blind man is encouraged (10:49; cf. Isa 35:4), receives his sight (10:52; cf. Isa 35:5), and is thus 'saved' (10:52; cf. Isa 35:4), C) they are on the 'Way' (10:52; cf. 46; Isa 35:8), D) they enter Zion with joy (11:1, 8f; cf. Isa 35:10), and E) declare the praises of God (11:10b, ὡσαννὰ ἐν τοῖς ὑψίστοις; cf. Isa 35:2, τὸ ὕψος τοῦ θεοῦ). What we seem to have here in the celebratory 'entry' of the Son of God and victorious Warrior accompanied by his 'healed' people into Jerusalem is the Markan equivalent of the climax of the INE.

However, Mark has already adumbrated on numerous occasions that all is not well. Kinman's original contribution to the discussion is to show, in terms of both the general 'entry' and more particular 'royal' and 'messianic' genres, the significance of Jesus not being met by city officials or leading citizens nor being escorted back to the city. Such a response, or lack thereof, to Jesus' παρουσία can only be interpreted as an intentional and blatant affront.[84] That their first meeting, when at last the authorities do appear, is one of confrontation (Mk 11:27-33) only heightens the insult and helps explain the severity of Jesus' response in the parable of the tenants (Mark 12:1-12). In keeping with Isaiah's promised INE and Malachi's warning, Israel's messianic-'servant'-deliverer and Son of God has at last

---

[82] As Duff recognises, 'March', 56, telling against Roth's suggestion, 'Cleansing', 177f; see Bauckham, 'Demonstration', 77f.

[83] The integration, or at least blurring, of roles of the Divine Warrior and the Messiah can be seen in e.g. 4 Ezra 13:1-3, cf. v. 37; Duff, 'March', 67n55.

[84] Kinman, *ibid.*, 121.

come to Zion. But in a stunning reversal of the INE hope, official Jerusalem has in a most pointed manner not welcomed him. What might transpire when he 'suddenly comes to his Temple' is not a happy thought.

III. Jesus and the Temple[85]

a) Introduction

Once again the themes of the INE expectation and the ancient formal 'entry' genre coincide. A standard feature of the formal 'entry' is that the processional entrance is followed by a ceremonial visit to a temple; Mark's account of Jesus' Temple visit is therefore true to type.[86] Duff's article offers an additional insightful nuance. To offer sacrifice or to participate in some sort of cultic activity amounted to an 'act of appropriation', and 'provided the conqueror the religious legitimation to rule'.[87] In Mark, however, we hear nothing of a regular cultic activity but instead of Jesus' condemnation of present practice. Here his presentation of Jesus as David's Son resonates with the aforementioned expectations of Temple cleansing (again, *Pss. Sol.* 17). Similarly, at the culmination of the INE, Yahweh is greatly concerned with the restoration of 'his house' (56:5, 7; 60:7; cf. Mk 11:17). In view of the implications of Mark's introductory appeal to Malachi 3:1, it is not hard see in Jesus, as T. A. Burkill suggests, 'the Lord of the temple and the God-sent guardian of its sanctity'.[88] Mark's account of Jesus' visiting the Temple and looking around seems intended to set the stage for his actions on the next day.[89] He also twice mentions that Jesus does not remain in Jerusalem (11:11b, 19), a withdrawal which may indicate the messianic King's awareness, on the basis of his snubbed entry, that he is unwelcome in his own city.[90]

---

[85] Although of some relevance, since they do not immediately involve allusions to Isaiah (e.g. Isa 56 in the Temple) or Malachi (the 'cursing'), we will not be examining the claims of the false witnesses at the trial, 14:58, nor the significance of the veil being torn, 15:38. On this see e.g. Donahue, *Kingship*, 103-38, 201ff; Juel, *Messiah*, 117-225; Lührmann, 'Zerstörung'; Matera, *Kingship*, 137ff; Vögtle, 'Tempelworte'; and Kim, 'Temple'.

[86] E.g. Archelaus' 'royal' entry into Jerusalem was also followed by a procession to the Temple, Jos. *Ant.* 17.194ff, Catchpole, 'Entry', 321; Duff, 'March', 60ff.

[87] 'March', 62.

[88] 'Strain', 37.

[89] Lane, 398; Gundry, 635.

[90] Pesch, 2.187, suggests lack of accommodation.

In terms of Mark's literary technique, it is commonly accepted that the intercalation of the cursing of the fig-tree and the Temple-'incident' reflects his characteristic method of indicating that the passages are mutually interpretive and symbolise the end of the cultic practice in the Temple, and even its physical destruction (cf. 13:2).[91] This has more recently been questioned on various grounds and will need to be examined.[92] A related issue is the apparent contradiction between the clear statements in Mark concerning the destruction of the Temple (e.g. 13:1ff) and the symbolism of Jesus' action in the 'cleansing', or better still 'incident' (to use M. D. Hooker's non-prejudicial term[93]), which seems not to signify destruction (11:15f).[94] Further, how is one to understand Jesus' aphoristic teaching in the outer court and his 'stone' saying at the end of the 'wicked tenants' parable?

b) The Fig-Tree and the Temple

Jesus' cursing the fig-tree has generated a good deal of discussion as W. R. Telford's extensive survey shows.[95] Many scholars have understood its relationship to the Temple incident as a mutually interpretative complex such that the cursing of the tree bespeaks the Temple's future. However, R. H. Gundry has recently devoted a entire subsection of his commentary to challenging this near-consensus, and particularly Telford, whose mono-graph has largely shaped present day debate.[96] Gundry's primary points, which may serve as a convenient summary of the major (and some

---

[91] See e.g. Dobschütz, 'Erzählerkunst'; Donahue, *Christ*, 58-63; Achtemeier, 23-26; Telford, *Barren*, in summary, 161ff; Burkill, 'Strain', 38; Schnellbächer, 'Theology'; Kelber, 97-102; Hooker, 'Traditions'; Edwards, 'Sandwiches'; Evans, 'Action', 239ff; and especially now Shepherd, *Sandwich*, 209ff. Dowd, *Prayer*, 39, notes that this interpretation of the fig tree goes back to Victor of Antioch's sixth cent. commentary on Mark.

[92] E.g. Räisänen, 24f (citing Werner, *Einfluß*, and Dschulnigg, *Sprache*), and Gundry, 671ff.

[93] 'Traditions', 7.

[94] This has engendered considerable debate concerning Jesus' historical intention. Our concern is with how Mark presents the idea.

[95] *Barren*, 1-38. Specialist studies continue to appear, most recently including e.g. a socio-economic approach in Oakman, 'Cursing'; Krause, 'Narrated', who argues for Hos 9:10-17 as the basic horizon; and the midrashic approach of Buchanan, 'Withering' (on Mt) who sees an evolutionary process beginning with Ps 1 through Jer 17, Ezek 47, and Zech 14.

[96] See Gundry, 671-82; and also Dowd, *Prayer*, 72-75. Interestingly, Gundry cites Dowd in support of his case, but fails to mention her argument that the fig tree incident both teaches about faith and symbolises judgement on Jerusalem, *Prayer*, 55.

minor) difficulties, are as follows.[97] A) While fruitlessness, fig-trees, and figs are undoubtedly common Jewish metaphors, Mark's need to explain Jewish practices in 7:2-4 'contradicts the argumentative presupposition that Mark's audience was steeped in Jewish lore'.[98] B) OT prophetic actions arose out of an intention to communicate, not out of hunger, and did not entail the miraculous. C) In the six OT examples cited by Telford,[99] the fig-tree does not represent the Temple but Israel, and even if one allows the Temple to represent Israel, Mark's use of the fig-tree image does not correspond to OT usages. D) Mark's text does not admit of a symbolic interpretation, since only a failure to have borne fruit constitutes religious sterility and Jesus is not looking for fruit. E) The events in the Temple do not correspond to the destructive implications of the cursing. For example, Jesus does not seek to stop sacrifices in the inner court, but instead simply prevents commercial traffic in the outermost court.[100] F) Telford's attempts to excise 11:24-25 being unconvincing, the second half of the fig-tree story teaches the power of prayer and indicates that the whole account does not concern the Temple. G) Finally, (although from this author's perspective not crucial), 'this mountain' cannot mean the Temple mount.

The array is impressive, but to borrow Gundry's question, how well do these arguments hold up? A) Mark 7:2-4 deals with extra-Torah practices[101] and implies nothing as to the familiarity of Mark's audience with OT imagery. In fact, Mark's frequent appeal to the OT suggests otherwise. On the other hand, Telford has recently produced an extensive overview of Græco-Roman views of fig-trees wherein he notes that several revered fig-trees were associated with Rome, the withering of one of which was regarded as an ominous portent.[102] On these latter grounds alone, the significance of Jesus' action for the city could easily have been divined. B) Whatever Jesus' original motivation in approaching the fig-tree, there is nothing to disallow him subsequently making a prophetic point if he so desired. Gundry's own argument assumes as much when he

---

[97] For a thorough survey of the issues raised over the past 150 years, again Telford, *Barren*, 1-38.

[98] *Ibid.*, 672.

[99] *Barren*, 142-56; namely, Jer 8:13; Isa 28:3-4; Hos 9:10, 16; Mic 7:1; Joel 1:7, 12.

[100] Following Hamilton, 'Temple'.

[101] See Gundry's discussion, 358f, and for considerable detail, Booth, *Purity*, 155-216.

[102] 'More', 299f.

states that the whole event arose out of Jesus' hunger, and only later resulted in a discourse on faith. Second, there is no logical necessity that non-miraculous OT prophetic symbolism must be determinative for Jesus' actions. C) Granted the importance of the Temple for Jerusalem, and Jerusalem for Israel—Jerusalem being something of a synecdoche for the nation—it is difficult to see why the fig-tree as a symbol for Israel could not also be used to symbolise the Temple and its establishment.[103] Furthermore, Telford produces numerous examples that link horticultural imagery of Israel flourishing, the 'mountain of the Lord', and the proper operation of the Temple and cultus.[104] With regard to how Mark's Jesus uses the fig-tree symbol over against the diverse usages in the OT (which diversity itself answers Gundry's objection), it is *context* that sets up the referent—in Mark at least the Temple establishment—just as is the case in the various OT passages. Gundry later happily allows that Mark 12:1-12 is based on Isaiah 5:1ff even though 'Jesus shifts the emphasis' by omitting the kind of produce the vine gives and, by introducing instead tenant farmers, making the point not the destruction of the vineyard but the tenants. D) However we handle the difficulty of Jesus' expectation of the tree,[105] even allowing that 'not the season ...' indicates that Jesus was looking for buds not figs,[106] the issue remains that Jesus expects something but does not find it. Either way, the symbolism of an outwardly productive plant that fails to meet the expectations it generates is retained. (Depending on the precise time of year, no buds may well indicate no future figs.) E) The lack of correspondence between the 'cursing' and the 'cleansing' has already been noted as a significant consideration. This will be dealt with in more detail below, but suffice to say here that they may not be as mutually exclusive as is sometimes suggested and, given our

---

[103] See Dowd, *Prayer*, 39, who notes the association of trees and temples in the ancient world. Von Kienle, 'Fiegenbaum', suggests that the fig tree represents that part of the Temple crowd which fails to respond to Jesus. While the basic distinction is right—obviously not every Israelite is condemned—Mark's concern seems more general, i.e. the passing of the old religious establishment and the reconstitution of the new.

[104] Telford, *Barren*, 140f. The texts are cited below in the subsequent discussion on the identity of the 'mountain' in Mk 11:22; see also Feldman, *Parables*, 151ff.

[105] Again see Telford, *Barren*, 1-38; and Gundry's brief review of more recent alternatives, 673f.

[106] Gundry, 636, citing, Bacon, *DCG*, 1.593; Christie, *Palestine*, 118-20; Bishop, *Jesus*, 217; and Carrington, 237.

argument to date regarding contextual awareness of OT texts, the Jeremiah 7 quotation could well imply judgement.

Point F) is more substantial. The second part of the story is indeed developed into a lesson on faith (vv. 22-25) and, because we are concerned with the text as it stands, verses 24-25 must be explained *in situ*.[107] (Incidentally, that Gundry seems to regard the defining influence of verses 22-25 as the most powerful element of his case almost implies that without them Telford's position would be quite strong.) The matter turns on one crucial issue: is the meaning of the fig-tree incident necessarily determined by the teaching on mountain-moving faith? Regardless of how the mountain-moving material is understood, can such a rigorously determinative link safely be assumed? In spite of Gundry's and Telford's agreement on this point, I think not. Mark's Jesus seems to me to be quite adept at changing tack if the situation offers a rationale for doing so.[108] The famous twists and turns of the 'salt-sayings' crux of 9:49-50 appear to be the result of a linkage forged solely on the basis of their common terminology and related if shifting themes.[109] Similarly, the disciples' forgetting bread leads to a warning about the leaven of Herod and the Pharisees, which then turns into a rebuke over hardness of heart (8:14-21). Jesus' teaching on the disciples' relationship to one another in 10:35-44 becomes the occasion to give the purpose behind his death (10:45). Perhaps, too, this tendency is reflected in the way Mark's Jesus often combines two OT texts in unusual ways.[110] Now these are clearly not well-flagged, nicely paced, scholarly discussions, but neither are they entirely unrelated, irrational lurches. And while in terms of mechanical issues such as the number or balance of words or verses none of these examples correspond precisely to Mark 11 or even to each other, they do, nevertheless, make the point.

It seems, then, not only possible but even typical that one kind of action or teaching by the Markan Jesus can give rise to instruction on another perhaps initially unrelated topic but which on reflection reveals a greater

---

[107] Redactional insertion or no, as Telford himself seems to appreciate, *Barren*, 49.

[108] This is not so much a question of redaction, but instead of what Mark, and perhaps his audience, was happy to regard as acceptable continuity.

[109] E.g. Lane, 350; and along similar lines, Gundry himself, 515. Whether Mark put these sayings together or not is immaterial at this point since he presents them as Jesus' words.

[110] Again, Kee, 'Function'.

continuity. And, unless one holds that Jesus was seeking out budless but leafy fig-trees so he could curse them as an opportunity to teach on mountain-moving faith, changing tack is exactly what he does here. This data suggests that the teaching on 'faith' (11:22-25) does not determine the meaning of the fig-tree cursing, and therefore it does not rule out metaphorical or symbolic significance for the fig-tree incident.[111] Granted this, Gundry's demurrals based on the identity of the 'mountain' (G) are no longer directly relevant, although they will be considered later when we discuss Mark 11:22ff.

Accordingly, Telford's arguments based on OT and later use of fig-tree imagery[112] and his recognition of the supporting role of Mark's intentional 'sandwich' structure[113] remain intact. Furthermore, we would suggest that additional support can be found in the thorough-going Markan matrix of Malachi imagery.[114] His opening Malachi 3:1 citation, as Telford notes (see below), implicitly warns of 'the Lord's sudden coming to his Temple'. This is not an inappropriate account of Jesus' arrival in Jerusalem, if 'suddenly' is taken to stress the need for preparedness, particularly in light of the leaders' absence at his παρουσία.[115] And it is perhaps even more so seeing that Jesus' activity in Jerusalem is centred on the Temple[116] and that he takes the initiative against his opposition 'in an unprecedented fashion' (11:15-18; 12:1-12, 38-40).[117]

Moreover, Mark's opening presentation of John suggests that he is Malachi's Elijah (1:6).[118] Granted Malachi's linking 'the coming Lord' and Elijah, it is noteworthy that Mark frequently links Jesus with John. Not only is John's imprisonment the catalyst for Jesus' beginning his ministry (1:14a; cf. 1:5 and 3:7f) but even in his death John is still, ominously both

---

[111] Dowd, *Prayer*, 37-55, appealing to rabbinic concerns about the efficacy of prayer in the face of the Temple's destruction, thinks that both fig tree panels combine judgment on the Temple and, as a natural correlative (for a Jew?), the efficacy of prayer. It is not clear, however, that the possible failure of prayer *per se* is the issue for Mark.

[112] *Barren*, 128-204.

[113] *Ibid.*, 48. To point out the sandwich structure is not thereby necessarily a rejection of history, but only to note that Mark could have chosen not to include the story or to do so in another way. Mark's setting, although somewhat similar to Matthew 21:21, is distinct from that of the other Gospels (Mt 17:19f; Lk 17:5-6).

[114] See Chapter 3, pp. 58ff, 87; and Chapter 7, pp. 184f, fn. 3, above.

[115] See Chapter 7, p. 185, fn. 4, above.

[116] Juel, *Messiah*, 127ff; Hooker, 'Traditions', 7ff.

[117] Burkill, 'Strain', 31, 39.

[118] See earlier, Chapter 3, p. 59, fn. 38; Chapter 7, p. 189, fn. 3.

for Jesus and Israel, functioning as Jesus' forerunner (6:14-29; 9:9-13). Further, 'Elijah' was to prepare the way, lest Yahweh at his appearing 'curse' the land (Mal 3:21 MT).   Given the pervasive theme of John's rejection, the symbolism of Jesus' cursing the fig-tree takes on greater significance.   Finally, in connection with the Temple incident, John is mentioned again—pointedly recorded, not immediately after the Temple scene itself, but after the intercalated fig-tree incident (11:27-33)—and is thereby directly connected with Jesus' authority to do and say what he does (again see below).

Mark's presuppositional use of the Malachi context seems evident. Jesus' action, as the Lord who after the long delay of his INE appearance now suddenly comes to his Temple, is predicated on the religious authorities' failure to hear 'Elijah' (11:31; cf. 1:4, 14; 9:13).[119] All of this strongly suggests that Jesus' cursing of the fig-tree, whatever its other meaning/s, in Mark's present setting carries considerable symbolic freight. As a result, in view of our argument for the programmatic character of 1:2f, we agree with Telford's almost passing comment that Mark intends that the cursing of the fig-tree should be read in light of Malachi's prophecy:

> Elijah the prophet *had* been sent before the great and terrible day of the Lord (Mal. 4.5; cf. Mk. 9.12) but they had done to him whatever they pleased (Mk. 9.13)! Therefore the Lord would come and smite the land with a curse (Mal. 4.5) and the blow *had* been struck against the barren fig-tree![120]

In light of this imagery there is a possible further connection with Isaiah, namely, the last great lament which we have aleady argued is

---

[119] Cf. Shae, 'Question', 23; Martin, 67f; but *pace* Hiers, 'Purification', 88f, who suggests that 11:30 indicates Jesus' authority is equivalent to John's, i.e. he too is an eschatological Elijah. Bowman, 221f, cites *Midr. Cant.* 2.13, which begins with a reference to Cant 2:11-13, on the fig tree putting forth its figs and then states that the second Exodus is expected to take place during the spring. Using this as background, Bowman suggests that the cursing of the fig tree is a demonstration that 'the Jewish view of the new Exodus ... is not to be'. Granted the lateness of the source, a less general and more precise implication seems rather that the present Temple establishment will no longer have a part in the NE.

[120] *Barren*, 163; cf. Hooker, 'Traditions', 8; Burkill, 'Strain', 39; Hiers, 'Purification', 88; Clark, 'Interpretation'; *pace* Gaston, *Stone*, 83. Barrett's observation, 'House', 20 (cf. Lindars' comment, *Apologetic*, 108) that the Malachi prophecy 'is so manifestly appropriate' that its omission is surprising, suggests that the reader is perhaps expected to understand it so. On the cursing of ground (Gn 3:17) and the destruction of trees (Ex 9:25; Ps 105:33; Jonah 4:6f) being acts of Yahweh, see Blackburn, *Theios*, 196f.

significant for Mark (1:10; 3:28ff; perhaps 5:25-34; and even 4:1 - 5:43).[121] Again, Isaiah 56-66 appears to be addressing Israel's situation after it failed through unbelief and rejection of Yahweh's wisdom in his choice of agent (i.e. Cyrus) to participate in the full hopes of the INE.[122] Now facing the aftermath, these chapters describe the nation's awful circumstances. Their sanctuary[123] has been burned and trodden down by their enemies (63:18; 64:12 MT) and Zion-Jerusalem and their cities have become like deserts (64:9 MT).[124] They have withered like a leaf (נָבֵל כֶּעָלֶה, 64:5 MT; cf. 1:30; 40:7[125]), and not only do Abraham and Israel (the patriarch) not recognise them (63:16) but they have become as if Yahweh, 'our father' (cf. first Exodus, Ex 4:22) and 'our redeemer', had never called them (63:16, 19).[126] It is possible that as desolation and being withered were the results of the first refusal to accept Yahweh's 'wise' choice of a deliverer, now in the fulfilment of the INE when there has again been a failure to repent and Yahweh's 'wise' choice has again been rejected, desolation and withering is again the result. (The objection that the desolation was there prior to the announcement of the INE does not detract from the symbolism.) But the language of being withered also points to another option.

R. A. Cantrell has suggested that the imagery of Yahweh seeking figs on his fig tree is found in Jeremiah 8:13, a text not far removed from Jeremiah's famous Temple sermon from which Jesus draws his subsequent pronouncement in the outer court (cf. Jer 7:11 in Mk 11:17).[127] The question of the literary structure of this section of Jeremiah is wide open[128] and the interpretation of the text in question, all are agreed, is particularly difficult.[129] The preceding verses lament the corruption of people, prophet, and priest (vv. 10-12); the latter echoing of the concerns of the Temple sermon and not unrelated to Jesus' critique of the activities in

---

[121] See respectively, Chapter 4, pp. 102-8; Chapter 6, pp. 150-51; p. 172, fn. 180; and p. 176, fn. 203.

[122] Once again, Watts, 'Consolation'.

[123] Westermann, 398.

[124] Cf. also Schnellbächer, 'Theology', 104.

[125] Westermann, 396.

[126] On the Exodus imagery here, Achtemeier, 113f.

[127] Cantrell, 'Cursed'.

[128] Thompson, 297, regards 8:4 - 10:25 as a miscellaneous collection following directly on from the Temple sermon, cf. Craigie, *et al*, 129. McKane, 187, seems content to address the text in small units without asking why the book eventually found the form it did.

[129] See the discussion in Holladay, 283-86.

the outer court (see below). In verse 13 the basic options are whether
A) Yahweh was seeking a harvest (a positive sense, cf. Isa 5:1ff) but found
the vine and the fig tree empty and the leaves withered, and thus ensures
judgement (v. 12b;[130] or B) because he found them empty Yahweh will
cause the leaves to wither;[131] or C) because of their sin Yahweh was going
to harvest them as an act of final destruction, so that there will be neither
grapes nor figs, and the leaves will be withered.[132] Although the second
alternative might be closest to Jesus' action, all three readily exhibit points
of contact. On this basis, Cantrell suggests that Jesus' cursing of the fig-tree
is a dramatic invocation of these verses, symbolising the judgement that
was to fall on account of the parlous state of the Temple (Jer 7:11).

This may raise a question about the necessity of Telford's appeal to
Malachi 3:1ff, but it need not. If, for Mark, Malachi serves to relate John
the Baptist and Jesus by providing the larger context of Jesus' coming to the
Temple and the reason for a curse in general (3:1, 24 MT), then the
Jeremiah background establishes both the particular basis on which the
curse is applied and the antecedent of Jesus' prophetic symbolism (Jer 7:11;
cf. 8:13). Once again Mark's Jesus brings together several OT perspectives
to make his point.

c) Jesus and the Temple Incident

(i) Introduction

In view of our primary interest in whether or not Mark is operating with
an INE paradigm, Jesus' use of Isaiah 56:7 will be our first concern. Again
we note the presence of a combined 'citation' which suggests something of
the importance of this scene for Mark.[133] There is also a certain ambiguity
to Jesus' action which, granted our reading of the cursing of the fig-tree,
raises questions as to the overall coherence of Mark's presentation. This is
especially so if the Temple incident is to be interpreted as a reforming act
and not one of judgement. Our second concern, then, will be to examine
the significance of Jesus' action and to determine whether or not it
contradicts the cursing of the fig-tree.

---

[130] Thompson, 301f.
[131] Craigie, *et al.*
[132] McKane, 189; Holladay, 283f; cf. LXX and *Tg. Jer.*
[133] Kee, 'Function', 173.

(ii) The INE and the Temple

Before turning to the explicit use of Isaiah 56 some brief comments on the role of the Temple in the INE are in order. Given the considerable emphasis on the return of Yahweh's presence in the INE, it is remarkable that there are so few references to the restoration of the Temple in Isaiah 40-55. Isaiah 44:28 makes the clearest statement when it unequivocally promises the Temple's rebuilding. The return of the sacred vessels is mentioned in Isaiah 52:11, but here the concern is apparently primarily one of purity and holiness.[134]

In almost direct contrast, when one moves into chapters 55-66 one of the signal aspects of their portrayal of Yahweh's return is their interest in the restoration of the Temple (בֵּיתִי: 56:5, 7; 60:7; מִקְדָּשִׁי מְקוֹם: 60:13; cf. הַר־קָדְשִׁי, 56:7; 57:13). Not only so, but in a striking indication of a radical inclusiveness, participation in worship is affirmed both for the eunuchs[135] and those foreigners who have joined themselves to Yahweh (56:2-7; cf. Isa 2:2-3), even to the point where the latter apparently partake in priestly service (66:19ff).[136] On the other hand, it is noteworthy that the only time the term הֵיכָל appears, as in 1-39, is in connection with Yahweh's judgement on the apostates among his people (66:6).[137]

(iii) The INE and the Nations

The mention of foreigners in Isaiah 56:7 opens up a pandora's box of seeming contradictions on the role of the nations in the INE. This is largely due to two apparently mutually exclusive features. On the one hand, there are clear denunciations of the nations. They are presented as foolish idolaters (40:15ff; 44:9-20) now under judgement (41:11f, 15f; 49:24ff; 51:7f, 12, 21ff; cf. 43:3f). This is particularly so in the case of arrogant daughter Babylon (43:14; 46:1ff; 47:1-15).[138] The nations come in abject surrender (45:14), bearing the exiles upon their shoulders and licking the

---

[134] Westermann, 252f, suggests that the silence concerning the temple indicates that the criteria for Yahweh's presence are to do with holiness, faithfulness, and purity of the people, not the cultus per se; cf. Stuhlmueller, 'Transitions', 8n29.

[135] Perhaps those, mentioned in 39:7, who had accepted this condition on entering official employment in exile, cf. Whybray, 198.

[136] See the discussion on pp. 321ff, below.

[137] The identity of these enemies is disputed. Westermann, 419, is convinced they are foreign nations, whereas for Achtemeier, 142f, they are apostate Jews. The context seems to support the latter.

[138] On this imagery in the context of the book, see Erlandsson, *Burden*, 135-42.

dust off the feet of their conquerors (49:22f). According to 52:1, the וְטָמֵא עָרֵל will not be permitted into Jerusalem. Just as Jacob-Israel's judgement occasioned the nation's victories, so her deliverance brings about their defeat. It is largely on the basis of this bellicose material that several scholars have denied any 'universalistic' tendencies in these chapters.[139]

On the other hand, there are texts which indicate a different future. While 40:5; 42:10ff; 44:5;[140] and 45:6[141] are ambiguous in this regard, D. W. Van Winkle has demonstrated that יחל in 51:5, where the nations wait for Yahweh's salvation, means 'to wait with eagerness' and never has negative connotations.[142]   He further shows that the אוֹר גּוֹיִם and בְּרִית עָם language is soteriological (cf. 49:6; 51:4f),[143] and hence Yahweh's invitation to the nations that they turn to him and be saved (45:22).[144]   Following G. F. Oehler, Van Winkle concludes that the visions of salvation and submission should be combined in that the attitude seems to be one of salvation yet not equality, 'This rule (i.e. Yahweh's) is both that for which the nations wait expectantly and to which they must submit'.[145]   This more positive element may not be so surprising if it is remembered that it is the pagan Cyrus who is mentioned as the agent of Babylon's defeat and Israel's deliverance (44:24; cf. 45:7; 41:2ff, 25).   Van Winkle's proposal may also find support if פְּלֵיטָה is synonymous with שְׁאֵרִית (cf. 37:32), in which case 45:20 describes a remnant from the nations who are summoned to turn to Yahweh.   If so, this equivalence suggests another way of resolving

---

[139] E.g. Snaith, 'Study'; Schoors, *Saviour*; and Orlinsky, 'So-Called'.

[140] Westermann, and Stuhlmueller, *Creative*, 129ff, see this as referring to proselytes.

[141] Snaith, 'Study', 154-65, tends to see passages that might otherwise be taken as positively referring to the nations as speaking of the Jewish exiles among the nations; cf. Schoors, *Saviour*, 302f.   Davies, 'Destiny', may assume too much in interpreting the language of 'seeing' and 'knowing' in e.g. 41:20 (?); 49:7 in a salvific light.   On 52:15f see Watts, 'Meaning'.

[142] 'Relationship', 447f; a similar case can be made for קוה, cf. 40:31 and 49:23.

[143] *Ibid.*, 452ff; Anderson, 'Covenant', 357; *pace* Snaith, 'Study', 157, and Orlinsky, 'So-Called', 97ff; cf. also Hollenberg, 'Nationalism', who argues that רַבִּים in 52:15 and 53:12 refers to the nations.   Lindars, 'Tidings', 485ff, argues that the message to the nations is not subsequent to, but one and the same with, the message to the exiles.

[144] Snaith, 'Study', 185, declares that כָּל־אַפְסֵי־אָרֶץ does not mean Gentiles, citing 43:5f. However, the context (a trial speech against the nations) implies the contrary, and elsewhere the expression appears synonymous with the nations, see 52:10; cf. Zech 9:10; Mic 5:3; Dt 33:17; and Pss 2:8; 22:28f; 72:8; etc.

[145] *Ibid.*, 457.   Davies, 'Destiny', 13f, sees instead an irreducible diversity deriving from a redactional mentality that saw the text as a 'billboard on which different political parties or religious groups daub their slogans'.

the tension. It could be that the remnant hermeneutic used of Israel, who had become like the nations and was thus under judgement, is also applied to the nations. Just as Yahweh offers to heal the bruises he inflicted on rebellious Israel (53:4f cf. 30:26; 1:5), so too the 'survivors' of the nations are invited to turn to him and be saved (45:20-22).

Inasmuch as the salvation and righteousness for which the nations wait is an expression of Yahweh's justice (51:4f), it is noteworthy that the revelation of Yahweh's מִשְׁפָּט is what unites the bulk of 40-55 with the various 'Servant Songs' which themselves present new insights into its true nature. In the songs Yahweh's justice includes light for the nations and so means not only deliverance for Jacob-Israel, but also, by the showing forth of his glory, light and salvation for the whole world.[146]

Similar kinds of themes are found in Isaiah 56-66 which also preserves both the particularism and universalism of 40-55.[147] On the one hand, the nations are judged (59:18f; 63:3f; 66:16, 24) and come in subjection to Israel (59:18; 60:10, 14; 61:5f) with any nation that refuses being destroyed (60:12; cf. 41:11ff). On the other hand, in perhaps the highest expression of universalism in the book and using language which is quite remarkable given the place of 'servants' terminology throughout these chapters,[148] the survivors of the nations not only come to Zion to worship (66:19; cf. 45:20-25; and 60:3, 6ff; cf. 2:1-4; 4:2-6; 42:6; 49:6; and 62:2f), but are even described as Yahweh's עֲבָדִים (56:6f).[149] The Temple, therefore, is to become a בֵּית־תְּפִלָּה לְכָל־הָעַמִּים (56:7).[150] Even more striking is the related text of 66:19. Although notoriously difficult, the antecedent of הֵם in verse 19 seems to be the nations in verse 18[151] and, therefore, indicates that some of these foreigners will become priests and Levites. This suggests that there will no longer be a distinction between the natural-born and the proselyte (66:21).[152] This does not, however, release the Gentiles 'of their task of assuring the return of the scattered Jews to their homeland' (60:4, 9; cf.

---

[146] Zimmerli and Jeremias, *TWNT*, 5.668f; = *TDNT*, 5.668ff; Beuken, '*MIŠPĀṬ* '.

[147] Muilenburg, 659.

[148] Again, see now especially Beuken, 'Main'.

[149] Westermann; Whybray; Smart; Blenkinsopp, 'Second'.

[150] In this context, it is difficult to determine if their ministry to Jerusalem (60:5-11) is willing or not, although 60:12 suggests that there is an element of threat involved, at least to those who refuse to serve.

[151] Westermann; Whybray.

[152] Achtemeier, 124f.

43:5).[153] But it may be that these פְּלֵיטִם will do so by declaring Yahweh's glory among the nations (66:19). Indeed, this could be the way in which the glory of Yahweh's work in Zion is 'seen' by the nations.[154]

In sum, while there is no doubt a message of judgement for the nations, there is also an offer of salvation. Not only so, but the more inclusive passages suggest the breaking down of distinctions such that even foreigners may serve as priests as Yahweh's Temple becomes 'a house of prayer for all nations'.

(iv) Jesus, Isaiah 56:7, and the Temple

Having cursed the fig-tree, Jesus enters the Temple or at least the outer court and drives out various groups. In view of the action and the Jeremiah allusion, the Isaiah 56 citation[155] is commonly understood as merely returning this court to its intended role as a place where Gentiles may pray unhindered.[156] This scenario is possible, but as C. K. Barrett noted some time ago and our immediately preceding discussion confirms something more is in view in Isaiah 56.[157] The evidence to date for a Markan INE hermeneutic, the eschatological slant given by the future κληθήσεται,[158] and the dative of benefit, πᾶσιν τοῖς ἔθνεσιν,[159] only increases one's doubts. Further, the nature of the circumstances—at best they would have constituted only a temporary disruption—and Mark's

---

[153] Whybray, 291.

[154] Cf. Conrad's analysis of Israel's role in the New Exodus, 'Oracles'.

[155] Apart from a slight change of word order, the form is almost identical to Isa 56:7 LXX, with the 'for all nations' differentiating it from Isa 60:7, LXX or 1 Macc 7:3. On the variations in wording, which are not of great significance, see Gundry, *Use*, 19f.

[156] E.g. Taylor; Lagrange; Lane; Kee, *Community*, 115, although he notes that Mark contrasts his inclusivist community with the exclusivist one of the Temple; Roloff, *Kerygma*, 97; France, *Jesus*, 93; Gnilka; Davies, *Gospel*, 350f; Eppstein, 'Cleansing', 56; Hurtado; Hooker. Both Gundry, 644, who sees here merely a demonstration of Jesus' authority, and surprisingly Grimm, 197f, barely address the significance of the Isaiah text.

[157] 'House', 15, where he asserts that the Temple never served such a function, and therefore Jesus' action cannot be construed as safeguarding Gentiles' present rights of worship. Others who see an eschatological dimension include Lightfoot, *Message*, 63; Gaston, *Stone*, 84, where Jesus has in mind an eschatological temple; Hiers, 'Purification', 89; Pesch, 2.199; cf. Kelber, *Kingdom*, 102f, who envisages the destruction of the Temple and its replacement with Mark's community.

[158] Lohmeyer, 'Reiningung', 261; Hiers, 'Purification', 89; Kelber, *Kingdom*, 102f.

[159] *Pace* Wellhausen, 90, and Kilpatrick, *Studies*, 157, on the basis of the immediate context in both Isa 56:7 and 60:7 (LXX), and also France, *Use*, 93, since this phrase indicates that for Mark it is not merely 'a house of prayer' versus 'a den of thieves' (see below).

intercalation with the symbolic cursing of the fig-tree, suggest this too is an acted parable.[160]

So what does Mark's Jesus intend, at least as far as his use of Isaiah 56:7 is concerned? E. Lohmeyer has noted the way in which Jesus' actions, beginning with the 'unclean' spirit in Capernaum (Mk 1:24), have on many occasions been to deal with uncleanness either by removing the stigma or redefining the terms, all of which are inclusive rather than exclusive in orientation.[161] It is significant, too, that Jesus' action is not directed against the inner, more sacred areas of the Temple proper. What he 'cleanses' is the outer court (or הר הבית, but commonly known in the literature by its more modern title, the 'Court of the Gentiles').[162] That business was conducted there without any record in extant sources of serious opposition to its location (apart from the account in question) suggests that this area was regarded in some way as less 'holy'.[163] It is this space which Jesus defines as a 'house of prayer'.[164]

The considerable implications of this statement are not immediately apparent unless several points are considered. First, the phrase 'house of prayer' although being for all nations in Isaiah 56:7 also appears later in 1 Maccabees 7:37, where it is explicitly delimited by 'τῷ λαῷ σου', namely, Israel. The point here is not that the Gentiles were not to have a place to pray, but that the Temple was not really for them. As Lloyd Gaston states, 'that the Gentiles may enter the outer court is occasionally mentioned, but only in the negative sense: they may not pass the *soreg* into the inner courts under penalty of death'.[165] Second, when one examines what is meant by the designation in Isaiah 56:7 and 60:7 (LXX), it clearly has to do

---

[160] Gaston, *Stone*, 84; cf. Sanders, *Jesus*, 70; Bauckham, 'Demonstration'; Hooker, 265.

[161] *Lord*, 24ff; citing also, the leper, 1:40-45; the forgiveness of sins, 2:1ff; the calling of Levi, 2:13-17; the woman with the flow of blood, 5:24b-34; and the parable on defilement, 7:15. One may also note here that the 'way' of the INE is also called in Isa 35:8 the 'Way of Holiness', in which case Lohmeyer's observation would suggest that Jesus' actions are aimed at opening up this holy 'way' to all.

[162] See Gaston, *Stone*, 87n2.

[163] Although Chilton, *Temple*, 107, emphasises the area's holiness, a distinction apparently remained, cf. 104-9, as the lack of contemporary sources criticising this innovation for impugning the Temple's holiness implies. His examples of Jewish outrage at Roman insensitivities, e.g. Jos. *B.J.* 2.224-27; *Ant.* 20.106-12, do not really address the issue of a differentiation in perceived holiness. Cf. Roth, 'Cleansing', 178, where Zech 14:21 may have provided justification for the exclusion of Gentiles from the inner courts.

[164] Lohmeyer, *ibid.*, 39.

[165] *Stone*, 87, citing Jos. *B.J.* 5.194; 6.124f; *Ant.* 15.417; and Acts 21:26ff; and on the prohibition, Bickerman, 'Warning'.

with the very heart of Temple practice, not just the periphery, since both instances mention offerings and sacrifices (cf. 1 Kgs 8:28ff).[166]

If this is so, then the Markan Jesus, as Israel's messianic king and inaugurator of the INE, is neither as many have assumed merely protecting the somewhat minimal access of Gentiles to the house of God, nor is he against the profanation *simpliciter* of the Temple,[167] nor is he making a statement about the eschatological replacement of the Temple.[168] Instead, the Lord of the Temple[169] having arrived, now orients the Temple toward its final goal. And this is not so much that the Gentiles would be permitted into the inner courts (although it may imply as much, see below),[170] but rather that the 'Court of the Gentiles' was to be considered not just a sacred space, but an equally sacred space.[171] By implication, given the inclusive theology of Isaiah 56-66, this indicates that the time is at hand when even Gentiles can belong to the 'kingdom of priests' (cf. 12:9; 15:39; cf. 13:27; Isa 66:18f; Zech 14:16; Mal 1:11).[172] As to whether the mention of 'prayer' constitutes an implicit critique of sacrifices, pointing forward to the time when his death would make them unnecessary,[173] Mark's account offers no observation.[174]

Likewise, there is no further comment in the larger context about Gentiles *per se*. Thus, although the statement is certainly consonant with an INE perspective on the nations, consistent with the Markan Jesus' hesitancy to actually inaugurate a 'mission to the Gentiles' (Mk 7:27), nothing more is done to elucidate this brief but pregnant declaration. On

---

[166] Also Gaston, *Stone*, 87, and the earlier literature cited therein; see Bauckham, 'Demonstration', 83f.

[167] E.g, France, *Jesus*, 93; Taylor, 463.

[168] E.g. Gaston, *ibid.*, 88; Kelber, *Kingdom*, 102f; Gnilka; Stock, *Method*, 298; Ernst.

[169] Several commentators deny a Mal 3 allusion here, e.g. Gaston, *Stone*, 82; and Barrett, 'House', 20, who is surprised at its omission. But given that the framing fig tree story has already alluded to it, and this within the larger Malachi matrix of the book, no further allusion is necessary.

[170] *Pace* Borg, *Conflict*, 171-77.

[171] Bauckham, 'Demonstration', 83f, makes the connection between sacrifice and prayer, but then goes on to see this merely as a statement about the primacy of prayer, which misses the point of 'for all nations' in both Isa 56 and Mark. That prayer may take the place of the defunct Temple is possible, see Dowd, *Prayer*, 37-55, but probably not Mark's immediate concern here since it puts 'my house' over against 'a place of prayer'.

[172] Lohmeyer, *ibid.*, 40. Hooker, 265, also sees the possibility of an eschatological dimension to the action.

[173] As e.g. in Schweizer, 233

[174] See Lightfoot, *Message*, 63; Taylor, 463.

the other hand, set in contrast to Isaiah 56's future hope is Jesus' indictment of the enterprise's current role as a 'den of thieves'—a critique whose
moment is heightened by the preceding cursing of the fig-tree.[175] It is to
this less encouraging aspect of Jesus' statement that we now turn.

(v) Jesus, Jeremiah 7:11, and the Temple

While scholarly consensus is agreed that the cursing of the fig-tree implies
judgement, the Markan Jesus' action in the Temple is more ambiguous
and has engendered a spirited debate. Does it imply cleansing and
therefore 'reformation'[176] (as per the common designation)[177] or
'disruption' and judgement?[178] Or is choosing either one beside the
point?[179] Given the extensive nature of the material, our aims here are
modest, namely, to outline the main options (and there are all manner of
minor variations), to note various problems, and to see if we can make
sense of what Mark is doing.

At first glance, the reforming or 'cleansing' idea is fairly obvious. Jesus
drives out the merchandisers in order that the outer court might return to
its proper use. Considering human nature, it would not be at all
surprising if unscrupulous vendors took advantage of their market
position and hence Jesus' allusion to Jeremiah 7. It used to be countered
that there was no hard evidence of such chicanery, but there is now
enough material to suggest the strong possibility of various levels of
corruption and unsavoury activity.[180] R. Bauckham offers a nuanced

---

[175] E.g. Lagrange, 296; France, *Jesus*, 93; Ernst; tend to make this the exclusive point.

[176] E.g. Taylor; Hiers, 'Purification'; Dowda, 'Cleansing', 231ff; Trocmé, *Formation*,
105n1; Pesch; Bilezikian, *Liberated*, 89; Hooker, 'Traditions', 17ff; Evans, 'Action', 269f,
although he seems to suggest otherwise in '"Cave"', 107f; Chilton, *Temple*, 100; and Gundry,
645.

[177] The word itself does not appear in Mark's account.

[178] E.g. Schweizer; Donahue, *Trial*, 114; Kelber, *Kingdom*, 102f; Gnilka; Dowd, *Prayer*,
45; Myers, 301; Geddart, *Watchwords*, 125; Sanders, *Jesus*, 61ff; Neusner, 'Money-Changers'.

[179] Lane, 407, in view of the fact that Jesus' words combine Isaiah and Jeremiah,
regards speculation on this matter as 'irrelevant'.

[180] For one of the most comprehensive accounts, see Evans, 'Action', 256-69; also
Bauckham, 'Demonstration'; Bockmuehl, 'Destruction', 15; Hooker, 264; and Eppstein,
'Cleansing', but noting Evans' criticisms, 'Action', 266f; cf. Hayward, ArB 12, *Jeremiah, ad
loc*. Seeley, 'Temple', has recently rejected Evans' data, but A) he seems to require evidence
of an order which most historical study simply cannot provide, B) his own case has
numerous historical assumptions, e.g. 'would probably', 'seems unlikely', for which he
offers very little concrete evidence, and C) his assumption that Jesus' acts must always be
transparently clear does not take into account the highly allusive and enigmatic nature of
e.g. Mark's presentation of Jesus' teaching.

approach when he sees, A) Jesus' action as constituting a wholesale attack on the fundamental concept of a Temple tax, B) the explicit mention of doves alludes to the abuse of the poor (citing *Ker.* 1:7), and C) the vessels and other animals refer to establishment profit taking.[181] On this view, the place had become a 'den of thieves' and so Jeremiah 7 is more than apt.[182] Not only so, but since the commercial interests are under the auspices of the Temple hierarchs the implications for them are not hard to see. It must be noted, however, that Jesus does not actually attack the sacrificial system itself,[183] in fact he keeps well away from the heart of the Temple proper.[184] Further, we have no evidence of messianic or prophetic figures coming to destroy the Temple, but 'cleansing' is common enough.[185] Finally, it would make little sense to speak of the Temple becoming a place of prayer (Isa 56:7) if it is already under sentence. One might also note here that the parable of the wicked tenants is not told against the Temple but those in charge.

Those taking the judgement or disruption view would argue that there are several problems with the cleansing position. Neusner maintains that Jesus' hindering the sale of sacrificial items in effect 'shuts down' the system.[186] According to *Sheqalim* 1:3 the money-changers were essential for the collection of the half-shekel Temple tax,[187] which funds were used for the maintenance of the public daily whole offerings which made atonement for the nation's sin (*t. Sheqal.* 1:6). The same applies to those buying and selling sacrificial animals[188] However, it is not clear that

---

181 'Demonstration', 75-81.

182 Catchpole, 'Entry', 333, suggests Zech as the primary background but Mark's λησταί is never used in the LXX or any of the Greek versions to render Zechariah's כנעני. Cf. also Roth, 'Cleansing'; followed by Gaston, *Stone*, 86; Duff, 'March', 65ff, citing Grant, 'Coming'; see also the discussion on p. 308 above, and pp. 333f, below.

183 *Pace* Juel, *Messiah*, 134, 12:33 only highlights the point at issue here in the 'cleansing': sacrifice without obedience is worthless. Chilton, *Temple*, argues that Jesus is engaged in a dispute about the purity of animals, but see the response of Evans, 'Jesus'.

184 See e.g. Gaston, *Stone*, 88; Taylor; Lightfoot, *Message*, 63.

185 Sanders, *Jesus*, 89f; Evans, 'Action', 249-56; cf. Gaston, *Stone*, 102-12.

186 'Money-changers'; cf. Sanders, *Jesus*, 66; Myers; also Eppstein, 'Cleansing', 45; and Ford, 'Money', who, citing *Ker.* 17:15; 18:2; 26:2; makes the interesting but finally unconvincing proposal that σκεῦος (v. 15) refers to money-containers used to transfer funds to the Temple deposits cf. Jos. *B.J.* 6.281. Neusner, *ibid.*, 290, offers the ingenious suggestion that the over-turning of the money-changer's 'table' signifies Jesus' intention to set up another 'table', that of the Eucharist.

187 See Bauckham, 'Demonstration'.

188 Cf. Eppstein, 'Cleansing', 43; Bauckham, 'Demonstration', 75.

expelling the sales from the outer court constitutes a crippling attack on the sacrificial system. Not only is there some evidence for competing markets,[189] but if Jesus wanted to attack the idea of sacrifices *per se* then this seems a particularly indirect way of doing so.[190] At the same time, based on the evidence cited above, the Temple hierarchy was very probably involved to some considerable extent in the business dealings. Jesus' action would, therefore, have constituted at the very least an indirect criticism of them,[191] as their response and the subsequent series of 'controversies' in Mark 11:27ff suggests.[192] But Jesus charge is not, as might initially be thought, merely directed at pecuniary malpractice; that is if we take the Jeremiah 7 allusion seriously.[193]

The expression σπήλαιον λῃστῶν comes from Jeremiah's famous 'Temple Sermon' (cf. 7:2b-15) which addresses the people's foolish misconception that they can commit all manner of sin and then 'flee' to the Temple like a brigand to his cave, hoping to escape the consequences of their actions through participation in the cult.[194] But, because they have disdained Yahweh's warnings and persisted in following the counsels of their rebellious hearts (vv. 13, 24ff), their sacrifices have no more significance than 'domestic meals' (v. 21)[195] and are therefore rejected.[196] As a result, judgement is irrevocable (vv. 13f, 16ff, 20)[197] and the Temple is to suffer a fate similar to that of the Shiloh shrine (v. 14). Since there has been no obedience, neither will there be sacrifices.

M. D. Hooker, recognising the appropriateness of Jeremiah 7:11ff, submits that the prophet also offers hope (7:5-7) and so Jesus' statement ought not be taken as indicating irrevocable judgement.[198] But, the verses which offer hope precede those from which Jesus' allusion is drawn. On the other hand, verse 11 leads directly through a series of connectives

---

[189] Eppstein, 'Cleansing', 55-56, although his theory concerning the recent institution of a market in the Temple has not been widely accepted; see Evans, 'Action', 265ff.

[190] Seeley, 'Act', 267; cf. Chilton, *Temple*, 110f.

[191] Gundry, 645, seems to underplay this.

[192] Burkill, 'Strain', 42, notes the similarities between this series of controversies and those at the beginning of the gospel. Both lead to climactic confrontations.

[193] The allusion to Jer 7 is on the basis of describing the Temple (בית הזה, MT; ὁ οἶκός μου, LXX) as a σπήλαιον λῃστῶν (so LXX; מערת פרצים, MT).

[194] Bright, 56; McKane, 163.

[195] Carroll, 215.

[196] Thompson, 287.

[197] Vv. 5-7 appear to be regarded as a vain hope, cf. v. 27.

[198] 'Traditions', 18.

(v. 12: כִּי לְכוּ־נָא; v. 13: וְעַתָּה יַעַן) to the message of judgement (vv. 14-20). This literary progression suggests that 7:11ff is a response to the people's refusal to listen, and therefore that judgment is inescapable.[199]

David Catchpole rejects this reading since it 'scarcely does justice to the situation described in verses 15f' of Mark 11.[200] But does it not? Although Josephus frequently describes the Zealots as λῃσταί and Mark 15:27 uses the word to mean 'insurrectionist',[201] it is sometimes argued that the behaviour envisaged in Mark 11:15 implies the sense of a common violent thief.[202] If taken in this latter sense, then as Bauckham argues, it is the rapacious behaviour of the priestly aristocracy that is at issue: 'they treat the temple ... as a base from which they go out on marauding raids and to which they return with their loot'.[203] For Bauckham, it is this very attitude, as in Jeremiah, that occasions their judgment.

Perhaps. But within the larger Markan schema Josephus' usage makes excellent sense, first, of Jesus' conflict with the authorities, particularly those from Jerusalem, second, of Mark's presentation of Jesus as both messianic King and Yahweh-Warrior, and third, given the highly nationalist connotations of the term. First, there are significant similarities between Mark's characterisation of the Jerusalem authorities and the attitudes displayed by the general populace and/or ruling class in Jeremiah 7. Both are portrayed as refusing to listen, as walking in the stubbornness of their own foolish counsels, and as confusing cultic practice with true obedience (whatever else might be said about their business dealings and thuggery[204]). In Mark's case, this equates to opposing God's present purposes in Jesus and so inviting judgement (Mk 4 and 7).[205] Both in Isaiah 6, and now also in the Jeremiah 7 allusion which is so appropriate to the Temple setting, this judgment entails the destruction of

---

[199] E.g. McKane, 163; cf. Craigie, *et al*, 122; Thompson, 282, who sees this as a response to not hearing. Cf. Juel, *Messiah*, 133f.

[200] 'Entry', 334; and e.g. Eppstein, 'Cleansing', 43; Seeley, 'Act', 267.

[201] Rengstorff, *TDNT*, 4.257-62; Roth, 'Cleansing'; Buchanan, 'Brigands'; cf. Seeley, 'Act', 269.

[202] So e.g. Josephus' derogatory usage is assumed to imply a common brigand, Pesch, 2.199; Bauckham, 'Demonstration', 84; Gundry, 644; cf. Kee, *Community*, 150.

[203] *Ibid.* Cf. Juel, *Messiah*, 133, although he argues that the phrase 'den of thieves' itself 'is inappropriate'.

[204] Bauckham, 'Demonstration', 84; Evans, 'Action', 259; Bockmuehl, 'Destruction', 15.

[205] Interestingly, the leaders' desire to destroy Jesus (v. 18) also echoes Jeremiah's experience (26:4-8).

Jerusalem. It should also be noted that Jesus' allusion to the OT undercuts the not uncommon objection that there was no popular expectation of a Messiah who destroys the Temple. That Peter has already fallen foul of assuming that Jesus' messiahship conformed to public expectation (Mk 8:31-33)[206] should alert us to the fact that the Markan Jesus draws his model from his own understanding of the OT, not popular conceptions nor those of contemporary or subsequent Jewish literature.[207]

Second, the stakes are clearly raised when all of this is put in the larger context of the Markan Jesus who proclaims the reign of God (1:14f), who functions as its inaugurating emissary and messianic king, and who also in a unique way is closely associated with the presence of Yahweh himself, namely as God's Son. To reject him can only be treasonous rebellion. This is nowhere so clear as in Jesus' 'triumphal' entry, when, as the king coming to his own city, he is pointedly snubbed by these very leaders of Jerusalem. And if the Temple, the next institution to be visited, is understood as Yahweh's own 'palace', then their questioning of his authority (11:28) is even more offensive; let alone their plot to kill him (11:18), hatched even while the Son of God is in his own 'house'.[208] 'Insurrectionists' are exactly what they are.

Third, it is the use of λῃστής which makes the point at issue 'the nationalist occupation of the house that was intended for international use';[209] and this is precisely what the Isaiah 56 allusion suggests. These insurrectionists have put their nationalist agendas ahead of Yahweh's INF intention that his house be a place of prayer for all nations.

On these twin bases, that A) Jesus' action was both an implicit attack on the Temple hierarchs and a challenge to their authority and B) his Jeremiah allusion in view of its immediate context constitutes a not-so-veiled threat of destruction, it is not difficult to see why immediately following in 11:18 Mark informs us that they plot his death.[210] From the

---

[206] Even more so if Jesus' actions are also considered to be parables.

[207] In the literature cited in Evans, 'Action', both Jer 7 and Ezek presuppose destruction. See further Bockmuehl, 'Destruction', 12ff; and Evans, 'Jesus'.

[208] Donahue, *Trial*, 114, observes that just as Jesus' 'bypassing of the Jewish cult and ritual in his healings and teachings' instigated a confrontation with the outcome that the authorities plot his death in 3:6, so too here.

[209] Barrett, 'House', 17; cf. Roth, 'Cleansing', 176f.

[210] Cf. Evans, 'Jesus', 105ff, and the story of Jesus, son of Ananias; Jos. *B.J.* 6.300-9.

Markan standpoint, Jesus has already accepted some form of messianic acclamation, and now threatens both their authority and their existence.

Returning to the juxtaposition of Isaiah 56 and Jeremiah 7, the one sets the standard for what the Temple should have become in the INE, a place of prayer for all nations, while the other shows what it has in fact become, a 'refuge of insurrectionists'. If the rebels will not allow the Temple to be a house of prayer for all nations, neither will it be permitted to remain a refuge for those who have consistently opposed God's INE purposes in Jesus.[211]   While Jesus' words may incidentally reveal the futility of a sacrificial system under these conditions (as was the case with Jeremiah and Isaiah; cf. 12:33),[212] they more clearly portend the Temple's coming destruction (cf. 15:38).[213]   Perhaps, then, Jesus' disruption of the institutional procedures adumbrate a greater and more permanent disruption to come. As indicated by the ensuing parable of the wicked tenants, God after prolonged sufferance and many emissaries will not long restrain his anger against the rebels (Mk 12:1-12).   Are we perhaps hearing the voice of Yahweh in the Temple dealing recompense to his enemies (Isa 66:6)?

It is essential to state at this point, as Mark 12 emphasises, that the central thrust of the material is directed against the Jerusalem leadership and Temple hierarchy.[214] The general populace, as we argued concerning Mark 4, stand in the balance. What will happen to the people depends on their response to their King—thus their clamour in Mark 15:6-15 is ominous indeed.[215]

An interesting adjunct to this interpretation is the Markan detail of the στιβάδας-bearing crowd so close to Jesus' cleansing action. When Judas and Simon Maccabaeus had come to Jerusalem their aim was to cleanse and rededicate the Temple and on both occasions they were accompanied by branch-carrying followers (1 Macc 4:36; 2 Macc 10:7; and 1 Macc 13:51).[216] The image of the palm and the inscription ציון לגאלת are also found on

---

[211] The Great Sanhedrin met regularly in the Chamber of Hewn Stone in the Temple, cf. Eppstein's discussion, 'Cleansing', 50f.

[212] Cf. Lohmeyer, *Lord*, 47. It is only on this basis that Juel's suggestion, *Messiah*, 134, of an opposition between 'house of prayer' and sacrificial cult is to be affirmed.

[213] See e.g. Best, *Temptation*, xlif.

[214] So also Juel, *Messiah*, 131.

[215] See also Marcus, 128f.

[216] Farmer, *Maccabees*, 136f, 155f; cited in Kinman, *Entry*, 116; cf. Catchpole, 'Entry', 320. Coakley, 'Messianic', 472, regards Mark's στιβάδας as defying explanation.

coins produced during the first Jewish revolt.[217] (One might be forgiven for pointing out again the importance of this term, גאל, in describing the hope of the INE.)[218]   Bearing in mind the differences—here the στιβάδας[219] are laid down, not carried, and the specific word 'palm' is not used, although one may inquire what the people thought they were doing in strewing the path in this way (cf. Jn 12:13)—nevertheless, the acclamation of the crowd suggests that they understood the entry in terms of such a 'deliverance' model.[220]   And, indeed, as with the Maccabean entries, the 'cleansing' of the Temple is the focal point.

From this perspective, Jesus, fresh from his victories as the Yahweh-Warrior in purging the land of the demonic, comes as the messianic King to effect the consummation in Jerusalem. The irony, of course, is that the cleansing/expulsion is directed not against the Romans but against the present Temple authorities and their functionaries and operatives, whom Jesus apparently regards as the true insurrectionists. Jerusalem has indeed been thrown into tumult as Yahweh's voice is heard 'dealing retribution to his enemies' (Isa 66:6, RSV). The fig-tree has been cursed, and recalling Mark's use of Malachi, Telford observes: 'The Lord whom they sought *had* suddenly come to his Temple (cf. Mal. 3.1 and Mk. 1.2) but had condemned rather than restored it!'[221]

W. W. Watty, however, rejects the Malachi identification because A) Jesus does not come suddenly but prefaces his action with a public entry (11:1ff) and an inspection of the Temple (11:11), B) the vendors not the priests are driven out, and C) there is no explicit reference to Malachi.[222] In response, 'suddenness' has also to do with the 'unexpected' and Jesus'

---

[217] Earlier attributed by Reifenberg, *Ancient*, to the Maccabees, the evidence now suggests the first revolt; see Hengel, *Zealots*, 117. Farmer, 'Palm', 63, cites Reifenberg, *Ancient*, 37, who notes that the palm is 'first and foremost' the symbol of the 'feast of tabernacles which so manifestly expresses the joy of deliverance'.

[218] See e.g. the discussion of Mk 10:45, Chapter 8, pp. 278ff; also Hengel, *Zealots*, 118, who sees especially Isa 52:1, with its picture of Yahweh as redeemer, as expressing the kernel of Jewish hopes, a text which we have suggested is closely related to the literary function of Isa 53.

[219] BAGD, 768, and BS, 3.276b, suggest something like 'leafy branches'. Gundry's comment, 629, that Mark says 'nothing about branches of any kind', assumes too much.

[220] On the messianic expectations for a 'war hero' Son of David, see Hengel, *Zealots*, 298ff, and the literature cited therein.

[221] *Barren*, 163; cf. fn. 120.

[222] 'Jesus', 235f; taken up by Gundry, 643.

actions were apparently that,[223] and, there is no need for explicit reference if other indicators make the allusion clear. But Watty is correct concerning the vendors. However, this may be accommodated if Jesus' symbolic and proleptic act is understood in more general terms, indirectly reflecting on those who permitted them to operate in the first place.

More to the point, does not Malachi speak of purging, rather than destruction?[224] Yes, ... and no. While it is true that Malachi 3 envisages purging, the purpose of Elijah's coming is so that Yahweh will not curse the land, which is the language of destruction. In the end, as it was in the prophets and as Jesus' implied in Mark 4, the purging is to be effected by means of judgment (cf. Isa 6:11-13).

d) Which Mountain?   The Meaning of the Mountain-Moving Saying
Numerous scholars have commented on what they feel to be the abrupt appearance of the 'mountain-moving' saying in Mark 11:22-25. In the preceding discussion we have already argued that such 'disjointed' materials are not uncommon in the teaching style of the Markan Jesus. Nevertheless, in view of the fig-tree symbolism, a common response has been to read this saying as an eschatological statement referring either to the Mount of Olives[225] or the Temple Mount.[226]

The first option takes the demonstrative to refer to the Mount of Olives and sees Zechariah 14:4's description of the earth-shattering (literally) consequences of the Messiah's arrival as the interpretive frame. For T. W. Manson, this 'striking background' explains the saying's Markan location.[227]   R. M. Grant, pointing out numbers of parallels between Zechariah 9-14 and Mark 11,[228] suggested that since the Hebrew 'to the west' (יָמָּה, Zech 14:4) means 'to the sea' Mark 11:23 alludes to Zechariah's

---

[223] Daube, *Sudden*, 74f; cf. Neusner, 'Money-changers', 289. It is also his first substantial act on arriving in Jerusalem, Hiers, 'Purification', 82.

[224] Hooker, 'Traditions', 8, sees a connection with the prologue but denies that the Malachi text is in view since Mark speaks of destruction not cleansing, *Message*, 83.

[225] E.g. Manson, *Messiah*, 29f, 39f; Grant, 'Coming', 300; Evans, 'Galilee', 7; Smith, 'Figs', 322; cf. Hurtado, 184. A number of scholars, not listed here, also see Jesus as indicating the Mount of Olives but without any eschatological implications.

[226] E.g. Abbott, *Fourfold*, 5.208; Dodd, *Parables*, 63n1; Lightfoot, *Message*, 78; Gaston, *Stone*, 454; Carrington, 242f; McKelvey, *Temple*, 65n3; Telford, *Barren*, 95-127; Trocmé, *Formation*, 105f; Kelber, *Kingdom*, 103f; Hooker, 'Traditions'; Broadhead, 'Mountain'.

[227] Manson, *ibid.*, 30.

[228] 'Coming', 298ff. E.g. v. 1: Zech 9:9; 14:4; v. 2: 9:9; vv. 8-10: 14:16-19; v. 11: 14:5; v. 13: cf. 14:8; v. 14: 14:4; v. 15: 14:21; v. 16: 14:20; v. 17: 14:16; v. 23: 14:4.

eschatological turmoil.[229] C. F. Evans, following Wright, noted additional parallels and argued that Mark 11:23 is 'not a general exhortation to faith, but a precise injunction ... to see that this is the period of the last days, and that Jerusalem is being judged'.[230]

Not all of these parallels are convincing, yet there are enough to suggest that Zechariah plays an influential role. But does Mark's Jesus have in mind the specifically eschatological tremors of the Mount of Olives? Probably not. In Zechariah, the setting is Yahweh's coming to rescue his people, which would certainly fit the overall INE thrust of Mark, but the immediate context of Mark 11:23 is one of warning and imminent judgement on the Temple establishment. Second, allowing that this might be eschatological imagery (but see Zech 14:5), the Mount of Olives is in fact 'divided', which sounds like a theophany of Yahweh's descent rather than judgement (e.g. Ex 19:16ff). On the other hand, being cast into the sea suggests total removal[231] and, since the sea represents chaos (e.g. Pss 18:16; 32:6; 46:2; 69:1, 14; Job 7:12; 26:12), evokes images of judgement and obliteration.[232] Third, Sharyn Dowd argues that it is inconceivable that the messianic dislocations should be dependent on just anybody's exercise of faith (11:23a: ὃς ἄν).[233] The case for a symbolic eschatological reference to the Mount of Olives is not strong.

More commonly, 'this mountain' is understood to refer to the Temple Mount. Telford, whose work is generally regarded as the standard exposition, has argued the case extensively.[234] First, since Mark has placed this material here, Telford argues that it must be related to the foregoing and, therefore, must somehow be connected to the fig-tree and Temple.[235] Next, turning to the OT, he notes that 'the mountain of the Lord' is a well known designation for the place where Yahweh will 'plant' his people so

---

[229] *Miracle*, 167.

[230] Evans, 'Galilee', 7, cf. 5ff, citing e.g. Zech 9:11 in the words of institution, Mk 14:24; and Zech 13:7 in the smiting of the shepherd, Mk 14:27.

[231] Marshall, *Faith*, 168, notes the difference between moving north and south and being cast into the sea.

[232] Cf. e.g. Mk 5:13 and 9:42, Mauser, 126; Schnellbächer, 'Temple', 104; Marshall, *Faith*, 168f; *pace* Gundry, 678, who fails to realise A) the Exodus background, and therefore judgment connotations, of Mk 5:31, and B) that Mk 9:42 is still an act of terrible judgment, if only to heighten the seriousness of the alternative.

[233] *Prayer*, 73f.

[234] *Barren*.

[235] See e.g. *ibid.*, 49, upon which the rest of the work is predicated.

that they might flourish (espec. Ex 15:17; Ps 78:54; Ezek 17:22f; Isa 2:2; = Mic 4:1; cf. Isa 27:6), although 'cultic aberration' results in judgement against both fig and vine (e.g. Jer 5:17; 8:13; Hos 2:12; 9:10, 16; Amos 4:9). Much the same relationship obtains for rabbinic literature.[236] There is already, then, in the OT and later literature a conjunction of Temple Mount, horticultural imagery (including the fig-tree), with blessing seen as flourishing, and judgment as withering. This would fit with Mark where although the fig-tree is clearly flourishing, the signs of fruitfulness to come are utterly absent.

Telford also cites rabbinic texts where 'the mountain of the Lord' is apparently shortened to 'this mountain' and as such refers to the Temple (*b. Pesah* 87b, and *b. Git.* 56b),[237] and notes a discussion in *b. Baba Bathra* 3b-4b which speaks of moving mountains in the context of theoretically destroying the Temple in order to build a new one.[238] Finally, it is a feature of the 'Messianic Age' that all obstacles to God's returning people will be removed, particularly mountains (Isa 40:4; 45:2; 49:11; cf. 64:1-3).[239] On this basis, the oddity of Mark 11:22ff being so closely attached to the preceding can be explained. Its function is to announce ...

> ... that 'the moving of mountains' expected in the last days was now taking place. Indeed, about to be removed was the mountain *par excellence*, the Temple Mount. The Temple, known to Jewish people as 'the mountain of the house' or 'this mountain' was not to be elevated, as expected, but cast down! As R. E. Dowda states: "The temple is the mountainous obstacle which is to vanish before the faith of the gospel movement. The temple system with its corrupt clericalism and vested interests, is to be removed in the eschatological era, which is now being experienced."[240]

Does this interpretation fare any better? Neither Sharyn Dowd, nor Gundry think so.[241] For Dowd, A) the rabbinic designations are too late and Telford has not demonstrated that 'this mountain' would have been understood as a reference to the Temple by Mark's readers, and in fact Telford is unable to adduce any ancient interpretation (unlike fig-tree cursing) to support this view. In terms of moving mountains, B) 'in Isa 2:2

---

[236] *Ibid.*, 134-41.
[237] *Ibid.*, 170n65.
[238] *Ibid.*, 112.
[239] *Ibid.*, 116, citing Derrett, 'Figtrees', 253; cf. Hahn, 'Wort', 157.
[240] *Ibid.*, 119, citing Dowda, 'Cleansing', p. 250; cf. Marshall, *Faith*, 168f; and Schnellbächer, 'Temple'.
[241] Respectively, *Prayer*, 72f; *Mark*, 677.

and Mic 4:1, "the mountain of the house of the Lord" will be *established* in the Messianic age, not removed', C) the mountains in Isaiah (40:4f; 45:2) are levelled, not removed or cast into the sea, D) in Zechariah 4:6-10 the 'mountain will be levelled so that the Temple can be *restored*', E) *b. Baba Bathra* 3b is not about removing the Temple but about solving impossible legal difficulties, and, finally, F) the demonstrative clearly refers to the Mount of Olives.[242]

Considering Dowd's concerns before going on to Gundry, A) granted the late date of the rabbinical material, she is correct in that 'this mountain' on its own is not unambiguously a reference to the Temple Mount.[243] However, it does occur hard on the heels of what appears to be a stunning reversal of eschatological expectation for the 'house on the mountain of the Lord', and this might be a contextual hint. And as Donald Juel notes, in *Tg. Isaiah* 5:1ff, a passage that provides the imagery for the parable of the tenants in Mark 12:1ff, Israel is given an inheritance בטור רם (5:1b).[244] On the other hand, that no ancient interpreter saw it this way is significant, but may in fact say more about Mark's interpreters' horizons than Mark. Given that the text occurs elsewhere without a Temple setting (Mt 17:19-20; 1 Cor 13:2), it is quite possible that ancient interpreters might have read their Mark through the eyes of Paul, or more likely Matthew, as did their scribes.[245] Moving now to points E) and F). Dowd is correct with regard to E) that, based on the rabbinic usage Telford himself cites, the metaphor concerns solving impossible legal problems, not removing Temples. On the other hand, F) having stood on the Mount of Olives and looked across at the Temple Mount, I see no reason why one pointing at it could not use the demonstrative 'this'. As to points C) and D), granted the language is 'levelled', the fundamental concept is obviously the removal of mountainous obstacles. The language of casting into the sea merely expresses the same idea. But, and this is the crucial connection, granted the negative connotations noted above of the sea as chaos and being cast into it as an act of judgment—which, by the way, is consistent with the withered fig-tree and Mark 13:2—'casting into the sea' only serves to

---

[242] *Prayer*, 72f.

[243] The language is in fact indeterminate, cf. Schmithals, 214.

[244] *Messiah*, 136f.

[245] On the well known phenomenon of scribes harmonising the texts of Mark and Luke to Matthew; see Aland, *Text*, 290f; Metzger, *Text*, 197.

heighten the irony of the extraordinary reversal of prophecies such as those mentioned in B). That is to say, removal is not antithetical to establishment when what is removed is a corrupt system in order that the new might be established in its stead. Here we have yet another example of Mark's Jesus bringing together two ideas to make a powerful point, namely, the idea of the removal of mountainous objects, with the idea of the sea as the place of chaos and judgment. And all this allusively, and with considerable irony, applied to Mount Zion.

Gundry, likewise rejects Telford's interpretation on the basis of a series of putative 'failures', some of which are similar to Dowd's concerns. We discuss only those not addressed above, *viz.* Telford's 'failure' A) 'to distinguish between the Temple and the mount on which it stands',[246] B) to realise that the Mount must remain as the site of the Temple ruin (13:2), C) 'to demonstrate' that the destruction of the Temple is to happen as the result of the disciples' faith, and finally, D) to account for that fact that Mark nowhere else uses 'mountain' to refer to the Temple site.

In response. A) if Jerusalem can be a synecdoche for Israel, then, given Telford's examples, it seems somewhat pedantic to deny that 'this mountain' could refer to what is on the mountain, and again, the immediate context both in terms of symbolism and literary structure suggests the Temple Mount. B) is only of concern on a literal reading which nobody, as far as I can tell, is proposing. Taking D) next, that Mark nowhere else uses the term in this way hardly disqualifies him from doing so now—unless he is not permitted a unique use of a term (but cf. e.g. ἅγιος in a title for Jesus only in 1:24). Finally, C) is of course the issue. First, two points. In this case, 'demonstration' is an impossibly unrealistic demand for either position (e.g. note the ambiguity of the demonstrative). A 'good likelihood' is more reasonable. Second, it is not clear from the above quote that Telford means that the disciples will effect the actual physical destruction of the Temple through their prayer, as Gundry suggests. On the contrary, suppose one allows an underlying eschatological (or apocalyptic) symbolism. Then, just as Jesus comes to a rebellious Jerusalem—characterised by a corrupt Temple system (cf. Mal 3:5; 1:6 - 2:16[247]) with whose masters he has been in constant conflict—and

---

[246] 677.
[247] See earlier, Chapter 3, pp. 68 and 70.

adumbrates judgement by cursing the fig-tree (cf. Mal 3:1f, 21 MT), is it not possible that his disciples, by their prayerful faith, might see the 'removal' of this 'obstacle' that is standing in the way not only of the Lord's INE coming but of the ἔθνεσιν coming to him (Isa 56:7 in Mk 11:17a; and also e.g. Acts 4:1-31; 13:44-50)?

Nevertheless, Dowd is surely correct in her intention to regain what seems to be the primary point of the passage. It is difficult from this distance to know whether Jesus meant his words to apply quite literally to physical mountains—as early tradition suggests some people took them[248]—or metaphorically, as for example in Mark 10:43-47. If the latter, then we have graphic hyperbole, not to be taken literally but understood as a memorable way of saying that all things are possible to those who have faith.[249] In any case, as Dowd points out, the early church took it as referring to the power of faith (1 Cor 13:2; Mt 17:19-20; 21:21; Lk 17:2-8).[250] Whatever the merits of an eschatological symbolic reading, it seems a mistake to make this predominant over, or even exclusive of, what appears to be the straightforward reading: believing prayer can achieve even the impossible.

So what about the symbolic reading? The solution seems straightforward. Just as Dowd is content to allow a dual function to the first fig-tree incident, is it not also possible for the second, with the mountain included? Mark already seems to do something like this with his healing-of-the-blind miracles which not only demonstrate that Jesus is Israel's INE healer but also say something, using typical wisdom imagery, about the need to see things in God's way. What if Mark has recorded the 'mountain-moving' here precisely because it too has a dual function? Yes, believing prayer can effect the ἀδύνατον, and, moreover, even deal with such formidable obstacles to the INE gospel as an entrenched, powerful, unrepentant, and hostile religious establishment (again espec. Acts 4:1-31). Even this οἶκος, taken over as it is by strong men, will be subject to the ἐξουσία of a stronger one (cf. 3:27, and 3:3).

---

[248] See the account in Dowd, *Prayer*, 74, of one St. Gregory Thaumaturgus, who reputedly demonstrated precisely this kind of faith.

[249] E.g. Taylor and Nineham who see it entirely as metaphor, and e.g. Lagrange, Grundmann, Cranfield, Lane, who, given that the fig tree is literal and on the basis of the demonstrative, see it as referring to the Mount of Olives but with metaphorical intent.

[250] *Prayer*, 74.

e) The Question About Jesus' Authority

We have already alluded to the importance of this event. Not only does it close off the fig-tree-Temple intercalation, but it serves to lead into the crucial parable of the wicked tenants. Jesus is approached by Israel's Jerusalem authorities in full array. Here, for the first time since Mark 4 and 7, those who ought to have welcomed him appear, but belatedly and yet again to confront him. In what seems on the surface to be an appropriate exercise of their lawful prerogative, they question him concerning his ἐξουσία 'to do these things',[251] which almost certainly refers to the preceding Temple 'incident' (cf. 11:18).[252]

The key issue here as far as this book is concerned is Jesus' response. He neither performs a miracle, as he did at the beginning of the first sequence of controversies (2:5-12), nor engages in a theological debate, as when those controversies were finally concluded (3:23-30; cf. 7:6-13). Instead, he asks a question about John's baptism: did it come from heaven or from man? Commentators generally construe this link with John in terms of John's God-given authority, taking Jesus to imply that his authority too comes from the same source. Thus, the leaders' unbelieving response to John is what ensures their rejection of Jesus; which in a general sense is true.[253] Gundry takes a different tack in contending that the issue is John's testimony which pointed to Jesus as the 'stronger one': if they had believed John they would have accepted Jesus.[254] Similarly, it may refer to John's affirmation of Jesus' as the messianic 'Spirit-baptizer' (1:8). But what has this to do with John's baptism in particular?

It is widely agreed that 'baptism' is a synecdoche for John's ministry; how is this to be understood? Hooker makes the tentative suggestion that since Mark links John with Malachi 3:1, Jesus is Malachi's Lord of the Temple and hence his authority.[255] This seems right, Jesus is indeed the Temple's Lord (cf. Mk 12:1-12). Can we be more specific?

---

[251] Ἐξουσία is mentioned in connection with Jesus' exorcisms (1:22, 27) which we have suggested were linked with the Yahweh-Warrior motif, and his claim to forgive sin (2:10).

[252] Lohmeyer, *Lord*, 43; Lane; Pesch; Shae, 'Question', 22.

[253] Taylor; Schweizer; Lane; Hurtado; Gnilka; Ernst; Hooker.

[254] Gundry, 658.

[255] *Mark*, 272.

Jesus' action in the Temple is not only a matter of acting in an authoritative way. Nor is it simply a statement about reforming the Temple. It specifically presages judgement. This is, we would urge, why they want to kill him. After all, Mark presents them as experts in the Scriptures who presumably well understood the implications of Jeremiah 7. On this view, in keeping with John's preaching (Mk 1:4) and thus the thrust of Malachi which was primarily concerned with priestly abuses and infidelities,[256] the authorities ought to have repented in preparation for the Lord of the Temple's delayed INE coming (cf. Isa 40:3). Their failure to do so, that is, to submit to John's 'baptism of repentance', amounted to a refusal to prepare themselves.[257] And so, as Telford rightly maintains, the Lord of the Temple has come, cursed the fig-tree (חֵרֶם, cf. Mal 3:24 MT), and announced sentence (Jer 7:11; cf. Jer 25:3-11; Isa 43:28; and Mk 12:2-5, 9). This is why Jesus points to John's baptism: their refusal to prepare through repentance is the grounds for his announcement of judgment.

So the authorities reason among themselves (vv. 31-32). Once again, wise in their own conceits, they cleverly extricate themselves by replying, with extraordinarily wonderful irony (perhaps some of the finest in Mark's Gospel), that they do not know. Quite so. The wheels of Isaiah 6 in Mark 4 and Isaiah 29 in Mark 7 have come full circle. How little they 'know', in the midst of their 'perception', will soon be revealed.

In conclusion, if we consider all this within the framework of the 'entry' genre, and considering Mark's cumulative presentation of Jesus as representative true Israel, messianic 'servant', Son of David, Son of Man, and even Yahweh-Warrior and Son of God, then to confront him concerning his authority is in effect to deny him the act of appropriation and to refuse him the right to rule. This is nothing if not mutiny.[258]

f) The Parable of the Vineyard and the Wicked Tenants

Following hard on the heels of the fig-tree/Temple 'incident' and the ensuing seditious confrontation over his authority (11:18 suggests that this would hardly be a polite request), Mark's Jesus presses the judgement

---

[256] See Chapter 3, p. 68, above.

[257] On the possible significance of this see Chapter 4, p. 104, fn. 72.

[258] Duff, 'March', 61f, cites the example of Alexander, who when refused this request by the Tyrians, laid siege to their city. Is it possible that a similar idea is in view here? The Jerusalem authorities' refusal to submit will lead to their city coming 'under siege', cf. Mk 13.

theme, by taking up the initiative in the vineyard parable.[259]   Although a well-known rabbinic image,[260] it is generally accepted that the Markan version owes much to Isaiah 5.[261]   The amount of literature of this passage is considerable,[262] but again our concerns are limited to its present Markan form and setting, and to its general significance in terms of an INE hermeneutic.

(i) The Isaiah Context

A piece of considerable literary merit, the so-called Vineyard Song (5:1-7) brings to a climax Yahweh's inauguration of his lawsuit against his people and appears just prior to his appearance as suzerain in the Temple (6:1ff).[263]   Although the form and genre of the poem has been debated at length—which probably reflects the need in the original setting initially to conceal the true significance of the parable so as to engage the listeners—it has been suggested that it is a 'Liebslied' whereby the 'best man' sings on behalf of his wronged friend, the aggrieved 'bridegroom'.[264]

The majority of commentators hold that after a brief introduction the song proper contains four elements: the owner's tender and thorough provision for his vineyard is contrasted with its obnoxious harvest (vv. 1b-2), an appeal for a verdict based on the disparity between the owner's unimpeachable faithfulness and the vineyard's inexcusable failure (vv. 3-4), a declaration of the verdict (vv. 5-6), and finally an interpretation: the vineyard is the nation and the sought-after fruit is justice and righteousness (v. 7).[265]

However, G. A. Yee, supported by G. T. Sheppard, has recently offered a more nuanced interpretation, based on a comparison with the form of Deuteronomy 32, contending that the structure is best analysed along the

---

[259] Burkill, 'Strain', 40.

[260] Feldman, *Parables*, 128-35; Jeremias, *Parables*, 88; Snodgrass, *Tenants*, 22ff; cf. Young, *Jesus*, 298ff; Stern, 'Rabbinic'.

[261] In addition to the major commentaries, Jeremias, *Parables*, 70; Juel, *Messiah*, 136f; Chilton, *Galilean*, 111ff; and Snodgrass, *Tenants*, 47ff, where his discussion presupposes as much.

[262] See the detailed study by Snodgrass, *Tenants*; also Young, *Jesus*, 282-316. Much of the discussion on parables, and in particular this one, has until recently been hamstrung by Jülicher's understandably reductionist reaction to earlier excessive allegorising.

[263] For a more detailed assessment of the literary structure, see Chapter 7, pp. 188ff, above. On the judicial nature of Isa 5:1-7, see Yee, 'Study', 33-36.

[264] Wildberger, 164; Clements, 57.

[265] Clements, 58; Kaiser, 59; cf. Whedbee, *Isaiah*, 44.

lines of a modified juridical parable,[266] consisting of A) a parable (vv. 1b-2),
B) call for judgment (v. 3), C) recital of God's benevolent actions (v. 4a),
D) indictment (v. 4b), E) sentence (vv. 5-6); and F), interpretation (v. 7).[267]
The main contribution of this analysis is that it highlights the central
point of the form which is to lure the hearers into passing judgment on
themselves (cf. Nathan's parable to David in 2 Sam 12:1-10).[268]

The vineyard imagery has occurred earlier, in 3:11f, where Yahweh
takes his stand in court against the elders and leaders of his people: 'it is
you who have ruined my vineyard ...' (3:11-15, LXX; cf. *Tg. Isa*). As
previously discussed,[269] this is in keeping with the consistent Isaianic
critique of the rebellious Jerusalemite leadership (cf. 1:2; 28). Here,
however, the vineyard signifies the whole people including the
leadership, who together are the elect of God and recipients of all the
privileges pertaining thereto.[270] Yahweh's planting of and provision for
his vineyard is imagery used in Psalm 80:9-19 (MT) to describe,
interestingly enough, Israel's deliverance in the Exodus and his provision
of the land in the conquest (see Jer 2:21 which seems to draw on Isa 5—
Yahweh plants שֹׂרֵק grapes—and also recalls Sinai where Yahweh gave
Israel birth, vv. 26-28; cf. Dt 32:10-14, 37[271]). Once again the importance of
the founding moment is evident.

The story itself is quite straightforward, expressing Yahweh's complaint
against his faithless people.[272] In spite of her special relationship to
Yahweh, the nation has not responded in kind. Yahweh, who has done
everything possible for his people, came seeking justice and righteousness
but found only bloodshed and the cry of suffering rising from the
oppressed. He calls for a decision, although he himself gives it. No doubt
the hearers would agree until they realise that they are, ironically, judging
themselves. Finally, in keeping with the juridical form, once the self-

---

[266] 'Study' and 'More' respectively, following the critique of Willis, 'Study'. See also
Simon, 'Poor', 220f, who cites five examples: 2 Sam 12:1-14; 14:1-20; 1 Kgs 20:35-43; Isa 5:1-7,
and Jer 3:1-5 (?).
[267] Yee, 'Study'; Sheppard, 'More'.
[268] Yee, 'Study', 38f, who also discusses the close parallels between the two.
[269] Chapter 7, pp. 189ff, above.
[270] Snodgrass, *Tenants*, 75, and literature cited therein.
[271] Yee, 'Study', 31ff, suggests that the song 'be studied in the light of the formal
aspects' of Dt 32; cf. Holladay, 104f; Craigie, *et al*, 37; Thompson, 180; and Carroll, 131.
[272] Whedbee, *Isaiah*, 47; Yee, 'Study'; Clements, 55.

judgment has occurred, the last verse brings the denouement: the failed vineyard is the hearers themselves.

(ii) The Parable in Mark[273]

Having been challenged by the Temple authorities, Jesus responds by means of a παραβολή—a term last used by Jesus in his previous meeting with the Jerusalem authorities' emissaries in Mark 7. In fact, on all three occasions where Jesus has been confronted by authorities from Jerusalem (3:22ff, 7:14ff, and here), his response has been in parables.[274] Whereas the first parable-rejoinder represented the culmination of a series of controversies (2:1ff) this one initiates another (12:13-40).[275]

Although using the imagery of the 'vineyard song' in Isaiah 5, there is a change of emphasis. No longer is the concern about the quality of the fruit nor is the vineyard *en toto* to be destroyed, but rather the tenants. In making this distinction between people and leaders Jesus appears to be influenced by Isaiah 3:11ff (cf. LXX, *Tg. Isa*). Based on standard OT imagery, a number of the referents are generally agreed.[276] The vineyard is Israel (Jer 2:21; Hos 10:1), the owner is God himself, and the servants are the prophets (cf. δοῦλοι in e.g. Jer 7:25; 25:4; Amos 3:7; Zech 1:6).

Based on rabbinic parallels (e.g. *Ex. Rab.* 30.17; 15.19), K. R. Snodgrass maintains that *'while* the story was being told' the tenants would have been more likely understood as either the earlier Canaanites or the present Roman forces of occupation and the servants who were killed Israel's leaders such as Judas Maccabaeus.[277] Apart from the question of whether Mark's hearers would have so understood it, given A) that in the vineyard imagery of Isaiah 3:11ff (LXX; cf. *Tg. Isa*) the national leadership is in view, B) that various Jewish traditions understood the tower and the vat in Isaiah 5 to refer to the Temple and the altar (e.g. *Tg. Isa* 5:1b; 4Q500[278]),[279]

---

[273] The most recent thorough examination of this parable in the Gospels is that of Snodgrass, *Tenants*, to whose work we will constantly refer.

[274] See Chapter 7, p. 224, above.

[275] Burkill, 'Strain', 42; cf. Telford, *Barren*, 48. Gundry, 665, mentions possible, if not entirely convincing, parallels between the two groups of controversies.

[276] Cf. Evans, 'Vineyard', 84f; Snodgrass, *ibid.*, 76f; Kingsbury, 115. Snodgrass' identification of the vineyard as the privileges of God's people, on the basis that the identity of Israel as a nation cannot be transferred, fails to recognise that the issue concerns the transference of leadership (cf. Lk 22:30).

[277] *Tenants*, 77f, 23f.

[278] See Baumgarten, 'Vineyard'.

[279] See also *t. Me'il.* 1:16; *t. Sukk* 3:15; cf. *1 Enoch* 89:56-73; *Barn.* 16:1-5.

C) that the Jewish authorities such as the Sanhedrin met there regularly,[280] and D) the immediate context, it seems clear that the tenants are the Temple authorities.[281]

On the other hand, if Snodgrass is right, then the surprise would have been even greater in that the expected Canaanite or Roman 'tenants' turn out to be Israel's leaders. This sits well with the earlier suggestion that the behaviour of the crowd at Jesus' entrance recalled aspects of the Maccabean entries. This time, however, it is not the Romans but the present Temple incumbents who are to be removed.

Further, in our discussion of the deeper significance of Jesus' casting out of demons, we have already suggested that part of Mark's concern is to show that Israel's problem is not the Romans but the idolatrous-demonic within (cf. Jesus' first miracle which was the casting out of an 'unclean' spirit in a Synagogue, 1:21-28; and the drowning of Legion in 5:1-20).[282] Granted the Isaianic link between idolatry and false wisdom, it is not surprising that Jesus' actions are directed not against the Romans but the idolatrous, and even demonic, character of the 'wisdom' that rejects Yahweh's purposes.

In the light of Mark's interest in John as Malachi's Elijah, the astounding 'patience' of the owner in the repeated sacrifice of his servants and the equally astonishing arrogance of the tenants makes good sense. This, for Mark's Jesus, is what has happened constantly and now finally even to Malachi's Elijah, namely, John (9:13).[283] What may have been surprising is the owner's reasoning in sending his son: if the tenants had not respected his servants, why should they the son?[284] (And herein the hearers accurately assess themselves). Further, this idea of obtaining the vineyard by murdering the heir has been criticised since, it is claimed, it is not a legal possibility.[285] But not only does the similarity with Ahab's

---

[280] Eppstein, 'Cleansing', 50f.

[281] *Pace* Pesch, 2.220 for whom they represent Israel's 'Halsstarrigkeit'.

[282] Chapter 6, pp. 163f, above.

[283] On various Jewish traditions on the nation's treatment of its prophets, see Snodgrass, *Tenants*, 79f, who cites *Pesiq. R.* 26 and Schoeps, 'Prophetenmorde'; also Steck, *Israel*. On it being the leaders of the nation who were largely responsible, Gundry, 689.

[284] Young, *Jesus*, 288.

[285] Carlston, *Parables*, 184f; but see Young, *Jesus*, 282f, who argues that, since γεωργοί probably renders אריסים, the tenants envisaged here could take over the land in the absence of an heir. However, his evidence, *Sipre Dt* § 312, appears ambiguous since the owner can still give the property to others.

murder of Naboth put the tenants in the worst possible light (1 Kgs 21:1-19, cf. ἐκληρονόμησας, v. 19; 2 Kgs 9:25f), but if their plan is utterly unrealistic, it only accentuates their indescribable folly. Everyone knows what an owner would do to the tenants in such a situation. How much more foolish their actions and perilous their plight when the owner is God?

In spite of the occasional doubt as to whether the son is Jesus,[286] he is undoubtedly so for Mark, since A) we already know that Jesus is God's υἱὸν ἀγαπητόν (1:11; 9:7), B) Mark has constantly signalled the impending death of only one figure, Jesus, (how he dies is not the point of the parable but merely reflects its inner narrative world), C) the immediate context has already informed us of the intentions of the Temple hierarchs (11:18; cf. 3:6; 12:12), and finally D) the combination of Mark's presentation of Jesus as the messianic King and the motif of the 'entry' genre combine to make him the true heir.[287]

The parable, then, announces that because the Jewish leaders have neither rendered Yahweh his proper due nor respected the heir to whom the vineyard ultimately belongs[288] they will be destroyed and the oversight of the vineyard given to others. The important point, as the majority of commentators agree, is that the parable is almost totally negative and, in keeping with the appeal to Isaiah 6 and 29 in Mark 4 and 7, directed primarily against the Jewish authorities, not Israel.[289] Here too the theme of Malachi's threatened judgment is continued.

Although the use of the Psalms in Mark is not part of our immediate concern, a brief word about Psalm 118:22-23 is in order since it functions as

---

[286] Milavec, 'Identity', has maintained that the last 'one' is not unambiguously Jesus because 'heir' is not a known title for the Messiah, 'last' does not fit Jewish Elijah expectations, and the son is murdered by the tenants and 'cast out' whereas Jesus is executed by the Romans and buried (on this last point so also Weder, *Gleichnisse*, 149n11; cf. Robinson, 'Wicked', 449). But Milavec fails to place these terms in the context of the parable. 'Heir' simply means the one who has ultimate claim and authority, which is exactly what the issue has been since Jesus arrived in Jerusalem; 'last' is in keeping with Mk 3:28f where Jesus is Israel's final and only option; and on 'killed and cast out' see point (B) below. That Israel is not to be destroyed is quite true, after all the 'twelve' are the new leaders (3:13-19).

[287] See also Snodgrass, *ibid.*, 80-87.

[288] It is important not to push the imagery too, the point is ownership and what is due to the owners, not issues about when the heir will inherit.

[289] Snodgrass, *ibid.*, 87-95; Trocmé, 207f, and literature cited therein; cf. Cornette, 'Vignerons'. Although he recognises the primacy of the Jewish leaders, Kingsbury's view, 115, that this is a statement about the 'church' assuming Israel's place needs clarification.

the 'capstone'[290] to the story. Numerous commentators feel the citation[291] to be incongruous since the parable concerns the punishment of the tenants while the 'citation' concerns the exaltation, probably, of the son.[292] However, a number of factors indicate that it is well-placed. First, as we have argued, this sort of juxtaposition is typical of the Markan Jesus' teaching style, and reflects his technique of citing together two previously unrelated texts at crucial junctures in his argument, in this case Isaiah 5:1f and Psalm 118.[293] He has already done something similar in the Temple (Isa 56 and Jer 7).

Second, juridical parables work by delaying the moment of self-identification until the hearers have passed judgment. This is commonly followed by a clarification or interpretation, as for example, Nathan's 'You are the man!' (2 Sam 12:7; cf. Isa 5:7). Jesus' citation of Psalm 118 functions analogously.[294] Third, the passion predictions constantly speak of Jesus' death and his subsequent rising again. The psalm is appropriate to the theme of reversal and subsequent vindication (cf. $\dot{\alpha}\pi o\delta o\kappa\iota\mu\dot{\alpha}\zeta\omega$ in 8:31).[295] This is even more so in the light of its messianic use in the 'entry' scene (11:9), with which it forms a neat *inclusio*. Fourth, if Matthew Black is right about a possible 'word play' on בנים/אבן/בן, then this would indicate its appropriateness here.[296] Finally, the term 'builders' is sometimes used in Qumran (CD 4:19-20; 8:12, cf. v. 3) and rabbinic literature (e.g. *b. Shabb.* 114a; *b. Ber.* 64a; *Tg. Pss* 118:22-29) to mean 'scholars' or 'religious leaders', and thus serves to tie in the verse to the preceding (cf. Acts 4:11).[297]

As to the significance of the psalm, the evidence is ambiguous.[298] Suffice to say that in rabbinic works, the reversal motif was applied to Abraham, Jacob, Israel, an unidentified figure, and David, and although there is no certain evidence of messianic application it does seem to have

---

[290] The meaning of $\kappa\epsilon\phi\alpha\lambda\dot{\eta}\nu$ $\gamma\omega\nu\iota\alpha\varsigma$ is disputed. Jeremias, '$\kappa\epsilon\phi\alpha\lambda\dot{\eta}$' and 'Eckstein', and Derrett, '"Stone"', argue for 'capstone', while for McKelvey, *Temple*, 194-204, it means foundational 'cornerstone'.

[291] On the inconsequential variations in wording, see Gundry, *Use*, 20.

[292] E.g. Nineham; Suhl, 141; Donahue, *Trial*, 124; Carlston, *Parables*, 190; Hooker; Marcus, 112; cf. Taylor. See also Gundry's arguments to the contrary, 690.

[293] See again Kee, 'Function', 176.

[294] Snodgrass, *ibid.*, 96f.

[295] So also Snodgrass, *ibid.*, 100; Str-B, 1.875-76.

[296] 'Christological', 12.

[297] Derrett, '"Stone"'; Snodgrass, *ibid.*, 96, citing Str-B, 1.876; Marcus, 124f. Cf. the Pauline imagery in 1 Cor 3:10-17 where Christian teachers also build God's temple.

[298] See the discussions in Derrett, '"Stone"'; Snodgrass, *ibid.*, 99ff; Marcus, 114f.

been understood eschatologically. In the light of the messianic overtones of the immediately following verses (118:25f) as used in 11:9, Mark probably means that these verses here should recall that acclamation and likewise be messianically construed (cf. Acts 4:11; 1 Pet 2:7). In any case, the immediate point seems clear: the son-stone who was killed-rejected by the tenants-builders will be vindicated by God and made the κεφαλὴν γωνίας of the people of God's future hopes.

Taking the imagery further, J. R. Donahue contends that the 'stone' imagery, in the light of the preceding anti-Temple material and the thematic unity of these chapters as whole, suggests more specifically that Jesus is to be either the capstone or foundation stone of the new Temple that will replace the old (cf. 1 Pet 2:4-7).[299] The charges brought against Jesus at his trial may lend support to this possibility (14:58; cf. 15:29, 38),[300] as do also perhaps the echoes of Temple, stone, οἰκοδομαί (cf. οἱ οἰκοδομοῦντες), and ποταπός (cf. θαυμαστή; see BAGD, 695) in Mark 13:1f.[301] This would suggest a progression through these materials from Jesus as the messianic King come to 'cleanse the Temple' (11:1-11), to the one who announces the present arrangement's demise (11:12-25), and finally to its eventual replacement based on himself (11:26 - 12:12). If so, then we may have here intimations that the Markan Jesus sees himself as the one who fulfils the NE hope of Isaiah 2:2 and 56:7 (cf. 11:16).[302]

The hierarchs' response to this declaration of Jesus' ascendancy and their final demise, is to seek his arrest (12:12). According to H. Räisänen, the leaders' perception contradicts Mark's so-called *Parabeltheorie*.[303] However, as argued earlier, this fails to do justice to Mark's sophistication either in terms of his view of parables or his fine irony.[304] The point is that on the one occasion when Mark's informs us that the Jerusalem authorities 'perceive' that the parable is told against them, it is their very 'perception' that sets in train their own demise. To reject Jesus and to seek to destroy him results in the destruction of the Temple. Yes, they have 'understood' the parable, much like Ahaz understood Isaiah. But they

---

[299] *Trial*, 122-27; cf. Marcus, 119-22.

[300] See further Donahue, *ibid.*, 103-38.

[301] Marcus, 120f.

[302] See also Marcus, 121, although he seems to go too far in reading 'others' (12:9) to either mean or include Gentiles. This is not evident in the text.

[303] *"Messianic"*, 88; cf. Lambrecht, *Astonished*, 132; Snodgrass, *ibid.*, 73; Gundry, 691.

[304] See Chapter 7, pp. 206ff, above.

have refused to accept that it is also the truth before which they must yield. This, after all, is what genuine wisdom is about. The parallels with the Isaianic paradigm are two-fold. First, Isaiah 5 is a juridical parable designed to lure the hearers into judging themselves, and that is exactly what is happening here. And second, in keeping with Mark's use of Isaiah 6 and 29, just as Yahweh used the Jerusalem leadership's reliance on their own wisdom to lead them into judgment, so also here.

Finally, the parable leads into an second series of confrontations and questions which, as Hooker has suggested, are generally related to the preceding matter of Jesus' authority.[305] The 'taxes' question put by some of the Herodians and the Pharisees not only highlights their failure to give to God that which is due him (loyalty to his Son; cf. 3:6), but perhaps adumbrates the Jerusalem leadership's greater loyalty to Caesar in getting Jesus executed as an insurrectionist. The Sadducees' question on the resurrection resonates with the Markan theme of the ultimate vindication of Jesus (the murdered 'son' and rejected stone), while keeping the great commandments—love God (whom in Jesus they have not) and your neighbour (including the nations)—are truly worth more than all the sacrifices in the Temple (cf. Isa 56:7 and Jer 7:11 in Mk 11:17).

The last of the controversies, now initiated by Jesus, deals again with Jesus' messiahship; a principle theme for Mark.[306] By starting with Psalm 110's affirmation of lordship, and couching the question in terms of being David's son, Jesus highlights the ambiguity of David's statement.[307] Since in Mark's account everyone seems agreed that the Messiah is David's son, the question would have at first perplexed. But if the second line was agreed, perhaps it was the first line of the syllogistic question that needed thought. What does David mean by Lord? What does Jesus mean? Exactly. He is not merely David's messianic Son, but also his (and therefore their) Lord (cf. 11:10) and once again we return to the question of

---

[305] 'Traditions', 9f. Dewey, *Debate*, 156-63, has suggested that the Jerusalem conflict stories counterbalance 2:1 - 3:6; but see Smith, 'Opponents', 175f. Daube, 'Earliest', 180ff, proposes that they correspond to a rabbinical classification of four questions closely related to Passover *Haggadah*, *viz*. questions of wisdom: about points of law; questions of vulgarity: mocking questions usually about resurrection; questions of the proper way of the land: about piety; and questions of interpretation: about apparent contradictions in Scripture.
[306] On Gundry's reading, 718, Jesus is merely engaged in point-scoring, and displays a rigidity and plodding literalism that is foreign to his own use of Scripture elsewhere.
[307] Matt 22:45 clarifies the intent but looses the impact of the destabilising logic.

authority.[308]   So then, at the conclusion of Jesus' verbal conflict with the Jerusalem authorities, Mark here brings together the two key components of Jesus' identity: he is both Messiah and Lord.

Following hard on the heels of the defeated silence of the Temple authorities, comes the denunciation of the scribes' insincere piety.   As Israel's teachers they have constantly been heading up Jesus' opposition (2:6, 11; 3:22; 7:1, 5; 9:14; 11:18; cf. 1:22) so the judgement language here probably serves as a final condemnation of the kind of 'building' activities in which they have been engaged. Blind and deaf to Yahweh's wisdom but more importantly refusing to follow a path not of their own under-standing, they are no longer fit to be Yahweh's servants and are Israel in name only (cf. Isa 48:1f). The results of 'building' in such a way are then openly revealed in Mark 13 where Jesus begins with an explicit statement of what to this point has only been expressed parabolically or implicitly, namely, the coming destruction of the Temple (13:1f).

g) Conclusion

The INE envisaged the coming of Yahweh, the victorious deliverer of his people to a liberated and soon-to-be gloriously restored Jerusalem. And on the surface, Jesus, as messianic Son of God and Yahweh-Warrior, does indeed come on the INE way, accompanied by the 'blind' and in procession with rejoicing crowds. So identified, Jesus bears the appropriate authority. However, the absence of any official welcome draws attention to the other main Markan narrative plot: the unpreparedness and hostility of the nation's leaders. Consequently, we are confronted not with signs of escha-tological blessing, but instead, in keeping with Malachi's threat, the cursing of the fig-tree.   This along with the 'cleansing' incident constitutes Jesus' climactic confrontation with his opponents and signifies the coming destruction of the Temple. Mark's account of Jesus' use of Isaiah 56 and Jeremiah 7 provides the rationale. Whereas in the INE the Temple should have become a 'house of prayer for all nations', the institution had instead engendered a false security and become a 'den of thieves' for an obdurate, nationalistic, and hostile leadership. As in Jeremiah, such practice was not only meaningless but subject to judgement. At this point, the much cited absence of material describing a messianic figure who will destroy the

---

[308] Chapter 8, pp. 288ff, above.

Temple is to some extent irrelevant. The Markan Jesus' is not coming to the Temple merely as Messiah—his multifaceted presentation of Jesus needs more to be taken into account—but on the basis of Malachi, and Isaiah's Yahweh-Warrior, also as its Lord (cf. Isa 66:6). This is why Jesus asks the religious establishment for their assessment of John. Because of their 'failure' (read 'refusal') to 'understand', Malachi's purging curse will be applied, and this in the terms of Jeremiah 7. In both cases something much more severe than mere renovation is in view. The parable of the tenants then comes full circle to the issue of Jesus' identity and authority. In spite of the tenants murderous' plans, their 'wisdom' will lead to their own destruction, and the heir's vindication. And predicated on Jesus, the true son and heir, a new leadership, and presumably a new Temple to which all nations will come, will emerge to take the place of the old.

IV. The Words of Institution: Jesus' Death and Isaiah's Servant?

a) Introduction

In Chapter 8 we argued that while not excluding the influence of other OT texts—Mark's Jesus characteristically combines ideas from several such sources—the primary background for Jesus' self-understanding of his coming death appears most likely to have been derived from the descriptions of the sufferings of the enigmatic Isaianic 'servant'. The aim of this section is to see if there is any evidence that the Markan Jesus understood his death in a similar way in this final part of his gospel, and if so, to make some suggestions as to its significance. As it is, numerous commentators have seen an allusion to Isaiah 53 in the words of institution in Mark 14:24, which also happens to be the only place in these last chapters where Jesus offers any indication of his perception of his coming death. A number of other allusions to Isaiah 53 (and 50) have also been proposed, but here opinion becomes increasingly divided (see below). We will therefore concentrate on Mark 14:24, and then offer some brief observations on several of the other candidate passages.

Before doing so, however, it is important to note some cardinal features of Mark's accounts of Jesus' self-understanding. In the first section of his gospel, although Mark frequently mentions the fact of Jesus' exorcisms—they could even be regarded as characteristic of Jesus' activity herein—he has only one instance where some explanation of their significance is offered (3:27). Likewise, in the 'Way' section with its focus on Jesus' impending passion—also perhaps the chief concern of the section as is suggested, for example, not only by the three similarly constructed predictions but also their careful placement within the overall structure—there is again only one brief statement as to the import of this future suffering (10:45). The same pattern apparently applies in this final section. Although much material is devoted to the events immediately leading up to and including Jesus' death, only 14:24 gives any specific indication of its significance.[309]

Second, in all three cases the explanations themselves exhibit some 'formal' similarities. They are quite brief, almost to the point of being terse. They are also characteristically highly allusive and, as we have seen, the majority of scholars have suggested some sort of OT background even if there has been debate as to its precise nature. Third, Mark seems to have placed these statements at crucial points in his developing narrative. The Beelzebul controversy stands at the juncture of the first series of controversies and the all-important parable materials. The ransom saying comes in the third and final passion prediction at the climax of the 'Way' section. Likewise, the cup saying is situated between the concatenated accounts of Jesus' various pronouncements—again in word and in deed—of the Temple's destruction, and the narratives of the Temple authorities' attempt to destroy him (i.e. Jesus' trial and execution).

All this appears too consistent to be co-incidental and suggests thoughtful design.[310] Why does Mark do this? It is difficult to tell, but the relative infrequency of explanations—one per section—and their apparently careful placement suggest that they ought to be given considerable weight. Consequently, although it represents only one verse, Mark 14:24 is more than likely of considerable importance.

---

[309] It is difficult to determine whether the saying in the Temple incident should also be considered here. Is Jesus' death the sole focus, or perhaps as our analysis might suggest, is it to be closely tied with his pronouncement in the Temple? If so, and although merely speculation, might it be that two key sayings, i.e. about the strong man and the ransom, find their respective fulfilment in the Temple material (11:17, summarising chs. 11-13) and in Jesus' death (14:24; summarising chs. 14-16) such that both the themes of the first and second sections come together in the final climactic section?

[310] Best, *Temptation*, liii.

b) Mark 14:24: The Cup Saying

In placing side by side the preparations for the Passover and the Jewish authorities' preparations to seize Jesus 'ἐν δόλῳ', Mark 14:1 continues the theme of the parable of the wicked tenants. (The intervening material of Mark 13, which contains several allusions to Isaiah but is so complex as to require its own additional Chapter and so is not dealt with in this book, could well be intended to explain the eschatological implications of Jesus' pronouncements concerning the Temple and its hierarchy.) The nation's leaders seek Jesus' death, but Yahweh will wondrously use their plans both to judge them and to effect his final INE purposes. Second, that all of this happens during the feast that recalls Israel's founding moment deliverance only heightens the irony, and even more so if, as is indicated by later tradition, this was the night on which Israel's next deliverance was expected to take place.[311] Furthermore, for Mark the meal at which these words are spoken is itself the Passover meal (14:12-16).[312] The Exodus-New Exodus paradigm could hardly be clearer.

The statement in question has commonly been treated in two parts: τοῦτό ἐστιν τὸ αἷμά μου τῆς διαθήκης and τὸ ἐκχυννόμενον ὑπὲρ πολλῶν. It is almost universally agreed that the first half alludes to Exodus 24:8.[313] If so, then we note at the outset that once again there is a combination of different motifs (i.e. iconic augmentation). The events at Sinai (Ex 24:3-8) are recalled within the context of a Passover meal. Passover, of course, remembers the night when Yahweh redeemed his people from bondage. But what is the significance of Exodus 24 and why add it here?

It generally agreed that Exodus 24:8 describes part of the blood ritual at the foot of Mount Sinai (cf. Ex 20:18-21) where, after setting up twelve stones representative of the tribes of Israel (v. 4), Moses takes half of the blood of the sacrifices and 'dashes' (זרק) it upon the altar (v. 6) and, after

---

[311] Chapter 2, p. 39, fn. 29. On the possible messianic significance of the bread saying, see Daube, *Cometh*; and Carmichael, 'Eucharist'.

[312] See further e.g. Jeremias, *Eucharistic*, 16ff. On the coherence of vv. 12-26 within a Passover context, see Pesch, 'Gospel,' 139-48.

[313] The two variants—the addition of καινῆς and εἰς ἄφεσιν ἁμαρτιῶν—are best seen as assimilations to Mt and/or later tradition; on the textual issues, see Gundry, *Use*, 57ff. Some see also an echo of Zech 9:11 which may have the Exodus in view (cf. *Tg.*), and in particular the remembrance of the Ex 24 covenant; cf. Taylor; Hooker, *Servant*, 82; and Marcus, 157, on the basis of the possessive pronoun but which may simply indicate that Jesus is speaking of his blood. However, Mark is closer to Ex 24:8; e.g. France, *Jesus*, 66. Later Judaism understood דַּם בְּרִית also to refer to the rite of circumcision, Jeremias, *ibid.*, 225nn4, 5.

reading from the book of the covenant (v. 7), 'dashes' (זרק) the other half upon the people (v. 8). All this is immediately followed by a covenant ratification meal on the mountain of God (vv. 9-11). From the perspective of the Book of Exodus, these events signal the fulfilment of Yahweh's promised deliverance whereby Israel is now able to 'sacrifier et servir YHWH «sur cette montagne»' (cf. Ex 3:12),[314] and mark the inauguration of Yahweh's covenant with Israel as his newly redeemed people.

The exact significance of the rite itself has been debated.[315] E. W. Nicholson, however, has cogently argued that its point is to convey holiness and thus serves to constitute Israel, in the language of Exodus 19:6, 'as Yahweh's "kingdom of priests and a holy nation" (cf. Isa. lxi 6)'.[316] That the same kind of procedure is followed in Leviticus 8, where during the sanctification of the priests blood is placed on them (vv. 23f) and the remainder 'dashed' on the altar (זרק, v. 24b), lends further support to Nicholson's suggestion. Along similar lines, R. S. Hendel in his treatment of the social function of sacrifice suggests that the whole Exodus event can be seen as 'an elaborate rite of passage' whereby Turner's tripartite scheme of separation, limen, and reaggregation is enunciated in Israel's escape from Egypt, her encounter with Yahweh, and journey homeward (i.e. to the promised land).[317] In this model, the ceremony of Exodus 24:3-8 becomes part of the means by which Israel's 'new religious and social identity is articulated' thereby consecrating her to Yahweh as his one people—hence the twelve stones.[318]

In terms of Mark, just as the first Exodus entailed a journey followed by the 'blood of the covenant' (and a meal) at the 'mountain of God', so too Mark's Jesus at the end of the 'Way' journey speaks of the blood of the covenant (in the context of a meal) in Jerusalem, that is, Mount Zion.[319] Perhaps it is coincidence, but one also notes that just as the twelve stones

---

[314] Schenker, 'Sacrifices', 491.

[315] See e.g. the more recent discussions in Kutsch, '"Bundesblut"'; Nicholson, 'Ritual'; Hendel, 'Sacrifice'; and Schenker, 'Sacrifices'.

[316] 'Ritual', 86.

[317] 'Sacrifice', 375. Although recognising that 'aspects of Turner's theory have been criticised', Hendel argues that his 'discussion nevertheless provides an important step toward an understanding of the ritual symbolism of Ex 24,3-8'.

[318] *Ibid.*, 376.

[319] Aalen, 'Opfermahl', 149ff, notes that Ex 24 is the only place in the OT where the blood of the covenant and the eating of a meal are explicitly joined.

in Exodus 24 represent all Israel whose leaders subsequently ascend the holy mountain to eat in Yahweh's presence, so Mark particularly records that 'the Twelve', whom he apparently views as Israel's new leadership (3:13-19), are with Jesus at this covenant moment (14:17; cf. v. 20).[320] Be that as it may, the Exodus allusion seems to imply that Jesus' death not only inaugurates a covenant but also articulates, if not a new covenant people, at least a new identity for them.

Several data point in this direction. First, Exodus 24 is itself precisely about this with the blood rite establishing the 'new religious and social identity' of the newly redeemed people as Yahweh's kingdom of priests, a holy people. Second, we have earlier suggested that Jesus' choosing of the Twelve (3:13-19) and his response to his family (3:20-30) indicates that being a member of true Israel is predicated, not on one's nationality or filial ties, but on one's response to Jesus.[321] This implies a redefinition of what it means to be Israel. Third, we have already seen how Lohmeyer viewed many of Jesus' actions either as removing the stigma of uncleanness or redefining uncleanness/holiness in an inclusive manner, again indicating a redefinition of God's people. At the same time, Jesus' pronouncement in the Temple implies that Gentiles too are now to be included in new ways among God's people.[322] When seen in this light, an appeal to Exodus 24 only underlines the point that Mark's Jesus is about the reconstitution of Israel.

Does this have any connection with the INE? Clearly so, first, in terms of the general Exodus/New Exodus pattern. After all, the Passover recalled Israel's redemption—and thereby provided what we have seen is a key motif in the INE, namely, יְהוה גָּאֵל יִשְׂרָאֵל—and this so that she might be constituted as God's people at the Mount of God. Second, as we have observed above, the INE also envisages a radical redefinition of Israel which not only sees a bifurcation within the nation but also offers unprecedented opportunities for Gentiles. Indeed, the only other place in the prophetic corpus where as part of the eschatological vision the nation is described in language reminiscent of Exodus 19:6 is in the crowning

---

[320] Cf. Myhre, 'Paktens'.
[321] See Chapter 7, pp. 185ff, above.
[322] See also Gnilka, 2.246.

declaration of Isaiah 61:6 (אַתֶּם כֹּהֲנֵי יהוה תִּקָּרֵאוּ).[323]   The goal of the INE, as with its precursor, is thus the reconstitution of God's priestly people, and this as suggested above also involves, at its most inclusive, a priestly role for Gentile proselytes (66:19).

Third, integral to this reconstitution is Yahweh's promised בְּרִית שְׁלוֹמִי that לֹא תָמוּט (54:10), which is likened both to that of the days of Noah (56:9-17; cf. 54:11-17) and to the Davidic בְּרִית עוֹלָם (55:3).   Because a renewal of the Mosaic covenant is not mentioned, particularly in view of the formative influence of the Exodus traditions, it is often assumed that it is thereby eschewed;[324] although P. M. Hoepers' and B. C. Ollenburger's analyses raises questions as to the validity of such a categorical exclusion.[325]   Nevertheless, the fundamental characteristic of this new covenant, to which the Noahic and Davidic ones testify and which is perhaps why the specific mention of a renewal of the Mosaic covenant is absent (but cf. 48:17ff), is commonly understood to be its everlasting, unilateral, and unconditional nature.   Hence Israel's salvation is described as a תְּשׁוּעַת עוֹלָמִים (45:17, 51:8) and her joy as a שִׂמְחַת עוֹלָם (51:11).[326]

With these characteristics in view, it seems significant that not only is the 'death' of the 'servant' linked to Israel's deliverance such that it apparently occasions the emergence of other 'servants of Yahweh' (54:17),

---

[323] Achtemeier, *Community*, 90. Itself in a context of an invitation to participate in Yahweh's covenant, Sweeney, *Isaiah*, 90.

[324] Cf. Rost, 'Sinaibund'. Anderson, 'Covenant', 342, observes that Isa 40-55 draws deeply from Israel's historic traditions yet seems hardly to mention Sinai or the conditional promises of the covenant. Mosaic traditions, although rarely referred to in first section (Sanders, *Torah*, 56f; Vriezen, 'Essentials', 128ff), are more apparent in chs. 40ff and suggest that the prophet mediates (as did Moses) between people and God (Evans, 'Use', 93n5). The same role could be attributed to the 'servant', e.g. Isa 42:6; 49:8.

[325] Hoepers, *Bund*, has argued that the Davidic covenant should not be regarded as altogether new and distinct from the Sinaitic one but is instead the same covenant with an additional enablement for the house of David. If this is the case, then it may be mistaken to set Exodus and David/Zion traditions in opposition. Ollenburger, *Zion*, 152ff, has also criticised this too-easy distinction between Jerusalem and Mosaic traditions on other grounds. Also Gunneweg, 'Sinaibund', 340; Anderson, 'Covenant', 344ff; Kraus, *Worship*, 188-200; Harner, *Grace*, 147ff.

[326] Anderson, 'Covenant', 342ff, 348, where in Isa 40-55 Israel's future salvation is not 'contingent on the renewal of the Mosaic covenant in the present'. In relating the Exodus and Covenant traditions, the prophet 'adopts the unconditional covenant with David, though separating it from the conditional Mosaic covenant with which it had been bound from the very first; and he adopts the unconditional covenant with David, though separating it from the unhappy history of the Davidic dynasty and transferring its promises of grace to the people', 357; McCarthy, 'Covenant', 236ff. The imminent covenant is of such an order that only the Noachic covenant is comparable, Muilenburg, 'Isaiah', 637.

that is, Israel's reconstitution, but on two occasions we are informed that the 'servant' is also to be אֹור גֹּויִם and בְּרִית עָם (Isa 42:6; 49:6, 8).[327] What is meant by these expressions is not entirely clear, but, as we have noted above, Van Winkle has shown that the language links the motifs of salvation for the nations with that of covenant. This is so at least for Israel (cf. Jer 31:31-33), if not, given the use of עַם in the immediately preceding context (Isa 42:5), the nations also (cf. Isa 2:2-4; 19:23f).[328] In light of the discussion of Exodus 24 above and the INE hope of a new covenant, such a role for the 'servant' would not be unexpected, especially if he is construed in some way as a new Moses.[329]

The crucial point, however, is that the Isaianic 'servant' is explicitly connected with the NE and covenant,[330] and furthermore is the only figure associated with the hope of a NE so conceived in the OT. If Mark's Jesus is construed within the context of the INE then the natural precursor to his covenant-inaugurating role would be that of the Isaianic 'servant'.[331] Jesus' use of covenant-inaugurating language in the context of his forthcoming death only strengthens the conceptual connection with the 'servant' whose 'death', we have already argued, is somehow central to the NE. That Mark's Jesus should choose to make such a heavily freighted declaration on Passover, whereby his violent death itself during Passover will be the instrumental means of the covenantal beginning of a newly defined Israel, is entirely fitting.

Nevertheless, although Hooker regards the idea of διαθήκη as the 'greatest similarity' between Mark 14:24 and 'the thought of the prophet', she argues that the concept of Jesus as 'the leader who was to be a covenant to his people' (cf. Isa 42:6 and 49:8) is 'clearly only a secondary one in this

---

[327] Duhm's original demarcation of the so-called Servant Songs has been much debated. They are here delimited as follows: 42:1-7(9); 49:1-9; 50:4-9; and 52:13 - 53:12. But cf. e.g. Mettinger, 'Farewell', who includes 49:8-13 and 42:18-25; North, *Suffering*, 132ff, who e.g. limits the first 'song' to vv. 1-4; and Orlinsky, 'So-Called', 17ff, who argues against the unity of 52:13 - 53:12.

[328] Although עַם is commonly used of Israel—frequently with a pronominal possessive suffix—in the 'song' from which the phrase is taken עַם is apparently used of humanity in general (cf. 40:7; plural in 49:22; 51:4f); see Westermann, 99f, and the numerous commentators listed there.

[329] See the literature cited above in Chapter 8, pp. 277f and fn. 219.

[330] France favourably cites Cullmann, *Christology*, 55, who regards covenant-making as 'one of the two "essential characteristics" of the Servant', *Jesus*, 122.

[331] Also e.g. Wolff, *Jesaja*, 65.

passage'.[332] Further, 'the complete absence of the idea of blood-shedding from both Isa. 42. 6 and 49. 8, as well as from the Servant Songs themselves' makes 'any connection between these passages and the words of Jesus ... extremely unlikely'.[333]

In response to the first objection, 'secondary' does not mean 'invalid', since surely function and identity are related. In the light of both Mark's INE hermeneutic—Hooker freely admits the general Deutero-Isaianic background to Jesus' ministry[334]—and the preceding discussion on the role of the 'servant' in the INE, what other interpretive paradigm might we propose? As we have argued above, only the figure of the Isaianic (Moses-like?) 'servant' combines the roles of effecting the NE, being a covenant, and 'dying' for others. An explicit identification may not be made in Mark, but it seems very much to be the underlying and foundational assumption. This leads to Hooker's second objection that 'the idea of blood-shedding' is completely absent from the 'servant' passages.[335] However, if $\alpha\hat{\iota}\mu\alpha\ \dot{\epsilon}\kappa\chi\dot{\epsilon}\omega$ merely means 'bloodshed', that is, the taking of life (see below), and since this on the basis of OT usage is often associated with violent and unjust death (e.g LXX: 2 Kgs 21:16; 24:4; Ps 13:3, 79:10; Prov 1:16; and 6:17), then surely the 'idea' is present, if not in Isaiah 42 and 49, then certainly in the suffering and 'death' of the innocent 'servant' as described in Isaiah 50 and 53.

The second phrase, $\tau\grave{o}\ \dot{\epsilon}\kappa\chi\upsilon\nu\nu\acute{o}\mu\epsilon\nu\upsilon\nu\ \dot{\upsilon}\pi\grave{\epsilon}\rho\ \pi\upsilon\lambda\lambda\hat{\omega}\nu$, describes both how this covenant is to be effected and on whose behalf. Many scholars have seen here an allusion to Isaiah 53, if not on account of the 'poured out' since $\dot{\epsilon}\kappa\chi\dot{\epsilon}\omega$ is never used of עָרָה in the LXX,[336] then usually in terms of the

---

[332] *Servant*, 82; so also Best, *Temptation*, 146, for whom 'covenant' is too wide a term in the OT to be linked with one figure.

[333] *Ibid.*; and also Best, *ibid.*

[334] Again, *Servant*, 66, 67f, 73, cf. 95.

[335] While true with regard to those texts that specifically mention covenant (42:1ff; 49:1ff), this argument assumes that Mark's Jesus could not have related the 'servant' figure of Isa 42:1ff and 49:1ff to that of Isa 53, with the latter explaining how the former were to occur. But if the tradition in some editions of *Tg. Isa* can see the Messiah mentioned in both (again Chapter 3, p. 115, fn. 137), then, given the creativity of Mark's Jesus, it is not impossible that he too saw some link between them, even if the majority of his contemporaries did not (also Chapter 8, p. 244, fn. 86). The issue of the uniqueness of this understanding over against contemporary understanding will be dealt with in Chapter 10 below.

[336] Pesch, 2.359, (cf. Whybray, fn. 340, below) who denies that it constitutes an allusion to Isa 53:12, whereas Gundry, *Use*, 59; France, *Jesus*, 122; and Moo, *Passion*, 131, assert that $\dot{\epsilon}\kappa\chi\dot{\epsilon}\omega$ exactly corresponds to עָרָה.

reference to 'the many' based on its frequent appearance in 53:11f.[337] But as in the case of Mark 10:45 both Hooker and Grimm have mounted separate challenges to this interpretation.[338]

Hooker raises two objections. First, pouring out blood (שָׁפַךְ דָּם / αἷμα ἐκχέω) simply means 'bloodshed' (i.e. 'to take life', e.g. Gn 9:6; Dt 19:10; Is 59:7; Ezek 22:3-12; Prov 1:16; Ps 106:38; but see below)[339] and therefore 'appears to have no connection' with Isaiah 53:12 where 'the Servant is laid bare to death' (הֶעֱרָה לַמָּוֶת נַפְשׁוֹ).[340] Second, having denied or minimised any other connection with Isaiah 53, the reference to the 'many' is alone insufficient to establish an Isaiah 53 allusion.[341]

On the first point, at a conceptual level and given the previously mentioned connotations of violence and injustice, it is difficult to see any substantial difference between 'bloodshed' and the experience of the innocent 'servant' who is at least under the threat of death, and probably worse. Moreover, הערה is 'a strange and mysterious metaphor' of which 'pour out' is a valid rendering, and in either case, Mark's 'poured out' 'blood' is hardly to be differentiated from Isaiah 53's 'laid bare' 'his soul to death', as the latter's context makes clear.[342] With regard to Hooker's

---

[337] Cf. Wolff, *Jesaja*, 66; Maurer, 'Knecht', 18; Lohse, *Märtyrer*, 124; France, *Jesus*, 122; Lane; Grimm, 297; Gnilka; Moo, *Passion*, 130f; Gundry, 832; Marcus, 187; on the basis of 'the many', espec. Pesch, 2.358.

[338] Suhl, 114-20, ingeniously proposes a gnostic origin.

[339] Also Lohse, *Märtyrer*, 125; France, *Jesus*, 122; Grimm, 297.

[340] *Servant*, 82; also Pesch, 2.358, (cf. *Abendmahl*, 94), who sees the expression as synonymous with δοῦναι τὴν ψυχήν in 10:45. Again, Whybray, *Thanksgiving*, 104f, has questioned whether the actual death of the 'servant' is in view. He argues that while 'pour out' or 'empty' most naturally suggest death, Ps 141:8, which is the only other place where ערה has נפשׁ as direct object, means 'to leave defenceless', i.e. 'lay bare', cf. Ps 137:7. Thus Isa 53:12 should read 'he left himself defenceless to the death' (or 'to the uttermost'); i.e. entirely 'at the mercy of his enemies or persecutors'. But since the contexts of both psalms imply that what is being risked is injury or death and destruction, why should Isa 53:12 add לַמָּוֶת since on Whybray's reading it contributes nothing other than what might reasonably be inferred? In view of the absence of לַמָּוֶת in parallel examples, its presence here strongly suggests that the defencelessness was maintained even 'to the point of death'. However, even if one accepts Whybray's reading, i.e. the 'servant' is willing to obey even if it means death but does not in fact die, that Mark's Jesus renders himself 'defenceless' even to actual death, hardly disqualifies the parallel. The LXX and the Greek versions appear to understand that the 'servant' dies.

[341] *Ibid.*

[342] France, *Jesus*, 122. Later, in 244n18, he cites Isa 32:15 where the single occurrence of the Niphal—described as the passive of the Hiphil 2 under which category Isa 53:12 is listed, BDB, 788—clearly means 'pour out'. The Targum's מסר, 'to surrender, deliver', may be an attempt to render the sense of 'to lay bare' (cf. Ps 137:7; 141:8) while the LXX's and the Greek versions', παρεδόθη, is more interpretive.

second objection, it is to be questioned whether all we have is a solitary reference to 'the many'. Hooker freely admits the point of the passage to be that Jesus' death establishes a new covenant between God and the 'many'[343] such that it is 'the redemptive act which brings the new community of God's people into being',[344] and, as noted earlier, that the general background to Jesus' ministry is 'Deutero-Isaianic'. Once again, Mark 9:12's linking of Jesus' death to the OT and the contextual correspondences outlined above considerably reduce the range of options: who else within the INE horizon 'dies' for the benefit of the 'many' and brings 'the new community of God's people into being', if not the 'servant'?

Werner Grimm, noting Mark 14:24's linguistic similarity to Matthew 23:35's πᾶν αἷμα δίκαιον ἐκχυννόμενον, also argues that 'blood ... poured out' is not sacrificial language but means merely death, although the covenant language in the context of a meal probably refers to Exodus 24.[345] In terms of Isaiah 53, while there is a conceptual parallel—Jeremias is right in seeing πολλῶν as a reference to Isaiah 53:12—the preposition ὑπέρ finds no correspondence because 53:12b's תַּחַת is 'eindeutig konjunktional und nicht präpositional verwendet' and ὑπέρ πολλῶν is distinct from לָרַבִּים and בָּרַבִּים.[346] Instead, the constructions תַּחְתֶּיךָ ... כָּפְרְךָ and נָתַתִּי תַּחְתֶּיךָ and אֶתֵּן ... תַּחְתֶּיךָ, (Isa 43:3a, b, 4) suggest that תַּחַת can be a shortened form of כֹּפֶר תַּחַת. Since in Isaiah 43:3 LXX, which stands behind Mark 10:45's λύτρον ἀντὶ πολλῶν, תַּחַת is rendered by ὑπέρ, then Mark 14:24's ὑπέρ πολλῶν is simply a parallel to 10:45's (λύτρον) ἀντὶ πολλῶν. Thus ὑπέρ again reflects Isaiah 43:3f not 53:12.[347]

In the light of Grimm's first assertion, it is of some interest that ἐκχέω αἷμα does in fact occur in sacrificial contexts in the LXX particularly as part of the ritual which both 'sanctifies' the altar and 'makes atonement' for it (וַיְקַדְּשֵׁהוּ לְכַפֵּר עָלָיו, Lev 8:15; cf. Ex 24:6) and as such is integral to acts of consecration of priests (Ex 29:12; Lev 8:15) and of Israel (cf. Ex 24:8), and of atonement as effected by the sin offering (e.g. Lev 4:7, 18, 25, 30, 34, for the priests and for Israel).[348] It is possible, given the allusion to Exodus 24 and

---

343 *Servant*, 82.
344 *Mark*, 343.
345 *Verkündigung*, 297.
346 *Ibid.*, 297, 298.
347 *Ibid.*
348 See also Moo, *Passion*, 130; citing Tödt, *Son*, 204f.

the modifying prepositional phrase ὑπὲρ πολλῶν which D. J. Moo argues
has sacrificial overtones,[349] that Jesus' concept of 'poured out blood'
functions as a metonymy for an act of consecration and atonement (cf. *Tgs.
Onq.* and *Yer.* on Ex 24:7-8 which seem to indicate that this particular
consecrating sacrifice was also atoning).[350] And even if not so specific, the
Passover meal context and the language of 'covenant' and 'blood' seems
clearly to imply the idea of sacrifice. Again, the only figure who is related
to the INE and who is in any way connected with sacrificial language is the
Isaianic 'servant'. Even if the unique expression in 53:10 is difficult, the
fact remains that he is described in terms of an אָשָׁם, the purpose of which
is to make atonement for sin (e.g. Lev 5:6f, 15-19; espec. 7:1ff which also
entails the act of blood being 'dashed' [זרק] upon the altar; cf. Ex 24:6-8).[351]
Allowing for the complexity of the sacrificial system and the allusive
nature of Jesus' statement, which may yet again reflect a creative
combination of older ideas, the common cluster of motifs suggests that
something along these lines is in view in Mark 14:24.[352] Nonetheless,
even if the expression refers only to violent death, the arguments put
forward under the previous discussion of Mark 10:45 still apply here.[353]
Namely, as Grimm apparently recognises, the idea of 'death' 'on behalf of
others' is far clearer in Isaiah 53 than in Isaiah 43. And this even more so
in the light of the 'covenant' language which in the INE is primarily
associated with the 'servant'.

Regarding the prepositional phrase, it may be added in support of
Grimm's position that Isaiah 43:3f is the only place in the book where ὑπέρ
is used with anything like the sense of Mark 14:24 (cf. Dt 24:16, the only
place in the Torah, but here translating עַל; par. 2 Kgs 14:6 and 2 Chron
25:4). Not only so, but Isaiah 43:3f is the only occurrence of ὑπέρ for תַּחַת in
the LXX—ἀντί is unquestionably the regular rendering of תַּחַת when the
latter has the sense of exchange, that is, 'in the place of'.

---

[349] *Passion*, 131, as it certainly does in the NT, see BAGD, 838; cf. LXX: 1 Esdr 8:63;
2 Macc 1:26; 3:32.

[350] E.g. Pesch, *Abendmahl*, 95f.

[351] See further the discussion in Chapter 8, pp. 275f, fn. 209.

[352] See e.g. Haag, 'Opfer'; Meyer, 'Expiation', who sees a covenant sacrifice and
expiatory offering. As with with Ex 24 atoning blood as a covenant sign is here linked with
a meal, Myhre, 'Paktens'.

[353] Chapter 8, pp. 281ff, above.

But how realistic is it to base an explicit allusion to Isaiah 43:3f solely on its unusual use of a single and very common NT preposition? Grimm seems to suggest that Isaiah 43 is already in view due to Mark 10:45. But, it can be countered, on the basis of that same text, *and* the *three* passion predictions, *and* Mark 9:12, that Isaiah 53 is more so. Allusions also tend to be established on the basis of a cluster of linguistic and/or conceptual similarities. The only point of contact with Isaiah 43 is the preposition; there are no linguistic parallels with 'death' or 'the many', nor is it easy to see how Isaiah 43 relates to the idea of covenant inauguration (Mk 14:24a). Further, that תַּחַת can be a shortened form of כֹּפֶר תַּחַת is based on Isaiah 43:3a, b and only works there because the complete expression occurs in the immediately preceding *stichos*. No such complete line appears in Mark 14 and therefore it is hardly evident that ὑπέρ stands for כֹּפֶר תַּחַת.

On the other hand, if ὑπέρ is taken at face value and not as an attempt to render either of the prepositions לְ or בְּ (Isa 53:11), then the integration of the motifs of the 'death' of an individual, the 'on behalf of', and 'the many' is far more congruent with the actions of the 'servant' in Isaiah 53 whose 'death' is more than adequately summarised as being 'on behalf' or 'for the benefit' 'of the many'.

It has also been observed that Qumran used 'the many' as a self-referent, which implies, in keeping perhaps with their self-designatory use of Isaiah 40:3, that they are the true covenant community, that is, faithful Israel.[354] This could well be its meaning here, which would fit with the Exodus 24 allusion and with those words and actions of Jesus elsewhere in Mark which indicate that he is the locus of the new covenant community.[355] The 'servant' having already been associated with the idea of covenant facilitates the conceptual link between Mark 14:24a and 24b.

So then, on this reading, whereas Mark 10:45's ἀντὶ πολλῶν might reflect the thought of Isaiah 43, it seems that ὑπέρ πολλῶν in Mark 14:24 owes more to the influence of Isaiah 53.

We have so far largely focussed only on Mark 14:24 itself, but as we have seen with Mark 10:45 merely examining isolated phrases or words without regard to larger contexts is both artificial and poor method. We

---

[354] Werner, 'Frage', citing the numerous occurrences in 1QS 6-7.

[355] See Schede, 'Fragen'; Gnilka, 2.245, who cites Isa 42:6; 49:7f, and the discussion of various Jewish traditions in Jeremias, *Eucharistic*, 227ff; cf. Chapter 8, p. 282, fn. 249, above.

have already argued that Mark's overarching INE hermeneutic provides us with indications as to the larger background within which these data are to be interpreted. More precisely, however, we have also argued that the passion predictions, in keeping with what 'is written' (Mark 9:12), point primarily to the sufferings associated with two 'servant' passages, namely, Isaiah 50 and 53. We would expect the same horizon here. And indeed, the clear echoes of Mark 10:45 which many scholars have noted in Mark 14:24—H. M. Wolff sees 10:45 as the 'Selbstvertretung' and 14:24 as the 'Frucht'[356]—strongly suggest that some sort of common interpretative framework is assumed.[357] It would appear, then, that we should at least begin with Isaiah 50 and 53 as interpretive frames for subsequent material, only going elsewhere if they fail to elucidate the texts at hand or if, on linguistic or conceptual grounds, they are clearly inapplicable. However, once an INE framework is assumed and in the case of Mark 14:24 particularly the career and role of the enigmatic 'servant' as described in Isaiah 50 and 53, not only do we see a good degree of coherence with other Markan themes, but it also makes considerable sense of the passage.

In the light of the preceding discussion, and since the Passover recalled the old Exodus and almost certainly in the first century looked forward to the New, it is hardly surprising that Mark 14:24 combines motifs associated with Israel's past and future deliverances. First, the allusion to Exodus 24's covenant-inaugurating 'blood' at Sinai, which appears to include atonement for and the consecration of Israel, captures the heart of the Exodus/Passover event whereby the nation becomes God's newly constituted people. But if this is in the past, the Isaiah 53 component looks forward. The 'servant' is not only the one figure associated with the New Exodus themes of covenant and the future reconstitution of God's people, but Isaiah 53 in particular is intimately related to the INE's movement of Israel from bondage (Isa 52) to a gloriously restored Jerusalem (Isa 54) with its description of 'servants' (plural).[358] Moreover, the 'servant' is the only figure whose 'death' is somehow connected with this future event. All this suggests that Mark's Jesus sees his death on Passover as effecting the

---

[356] *Jesaja*, 64ff.

[357] Cf. e.g. Lane, 507; Grimm, 297; Gnilka, 2.242; Marcus, 187.

[358] As in Chapter 8, p. 279, and this Chapter, p. 303 above.

INE's promised covenantal reconstitution of 'true' Israel and as such marks her 'rite of passage' from bondage to the presence of God.

Finally, once again there are hints of the operation of an innovative hermeneutic that takes up and combines several distinct motifs (cf. e.g. the prologue which seems to present Jesus as Messiah, true Israel, and yet closely identifies him with Yahweh's very presence, and 10:45 where he is both SoM and 'servant'). The reference to his coming death in the setting of a Passover meal may suggest, although this is open to some question, that Mark's Jesus sees himself in terms of the Passover lamb and thus as the one whose death inaugurates Israel's deliverance (cf. 1 Cor 5:7f).[359] More likely perhaps, the imagery of Exodus 24 indicates that the Markan Jesus sees his death as analogous to the sacrifice at the foot of Sinai which both constituted and consecrated Israel in her new identity. Lastly, perhaps itself reflecting on Moses' offer in Exodus 32:30ff, the allusion to Isaiah 53 suggests that he is also to be seen as the אשם which deals with Israel's guilt and is somehow related to effecting the INE.

c) Other Possible Allusions to Isaiah 50 and 53

In addition to Isaiah 53 in Mark 14:24, other possible allusions to the suffering of the Isaianic 'servant' in the passion narrative have been proposed. For example, NA[26] suggests Isaiah 53:7 in 14:49 and 14:61, and 53:12 in 15:27. Kee grants first place to Isaiah 50:6 in Mark 14:65, then sees allusions to Isaiah 53:12 in 14:21 (possible), 53:5 (*Tg. Isa*) in 14:58, 53:7 in 14:60 (possible), 53:6 (LXX) in 15:15, 50:2f in 15:33, 53:9 in 15:43 and 46, and finally suggests the 'influence' of 53:3-5 in 14:65.[360] Surprisingly, he does not mention Isaiah 53:12 in Mark 14:24. Moo discusses 53:3 in 14:8, 53:7 in 14:61, 50:7 and 53:7 in 14:65 and 15:19, 53:7 in 15:5, and 53:12 in 15:27. He finds favourably for all except Mark 14:8 and 15:27.[361] Obviously there is more debate about some of these proposed allusions than others—Hooker and A. Suhl, for example, would question most if not all of these supposed parallels—and it is not our intention to examine every case. A few of these texts do, however, seem to confirm the presence of the larger pattern

---

[359] Cf. Jeremias, *Eucharistic*, 220-24; but see Marshall's criticisms, *Supper*, 87ff.

[360] 'Function', 169-71.

[361] *Passion*, 127-72. Maurer, 'Knecht', suggests far more possibilities; and see now also Marcus, 186-96. Of these, Moo's work is the most detailed.

already suggested by Mark 9:12, the passion predictions, Mark 10:45, and the 'cup saying'.

Probably the clearest case is the 'spitting' and 'slapping' in 14:65 (cf. 15:19). Moo has pointed out that ἐμπτύω and its cognate noun is found only three times in the LXX (Num 12:14, Dt 25:9, Isa 50:6) and that ῥάπισμα is mentioned in the LXX only in Isaiah 50:6 and the verb only in Hosea 11:4 and Judges 16:25 (in B).[362] Of these references, again given Mark 9:12's 'it is written', only Isaiah 50:6 offers a genuine parallel.

While Hooker allows that these passages 'quite evidently echo words in the LXX version of Isa. 50. 6', she doubts an intentional connection since the writer 'would surely have kept more closely to the original'.[363] But why should he? Hooker's point might be tenable if Mark's aim was to draw direct attention to each and every parallel. But what if Mark, having already established an OT context, chose instead to stay with the narrative, expecting that his audience would notice the allusions, especially given his preceding material? After all, as Joel Marcus has observed, if Mark 14:65 is read in the light of 10:34, then these two passages together 'contain the three essential elements of Isa. 50:6'.[364] It is difficult then, given influence of Isaiah 53 on the passion predictions, not to see in 14:65 an allusion to the suffering of the 'servant'.

The 'silence' of Jesus (14:61; 15:5) has been recognised as a definite Markan pattern and has been proposed as an allusion to Isaiah 53.[365] However, Hooker argues that A) the 'silence' is only partial since he answers Pilate,[366] B) if Mark had intended an allusion to the 'suffering servant' it would have been more explicit, C) there is 'no indication' that Jesus' was 'consciously acting in accordance with that picture',[367] and D) it is 'inconceivable that (Jesus) ... should now wrangle with his accusers' since all along he 'is prepared to answer an honest question but ignores partisan assertions'.[368]

---

[362] *Passion*, 88 and 139; see Maurer, 'Knecht', 7f.

[363] *Servant*, 90f.

[364] *Way*, 190.

[365] Maurer, 'Knecht', 9; Hooker, *Servant*, 88f; Moo, *Passion*, 148ff; cf. Haenchen, *Weg*, 514, who sees this as a later insertion.

[366] *Servant*, 89.

[367] *Ibid.*, 88f.

[368] *Ibid.*, 89.

Taking A) first, even given occasional 'lapses', the 'silence' motif appears intentional and still needs to be explained. (On the other hand, it could perhaps be argued that in Isaiah the 'silence' is closely related to the perversion of justice (53:7, 8)[369] and thus Jesus' silence is only in response to false accusations.) Turning next to D), Jesus' actions in several instances would indicate otherwise. In Mark 7:6ff the Markan Jesus describes his questioners as 'hypocrites' which hardly suggests that he regards their question as 'honest'. Similarly, in 12:13ff it is evident that he recognises their attempt at entrapment as hypocrisy (v. 15), but still engages in debate. Jesus' silence is to be explained on other grounds. Any assessment of B) necessarily involves a subjective judgement as to what constitutes a 'clear' allusion and this includes an assumption of how much emphasis Mark ought to have put on an intended allusion. Nevertheless, if for the moment we hold the objection in abeyance, what of C), which introduces the matter of the larger context? On the basis of the preceding argument of this book and particularly in light of Mark's accounts of Jesus' own words in 9:12, the passion predictions, the 'ransom' saying (10:45), and the 'cup' saying (14:24), we would urge to the contrary that there is considerable indication that if any OT pattern informed the Markan Jesus' understanding of his suffering and death, it was that of the Isaianic 'servant'. Since the 'silence' motif appears intentional and coheres well with Isaiah 53, there seems little objective reason to deny that it too derives from the description of the 'servant'.

Other parallels have been proposed: for example, the motif of exchange in the Barabbas incident (cf. Isa 53:6, 12),[370] the prominence of παραδίδωμι throughout (14:10f, 18, 21, 41f, 44; 15:1, 10, 15),[371] the amazement of Pilate (15:5; θαυμάζω, cf. Isa 52:15, LXX; but not the MT), and perhaps the implied awe of the centurion (15:39).[372] The latter two suggestions are largely unconvincing since the responses in Mark and Isaiah have different causes.[373] Nor do either of the former, in their own right, establish a link with the Isaianic 'servant'. However, if the passion predictions are

---

[369] Both Westermann, 257, and Whybray, *Thanksgiving*, 118f, suggest that the context envisaged here is a trial.

[370] So Gnilka, 2.303.

[371] Moo, *Passion*, 92-96; Gnilka, *ibid.*; Marcus, 188.

[372] Maurer, 'Knecht', 9; Moo, *Passion*, 148ff; and Marcus, 185.

[373] See Moo, *Passion*, 148n2.

influenced by Isaiah 53—both 9:31 and 10:33 use παραδίδωμι—and are intended to set the context for the passion narrative, then it seems reasonable to suppose that Mark intended παραδίδωμι throughout this section to be read in their light and thus also to echo Isaiah 53:6 and 12.

If the preceding arguments commend themselves, then, *prima facie*, they raise the possibility that Jesus' trial and execution, as a whole, is to be read in the light of Isaiah 50 and 53. This may then, on the grounds of consanguinity, suggest that some of the other allusions proposed above, which by themselves do not immediately evoke these chapters, are to be so understood. But this is another matter and we shall pursue it no further.

c) Conclusion

We argued in the previous Chapter that the numerous references to Jesus' suffering and death in Mark's 'Way' section and particularly the ransom saying in 10:45, when read within the parameters established by Mark 9:12, appear to have been influenced primarily by Isaiah 53. In spite of some arguments to the contrary, the same seems to apply to the cup saying and to other features in the passion narrative itself.

If so, then on the eve of the Passover, which both commemorated the first Exodus and in all probability looked forward to a new deliverance under the Messiah, and in the only place in this section where there is any indication of the significance of his coming death, Mark's Jesus creatively integrates Israel's founding moment—the covenantal formation of God's people at Sinai—with the prophetic hope of the NE—the self-offering of the Isaianic 'servant', itself perhaps derived from Moses' offer on Mount Sinai. Thus the INE in Mark comes to its climax, as in Isaiah, in the final 'self-offering' of the 'servant', who is not only to be a 'covenant' but whose 'death' is somehow integral to facilitating the NE.

V. The Short Ending of Mark

a) 'For they were afraid ...'

The sudden and almost anti-climactic ending of Mark continues to be a source of fascination and has spawned a considerable literature. Although we do not intend entering this debate in any detail, we will nevertheless briefly mention an interesting parallel with the message of Isaiah 40-55.

Generally Isaiah 40-55 is seen as announcing Israel's deliverance from exile, and this is borne out by the prologue and the content of the various oracles, proclamations, and hymns which announce, detail, and celebrate the nation's imminent salvation.[374] But, as we have argued elsewhere, there is also an on-going and increasingly polarised altercation between Yahweh and Jacob-Israel concerning his power, his faithfulness, and his wisdom.[375] One of the issues underlying this tension seems to be Jacob-Israel's fear as is evident in the constant refrain of 'fear not' as Yahweh encourages his people to trust him and to accept that their salvation is near (Isa 40:9; 41:10, 13, 14; 43:1, 5; 44:2; 44:8; cf. 51:7, 13; 54:4, 14).[376] We also argued that it was ultimately because of Jacob-Israel's 'fear' and refusal to accept, to believe, and to act on the 'good news' of the prophet's message that the INE was delayed.

Apparently not much had changed in Malachi's day nor, if our reading is correct, in that of the Markan Jesus. If we are right in seeing Mark's Jesus as the one who inaugurates the long-awaited INE it is perhaps not surprising, as Chris Marshall has shown, that the question of 'faith and unbelief' is a central issue for Mark.[377] It figures prominently in Jesus' opening invitation to repent and believe,[378] and also in the unbelief and lack of repentance that characterises Israel's leadership.[379] The disciples, too, respond in a mixture of 'faith' and 'fear'.[380] In commenting on the latter in Mark 4:34 Marshall observes that 'when believers fail to act in faith, they are not merely "small in faith"; they are actually succumbing to

---

[374] Using the formal categories of Westermann, 'Heilswort'; Schoors, *Saviour*; and Melugin, *Formation*; cf. Harner, 'Salvation'; and also e.g. the criticisms of Schüpphaus, 'Stellung'; von Waldow, 'Meaning', 267; and especially Conrad, 'Oracles'. However, as all parties recognise, many of the texts in Isa 40-55 do not adhere to standard *Gattungen*, and thus even Conrad must admit 'inconsistencies' in his alternative proposal. Ultimately, it is not clear that Conrad has so much delineated different forms as detected the influence of older traditions on their content.

[375] Watts, 'Consolation', 35-49.

[376] See also e.g. 42:10-17 and 44:23 where Yahweh himself cries out and summons creation to cry aloud and sing songs of praise.

[377] *Faith*.

[378] On the literary function of 1:14-15 from this perspective, see e.g. Marshall, *Faith*, 36ff, who also argues for a link between 1:14-15 and 16:7-8, see 41f.

[379] As in Chapter 7 above, and Marshall, *ibid.*, 179-208.

[380] Chapters 7 and 8 above, and Marshall, *ibid.*, 208-25.

the power of the γενέα ἄπιστος that stands opposed to God's rule'.[381] Nevertheless, their unbelief does not prevent Jesus exercising his authority, even in the face of what appears to be a demonically inspired onslaught. Jesus calms the fearfully chaotic sea just as he heals the demonised lad.

If we are on the right track, this may explain why Mark's gospel concludes rather abruptly with a statement about a 'fear' that results in silence. At the outset of the INE's announcement, there is the urgent command to proclaim, to not hold back, to not be afraid in announcing the 'good news' (Isa 40:9;[382] cf. 52:7-9). But in the end, it was 'fear' that threatened the full realisation of Yahweh's promised deliverance. Perhaps Mark, recalling that these first witnesses of true Israel's 'resurrection' where silenced by their fear, also has in mind the possibility that members of his audience might also be tempted, out of fear, to be silent, to succumb to the unbelief of the 'faithless generation'. On the other hand, Mark has already explained that it was in Galilee (cf. 16:7) that Jesus prevailed over the power of the watery deep (4:35ff), with all of its deathly connotations, and this in spite of the fear of the disciples. Perhaps, then, in addition to the warning, there is also a word of encouragement to his audience. Even if they too have been tempted to be silent, they need to recognise that Jesus has still conquered. And if, for Mark, 'discipleship evidently involves a continuing struggle for the victory of faith over unbelief'[383] (and we would add 'fear'), then maybe being reminded of Jesus' great victory will provide the added strength and encouragement they need to proclaim the gospel in the face of hostility and rejection.

VI. Conclusion

Corresponding to the INE hope of Yahweh's coming to Zion, the last section of Mark begins with Jesus' victorious arrival at Jerusalem as both Messiah and Son of God/Yahweh-Warrior. Not unexpectedly given the rising hostility in the first section, Jesus' entry is snubbed by the Jerusalem authorities. Nevertheless, true both to Malachi and to the ancient 'entry'

---

[381] *Ibid.*, 219.
[382] See fn. 7 above.
[383] Marshall, *ibid.*, 224.

genre, Jesus next visits the Temple both as its Lord and guardian, and as its deliverer undertaking an act of purification and appropriation. On the one hand, the intercalatory cursing of the fig-tree echoes Malachi's threat and adumbrates the judgement expressed in Jesus' citation of Jeremiah 7:11. On the other, both the entry and 'cleansing' motifs cohere with the Maccabean entries, but this time it is the insurrectionist Temple hierarchs and not foreigners who are 'cleansed'. Similarly, the saying about mountain-moving faith seems to adumbrate the ultimate removal of the present Temple establishment which, in its present form, constitutes such a formidable obstacle to the fulfilment of the INE. On a more positive note, the citation of Isaiah 56:7 presages the fulfilment of Isaiah's vision for the Temple and given the 'outer court' setting echoes the INE hope of a more inclusive role for Gentiles. When challenged over his authority to do these things, Mark's Jesus alludes to the authorities' rejection of John the Baptist—Malachi's Elijah—thereby evoking Mark's opening sentence. This leads directly into the Isaiah 5 derived parable of the wicked tenants parable which pronounces their demise (cf. Mk 13).

After dealing with Jesus' threats to the present Temple institution, Mark turns to the realisation of the institutional threat to Jesus, again interpreted within the INE horizon. Mark's story, after the emphatic repetition of the passion predictions contained in the 'Way' section, now reaches it climax in an extended account of Jesus' suffering and death, much of the substance and purpose of which coheres with that of the Isaianic 'servant' whose suffering and death provides the catalytic moment for the NE. In keeping with the two preceding sections, the Markan Jesus offers only one brief and highly allusive statement as to the central significance of this final part, the 'cup saying' in Mark 14:24. Jesus' death is nothing other than the self-offering of the Messiah and true 'servant' Israel (who is both S/son of God and SoM), by which he effects a covenant for the people (v. 24a, cf. Ex 24:8; Isa 42:6; 49:6) and thus initiates the INE for 'the many' (v. 24b; Isa 53:11f), both Jews and Gentiles, who will now constitute the new people of God.

Finally, the undoubtedly enigmatic short ending of Mark may serve both as stark reminder of the deblitating role that fear had once played in the delay of the NE, and as a warning against allowing it to do so again.

Chapter 10: Conclusions

While not suggesting that everything in Mark must fit the proposed model,
nevertheless the INE seems to provide the best integrative paradigm for
the Gospel as a whole. Whewell's 'theory of consilience' and social theory
offer further confirmation.

I. Observations

We began this study by noting the current hiatus in Markan research with
regard to that 'aim ... and ... perspective which gives coherence to all the
features of the Second Gospel'.[1] Rejecting the idea that no such coherence
exists as both premature and a counsel of despair—Mark's literary achievement has increasingly been noted even if occasionally overplayed—our
line of research was prompted both by the thorough-going influence of the
OT on Mark's work and the idea that texts can function as indicators of
larger hermeneutical frameworks. In the light of the suggestive proposals
of C. H. Dodd and Francis Foulkes on the impress of the OT *Weltanschauung* on the NT, we surveyed earlier analyses on the OT's influence
on the Mark. Although in many places we found that certain OT events
appeared paradigmatic for particular episodes within Mark's story, we
concluded that former proposals of larger overarching syntheses failed on
one or more of the following grounds: so complex or subtle as to defy
credibility, unable to integrate adequately Markan structure and themes,
reliant on questionable or overly subtle OT allusions, and/or failure to
integrate the proposed structural paradigm with the emphases of Mark's
actual OT citations, in particular, his opening appeal to a putative
quotation of Isaiah.

We then examined the role of ideology's schematised representation of
a group's history in structuring and inculcating that group's self-
understanding. It was proposed that while earlier attempts at analysing
Mark's theological structure rightly discerned the importance of Israel's

---

[1] Kee, 'Recent', 353.

founding moment, they singularly failed to appreciate the prophetic transformation of the first Exodus into the future hope of a New Exodus. Recognising that applying the findings of modern social theory to an ancient document runs the risk of severe anachronism, there nevertheless seemed sufficient *prima facie* evidence to warrant examining Mark through the lens of this social heuristic. It was hoped, in conceiving of Mark's OT citations and allusions as iconic indicators of his hermeneutical framework, that a more fundamental underlying organising principle might be discovered. We are now in a position to offer the following observations:

1. In keeping with ancient literary practice, Mark's introductory sentence (1:1-3) indicates his Gospel's conceptual framework. After examining the OT backgrounds and something of the social function of the texts involved, we proposed that Mark's opening composite citation is intended to evoke two different but closely related schemata. First, the appeal to Isaiah 40 evinces Israel's great hope of Yahweh's coming to initiate her restorational NE. Second, the allusion to Malachi not only recalls the delay of this NE but also sounds an ominous note of warning in that the nation must be prepared or else face purging judgement. (Since Malachi is concerned with the delay of the NE, it is in a sense subsumed within the NE schema, although due to the new historical situation the focus is not so much on Yahweh's initial coming to Babylon (Isa 40:1ff) as on his coming to Jerusalem, cf. Isa 65-66). These twin themes of the fulfilment of the delayed INE promise and possible judgement due to lack of preparedness are fused in Mark's opening citation and together seem to establish the basic thematic contours for his presentation of Jesus.

2. The prologue's innovative integration of motifs and allusions is not only consistent with both of these schemata but elaborates them. In terms of the INE, the content of εὐαγγέλιον (1:1, 14) concerns Yahweh's Warrior-Shepherd delivering activities on Israel's behalf. Echoing the integration of Exodus motifs as found in Isaiah 63:7 - 64:11's lament over the NE's delay, the rent heavens and descent of the Spirit (1:10) signals the beginning of Yahweh's saving intervention. In this setting, the allusions in the divine attestation (1:11), particularly given the descent of the Spirit, designate Jesus as Israel's messianic-'servant' deliverer (cf. Ps 2:7 and Isa 42:1). Equally, the iconic augmentation of the 'my son' language with the

Exodus echoes of passing through the water and the subsequent journey into the desert (1:10-12) present Jesus as 'true' Israel (cf. Ex 4:22, with ἀγαπητός indicating his unique Sonship, cf. Gn 22). The paradigm which appears to have facilitated the convergence of these two identifications is also Isaianic. The ambiguity inherent in the enigmatic 'servant' motif— alluded to in the voice and the descent of the Spirit (cf. Isa 42:1)—enables Jesus to be at once true 'servant'-Israel and 'blind-and-deaf' Jacob-Israel's messianic-'servant' deliverer. (One notes in passing that in spite of the Markan Jesus' thorough-going use of 'SoM' there is nothing in the prologue that particularly evokes Daniel 7; perhaps reflecting the early church's non-utilisation of the term.) Finally, the language of Jesus' programmatic announcement (1:14-15) is not only consistent with an INE hermeneutic, but there is some suggestion that Mark also construes Jesus' declaration in terms of the 'messenger' tradition of Isaiah 61:1.

Concerning Malachi's warning, Mark's presentation of John the Baptist (1:6) is consonant with his being Malachi's Elijah to whom Israel must respond if she is to participate in the long-delayed NE. It hardly augurs well that the beginning of Jesus' preaching (1:14a and 14b) is immediately preceded by the abrupt notification of John's imprisonment.

3. The Gospel's basic literary structure is consistent with the INE schema. A survey of a diverse range of literary analyses reveals two major 'breaks' in Mark's narrative (8:21-27 and 10:45 - 11:1) which suggest that he uses a three-part macro-structure. These three sections may be sum-marised as describing A) Jesus' 'evangelistic' ministry of powerful words and deeds in Galilee and beyond, B) a journey with his 'blind' disciples ἐν τῇ ὁδῷ, and C) arrival in Jerusalem, which structure displays broad parallels with the INE schema of A) Yahweh's deliverance and healing of his exiled people, B) a journey where 'blind' Israel is led along 'a way they do not know', and C) arrival in Jerusalem.

Likewise, the Malachi schema is reflected in A) Mark's opening account of an Elijah-like forerunner and his rejection, and B) the concluding crisis precipitated by Jesus' arrival in Jerusalem which is characterised both by the emphatic intercalation of the cursing of the fig-tree with the 'cleansing' and a preoccupation with the Temple (cf. Mal 3:1, 24, MT).

4. In Mark's first section, his presentation of Jesus' exorcisms, healings, and storm-stilling/sea-walking recapitulate the images and actions associ-

ated with Yahweh's INE deliverance of the exiles. The concentration of Jesus' miracles in this section also accords with their distribution in the INE. That Mark regards the exorcisms as the hallmark of Jesus' mighty deeds is evident in their frequent mention and structural prominence (1:21-28, 34, 39; 3:10f, 15, 22ff; 5:1-20; 6:13; 7:24-30, 9:14-29). It is, therefore, noteworthy that on the one climactic occasion when the Markan Jesus comments on their significance it is apparently in terms of the Isaianic Yahweh-Warrior (Isa 49:24f in Mk 3:27). But whereas in Isaiah the captives were in bondage to Babylon whose idols epitomised her power, in Mark it is the unclean spirits/demons, understood to be the powers behind the idols, who are the oppressors. From this standpoint, Jesus' exorcisms are the Markan equivalent of Yahweh's promised release of the Isaian exile. And just as Yahweh in Isaiah appealed to the *Chaoskampf* to demonstrate his ability to effect the NE, so too Mark's Exodus-like juxtaposition of the storm-stilling and the drowning of the demonic legion demonstrates not only Jesus' power to effect the INE but also something of his identity (4:35 - 5:20). Jesus' healings of the blind, deaf, and lame likewise echo Yahweh's healing of the exiles in the INE. Finally, the feedings evoke Yahweh's provision for his people in the Exodus and its Isaianic transformation (6:34-44; 8:1-10). Noting that we might have expected the feedings to occur in Mark's 'Way' section, we suggested that their 'displacement' indicates that genuine participation in the INE requires more than mere involvement in the signs of its presence.

5. Alongside this, Mark's presentation of the religious authorities' hostility toward Jesus continues the threatening undercurrent implicit in Malachi's warning. After a series of confrontations (2:1 - 3:6), the blasphemy warning in the pivotal Beelzebul controversy (3:22-30) is reminiscent of Isaiah 63 (cf. Mk 1:10f) and its recounting of rebellious Israel's 'grieving' the Spirit during the first Exodus. Now, as then, Yahweh becomes their enemy (Isa 63:10 cf. Mk 3:28f). The immediately following and programmatic material on the purpose of the parables (4:1-34) cites the hardening text of Isaiah 6 (4:12) and, in drawing upon the terminology of the Isaianic 'wisdom' polemic, suggests that Jesus' rejection is similarly due to the self-reliant 'wisdom' of the Jerusalemite leadership. The same theme continues in the only other place in the first two sections of Mark where Jesus is confronted by leaders 'from Jerusalem' (Isa 29:13 in Mk 7:6f).

In keeping with the later chapters of Isaiah (espec. Isa 65:1-15), a bifurcation is now being effected within Israel. Those who adhere to Jesus' teaching are 'insiders' and so 'true' members of his family (and hence also of true Israel?; 4:11, cf. 3:13-19, 20-21, 31-35) while those leaders who have ranged themselves against him (4:11b-23; cf. 3:22-30) are 'outsiders'. In between stand the vast and as-yet-undecided crowds whose fate depends on how 'carefully' they 'hear' (4:1, 3, 9, 23, 33).

6. Turning to Mark's second section, his account of Jesus' leading his 'blind' disciples along the 'Way' of the suffering SoM parallels the action of Yahweh and his true 'servant' on behalf of 'blind' Jacob-Israel in the second part of the INE schema. Just as in the INE the 'way' of return involved two components, spatial—to Jerusalem—and sapiential—accepting Yahweh's wisdom, so also in Mark the 'Way' to Jerusalem is a 'Way' of instruction, namely, that the Messiah must suffer. Arising from the use of Isaiah 6 in Mark 4, Mark's 'blindness' and 'deafness' language invokes the Isaianic 'wisdom' polemic which, as amplified in the INE materials, concerns Jacob-Israel's inability to accept the unconventional nature of Yahweh's plan for her deliverance. Symbolising the disciples' condition (4:13, 41; 6:52; 7:18f; 8:14-21), Mark's only healing-of-the-blind miracles bracket his 'Way' section (8:22-26; 10:46-52) and thereby evoke the Isaianic picture of Yahweh, through his 'servant', leading the 'blind' along a path they do not know (cf. Isa 42:16). Just as in Isaiah Yahweh's purposes were ultimately to be accomplished through the astonishing career of a suffering 'servant', so in Mark the three-fold passion predictions (8:31; 9:31; 10:33-34; cf. 9:12; Isa 53, 50) emphasise that the way of wise Yahweh's NE deliverance finds it supreme expression in the 'Way' of a crucified faithful 'servant' Israel-SoM-Messiah (also 10:45; cf. Isa 53).

7. In Mark's final section, the two schemata introduced by his opening sentence come to their respective conclusions. The Malachi/Exodus allusion, intimating the dark side of Yahweh's INE coming, projects the interpretive framework for Mark's intercalation of Jesus' cursing of the fig tree and 'cleansing' of the Temple. Since the insurrectionist leadership had earlier rejected John's preparatory baptism (1:14a; 11:30-33) it is not surprising that they should disregard the entry of Jesus, the Temple's Lord and their messianic king, and question his authority (11:28; cf. 3:6, 22). Consequently, the 'land' is cursed (11:12-25) and the Temple, intended to

be a house of prayer for all nations (Isa 56:7) but now a den of thieves (Jer 7:11), is placed under sentence of destruction (13:1ff; cf. 11:23).

At the same time and quite confounding the hierarchs' murderous intentions, Jesus announces that they will be deposed and that he himself will become the 'cornerstone/capstone' of a new building (12:1-11; a new Temple?).   And here the INE paradigm, already evident in Jesus' messianic entry into the city in as much as it echoes the arrival of the victorious Warrior-Shepherd Yahweh in Jerusalem, emerges again. Yahweh's deliverance of his people will come to pass but only through the suffering of his 'servant' Messiah.   Just as the self-offering of the Isaianic 'servant', who was also to be 'a covenant for the people', is integral to effecting Israel's INE deliverance, so too Mark's Jesus at the climax of his inauguration of the INE establishes through his death the new covenant for the newly reconstituted people of God (14:24, cf. Ex 24:8 and Isa 42:6; 49:8; 53:10-12).

II. Assessment

a) Introduction

Obviously, the first concern is the validity of each, or part thereof, of the observations offered above.   The more convincing each observation, the more compelling their combined effect.   If we grant that these individual observations are substantially correct, how is their overall coherence to be interpreted?

It may of course be argued that Mark intends no further significance than is contained in the face value of the words he actually quotes, that he intends neither linkage between them nor any larger schema overall, and that all of the above is merely the result of reading too much into the material and the occasional happy coincidence.   This is, it is not to be denied, a possibility.   On the other hand, one must ask at what point coincidences become both so numerous and so happy as to suggest design. Perhaps these congruities, given that they appear in the one book, and in this particular order, and with such comfortable collusion, are no more a matter of happenstance than the appearance of Mark's Gospel itself.   This, it may be countered is 'merely' a matter of personal judgement, but as

Michael Polanyi has demonstrated personal judgement is to a greater or
lesser degree quite central to the acquisition of all growth in knowledge;[2]
and hardly to be dismissively assigned a lesser epistemological status (*viz.*
'merely').   But if personal judgement is the key, how then are these
correlations to be evaluated?

b) The Argument from the Philosophy of Science[3]

In evaluating the truth value of inductions to possible causes, the
philosopher of science William Whewell postulated his theory of
Consilience:

> The Consilience of Inductions takes place when an Induction, obtained from one class
> of facts, coincides with an Induction, obtained from another class. This Consilience
> is a test of the truth of the Theory in which it occurs.[4]

In other words, when two chains of inductive reasoning from different
classes of phenomena lead to the same 'conclusion', then a consilience of
inductions has occurred.   The greater the number of inductions, the
greater the possibility that the theory is true. For example, on the basis of
the role of prologues in literary antiquity, we 'induce' that the Isaianic NE
is of importance for Mark. With regard to another class of phenomena, for
example, literary structure, we find that the overall literary structure of
Mark also coincides with an INE schema. Or, with regard to thematic
concerns, for example Jesus' exorcisms, we find that Mark in the crucial
Beelzebul controversy records an allusion to Isaiah 49:24f which describes
the Yahweh-Warrior's NE deliverance of bound Israel. The conjunction
of these three chains of reasoning from three different classes of
phenomena constitutes a consilience of inductions, and thus tends to
corroborate the theory.

I suggest that in Mark we have numerous classes of phenomena, A) the
function of opening sentences in literary antiquity, B) the content of the
prologue, C) Mark's overall structural outline, D) the relationship between
certain sub-units of Markan structure (e.g. 3:20ff, 4:1ff and 4:35ff), E) various
allusions to OT motifs (e.g. 1:9ff; 3:27; 10:45), F) specific citations of the OT
(e.g. Isa 6:9f; 29:13; 56:7), and G) various Markan themes (these could count

---

[2] See the outstanding summation of his thought in Scott, *Everyman*.

[3] I am indebted to my former fellow-student, now Dr. Steven Myer, for drawing my
attention to this material.

[4] Whewell, *Philosophy*, 469. On consilience in modern philosophy of science: Thagard,
'Criteria'; Laudan, 'Consilience'; Hesse, 'Consilience'; cf. Gould, 'Homology', 65.

as separate classes of phenomena but we will lump them together), for example, Jesus' exorcisms, his healing miracles, the stilling of the storm, Jesus as teacher, Jesus as 'Messiah', Jesus' 'suffering' being described in language best explained in terms of the Isaianic 'servant', and the incomprehension of the 'blind' disciples both prior to and within Mark's 'Way' section.   All these different classes of phenomena seem best elucidated in terms in the INE.   Moreover, the appeal to imagery from Malachi also fits in that this book itself likewise appears to address the delay of the INE.[5]   Again, the harmony of this induction, from yet another class of data, with the primary theory further strengthens the proposal. The hypothesis of an INE framework (including the Malachi subset), we suggest, leads to a greater degree of consilience than any other literary theory yet proposed for Mark in that it explains and integrates a large number of previously separate classes of recognised phenomena.

Second, Whewell's system also implied another controlling criterion, that of 'simplicity'.   The more consilient a theory, the more it explains and systematises.[6]   Inherent in this idea is the restriction of the number of auxiliary hypotheses which are required to enable a given theory to fit the data.   That is, a characteristic of a theory's accuracy is that it leaves less that needs to be explained by other means.   For example, given the usual expectation of the INE—the Messiah would be welcomed—Mark must offer his own auxiliary hypothesis to explain Jesus' rejection (e.g. Isa 6 in Mk 4).   In our case such hypotheses would include, for example, the explanations required for the feeding narratives' unexpected position, or those few miracles that occur outside the first section.   These hypotheses are not in themselves negative, but the fewer required the more comprehensive the main theory is shown to be.   An INE model, because it requires few auxiliary hypotheses, meets the criterion of simplicity.

Third, the final guideline advanced for theory selection is the principle of analogy.[7]   This principle holds that if two phenomena exhibit a range of similar properties then comparable causes should have comparable effects. For example, Darwin argued that since artificial selection results in changes in animal morphology so then might natural selection.   In our

---

[5] See the discussion in Chapter 3, pp. 67-74, above.

[6] See further especially Thagard, 'Criteria'.

[7] Thagard, *ibid.*

case, and as many scholars have suggested, if Israel understood her
founding moment in terms of an Exodus, so then might New Israel appeal
to a New Exodus; as Israel's early documents reflect an Exodus ideology, so
then might those of New Israel assume a New Exodus perspective.

Consequently, although these criteria by the nature of the case do not
constitute 'proof', nevertheless, high consilience, simplicity, and analogy
together comprise an argument of considerable force that Mark did indeed
have in mind an Isaianic NE framework.

c) The Argument from Social Science

But even so, what evidence is there that suggests not merely the possibility
but the plausibility of the existence of such a conceptual framework? The
criterion of analogy raises again the previously discussed matter of the role
ideology.   It is worthwhile then briefly to review the material from
Chapter 2, particularly since it concerns that which is implicit and
assumed. The nature of ideology is complex but its essential function is to
justify and explain a community's existence vis-á-vis other communities.[8]
Ideology provides the interpretive framework through which a given
community both understands and shapes its internal relations, its history
and its environment; that is, ideology provides a total world view.[9] It is
not a proposition thought through, but an assumption thought from.

As we saw, recent studies have highlighted the role of a community's
founding moment in shaping its ideology, which in turn seeks to keep the
founding moment alive. Through ritual re-enactments a community's
history is retold and the values and energies enshrined in that
community's founding moment are inculcated, thereby re-constituting the
community throughout succeeding generations. Israel's Exodus and its
remembrance in the Passover haggadah are exemplary. The great event is
retold, values explained, and the nation's special identity reinforced.
However, to facilitate this inculcation the re-enactment must be simplified
and schematised. A too-complex accounting, while satisfying scholars,

---

[8] The 'vis-á-vis' is important because it expresses the possibility of legitimating an
asymmetric distribution of power, e.g. Israel's Exodus ideology justifies their hegemony
over Canaanite land. *Pace* Geertz's cultural systematic, 'Ideology', and Seliger's
ecumenical approach, *Ideology*, which are too omnipresent, thereby robbing the concept of
its critical edge.

[9] Again, this is simplistic—realistically there is actually a hierarchy of competing
and overlapping ideologies—but must suffice due to space limitations.

would be inaccessible to the vast majority and too cumbersome to function.   Its medium is the symbol and icon—whether visual or linguistic—compact and full of meaning.   Since it is reinforced from youth, very little is required to invoke ideology's interpretive framework. By the same token, 'untrained' participants will often fail to make the connections.

Given that the remembrance of the past provides the categories for understanding the present and projecting the future, Foulkes and Dodd were right in recognising that Israel understood its history in terms of the consistent and repeated acts of God. As noted earlier, this is especially true of the Exodus whose influence on several prophetic movements in the New Testament era (e.g. Theudas, the unnamed prophet, and the weaver Jonathan) and the rabbis is well attested.   Numerous studies likewise confirm the influence of Exodus traditions on the NT.

This provided some justification for the theories discussed in Chapter 1 which posited the Exodus as Mark's guiding principle. The inadequacy of these studies was their failure to recognise that during the exilic period the prophets not only drew on the Exodus experience as a model for future deliverance (as social theory would lead us to expect), but transformed the earlier founding-moment ideology into the future hope of a new and greater Exodus.

What are the implications for our thesis, given the observations offered above? First, social theory suggests that the existence of integrating conceptual frameworks are integral to the maintenance of any community. Second, it almost axiomatic that Mark should wish to present his account of God's great act of salvation in terms of an Isaianic NE, not least since Isaiah is perhaps the greatest prophet of Israel's restoration. Mark's basic three-fold outline also displays the simple clarity inherent in ideological formulations. His unaffected 'allusive' and symbolic references to the icons of Israel's memory (e.g. Yahweh-Warrior, storm-stilling, feedings) are also perfectly at home with one immersed in Israel's ideologically-shaped recounting of her history.   That we do not immediately recognise them is more likely due to our being outsiders than Markan ineptitude or lack of intention. Social theory also explains how Mark's opening sentence could invoke an INE framework—the first line of Lincoln's Gettysburg address functions in much the same way.

Once established as his fundamental hermeneutic, more detailed parallels could be added as Mark reflected on the significance of Jesus' life in the light of INE expectations—a plausible epistemological development from a relatively simple idea to Mark's complex presentation can thereby be postulated.

Related to this is one final and important consideration. When a community divides over an issue, a struggle may quickly develop over who are the true heirs to the mores and ideals of the founding moment. We mentioned in this regard, for example, Jeroboam who set up golden calves declaring, 'These are the gods who brought you out of Egypt', and Lincoln who appealed to the Founding Fathers. If a major issue in the NT is that of self-definition in the light of division over which group can legitimately claim to constitute faithful Israel, it is not surprising that Mark should seek to show the continuity of his story with Israel's prophetically transformed founding moment to make his case. There is now even further consilience: inductions from the literary data and the expectation of social theory also coincide.

d) *Mark's Audience and OT Awareness*

Having said all this, a common question arises: what evidence do we have that Mark's audience[10] would have understood the intention of these citations and allusions, particularly given the absence of explicit promise and fulfilment motifs such as those found in Matthew and, to a lesser extent, Luke? Can we reasonably expect such awareness on the part of Mark's readership?

Again, as argued earlier, Mark's frequent if not ubiquitous use of OT texts and motifs, often at crucial points in his narrative, is *prima facie* evidence of an intentionality which strongly suggests that he assumed at least some of his audience were reasonably familiar with parts of the OT.[11] One notes here the vastly different approach of the Lucan Paul in Acts 17 compared to, for example, the Synagogue Sermon in Acts 13 with its thorough-going use of OT themes. That Mark's Gospel appears more in keeping with the latter suggests that it too presupposes an audience containing some Jews or at the very least Gentile 'god-fearers' and that he

---

[10] On the question of whether the Evangelists write to particular communities, see now the unpublished paper by Bauckham, 'Whom'.
[11] See Chapter 4, p. 94, above.

could reasonably expect on the basis of their previous synagogue experience some familiarity with the OT and its themes.[12]

It is hardly less probable that Mark also intended fellow Christians to benefit from his work. Since the OT was no doubt from the very beginning the foundation of both their catechism and apologetic, it is surely reasonable to expect more than a passing acquaintance with those OT materials with which Mark deals.[13] Again, it seems highly unlikely that Mark's Gospel appeared 'out of the blue' like some theological supernova. Instead, it more likely represents a compendium of the teaching with which his community was already *au fait*. In other words, perhaps there was not a great deal in Mark's book that was particularly new at all and that at least part of his intended audience were just as likely to be reading his gospel making sure he had it right as gaping in wonder at his new insights. In this respect we recall Christopher Stanley's findings which given the obvious way in which Mark uses and adapts his texts suggests that he assumes some degree of acquaintance with the OT source material.[14]

Ultimately, however, the only hard data we have is the evidence of the document itself. On the basis of the arguments propounded here—if they are judged successful—of consilience (i.e. overall coherence, simplicity, analogy) and the role of ideology in shaping group consciousness, it would appear that Mark's Gospel has been structured along the lines proposed. If so, I would urge that the most natural conclusion is that Mark produced his work in this way on the assumption that he would be understood.

It is appropriate to ask, why then did not this understanding survive to the present? A brief response, more indicative than complete, must suffice. On the one hand, in some respects it did survive: many have noted the general Isaianic background to Jesus' life and ministry. On the other, clearly the overall structure and many of the details outlined here have not been carried over into the teaching tradition of the church. This should not, however, be regarded as surprising. Even a cursory examination of the history of the interpretation of Jesus' parables reveals how, with the changing centre of gravity of the early church from its

---

[12] On the question of Mark's readership, see e.g. Martin, 61ff; Hengel, 'Origin'.
[13] Cf. Dodd, *According*; Lindars, *Apologetic*.
[14] See Chapter 2, pp. 51f.

Jewish roots to a Gentile constituency, their interpretation reflected the literary and hermeneutical context of the prevailing culture. Consequently, the original force of the parables dissipates relatively quickly within the horizon of the Græco-Roman world. By the same token it is not difficult to see how, as the church became increasingly Gentile and found itself interacting more and more with others from that milieu, the riches of its Jewish roots which lay at the heart of her Gospels should also come gradually to be misunderstood or neglected.

III. Conclusions

a) In Response to the Survey of Recent Scholarship

1. Mark has not abandoned *Heilsgeschichte*, but on the contrary it is his 'indispensable presupposition'. Given the contemporary interpretations of the OT materials he appeals to, and as he offers no clear indication of his rejection of the eschatological orientation of those interpretations, it is affirmed that Mark presents Jesus in terms of the fulfilment of Israel's hopes for a NE, especially as described in the book of Isaiah. His Gospel is therefore to be seen in continuity with God's historic dealings with his people, but now also including Gentiles *qua* Gentiles (cf. e.g. Mk 7:19).

2. Kee's observations on the Markan tendency to conflate OT references and to place them at critical points in his argument are to be confirmed. Aspects of this tendency are particularly evident in Mark's opening citation and in his accounts of Jesus' use of the OT, and as such reflects the literary conventions of his day (cf. Stanley).

3. If this thesis is deemed convincing, the weakness of earlier attempts to relate Israel's founding moment to that of reconstituted Israel resides not in the deficiency of their basic intuition, which was correct in essence, but rather in their failure to apprehend the significance of the prophetic transformation of the past Exodus into the future hope of the NE.

4. In the cases we examined Mark does appear to be aware of the OT context, although what we mean by 'context' may need modification (see 5 below). In fact, in several places some familiarity with the OT context seems essential to understanding correctly Mark's point (e.g. Isa 6 in Mk 4).

5. Dodd's conception of citations as pointers to 'text plots' may benefit from a more nuanced articulation. Although perhaps somewhat subtle, the perspective of social theory suggests that it is not only the 'literary setting' *per se* which is in view—although it is clearly important—but also the underlying ideological and, therefore, schematised representation of Israel's on-going 'story' which those texts not only record but also presume and with which they interact. The same applies to the NT's use of OT motifs. That is, the citations or motifs themselves, by means of the 'text plots' to which they point, function as symbols or icons and so provide a shorthand method of referring to whole fields of meaning which themselves are located within the on-going schema of Israel's 'story'. Equally important, this 'story' seems best understood from the perspective of the larger on-going dynamic of Israel's relationship with her God: A) as Yahweh had acted to save his people in the past, so he does now, but B) as his people in the light of their own wisdom had in the past frequently questioned Yahweh's methods and/or agents of salvation, so also now.

b) In Relation to the Thesis Proper

1. To the extent that each individual observation listed above is accepted, either fully or in part, it offers its own statement of findings concerning Mark's presentation. These will not be reiterated here.

2. The greater the number of observations accepted, the more the criteria of theory selection and the logic of social theory's understanding of the ideology will suggest that Mark is operating with a consistent Isaianic NE framework. If so, the argument from social theory also suggests that it is Mark's ideologically-shaped understanding of Israel's future hopes which provides the major structural clue to the shape of his gospel. Mark's selection, editorial arrangement, and/or composition of pericopae, derives primarily from the interaction between an INE fulfilment framework and his understanding of Jesus' teaching and deeds, rejection by the Jewish leadership, death, and resurrection.

3. It is often urged that the purpose of Mark is to be found in his theology rather than any historical concern. Although such a radical discontinuity implied is hardly sustainable today,[15] we propose that Mark wishes to show in the broadest terms that:

---

[15] Cf. Wright, *People*, 31-144.

a) Jesus' ministry was the inauguration of the fulfilment of Isaiah's long-awaited NE developed in accordance with the observations above.

b) Jesus' rejection, particularly by the Jewish leadership, is explained by their 'blind' reliance on their own wisdom. This is not unforeseen since they had already rejected John, Malachi's Elijah, and in any case such 'blindness' has characteristically plagued the nation's leaders in the past. But Jesus had also been misunderstood by Israel in general. This, too, is not as incomprehensible as might initially be supposed, since even Jesus' closest followers were blinded by their own expectations to the full significance of his ministry. In a word, Mark is 1 Corinthians 1:18-25 writ large.

4. However, positing the INE hermeneutic as the major concern of Mark does not require that it was Mark's only interest. We can happily accept that Mark was influenced by additional concerns. For instance, he could equally use Jesus' teaching on the 'Way' to address the question of suffering discipleship, and choose his selection of Jesus' teaching, and even make use of the disciples' obduracy, for more pastoral purposes. Such aims can be integrated within a larger INE rubric without damaging the overall thesis.

5. At the turn of the century, A. E. Garvie wrote:

> The Christian religion was spoken of simply as the way, either because Christ claimed to be the Way, or because he had spoken of the narrow way unto life, or lastly because in him was fulfilled the prophetic sayings regarding the way (Isa 40[3]; Mal 3[1]).[16]

S. V. McCasland, affirming this suggestion, went on to argue that 'the Way ... as a designation of Christianity was derived from Isa 40 3 and that it is an abbreviated form of "the way of the Lord"'.[17] This book would confirm these views with the added comment that the 'Way' may well be a shorthand reference to the INE way of Yahweh's eschatological salvation for his people (accomplished through a crucified Messiah) and that it also shares the 'wisdom' connotations of this language.

6. Finally, in regard to Christology. The primary datum for Mark seems to be that Jesus is to be understood as S/son of God. While not at all down-playing Mark's interest in Jesus' unique filial relationship to the

---

[16] "'Way'", 230.
[17] *Ibid.*

Father, this language must first be seen in terms of Jesus being 'true Israel', who after all was intended to be Yahweh's 'son' (Ex 4:22) and in which category Israel's messianic kingship was likewise understood (Ps 2). At the same time, Israel was intended to be Yahweh's faithful 'servant'. But since she had failed, a new 'servant' was to be installed (Isa 42, 49; cf. *Tg. Isa*), revealed now in Jesus. And given the 'servant's' role, Jesus is not only 'true' Israel but also 'blind and deaf' Israel's messianic deliverer (*Tg. Isa* 42; Ps 2). This much seems established at the outset in Mark's story (Mk 1:9-15). As such Jesus is also the 'genuinely human one', that is, 'one like a Son of Man', who truly bears the image of God and who presides over the people of God's vindication in their new-creational New Exodus (cf. Dn 7). This SoM also exercises authority such as has heretofore been the sole prerogative of Yahweh himself (forgiving sins, Mk 2:10; subduing the chaotic sea, Mk 4:39-41). For Mark, there is clearly more to Jesus' particular sonship than mere metaphor: his is indeed Yahweh's 'unique' Son.

We have also argued that the Markan Jesus apparently understood his death in terms of the Isaianic 'servant' in that his descriptions of his future sufferings are drawn largely from the so-called 'Servant Songs', primarily Isaiah 53 but also 50. This naturally raises questions as to the significance of this language, not only for Mark, who may have understood one thing, but also for Jesus, who may have intended another. It is possible that the terminology is used simply because it most clearly and fully expresses the suffering of a righteous figure, and was, after all, near to hand given that much of the Markan Jesus' ministry was shaped by reflection on the Isaianic expectation. However, such an interpretation does not, we have argued, adequately take into account the strongly purposive nature of this suffering both in Isaiah and in Mark. Not only is the idea of suffering linked with NE deliverance solely, in the OT (cf. Mk 9:12), in Isaiah, it is also a suffering that is clearly on behalf of others. Those who wish to argue that only the fact of the suffering is in view, need to show why the Markan Jesus did not intend a direct link between the purpose which is clearly an irreducible element of his perception of his death and the purpose implied in Isaianic texts from which, we have argued, he almost certainly draws his suffering language. And this especially given Mark's INE framework. It may be argued that if this connection was intended why was it not clearer? But this expectation quite runs counter to the

Markan Jesus who apparently delights in the oblique and the allusive and in 'dark sayings' that were anything but immediately obvious. Given the sheer evocative power inherent in the Markan INE pattern, the argument from lack of specificity is not only weak but is also out of character with the Markan Jesus.

This is not to say that Mark's Jesus saw himself as the 'Suffering Servant' of modern invention, but on the other hand one should not rule out the possibility that in meditating on the hopes of the INE he interpreted Yahweh's faithful 'servant' as integral to effecting the INE—parts of *Tg. Isaiah* 42 and 53 are linked with the Messiah and these traditions may well go back to Jesus' day. Having so identified himself, it is not impossible that, perhaps also under the influence of a new exegesis of Daniel 7 (whereby the one like a son of man characterises Israel not only in her vindication but also in her suffering, cf. Dn 3 and 6), he thereby also broke new ground in deriving primarily from Isaiah 53 the necessity of own his suffering and death for the many—which after all is the natural implication of his drawing his language primarily from this text. And this irrespective of contemporary interpretations—Mark's Jesus is hardly one who gives the impression of being beholden to traditional exegesis whether of Daniel or Isaiah.

What the early church (or even Mark) did with this, and whether or not they fully appreciated its implications, is a separate issue and cannot be entered into here in any detail. However, we may at least canvas the question: if Jesus did conceive of his death in this way, why was it not taken up earlier and more clearly in the primitive church? First, the Markan Jesus' sayings, and not only on this subject, are characteristically highly allusive and hardly immediately obvious. Any reservations as to messianic suffering, and especially if no concept of an individual Isaianic 'servant' was current, would only have made the easy interpretation of the passion predictions, *et al*, along such lines intrinsically unlikely. Second, the disciples in Mark are regularly portrayed as failing to comprehend the manner in which Jesus transforms OT hopes even as he fulfils them. Irrespective of the question of any polemical intent, this may be evidence of a genuine bewilderment, not only among the disciples but the people at large (Mk 8:27-28). It is not unrealistic to allow some time for a fuller appreciation of these allusions to develop.[18] Third, there is little evidence to suggest that the concept of the 'servant' of Isaiah as an independent eschatological or redemptive figure existed in Judaism—although as noted earlier parts of these 'songs' appear to have been interpreted messianically. Even if the disciples had made the connection earlier, what profit was there for primitive Christians to offer a "redemption through 'servant' suffering" apologetic based on texts that were not popularly so understood, let alone as requiring fulfilment? (It is significant that it is Justin Martyr, a Gentile and who therefore may be less sensitive to this situation, who first clearly seeks to use Isaiah 53 in an apologetic sense.)

This of course does not deal with catechetical or paraenetic materials (if we can make such a distinction). But how much catechesis do we have, in terms of the life of Jesus, outside the Gospels? In regard to what we might describe as paraenetic writings, M. D. Hooker has argued that the only references to Isaiah 53 in primitive materials are concerned with *imitatio Christi*.[19] However, this argument cuts both ways. If an author's purpose is to encourage Christians to stand firm in the face of suffering, it is hardly surprising that they should speak only of the exemplary model of Jesus without feeling the necessity to expound on the 'prophetic' necessity or significance of Jesus' death. But even so 1 Peter suggests by its very casualness that such an idea may not have been far away (cf. *Barn.* 5:1f; 5:13 - 6:2). This is significant. Whatever else we might say it is crucial not to gloss over the entirely unaffected manner in which 1 Peter 2:22ff so easily articulates the 'full identification of Jesus with the Servant in all its Christological significance'.[20] It might be the 'earliest definite proof',[21] but the fact that it appears almost as an afterthought strongly suggests that not only was the notion not novel, it could apparently be assumed to be common currency at least among the intended audience of the Epistle.[22] What might be more fruitful, and what of course cannot be carried out

---

[18] Hooker, *Servant*, 154ff, proposes a similar development on the basis of later reflection on Jesus' ministry, but does not allow that Jesus himself or the primitive church had made the connection.

[19] *Ibid.*, 130ff; citing e.g. *1 Clem* 16:1-7; Pol. *Phil.* 8:1-2; etc.

[20] To use the words of Hooker, *ibid.*, 127.

[21] *Ibid.*

[22] If there is some truth to the link between Mark and Peter, then the fact that it is 1 Peter who has this Christological understanding may suggest that Mark's use of Isa 53 was indeed understood in this way.

here, is an analysis of those passages where OT texts are cited to explain the necessity and significance of Jesus' death, not in early apologetic or kerygmatic contexts since presumably the Jewish context and theological milieu of the primitive church would have meant that an appeal to Isaiah 53 may not have been terribly meaningful, but instead in catechesis.

IV. Implications and Suggestions for Further Research

In conclusion, we offer some very brief comments on the possible implications of this study for further research.

1. An INE reading may provide additional support for a Roman provenance for Mark. One of the major issues of Romans appears to be national Israel's rejection of the fulfilment of God's promises in Jesus (Rom 9-11): just how trustworthy is this gospel if the very people whose history and covenant it fulfils reject it?[23] At the moment when Paul turns to face the issue squarely he draws on Exodus/new Exodus imagery (9:14ff, 24ff; 10:15, 16, 20, 21; 11:34).[24] One also notes echoes of Isaianic anti-wisdom polemics (e.g. 9:20, 33; 11:34; cf. Isa 29:16; 45:9; 40:13).[25] In other words, Paul's gospel of 'faith in Jesus' is indeed the fulfilment of Israel's hopes, and yet, apart from a remnant, Israel has rejected it, choosing her own path instead. Mark may be addressing the same problem. He too presents Jesus and his summons to believe in terms of Israel's New Exodus hopes. At the same time, he also asserts that the reason for Jesus' rejection was the 'blindness' of the nation's leadership to God's purposes, arguing that this too is in 'accordance with the Scriptures'. That the Jewish people by and large join in that rejection is not to be wondered, since even Jesus' closest disciples did not understand. These similarities suggest that Mark's Gospel (and perhaps his account of Peter's preaching while in Rome if the tradition holds true) also addresses a similar concern, and therefore perhaps, has in view a similar constituency. However, since this issue in all likelihood concerned the church at large and not merely Rome, some care should be taken.

---

[23] Wright, *Messiah*, 220; Dunn, *Romans*, 2.518ff.
[24] Hays, *Echoes*, 66f.
[25] Evans, 'Paul'; Maillot, 'Essai'; cf. Chapters 6 and 7.

2. As we have primarily restricted ourselves to Isaianic texts, there is room for further research to examine this proposal by investigating the consilience of Mark's use of other OT motifs and texts with the INE theory. For example, in earlier works the role of Zechariah was considered to be important; if so, what might appeals to Zechariah contribute to this approach? Or the Psalms?

3. In terms of Christology, given, for example, Mark's apparent application of the Yahweh-Warrior motif to Jesus and his use of Isaiah and Malachi in his opening sentence—both of which seem to deal with the very coming of Yahweh himself—an interesting line of endeavour might be to assess whether or not a high Christology is already in place, perhaps even presupposed, at this early stage.

4. The focus of this study has been with Mark as it presently stands. If an INE hermeneutic has been convincingly argued, a further project could be to seek to discover how much of this perspective goes back to Jesus himself.

Bibliography of Works Cited

Primary Sources

Ante-Nicene Christian Library: Translations of the Writings of the Fathers down to A. D. 325 eds. A. Roberts and J. Donaldson 24 vols. (Edinburgh: T. & T. Clark, 1867-72).

The Apocryphal Old Testament ed. H. F. D. Sparks (Oxford: Clarendon, 1984).

Biblica Hebraica Stuttgartensia eds. K. Elliger and W. Rudolph, New Ed. (Stuttgart: Deutsche Biblegesellschaft, 1977).

Aramaic Texts from Qumran with Translations and Annotations B. Jongeling, C. J. Labuschagne, and A. S. van der Woude vol. 1 SSS 4 (Leiden: Brill, 1976).

Aristotle, *Aristotelis. Ars Rhetoria* ed. W. D. Ross (Oxford: Clarendon, 1959).

Baillet, M., *et al., Discoveries in the Judean Desert* 7 vols. (Oxford: Clarendon, 1955-82).

The Bible in Aramaic: ed. A. Sperber 4 vols. (Leiden: Brill, 1959-68).

Biblica Sacra luxta Vulgatam Versionem ed. R. Weder 2 vols. (Stuttgart: Württembergische Bibelanstalt, 1969).

Black, M., *The Book of Enoch or I Enoch: A New English Edition with Commentary and Textual Notes* SVTP 7 (Leiden: Brill, 1985).

Box, G.H., *The Ezra-Apocalypse, Being Chapters 3-14 of the Book Commonly Known as 4 Ezra (or II Esdras)* (London, 1912).

Burrows, M., *The Dead Sea Scrolls of St. Mark's Monastry* vol. 2 (New Haven: ASOR, 1951).

Corpus Christianorum; Series Latina vol. 1- (Turhalti: Brepols Editores Pontificii, 1953-).

Davies, P. R., *The Damascus Covenant* JSOTSupp 25 (Sheffield: JSOT, 1983).

The Dead Sea Scrolls in English ed. and trans. G. Vermes (Harmondsworth: Penguin, 1987³).

The Dead Sea Scrolls Translated: The Qumran Texts in English F. R. Martínez trans. Wilfred G. E. Watson (Leiden: Brill, 1994).

Dupont-Sommer, A., *The Essene Writings from Qumran* trans. G. Vermes (Gloucester, MA.: Peter Smith, 1973).

Eusebius: The Ecclesiastical History trans. K. Lake and J. E. L. Oulton, 2 vols., Loeb (Cambridge, MA.: Harvard University, 1926-32).

Hebrew-English Edition of the Babylonian Talmud ed. I. Lévi SSS 20 vols. (London: Soncino, 1972-84).

Hennecke, E., *New Testament Apocrypha* 2 vols. ed. W. Schneemelcher, trans. and ed. R. McL. Wilson (rev. ed., Cambridge: James Clark & Co. Ltd./Louisville, KY: Westminster and John Knox, 1991-92).

Irenaeus, *Contra Hæreses* in *Sancti Irenæi* ed. W. W. Harvey, 2 vols. (Cambridge, 1958).

The Isaiah Targum: Introduction, Translation, Apparatus and Notes ArB 11 B. D. Chilton (Edinburgh: T. & T. Clarke, 1987).

James, M. R., *The Biblical Antiquities of Philo* (London: SPCK, 1917).

The Targum of Jeremiah: Introduction, Translation, Apparatus and Notes ArB 12 R. Hayward (Edinburgh: T. & T. Clarke, 1987).

Josephus trans. H. St. J. Thackery (vols. 1-5), R. Marcus (vols. 5-8) with A. Wikgren (vol. 8) and L. H. Feldman (vols. 9-10) LCL (London: Heinemann, 1926-65).

Klein, M. L., *The Fragment-Targums of the Pentateuch: According to their Extant Sources* AnBib 76, 2 vols. (Rome: Biblical Institute, 1980).

Knibb, M. A., *The Book of Enoch: A New Edition in Light of the Aramaic Dead Sea Fragment* 2 vols. (Oxford: Clarendon, 1978).

Kuhn, K. G., *Der tannaitische Midrasch Sifre zu Numeri* Rabbinsiche Texte 2:3 (Stuttgart: Kohlhammer, 1959).

Le Déaut, R., *Targum du Pentateuque: Tradition des Deux Recensions Palestinennes Complètes avec Introduction, Parallèlles, Notes et Index* 5 vols. Sources Chrétiennes 245, 256, 261, 271, 282 (Paris: Cerf, 1978-81).

Licht, J., *The Thanksgiving Scroll. A Scroll from the Wilderness of Judaea. Text, Introduction and Commentary* (Jerusalem: Bialik Institute, 1957).

Lucian, *How to Write History* in *Lucian* 8 vols. Loeb, trans. K. Kilburn (Cambridge, Mass.: Harvard, 1958) vol. 6:1-73.

Mekilta, The Song of the Sea ed. J. Goldin (New Haven: Yale, 1971).

Mekilta de-Rabbi Ishmael ed. J. Z. Lauterbach 3 vols. (Philadelphia: Jewish Publication Society of America, 1933-35).

Midrasch Tanchuma: Ein agadischer Commentar zum Pentateuch von Rabbi Tanchuma den Rabi Abba ed. S. Buber (Wilna: Romm, 1885).

Midrash Rabbah eds. H. Freedman and M. Simon, 10 vols. (London: Soncino, 1939).

The Midrash on the Psalms ed. by W. G. Braude, YJS 13, 2 vols. (New Haven: Yale, 1959).

Midrasch Tehillim ed. S. Buber (Wilna: Romm, 1891).

Milik, J. T., ed., with M. Black, *The Books of Enoch: Aramaic Fragments of Qumran Cave 4* (Oxford: Clarendon, 1976).

The Mishnah trans. H. Danby (Oxford: University, 1933).

Mishnayoth ed. P. Blackman, 7 vols. (New York: Judaica Press, 1964).

Neophyti 1: Targum Palestinense MS de la Biblotheca Vaticana ed. A. Diez Macho, 6 vols. (Madrid: Consejo Superior de Investigaciones Cientificas, 1968-79).

Novum Testament Graece ed. E. Nestle *et al.* (rev. ed., Stuttgart: Deutsche Biblestiftung, 1981^{26}).

Old Testament Pseudepigrapha ed. J. H. Charlesworth, 2 vols. (New York: Doubleday, 1983, 1985).

Origenis Hexaplorum quae Supersunt; sive veterum interpretum graecorum in totum Vetus Testamentum fragmenta ed. F. Field, 2 vols. (Oxonii: Clarendoniano, 1875).

Pesikta. Die älteste Hagada, redigirt in Palästina von Rab Kahana (Lyck: Silbermann, 1868).

Pesikta Rabbati: discourses for Feasts, Fasts, and Special Sabbaths trans. W. G. Braude, YJS 18, 2 vols. (New Haven: Yale University, 1968).

Philo Judaeus: Opera Quae Supersunt ed. L. Cohn and P. Wendland, 6 vols. + vol. 7: *Indices ad Philonis Alexandrini Opera* (by J. Leisegang) (Berlin: de Gruyter, 1896-1926).

Philo trans. F. H. Colson (vols. 2, 6-10) with G. H. Whitaker (vols. 1, 3-5); and by R. Marcus (Supplements 1-2) LCL (London: Heinemann, 1929-53).

Pritchard, J. B., *Ancient Near Eastern Texts Relating to the Old Testament* (Princeton: University, 1969^3).

Pseudo-Jonathan (Thargum Jonathan ben Usiël zum Penteteuch) ed. M. Ginsberger (Berlin: Calvary, 1903).

Quintilian, *M. Fabi Qunitiliani. Institutionis Oratoriae, Libri Duodecim* ed. M. Winterbottom, 2 vols. (Oxford: Clarendon, 1970).

Quinti Septimii florentis Tertulliani Quae Supersunt Opera ed. F. Oehler, 3 vols. (Leipzig: Weigel, 1853).

Russell, D. A., and Winterbottom, M., *Ancient Literary Criticism. The Principal Texts in New Translations* (Oxford: Clarendon, 1972).

Santos, E. C. D., *An Expanded Index for the Hatch-Redpath Concordance to the Septuagint* (Jerusalem: Dugith, Baptist House, n.d.).

Septuaginta: Id est Vetus Testamentum graece iuxta LXX interpretes ed. A. Ralphs, 2 vols in 1 (Stuttgart: Deutsche Bibgesellschaft, c. 1935).

Septuaginta: Vetus Testamentum Graecum Auctoritate Academiae Scientiarum Gottingensis editum 16 vols. (Göttingen: Vandenhoeck & Ruprecht, 1931-).

Sifre on Deuteronomy ed. L. Finklestein, YJS 24 (New York: Jewish Theological Seminary of America, 1969).

Sifre to Numbers eds. W. S. Green and J. Neusner, 2 vols., BJS 118-9 (Atlanta: Scholars, 1986).

Sifre: A Tannaitic Commentary on the Book of Deuteronomy trans. R. Hammer (New Haven: Yale, 1986).

Sophocles: The Theban Plays trans. E. F. Watling (Middlesex: Penguin, 1947).

Talmud Yerushalmi Krotoshin: 1866 (reprint, Jerusalem: Shiloh, 1967).

The Targum of Isaiah ed. and trans. J. F. Stenning (Oxford: Clarendon, 1949).

The Targums of Onkelos and Jonathon ben Uzziel on the Pentateuch with the Fragments of the Jerusalem Targum: From the Chaldee trans. J. W. Etheridge (New York: Ktav, 1968).

Targum de Salmos, ed. I. Diez Merino, BHB 6 (Madrid: Instituto 'Francisco Suárez', 1982).

Tosefta: Based on the Erfurt and Vienna Codices ed. M. S. Zuckermandel (Jerusalem: Bamberger & Wharmann, 1937²).

Yadin, Y., *The Temple Scroll* 3 vols. (Jerusalem: Israel Exploration Society, 1983).

The Wisdom of Ben-Sira: A New Translation with Notes, Skehan, P. W., intro. by Di Lella, A. A. (Garden City, New York: Doubleday, 1987).

Secondary Sources

Aalen, S., 'Das Abendmahl als Opfermahl,' *NovT* 6 (1963) 128-52.

Abbott, E. A., *The Fourfold Gospel* 5 vols. (Cambridge: University, 1914-18).

Abrahams, I., 'Rabbinic Aids to Exegesis' in *Cambridge Biblical Essays* ed. H. B. Swete (London: Macmillan, 1909) 159-92.

Achtemeier, E., *The Community and Message of Isaiah 56-66* (Minneapolis: Augsburg, 1982).

Achtemeier, P. J., '"And He Followed Him": Miracles and Discipleship in Mark 10:46-52,' *Semeia* 11 (1978) 115-45.

_____ '"He Taught Them Many Things": Reflections on Marcan Christology,' *CBQ* 42 (1980) 465-81.

_____ 'Mark as Interpreter of the Jesus Traditions,' *Int* 32 (1978) 339-52.

_____ 'The Origin and Function of the Pre-Marcan Miracle Catenae,' *JBL* 91 (1972) 198-221.

_____ 'Toward the Isolation of Pre-Markan Miracle Catenae,' *JBL* 89 (1970) 265-91.

Ackroyd, P. J., 'The Death of Hezekiah - A Pointer to the Future?' in *De la Torah au Messie*, FS. H. Cazelles, ed. M. Carrez *et al* (Paris: Desclée, 1981) 219-226.

_____ *Exile and Restoration* (London: SCM, 1968).

_____ 'An Interpretation of the Babylonian Exile: A Study of 2 Kings 20, Isaiah 38-39,' *SJT* 27 (1974), 329-52.

_____ 'Isaiah I-XII: Presentation of a Prophet,' *Congress Volume* SuppVT 29 (1977) 16-48.

_____ 'Isaiah 36-39: Structure and Function' in *Von Kanaan bis Kerala*, FS. Prof. Mag. Dr. Dr. J. P. M. van der Ploeg O. P., ed. J. R. Nelis *et al*, AOAT 211 (Neukirchen-Vluyn: Neukirchener, 1982) 3-21.

_____ 'A Note on Isaiah 2:1,' *ZAW* 75 (1963) 320-21.

Adams, J. L., 'Religion and Ideologies,' *Confluence* 4 (1955) 72-84.

Ahlström, G., *Joel and the Temple Cult of Jerusalem* SupVT 21 (Leiden: Brill, 1971).

Aland, K. and B., *The Text of the New Testament: An Introduction to the Critical Editions and the Theory and Practice of Modern Textual Criticism* trans. E. F. Rhodes (Grand Rapids: Eerdmans, 1989²).

Albrektson, B., *History and the Gods* CB 1 (Lund: CWK Gleerup, 1967).

Allegro, J. M., *Discoveries in the Judean Desert* vol. V. (Oxford: Clarendon, 1968).

_____ 'Fragments of a Qumran Scroll of Eschatological Midrashim,' *JBL* 77 (1958) 350-54.

_____ 'Further Messianic References in Qumran Literature,' *JBL* 75 (1956) 174-87.

____ 'More Isaiah Commentaries from Qumran's Fourth Cave, ' *JBL* 77 (1958) 215-21.

Allen, E. L., 'Jesus and Moses in the New Testament,' *ExpT* 67 (1956) 104-6.

Allison, D. C., 'Elijah Must Come First,' *JBL* 103 (1984) 256-58.

____ *The End of the Ages has Come* SNTW (Edinburgh: T. & T. Clarke, 1987).

Alt, A., *Where Jesus Worked* trans. K. Grayston (London: Epworth, 1961).

____ 'Mark's Concept of Parable. Mark 4, 11f. in the Context of the Second Gospel,' *CBQ* 29 (1967) 220-27.

Ambrozic, A. M., *The Hidden Kingdom: A Redaction-critical Study of the References to the Kingdom of God in Mark's Gospel* CBQMS 2 (Washington, DC: Catholic Biblical Association of America, 1972).

Anderson, B. W., *Creation versus Chaos* (Philadelphia: Fortress, 1987).

____ 'Exodus and Covenant in Second Isaiah and Prophetic Tradition' in *Magnalia Dei: the Mighty Acts of God* eds. F. M. Cross, W. E. Lemke, and P. D. Miller, Jr. (New York: Doubleday, 1976) 339-60.

____ 'Exodus Typology in Second Isaiah' in *Israel's Prophetic Heritage* eds. B. W. Anderson and W. Harrelson (New York: Harper, 1962) 177-95.

____ *Understanding the Old Testament* (Englewood Cliffs: Prentice-Hall, 1975³).

Anderson, H., *The Gospel of Mark* NCB (London: Oliphants, 1976).

____ 'The Old Testament in Mark's Gospel' in *The Use of the Old Testament in the New and Other Essays: Studies in the Honor of William Franklin Stinespring*, ed. J. M. Efird (Durham, NC: Duke University, 1972) 280-306.

Annen, F., *Heil für die Heiden: Zur Bedeutung und Geschichte der Tradition vom bessessenen Gerasener (Mk 5,1-20 parr.)* FTS 20 (Frankfurt am Main: Joseph Knecht, 1976).

Arbesmann, P. R., *Das Fasten bei den Griechen und Römern* (Gießen: Töpelmann, 1929).

Arendt, A., *Origins of Totalitarianism* (NY: Harcourt, Brace and Jovanovich, 1973).

Arens, E., *The HΛΘON-Sayings in the Synoptic Tradition: A Historical-Critical Investigation* OBO 10 (Vandenhoeck & Ruprecht: Göttingen, 1976).

Arnold, G., 'Mk 1,1 und Eröffnungswendungen in griechischen und lateinischen Schriften,' *ZNW* 68 (1977) 123-27.

Aune, D. E., 'A note on Jesus' Messianic Consciousness and the 11Q Melchizedek,' *EvQ* 45 (1973) 161-5.

Avi-Yonah, M., *The Jews of Palestine: A Political History from the Bar Kokhba War to the Arab Conquest* (Oxford: Blackwell, 1976).

Aytoun, R. A., 'The Servant of the Lord in the Targum,' *JTS* 23 (1922) 172-80.

Baarda, T., 'Gadarenes, Gerasenes, Gergesenes and the "Diatesseron" Tradition' in *Neotestimentica et Semetica* FS M. Black, eds. E. Ellis and M. Wilcox (Edinburgh: T. & T. Clark, 1969) 181-97.

Baarlink, H., *Anfängliches Evangelium. Ein Beitrag zur näheren Bestimmung der theologischen Motive im Markusevangelium* (Kampen, Nether-lands: J. H. Kok, 1977).

Bächli, O., 'Was habe ich mit Dir zu schaffen?,' *TZ* 33 (1977) 69-80.

Bacon, B. W., 'Supplementary Note on the Aorist εὐδόκησα,' *JBL* 20 (1901) 28-30.

Bailey, K. E., *Through Peasant Eyes* (Grand Rapids: Eerdmans, 1980).

Baird, J. A., 'A Pragmatic Approach to Parable Exegesis: Some New Evidence on Mark 4: 11, 33-4,' *JBL* 76 (1957) 201-7.

Baird, M. M., 'The Gadarene Demoniac (Mk. 5),' *ExpT* 31 (1919-20) 189.

Baldwin, J. G., *Haggai, Zechariah, Malachi* TOTC 24 (London: Tyndale, 1972).

Ball, D. R., *The Seven Pillories of Wisdom* (Macon, Georgia: Mercer, 1990).

Ball, T., and Dagger, R., *Ideals and Ideologies: A Reader* (NY: Harper Collins, 1991).

Bamptfylde, G., 'The Similitudes of Enoch: Historical Allusions,' *JSJ* 15 (1984) 9-13.

Barnes, W. E., 'Cyrus the "Servant of Jehovah",' *JTS* 32 (1931) 32-39.

Barnett, P. W., 'The Jewish Sign Prophets - A.D. 40-70 - Their Intentions and Origin,' *NTS* 27 (1981) 679-97.

Barrett, C. K., 'The Background of Mark 10:45' in *New Testament Essays: Studies in Memory of T. W. Manson* ed. A. J. B. Higgins (Manchester: University, 1959) 1-18.

_____ *The Gospel According to St. John* (London: SPCK, 1960²).

_____ *The Holy Spirit and the Gospel Tradition* (London: SPCK, 1970).

_____ 'The House of Prayer and the Den of Thieves' in *Jesus und Paulus* FS W. G. Kümmel, eds. E. E. Ellis and E. Gräßer (Göttingen: Vandenhoeck & Ruprecht, 1975) 13-20.

_____ 'Mark 10.45: A Ransom for Many' in *New Testament Essays* (London: SPCK, 1972) 20-26.

Barstad, H. M., *A Way in the Wilderness. The «Second Exodus» in the Message of Second Isaiah* JSSM 12 (Manchester: University, 1989).

Barth, G., 'Matthew's Understanding of the Law' in G. Bornkamm, G. Barth, and H. J. Held, *Tradition and Interpretation in Matthew* NTL trans. P. Scott (London: SCM, 1963), 58-164.

Barth, H., *Die Jesaja-Worte in der Josaizeit* WMANT 48 (Neukircken-Vluyn: Neukirchener, 1977).

Bater, B. R., 'The Church in the Wilderness. A Study in Biblical Theology', Th.D. diss.: Union Theological Seminary, New York, 1963.

Bauckham, R., 'For Whom were Gospels Written?' unpublished paper presented to the British NT Conference, Bangor, Wales, 1995 (?).

_____ 'Jesus' Demonstration in the Temple' in *Law and the Temple: Essays on the Place of the Law in Israel and Early Christianity* ed. B. Lindars (Cambridge: James Clarke, 1988) 72-89.

Bauernfeind, O., *Die Worte der Dämonen im Markusevangelium* BWANT 3,8 (Stuttgart: Kohlhammer, 1927).

Baumgarten, J. M., '4Q500 and the Ancient Conception of the Lord's Vineyard,' *JJS* 40 (1989) 1-6.

Baumgartner, W., 'Zum Problem des Jahwe-Engels' in *Zum Alten Testament und seiner Umwelt* (Leiden: Brill, 1959) 240-46.

Baxandall, M., *Painting and Experience in the Fifteenth Century Italy: A Primer in the Social History of Pictorial Style* (Oxford: University, 1988²).

Bayer, H. F., *Jesus' Predictions of Vindication and Resurrection: The provenance, meaning and correlation of the Synoptic predictions* WUNT 2:20 (Tübingen: J. C. B. Mohr (Paul Siebeck), 1986).

Beach, C., *The Gospel of Mark: Its Making and Meaning* (New York: Harper, 1959).

Beale, G., 'An Exegetical and Theological Consideration of the Hardening of Pharaoh's Heart in Exodus 4-14 and Romans 9,' *TrinJ* 5 NS (1984) 129-54.

_____ 'Isaiah vi 9-13: A Retributive Taunt Against Idolatry' *VT* 41 (1991) 257-78.

_____ 'The Old Testament Background of Reconciliation in 2 Corinthians 5-7 and Its Bearing on the Literary Problem of 2 Cor. 6:14-7:1,' *NTS* 35 (1989) 550-81.

_____, ed., *The Right Doctrine from the Wrong Texts? Essays on the Use of the Old Testament in the New* (Grand Rapids: Baker, 1994).

Beasley-Murray, G. R., *Jesus and the Kingdom of God* (Exeter: Paternoster, 1986).

_____ 'The Two Messiahs in the Testaments of the Twelve Patriarchs,' *JTS* 48 (1947) 1-17.

Beaudet, R., 'La typologie de l'Exode dans le Second-Isaie,' *LavalTPh* 19 (1963) 12-21.

Beavis, M. A., *Mark's Audience: The Literary and Social Setting of Mark 4.11-12* JSNTSupp 33 (Sheffield: JSOT, 1989).

Beck, N. A., "Reclaiming a Biblical Text: the Mark 8:14-21 Discussion about Bread in the Boat,' *CBQ* 43 (1981) 49-56.

Becker, J., *Das Heil Gottes* SUNT 3 (Göttingen: Vandenhoeck & Ruprecht, 1964).

Beckwith, R., *The Old Testament Canon of the New Testament Church* (London: SPCK, 1985).

Begrich, J., *Studien zu Deuterojesaja* TBü 20 (reprint, Münich: Kaiser, 1969).

Belo, F., *A Materialist Reading of the Gospel of Mark* (Maryknoll, NY: Orbis, 1981).

Bentzen, A., *Jesaja* (Copenhagen, 1944).

_____ *Messias, Moses redivivus, Menschensohn* (Zürich, 1948).

Berger, K., 'Die königlichen Messiastraditionen des Neuen Testaments,' *NTS* 20 (1973) 1-44.

Berkey, R. F., 'ΕΓΓΙΖΕΙΝ, ΦΘΑΝΕΙΝ, and Realized Eschatology,' *JBL* 82 (1963) 177-87.

Best, E., 'Discipleship in Mark: Mark viii.22- x.52,' *SJT* 23 (1970) 323-37.

_____ *Following Jesus: Discipleship in the Gospel of Mark* (Sheffield: JSOT, 1981).

_____ 'Mark III. 20, 21, 31-35,' *NTS* 22 (1976) 309-19.

_____ *Mark: The Gospel as Story* SNTW (Edinburgh: T. & T. Clarke, 1983).

_____ 'Mark's Use of the Twelve,' *ZNW* 69 (1978) 11-35.

_____ 'The Miracles in Mark,' *RevExp* 75 (1978) 539-54.

_____ 'Peter in the Gospel according to Mark,' *CBQ* 40 (1978) 547-58.

_____ 'The Role of the Disciples in Mark,' *NTS* 23 (1977) 377-401.

_____ *The Temptation and the Passion: The Markan Soteriology* SNTS 2 (Cambridge: University, 1990²).

Betz, O., 'The Eschatological Interpretation of the Sinai-Tradition in Qumran and in the New Testament,' *RvQ* 6 (1967-8) 89-107.

_____ 'Die Frage nach dem messianischen Bewusstsein Jesu,' *NovT* 6 (1963) 20-48.

_____ 'Jesu Evangelium vom Gottesreich' in *Das Evangelium und die Evangelien* WUNT 28, hrsg. P. Stuhlmacher (Tübingen: J. C. B. Mohr (Paul Siebeck), 1983) 55-77.

_____ 'Jesu Heiliger Krieg,' *NovT* 2 (1958) 116-37.

_____ 'Miracles in the Writings of Flavius Josephus' in *Josephus, Judaism and Christianity* eds. L. H. Feldman and G. Hata (Leiden: Brill, 1987) 212-35.

_____ 'The Concept of the So-called "Divine Man" in Mark's Christology' in *Studies in the New Testament and Early Christian Literature: Essays in Honor of Allen P. Wikgren* ed. D. E. Aune, NovTSupp 33 (Leiden: Brill, 1972) 229-40.

_____ *What do we know about Jesus?* trans. M. Kohl (London: SCM, 1968).

Beuken, W. A. M., 'The Main Theme of Trito-Isaiah "The Servants of Yahweh",' *JSOT* 47 (1990) 67-87.

_____ '*MIŠPĀṬ* The First Servant Song and its Context,' *VT* 22 (1972) 1-30.

_____ 'Servant and Herald of Good Tidings. Isaiah 61 as an Interpretation of Isaiah 40-55' in *The Book of Isaiah—Le Livre d'Isaïe. Les oracles et leur relectures. Unité et complexité de l'ouvrage* ed. J. Vermeylen, BETL 81 (Leuven: Leuven University/ Peeters, 1989) 411-42.

Bickerman, E. J., 'The Warning Inscription of Herod's Temple,' *JQR* 37 (1946-47) 387-405.

Bieler, L., *ΘΕΙΟΣ ANHP. Das Bild des 'göttlichen Menschen' in Spätantike und Frühchristentum* 2 vols. (Wein: Buchhandlung Oskar Höfels, 1935-36); (reprint, Darmstadt: Wissenschaftliche Buchgelleschaft, 1967).

Bietenhard, H., 'Die Dekapolis von Pompeius bis Traian. Ein Kapitel aus der neutestamentlicher Zeitgeshichte,' *ZDPV* 79 (1963) 24-58.

Bilezikian, G. G., *The Liberated Gospel: A Comparison of the Gospel of Mark and Greek Tragedy* (Grand Rapids: Baker, 1977).

Bishop, E. F. F., *Jesus of Palestine* (London: Lutterworth, 1955).

_____ 'Why "Son of David"?,' *ExpT* 47 (1935-6) 21-25.

Black, M., *An Aramaic Approach to the Gospels and Acts* (Oxford: Clarendon, 1967³).

_____ *The Book of Enoch or I Enoch: A New English Edition with Commentary and Textual Notes* SVTP 7 (Leiden: Brill, 1985).

_____ 'The Christological Use of the Old Testament in the New Testament,' *NTS* 18 (1971) 1-14.

_____ 'The Kingdom of God Has Come,' *ExpT* 63 (1951-2) 289-90.

_____ 'The Messiah in the Testament of Levi xviii,' *ExpT* 60 (1949) 321-22.

_____ 'The "Son of Man" Passion Sayings in the Gospel Tradition,' *ZNTW* 60 (1969) 1-8.

_____ 'The "Two Witnesses" of Rev. 11:3f. in Jewish and Christian Apocalyptic Tradition' in *Donum Gentilicium: New Testament Studies in honour of David Daube* eds. C. K. Barrett *et al* (Oxford: Clarendon, 1978) 227-37.

Blackburn, B., *Theios Aner and the Markan Miracle Traditions. A Critique of the Theios Aner Concept as an Interpretative Background of the Miracle Traditions Used by Mark* WUNT 2, 40 (Tübingen: J. C. B. Mohr (Paul Siebeck), 1991).

Blake, R. P., 'The Georgian Version of Fourth Esdras from the Jerusalem Manuscript,' *HTR* 19 (1926) 299-375.

Blanchette, O., 'The Wisdom of God in Isaia,' *AER* 145 (1961) 413-23.

Blatherwick, D., 'The Markan Silhouette?,' *NTS* 17 (1970/71) 184-92.

Blenkinsopp, J., 'Deuteronomy' in *New Jerome Bible Commentary* eds. R. E. Brown, J. A. Fitzmyer, R. E. Murphy (London: Geoffery Chapman, 1989).

_____ 'The Oracle of Judah and the Messianic Entry,' *JBL* 80 (1961) 55-64.

_____ 'Scope and Depth of the Exodus Tradition in Deutero-Isaiah, 40-55' in *The Dynamism of Biblical Tradition*, Concilium 20 (Paramus, N.J.: 1966) 41-50.

Blevins, J. L., *The Messianic Secret in Markan Research, 1901-1976* (Washington: University Press of America, 1981).

Blidstein, G., *Honor thy Father and Mother* (New York: KTAV, 1973).

Bligh, P. H., 'A Note on Huios Theou in Mark 15[39],' *ExpT* 80 (1968-69) 51-53.

Blomberg, C. L., 'The Miracles as Parables' in *Gospel Perspectives 6: The Miracles of Jesus* eds. D. Wenham and C. Blomberg (Sheffield: JSOT, 1986) 327-59.

Bluhm, W., *Ideologies and Attitudes* (Englewood Cliffs: Prentice-Hall, 1974).

Böcher, O., *Dämonenfurcht and Dämonenabwehr. Ein Beitrag zur Formgesechichte der christlichen Taufe* BWANT V/10 (Stuttgart: Kohlhammer, 1970).

_____ 'Johannes des Täufer in der neutestamentlichen Überlieferung' in *Kirke in Zeit und Endzeit* (Neukirchen-Vluyn: Neukirchener, 1983) 70-89.

Bock, D., *Proclamation from Prophecy and Pattern: Lucan Old Testament Christology* JSNT 12 (Sheffield: Academic, 1987).

Bockmuehl, M. N. A., *Revelation and Mystery in Ancient Judaism and Pauline Christianity* WUNT 2 (Tübingen: J.C.B. Mohr (Paul Siebeck), 1990).

Boecker, H. J., 'Bemerkungen zur formgeschichtlichen Terminologie des Buches Maleachi,' *ZAW* 78 (1966) 78-80.

Bokser, B. M., 'Messianism, The Exodus Pattern, and Early Rabbinic Judaism' in *The Messiah* ed. J. H. Charlesworth (Minneapolis: Fortress, 1992) 239-58.

Bonnard, P. E., *Le Second Isaïe, son disciple et leurs éditeurs* SB. (Paris: J. Gabalda, 1972).

Bonner, C., *The Last Chapters of Enoch in Greek* StD 7 (London: Christophers, 1937).

Bonnet, C., 'Le désert: sa significiation dans l'evangile de Marc,' *Hokhma* 13 (1980) 20-34.

Boobyer, G. H., 'Galilee and Galileans in St. Mark's Gospel,' *BJRL* 35 (1952) 334-48.

_____ 'The Miracles of the Loaves and the Gentiles in St. Mark's Gospel,' *SJT* 6 (1953) 77-87.

_____ 'The Secrecy Motif in St. Mark's Gospel,' *NTS* 6 (1959-60) 225-35.

_____ *St. Mark and the Transfiguration Story* (Edinburgh: T. & T. Clarke, 1942).

_____ 'The Redaction of Mark IV.1-34,' *NTS* 8 (1962) 59-70.

Booth, R. P., *Jesus and the Laws of Purity: Tradition History and Legal History in Mark 7* JSNTSup 13 (Sheffield: University, 1986).

Borg, M. J., *Conflict, Holiness and Politics in the Teachings of Jesus* (New York/Toronto: Edwin Mellen, 1984).

Boring, M. E., 'Mark 1:1-15 and the Beginning of the Gospel,' *Semeia* 52 (1990) 43-81.

Boucher, M., *The Mysterious Parable* CBQMS 6 (Washington: Catholic Biblical Commission, 1977).

Boudon, R., *The Analysis of Ideology* trans. M. Slater (Cambridge: Polity, 1989).

Bousset, W., *Kyrios Christos* (Göttingen: Vandenhoeck & Ruprecht, 1926[3]).

Bowker, J. W., 'Mystery and Parable,' *JTS* 25 (1974) 300-17.

Bowman, J., *The Gospel of Mark: The New Christian Jewish Passover Haggadah* SPB 8 (Leiden: Brill, 1965).

Bowman, J. W., 'The Term "Gospel" and its Cognates in Palestinian Syriac' in *New Testament Essays. Studies in Memory of T. W. Manson* ed. A. J. B. Higgins (Manchester: University, 1959) 54-67.

Brady, J. R., 'The Role of Miracle-Working as Authentication of Jesus as "Messiah",' *Churchman* 103 (1989) 32-39.

Branscomb, B. H., *The Gospel of Mark* (London: Hodder & Staughton, 1952[6]).

Bretscher, P. G., 'Exodus 4: 22-23 and the Voice from Heaven,' *JBL* 87 (1968) 301-11.

_____ '"Whose Sandals"? (Matt. 3; 11),' *JBL* 86 (1967) 81-7.

Brett, L. F. X., 'Suggestions for an Analysis of Mark's Arrangement' in C. S. Mann *Mark* AB 27 (Garden City, New York: Doubleday, 1986) 174-90.

Brierre-Narbonne, J.-J., *Exégèse targumique des prophéties messianique* (Paris: Geuthner, 1936).

Bright, J., *Jeremiah* AB 21 (New York: Doubleday, 1965).

Broadhead, E. K., 'Which Mountain is "This Mountain"? A Critical Note on Mark 11:22-25,' *Paradigms* 2 (1986) 33-38.

Brooke, G. J., *Exegesis at Qumran: 4QFlorilegium in its Jewish Context* JSOTSupp 29 (Sheffield: University, 1985).

_____ 'Isaiah 40:3 and the Wilderness Community' in *New Qumran Texts and Studies: Proceedings of the First Meeting of the International Organisation for Qumran Studies, Paris 1992* STDJ 15 (Leiden/New York: Brill, 1994) 117-32.

Brown, R. E., *The Gospel According to John* AB 29/29a, 2 vols (New York: Doubleday, 1966, 70).

_____ 'The Gospel Miracles' in *The Bible in Current Catholic Thought* (New York, 1962) 184-201.

_____ 'Jesus and Elisha,' *Pers* 12 (1971) 85-104.

_____ 'The Messianism of Qumran,' *CBQ* 19 (1957) 53-82.

_____ *The Semitic Background of the Term 'Mystery' in the New Testament* (Philadelphia: Fortress, 1968).

Brownlee, W. H., 'The Background of Biblical Interpretation at Qumran' in *Qumran: Sa piété, sa théologie et son milieu* ed. M. Delcor, BETL 46 (Leuven/Paris: University/Gembloux, 1978) 183-93.

_____ *The Meaning of the Qumran Scrolls for the Bible* (New York: Oxford University, 1964).

Bruce, F. F., 'When is a Gospel not a Gospel?,' *BJRL* 45 (1963) 319-39.

_____ *This is That: The New Testament Development of Some Old Testament Themes* (London: Paternoster, 1968).

Brunner, H., *Altägyptische Erziehung* (Wiesbaden: Otto Harrassowitz, 1957).

Buchanan, G. W., 'Mark 11.15-19: Brigands in the Temple,' *HUCA* 30 (1959) 169-77.

_____ 'Withering Fig Trees and Progression in Midrash' in *The Gospels and the Scriptures of Israel* eds. C. A. Evans and W. R. Stegner, JSNTSupp 104, SSEJC 3 (Sheffield: Academic, 1994) 249-69.

Budesheim, T. L., 'Jesus and the Disciples in Conflict with Jerusalem,' *ZNTW* 62 (1971) 190-209.

Bultmann, R., *The History of the Synoptic Tradition* trans. J. Marsh (Oxford: Blackwell, 1972[2]).

Burger, C., *Jesus als Davidssohn. Eine traditionsgeschichtliche Untersuchung* FRLANT 98 (Göttingen: Vandenhoeck & Ruprecht, 1970).

Burgon, W. J., and Miller, E., *The Causes of the Corruption of the Traditional Text of the Holy Gospels* (London: George Bell, 1896).

Burke, D. G., *The Poetry of Baruch: A Reconstruction and Analysis of the Original Hebrew Text of Baruch 3:9 - 5:9* SBLSCS 10 (Chico: Scholars, 1982).

Burkill, T. A., 'Blasphemy: St. Mark's Gospel as Damnation History' in *Christianity, Judaism and Other Greco-Roman Cults. Studies for Morton Smith at Sixty* ed. J. Neusner, vol. 1 of 4 (Leiden: Brill, 1975).

_____ 'Mark 3:7-12 and the Alleged Dualism in the Evangelist's Miracle Material,' *JBL* 87 (1968) 409-17.

_____ *Mysterious Revelation. An Examination of the Philosophy of St. Mark's Gospel* (Ithaca: Cornell University, 1963) .

_____ *New Light on the Earliest Gospel* (Ithaca: Cornell University, 1972).

_____ 'Strain on the Secret: An Examination of Mark 11:1-13:37,' *ZNW* 51 (1960) 31-46.

Burridge, R. A., *What are the Gospels? A Comparison with Graeco-Roman Biography* SNTSMS 70 (Cambridge: University, 1992).

Burrows, M., *More Light on the Dead Sea Scrolls* (London: Secker and Warburg, 1958).

_____ 'The Origin of the Term "Gospel",' *JBL* 44 (1925) 21-33.

Buse, I., 'The Markan Account of the Baptism of Jesus and Isaiah LXIII,' *JTS* 7 (1956) 74-5.

Byrne, B., *'Sons of God' - 'Seed of Abraham'* AnBib 83 (Rome: Biblical Institute, 1979).

Cadbury, H. J., *The Making of Luke-Acts* (London, 1927).

Cadoux, C. J., 'The Imperatival Use of *dei* in the New Testament,' *JTS* 42 (1941) 165-73.

Caird, G. B., *A Commentary on the Revelation of St. John the Divine* (London: Black, 1966).

Camery-Hoggath, J., *Irony in Mark's Gospel* SNTSMS 72 (Cambridge: University, 1992).

Campbell, J., 'The Kingdom of God has Come,' *ExpT* 48 (1936-7) 91-94.

Cancik, H., 'Die Gattung Evangelium: Das Evangelium des Markus im Rahmen der antiken Historiographie' in *Markus-Philologie, Historische, literargeschichtliche und stilistische Untersuchungen zum zweiten Evangelium* ed. H. Cancik (Tübingen: J. C. B. Mohr (Paul Siebeck), 1984) 85-113.

Cantrell, R. A., 'The Cursed Fig Tree,' *BibToday* 29 (1991) 105-8.

Caragounis, C. C., *The Son of Man* WUNT 38 (Tübingen: J. C. B. Mohr (Paul Siebeck), 1986).

Carlson, R. A., *David, The Chosen King* (Uppsala: Almquist and Wiksells Boktryokeri A. B., 1964).

Carlston, C. E., *The Parables of the Triple Tradition* (Philadelphia: Fortress, 1975).

_____ 'Transfiguration and Resurrection,' *JBL* 80 (1961) 233-40.

Carmichael, D. B., 'David Daube on the Eucharist and the Passover Seder,' *JSNT* 42 (1991) 45-67.

Carmignac, J., 'Les citations de l'Ancien Testament dans "La Guerre des fils de lumière contre les fils de ténèbres",' *RB* 63 (1965) 234-60, 375-90.

Carrington, P., *According to Mark: A Running Commentary on the Oldest Gospel* (Cambridge: University, 1960).

_____ *Primitive Christian Calender: A Study in the Making of the Marcan Gospel* (Cambridge: University, 1952).

Carroll, R. P., *Jeremiah* OTL (London: SCM, 1986).

_____ 'Rebellion and Dissent in Ancient Israelite Society,' *ZAW* 89 (1977) 176-204.

Carson, D. A., 'Matthew' in *EBC* 8 (Grand Rapids: Zondervan, 1984) 3-599.

Casey, M., 'Idiom and Translation: Some Aspects of the Son of Man Problem,' *NTS* 41 (1995) 164-82.

_____ *Son of Man. The Interpretation and Influence of Daniel 7* (London: SPCK, 1979).

Cassuto, U., *A Commentary on the Book of Exodus* trans. I. Abrahams (Jerusalem: Magnes, 1967).

Castoriadis, C., *The Imaginary Institutions of Society*, trans. K. Blamey (Cambridge: University, 1987).

Catchpole, D. R., 'The "Triumphal" Entry' in *Jesus and the Politics of His Day* eds. E. Bammel and C. F. D. Moule (Cambridge: University, 1984) 319-34.

Cave, C. H., 'The Obedience of the Unclean Spirits,' *NTS* 11 (1964) 93-7.

Ceresko, A.R., 'The Rhetorical Strategy of the Fourth Servant Song (Isaiah 52:13-53:12): Poetry and the Exodus-New Exodus,' *CBQ* 56 (1994) 42-55.

Cerfaux, L., 'La connaissance des secrets du Royaume d'après Mt., XIII, 11 et parallèles,' *NTS* 2 (1955-6) 238-49.

Chamblin, K., 'John the Baptist and the Kingdom of God,' *TynBul* 15 (1964) 10-16.

Charlesworth, J. H., 'From Messianology to Christology: Problems and Prospects' in *The Messiah* ed. J. H. Charlesworth (Minneapolis: Fortress, 1992) 3-35.

_____ 'The Concept of the Messiah in the Pseudigrapha' in *ANRW* II, 19.1, 188-218.
_____ 'The Historical Jesus in the Light of Writings Contemporaneous with Him' in *ANRW* II, 25.1, 451-76.
_____ *Jesus Within Judaism* ABRL (New York: Doubleday, 1988).
Charlesworth, J. H., ed., *The Messiah* (Minneapolis: Fortress, 1992).
Charpentier, E., *Jeunesse du Vieux Testament* (Paris: Fayard, 1963).
Chary, Th., *Les prophètes et le culte à partir de l'exil* (Tournai: Desclé, 1954).
Chavasse, C. , 'Jesus: Christ and Moses,' *Th* 54 (1951) 244-50, 289-96.
Chevallier, M. A., *L'Esprit et le messie dans le bas-judaïsme et le Nouveau Testament* (Paris: Presses universitaires de France, 1958).
_____ *Souffle de Dieu: Le saint-esprit dans le Nouveau Testament* PT 26 (Paris: Beauchesne, 1978).
Cheyne, T. K., *The Prophecies of Isaiah* 2 vols. (London: Kegan Paul, Trench and Co., 1889⁵).
Childs, B. S., *Exodus* OTL (London: SCM, 1974).
_____ *Introduction to the Old Testament as Scripture* (Philadelphia: Fortress, 1979).
Chilton, B. D., 'Commenting on the Old Testament' in *It Is Written: Scripture Citing Scripture, Essays in Honour of Barnabas Lindars SSF* eds. D. Carson and H. G. M. Williamson (Cambridge: University, 1988) 122-40.
_____ *A Galilean Rabbi and his Bible: Jesus' Own Interpretation of Isaiah* (London: SPCK, 1984).
_____ *The Glory of Israel. The Theology and Provenience of the Isaiah Targum* JSOTSupp 23 (Sheffield: JSOT, 1982).
_____ *God in Strength* SNTU: B. 1 (Freistadt: F. Plöchl, 1979).
_____ 'Introduction' in *The Kingdom of God* ed. B. Chilton (London: SPCK, 1984) 1-26.
_____ 'Jesus and the Repentance of E. P. Sanders,' *TynBul* 39 (1988) 1-18.
_____ 'Jesus *ben David*: Reflections on the *Davidssohnfrage*,' *JSNT* 14 (1982) 88-112.
_____ *The Temple of Jesus: His Sacrificial Program Within a Cultural History of Sacrifice* (University Park, Penn.: Pennsylvania State University, 1992).
_____ 'The Transfiguration,' *NTS* 27 (1980) 115-24.
Chirichigno, G. C., 'The Narrative Structure of Exod 19-24,' *Bib* 68 (1987) 457-79.
Christie, W. M., *Palestine Calling* (London: Pickering, n.d.).
Citron, B., 'The Multitudes in the Synoptic Gospels,' *SJT* 7 (1954) 408-18.
Clark, A., 'The Interpretation of the Cursing of the Fig Tree Pericope in Mark's Gospel,' *CGST Journal* 12 (1992) 96-114.
Clark, K. W., 'Realized Eschatology,' *JBL* 59 (1940) 367-83.
Clark, W. K. L., 'What is the Gospel?' in *Divine Humanity* (New York: McMillan, 1936) 86-100.
Clements, R. E., 'Beyond Tradition-History: Deutero-Isaianic Development of First Isaiah's Themes,' *JSOT* 31 (1985) 95-113.
_____ *Isaiah 1-39* NCBC (London: Marshall, Morgan & Scott, 1980).
_____ 'The Prophecies of Isaiah and the Fall of Jerusalem in 587 B.C.,' *VT* 30 (1980) 421-36.
_____ 'The Unity of the Book of Isaiah,' *Int* 36 (1982) 117-29.
Clifford, R. J., 'Isaiah' in *Harper's Bible Commentary* ed. J. L. Mays (San Francisco: Harper, 1988) 571-96.
_____ *Fair Spoken and Persuading: An Interpretation of Second Isaiah* (New York: Paulist, 1984).
_____ 'The Function of Idol Passages in Second Isaiah,' *CBQ* 42 (1980) 450-64.
Clines, D. J. A., *I, He, We, and They—A Literary Approach to Isaiah 53* JSOTSupp 3 (Sheffield: JSOT, 1976).
Coakley, J. F., 'Jesus' Messianic Entry into Jerusalem (John 12: 12-19 par.),' *JTS* 46 (1995) 461-82.
Coats, G. W., *Rebellion in the Wilderness* (Nashville: Abingdon, 1968).
Collins, J. J., *Daniel* Hermeneia (Minneapolis: Fortress, 1993).
_____ 'A Pre-Christian "Son of God" Among the Dead Sea Scrolls,' *BibRev* 9 (1993) 34-38.

_____ 'The Works of the Messiah,' *DSD* 1 (1994) 98-112.

Colon, J. B., 'Marc (Évangile selon Saint)' in *DBSuppl* V (1957) col. 838.

Conrad, E. W., 'The "Fear Not" Oracles in Second Isaiah,' *VT* 34 (1984) 127-52.

Conzelmann, H., 'Gegenwart und Zukunft in der synoptischen Tradition,' *ZTK* 54 (1957) 277-96.

Cooke, G., 'The Israelite King as Son of God,' *ZAW* 73 (1961) 202-25.

Coole, D., 'Phenomenology and Ideology in Merleau-Ponty' in *The Structure of Modern Ideology: Critical Perspectives on Social and Political Theory* ed. N. O'Sullivan (Aldershot, UK: Edward Elgar/Brookfield, Vermont: Gower, 1989) 122-50.

Coppens, J., 'L 'Élu et les élus dans les Écritures Saintes et les Écrits de Qumrān,' *EphTheolLou* 57 (1981) 120-24.

_____ *Le Fils d'Homme Vétéro- et Intertestamentaire* (Leuven: University, 1983).

_____ 'La logia du Fils de l'homme dans l'évagile de Marc' in *L'Évangile selon Marc. Tradition et Rédaction* ed. M. Sabbe BETL 34 (Leuven: University, 1988²) 487-528.

_____ *Le Messianisme Royal* LD 54 (Paris: Cerf, 1968).

Cornette, A., 'Notes sur la Parabole des Vignerons: Marc 12/5-12,' *FoiVie* 84 (1985) 42-8.

Countryman, L. W., 'How Many Baskets Full? Mark 8: 14-21 and the Value of Miracles in Mark,' *CBQ* 47 (1985) 643-55.

Court, J. M., 'The Philosophy of the Synoptic Miracles,' *JTS* 23 (1972) 1-15.

Coutts, J., '"Those Outside" (Mark 4, 10-12),' *SE* 2, 155-57.

Craghan, J. F., 'The Gerasene Demoniac,' *CBQ* 30 (1968) 522-36.

Craigie, P. C., *Psalms 1-50* WBC 19 (Waco, Texas: Word, 1983).

Craigie, P. C., Kelly, P. G., and Drinkard, J. F., Jr., *Jeremiah 1-12* WBC 26 (Dallas: Word, 1991).

Cranfield, C. E. B., 'The Baptism of our Lord—A Study of St. Mark 1: 9-11,' *SJT* 8 (1955) 53-63.

_____ *The Gospel According to St. Mark* CGTC (Cambridge: University, 1959).

_____ 'Mark 4:1-34,' *SJT* 4, 5 (1955/1956) 398-414, 49-66.

_____ 'A Study of St. Mark 1.9-11,' *SJT* 8 (1955) 53-63.

Cross, F. M., *The Ancient Library of Qumran* AA 272 (rev. ed., Garden City: Doubleday, 1961).

_____ *Canaanite Myth and Hebrew Epic* (Cambridge, Mass.: Harvard, 1973).

Crossan, J. D., *The Historical Jesus. The Life of a Mediterranean Jewish Peasant* (Edinburgh: T. & T. Clarke, 1991).

_____ 'Mark and the Relatives of Jesus,' *NovT* 15 (1973) 81-113.

_____ 'Redaction and Citation in Mark 11:9-10 and 11:17,' *BR* 17 (1972) 33-50.

Crüsemann, F., *Studien zur Formgeschichte von Hymnus und Danklied in Israel* WMANT 32 (Neukirchen-Vluyn: Neukirchener, 1969).

Cullmann, O., *Baptism in the New Testament* trans. J. K. S. Reid, SBT 1 (London: SCM, 1950).

_____ *The Christology of the New Testament* trans. S. L. Guthrie and Charles A. M. Hall (London: SCM, 1959).

Dahl, N. A., 'The Atonement—An Adequate Reward for the Aqedah? (Ro. 8: 32)' in *Neotestamentica et Semitica. Studies in Honour of Matthew Black*, eds. E. E. Ellis and M. Wilcox (Edinburgh: T. & T. Clark, 1969) 15-29.

_____ *Jesus in the Memory of the Early Church* (Minneapolis: Augsburg, 1976).

_____ *Das volk Gottes* Norske Videnskapsakad Skrifter 1941/1 (Oslo: Jacob Dybwad, 1941).

Dalman, G., *Jesus-Yeshua: Studies in the Gospels* trans. P. Levertoff (London: SPCK, 1929).

_____ *The Words of Jesus: Considered in the Light of Post-Biblical Jewish Writings and the Aramaic Language* trans. D. M. Kay (Edinburgh: T. & T. Clarke, 1902).

Daly, R. J., 'The Soteriological Significance of the Sacrifice of Isaac,' *CBQ* 39 (1977) 45-75.

Daniélou, J., 'La typologie d'Isaak dans le chrisianisme primitif,' *Bib* 28 (1947) 363-93.

Daniels, D. R., *Hosea and Salvation History: The Early Traditions of Israel in the Prophecy of Hosea* BZAW 191 (Berlin and New York: de Gruyter, 1990).

Danker, F. W., 'The Demonic Secret in Mark: A Reexamination of the Cry of Dereliction (15:34),' *ZNW* 51 (1970) 48-69.

Daube, D., 'The Earliest Structure of the Gospels,' *NTS* 5 (1959) 174-87.

_____ *The Exodus Pattern in the Bible* (London: Faber and Faber, 1963).

_____ *He That Cometh* (London: Diocesan Council, 1966).

_____ 'Rabbinic Methods of Interpretation and Hellenistic Rhetoric,' *HUCA* 22 (1949) 239-64.

_____ *The Sudden in the Scriptures* (Leiden: Brill, 1964).

Dautzenberg, G., 'Die Zeit des Evangeliums. Mk 1, 1-15 und die Konzeption des Markus-evangeliums,' *BZ* 21 (1977) 219-34.

Davenport, G. L., 'The "Anointed of the Lord" in Psalms of Solomon 17' in *Ideal Figures in Ancient Judaism* eds. J. J. Collins and G. W. E. Nickelsburg, SBLSCS 12 (Chico: Scholars, 1980) 67-92.

Davies, G. I., 'The Destiny of the Nations in the Book of Isaiah' in *The Book of Isaiah—Le Livre d'Isaïe. Les oracles et leur relectures. Unité et complexité de l'ouvrage* ed. J. Vermeylen, BETL 81 (Leuven: Leuven University/Peeters, 1989) 93-120.

Davies, P. R., and Chilton, B. D., 'The Aqedah: A Revised Tradition History,' *CBQ* 40 (1978) 514-46.

Davies, W. D., *Gospel and Land* (Berkeley: University of California Press, 1974).

_____ 'Reflections on Archbishop Carrington's "The Primitive Christian Calender"' in *The Background to the New Testament and its Eschatology*, eds. W. D. Davies and D. Daube (Cambridge: University, 1956) 124-52.

_____ *The Setting of the Sermon on the Mount* (Cambridge: University, 1964).

Davies, W. D., and Allison, D. C. Jr., *The Gospel According to Saint Matthew* vol. 1 of 3, ICC (Edinburgh: T. & T. Clark, 1988).

Davis, K. L., 'The Literary History and Theology of the Parabolic Material in Mark 4 in Relation to the Gospel as a Whole', Ph.D. diss.: Union Theological Seminary, Virginia, 1966.

Day, J., 'DAʿAT "Humiliation" in Isaiah liii 11 in the Light of Isaiah liii 3 and Daniel xii 4, and the Oldest Interpretation of the Suffering Servant,' *VT* 30 (1980) 97-103.

_____ *God's Conflict with the Dragon and the Sea. Echoes of a Canaanite Myth in the Old Testament* UCOP 35 (Cambridge: University, 1985).

Déaut, R. Le., *La Nuit Pascale* AnBib 22 (Rome: Institut Biblique Pontifical, 1963).

Dehn, G., *Der Gottessohn. Einführung in das Evangelium des Markus* (Hamburg: Furche, 1953).

Deissler, A., *Zwölfpropheten III, Zefanja, Haggai, Sacharia, Maleachi* Neue Echter Bibel (Würzburg: Echter, 1988).

Deissmann, A., *Light From the Ancient East* trans. L. R. M. Strachan (London: Hodder and Stoughton, 1927⁴).

De Jonge, M., 'Christian Influences on the Testament of the Twelve Patriarchs,' *NovT* 4 (1960) 99-117.

_____ 'Jesus, Son of David and Son of God' in *Intertextuality in Biblical Writings: Essays in Honour of Bas van Iersel* ed. S. Draisma (Kampen: Kok, 1989) 95-104.

_____ *The Testaments of the Twelve Patriarchs* (Assen: van Gorcum, 1953).

_____ 'The Use of the Word "Anointed" in the Time of Jesus,' *NovT* 8 (1966) 132-48.

De Jonge, M., and v. der Woude, A. S., '11Q Melchizedek and the New Testament,' *NTS* 12 (1965-66) 301-26.

Delcor, M., 'Psaumes de Salomen' in *SDB* 48 (1973) Cols. 214-45.

Delitzsch, F., *Jesaja* (Giessen/Basel: Brunnen, 1984⁵).

Delling, G., 'Die Bezeichnung «Söhne Gottes» in der jüdischen Literatur der hellenistisch-römanischen Zeit' in *God's Christ and His People* eds. J. Jervell and W. Meeks FS N. A. Dahl (Oslo: Universitetsforlaget, 1977) 18-28.

_____ 'Das Verständnis des Wunders im Neuen Testament' in *Studien zum NT* eds. F. Hahn *et al* (Göttingen: Vandenhoeck & Ruprecht, 1970) 146-59.

Derrett, J. D. M., 'Contributions to the Study of the Gerasene Demoniac,' *JSNT* 3 (1979) 2-17.

_____ 'Figtrees in the New Testament,' *HeyJ* 14 (1973) 249-65.

_____ 'The Law in the New Testament: the Palm Sunday Colt,' *NovT* 13 (1971) 248-53.

_____ 'Legend and Event: The Gerasene Demoniac: An Inquest into History and Liturgical Projection' in *Studia Biblica 1978* II, ed. E. H. Livingstone JSNTSup 2 (Sheffield: University, 1980) 63-73.

_____ *The Making of Mark: The Scriptural Bases of the Earliest Gospel* 2 vols. (Shipston-on-Stour, England: Drinkwater, 1985).

_____ 'Mark's Technique: The Haemorrhaging Woman and Jairus' Daughter,' *Bib* 63 (1982) 474-505.

_____ '"The Stone that the Builders Rejected"' in *Studies in the New Testament* vol. 2 (Leiden: Brill, 1978) 60-67.

_____ *Studies in the New Testament* vols. 1-4 (Leiden: Brill, 1977-86).

_____ 'Trees Walking, Prophecy, and Christology (Mk 8:22-26),' *StTh* 35 (1981) 33-54.

Deubner, L., *Attische Feste* (Berlin, 1956).

Dewey, J., *Markan Public Debate* SBLDS 48 (California: Scholars Press, 1977).

Dibelius, M., *From Tradition to Gospel* trans. B. L. Woolf (London: Nicholson and Watson, 1934).

Dietrich, W., *Jesaja und die Politik* BEvT 74 (Münich: Kaiser, 1976).

Dobschütz, E. von., 'A Collection of Old Latin Bible Quotations,' *JTSt* 16 (1915) 1-27.

_____ 'Zur Erzählerkunst des Markus,' *ZNTW* 27 (1928) 193-98.

Dodd, C. H., *According to the Scriptures* (London: Nisbet, 1952).

_____ 'The Appearances of the Risen Christ: An Essay in Form-Criticism of the Gospels' in *Studies in the Gospels. Essays in Memory of R. H. Lightfoot* ed. D. E. Nineham (Oxford: Blackwell, 1955) 9-35.

_____ 'The Framework of the Gospel Narrative' in *New Testament Studies* (Manchester: University, 1967; orig., 1932) 1-11.

_____ *The Parables of the Kingdom* (London: Nisbet, 1935).

Donahue, J. R., *Are You the Christ? The Trial Narrative in the Gospel of Mark* SBDLS 10 (Missoula: Scholars, 1973).

_____ 'Jesus as the Parable of God in the Gospel of Mark,' *Int* 32 (1978) 369-86.

_____ 'Recent Studies on the Origin of "Son of Man" in the Gospels,' *CBQ* 48 (1986) 484-98.

Donner, H., 'Adoption oder Legitimation,' *OA* 8 (1969) 87-119.

Dormeyer, D., 'Die Kompositionsmetapher "Evangelium Jesu Christi, des Sohnes Gottes" Mk 1.1. Ihre Theologische und Literarische Aufgabe in der Jesus-Biographie des Markus,' *NTS* 33 (1987) 452-68.

Doron, P., 'The Motif of the Exodus in the Old Testament,' *SciptBull* 13 (1982) 5-8.

Dowd, S. E., *Prayer, Power and the Problem of Suffering* SBLDS 105 (Atlanta: Scholars, 1988).

Dowda, R. E., 'The Cleansing of the Temple in the Synoptic Gospels', Ph.D. diss.: Duke University, 1972.

Driver, G. R., *The Judean Scrolls* (Oxford: Blackwell, 1965).

Driver, S. R., *The Minor Prophets* CB (Edinburgh: T. C. and E. J. Jack, 1906).

Drummond, J., *The Jewish Messiah: A Critical History of the Messianic Idea Among the Jews from the Rise of the Maccabees to the Closing of the Talmud* (London: Longmans, 1877).

Drury, J., 'Mark 1.1-15: An Interpretation' in *Alternative Approaches to New Testament Study* ed. A. E. Harvey (London: SPCK, 1985).

_____ 'The Sower, the Vineyard, and the Place of Allegory in the Interpretation of Mark's Parables,' *JTS* 24 (1973) 367-79.

Dschulnigg, P., *Sprache, Redaktion und Intention des Markus-Evangeliums. Eingentümlich-keiten der Sprache des Markus-Evangeliums und ihre Bedeutung für die Redaktion-skritik* (Stuttgart, 1984).

Duff, P. B., 'The March of the Divine Warrior and the Advent of the Greco-Roman King: Mark's Account of Jesus' Entry into Jerusalem,' *JBL* 111 (1992) 55-71.

Duling, D. C., 'Solomon, Exorcism, and the Son of David,' *HTR* 68 (1975) 235-52.

Dumbrell, W. J., 'Malachi and the Ezra-Nehemiah Reforms,' *RTR* 35 (1976) 42-52.

_____ 'The Purpose of the Book of Isaiah,' *TynBul* 36 (1985) 111-28.

_____ 'Worship in Isaiah 6,' *RTR* 43 (1984) 1-8.

Duncan, G. S., *Jesus, Son of Man. Studies contributing to a modern protrait* (London: Nisbet, 1947).

Dunn, J. D. G., *Christology in the Making: An Inquiry into the Origins of the Doctrine of the Incarnation* (London: SCM, 1989²).

_____ 'Messianic Ideas and Their Influence on the Jesus of History' in *The Messiah* ed. J. H. Charlesworth (Minneapolis: Fortress, 1992) 365-381.

_____ 'The Messianic Secret in Mark,' *TynBul* 21 (1970) 92-117.

_____ *Romans 1-8, 9-16* 2 vols., WBC 38:I, II (Dallas: Word, 1988).

_____ 'Spirit and Fire Baptism,' *NTS* 14 (1972) 81-92.

Dupont, J., '"Filius meus es tu" Interpétation de Ps. 2:7 dans le NT,' *RSR* 35 (1948) 522-43.

_____ 'Les Transmission des Paroles de Jésus sur la Lampe et la Mesure dans Marc 4:21-25 et dans la Tradition Q' in *Logic Les Paroles de Jésus—The Sayings of Jesus* ed. J. Delobel, BETL 59 (Leuven: University, 1982) 201-36.

Durham, J. I., *Exodus* WBC vol. 3 (Waco, Texas: Word, 1987).

Earl, D., 'Prologue-form in Ancient Historiography' in *ANRW* I:22, 842-56.

Eaton, J. H., *Kingship and the Psalms* SBT 2/32 (London: SCM, 1976).

Ebeling, H. J., *Das Messiasgeheimnis und die Botschaft des Marcus-Evangelisten* BZNW 19 (Berlin: Töpelmann, 1939).

Edersheim, A., *The Life and Times of Jesus the Messiah* (London: Longmans, 1906).

Edgar, S. L., "Respect for Context in Quotations from the Old Testamet,' *NTS* 10 (1964) 277-89.

Edwards, J. R., 'Markan Sandwiches. The Significance of Interpolations in Markan Narra-tives,' *NovT* 31 (1989) 193-216.

Egger, W., *Frohbotschaft und Lehre: Die Sammelberichte des Wirkens Jesu in Markusevangelium* (Frankfurt: Knecht, 1976).

Eichrodt, W., *Ezekiel* OTL trans. C. Quinn (London: SCM, 1970).

_____ *Theology of the Old Testament* OTL, 2 vols., trans. J. A. Baker (Philadelphia: Westminster, 1961, 1967).

Eisenman, R., and Wise, M., *The Dead Sea Scrolls Uncovered* (Dorset, Shaftesbury, *et al*: Element, 1992).

Eissfeldt, O., 'Jahwe als König,' *ZAW* 46 (1928) 81-105.

Elliger, K., 'Der Begriff "Geschichte" bei Deuterojesaja' in *Kleinen Schriften zum A. T.* TBü 32 (München: Kaiser, 1966) 199-211.

_____ *Deuterojesaja* vol.1 BKAT XI,1 (Neukirchen-Vluyn: Neukirchener, 1978).

_____ *Deuterjesaja in seinem Verhältnis zu Tritojesaja* BWANT 63 (Stuttgart: Kohlhammer, 1933).

_____ *Die Propheten Nahum, Habakuk, Zephanja, Haggai, Sacharja, Maleachi* ATD 25/II (Göttingen: Vandenhoeck & Ruprecht, 1982).

Elliott-Binns, L. E., *Galilean Christianity* SBT 16 (London: SCM, 1956).

Ellis, E. E., *Paul's Use of the Old Testament* (reprint, Michigan: Baker, 1981).

_____ *The Old Testament in Early Christianity* (Grand Rapids: Baker, 1991).

Ellul, J., 'Le rôle médiateur de l'idéologie' in *Demythisation et idéologie* ed. E. Castelli (Paris: Aubier, 1973) 335-54.

Emerton, J. A., 'Some New Testament Notes: III. The Aramaic Background of Mark 10:45,' *JTS* 11 (1960) 334-35.

Emmerson, G. I., *Isaiah 56-66* OTG (Sheffield: JSOT, 1992).

Engels, F., *Anti-Dühring* (Moscow: Foreign Languages Publishing House, 1971).

Eppstein, V., 'The Historicity of the Gospel Account of the Cleansing of the Temple,' *ZNW* 55 (1964) 42-58.

Erlandsson, S., *The Burden of Babylon: A Study of Isaiah 13:2-14:23* (Lund: Berlingska Boktrycheriet, 1970).

Ernst, J., *Das Evangelium nach Markus* (Germany: Friedrich Pustet Regensburg, 1981).

Evans, C. A., 'A Note on the Function of Isaiah, VI, 9-10 in Mark, IV,' *RB* 88 (1981) 234-5.

_____ 'Jesus' Action in the Temple: Cleansing or Portent of Destruction?,' *CBQ* 51 (1989) 237-70.

_____ 'Jesus and the "Cave of Robbers": Toward a Jewish Context for the Temple Action,' *BBR*3 (1993) 93-110.

_____ 'On Isaiah's Use of Israel's Sacred Tradition,' *BZ* 30 (1986) 92-99.

_____ 'On the Isaianic Background of the Sower Parable,' *CBQ* 47 (1985) 464-68.

_____ 'On the Unity and Parallel Structure of Isaiah,' *VT* 38 (1988), 131-47.

_____ 'On the Vineyard Parables of Isaiah 5 and Mark 12,' *BZ* 28 (1984) 82-86.

_____ 'Paul and the Hermeneutics of "True Prophecy",' *Bib* 65 (1984) 560-70.

_____ *To See and Not Perceive. Isaiah 6.9-10 in Early Jewish and Christian Interpretation* JSOTSup 64 (Sheffield: University, 1990).

Evans, C. F., *The Beginning of the Gospel* (London: SPCK, 1968).

_____ 'I will go before You into Galilee,' *JTS* 5 (1954) 3-18.

Eversan, A. J., 'The Days of Yahweh,' *JBL* 93 (1974) 329-37.

Exum, J. C., 'Isaiah 28-32: A Literary Approach' in *SBL 1979 Sem. Papers* vol. 2, ed. P. Achtemeier (Missoula: Scholars, 1979) 123-51.

_____ 'Of Broken Pots, Fluttering Birds and Visions in the Night: Extended Similie and Poetic Technique in Isaiah,' *CBQ* 43 (1981) 331-52.

Fabry, H. J., 'Die Wurzel שוב in der Qumranliteratur' in *Qumran: Sa piété, sa théologie et son milieu* ed. M. Delcor, BETL 46 (Leuven/Paris: University/Gembloux, 1978) 285-93.

Faierstein, M. M., 'Why Do the Scribes Say That Elijah Must Come First?,' *JBL* 100 (1981) 75-86.

Farmer, W. R., *Maccabees, Zealots, and Josephus* (NY: Columbia University, 1956).

_____ 'The Palm Branches in John 12, 13,' *JTS* 3 (1952) 62-66.

Farrer, A. M., *St. Matthew and St. Mark* (Westminster: Dacre, 1954).

_____ *A Study in Mark* (Westminster: Dacre, 1951).

Fascher, E., 'Theologische beobachtungen zu δεῖ' in *Neutestamentliche Studien für Rudolf Bultmann* BZNTW 21 (Berlin: Töpelmann, 1957) 228-54.

Faw, C. E., 'The Outline of Mark,' *JBR* 25 (1957) 19-23.

Fay, G., 'Introduction to Incomprehension: The Literary Structure of Mark 4.1-34,' *CBQ* 51 (1989) 65-81.

Feldman, A., *The Parables and Similes of the Rabbis* (Cambridge: University, 1924).

Feneburg, W., *Der Markusprolog: Studien zur Formbestimmung des Evangeliums* SANT 36 (Munich: Kosel, 1974).

Feuillet, A., 'Le bapteme de Jésus d'après selon Saint Marc (1,9-11),' *CBQ* 21 (1959) 468-90.

_____ 'La coupe et le bapteme de la passion (Mc, x, 35-40; cf. Mt, xx, 20-23; Lc, xii, 50),' *RB* 74 (1967) 356-91.

_____ 'La personnalité de Jésus entrevue à partir de sa soumission au rite de repentance du Précurseur,' *RB* 77 (1970) 30-49.

_____ 'Le Symbolisme de la Colombe dans les récits évangéliques de bapteme,' *RSR* 46 (1958) 524-44.

Fichtner, J., 'Jahves Plan in der Botschaft des Jesaja,' *ZAW* 63 (1951) 16-33.

_____ 'Jesaja unter den Weisen,' *TL* 74 (1949) 75-80; ET: 'Isaiah Among the Wise' in *Studies in Ancient Israelite Wisdom* ed. J. L. Crenshaw (New York: KTAV, 1976) 429-38.

Fischer, J., *Das Buch Isaias* 2 vols. (Bonn: Peter Hanstein, 1939).

_____ 'Das Problem des neuen Exodus in Is 40-55,' *TübTQ* 110 (1929) 313-24.

Fischer, J. A., 'Notes on the Literary Form and Message of Malachi,' *CBQ* 34 (1972) 315-20.

Fischer, I., *Wo ist Jahwe? Das volksklagelied Jes 63,7-64,11 als Ausdruck des Ringens um eine gebrochene Bezeihung* SBB 19 (Stuttgart: Katholisches Biblewerk, 1989).

Fishbane, M., *Biblical Interpretation in Ancient Israel* (Oxford: Clarendon, 1985).

_____ 'The "Exodus" Motif/Paradigm for Renewal' in *Text and Texture. Close Readings of Selected Biblical Texts* (New York: Schocken, 1979) 121-51.

Fisher, L., 'Can This be the Son of David?' in *Jesus and the Historian. Written in Honor of Ernest Cadman Colwell* ed. F. T. Trotter (Philadelphia: Westminster, 1968) 82-97.

Fisher, M. K., and von Wahlde, U. C., 'The Miracles of Mark 4:35-5:43: Their Meaning and Function in the Gospel Framework,' *BTB* 11 (1981) 13-16.

Fitzmyer, J. A., 'The Aramaic 'Elect of God' Text from Qumran Cave IV,' *CBQ* 27 (1965) 348-72.

_____ 'Aramaic Evidence Affecting the Interpretation of *Hosanna* in the New Testament' in *Tradition and Interpretation in the New Testament* FS E. Earle Ellis, eds. G. F. Hawthorne and O. Betz (Grand Rapids: Eerdmans/Tübingen: J.C.B. Mohr (Paul Siebeck), 1987) 110-18.

_____ 'The Contribution of Qumran Aramaic to the Study of the New Testament,' *NTS* 20 (1973-4) 382-407.

_____ 'Further Light on Melchizedek from Qumran Cave 1,' *JBL* 86 (1967) 25-41.

_____ *The Gospel According to Luke* AB 28/28a, 2 vols. (New York: Doubleday, 1981).

_____ 'Jewish Christianity in Acts in Light of the Qumran Scrolls' in *Studies in Luke-Acts. Essays presented in honor of Paul Schubert* eds. L. E. Keck and J. Louis Martyn (New York: Abingdon, 1986) 233-57.

_____ 'Judaic Studies and the Gospels: The Seminar' in *The Relationships Among the Gospels: An Interdisciplinary Dialogue* ed. O. A. Walker, Jr. (San Antonio: Trinity University, 1978) 237-58.

_____ 'More About Elijah Coming First,' *JBL* 104 (1985) 295-96.

_____ '"4Q Testimonia" and the New Testament,' *ThSt* 18 (1957) 513-37.

_____ 'The Son of David Tradition and Matt. 22:41-46 and parallels (Mark 12:35-7)' in *Essays on Semitic Background of N.T.* (London: Chapman, 1971) 113-26.

_____ 'The Use of Explicit Old Testament Quotations in Qumran Literature and in the New Testament,' *NTS* 7 (1961) 297-333.

_____ *A Wandering Aramean: Collected Aramaic Essays* SBLMS 25 (Ann Arbor, Michigan: Scholars, 1979).

Flammer, B., 'Die Syrophoenizerin,' *TQ* 148 (1968) 463-78.

Flusser, D., 'Two Notes on the Midrash on 2 Sam vii,' *IEJ* 9 (1959) 195-205.

Focant, C., 'L'incompréhension des disciples dans le deuxième évangile,' *RevBib* 82 (1975) 161-85.

Fohrer, G., *Introduction to the Old Testament* trans. D. Green (London: SPCK, 1970).

_____ 'Zion-Jerusalem im Alten Testament' in *Studien zur alttestamentlichen Theologie und Geschichte (1949-1966)* BZAW 115 (Berlin: de Gruyter, 1969) 195-241.

Fokkelman, J. P., 'Stylistic analysis of Isaiah 40:1-11,' *OTS* 21 (1981) 68-90.

Ford, J. M., 'Money "bags" in the Temple (Mk 11,16),' *Bib* 57 (1976) 249-53.

Fortna, R. T., *The Gospel of Signs* SNTSMS 11 (Cambridge: University, 1970).

Foucart, P., *Les mystères d'Eleusis* (Paris, 1914).

Foulkes, F., *The Acts of God* (London: Tyndale, 1958).

Fowler, R. M., *Let the Reader Understand* (Minneapolis: Fortress, 1991).

France, R. T., *Jesus and the Old Testament* (reprint, Grand Rapids: Baker, 1982).

_____ 'Mark and the Teaching of Jesus' in *Gospel Perspectives 1: Studies of History and Tradition in the Four Gospels* eds. R. T. France and D. Wenham (Sheffield: JSOT, 1980) 101-36.

_____ *Matthew—Evangelist and Teacher* (Exeter: Paternoster, 1989).

_____ 'The Servant of the Lord in the Teaching of Jesus,' *TynBul* 19 (1968) 26-52.

Frankemölle, H., 'Evangelium als theologischer Begriff und sein Bezug zur literarischen Gattung "Evangelium",' *ANRW* II 25.2, 1635-1704.

_____ 'Jesus als deuterojesanischer Freudenbote?' in *Vom Urchristentum zu Jesus. FS. Joachim Gnilka zum 60 Geburtstag* hrsg. von H. Fankemölle und K. Kertelge (Breisgau, Basel, Wein: Herder, 1989) 34-67.

Fredriksson, H., *Jahwe als Krieger* (Lund: C. W. K. Gleerup, 1945).

Freedman, D. N., 'Pottery, Poetry, and Prophecy,' *JBL* 96 (1977) 5-26.

Freyne, S., 'Disciples in Mark and the *Maskilim* in Daniel,' *JSNT* 16 (1982) 7-23.

_____ 'Galilean Religion of the First Century C.E. against its Social Background,' *ProcIrBibAssoc* 5 (1981) 98-114.

_____ *Galilee, Jesus and the Gospels. Literary Approaches and Historical Investigations* (Dublin: Gill and Macmillan, 1988).

Friedrich, G., 'Die beiden Erzählungen von der Speisung in Mark 6,31-44, 8,1-9,' *TZ* 20 (1964) 10-22.

Fuller, R. H., *Foundations of New Testament Christology* (New York: Scribner's, 1965).

_____ *Interpreting the Miracles of Jesus* (Philadelphia: Westminster, 1963).

_____ *The Mission and Achievement of Jesus* SBT 12 (London: SCM, 1954).

Funk, R., *Language, Hermeneutic and the Word of God* (New York: Harper and Row, 1966).

Fusco, V., *Paraola et Regno: La Sezione delle Parabole (Mc. 4, 1-34) nella Prospettive Marciana* (Brescia: Morcelliana, 1980).

Gaboury, A., 'Deux fils uniques: Isaac et Jésus. Connexions vétéro-testamentaires de Mc 1,11 (et Parallèles),' *SE IV, 1* :198-204.

Gage, W., *The Gospel of Genesis: Studies in Protology and Eschatology* (Winona Lake, Indiana: Carpenter, 1984).

Gärtner, B., *The Temple and the Community in Qumran and the New Testament: A Comparative Study in the Temple Symbolism of the Qumran Texts and the New Testament*, SNTSMS 1 (Cambridge: University, 1965).

Garvie, A. E., '"Way"' in *Dictionary of the Bible* vol. 4, ed. J. Hastings (Edinburgh: T. & T. Clarke, 1902) 899.

Gaston, L., 'Beelzebul,' *TZ* 18 (1962) 247-55.

_____ *No Stone Upon Another: Studies in the Significance of the Fall of Jerusalem in the Synoptic Gospels* NovTSupp 23 (Leiden: Brill, 1970).

Geddart, T. J., *Watchwords: Mark 13 in Markan Eschatology* JSNTSupp 26 (Sheffield: JSOT, 1989).

Geertz, C., 'Ideology as a Cultural System' in *The Interpretation of Cultures* (NY: Basic, 1973) 193-233.

Gelston, A., 'Knowledge, Humiliation or Suffering: A Lexical, Textual and Exegetical Problem in Isaiah 53' in *Of Prophets' Visions and the Wisdom of the Sages* eds. H. A. McKay and David J. A. Clines JSOTSupp 162 (Sheffield: JSOT, 1993) 126-41.

Gerhardsson, B., 'The Parable of the Sower and its Interpretation (Mark 4,1-20),' *NTS* 14 (1967-8) 165-93.

_____ *The Testing of God's Son* (Lund: CWK Gleerup, 1966).

Gerleman, G., 'Bemerkungen zur Terminology der 'Blindheit' im Alten Testament,' *SEÅ* 41 (1976-7) 77-80.

Gero, S., '"My Son the Messiah": A Note on 4 Ezra 7:28-29,' *ZNW* 66 (1975) 264-67.

Gibbs, J. M., 'Mark 1.1-15, Matthew 1.1-4.16, Luke 1.14.30, John 1.1-51: The Gospel Prologues and Their Function,' *SE* 6 ed. E. A. Livingstone (Berlin: Akadamie, 1973) 154-88.

Gibson, J. B., 'The Rebuke of the Disciples in Mark 8. 14-21,' *JSNT* 27 (1986) 31-47.

Gillet, G., 'Evangelium. Studien zur urchristlichen Missionssprache', diss.: Heidelberg, 1924.

Gils, F., *Jésus prophète d'après les évangiles synoptiques* OBL 2 (Louvain: University, 1957).

Ginsberg, H. L., 'The Oldest Interpretation of the Suffering Servant,' *VT* 3 (1953) 400-4.

Ginzberg, L., *An Unknown Jewish Sect?* (New York: Jewish Theological Seminary, 1976).

Gitay, Y., *Isaiah and his Audience: The Struture and Meaning of Isaiah 1-12* SSN (Assen/ Maastricht: Van Gorcum, 1991).

Glasswell, M. E., 'The Use of Miracles in the Markan Gospel' in *Miracles* ed. C. F. D. Moule (London: Mowbray, 1965) 151-62.

Glazier-McDonald, B., *Malachi: The Divine Messenger* SBLDS 98 (Altanta: Scholars, 1987).

Gnilka, J., *Das Evangelium Nach Markus* EKK II/1, 2 (Zürich: Benziger/Neukirchener, 1978, 79).

_____ *Das Matthäusevangelium* HTKNT I.1/2 (Freiburg: Herder, 1986, 1988).

_____ *Der Verstockung Israels: Isaias 6, 9-10 in der Theologie der Synoptiker* SANT 3 (Münich: Kösel, 1961).

Goguel, M., *L'évangile de Marc* (Paris: Leroux, 1909).

Goldsmith, D., 'Acts 13:33-37: A *Pesher* on II Sam 7,' *JBL* 87 (1968) 321-24.

Goodman, M., *State and Society in Roman Galilee, A.D.. 132-212* (Totowa, NJ: Rowman & Allenheld, 1983).

Goppelt, L., *Typos: The Typological Interpretation of the Old Testament* trans. D. H. Madvig (Grand Rapids: Eerdmans, 1982).

Gordis, R., 'The "Begotten Messiah" in the Qumran Scrolls,' *VT* 7 (1957) 191-94.

Gottwald, N., *The Hebrew Bible: A Socio-Literary Introduction* (Philadelphia: Fortress, 1985).

Gould, E. P., *A Critical and Exegetical Commentary on the Gospel according to St. Mark* ICC (Edinburgh: - Clark, 1955).

Gould, S., 'Evolution and the Triumph of Homology, Or Why History Matters,' *The American Scientist* 74 (1986) 60-69.

Goulder, M. D., *The Evangelists Calender* (London: SPCK, 1978).

_____ *Midrash and Lection in Matthew* (London: SPCK, 1964).

_____ 'Those Outside (MK. 4:10-12),' *NovT* 33 (1991) 289-302.

Grant, F. C., *The Earliest Gospel* (New York: Abingdon, 1943).

_____ 'The Gospel According to St. Mark,' *IB* 7 (New York: Abingdon, 1951) 627-917.

_____ *The Gospels. Their Origin and Growth* (London: Faber & Faber, 1957).

_____ *Miracle and Natural Law in Graeco-Roman and Early Christian Thought* (Amsterdam: North-Holland, 1952).

Grant, R. M., 'The Coming of the Kingdom,' *JBL* 67 (1948) 297-303.

Gray, G. B., *The Book of Isaiah I-XXXIX* 2 vols. ICC (Edinburgh: T. & T. Clarke, 1928).

_____ 'The Kingship of God in the Prophets and the Psalms,' *VT* 11 (1961) 1-29.

Greenberg, M., *Ezekiel 1-20* AB 22 (New York: Doubleday, 1983).

_____ 'Some Postulates of Biblical Law' in *Yehezkel Kaufmann Jubilee Volume* ed. M. Haran (Jerusalem: Magnes, 1960) 5-28.

Greenfield, J. C. and Stone, M. E., 'The Enochic Pentateuch and the Date of the Similitudes,' *HTR* 70 (1977) 51-65.

Grelot, P., *La venue du Messie: Messianisme et eschatologie* RB 6 (Bruges: Desclée de Brouwer, 1962).

_____ 'L'exégèse messianique de'Isaïe, LXIII,1-6,' *RB* 70 (1963) 371-80.

_____ 'L'interprétation messianique d'Isaïe 9, 5 dans le Targoum des prophètes' in *De la Torah au Messia. Mélanges H. Cazelles* eds. J. Doré, P. Grelot, M. Carrez (Paris: Desclée, 1981) 535-43.

Gressman, H., 'Die literarische Analyse Deuterojesajas,' *ZAW* 34 (1914) 254-97.

Grimes, A., 'Ideology and Religion' in *The Form of Ideology* ed. by D. J. Manning (London: Unwin and Allen, 1980) 22-37.

Grimm, W., *Die Verkündigung Jesu und Deuterojesaja* ANTI 1 (Frankfurt am Main, Bern: Peter Lang, 1981[2]).

Grindel, J., 'The Origin and the Use of Isaiah 40:3 in the Gospels,' *Vincentia Studies* 1 (1968) 25-32.

Gross, H., 'Doch für Sion kommt er als Erlöser,' *Conc* 3 (1967) 812-18.

Grundmann, W., *Der Begriff der Kraft in der neutestamentlichen Gedankenwelt* BWANT 4/8 (Stuttgart: Kohlhammer, 1932).

_____ *Das Evangelium nach Markus* ThHK 2 (Berlin: Evangelische Verlaganstalt, 1959[2]).

_____ 'Die Frage nach der Gottessohnschaft des Messias im Lichte von Qumran' in *Bible und Qumran: Beiträge zur Erforschung der Beziehungen zwischen Bibel- und Qumranwissenschaft: Hand Bardtke zum 22. 9. 1966* (Berlin: Evangelische Haupt-Bibelgesellschaft, 1968) 86-111.

Guelich, R., '"The Beginning of the Gospel" Mark 1: 1-15,' *BibRes* 27 (1982) 5-15.

_____ 'The Gospel Genre' in *Das Evangelium und die Evangelien* WUNT 28, hrsg. P. Stuhlmacher (Tübingen: J. C. B. Mohr (Paul Siebeck), 1983) 183-219.

_____ *Mark* vol. 1, WBC 34a (Dallas: Word, 1989).

Gundry, R. H., *Mark: A Commentary on His Apology for the Cross* (Grand Rapids: Eerdmans, 1993).

_____ *The Use of the Old Testament in St. Matthew's Gospel* NovTSup 18 (Leiden: Brill, 1967).

Gunkel, H., *Schöpfung und Chaos in Urzeit und Endzeit, Eine religionsgeschichtliche Untersuchung über Genesis 1 und Ofenbarung 12* (Göttingen: Vandenhoeck & Ruprecht, 1894).

Gunneweg, A. H., 'Sinaibund und Davidsbund,' *VT* 10 (1960) 335-41.

Güttgemanns, E., *Candid Questions Concerning Gospel Form Criticism: A Methodological Sketch of the Fundamental Problematics of Form and Redaction Criticism* PTMS 26 trans. W. G. Doty (Pittsburgh: Pickwick, 1979).

Haag, E., 'Das Opfer des Gottesknechtes (Jes 53,10),' *TrThZ* 86 (1977) 81-98.

_____ 'Der Weg zum Baum des Lebens: Ein Pradiesmotiv im Buch Jesaja' in *Künder des Wortes: Beiträge zur Theologie der Propheten*, hrsg. L. Ruppert *et al.*, FS J. Schreiner (Würzburg: Echter, 1982) 35-52.

Habel, N. C., '"Yahweh, Maker of Heaven and Earth": A Study in Tradition Criticism,' *JBL* 91 (1972) 321-37.

Habermas, J., *Towards a Rational Society* trans. J. J. Shapiro (London: Heinemann, 1971).

Hadas, M., and Smith, M., *Heroes and Gods. Spiritual Biographies in Antiquity* (New York: Harper and Row, 1963).

Haenchen, E., 'Die Komposition von Mk VIII:27-IX:1,' *NovT* 6 (1963) 81-109.

_____ *Der Weg Jesu: Eine Erklärung des Markus-Evangeliums und der kanonischen Parallelen* (Berlin: de Gruyter, 1968).

Hahn, F., 'Jesu Wort vom bergeverstzenden Glauben,' *ZNTW* 76 (984) 149-69.

_____ *Mission in the New Testament* SBT 47 trans. F. Clark (London: SCM, 1965).

_____ *The Titles of Jesus in Christology: Their History in Early Christianity* trans. H. Knight and G. Ogg (London: Lutterworth, 1969).

Halpern, B., '"Myth" and "Ideology" in Modern Usage,' *History and Theory* 1 (1961) 129-49.

Hamborg, G. R., 'Reasons for the Judgement in the Oracles Against the Nations of the Prophet Isaiah,' *VT* 31 (1981) 145-59.

Hamilton, N. Q., 'Temple Cleansing and Temple Bank,' *JBL* 83 (1964) 365-72.

Hamilton, R., 'The Gospel of Mark: Parable of God Incarnate,' *Theol* 86 (1986) 438-41.

Hanhart, R., 'Die Bedeutung der Septuaginta in neutestamentlicher Zeit,' *TheolKirch* 81 (1984) 395-416.

Hanninen, S., and Paldan, L., eds., *Rethinking Ideology* (Berlin/NY, 1983).

Hanson, P. D., *The Dawn of Apocalyptic* (rev. ed., Philadelphia: Fortress, 1979).

_____ 'Messiahs and Messianic Figures in Proto-Apocalypticism' in *The Messiah* ed. J. H. Charlesworth (Minneapolis: Fortress, 1992) 67-78.

Hare, D. R. A., *The Theme of Jewish Persecution of Christians in the Gospel according to St. Matthew* (Cambridge: University, 1967).

Harnack, A., 'The Conflict with Dæmons' in *The Mission and Expansion of Christianity in the First Three Centuries* ed. and trans. J. Moffat, TTL 19, 20 (London: Williams and Norgate, 1908) 125-46.

_____ *Reden und Aufsätze* I (Giessen: Töpelmann, 1906²).

Harner, P. B., 'Creation Faith in Deutero-Isaiah,' *VT* 17 (1967) 298-306.

_____ *Grace and Law in Second Isaiah* ANETS 2 (Queenston, Ontario: Edwin Mellen, 1988).

_____ 'The Salvation Oracle in Second Isaiah,' *JBL* 88 (1969) 418-23.

Harris, M., *Exodus and Exile*. (Minneapolis: Fortress, 1992).

Harris, R. J., *Testimonies* 2 vols. (Cambridge: University, 1916, 1920).

Hartman, L., 'Dop, and och barnaskap. Några traditionshistoriske överväganden till Mk 1:9-11 par,' *SvenskExegÅrs* 37-8 (1972-73) 88-106, [see NTA 18, 1973-4, # 869].

_____ *Prophecy Interpreted: The Formation of Some Jewish Apocalyptic Texts of the Eschatological Discourse Mark 13 par.* ConBNT 1 (Uppsala: CWK Gleerup, 1966).

Hartmann, G., *Der Aufbau des Markusevangeliums* (Münster: Aschendorff, 1936).

Harvey, A. E., 'The Use of Mystery Language in the Bible,' *JTS* 31 (1983) 320-36.

Harvey, J., 'La typologie de l'Exode dans les Psaumes,' *ScE*15 (1963) 383-406.

Hasel, G., *The Remnant* (Berrien Springs: Andrews University, 1974).

Hatch, E., *Essays in Biblical Greek* (Oxford: Clarendon, 1889).

Hays, R. B., *Echoes of Scripture in the Letters of Paul* (New Haven-London: Yale, 1989).

Hawkin, D. J., 'The Incomprehension of the Disciples,' *JBL* 91 (1972) 491-500.

_____ 'The Symbolism and Structure of the Markan Redaction,' *EvQ* 49 (1977) 49-50, 98-110.

Hayward, R., 'The Present State of Research into the Targumic Account of the Sacrifice of Isaac,' *JJS* 32 (1981) 127-50.

Head, P. M., 'A Text-Critical Study of Mark 1.1 "The Beginning of the Gospel of Jesus Christ",' *NTStud* 37 (1991) 621-29.

Hedrick, C. W., 'The Role of "Summary Statements" in the Composition of the Gospel of Mark: A Dialog with Karl Schmidt and Norman Perrin,' *NovT* 26 (1984) 289-311.

Heil, J. P., *Jesus Walking on the Sea. Meaning and Gospel Functions of Matt 14:22-33, Mark 6:45-52 and John 6:15b-21* AnBib 87 (Rome: Pontifical Biblical Institute, 1981).

Heising, A., *Die Botschaft der Brotvermehrung* SBS 15 (Stuttgart: Katholische Bibelwerk, 1967²).

_____ 'Exegese und Theologie der alt- und neutestamentlichen Speisewunder,' *ZTK* 86 (1964) 80-96.

Heitmüller, W., 'Zum Problem Paulus und Jesus,' *ZNW* 13 (1912) 320-37.

Held, J. H., 'Matthew as Interpreter of the Miracle Stories' in G. Bornkamm, G. Barth and H. J. Held *Tradition and Interpretation in Matthew* trans. P. Scott (London: SCM, 1963) 165-299.

Hempel, J., 'Licht, Heil und Heilung,' *Antaios* 2 (1961) 375-88.

Hendel, R. S., 'Sacrifice as a Cultural System: The Ritual Symbolism of Exodus 24,3-8,' *ZATW* 101 (1984) 366-90.

Hengel, M., *The Atonement. The Origins of the Doctrine in the New Testament* trans. J. Bowden, (Philadelphia: Fortress, 1981).

_____ 'Between Jesus and Paul' in *Between Jesus and Paul* trans. J. Bowden (London: SCM, 1983) 1-29.

_____ *The Charismatic Leader and His Followers* SNTW trans. J. Grieg (New York: Crossroad, 1981).

_____ 'Christology and New Testament Chronology. A Problem in the History of Earliest Christianity' in *Between Jesus and Paul* trans. J. Bowden (London: SCM, 1983) 30-47.

_____ ' 'Christos' in Paul' in *Between Jesus and Paul* trans. J. Bowden (London: SCM, 1983) 65-77.

_____ *Gewalt und Gewaltlosigkeit* (Stuttgart: Calwer, 1971).

_____ 'Literary, Theological and Historical Problems in the Gospel of Mark' in *Studies in the Gospel of Mark* trans. J. Bowden (Philadelphia: Fortress, 1985).

_____ 'The Gospel of Mark: Time of Origin and Situation' in *Studies in the Gospel of Mark* trans. J. Bowden (Philadelphia: Fortress, 1985) 1-30.

_____ *The Son of God* trans. J. Bowden (Philadelphia: Fortress, 1976).

_____ *De Zeloten: Untersuchungen zur Jüdischen Freuiheitsbewegung in der Zeit von Herodes I. bis 70 n. chr.* AGSJU 1 (Leiden: Brill, 1961); ET: *The Zealots* trans. D. Smith (Edinburgh: T. & T. Clarke, 1989).

Herion, G. A., 'The Impact of Modern and Social Science Assumptions on the Reconstruction of Israelite History,' *JSOT* (1986) 3-33.

Hermann, I., *Das Markus Evangelium I* (Düsseldorf: Patmos, 1965).

Herrman, S., *Die prophetischen Heilserwartungen im A.T.* BWANT 5/5 (Stuttgart: Kohlhammer, 1965).

Hesse, F., *Das Verstockungsproblem im Alten Testament* BZAW 74 (Berlin: Töpelmann, 1955).

Hesse, M., 'Consilience of Inductions' in *The Problem of Inductive Logic* ed. I. Lakatos (Amsterdam: North Holland, 1968) 232-46.

Hessler, E., *Gott der Schöpfer. Ein Beitrag zur Komposition und Theologie Deuterojesajas* diss.: Greifswald, 1961.

Hiers, R., 'Purification of the Temple: Preparation for the Kingdom of God,' *JBL* 90 (1971) 82-91.

Higgins, A. J. B., *Jesus and the Son of Man* (London: Lutterworth, 1964).

Hill, D., *Greek Words with Hebrew Meanings* (Cambridge: University, 1967).

Hobbs, E. C., 'The Gospel of Mark and the Exodus,' Ph.D. diss.: University of Chicago, 1958.

Hoepers, P. M., *Der neue Bund bei den Propheten* (Freiburg: Herder & Co., 1933).

Hofius, O., 'Vergebungszuspruch und vollmachtsfrage Mk 2,1-12 und das Problem priesterlicher Absolution im antiken Judentum' in *»Wenn nich jetzt, wann dann?« Aufsätze für Hans-Joachim Kraus zum 65* hrsg. H.-G. Geyer *et al* (Neukirchener-Vluyn: Neukirchener, 1983) 115-27.

Holladay, W. L., *Jeremiah 1: A Commentary of the Book of the Prophet Jeremiah Chapters 1-25* Hermeneia (Philadelphia: Fortress, 1986).

Hollenbach, P., 'Jesus, Demoniacs, and Public Authorities,' *JAAR* 49 (1981) 567-88.

Hollenberg, D. E., 'Nationalism and "The Nations" in Isaiah XL-LV,' *VT* 19 (1969) 23-36.

Holmgren, F., 'Yahweh the Avenger: Isaiah 63:1-6' in *Rhetorical Criticism* eds. J. J. Jackson and M. Kessler (Pittsburg: Pickwick Press, 1974) 133-48.

Holm-Nielsen, S., 'The Exodus Traditions in Ps. 105,' *ASTI* 11 (1978) 22-30.

Holtzmann, H. J., *Der Synoptiker* HKNT I.1 (Tübingen: Mohr, 1901³).

Holzmeister, U., 'Vom angeblichen Verstockungszweck der Parabeln des Herrn,' *Bib* 15 (1934) 321-64.

Hommes, N. J., *Het Testimoniaboek* (Amsterdam, 1935).

Hooker, M. D., *The Gospel According to St. Mark* BNTC (London: A. & C. Black, 1991).

_____ *Jesus and the Servant* (London: SPCK, 1959).

_____ 'Mark' in *It Is Written: Scripture Citing Scripture, Essays in Honour of Barnabas Lindars SSF* eds. D. Carson and H. G. M. Williamson (Cambridge: University, 1988) 220-30.

_____ *The Message of Mark* (London: Epworth, 1983).

_____ *The Son of Man in Mark* (London: SPCK, 1967).

_____ 'What Doest Thou Here Elijah?' in *The Glory of Christ in the New Testament: Studies in Christology* FS G. B. Caird, eds. L. D. Hunt and N. T. Wright (Oxford: Clarendon, 1987) 59-70.

_____ 'Traditions about the Temple in the Sayings of Jesus,' *BJRL* 70 (1988) 7-20.

van Hoonaker, A., *Les douze petits prophètes* (Paris: Gabalda, 1908).

Horbury, W., 'The Messianic Associations of the "Son of Man", ' *JTS* 36 (1985) 34-55.

Horsley, R. A., *Sociology and the Jesus Movement* (New York: Crossroad, 1989).
Horsley, R. A., and Hanson, J. S., *Bandits, Prophets and Messiahs: Popular Movements at the Time of Jesus* (Minneapolis: Winston/Edinburgh: T&T Clarke, 1985).
Horstmann, M., *Studien zur Markinischen Christologie* NA 6 (Münster: Aschendorff, 1969).
Horton, F. L., Jr., *The Melchizedek Tradition* SNTSMS 30 (Cambridge: University, 1976).
Hoskyns, E. C., 'Jesus the Messiah' in *Mysterium Christi* ed. G. K. A. Bell and D. A. Deissmann (London: Longmans, 1930) 69-89.
Hoskyns, E. C., and Davey, N., *The Riddle of the New Testament* (London: Faber & Faber, 1947).
Howard, W. F., 'John the Baptist and Jesus: A Note on Evangelic Chronology' in *Amicitiae Corolla* FS. R. Harris, ed. H. G. Wood (London: University, 1933) 118-32.
Hubaut, M., 'Le "mystère" révélé dans les paraboles,' *RTL* 5 (1974) 454-61.
Huby, J., *L'évangile selon Saint Marc* VS 2 (Paris: Beauchesne, 1948).
Hugenberger, G.P., 'The Servant of the Lord in the "Servant Songs" of Isaiah: A Second Moses Figure' in *The Lord's Anointed*, eds. P. E. Satterthwaite, R. S. Hess, G. J. Wenham (Michigan: Baker; Carlisle: Paternoster, 1995) 105-40.
Hughes, J., 'John the Baptist: the Forerunner of God Himself,' *NovT* 14 (1972), 191-218.
Hultgard, A., 'The Ideal "Levite", the Davidic Messiah and the Saviour Priest in the Testaments of the Twelve Patriarchs' in *Ideal Figures in Ancient Judaism* ed. J. J. Collins and G. W. E. Nickelsburg, SBLSLS 12 (Chico: Scholars, 1980) 93-110.
Humbert, P., 'Le Messie dans le Targoum des Prophètes,' *RTP* 43, 44 (1910, 11) 420-447, 5-46.
Humphrey, H. M., 'Jesus as Wisdom in Mark,' *BTB* 19 (1989) 48-53.
Hunt, P. B. W. S., *Primitive Gospel Sources* (London, 1951).
Hunter, A. M., *Paul and his Predecessors* (rev. ed., London: SCM, 1961).
Huntress, E., '"Son of God" in Jewish Writings Prior to the Christian Era,' *JBL* 54 (1933) 117-23.
Huppenbauer, H. W., '*ṬHR* und *ṬHRh* in der Sektenregel von Qumran,' *ThZ* 13 (1957) 350-51.
Hurtado, L. W., *Mark* GNCS (San Francisco: Harper and Row, 1983).
____ *One God, One Lord: Early Christian Devotion and Ancient Jewish Monotheism* (London: SCM, 1988).
Hutton, W., 'The Kingdom of God has Come,' *ExpT* 64 (1952-3) 89-91.
Hyatt, J. P., *Exodus* NCB (London: Oliphants, 1971).

van Iersel, B., 'De betekenis van Marcus vanuit zijn topografische structuur,' *Tijdschrift voor Theologie* 22 (1982) 117-38.
____ 'Fils de David et fils de Dieu. La venue du Messie,' *ReichBibl* 6 (1962) 113-32.
____ 'Locality, Structure, and Meaning in Mark,' *LingBib* 53 (1983) 45-54.
____ 'Die wunderbare Speisung und das Abendmahl in der synoptischen Tradition,' *NovT* 7 (1964-5) 167-94.
____ 'The Reader of Mark as Operator of a System of Connotations,' *Semeia* 48 (1989) 83-114.
Instone-Brewer, D., *Techniques and Assumptions in Jewish Exegesis before 70 CE* TSAJ 30 (Tübingen: J. C. B. Mohr (Paul Siebeck), 1992).
Isbell, C. D., *Malachi* (Grand Rapids: Zondervan, 1980).

Jackson, F. and Lake, S., eds., *The Beginnings of Christianity*, part I; 5 vols., (London: Macmillan, 1920-33).
Janowski, B., and Lichtenberger, H., 'Enderwartung und Reinheitsidee: Zur eschatologischen Deutung von Reinheit und Sühne in der Qumrangemeinde,' *JJS* 34 (1983) 31-62.
Jellicoe, S., *The Septuagint and Modern Study* (Oxford: University, 1968).
Jenni, E., 'Die rolle des Kyros dei Deuterojesaja,' *TZ* 10 (1954) 241-56.
Jensen, J., *The Use of tôrâ by Isaiah* CBC Mono. 3 (Arlington, Va.: Information Products and Services Corp., 1973).
Jeremias, Joachim, 'Eckstein—Schlußstein,' *ZNTW* 36 (1937) 154-57.

____ *The Eucharistic Words of Jesus* trans. N. Perrin (Philadelphia: Fortress, 1966).

____ *Jerusalem in the Time of Jesus: An Investigation into Economic and Social Conditions During the New Testament Period* trans. F. H. and C. H. Cave (Philadelphia: Fortress, 1969).

____ 'Jesus and the Servant' review of M. D. Hooker, *Jesus and the Servant, JTS* 11 (1960) 140-44.

____ *Jesus' Promise to the Nations* trans. S. H. Hooke, SBT 24 (Philadelphia: Fortress, 1982).

____ *Jesus als Weltvollender* BFCT 33 (Gütersloh: 'Der Rufer' Evangelischer, 1929).

____ 'κεφαλὴ γωνίας—ἀκρωγωνιαῖος,' *ZNTW* 29 (1930) 264-80.

____ *New Testament Theology: The Preaching of Jesus* trans. J. Bowden (New York: Scribners, 1971).

____ *The Parables of Jesus* trans. S. H. Hooke (rev. ed., London: SCM, 1963).

____ *The Prayers of Jesus* (Philadelphia: Fortress, 1978).

Jeremias, Joachim, and Zimmerli, W.,*The Servant of God* (rev. ed., London: SCM, 1965).

Jeremias, Jorge, *Theophanie. Die Geschichte einer alttestamentlichen Gattung* WMANT 10 (Neukirchen: Neukirchener, 1977²).

Jervell, J., 'The Lost Sheep of Israel' in *Luke and the People of God* (Minneapolis: Augsburg, 1972) 113-32.

____ 'The Twelve on Israel's Thrones: Luke's Understanding of the Apostolate' in *Luke and the People of God* (Minneapolis: Augsburg, 1972) 75-112.

Johnson, D. G., *From Chaos to Restoration* JSOTSupp 61 (Sheffield: JSOT Press, 1988).

Johnson, E. S., 'Mark VIII.22-26: The Blind Man from Bethsaida,' *NTS* 25 (1978-79) 370-83.

____ 'Mark 10:46-52: Blind Bartimaeus,' *CBQ* 40 (1978) 191-204.

____ 'The Theme of Blindness and Sight in the Gospel of Mark', Ph.D. diss.: University of St. Andrews, 1976.

Johnson, S. E., *A Commentary on the Gospel According to St. Mark* (London: Adam & Charles Black, 1960).

Johnstone, W., 'YD' II, "Be Humbled, Humiliated"?,' *VT* 41 (1991) 49-62.

Jones, G. H., 'Abraham and Cyrus: type and anti-type?,' *VT* 22 (1972) 304-19.

Judge, E. A., 'Decrees of Caesar at Thessalonika,' *RTR* 30 (1971) 1-7.

Juel, D., *Messiah and Temple: The Trial of Jesus in the Gospel of Mark* SBLDS 31 (Missoula: Scholars Press, 1977).

____ *Messianic Exegesis. The Christological Interpretation of the Old Testament in Early Christianity* (Philadelphia: Fortress, 1988).

Jülicher, A., *Die Gleichnisreden Jesu* (Tübingen: Mohr, 1910 [1899]).

Kähler, M., *The So-Called Historical Jesus and the Historic, Biblical Christ* trans. C. E. Braaten (Philadelphia: Fortress Press, 1964).

Kaiser, O., *Isaiah 1-12, Isaiah 13-39* trans. R. A. Wilson, OTL (London: SCM, 1972², 1974²).

____ 'Die Verkündigung des Propheten Jesaja im Jahre 701,' *ZAW* 81 (1969) 304-15.

Kallas, J., *The Significance of Miracles in the Synoptic Gospels* (London: SPCK, 1961).

Kang, S.-M., *Divine War in the Old Testament and in the Ancient Near East* BZAW 177 (Berlin, New York: Walter de Gruyter, 1989).

Kapelrud, A. S., 'The Main Concern of Second Isaiah,' *VT* 32 (1982) 51-58.

Keck, L. E., *A Future for the Historical Jesus* (London: SCM, 1972).

____ 'The Introduction to Mark's Gospel,' *NTS* 12 (1966) 352-70.

____ 'Mk 3,7-12 and the Mark's Christology,' *JBL* 84 (1965) 341-58.

____ 'The Spirit and the Dove,' *NTS* 17 (1970-1) 41-67.

Kee, H. C., *Community of the New Age* NTL (London: SCM, 1977).

____ 'The Function of Scriptural Quotations and Allusions in Mark 11-16' in *Jesus und Paulus* eds. E. Earle Ellis and E. Grässer (Göttingen: Vandenhoeck & Ruprecht, 1975) 165-85.

____ 'Mark's Gospel in Recent Research,' *Int* 32 (1978) 353-68.

_____ *Medicine, Miracle and Magic in New Testament Times* (Cambridge: University, 1986).

_____ *Miracle in the Early Christian World* (New Haven and London: Yale University, 1983).

_____ 'The Terminology of Mark's Exorcism Stories,' *NTS* 14 (1967-8) 232-46.

Keegan, T. J., 'The Parable of the Sower and Mark's Jewish Leaders,' *CBQ* 56 (1994) 501-18.

Kelber, W. H., 'Apostolic Tradition and the Form of the Gospel' in *Discipleship in the New Testament* ed. Fernando F. Segovia (Philadelphia: Fortress, 1985) 24-46.

_____ *The Kingdom in Mark* (Philadelphia: Fortress, 1974).

_____ 'The Kingdom and Parousia in the Gospel of Mark' Ph.D. diss.: University of Chicago, 1970.

_____ *Mark's Story of Jesus* (Philadelphia: Fortress, 1979).

_____ *The Oral and Written Gospel* (Philadelphia: Fortress, 1983).

Keller, J., 'Jesus and the Critics: A Logico-Critical Analysis of the Marcan Confrontation,' *Int* 40 (1986) 29-38.

Kermode, F., *The Genesis of Secrecy: On the Interpretation of Narrative* (Cambrige, MA: Harvard, 1979).

Kertelge, K., 'Die Funktion der "Zwölf" im Markusevangelium: Eine redaktionsgeschichtliche Auslegung, zugliech ein Beitrag zur Frage nach dem neutestamentlichen Amtsverständnis,' *TTZ* 78 (1969) 193-206.

_____ *Die Wunder Jesu im Markusevangelium: Eine redaktionsgeschichtliche Untersuchung* SANT 23 (Munich: Kösel, 1970).

von Kienle, B., 'Mk 11:12-14:20-25: der verdorrte Feigenbaum,' *BibNot* 57 (1991) 17-25.

Kiesow, K., *Exodustexte im Jesajabuch: Literarkritische und motivegeschichtliche Analysen* (Göttingen: University/Vandenhoech & Ruprecht, 1979).

Kiilunen, J., *Die Vollmacht in Widersteit: Untersuchungen zum Werdegang von Mk 2,1-3,6.* (Helsinki: Suolmalainen Tiedeakatemia, 1985).

Kilian, R., '"Baut eine Strasse für unseren Gott!" Überlegungen zu Jes. 40,3-5' in *Künder und Wortes* FS J. Schreiner, ed. L. Ruppert *et al* (Würzburg: Echter, 1982) 53-60.

Kilpatrick, G. D., 'The Gentile Mission in Mark and Mark 13:9-11' in *Studies in the Gospels. Essays in Memory of R. H. Lightfoot* ed. D. E. Nineham (Oxford: Blackwell, 1955) 145-58.

_____ 'The Order of Some Noun and Adjective Phrases in the New Testament,' *NovT* 5 (1962) 112-13.

_____ 'The Punctuation of John VII. 37-8,' *JTS* 11 (1960) 340-41.

Kim, J. C., *Verhältnis Jahwes zu den anderen Göttern in Deuterojesaja* diss.: Heildelberg, 1962.

Kim, S., 'Jesus and the Temple,' *ACTS Theological Journal* 3 (1988) 87-131.

_____ *'The "Son of Man"' as the Son of God* WUNT 30 (Tübingen: J. C. B. Mohr (Paul Siebeck), 1983).

Kingsbury, J. D., *The Christology of Mark's Gospel* (Philadelpia: Fortress, 1983).

_____ *Conflict in Mark* (Minneapolis: Fortress, 1989).

_____ 'The Religious Authorities in the Gospel of Mark,' *NTS* 36 (1990) 42-65.

Kinman, B., *Jesus' Entry into Jerusalem: In the Context of Lukan Theology and the Politics of His Day* (Leiden: Brill, 1995).

Kirkland, J. R., 'The Earliest Understanding of Jesus' Use of Parables: Mark IV 10-12 In Context,' *NovT* 19 (1976-7) 1-21.

Kirkpatrick, A. F., *The Book of Psalms* (Cambridge: University, 1902).

Kissane, E. J., *The Book of Isaiah* 2 vols. (Dublin: Brown and Nolan, 1941, 43).

_____ *The Book of the Psalms* 2 vols. (Dublin: Brown and Nolan, 1953, 54).

Kitchen, K. A., 'The Fall and Rise of Covenant, Law and Treaty,' *TynBul* 40 (1989) 118-135.

Kittel, B., *The Hymns of Qumran* SBLDS 50 (Chico: Scholars, 1981).

Kiuchi, N., *The Purification Offering in the Priestly Literature* JSOTSupp 56 (Sheffield: JSOT, 1987).

Klauck, H.-J., *Allegorie und Allegorese in synoptischen Gleichnistexten* (Münster: Aschendorf, 1978).

____ 'Die erzählerische Rolle der Jünger im Markusevangelium. Eine narrative Analyse,' *NovT* 24 (1982) 1-26.

____ 'Die Frage der Sündenvergebung in der Perikope von der Heilung des Gelähmten,' *BZ* 25 (1981) 223-48.

Klausner, J., *The Messianic Idea in Israel* trans. W. F. Stinespring (New York: MacMillan, 1955).

Kline, M., 'The Old Testament Origins of the Gospel Genre,' *WTJ* 38 (1975-76) 1-27.

Klinzing, G., *Die Umdeutung des Kultus in der Qumrangemeinde und im Neuen Testament* SUNT 7 (Göttingen: Vandenhoeck & Ruprecht, 1971).

Klostermann, E., *Das Markus Evangelium* HNT 3 (Tübingen: Mohr, 1940[4]).

____ *Das Matthäusevangelium* HNT 4 (Tübingen: Mohr, 1938[3]).

Knibb, M. A., 'Commentary on 2 Esdras' in R. J. Coggins and M. A. Knibb *The First and Second Books of Esdras* (Cambridge: University, 1979) 76-307.

____ 'The Date of the Parables of Enoch: A Critical Review,' *NTS* 25 (1978-79) 344-57.

____ *The Ethiopic Book of Enoch* 2 vols. (Oxford: University, 1978).

Knierim, R., 'The Vocation of Isaiah,' *VT* 18 (1968), 47-68.

Knigge, H.-D., 'The Meaning of Mark,' *Int* 22 (1968) 53-70.

Knight, G. A. F., *Theology as Narration: A Commentary on Exodus* (Edinburgh: Handsel, 1976).

Knox, J., 'The "Prophet" in the New Testament Christology' in *Lux in Lumine: Essays to Honor W. Norman Pittenger* ed. R. A. Norris (New York: Seabury, 1966) 23-34.

Koch, D. A., 'Inhaltliche Gliederung und geographischer Aufriss im Markusevangelium,' *NTS* (1983) 145-66.

____ *Die Bedeutung der Wundererzählungen für die Christologie des Markus-Evangeliums* BZNW 42 (Berlin/New York: de Gruyter, 1975).

____ *Die Schrift als Zeuge des Evangeliums* (Tübingen: J.C.B. Mohr (Paul Siebeck), 1984).

Koch, K., 'Messias und Sündenvergebung in Jesaja 53 - Targum,' *JSJ* 3 (1972) 117-48.

____ 'Die Stellung des Kyuros im Geschichtsbild Deuterojesajas und ihre überlieferungsgeschichtliche Verankerung,' *ZAW* 84 (1972) 352-56.

Koester, H., 'One Jesus and Four Primitive Gospels,' *HTR* 61 (1968) 203-47.

Koch, R., 'Der Gottesgeist und der Messias,' *Bib* 27 (1946) 396-401.

Köhler, L., *Deuterojesaja (40-55) stilistisch untersucht* BZAW 37 (Giessen: Töpelmann, 1923).

____ *Hebrew Man* (New York: Abingdon, 1946).

____ *Old Testament Theology* (Philadelphia: Westminster, 1957).

Kolenkow, A. B., 'Beyond Miracles, Suffering and Eschatology (on the purpose of Mark)' in *SBL Seminar Papers* vol. 2, ed. G. MacRae (Cambridge, MA.: SBL, 1973) 155-202.

____ 'Relationships between Miracle and Prophecy in the Greco-Roman World and Early Christianity' in *ANRW* II. 23.2, 1470-1506.

Koole, J. L., 'De beeldenstorm van deuterojesaja' in *Loven en geloven*, opstellen aangeboden aan Prof. Dr. Nic. H. Ridderbos, (Amsterdam, 1975).

Kraeling, C. H., *John the Baptist* (New York/London: Scribner's, 1951).

Kraus, D., 'Narrated Prophecy in Mark 11.12-21: The Divine Authorization of Judgment' in *The Gospels and the Scriptures of Israel* eds. C. A. Evans and W. R. Stegner, JSNTSupp 104, SSEJC 3 (Sheffield: Academic, 1994) 235-48.

Kraus, H-J., 'Die ausgebliebene Endtheophanie: Eine Studie zu Jes 56-66,' *ZAW* 78 (1966) 317-32.

____ *Psalmen* BKAT 15, 2 vols. (Neukircken-Vluyn: Neukirchener, 1978).

____ *Worship in Israel* (Oxford, 1966).

Kremer, J., 'Jesu Wandel auf dem See nach Mk 6,45-52,' *BibLeb* 10 (1969) 221-32.

Krupp, K., *Das Verhältnis Jahwe-Israel im Sinne eines Ehebundes* diss.: Freiburg, 1972.

Kruse, H., 'Das Reich Satans,' *Bib* 58 (1977) 29-61.

Kuby, A., 'Zur Konzeption des Markus-Evangeliums,' *ZNW* 49 (1958) 52-64.

Kuhn, K. G., 'The Two Messiahs of Aaron and Israel' in *The Scrolls and the New Testament* ed. K. Stendahl (rev. ed., London: SCM, 1958) 54-64.

Kümmel, W. G., *Heilsgeschehen und Geschichte. Gesammlte Aufsätze 1933-* MTS 3/16 eds. E. Grässer, O. Merk und A. Fritz (Marburg: Elwert, 1963).

_____ *Introduction to the New Testament* trans. K. C. Kee (rev. ed., New York and Nashville: Abingdon, 1973).

_____ *Verheissung und Erfüllung* (Zürich: Zwingli, 1956³), ET *Promise and Fulfilment: The Eschatological Message of Jesus* SBT 23 trans. D. M. Barton (London: SCM, 1957).

Kuthirakkattel, S., *The Beginning of Jesus' Ministry According to Mark's Gospel (1,14-3,6): A Redactional Critical Study* AnBib 36 (Rome: Pontifico Istituto Biblico, 1990).

Kutsch, E., 'Das sog. "Bundesblut" in Ex XXIV 8 und Sach IX 11,' *VT* 23 (1973) 25-30.

Lack, R., *La Symbolique du Livre d'Isaïe* AnBib 59 (Rome: Biblical Institute Press, 1973).

Lagrange, M.-J., *L'evangile selon Saint Marc* (rev. ed., Paris: Gabalda, 1947).

_____ 'Le but des paraboles d'après l'Evangile selon Saint Marc,' *RB* 7 (1910) 5-35.

_____ 'Notes sur les prophètes messianiques des derniers prophètes,' *RB* 15 (1906) 67-83.

Lamarche, P., 'Les Miracles de Jésus selon Marc' in *Les Miracles de Jésus selon le Nouveau Testament* ed. X. Léon-Dufour (Paris: Seuil, 1977) 213-26.

Lambrecht, J., *Once More Astonished: The Parables of Jesus* (New York: Crossroad, 1981).

_____ 'Redaction and Theology in Mk. IV' in *L'Évangile selon Marc: tradition et Rédaction* ed. M. Sabbe, BETL 34 (Louvain: University, 1974) 269-307.

_____ 'The Relatives of Jesus in Mark,' *NovT* 16 (1974) 241-58.

Lampe, G. W. H., 'The Holy Spirit in the writings of St Luke' in *Studies in the Gospels: Essays in memory of R. H. Lightfoot* ed. D. E. Nineham (Oxford: Blackwell, 1955) 159-200.

_____ *The Seal of the Spirit: A Study in the Doctrine of Baptism and Confirmation in the New Testament and the Fathers* (London: SPCK, 1967²).

Lane, W. L., *The Gospel of Mark* NICNT 2 (Grand Rapids: Eerdmans, 1974).

Lampe, P., 'Die markinsiche Deutung des Gleichnisses vom Sämann Markus 4:10-12,' *ZNW* 65-66 (1974-5) 140-50.

_____ 'A New Commentary Structure in 4QFlorilegium,' *JBL* 78 (1959) 343-46.

_____ 'The Present State of Markan Studies' in *The Gospels Today. A Guide to Some Recent Developments* ed. J. H. Skilton *et al.* (Philadelphia: Skilton House, 1990).

Lang, F. G., 'Kompositionsanalyse des Markusevangelium,' *ZTK* 74 (1977) 1-24.

_____ '"Über Sidon mitten ins Gebiet der Dekapolis" Geographie und Theologie in Markus 7,31,' *ZDPV* 94 (1978) 145-60.

Langdon, E., *The Essentials of Demonology* (London, 1949).

Larfeld. W., *Die neutestamentliche Evangelien nach ihrer Eigenart und Abhängigkeit* (Gütersloh: Bertelsmann, 1925).

LaRondelle, H. K., *The Israel of God in Prophecy* (Michigan: Andrews University, 1983).

Lash, N., 'Ideology, Metaphor and Analogy' in *The Philosophical Frontiers of Christian Theology* eds. Hebblethwaite and Sutherland (Cambridge: University Press, 1982) 68-94.

Laudan, L., 'William Whewell on the Consilience of Inductions,' *The Monist* 55 (1971) 368-91.

LaVerdiere, E. A., 'Feed My Sheep: Eucharistic Tradition in Mark 6:34-44' in *Bread from Heaven*, ed. P. Bernier (New York: Paulist, 1977) 45-58.

Leaney, A. R. C., 'The Gospels Evidence for First-Century Judaism' in D. E. Nineham *et al. Historicity and Chronology in the NT* TC 6 (London: SPCK 1965) 28-45.

_____ *The Rule of Qumran and Its Meaning* NTL (London: SCM, 1966).

Leenhardt, F. J., *Le Baptême Chrétien: son Origine, sa Signification* (Neuchatel and Paris: Delachaux & Niestlé, 1946).

Legasse, S., 'L'„Homme fort" de Luc. xi 21-22,' *NovT* 5 (1962) 5-9.

Leivestad, R., *Christ the Conqueror* (London: SPCK, 1954).

Lemcio, E. E., 'External Evidence for the Structure and Function of Mark iv. 1-20, vii. 14-23 and viii. 14-21,' *JTS* 29 (1978) 323-38.

____ 'The Intention of the Evangelist, Mark,' *NTS* 32 (1986) 187-206.

Lenglet, A., 'The structure littéraire de Daniel 2-7,' *Bib* 53 (1972) 169-90.

Lentzen-Deis, F., *Die Taufe Jesu nach den Synoptikern* FTS 4 (Frankfurt: Knecht, 1970).

Leupold, H. C., *Isaiah* (reprint, Welwyn, England: Evangelical Press, 1977).

Levey, S. H., *The Messiah: An Aramaic Interpretation. The Messianic Exegesis of the Targum* MHUC 2 (New York: Hebrew Union College, 1974).

Lichteim, M., *Ancient Egyptian Literature, vol.1: The Old and Middle Kingdoms* 3 vols. (Berkeley *et al.*: University of California Press, 1973).

Liebreich, L. J., 'The Position of Chapter Six in the Book of Isaiah,' *HUCA* 25 (1954) 37-40.

Lightfoot, R. H., *The Gospel Message of St. Mark* (Oxford, 1950).

____ *History and Interpretation in the Gospels* (London: Hodder and Stoughton, 1934).

____ *Locality and Doctrine* (London: Hodder and Stoughton, 1938).

Limbeck, M., 'Beelzebul—eine ursprüngliche Bezeichnung für Jesus?' in *Wort Gottes in der Zeit* FS H. Schelkle (Düsseldorf: Patmos, 1973) 31-42.

Lind, M. C., *Yahweh is a Warrior* (Cambridge, MA: Harvard, 1980).

Lindars, B., 'Elijah, Elisha and the Gospel Miracles' in *Miracles* ed. C. F. D. Moule (London: Mowbray, 1965) 63-79.

____ 'Good Tidings in Zion: Interpreting Deutero-Isaiah Today,' *BJRL* 68 (1986) 473-97.

____ *New Testament Apolgetic: The Doctrinal Significance of the Old Testament Quotations* (London: SCM, 1961).

____ *Jesus Son of Man* (London: SPCK, 1983).

____ 'Salvation Proclaimed: VII. Mark 10[45]: A Ransom for Many,' *ExpT* 93 (1981-2) 292-95.

Lindblom, J., 'Wisdom in the Old Testament Prophets' in *Wisdom in Israel and the Ancient Near East* eds. M. Noth and D. Winton Thomas, FS H. H. Rowley, SuppVT3 (1955) 192-204.

Lindeskog, G., 'Logia-Studien,' *ST* 4 (1950) 129-84.

Loader, B., 'The New Dea Sea Scrolls: New Light on Messianism and the History of the Community,' *Colloq* 25 (1993) 67-85.

von Loewanclau, I., 'Zur Auslegung von Jesaja 1, 2-3,' *EvT* 26 (1966) 294-308.

Loewenstamm, S. E., *The Evolution of the Exodus Tradition* trans. B. J. Schwartz (Jerusalem: Magnes, 1992).

Lohmeyer, E., *Das Evangelium des Markus. Übersetzt und erklärt* KKNT 1,2 (Göttingen: Vandenhoeck & Ruprecht, 1953).

____ *Das Evangelium des Matthäus* (rev. by W. Schauch, Göttingen: Vandenhoeck & Ruprecht, 1967).

____ *Galiläa und Jerusalem* (Göttingen, 1936).

____ *Lord of the Temple: A Study of the Relation Between Cult and Gospel* trans. S. Todd (Edinburgh-London: Oliver & Boyd, 1962).

____ 'Die Reinigung des Tempels,' *ThBl* 20 (1941) 257-64.

Lohse, E., *Märtyrer und Gottesknecht. Untersuchungen zur urchristlichen Verkündigung vom Sühntod Jesu Christ* FRLANT 64 (Göttingen: Vandenhoeck & Ruprecht, 1963[2]).

Loisy, A., *The Birth of the Christian Religion* trans. L. P. Jacks (London: Allen & Unwin, 1948).

____ *Les Evangels Synoptiques* 2 vols. (Paris, 1907).

Longenecker, R., *Biblical Exegesis in the Apostolic Period* (Eerdmans, 1975).

Longman, T., III, 'The Divine Warrior: The New Testament Use of an Old Testment Motif,' *WTJ* 44 (1982) 290-307.

Longman, T., and Reid, D. G., *God is a Warrior* SOTBT (Grand Rapids: Zondervan, 1995).

van der Loos, H., *The Miracles of Jesus* NovTSupp 9 (Leiden: E. J. Brill, 1968).

Louw, J., 'De bezetene en de kudde, Marc 5:1-20. Een hypothese,' *NTT* 13 (1958-9) 59-61, [see NTA 3, 1959, # 591]

Love, J. P., 'The Call of Isaiah,' *Int* 11 (1957) 282-296.

Lövestam, E., 'Jésus Fils et David chez les Synoptiques,' *StTh* 28 (1974) 97-109.

_____ *Son and Saviour. A Study of Acts 13, 32-37* trans. M. J. Petry *ConNT* XVIII (Lund-Copenhagen: G. W. K. Gleerup and Ejnar Munksgaard, 1961).

_____ *Spiritus Blasphemia* (Lund: Gleerup, 1968).

Lubsczyk, J. R., *Der Auszug aus Egypten, seine theologische Bedeutung in prophetischer und priestlischer Überlieferung* ETS 11 (Leipzig, 1963).

Lührmann, D., 'Biographie des Gerechten als Evangelium' in *Wort und Dienst* 14 (1977) 25-50.

_____ 'Markus 14.53-64: Christologie und Zerstörung des Tempels im Markusevangelium,' *NTS* 27 (1980-1) 457-75.

_____ *Das Markusevangelium* HNT 3 (Tübingen: J. C. B. Mohr (Paul Siebeck), 1987).

Luz, U., 'Das Geheimnismotiv und die markinische Christologie,' *ZNW* 56 (1965) 9-30.

MacIntrye, A., *Against the Self Images of the Age* (NY: Schloken Books, 1971).

MacLaurin, E. C. B., 'Beelzeboul,' *NovT* 20 (1978) 156-60.

McCarthy, D. J., 'Covenant in the Old Testament: the Present State of Inquiry,' *CBQ* 27 (1965) 217-40.

McCasland, S. V., 'Signs and Wonders,' *JBL* 76 (1957) 149-52.

_____ '"The Way",' *JBL* 77 (1958) 222-30.

McCurley, F. R., '"And After Six Days" (Mark 9:2): A Semitic Literary Device,' *JBL* 93 (1974) 67-81.

McKane, W., *Jeremiah* vol. 1 ICC (Edinburgh: T. & T. Clarke, 1986).

_____ *Prophets and Wise Men* SBT 1/44 (London: SCM, 1965).

McKelvey, R. J., *The New Temple* OTM 3 (Oxford: University, 1969).

McKenzie, S. L., *Second Isaiah* AB 20 (Garden City, New York: Double Day, 1968).

McKenzie, S. L., and Wallace, H. N., 'Covenant Themes in Malachi,' *CBQ* 45 (1983) 549-63.

McLellan, D., *Ideology* (Minneapolis: University of Minnesota Press) 1986.

Maag, V., *Malkût YHWH* VTSup 7 (Leiden: Brill, 1960).

Mack, B. L., *A Myth of Innocence: Mark and Christian Origins* (Philadelphia: Fortress, 1988).

Maillot, A., 'Essai sur les citations vétérotestamentaires contenues dans Romains 9 à 11, ou comment se servir de la torah pour montrer que le "Christ est la fin de la Torah",' *ETR* 57 (1982) 55-73.

Maisch, I. M., *Die Heilung des Gelähmten. Eine exegetisch-traditionsgeschichtliche Unter-suchung zu Mk 2,1-12* SBS 52 (Stuttgart: Katholisches Bibelwerk, 1971).

Malbon, E. S., 'Disciples/Crowds/Whoever: Markan Characters and Readers,' *NovT* 28 (1986) 104-30.

_____ 'Echoes and Foreshadowings in Mark 4-8: Reading and Rereading,' *JBL* 112 (1993) 211-30.

_____ 'Fallible Followers: Women and Men in the Gospel of Mark,' *Semeia* 28 (1983) 29-48.

_____ 'Galilee and Jerusalem,' *CBQ* 44 (1982) 242-55.

_____ 'The Jewish Leaders in the Gospel of Mark: A Literary Study of Marcan Character-ization,' *JBL* 108 (1989) 259-81.

_____ *Narrative Space and Mythic Meaning in Mark* (New York: Harper and Row, 1986).

_____ 'Text and Contexts: Interpreting the Disciples in Mark,' *Semeia* 62 (1993) 81-102.

Malchow, B. V., 'The Messenger of the Covenant in Mal. 3:1,' *JBL* 103 (1984) 252-55.

Malina, B., *The New Testament World: Insights from Cultural Anthropology* (Atlanta: John Knox, 1981).

Maloney, F. E., 'The Vocation of the Disciples in the Gospel of Mark,' *Salesianum* 43 (1981) 487-516.

Manek, J., 'The New Exodus in the Books of Luke,' *NovT* 2 (1955) 8-23.

Mann, C. S., *Mark* AB 27 (Garden City, New York: Doubleday, 1986).

Mann, J., *The Bible as Read and Preached in the Old Synagogue* 2 vols. (Cincinatti: Jewish Publication Society, 1940; Maurice Jacobs, 1966).

Mannheim, K., *Ideology and Utopia* trans. L. Wirth and E. Shils (London: Routeledge and Kegan Paul, 1936).

Manning, D. J.,, 'Ideology and Political Reality,' in *The Structure of Modern Ideology* ed. N. O'Sullivan (Brookfield, VN: Gower, 1989) 54-88.

Mansfield, M. R., *'Spirit and Gospel' in Mark* (Peabody, Mass.: Hendrickson, 1987).

Manson, T. W., '2 Cor. 2: 14-17: Suggestions Towards an Exegesis' in *Studia Paulina in honorem J. de Zwaan* eds. J. N. Sevenster and W. C. van Unnik (Haarlem: Bohn, 1953) 155-62.

_____ 'The Old Testament in the Teaching of Jesus,' *BJRL* 34 (1951-52) 312-32.

_____ *The Sayings of Jesus* (reprint, London: SCM, 1950).

_____ *The Teaching of Jesus* (Cambridge: University, 1948).

Manson, W., *Jesus the Messiah* (London: Hodder and Stoughton, 1943).

_____ 'Mark 4;10-12,' *ExpT* 68 (1956-57) 132-35.

Marcus, J., 'Mark 4:10-12 and Marcan Epistemology,' *JBL* 103 (1984) 557-74.

_____ 'Mark 9,11 - 13: "As It Has Been Written",' *ZNW* 80 (1989) 42-83.

_____ *The Mystery of the Kingdom of God* SBLDS 90 (Atlanta: Scholars, 1986).

_____ *The Way of the Lord: Christological Exegesis of the Old Testament in the Gospel of Mark* (Louisville, Kentucky: Westminster/John Knox, 1992).

Marshall, C. D., *Faith as a Theme in Mark's Gospel* SNTSMS 64 (Cambridge: Univ., 1989).

Marshall, I. H., 'An Assessment of Recent Developments' in *It Is Written: Scripture Citing Scripture, Essays in Honour of Barnabas Lindars SSF* eds. Carson and Williamson (Cambridge: University, 1988) 1-21.

_____ *The Gospel of Luke* NIGTC (Grand Rapids: Eerdmans, 1978).

_____ *Last Supper and Lord's Supper* (Grand Rapids: Eerdmans, 1980).

_____ 'Son of God or Servant of Yahweh? - A Reconsideration of Mark 1:11,' *NTS* 15 (1968-69) 326-36.

Marti, D. K., *Das Dodekapropheton* KHAT XIII (Tübingen: Mohr, 1904).

Martin, R. P., *Mark: Evangelist and Theologian* (Grand Rapids: Zondervan, 1972).

Martin-Achard, R., 'Sagesse de dieu et sagesse humaine chez ésaie' in *Hommage a Wilhelm Vischer* (Montpellier: Causse Graille Castelnau, 1960).

Martínez, F. G., 'Nuevos Textos Mesiánicos de Qumran y el Mesías del Nuevo Testamento,' *Cmio* 26 (1993) 3-31.

_____ 'Salmos Aprócrifos en Qumran,' *EstBib* 40 (1982) 197-220, [see NTA 28, 1975, # 747].

Martyn, J. L., *History and Theology in the Fourth Gospel* (New York: Harper and Row, 1968).

Marxsen, W., *Der Evangelist Markus: Studein zur Redaktionsgeschichte des Evangeliums* FRLANT 49 (Göttingen: Vandenhoeck & Ruprecht, 1959[2]); ET: *Mark the Evangelist: Studies on the Redaction History of the Gospel* trans J. Boyce *et al* (New York/Nashvile: Abingdon, 1969).

Mason, R., *Preaching the Tradition* (Cambridge: University, 1990).

Masuda, S., 'The Good News of the Miracle of the Bread,' *NTS* 28 (1982) 191-219.

Matera, F. J., 'The Incomprehension of the Disciples and Peter's Confession (Mark 6,14-8,30),' *Biblica* 70 (1989) 153-172.

_____ 'Interpreting Mark—Some recent theories of Redaction Criticism,' *LouvStud* 2 (1968) 113-31.

_____ *The Kingship of Jesus* SBLDS 66 (Chico: Scholars, 1982).

_____ 'The Prologue as the Interpretative Key to Mark's Gospel,' *JSNT* 34 (1988) 3-20.

Maurer, C., 'Knecht Gottes und Sohn Gottes im Passionsbericht des Markusevangeliums,' *ZTK* 50 (1953) 1-38.

Mauser, U., *Christ in the Wilderness: The Wilderness Theme in the Second Gospel and Its Basis in the Biblical Tradition* SBT 39 (London: SCM, 1963).

May, D. M., 'Mark 3:20-35 from the Perspective of Shame/Honor,' *BTB* 17 (1987) 83-7.

Mayer, R., 'Der Anfang des Evangeliums in Galiläa,' *BibKirch* 36 (1981) 213-21.
Meagher, J. C., *Clumsy Construction in Mark's Gospel. A Critique of Form- and Redaktions-geschichte* TST 3 (Toronto: Edwin Mellen, 1979).
Mearns, C. L., 'Dating the Similitudes of Enoch,' *NTS* 25 (1978-79) 360-69.
Meeks, W. A., *The Prophet-King. Moses Traditions and the Johannine Christology* NovTSup 14 (Leiden: Brill, 1967).
Melugin, R. F., *The Formation of Isaiah 40-55* (Berlin, New York: Walter de Gruyter, 1976).
_____ 'Isaiah 52:7-10,' *Int* 36 (1982) 176-81.
Mendels, D., 'Pseudo-Philo's *Biblical* Antiquities, the "Fourth Philosophy," and the Political Messianism of the First Century C.E.' in *The Messiah* ed. J. H. Charlesworth (Minneapolis: Fortress, 1992) 261-75.
Menoud, Ph. H., 'La signification du miracle dans le Nouveau Testament,' *RThPh* 48-9 (1948-9) 173-92.
Merrill, E. H., 'The Language and Literary Characteristics of Isaiah 40-55 as Anti-Babylonian Polemic', PhD. diss.: Columbia University, 1984.
van der Merwe, B. J., *Pentateuchtradisies in die prediking van Deuterojesaja* diss.: Groningen, 1955.
Meszaros, I., *Philosophy, Ideology and Social Science* (Brighton, UK: Wheatsheaf, 1986).
Mettinger, T., *A Farewell to the Servant Songs* (Lund: CWK Gleerup, 1983).
_____ 'YHWH SABAOTH—The Heavenly King in the Cherubim Throne' in *Studies in the Period of David and Solomon and Other Essays*, ed. T. Ishida (Winona Lake, Indiana: Eisenbrauns, 1982) 109-38.
Metzger, B. M., 'The Formulas Introducing Quotations of Scripture in the NT and the Mishnah,' *JBL* 70 (1951) 297-307.
_____ *A Textual Commentary on the Greek New Testament* (corrected ed., London: Bible Societies, 1975).
_____ *The Text of the New Testament: Its Transmission, Corruption, and Restoration* (Oxford: University, 1992³).
Meye, R. P., *Jesus and the Twelve. Discipleship and Revelation in Mark's Gospel* (Grand Rapids: Eerdmans, 1968).
_____ 'Mark 4, 10: "Those About Him with the Twelve"' in *StEv* 2 (1964) 211-18.
_____ 'Psalm 107 as "Horizon" for Interpreting the Miracle Stories of Mark 4:35-8:26' in *Unity and Diversity in New Testament Theology: Essays in Honor of George E. Ladd* ed. R. A. Guelich (Grand Rapids: Eerdmans, 1978) 1-13.
Meyer, A., 'Die Entstehung des Markusevangeliums' in *Festgabe für Adolf Jülicher* (Tübingen: Mohr, 1927) 35-60.
Meyer, B. F., 'The Expiation Motif in the Eucharistic Words: A Key to the History of Jesus?,' *Gregorianum* 69 (1988) 461-87.
Meyer, H. A. W., *Critical and Exegetical Handbook to the Gospel of Mark and Luke* I (Edinburgh: T. & T. Clarke, 1880).
Meynet, R., 'Qui donc est "le plus fort"? Analuse thetorique de Mc 3, 22-30; Mt 12, 22-37; Lc 11, 14-26,' *RB* 90 (1983) 334-50.
Michaelis, W., *Engelchristologie im Urchristentum* GBT 1 (Basel: Mäjer, 1942).
_____ *Das Evangelium nach Matthäus* 2 Teil. (Zürich: Zwingli, 1948-9).
Michaels, J. R., *Servant and Son: Jesus in Parable and Gospel* (Atlanta: John Knox, 1981).
Michel, O., 'Eine philologische Frage zur Einzugsgeschichte,' *NTS* 6 (1959-60) 81-82.
_____ *Paulus und seine Bibel* BFCT 2/18 (Gütersloh: Bertelsmann, 1929).
Michel, O., and Betz, O., 'Von Gott gezeugt' in *Judentum, Urchristentum, Kirche* FS J. Jeremias, hrsg. W. Eltester BZNW 26 (Berlin: Topelmann, 1960) 3-32.
Milavec, A., 'The Identity of "The Son" and "The Others": Mark's Parable of the Wicked Husbandmen Reconsidered,' *BTB* 20 (1990) 30-37.
Milgrom, J., *Cult and Conscience: The Asham and the Priestly Doctrine of Repentance* SJLA (Leiden: Brill, 1976).
_____ *Levitcus* AB 3 (New York: Doubleday, 1991).

Milik, J. T., '*Milkî-ṣedeq* et *Milkî-reša*' dans les anciens écrits juifs et chrétiens,' *JJS* 23 (1972) 95-144.

Milikowsky, C., '*ʾlyhw whmšyḥ* (Elijah and the Messiah),' *JSJT* 2 (1982-3) 491-96.

_____ '*Sdr-ʿwlm whtwspt*' (*Seder ʿOlam* and the Tosefta),' *Tarbiz* 49 (1980) 246-63.

Miller, J. W., 'Prophetic Conflict in Second Isaiah' in *Wort-Gebot-Glaube* ed. H. J. Stoebe (Zürich: Zwingli, 1971) 77-85.

Miller, P. D., 'The Divine Council and the Prophetic Call to War,' *VT* 18 (1968) 100-7.

_____ *The Divine Warrior in Early Israel* HSM 5 (Cambridge, MA: Harvard, 1973).

_____ 'Faith and Ideology in the Old Testament' in *Magnalia Dei: The Mighty Acts of God* eds. F. M. Cross, W. E. Lemke and P. D. Miller Jr. (New York, 1976) 464-79.

Miller, D., and Miller, P., *The Gospel of Mark as Midrash on Earlier Jewish and New Testament Literature* SBEC 21 (Lewiston, N.Y.: Edwin Mellen, 1990).

Minear, P. S., 'Audience Criticism and Markan Ecclesiology' in *Neues Testament und Geschichte* (Zürich/Tübingen: J. C. B. Mohr (Paul Siebeck), 1972) 79-89.

Minette de Tillesse, G., *Le secret messianique dans l'Évangile de Marc* LD 47 (Paris: Cerf, 1968).

Montefiore, C., 'Rabbinic Conceptions of Repentance,' *JQR* 16 (1903-4) 209-57.

Moo, D. J., *The Old Testament in the Gospel Passion Narratives* (Sheffield: Almond, 1983).

_____ 'Tradition and the Old Testament in Matt. 27: 3-10' in *Gospel Perspectives* 3 eds. R. T. France and D. Wenham (Sheffield: JSOT, 1983) 157-75.

Moore, C. A., 'Mark 4:12: More Like the Irony of Micaiah than Isaiah' in *A Light unto My Path* GTS 4 FS J. M. Myers ed. H. N. Bream *et al* (Philadelphia: Temple, 1974) 335-44.

Moore, G. F., *Judaism* 3 vols. (Cambridge: Harvard, 1932).

Morgenstern, J., 'Deutero-Isaiah's Terminology for Universal God,' *JBL* 62 (1943) 269-80.

Morris, L., *The Gospel According to John* NIC (Grand Rapids: Eerdmans, 1971).

_____ 'The Gospels and Jewish Lectionaries' in *Gospel Perspectives* 3 eds. R. T. France and D. Wenham (Sheffield: JSOT, 1983) 129-56.

_____ *The New Testament and Jewish Lectionaries* (London: Tyndale, 1964).

Mosley, A. W., 'Jesus' Audiences in the Gospels of St Mark and St Luke,' *NTS* 10 (1963) 139-49.

Moulder, W. J., 'The Old Testament Background and the Interpretation of Mark x. 45,' *NTS* 24 (1978) 120-27.

Moule, C. F. D., 'Fulfilment-Words in the New Testament, Use and Abuse,' *NTS* 14 (1967-8) 293-320.

_____ *The Gospel According to Mark* CBC (Cambridge: University, 1965).

_____ 'Mark 4:1-20 Yet Once More' in *Neotestimentica et Semetica* FS M. Black, eds. E. Ellis and M. Wilcox (Edinburgh: T. & T. Clark, 1969) 95-113.

_____ '"The Son of Man": Some of the Facts,' *NTS* 41 (1995) 277-79.

Mowinckel, S., *He That Cometh* trans. G. W. Anderson (Oxford: Blackwell, 1956).

_____ 'Die Komposition des deuterojesajanischen Buches,' *ZAW* 49 (1931) 87-112, 242-260.

_____ *Psalmenstudien* Bd. 1-6 (Oslo: Kristiane, 1921-24).

_____ *The Psalms in Israel's Worship*, 2 vols, trans. D. R. Ap-Thomas (Oxford: Blackwells, 1962).

Mühlmann, W. E., *Chiliasmus und Nativismus. Studien zur Psychologie, Soziologie und historischen Kasuistik der Umsturzbewegungen. Studien zur Soziologie der Revolution* vol. 1 (Berlin: Dietrich Reimer, 1961).

Muilenburg, J., 'The Book of Isaiah,' *IB* vol 5 (New York/Nashville: Abingdon, 1956) 381-773.

Müller, D., *Die Propheten in ihrer ursprünglichen Form* (Vienna: Hölder, 1896).

Müller, M., *Der Ausdruck 'Menschensohn' in der Evangelium. Voraussetzungen und Bedeutung* ATD 17 (Leiden: Brill, 1984).

Mullins, W. A., 'On the Concept of Ideology in Political Science,' *American Political Science Review* 66 (1972) 498-510.

Mußner, F., 'Die Bedeutung und Heilsgeschichte: Dargetan am Gleichnis von der selbtswachsenden Saat (Mk. 4,26-29),' *TTZ* 64 (1955) 257-66.

_____ 'Gottesherrschaft und Sendung Jesu nach Mk 1,14f.: Zugleich ein Beitrag über die inner Struktur des Markusevangeliums' in ed. F. Mußner *Praesentia Salutis: Gesammelte Studien zu Fragen und Themen des Neuen Testaments* (Düsseldorf: Patmos, 1967) 81-91.

Myers, C., *Binding the Strong Man. A Political Reading of Mark's Story of Jesus* (New York: Orbis, 1988).

Myers, J. M., *I and II Esdras* AB 42 (Garden City: Doubleday, 1974).

Myhre, K., 'Paktens blod i vinordet. En undersokelse av herspillingen på Ex 24,8 i Mark 14,24 / Matt 26,28,' *TidsTheolKirk* 55 (1984) 271-86, [see NTA 29, 1985, # 964].

Neusner, J., 'Geschichte und rituelle Reinheit im Judentum des 1. Jahrhunderts n. Chr.,' *Kairos* 21 (1979) 119-32.

_____ ed., with W. S. Green and E. Frerichs, *Judaisms and Their Messiahs at the Turn of the Christian Era* (Cambridge: Univ., 1987).

_____ *Messiah in Context: Israel's History and Destiny in Formative Judaism* (Philadelphia: Fortress, 1984).

_____ 'Money-changers in the Temple: the Mishnah's Explanation,' *NTS* 35 (1989) 287-90.

_____ *The Pharisees: Rabbinic Perspectives* SAJ (Hoboken, N.J.: Ktav, 1973).

Neyrey, J. H., 'The Idea of Purity in Mark's Gospel,' *Semeia* 35 (1986) 91-128.

Nicholson, E. W., 'The Covenant Ritual in Exodus XXIV 3-8,' *VT* 332 (1982) 74-86.

Nickelsburg, G. W. E., *Resurrection, Immortality and Eternal Life in Intertestamental Judaism* HTS 26 (Cambridge, MA: Harvard, 1972).

Niditch, S., 'The Composition of Isaiah 1,' *Bib* 61 (1981) 509-29.

Nielsen, K., 'Das Bild des Gerichts (*rib*-pattern) in Jes. i-xii,' *VT* 29 (1979) 309-24.

_____ 'Is 6:1-8:18* as Dramatic Writing,' *StTh* 40 (1986) 1-16.

Nilsson, M. P., *Griechische Feste von religiöser Bedeutung* (Leipzig, 1906).

Nineham, D. E., *The Gospel of St Mark* PGC (London: Adam and Charles Black, 1963).

Nixon, R. E., *The Exodus in the New Testament* (London: Tyndale, 1963).

Noch, A. D., 'The Apocryphal Gospels,' *JTS* 11 (1960) 63-70.

North, C. R., *The Second Isaiah* (London: Clarendon, 1964).

_____ *The Suffering Servant in Deutero-Isaiah* (London: Oxford University, 1948).

North, R., 'Angel-Prophet or Satan-Prophet?,' *ZAW* 82 (1970) 31-67.

_____ 'Separated Spiritual Substances in the Old Testament,' *CBQ* 29 (1967) 419-49.

Noth, M., *Exodus* OTL trans. J. S. Bowden (London: SCM, 1962).

Nötscher, F., *Gotteswege und Menschenwege in der Bibel und Qumran* BBB 15 (Bonn: Peter Hanstein, 1958).

Nützel, J. M., *Die Verklärungserzahlung im Markusevangelium* (Würzburg: Echter, 1973).

Oakman, D. E., 'Cursing Fig Trees and Robbers' Dens: Pronouncement Stories Within Social-Systemic Perspective: Mark 11:12-25 and Parallels,' *Semeia* 64 (1994) 253-72.

_____ 'Rulers' Houses, Thieves, and Usurpers,' *Forum* 4 (1988) 109-23.

Ogden, G. S., 'Moses and Cyrus. Literary Affinities between the Priestly Presentation of Moses in Exodus vi-viii and the Cyrus Song of Isaiah xliv 24 -xlv 13,' *VT* 28 (1978) 195-203.

Ollenburger, B. C., *Zion, City of the Great King* JSOTSupp 41 (Sheffield: JSOT Press, 1987).

Olmstead, A. T., 'II Isaiah and Isaiah Chapter 35,' *AJSL* 53 (1936-37) 251-53.

O'Neill, J. C., 'Did Jesus teach that his Death would be Vicarious as well as Typical?' in *Suffering and Martyrdom in the New Testament* eds. W. Horbury and B. McNeil (Cambridge: University, 1981) 9-27.

Orlinsky, H. M., 'The So-Called "Servant of the Lord" and "Suffering Servant" in Second Isaiah' in N. H. Snaith and H. M. Orlinsky, *Studies on the Second Part of the Book of Isaiah* SupVT 14 (rev. ed., Leiden: Brill, 1977) 1-133.

Osborne, B. A. E., 'Peter: Stumbling-Block and Satan (Mk. viii 33),' *NovT* 15 (1973) 187-90.
van der Osten-Sacken, P., *Gott und Belial: Traditionsheschichtliche Untersuchungen zum Dualismus in den Texten aus Qumran* SUNT 6 (Göttingen: Vandenhoeck & Ruprecht, 1969).
_____ 'Streitgespräch und Parabel als Formen markinsicher Christologie' in *Jesus Christus in Historie und Geschichte* FS H. Conzelmann, ed. G. Strecker (Tübingen: J. C. B. Mohr (Paul Siebeck), 1975) 375-93.
O'Sullivan, N., ed., *The Structure of Modern Ideology: Critical Perspectives on Social and Political Theory* (Aldershot, UK: Edward Elgar/Brookfield, Vermont: Gower, 1989).
Oswalt, J. N., *The Book of Isaiah Chapters 1-39* NIC (Grand Rapids: Eerdmans, 1986).
_____ 'The Golden Calves and the Egyptian Concept of Deity,' *EvQ* 45 (1973)13-20.
Otto, R., *The Kingdom of God and the Son of Man* (London: Redhill, 1943).

Pannenberg, W., ed., *Revelation as History* (London: Sheed and Ward, 1969).
Parunak, H., 'Oral Typesetting: Some Uses of Biblical Structure,' *Bib* 62 (1981) 153-68.
_____ 'Transitional Techniques in the Bible,' *JBL* 102 (1983) 525-48.
Patri k, D., 'The Covenant Code Source,' *VT* 27 (1977) 145-57.
_____ 'Epiphanic Imagery in Second Isaiah's Portrayal of a New Exodus,' *HTR* 8 (1984) 125-41.
Patten, P., 'The Form and Function of Parables in Select Apocalyptic Literature and their Significance for Parables in the Gospel of Mark,' *NTS* 29 (1983) 246-58.
Paul, S. M., *Studies in the Book of the Covenant in the Light of Cuneiform and Biblical Law* VTSup 18 (Leiden: Brill, 1970).
Pauritsch, K., *Die neue Gemeinde: Gott Sammelt Ausgestossene und Arme* AnBib 47 (Rome: Biblical Institute Press, 1971).
Peacock, H. P., 'Discipleship in the Gospel of Mark,' *RevExp* 75 (1978) 555-64.
Peisker, C. H., 'Konsekutives ἵνα in Markus 4:12,' *ZNW* 59 (1968) 126-27.
Perrin, N., 'The Creative Use of the Son of Man Traditions by Mark,' *USQR* 23 (1967-68) 357-65.
_____ 'The Christology in Mark: A Study in Methodology' in *A Modern Pilgrimage in New Testament Christology* (Philadelphia: Fortress, 1974) 84-93.
_____ 'The Literary *Gattung* "Gospel"—Some observations,' *ExpT* 82 (1970) 4-7.
_____ 'Towards an Interpretation of the Gospel of Mark' in *Christology and a Modern Pilgrimage* ed. H. D. Betz (SBL, 1971) 7-30.
Perrin, N., and Duling, D. C., *The New Testament: An Introduction; Proclamation and Parenesis, Myth and History* (New York, et al.: Harcourt and Brace, 1982[2]).
Pesch, R., *Das Abendmahl und Jesu Todesverständnis* (Freiburg: Herder, 1978).
_____ 'Anfang des Evangeliums Jesu Christi: Eine Studie zum Prolog des Marjusevangeliums (Mk 1.1-15)' in *Die Zeit Jesu: Festschrift für Heinrich Schlier* eds. G. Bornkamm and K. Rahner (Freiburg: Herder, 1970) 108-44.
_____ *Der Besessene von Gerasa. Enstehung und Überlieferung einer Wundergeschichte* SB 56 (Stuttgart: KBW, 1972).
_____ 'The Gospel in Jerusalem: Mark 14:12-26' trans. J. Vriend, in *The Gospel and the Gospels* ed. P. Stuhlmacher (Grand Rapids: Eerdmans, 1991) 106-48.
_____ 'The Markan Version of the Healing of the Gerasene Demoniac,' *EcumRev* 23 (1971) 349-76.
_____ *Das Markusevangelium* HTKNT II.1/2 (Freiburg: Herder, 1976, 77).
_____ 'Das Messiasbekenntnis des Petrus (Mk.8, 27-30) Neuverhandlung einer alten Frage,' *BZ* 18 (1974) 20-31.
_____ *Naherwartungen: Tradition and Redaktion in Mk. 13* (Düsseldorf: Patmos, 1968).
Pesch, W., 'Die Abhängigkeit des 11 Salomonischen Psalms vom letzten Kapital des Buches Baruch,' *ZAW* 26 (1955) 251-63.
Petersen, N. R., 'The Composition of Mark 4:1-8:26,' *HTR* 73 (1980) 185-217.

_____ Literary Criticism for New Testament Critics GBS (Philadelphia: Fortress, 1978).

Peterson, D. L., Late Israelite Prophecy: Studies in Deutero-Prophetic Literature and in Chronicles SBLMS 23 (Missoula: Scholars, 1977).

Peterson, E., 'Die Einholung des Kyrios,' ZSTh 7 (1929-30) 682-702.

Petzke, G., Die Traditionen über Apollonius von Tyana und das Neue Testament SCHNT 1 (Leiden: Brill, 1970).

Pfeiffer, E., 'Die Disputationsworte im Buche Maleachi (Ein Beitrag zur formgeschicht- lichen Struktur),' EvTh 19 (1959) 546-68.

Phillips, A., Ancient Israel's Criminal Law (Oxford: Blackwell, 1970).

Pilch, J. J., and Malina, B. J., eds. Biblical and Social Values and Their Meaning (Peabody, MA: Hendrickson, 1993).

Pimental, P., 'The "unclean spirits" of St. Mark's Gospel,' ExpT 99 (1988) 173-75.

Piper, O., 'The Origin of the Gospel,' JBL 78 (1959) 115-24.

_____ 'Unchanging Promises: Exodus in the New Testament,' Int 11 (1957) 3-22.

Pirot, L., and Leconte, R., L'évangile selon saint Marc P-C 9 (Paris, 1950).

Plooij, D., 'The Baptism of Jesus' in Amicitiae Corolla FS. R. Harris, ed. H. G. Wood (London: University, 1933) 239-52.

Pokorny, P., Der Gottessohn TS 109 (Zürich: Theologische, 1971).

_____ 'Das Markusevangelium. Literarische und theologische Einleitung mit Forschungs- bericht,' ANRW II.52.3, 1969-2035.

Polan, G. J., 'Salvation in the midst of Struggle,' TBT 23 (1985) 90-97.

_____ In the Ways of Justice Toward Salvation AUS 13 (Series VII) (New York, et al: Peter Lang, 1986).

Porter, S. E., Verbal Aspect in the Greek of the New Testament with Reference to Tense and Mood SBG 1 (New York, et al: Peter Lang, 1989).

Potterie, I. de la, 'De compositione evangelii Marci,' VD 44 (1966) 135-41.

Preuß, H. D., Deuterojesaja. Eine Einführung in seine Botschaft (Neukircken-Vluyn: Neukirchener, 1976).

_____ Verspottung fremder Religionen im Alten Testament BWANT 12 (Stuttgart: Kohl- hammer, 1971).

Pritchard, J. B., 'The Theology of Memphis' in Ancient Near Eastern Texts (Princeton: University, 1969).

Pryke, E. J., Redactional Style in the Markan Gospel SNTSMS 33 (Cambridge: University, 1978).

Quesnell, Q., The Mind of St. Mark: Interpretation and Method through the Exegesis of Mark 6.52 AnBib 38 (Rome: Pontifical Biblical Institute, 1969).

Rabin, C, The Zadokite Documents (Oxford: Clarendon, 1954).

von Rad, G., Der heilige Krieg im alten Israel ATANT 20 (Zürich: Zwingli, 1951).

_____ 'Das judäische Königsritual' in Gesammelte Studien zum Alten Testament I, TBü 8 (Munich: Chr. Kaiser, 1958) 205-13.

_____ 'The Levitical Sermon in I and II Chronicles' in The Problem of the Hexateuch and Other Essays (London: SCM, 1966).

_____ Old Testament Theology 2 vols., trans. D. M. G. Stalker (New York: Harper and Row, 1962, 1965).

Rademakers, J., La bonne nouvelle de Jesus selon Saint Marc 2 vols. (Brussels: Inst. et Theol., 1974).

Räisänen, H., The Idea of Divine Hardening PFES 25 (Helsinki, 1976).

_____ The 'Messianic Secret' in Mark's Gospel trans. C. Tuckett, SNTW (Edinburgh: T. & T. Clarke, 1990).

Rawlinson, A. E. J., St. Mark (London: Meuthen, 1936⁴).

Reedy, C. J., 'Mk. 8: 31-11: 10 and the Gospel Ending: A Redaction Study,' CBQ 34 (1972) 188- 97.

Reifenberg, A., *Anceint Jewish Coins* (2nd. and rev. ed., Jerusalem: Rubin Mass, 1947).

Reiterer, F. V., *Gerechtigkeit als Heil* (Graz, Austria: Akademische Verlagsanstalt, 1976).

Rendtorff, R., *Das Alte Testament: Eine Einführung* (Neukirchen-Vluyn: Neukirchener, 1983[2]).

_____ 'Zur Komposition des Buches Jesaja,' *VT* 34 (1984) 295-320.

_____ 'Die theologische Stellung des Schöfungsglaubens bei Deutero-Isaiah,' *ZTK* 51 (1954) 3-13.

Reploh, K. G., *Markus — Lehrer der Gemeinde: eine redaktionsgeschichtliche Studie zu den Jüngerperikopen des Markusevangeliums* SBM 9 (Stuttgart: Katholisches Bibelwek, 1969).

Repo, E., *Der 'Weg' als Selbsterzeichnung des Urchristentums: Eine traditionsgeschichtliche und semasiologische Untersuchung* (Helsinki: Suomalainen Tudeakatemia, 1964).

Reymond, P., *L'eau. Sa vie et signification dans l'Ancien Testament* SVT 6 (Leiden: Brill, 1952).

Rhoads, D., and Michie, D., *Mark as Story: An Introduction to the Narrative of a Gospel* (Philadelphia: Fortress, 1982).

Richardson, A., *An Introduction to the Theology of the New Testament* (London: SCM, 1958).

_____ *The Miracle Stories of the Gospels* (London: SCM, 1959).

Richardson, H., 'Some Notes on 1QSa,' *JBL* 76 (1957) 108-22.

Ricoeur, P., 'The Function of Fiction in Shaping Reality,' *Man and World* 12 (1979) 123-141.

_____ 'Science and Technology' in *Hermeneutics and the Human Sciences*, ed. and trans. J. Thompson (Cambridge: University, 1981) 222-46.

Ridderbos, H., *The Coming of the Kingdom* (Philadelphia: Fortress, 1962).

Riesenfeld, H., *Jésus Transfiguré* (Copenhagen: Ejnar Munksgaard, 1947).

_____ 'On the Composition of Mark' in *The Gospel Traditions* (Philadelphia: Fortress, 1954) 51-74.

Riesner, R., *Jesus als Lehrer* (Tübingen: J. C. B. Mohr (Paul Siebeck), 1981).

Rigaux, B., *The Testimony of St. Mark* trans. M. Carroll (Chicago: Franciscan Herald, 1966).

Ringgren, H., *The Faith of Qumran: Theology of the Dead Sea Scrolls* trans. E. T. Sander (Philadelphia: Fortress, 1963).

_____ *Word and Wisdom* (Lund: Haken Ohlssons Boktryckeri, 1947).

Robbins, V. K., 'Dynamis and Semeia in Mark,' *BR* 18 (1973) 5-20.

_____ *Jesus the Teacher* (Philadelphia: Fortress, 1984).

_____ 'Mark 1.14-20: An Interpretation at the Intersection of Jewish and Graeco-Roman Traditions,' *NTS* 28 (1982) 220-36.

Robbins, V. K., and Mack, B. L., *Patterns of Persuasion in the Gospels* (Sonoma, CA: Polebridge, 1989).

Roberts, C. H., 'Two Biblical Papyri in the John Rylands Library,' *BJRL* 20 (1936) 219-44.

Roberts, J. J. M., 'The Davidic Origin of the Zion Tradition,' *JBL* 92 (1973) 329-44.

_____ 'The Divine King and the Human Community in Isaiah's Vision of the Future' in eds. A. Green, *et al*, *The Quest for the Kingdom of God: Essays in Honor of George E. Mendenhall* (Winona lake, Indiana: Eisenbrauns, 1983) 127-36.

_____ 'Isaiah in Old Testament Theology,' *Int* 36 (1982) 130-43.

_____ 'Zion in the Theology of the Davidic-Solomonic Empire' in *Studies in the Period of David and Solomon and Other Essays*, ed. T. Ishida (Winona Lake, Indiana: Eisenbrauns, 1982) 93-108.

Robinson, J. A., *St. Paul's Epistle to the Ephesians* (London: Macmillan, 1904[2]).

Robinson, J. A. T. , 'Elijah, John and Jesus: An Essay in Detection,' *NTS* 4 (1957-58) 265-81.

_____ 'Gnosticism and the New Testament' in *Gnosis* FS for H. Jonas, ed. B. Aland (Göttingen: Vandenhoeck & Ruprecht, 1978).

_____ 'The Parable of the Wicked Husbandmen: A Test of Synoptic Relationships,' *NTS* 21 (1975) 443-61.

Robinson, J. M., *The Problem of History in Mark* SBT 21 (London: SCM, 1957).

Rogerson, J. W., and MacKay, J. W., *Psalms 1-150* 3 vols. CBC (Cambridge: University, 1977).

Roloff, J., *Der Kerygma und der irdische Jesus historische Motive in den Jesus-Erzählungen der Evangelien* (Göttingen: Vandenhoeck & Ruprecht, 1970).

Romaniuk, K., 'Exégèse du Nouveau Testament et ponctuation,' *NovT* 23 (1981) 195-209.

Ropes, J. H., *The Synoptic Gospels* (reprint, London: Oxford University, 1960).

Rose, D. G., 'The Use of Exodus Imagery in Second Isaiah', Ph.D. diss.: Yale, 1959.

Ross, J. F., 'The Prophet as Yahweh's Messenger' in *Israel's Prophetic Heritage* eds. B. W. Anderson and W. Harrelson (New York: Harper and Bros., 1962) 98-107.

Rost, L., 'Sinaibund und Davidsbund,' *TLZ* 72 (1947) 129-34.

Roth, C., 'The Cleansing of the Temple According to Zechariah xiv 21,' *NovT* 4 (1960) 174-81.

Roth, W. M. W., 'For Life, He Appeals to Death (Wis 13:18): A Study of Old Testament Idol Parodies,' *CBQ* 37 (1975) 21-47.

Roth, W., *Hebrew Gospel: Cracking the Code of Mark* (Oak Park, IL: Meyer-Stone, 1988).

Rowland, C., *The Open Heaven* (London: SPCK, 1982).

Ruckstuhl, E., 'Jesus als Gottessohn im Spiegel des markinischen Taufberichts' in *Die Mitte des Neuen Testaments. Einheit und Vielfalt neutestamentlicher Theologie* FS Eduard Schweizer, eds. U. Luz und H. Weder (Göttingen: Vandenhoeck & Ruprecht, 1983) 193-220.

Rudolph, W., *Haggai - Sacharja 1-8 - Sacharja 9-14, Malachi* KAT 13/4 (Gütersloh: Mohn. 1976).

Ruppert, L., *Jesus als der leidende Gerechte?* SBS 59 (Stuttgart: Katholisches Bibelwerk, 1972).

Ryle, E. H., and James, M. R., *Psalms of the Pharisees, commonly called The Psalms of Solomon* (Cambridge: University, 1891).

Sahlin, H., 'The New Exodus of Salvation according to St. Paul' in *The Root of the Vine* eds. A. Fridrichsen *et al* (New York, 1953) 81-95.

_____ 'Die Perikope von gerasenischen Bessessen und der Plan des Markusevangeliums,' *StudTheol* 18 (1964) 159-72.

_____ *Zur Typologie des Johannesevangeliums* UUA 4 (Uppsala: Lundaquistaka, 1950).

Saldarini, A. J., 'The Pharisees, Scribes and Sadducees in Mark', unpublished paper; in shortened form, 'The Social Class of the Pharisees' in *The Social World of Formative Christianity and Judaism: Essays in Tribute to Howard Clarke Kee* eds. J. Neusner *et al* (Philadelphia: Fortress, 1988) 69-77.

Sanders, E. P., *Paul and Palestinian Judaism: A Comparison of Patterns of Religion* (London: SCM/Philadelphia: Fortress, 1977).

_____ *Jesus and Judaism* (London: SCM, 1985).

Sanders, J. A., *Torah and Canon* (Philadelphia: Fortress, 1972).

Saner, G., 'Umkehrforderung in der Verkündigung Jesajas,' *Wort-Gebot-Glaube* FS W. Eichrodt ATANT 59 (Zürich: Zwingli, 1970) 279-84.

Sawyer, J. F. A., *From Moses to Patmos* (London: SPCK, 1977).

_____ *Isaiah* vol. 2 DSB (Philadelphia: Westminster, 1986).

Schaberg, J., 'Daniel 7, 12 and the New Testament Passion-Resurrection Predictions,' *NTS* 31 (1985) 208-22.

Schede, C., 'Fragen zur revidierten Einheitsuberstzung Nochmals "für die Vielen" oder "für alle"?,' *BibLiturg* 54 (1981) 226-8.

Schelke, K. H., 'Der Zweck der Gleichnisreden (Mk 4,10-12)' in *Neues Testament und Kirche: Festschrift R. Schnackenburg* ed. J. Gnilka (Freiburg-Basel-Vienna: Herder, 1974) 71-75.

Schenke, L., *Die Wundererzählungen des Markusevangeliums* SBB (Stuttgart: Katholisches Bibelwerk, 1974).

Schenker, A., 'Les sacrifices d'alliance, Ex XXIV, 3-8, dans leur portée narrative et re-
ligieuse: Contribution à l'étude de la *berît* dans l'Ancien Testament,' *RevB* 101
(1994) 481-94.

Schlatter, A., *Der Evangelist Matthäus* (Stuttgart: Calwer, 1959[5]).

＿＿＿ *Johannes der Täufer* ed. W. Michaelis (Basel: Reinhart, 1956).

＿＿＿ *Der Glaube im Neuen Testament* (Stuttgart: Calwer, 1927[4]).

Schmahl, G., *Die Zwölf im Markusevangelium—Eine redaktionsgeschichtliche Untersuchung* TTS 30 (Trier: Paulinus, 1974).

Schmauch, W., *Orte der Offenbarung und Offenbarungswort im Neuen Testament* (Göttingen:
Vandenhoeck & Ruprecht, 1956).

Schmid, J., *Das Evangelium nach Markus* RNT 2 (Regensburg: F. Pustet, 1958[4]).

Schmidt, J.M., "Gedanken zum Verstockungsaufrag Jesajas (Is 6),' *VT* 21 (1971) 68-90.

Schmidt, K., *Der Rahmen der Geschichte Jesu: Literarkritische Untersuchungen zur ältesten
Jesusüberlieferung* (Berlin: Trowitzsch, 1919).

Schmithals, W., *Das Evangelium nach Markus* 2 vols. OKNT 2/1-2 (Gütersloh: Echter,
1979)

Schnackenburg, R., *Das Evangelium nach Markus* GS 2/1,2 (Düsseldorf: Patmos, 1984[3]).

＿＿＿ '"Das Evangelium" im Verständnis des ältesten Evangelisten' in *Orientierung an
Jesus. Zur Theologie der Synoptiker* ed. P. Hoffman (Freiburg *et al*: Herder, 1973)
309-24.

＿＿＿ *The Gospel According to St. John* 3 vols. HTCNT trans. K. Smyth (New York: Herder
and Herder, London: Burns and Oates; 1968, 1980, 1982).

Schneck, R., *Isaiah in the Gospel of Mark, I-VII* BDS 1 (Vallejo, CA: BIBAL, 1994).

Schneider, G., 'Die Davidssohnfrage (Mk. 12:35-7),' *Bib* 53 (1972) 65-90.

Schnellbächer, E. L., 'The Temple as the Focus of Mark's Theology,' *HBT* 5 (1983) 92-112.

Schniewind, J., *Euangelion, Ursprung und erste Gestalt des Begriffs Evangelium* 2 vols.
(Güttersloh: Bertelsmann, 1927, 1931).

＿＿＿ *Das Evangelium nach Markus* NTD 1 (Göttingen: Vandenhoeck & Ruprecht, 1952[6]).

Schoeps, G. J., 'The Sacrifice of Isaac in Paul's Theology,' *JBL* 65 (1946) 385-92.

Schoeps, J., 'Die jüdischen Prophetenmorde' in *Aus frühchristlicher Zeit* (Tübingen: J. C. B.
Mohr (Paul Siebeck), 1950) 126-43.

Schoneveld, J., 'Ezekiel XIV 1-8,' *OTS* 15 (1969) 193-204.

Schoors, A., *I am God Your Saviour* SupVT 24 (Leiden: Brill, 1973).

＿＿＿ 'שבי and גלות in Isa. 40-55; Historical Background' in *Proceedings of the 5th World
Congress of Jewish Studies* (Jerusalem, 1969) 90-101.

Schreiber, J., 'Die Christologie des Markusevangeliums. Beobachtungen zur Theologie und
Komposition des zweiten Evangeliums,' *ZTK* 58 (1961) 154-83.

＿＿＿ *Theologie des Vertrauens: Eine redaktionsgeschichtliche Untersuchung des Markus-
evangeliums* (Hamburg: Furche, 1967).

Schreiner, J., 'Das Buch jesajanischer Schule' in *Wort und Botschaft* ed. J. Schreiner
(Würzburg: Echter, 1967) 142-62.

Schulz, S., 'Markus und des Alte Testament,' *ZTK* 58 (1961) 184-97.

＿＿＿ *Die Stunde der Botschaft* (Hamburg: Furche, 1967).

Schüpphaus, J., *Die Psalmen Salomos: Ein Zeugnis Jerusalemer Theologie und Frömmigkeit
in der Mitte des vorchristlichen Jahrhunderts* (Leiden: Brill, 1977).

＿＿＿ 'Stellung und Funktion der sogannten Heilsankündigung bei Deuterojesaja,' *ThZ* 27
(1971) 161-81.

Schürer, E., *The History of the Jewish People in the Age of Jesus Christ (175 B.C.-A.D. 135)*
rev. and ed. by G. Vermes *et al*, 3 vols. (Edinburgh: T. & T. Clarke, 1973-1987).

Schürmann, H., *Gottes Reich — Jesu Geschick. Jesu ureigener Tod im Licht seiner Basileia —
Verkündigung* (Freiburg *et al*: Herder, 1983).

Schwartz, D. R., 'The Three Temples of 4QFlorilegium,' *RQ* 10 (1979-81) 83-91.

Schweitzer, A., *The Mystery of the Kingdom of God* trans. W. Lowrie (London: Adam &
Charles Black, 1914).

_____ *The Quest for the Historical Jesus* trans. W. Montgomery (London: Black, 1911²).

Schweizer, E., 'Mark's Contribution to the Quest of the Historical Jesus,' *NTS* 10 (1964-5) 421-32.

_____ *The Good News According to Mark* trans. D. H. Madvig (London: SPCK, 1971).

_____ 'The Portrayal of the Life of Faith in the Gospel of Mark,' *Int* 32 (1978) 387-99.

_____ 'The Spirit of Power,' *Int* 6 (1952) 259-78.

_____ 'Die theologische Leistung des Markus,' *EvTh* 24 (1964) 337-55.

Scobie, C. H. H., *John the Baptist* (London: SCM, 1964).

Scott, D., *Everyman Revived: The Common Sense of Michael Polanyi* (Grand Rapids: Eerdmans, 1995).

Scott, M. P., 'Chiastic Structure: A Key to the Interpretation of Mark's Gospel,' *BTB* 15 (1985) 17-26.

Scott, R. B. Y., 'The Relation of Isaiah, Chapter 35, to Deutero-Isaiah,' *AJSL* 52 (1936-7) 178-91.

Seccombe, D. P., *Possessions and the Poor in Luke-Acts* SNTU 6 (Linz: Albert Fuchs, 1982).

Seeley, D., 'Jesus' Temple Act,' *CBQ* 55 (1993) 263-83.

Segal, A., '"He who did not spare his own son ...": Jesus, Paul, and the Akedah' in *From Jesus to Paul* eds. P. Richardson and J. C. Hurd, FS F. W. Breare (Ontario: Wilfred Laurier University, 1984) 169-84.

_____ *Rebecca's Children* (Cambridge, MA: Harvard University, 1985).

Seidelin, P., 'Der Ebed Jahwe und die Messiasgestalt im Jesajatargum,' *ZNTW* 35 (1936) 389-96.

Seidl, T., 'Yahwe der Krieger—Jahwe der Tröster (Jesaja 51,9-16),' *BN* 21 (1983) 116-34.

Seitz, C., 'The Divine Council: Temporal Transition and New Prophecy in the Book of Isaiah,' *JBL* 109 (1990) 229-47.

Seitz, O., 'The Future Coming of the Son of Man: Three Midrashic Formulations in the Gospel of Mark,' *StEv* 4 (1973) 478-88.

_____ 'Praeparatio Evangelica in the Markan Prologue,' *JBL* 82 (1963) 201-6.

Seliger, M., *Ideology and Politics* (London: Allen and Unwin, 1976).

Sellin, E., *Das Zwölfprophenbuch übersetz und erlkärt* KAT 12/2 (Leipzig: Deichertsche, 1930).

Selvidge, M. J., '"And Those Who followed Feared" (Mark 10.32),' *CBQ* 45 (1983) 396-400.

_____ *Woman, Cult, and Miracle Recital* (Cranbury, NJ: Associated University Presses, 1990).

Senior, D.,· *The Passion Narrative According to Matthew: A Redactional Study* BETL 39 (Leuven: University, 1975).

Sergeant, J., *Lion Let Loose: The Structure and Meaning of St. Mark's Gospel* (Exeter: Paternoster, 1988).

van Seters, J., *In Search of History. Historiography in the Ancient World and Origins of Biblical History* (Yale: University, 1983).

Shae, G. S., 'The Question on the Authority of Jesus (Mk.11:27-33),' *NovT* 16 (1974) 1-29.

Shepherd, T., *Markan Sandwich Stories: Narration, Definition, and Function* AUSDSS (Berrien Springs, Michigan: University, 1992).

Sheppard, G. T., 'The Anti-Assyrian Redaction and the Canonical Context of Isaiah 1-39,' *JBL* 104 (1985) 193-216.

_____ 'More on Isaiah 5, 1-7 as a Juridical Parable,' *CBQ* 44 (1982) 45-47.

Siegman, E. F., 'Teaching in Parables (Mk 4, 10-12; Lk 8, 9-10; Mt 13, 10-15),' *CBQ* 23 (1961) 161-81.

Silva, M., *Biblical Words and Their Meaning* (rev. ed., Grand Rapids: Zondervan, 1994).

Simcox, C. E., 'The rôle of Cyrus in Deutero-Isaiah,' *JAOS* 57 (1937) 158-71.

Simon-Yofre, H., 'Exodo en Deuteroisaias,' *Bib* 61 (1980) 530-53.

Simon, M., *Versus Israel: Étude sur les relations entre chrétiens et juifs dans l'empire romain (135-425)* (Paris: Boccard, 1964).

Simon, U., 'The Poor Man's Ewe Lamb: An Example of a Juridical Parable,' *Bib* 48 (1967) 207-42.

Sjöberg, E., 'Neuschöpfung in den toten-Meer-Rollen,' *StTh* 9 (1955) 131-36.

——— 'Wiedergeburt und Neuschöfung im palästinischen Judentum,' *StTh* 4 (1950) 44-85.

Skinner, J., *The Book of the Prophet Isaiah in the Revised Version* 2 vols., CBib. (rev. ed., Cambridge: University, 1929).

Slater, T. B., 'One like a Son of Man in First-century CE Judaism,' *NTS* 41 (1995) 183-98.

Smart, J. D., *History and Theology in Second Isaiah* (London: Epworth, 1967).

Smith, C. W. F., 'No Time for Figs,' *JBL* 79 (1960) 315-27.

——— 'Tabernacles in the Fourth Gospel and Mark,' *NTS* 9 (1963) 130-46.

Smith, D. E., 'Narrative Beginnings in Ancient Literature and Theory,' *Semeia* 52 (1990) 1-9.

Smith, J. M. P., 'Malachi' in *Haggai, Zechariah, Malachi and Jonah* ICC (Edinburgh: T. & T. Clark, 1951).

Smith, J. Z., 'Good News is No News. Aretalogy and Gospel' in *Christianity, Judaism and Other Greco-Roman Cults. Studies for Morton Smith at 60. Part One, New Testament* SJLA 12 (Leiden: Brill, 1975) 21-38.

Smith, M., *Clement of Alexandria and a Secret Gospel of Mark* (Cambridge, MA: Harvard, 1973).

——— '"God's Begetting the Messiah" in 1QSa,' *NTS* 5 (1958-9) 218-24.

——— 'The Occult in Josephus' in *Josephus, Judaism and Christianity* eds. L. H. Feldman and G. Hata (Leiden: Brill, 1987) 236-56.

Smith, R. H., 'Exodus Typology in the Fourth Gospel,' *JBL* 81 (1962) 329-42.

Smith, R. L., *Micah-Malachi* WBC 32 (Waco, Texas: Word, 1984).

Smith, S. H., 'The Literary Structure of Mark 11:1-12:40,' *NovT* 31 (1989) 104-24.

——— 'The Role of Jesus' Opponents in the Markan Drama,' *NTS* 35 (1989) 161-82.

Smolar, L., and Auerbach, M., *Studies in Targum Jonathan to the Prophets* LBS (New York: KTAV, 1983).

Snaith, N. H., *Five Psalms (1; 27; 51; 107; 134). A New Translation with Commentary and Questionary* (London: Epworth, 1938).

——— 'Isaiah 40-66. A Study of the Teaching of the Second Isaiah and Its Consequences' in N. H. Snaith and H. M. Orlinsky, *Studies on the Second Part of the Book of Isaiah* SupVT 14 (rev. ed., Leiden: Brill, 1977) 139-264.

Snodgrass, K. R., *The Parable of the Wicked Tenants* WUNT 27 (Tübingen: J. C. B. Mohr (Paul Siebeck), 1983).

——— 'Streams of Tradition Emerging from Isaiah 40:1-5 and Their Adaptation in the New Testament,' *JSNT* 8 (1980) 24-45.

Souter, A., 'ΑΓΑΠΗΤΟΣ,' *JTS* 28 (1927) 59-60.

Spykerboer, H. C., 'Isaiah 55:1-5: The Climax of Deutero-Isaiah. An Invitation to Come to the New Jerusalem' in *The Book of Isaiah—Le Livre d'Isaïe. Les oracles et leur relectures. Unité et complexité de l'ouvrage* ed. J. Vermeylen, BETL 81 (Leuven: Leuven University/Peeters, 1989) 357-59.

——— *The Structure and Composition of Deutero-Isaiah* diss.: University of Groningen, 1976.

Standaert, B. H., *L'évangile selon Marc: Composition et genre littéraire* (Brugge: Sint-Andriesabdij, 1978).

Stanley, C. D., 'The Importance of 4QTanhumim (4Q176),' *RevQum* 15 (1992) 569-82.

——— *Paul and the Language of Scripture: Citation Technique in the Pauline Epistles and Contemporary Literature* SNTSMS 74 (Cambridge: University, 1992).

Starcky, J., 'Les quatre étapes du messianisme à Qumran,' *RB* 70 (1963) 481-505.

Starkova, K. B., 'The Ideas of Second and Third Isaiah as Reflected in the Qumran Literature,' *Qumran Chronicle* 2 (1992) 51-62.

Stauffer, E., 'Messias oder Menschensohn?,' *NovT* (1956) 81-102.

Steck, O. H., 'Beiträge zum Verständnis von Jesaja 7, 10-7 und 8, 1-4,' *TZ* 29 (1973) 161-78.

——— 'Bermerkungen zu Jesaja 6,' *BZ* 16 (1972), 188-206.

_____ *Bereitete Heimkehr. Jesaja 35 als redaktionelle Brücke zwischen dem Ersten und dem Zweiten Jesaja* SBS 121 (Stuttgart: Katholische Bibelwerk, 1985).

_____ *Israel und das gewaltsame Geschick der Propheten* (Neukirchen: Neukirchener, 1967).

_____ *Gottesknecht und Zion* FAT 4 (Tübingen: J. C. B. Mohr (Paul Siebeck), 1992).

Stegner, W. R., 'The Baptism of Jesus. A Story Modeled on the Binding of Isaac,' *BibRev* 1 (1985) 36-46.

_____ 'Jesus' Walking on the Water: Mark 6.45-52' in *The Gospels and the Scriptures of Israel* eds. C. A. Evans and W. Richard Stegner JSNTS 104 (Sheffield: JSOT, 1994) 212-34.

_____ 'Romans 9: 6-29—A Midrash,' *JSNT* 22 (1984) 37-52.

Steichele, H-J., *Die liedende Sohn Gottes: Eine Untersuchung einiger alttestamentlicher Motive in der Christologie des Markus Evangeliums* BU 14 (Regensburg: Pustet, 1980).

Stein, R.H., 'Proper Methodology for Ascertaining a Markan Redaction History,' *NovT* 13 (1971) 181-98.

Stemberger, G., 'Galilee—Land of Salvation' in W. D. Davies *Gospel and Land* (Berkeley: University of California Press, 1974) 409-38.

Stendahl, K., *The School of St. Matthew and Its Use of the Old Testament* ASNU 20 (Philadelphia: Fortress Press, 1968[2]).

Stendebach, F. J., 'Das Schweineopfer im Alten Orient,' *BZ* 18 (1974) 263-71.

Stern, D., 'Jesus' Parables from the Perspective of Rabbinic Literature: the Example of the Wicked Husbandmen' in *Parable and Story in Judaism and Christianity* eds. C. Thoma and M. Wyschogrod (New York: Paulist, 1989) 42-80.

Stevens, B. A., 'Divine Warrior in Mark,' *BZ* 31 (1987) 101-9.

_____ 'Jesus as the Divine Warrior,' *ExpT* 94 (1982-3) 326-29.

Stock, A., *Call to Discipleship* GNS 1 (Dublin: Veritas, 1982).

_____ 'Hinge Transitions in Mark's Gospel,' *BTB* 15 (1985) 27-31.

_____ *The Method and Meaning of Mark* (Wilmington, Delaware: Michael Glazier, 1989).

_____ 'The Structure of Mark,' *BibToday* 23 (1985) 291-96.

Stock, K., *Boten aus dem Mit-Ihm-Sein: Das Verhältnis zwischen Jesus und den Zwölf nach Markus* AnBib 70 (Rome: Pontifical Biblical Institute, 1975).

Stolz, F., *Jahwes und Israel's Kreige: Kriegtheorien und Kriegserfahrungen im Glauben des alten Israels* ATANT 60 (Zürich: Theologischer, 1972).

Stone, M. E., 'The Concept of the Messiah in IV Ezra' in *Religions in Antiquity: Essays in Memory of Erwin Ramsdell Goodenough* ed. J. Neusner, SHR 14 (Leiden: Brill, 1968) 295-312.

_____ 'Features of the Eschatology of IV Ezra', Ph.D. diss., Harvard: 1965.

Stonehouse, N. B., *The Witness of Matthew and Mark to Christ* (Philadelphia: Presbyterian Guardian, 1944).

Strecker, G., 'Das Evangelium Jesu Christi' in *Jesus Christus in Historie und Theologie* FS for H. Conzelmann zum 60. Geburtstag, eds. G. Strecker *et al* (Tübingen: J. C. B. Mohr (Paul Siebeck), 1975) 503-48.

_____ 'The Passion and Resurrection Predictions in Mark's Gospel (Mark 8:31; 9:31; 10:32-34),' *Int* 22 (1968) 421-42.

Strugnell, J., 'Notes en marge du volume V des Discoveries in the Judean Desert of Jordan,' *RQ* 29 (1970) 220-22.

Stuhlmacher, P., 'Das Evangelium von der Versöhnung in Christus' in *Das Evangelium von der Versöhnung in Christus*, eds. P. Stuhlmacher and H. Class (Stuttgart: Calwer, 1979), 44-49.

_____ *Die paulinische Evangelium: I Vorgeschichte* (Göttingen: Vandenhoeck & Ruprecht, 1968).

_____ 'Die neue Gerechtigkeit in der Jesusverjündigung' in *Versöhnung, Gesetz und Gerechtigkeit* (Göttingen: Vandenhoeck und Ruprecht, 1981) 43-65.

_____ '"He is our Peace" (Eph. 2:14). On the Exegesis and Significance of Eph. 2:14-18' in *Reconciliation, Law, & Righteousness. Essays in Biblical Theology* trans. E. Kalin (Philadelphia: Fortress, 1986) 182-200.

_____ 'The New Righteousness in the Proclamation of Jesus' in *Reconciliation, Law, & Righteousness. Essays in Biblical Theology* trans. E. Kalin (Philadelphia: Fortress, 1986) 30-49.

_____ 'Zum Thema: Das Evangelium und die Evangelien' in *Das Evangelium und die Evangelien* WUNT 28, hrsg. P. Stuhlmacher (Tübingen: J. C. B. Mohr (Paul Siebeck), 1983) 1-26.

_____ 'Vicariously Giving His Life for Many, Mark 10:45 (Matt. 20:28)' in *Reconciliation, Law, & Righteousness. Essays in Biblical Theology* trans. E. Kalin (Philadelphia: Fortress, 1986) 16-29.

Stuhlmueller, C., *Creative Redemption in Deutero-Isaiah* AnBib 43 (Rome: Pontifical Biblical Institute, 1970).

_____ 'Deutero-Isaiah: Major Transitions in the Prophet's Theology and in Contemporary Scholarship,' *CBQ* 42 (1980) 1-29.

_____ '"First and Last" and "Yahweh-Creator" in Deutero-Isaiah,' *CBQ* 29 (1967) 189-205.

_____ 'The Theology of Creation in Second Isaias,' *CBQ* 21 (1959) 429-67.

_____ 'Yahweh King and Deutero-Isaiah,' *BR* 15 (1970) 32-45.

Stummer, F., 'Einige keilschriftliche Parallelen zu Jes 40-66,' *JBL* 45 (1926) 171-89.

Suhl, A., *Die Funktion der alttestamentlichen Zitate und Anspielungen in Markusevangelium* (Gütersloh: Gerd Mohn, 1965).

Sundberg, A. C., 'On Testimonies,' *NovT* 3 (1959) 268-81.

Sundwall, J., *Die Zusammensetzung des Markusevangeliums* ΑΛΑΗ 9/2 (Abo: Abo Akademi, 1934).

Sutcliffe, E. F., 'The Rule of the Congregation (1QSa) II, 11-12: Text and Meaning,' *RQ* 2 (1960) 541-47.

Swartley, W. M., *Israel's Scripture Traditions and the Synoptic Gospels: Story Shaping Story* (Peabody, MA: Hendrickson, 1994).

_____ 'The Structural Function of the Term "Way" (Hodos) in Mark's Gospel' in *The New Way of Jesus: Essays Presented to Howard Charles*, ed. W. Klassen (Kansas: Faith and Life Press, 1980), 73-86.

_____ 'A Study in Markan Structure: The Influence of Israel's Holy History Upon the Structure of the Gospel of Mark', Ph.D. diss.: Princeton Theological Seminary, 1973.

Sweeney, M. A., *Isaiah 1-4 and the Post-Exilic Understanding of the Isaianic Tradition* BZAW 171 (Berlin and New York: de Gruyter, 1988).

Sweet, J., *Revelation* (London: SCM/Philadelphia: Trinity, 1990).

Swete, H. B., *The Gospel According to St. Mark* (London: Macmillan, 1920³).

Tagawa, K., *Miracles et Évangile: La pensée personelle de l'evangeliste Marc* (Paris: Presses Universitaires de France, 1966).

Talbert, C. H., 'Biographies of Philosophers and Rulers as Instruments of Religious Propandanda in Mediterranean Antiquity,' *ANRW* II, 16:2, 1619-57.

_____ *What is a Gospel? The Genre of the Canonical Gospels* (Philadelphia: Westminster, 1987).

Talmon, S., 'The "Desert Motif" in the Bible and in Qumran Literature' in *Biblical Motifs*, ed. A. Altmann (Cambridge, MA: Harvard, 1966) 31-64.

Tannehill, R., 'The Disciples in Mark: The Function of a Narrative Role,' *JR* 57 (1977) 386-405.

_____ 'The Gospel of Mark as a Narrative Christology,' *Semeia* 16 (1975) 57-95.

Taylor, V., *The Gospel According to Mark* TC (Grand Rapids: Baker, 1981²).

_____ 'The Origin of the Markan Passion-Sayings,' *NTS* 1 (1954-55) 159-67.

_____ *Person of Christ in New Testament Teaching* (London: MacMillan, 1963²).

Teeple, H. M., *The Mosaic Eschatological Prophet* JBLMS 10 (Ann Arbor, Mich.: Cushing-Malloy, 1957).

Telford, W. R., *The Barren Temple and the Withered Tree* JSNTSup 1 (Sheffield: JSOT, 1980).

—— 'Introduction: The Gospel of Mark' in *The Interpretation of Mark* ed. W. R. Telford, IRT 7 (Philadelphia: Fortress/London: SPCK, 1985) 1-41.

—— 'More Fruit from the Withered Tree' in *Templum Amicitiae: Essays on the Second Temple presented to Ernst Bammel* FS E. Bammel, ed. W. Horbury JSNTSS 48 (Sheffield: Sheffield Academic, 1991) 264-304.

Terrien, S., 'Quelques remarques sur les affinités de Job avec le Deutéro-Esaïe' in *Volume du Congrès, Genève 1965* VTSupp 15 (Leiden: Brill, 1966) 295-310.

Thagard, P., 'The Best Explanation: Criteria for Theory Choice,' *Journal of Philosophy* 75 (1978) 76-92.

Theisohn, J., *Der auserwählte Richter* SUNT 12 (Göttingen: Vandenhoeck & Ruprecht, 1975).

Theissen, G., *The Miracle Stories of the Early Christian Tradition* SNTW trans. F. McDonagh (Philadelphia: Fortress, 1983).

—— *Sociology of Early Palestinian Christianity* trans. J. Bowden (Philadelphia: Fortress, 1978).

Thiselton, A. C., *The Two Horizons* (Grand Rapids: Eerdmans, 1980).

Thompson, J. A., *Jeremiah* NICOT (Grand Rapids: Eerdmans, 1980).

Thompson, J. B., *Surveys in the Theory of Ideology* (Cambridge: Polity, 1984).

Thompson, K, ed., *Beliefs and Ideology* (Chichester, Sussex: Ellis Horwood/London: Tavistock, 1986).

Thompson, M. B., *Clothed with Christ: The Example and Teaching of Jesus in Romans 12.1-15.13* JSNTSupp 59 (Sheffield: JSOT, 1991).

Thompson, R. C., *The Devils and Evil Spirits of Babylonia* 2 vols. (London: Lazac, 1903, 1904).

Thrall, M. E., 'Elijah and Moses in Mark's Account of the Transfiguration,' *NTS* 16 (1970) 305-17.

Thurston, B. B., 'Faith and Fear in Mark's Gospel,' *BibToday* 23 (1985) 305-10.

Tiede, D. L., *The Charismatic Figure as Miracle Worker* SBLDS 1 (Missoula: Montana University, 1972).

—— 'Religious Propaganda and the Gospel Literature of Early Christian Mission' in *ANRW* II 25:2, 1705-29.

Tilly, M., 'Kanaanäner, Händler und der Tempel in Jerusalem,' *BibNotiz* 57 (1991) 30-36.

Tödt, H. E., *The Son of Man in the Synoptic Tradition* trans. D. M. Barton (London: SCM, 1965).

Tolbert, M. A., *Sowing the Gospel: Mark's World in Literary-Historical Perspective* (Minneapolis: Fortress, 1989).

Tomasino, A. J., 'Isaiah 1:1-2:4 and 63-66, and the Composition of the Isaianic Corpus,' *JSOT* 57 (1993) 81-98.

Tooley, W., 'The Shepherd and the Sheep Image in the Teaching of Jesus,' *NovT* 7 (1964) 15-25.

Torrey, C. C., *The Second Isaiah* (New York: Scribners, 1928).

Towner, W. S., *The Rabbinic 'Enumeration of Scriptural Example.' A Study of a Rabbinic Pattern of Discourse with Special Reference to Mekilta d'R.Ishmael* SPB (Leiden: Brill, 1973).

Toy, C. H., *Quotations in the New Testament* (New York: Scribner's, 1884).

Trench, R. C., *Notes on the Miracles of Our Lord* (rev. ed., London: Kegan Paul, Trench & Co., 1886[13]).

Trilling, W., 'Die Botschaft vom Reiche Gottes (Mk 1, 14.15)' in *Christusverkündigung in den synoptischen Evangelien* (München: Kösel, 1969) 40-63.

Trocmé, É., *The Formation of the Gospel According to Mark* trans. P. Gaughan (London: SPCK, 1975).

____ 'Pour un Jésus public: Le evangélistes Marc et Jean aux prises avec l'intimisme de la tradition' in *OIKONOMIA: Heilsgeschichte als Thema der Theologie* FS O. Cullmann ed. F. Christ (Hamburg-Berstedt: Herbert Reich, 1957) 42-50.

____ 'Why Parables? A Study of Mark IV,' *BJRL* 59 (1976-77) 458-71.

Trumbower, J. A., 'The Role of Malachi in the Career of John the Baptist' in *The Gospels and the Scriptures of Israel* eds. C. A. Evans and W. Richard Stegner JSNTS 104 (Sheffield: JSOT, 1994) 28-41.

Tuckett, C. M., 'Mark's Concerns in the Parables Chapter (Mark 4,1-34),' *Bib* 69 (1988) 1-26.

____ ed., *The Messianic Secret* IRT 1 (Philadelphia: Fortress/London: SPCK, 1983).

Tunyogi, A. C., 'The Rebellions of Israel,' *JBL* 81 (1962) 385-90.

Turner, C. H., 'Ο ΥΙΟΣ ΜΟΥ Ο ΑΓΑΠΗΤΟΣ,' *JTS* 27 (1926) 113-29.

____ 'Text of Mark I,' *JTS* 28 (1927) 150-58.

Turpie, D. Mc.C., *The Old Testament in the New* (London: Williams and Norgate, 1868).

Tyson, J., 'The Blindness of the Disciples in Mark,' *JBL* 80 (1961) 261-68.

von Ungern-Sternberg, A., *Der traditionelle alttestamentliche Schriftbeweis 'de Christo' un 'de Evangelio' in der alten Kirche bis zur Zeit Eusebs von Caesarea* (Halle, 1913).

van Unnick, W. C., '"Die geöffneten Himmel" in der Offenbarungsvision des Apokryphons Johannes' in *Apophoreta* BZNW 30 FS. E. Haenchen, hrsg. W. Eltester (Berlin: Töpelmann, 1964) 269-80.

Urbach, E. E., *The Sages* 2 vols., trans. I. Abrahams (Jerusalem: Magnes, 1979).

Van Cangh, J.-M., *La multiplication des pains et l'eucharistie* (Paris: Cerf, 1975).

VanderKam, J., 'Righteous One, Messiah, Chosen One, and Son of Man in 1 Enoch 37-71' in *The Messiah* ed. J. H. Charlesworth (Minneapolis: Fortress, 1992) 169-91.

Van Winkle, D. W., 'The Relationship of the Nations to Yahweh and to Israel in Isaiah XL-LV,' *VT* 35 (1985) 446-58.

de Vaux, R., 'Les sacrifices de porcs en Palestine et dans l'Ancien Orient' in *Von Ugarit nach Qumran* BZAW 77, FS O. Eissfeldt (Berlin: de Gruyter, 1958) 250-65.

Verhoff, P. A., *The Books of Haggai and Malachi* NICOT 15 (Grand Rapids: Eerdmans, 1987).

Vermes, G., *Jesus the Jew* (London: Collins, 1973).

____ *Scripture and Tradition in Judaism* (Leiden: Brill, 1961).

Vermeylen, J., *Du Prophète Isaïe a l'apocalyptique* 2 vols. (Paris: Gabalda, 1978).

Verseput, D. J., 'The Role and the Meaning of the "Son of God" Title in Matthew's Gospel,' *NTS* 33 (1987) 532-56.

Via, D. O., Jr., *The Ethics of Mark's Gospel: in the Middle of Time* (Philadelphia: Fortress, 1985).

Vielhauer, P., 'Erwägungen zur Christologie des Markus-evangeliums' in *Zeit und Geschichte* Dnksgbe. R. Bultmann hrsg. E. Dinkler (Tübingen: J. C. B. Mohr (Paul Siebeck), 1964) 155-69.

____ 'Tracht und Speise Johannes des Täufers' in *Aufsätze zum Neuen Testament* TBü 31 (München: Kaiser, 1965) 47-54.

Violet, B., *Die Apokalypsen des Esra und des Baruch in deutscher Gestalt* (Leipzig, 1924).

Viteau, J., *Les psaumes de salomon* (Paris: Letouzey et Ané, 1911).

Vögtle, A., 'Das markinische Verständnis der Tempelworte' in *Die Mitte des Neuens Testaments* FS E. Schweizer, eds. U. Luz and H. Weder (Göttingen: Vandenhoeck & Ruprecht, 1983) 362-83.

Volz, P., *Die Eschatologie der jüdischen Gemeinde im neutestamentlichen Zeitalter* (Tübingen: Mohr, 1934²).

Vorster, W. S., 'The Function of the Use of the Old Testament in Mark,' *NeoT* 14 (1981) 62-72.

Vriezen, T. C., 'Essentials of the Theology of Isaiah' in *Israel's Prophetic Heritage* eds. B. W. Anderson and W. Harrelson. (New York: Harper, 1962) 126-46.

Vuilleumier, R., 'Malachie' in *Aggé, Zacharie, Malachie* CAT XIc (Neuchatel-Paris: Delachaux & Niestlé, 1981).

Waetjen, H. C., *A Reordering of Power. A Socio-Political Reading of Mark's Gospel* (Minneapolis: Fortress, 1989).

von Waldow, H. E., *Die traditionsgeschichtliche Hintergrund der prophetischen Gerichtsreden* BZAW 85 (Berlin: Töpelmann, 1963).

_____ 'The Message of Deutero-Isaiah,' *Int* 22 (1968) 259-87.

Walker, W. O., 'The Son of Man Question and the Synoptic Problem,' *NTS* 28 (1982) 374-88.

_____ 'The Son of Man: Some Recent Developments,' *CBQ* 45 (1983) 584-607.

Wansbrough, H., 'Mark 3,21—Was Jesus out of his Mind?,' *NTS* 18 (1972) 233-35.

Ward, J. M., 'The Servant's Knowledge in Isaiah 40-50' in *Israelite Wisdom* FS S. Terrien ed. J. G. Gammie *et al* (New York: Scholars Press, 1978) 121-36.

Watson, F., 'The Social Function of Mark's Secrecy Theme,' *JSNT* 24 (1985) 49-69.

Watts, J. D. W., 'The Formation of Isaiah Ch. 1: Its Context in chs. 1-4' in *SBL 1978 Sem. Papers* vol. 1, ed. P. Achtemeier (Missoula: Scholars, 1978) 109-19.

_____ *Isaiah 1-33, Isaiah 34-66* WBC vol. 24, 25 (Waco, Texas: Word, 1985, 1987).

Watts, R. E., 'Consolation or Confrontation? Isaiah 40-55 and the Delay of the New Exodus,' *TynBul* 41 (1990) 31-59.

_____ 'The Meaning of 'ālāw yiqpǝṣû mǝlākîm pîhem in Isaiah lii 15,' *VT* 40 (1990) 327-35.

Watty, W. W., 'Jesus and the Temple—Cleansing or Cursing?,' *ExpT* 93 (1982) 235-39.

Weber, M., *The Theory of Social and Economic Organization* trans. A. M. Henderson and Talcott Parsons (Glencoe, Il.: Free Press, 1947).

Webb, R. L., *John the Baptizer and Prophet: A Socio-Historical Study* JSNTSupp 62 (Sheffield: JSOT, 1991).

Webster, E. L., 'The Rhetoric of Isaiah 63-65,' *JSOT* 47 (1990) 89-102.

Weder, H., *Die Gleichnisse Jesu als Metaphern* (Göttingen: Vandenhoeck & Ruprecht, 1978).

Weeden, T. J., 'The Heresy that Necessitated Mark's Gospel,' *ZNW* 59 (1968) 145-58.

_____ *Mark—Traditions in Conflict* (Philadelphia: Fortress, 1971).

Weippert, M., '»Heiliger Kriege« in Israel und Assyrien,' *ZAW* 84 (1972) 460-93.

Weiser, A., *The Psalms*, trans. H. Hartnell. OTL (Philadelphia: Westminster Press, 1962).

Weiss, B., *Die Evangelien des Markus und Lukas* KKNT 1/2 (Göttingen: Vandenhoek und Ruprecht, 1901⁹).

Weiss, J., *Das älteste Evangelium. Ein Beitrag zum Verstandnis des Markusevangeliums und der älteste evangelischen Überlieferung* (Göttingen: Vandenhoeck & Ruprecht, 1903).

_____ *The History of Primitive Christianity* 2 vols. ed. F. C. Grant (London: McMillan, 1937).

_____ *Jesus' Proclamation of the Kingdom of God* trans. and eds. R. H. Hiers and D. L. Holland (Philadelphia: Fortress, 1971).

Weiss, K., 'Ekklesiologie, Tradition, und Geschichte in der Jüngerunterweisung Mark viii: 27-x: 52' in *Der historische Jesus und der kerygmatische Christus* eds. H. Ristow and K. Matthiae (Berlin: Evangelische Verlangsanstalt, 1960) 413-38.

Wellhausen, J., *Das Evangelium Marci* (Berlin: G. Reimer, 1903).

Wendland, E., 'Linear and Concentric patterns in Malachi,' *BT* 36 (1985) 108-21.

Wendling, E., *Die Entstehung des Markusevangeliums* (Tübingen: Mohr, 1908).

Wenham, D., 'The Meaning of Mark iii. 21,' *NTS* 21 (1974-5) 295-300.

_____ 'The Synoptic Problem Revisited: Some New Suggestions about the Composition of Mark 4: 1-34,' *TynBul* 23 (1972) 3-38.

Wenham, J., *Redating Matthew, Mark & Luke: A Fresh Assault on the Synoptic Problem* (London: Hodder & Stoughton, 1991).

Werner, E., '"Hosanna" in the Gospels,' *JBL* (1946) 97-122.

Werner, F., '"Theologie" und "Philologies"—Zur Frage der Überseztung von Mk 14, 24 "für die Vielen" oder "für alle"?,' *BibLiturg* 54 (1981) 228-30.

Werner, M., *Der Einfluß paulinischer Theologie im Markusevanglium* (Berlin, 1923).

Westermann, C., *Isaiah 40-66*, trans. D. M. G. Stalker (London: SCM, 1969).

———— 'Das Heilswort bei Deuterojesaja,' *EvTh* 24 (1964) 355-73.

———— 'Sprache und Struktur der Prophetie Deuterojesajas' in *Forshung am A.T.* TBü 24 (Munich: Kaiser, 1964) 92-170.

Whedbee, J. W., *Isaiah and Wisdom* (New York and Nashville: Abingdon, 1971).

Whewell, W., *Philosophy of the Inductive Sciences founded upon their History* vol. 2 (London: J. W. Parker, 1847[2]).

Whybray, R. N., *The Heavenly Counsellor in Isaiah xl 13-14* (Cambridge: University, 1971).

———— *The Intellectual Tradition of the Old Testament* BZAW 135 (New York and Berlin: Wlater de Gruyter, 1974).

———— *Isaiah 40-55* NCB (London: Oliphants, 1975).

———— *Thanksgiving for a Liberated Prophet: An Interpretation of Isaiah Chapter 53* JSOTSupp 4 (Sheffield: JSOT Press, 1978).

———— *Wisdom in Proverbs: The Concept of Wisdom in Proverbs 1-9* SBT 1/45 (London: SCM, 1965).

Wikenhäuser, A., *Einleitung in das neue Testament* (Freiburg: Herder, 1963[5]).

Wikgren, A., 'ΑΡΧΗ ΤΟΥ ΕΥΑΓΓΕΛΙΟΥ,' *JBL* 41 (1942) 11-20.

Wilcox, M., '"Upon the Tree"—Deut. 21: 22-23 in the New Testament,' *JBL* 96 (1977) 97-99.

Wilcox, P., and Paton-Williams, D., 'The Servant Songs in Deutero-Isaiah,' *JSOT* 42 (1988) 79-102.

Wildberger, H., *Jesaja 1-12, Jesaja 13-27, Jesaja 28-39*, BKAT X/1,2,3 (Neukichen-Vulyn: Neukirchener, 1972, 1978, 82). ET: *Isaiah 1-12* trans. T. H. Trapp (Minneapolis: Fortress, 1991).

Williams, A. L., *Adversus Judaeous* (Cambridge: University, 1935).

Williams, J. G., *Gospel against Parable: Mark's Language of Mystery* (Sheffield: Almond, 1985).

Williams, S. K., *Jesus' Death as Saving Event* HTRHDR 2 (Missoula: Scholars, 1975).

Williamson, H. G. M., 'The Concept of Israel in Transition' in *The World of Ancient Israel* ed. R. E. Clements (Cambridge: University, 1989) 141-61.

Willis, J. T., 'The Genre of Isaiah 5:1-7,' *JBL* 96 (1977) 337-62.

Windisch, H., 'Die Sprüche vom Eingehen in das Reich Gottes,' *ZNW* 27 (1928) 163-92.

———— 'Die Verstockungsidee in Mc 4:12 und das Kausale ἵνα in der spätern Koine,' *ZNW* 25 (1927) 203-9.

Wink, W., *John the Baptist in the Gospel Tradition* (Cambridge: University, 1968).

———— *Naming the Powers: The Language of Power in the New Testament* The Powers: vol. I (Philadelphia: Fortress, 1984).

———— *Unmasking the Powers. The Invisible Forces that Determine Human Existence* The Powers vol. 2 (Philadelphia: Fortress, 1986).

———— *Wisdom in Proverbs: The Concept of Wisdom in Proverbs 1-9* SBT 1/45 (London: SCM, 1965).

Wirkenhauser, A., *New Testament Introduction* trans. J. Cunningham (New York: Herder and Herder, 1958).

Wohlenburg, G., *Das Evangelium des Markus* (Leipzig: Deichert, 1930[3]).

Wolff, H. W., *Jesaja 53 im Urchristentum* (Berlin, 1953[3]).

———— 'Das Thema "umkehr" in der alttestamentlichen Propheten' in *Gesammelte Studien Zum Alten Testament* TBü 22 (München: Kaiser, 1964) 130-50.

Woods, E. J., 'Jesus and Beelzebub: The Meaning of "Finger of God" within Luke 11:14-26', D. Litt. et Phil. diss.: University of South Africa, Pretoria, 1989.

Wood, J. E., 'Isaac Typology in the New Testament,' *NTS* 14 (1968) 583-89.

van der Woude, A. S., 'Der Engel des Bundes' in *Die Botschaft und die Boten* FS H. W. Wolff. hrsg. J. Jeremias and L. Perlitt. (Neukirchen-Verlyn: Neukirchener, 1981) 289-300.

Wrede, W., *The Messianic Secret* trans. J. C. G. Greig (London: James Clarke, 1971).

Wright, G. E., 'The Lawsuit of God' in *Israel's Prophetic Heritage*, FS J. Muilenburg, eds. B. Anderson and W. Harrelson (New York: Harper and Row, 1962) 62-67.

_____ *The Old Testament and Theology* (New York, *et al*: Harper & Row, 1969).

Wright, J., 'Spirit and Wilderness: The Interplay of Two Motifs within the Hebrew Bible as a Background to Mark 1:2-13' in *Perspective on Language and Text Essay in Honnor of Francis I. Andersen's Sixtieth Birthday* eds. E. W. Conrad and E. G. Newing (Winona Lake: Eisenbrauns, 1987) 269-98.

Wright, J. W., *And Then There Was One: A Search for True Discipleship in the Gospel of Mark* (Kansas City: Beacon Hill, 1985).

Wright, N. T., 'The Messiah and the People of God', D.Phil. diss.: Oxford, 1980.

_____ *The New Testament and the People of God*(Minneapolis: Fortress, 1992).

Würthwein, E., *The Text of the Old Testament: An Introduction to the Biblica Hebraica* trans. E. F. Rhodes (Grand Rapids: Eerdmans, 1979).

Yadin, Y., 'A Midrash on 2 Sam. VII and Ps. I-II (4Q Florilegium),' *IEJ* 9 (1959) 95-98.

_____ 'Le Rouleau du Temple' in *Qumrān: sa piété, sa théologie et son milieu* ed. M. Delcor, BETL 46 (Paris: Duclot, Leuven: University, 1978) 115-19.

Ben-Yashar, M., 'Noch zum Miqdaš-'Adam in Florilegium,' *RevQ* 10 (1981) 587-88.

Yates, J. E., 'The Form of Mark i. 8b,' *NTS* 4 (1957-8) 334-38.

Yee, G. A., 'A Form-Critical Study of Isaiah 5:1-7 as a Song and a Juridical Parable,' *CBQ* 43 (1981) 30-40.

York, A. D., 'The Dating of Targumic Literature,' *JSJ* 6 (1979) 49-62.

Young, B. H., *Jesus and His Jewish Parables* (Mew York: Paulist, 1989).

Young, E. J., *The Book of Isaiah* 3 vols. NICOT (Grand Rapids: Eerdmans, 1965-72).

Young, F., 'Two Roots or a Tangled Mass?' in *The Myth of God Incarnate* ed. J. Hick (London: SCM, 1977) 87-121.

Ysebart, J., *Greek Baptismal Terminology: Its Origin and Early Development* GCP I (Nijmegen: Dekker & van de Vegt, 1962).

Zahn, Th., *Einleitung in das NT* (Leipzig: Deichert, 1900²).

_____ *Das Evangelium des Lucas* (Leipzig: Deichert, 1913).

Ziener, G., 'Die Brotwunder im Markusevangelium,' *BZ* 4 (1960) 282-85.

Ziesler, J. A., 'The Transfiguration Story and the Markan Soteriology,' *ExpT* 81 (1970) 263-68.

Zillessen, A., 'Der alte und der neue Exodus,' *ARW* 30 (1903) 289-304.

Zimmerli, W., *Ezekiel* 2 vols. trans. R. E. Clements (Philadelphia: Fortress, 1979).

_____ 'Gnadenjahr des Herrn' in *Archäologie und Altes Testament*, FS K. Galling, ed. A. Kuschke (Tübingen: J. C. B. Mohr (Paul Siebeck), 1970) 299-319.

_____ 'Ich bin Jahwe' in *Gottes Offenbarung*, TBü 19 (reprint, Munich: Kaiser, 1963) 11-40.

_____ 'Der "neue Exodus" in der Verkündigung der beiden grossen Exilspropheten' in *Gottes Offenbarung*, TBü 19 (reprint, Munich: Kaiser, 1963) 192-204.

Zimmerli, W., and Jeremias, J., *The Servant of God* (rev. ed., London: SCM, 1965).

Index of Passages

I. Old Testament

II. Old Testament Apocrypha

III. Pseudepigrapha

IV. Qumran Writings

V. New Testament

VII. Rabbinic Writings

VII. Hellenistic-Jewish Writings

VIII. Graeco-Roman

IX. Early Christian and Gnostic Writings

Index of Modern Authors

Index of Names and Subjects

Rikki E. Watts (Ph. D., Cambridge University) is associate professor of New Testament at Regent College in Vancouver, British Columbia.

Wissenschaftliche Untersuchungen zum Neuen Testament

Alphabetical Index of the First and Second Series

Anderson, Paul N.: The Christology of the Fourth Gospel. 1996. *Volume II/78.*
Appold, Mark L.: The Oneness Motif in the Fourth Gospel. 1976. *Volume II/1.*
Arnold, Clinton E.: The Colossian Syncretism. 1995. *Volume II/77.*
Avemarie, Friedrich und *Hermann Lichtenberger* (Ed.): Bund und Tora. 1996. *Volume 92.*
Bachmann, Michael: Sünder oder Übertreter. 1992. *Volume 59.*
Baker, William R.: Personal Speech-Ethics in the Epistle of James. 1995. *Volume II/68.*
Balla, Peter: Challenges to New Testament Theology. 1997. *Volume II/95.*
Bammel, Ernst: Judaica. Volume I 1986. *Volume 37* – Volume II 1997. *Volume 91.*
Bash, Anthony: Ambassadors for Christ. 1997. *Volume II/92.*
Bauernfeind, Otto: Kommentar und Studien zur Apostelgeschichte. 1980. *Volume 22.*
Bayer, Hans Friedrich: Jesus' Predictions of Vindication and Resurrection. 1986. *Volume II/20.*
Bell, Richard H.: Provoked to Jealousy. 1994. *Volume II/63.*
Bergman, Jan: see *Kieffer, René*
Betz, Otto: Jesus, der Messias Israels. 1987. *Volume 42.*
– Jesus, der Herr der Kirche. 1990. *Volume 52.*
Beyschlag, Karlmann: Simon Magus und die christliche Gnosis. 1974. *Volume 16.*
Bittner, Wolfgang J.: Jesu Zeichen im Johannesevangelium. 1987. *Volume II/26.*
Bjerkelund, Carl J.: Tauta Egeneto. 1987. *Volume 40.*
Blackburn, Barry Lee: Theios Aner and the Markan Miracle Traditions. 1991. *Volume II/40.*
Bockmuehl, Markus N.A.: Revelation and Mystery in Ancient Judaism and Pauline Christianity. 1990. *Volume II/36.*
Böhlig, Alexander: Gnosis und Synkretismus. Teil 1 1989. *Volume 47* –Teil 2 1989. *Volume 48.*
Böttrich, Christfried: Weltweisheit – Menschheitsethik – Urkult. 1992. *Volume II/50.*
Büchli, Jörg: Der Poimandres – ein paganisiertes Evangelium. 1987. *Volume II/27.*
Bühner, Jan A.: Der Gesandte und sein Weg im 4. Evangelium. 1977. *Volume II/2.*
Burchard, Christoph: Untersuchungen zu Joseph und Aseneth. 1965. *Volume 8.*
Cancik, Hubert (Ed.): Markus-Philologie. 1984. *Volume 33.*
Capes, David B.: Old Testament Yaweh Texts in Paul's Christology. 1992. *Volume II/47.*
Caragounis, Chrys C.: The Son of Man. 1986. *Volume 38.*
– see *Fridrichsen, Anton.*
Carleton Paget, James: The Epistle of Barnabas. 1994. *Volume II/64.*
Crump, David: Jesus the Intercessor. 1992. *Volume II/49.*
Deines, Roland: Jüdische Steingefäße und pharisäische Frömmigkeit. 1993. *Volume II/52.*
– Die Pharisäer. 1997. *Volume 101.*
Dietzfelbinger, Christian: Der Abschied des Kommenden. 1997. *Volume 95.*
Dobbeler, Axel von: Glaube als Teilhabe. 1987. *Volume II/22.*
Du Toit, David S.: Theios Anthropos. 1997. *Volume II/91*
Dunn , James D.G. (Ed.): Jews and Christians. 1992. *Volume 66.*
– Paul and the Mosaic Law. 1996. *Volume 89.*
Ebertz, Michael N.: Das Charisma des Gekreuzigten. 1987. *Volume 45.*
Eckstein, Hans-Joachim: Der Begriff Syneidesis bei Paulus. 1983. *Volume II/10.*
– Verheißung und Gesetz. 1996. *Volume 86.*
Ego, Beate: Im Himmel wie auf Erden. 1989. *Volume II/34.*
Ellis, E. Earle: Prophecy and Hermeneutic in Early Christianity. 1978. *Volume 18.*
– The Old Testament in Early Christianity. 1991. *Volume 54.*
Ennulat, Andreas: Die 'Minor Agreements'. 1994. *Volume II/62.*
Ensor, Peter W.: Paul and His 'Works'. 1996. *Volume II/85.*
Feldmeier, Reinhard: Die Krisis des Gottessohnes. 1987. *Volume II/21.*
– Die Christen als Fremde. 1992. *Volume 64.*
Feldmeier, Reinhard and *Ulrich Heckel* (Ed.): Die Heiden. 1994. *Volume 70.*

Fletcher-Louis, Crispin H.T.: Luke-Acts: Angels, Christology and Soteriology. 1997. *Volume II/94.*

Forbes, Christopher Brian: Prophecy and Inspired Speech in Early Christianity and its Hellenistic Environment. 1995. *Volume II/75.*

Fornberg, Tord: see *Fridrichsen, Anton.*

Fossum, Jarl E.: The Name of God and the Angel of the Lord. 1985. *Volume 36.*

Frenschkowski, Marco: Offenbarung und Epiphanie. Volume 1 1995. *Volume II/79* – Volume 2 1997. *Volume II/80.*

Frey, Jörg: Eugen Drewermann und die biblische Exegese. 1995. *Volume II/71.*

– Die johanneische Eschatologie. Volume I. 1997. *Volume 96.*

Fridrichsen, Anton: Exegetical Writings. Ed. by C.C. Caragounis and T. Fornberg. 1994. *Volume 76.*

Garlington, Don B.: 'The Obedience of Faith'. 1991. *Volume II/38.*

– Faith, Obedience, and Perseverance. 1994. *Volume 79.*

Garnet, Paul: Salvation and Atonement in the Qumran Scrolls. 1977. *Volume II/3.*

Gräßer, Erich: Der Alte Bund im Neuen. 1985. *Volume 35.*

Green, Joel B.: The Death of Jesus. 1988. *Volume II/33.*

Gundry Volf, Judith M.: Paul and Perseverance. 1990. *Volume II/37.*

Hafemann, Scott J.: Suffering and the Spirit. 1986. *Volume II/19.*

– Paul, Moses, and the History of Israel. 1995. *Volume 81.*

Heckel, Theo K.: Der Innere Mensch. 1993. *Volume II/53.*

Heckel, Ulrich: Kraft in Schwachheit. 1993. *Volume II/56.*

– see *Feldmeier, Reinhard.*

– see *Hengel, Martin.*

Heiligenthal, Roman: Werke als Zeichen. 1983. *Volume II/9.*

Hemer, Colin J.: The Book of Acts in the Setting of Hellenistic History. 1989. *Volume 49.*

Hengel, Martin: Judentum und Hellenismus. 1969, ³1988. *Volume 10.*

– Die johanneische Frage. 1993. *Volume 67.*

– Judaica et Hellenistica. Volume 1. 1996. *Volume 90.*

Hengel, Martin and *Ulrich Heckel* (Ed.): Paulus und das antike Judentum. 1991. *Volume 58.*

Hengel, Martin and *Hermut Löhr* (Ed.): Schriftauslegung im antiken Judentum und im Urchristentum. 1994. *Volume 73.*

Hengel, Martin and *Anna Maria Schwemer* (Ed.): Königsherrschaft Gottes und himmlischer Kult. 1991. *Volume 55.*

– Die Septuaginta. 1994. *Volume 72.*

Herrenbrück, Fritz: Jesus und die Zöllner. 1990. *Volume II/41.*

Hoegen-Rohls, Christina: Der nachösterliche Johannes. 1996. *Volume II/84.*

Hofius, Otfried: Katapausis. 1970. *Volume 11.*

– Der Vorhang vor dem Thron Gottes. 1972. *Volume 14.*

– Der Christushymnus Philipper 2,6-11. 1976, ²1991. *Volume 17.*

– Paulusstudien. 1989, ²1994. *Volume 51.*

Hofius, Otfried und *Hans-Christian Kammler:* Johannesstudien. 1996. *Volume 88.*

Holtz, Traugott: Geschichte und Theologie des Urchristentums. 1991. *Volume 57.*

Hommel, Hildebrecht: Sebasmata. Volume 1 1983. *Volume 31* – Volume 2 1984. *Volume 32.*

Hvalvik, Reidar: The Struggle for Scripture and Covenant. 1996. *Volume II/82.*

Kähler, Christoph: Jesu Gleichnisse als Poesie und Therapie. 1995. *Volume 78.*

Kammler, Hans-Christian: see *Hofius, Otfried.*

Kamlah, Ehrhard: Die Form der katalogischen Paränese im Neuen Testament. 1964. *Volume 7.*

Kieffer, René und *Jan Bergman (Ed.):* La Main de Dieu / Die Hand Gottes. 1997. *Volume 94.*

Kim, Seyoon: The Origin of Paul's Gospel. 1981, ²1984. *Volume II/4.*

– „The 'Son of Man'" as the Son of God. 1983. *Volume 30.*

Kleinknecht, Karl Th.: Der leidende Gerechtfertigte. 1984, ²1988. *Volume II/13.*

Klinghardt, Matthias: Gesetz und Volk Gottes. 1988. *Volume II/32.*

Köhler, Wolf-Dietrich: Rezeption des Matthäusevangeliums in der Zeit vor Irenäus. 1987. *Volume II/24.*

Korn, Manfred: Die Geschichte Jesu in veränderter Zeit. 1993. *Volume II/51.*

Koskenniemi, Erkki: Apollonios von Tyana in der neutestamentlichen Exegese. 1994. *Volume II/61.*

Kraus, Wolfgang: Das Volk Gottes. 1996. *Volume 85.*

– see *Walter, Nikolaus.*

Kuhn, Karl G.: Achtzehngebet und Vaterunser und der Reim. 1950. *Volume 1.*
Laansma, Jon: '1 Will Give You Rest'. 1997. *Volume II/98.*
Lampe, Peter: Die stadtrömischen Christen in den ersten beiden Jahrhunderten. 1987, ²1989. *Volume II/18.*
Lau, Andrew: Manifest in Flesh. 1996. *Volume II/86.*
Lichtenberger, Hermann: see *Avemarie, Friedrich.*
Lieu, Samuel N.C.: Manichaeism in the Later Roman Empire and Medieval China. ²1992. *Volume 63.*
Loader, William R.G.: Jesus' Attitude Towards the Law. 1997. *Volume II/97.*
Löhr, Gebhard: Verherrlichung Gottes durch Philosophie. 1997. *Volume 97.*
Löhr, Hermut: see *Hengel, Martin.*
Löhr, Winrich Alfried: Basilides und seine Schule. 1995. *Volume 83.*
Maier, Gerhard: Mensch und freier Wille. 1971. *Volume 12.*
– Die Johannesoffenbarung und die Kirche. 1981. *Volume 25.*
Markschies, Christoph: Valentinus Gnosticus? 1992. *Volume 65.*
Marshall, Peter: Enmity in Corinth: Social Conventions in Paul's Relations with the Corinthians. 1987. *Volume II/23.*
Meade, David G.: Pseudonymity and Canon. 1986. *Volume 39.*
Meadors, Edward P.: Jesus the Messianic Herald of Salvation. 1995. *Volume II/72.*
Meißner, Stefan: Die Heimholung des Ketzers. 1996. *Volume II/87.*
Mell, Ulrich: Die „anderen" Winzer. 1994. *Volume 77.*
Mengel, Berthold: Studien zum Philipperbrief. 1982. *Volume II/8.*
Merkel, Helmut: Die Widersprüche zwischen den Evangelien. 1971. *Volume 13.*
Merklein, Helmut: Studien zu Jesus und Paulus. 1987. *Volume 43.*
Metzler, Karin: Der griechische Begriff des Verzeihens. 1991. *Volume II/44.*
Metzner, Rainer: Die Rezeption des Matthäusevangeliums im 1. Petrusbrief. 1995. *Volume II/74.*
Mittmann-Richert, Ulrike: Magnifikat und Benediktus. *1996. Volume II/90.*
Niebuhr, Karl-Wilhelm: Gesetz und Paränese. 1987. *Volume II/28.*
– Heidenapostel aus Israel. 1992. *Volume 62.*
Nissen, Andreas: Gott und der Nächste im antiken Judentum. 1974. *Volume 15.*
Noormann, Rolf: Irenäus als Paulusinterpret. 1994. *Volume II/66.*
Obermann, Andreas: Die christologische Erfüllung der Schrift im Johannesevangelium. 1996. *Volume II/83.*
Okure, Teresa: The Johannine Approach to Mission. 1988. *Volume II/31.*
Park, Eung Chun: The Mission Discourse in Matthew's Interpretation. 1995. *Volume II/81.*
Philonenko, Marc (Ed.): Le Trône de Dieu. 1993. *Volume 69.*
Pilhofer, Peter: Presbyteron Kreitton. 1990. *Volume II/39.*
– Philippi. Volume 1 1995. *Volume 87.*
Pöhlmann, Wolfgang: Der Verlorene Sohn und das Haus. 1993. *Volume 68.*
Pokorný, Petr und *Josef B. Souček:* Bibelauslegung als Theologie. 1997. *Volume 100.*
Prieur, Alexander: Die Verkündigung der Gottesherrschaft. 1996. *Volume II/89.*
Probst, Hermann: Paulus und der Brief. 1991. *Volume II/45.*
Räisänen, Heikki: Paul and the Law. 1983, ²1987. *Volume 29.*
Rehkopf, Friedrich: Die lukanische Sonderquelle. 1959. *Volume 5.*
Rein, Matthias: Die Heilung des Blindgeborenen (Joh 9). 1995. *Volume II/73.*
Reinmuth, Eckart: Pseudo-Philo und Lukas. 1994. *Volume 74.*
Reiser, Marius: Syntax und Stil des Markusevangeliums. 1984. *Volume II/11.*
Richards, E. Randolph: The Secretary in the Letters of Paul. 1991. *Volume II/42.*
Riesner, Rainer: Jesus als Lehrer. 1981, ³1988. *Volume II/7.*
– Die Frühzeit des Apostels Paulus. 1994. *Volume 71.*
Rissi, Mathias: Die Theologie des Hebräerbriefs. 1987. *Volume 41.*
Röhser, Günter: Metaphorik und Personifikation der Sünde. 1987. *Volume II/25.*
Rose, Christian: Die Wolke der Zeugen. 1994. *Volume II/60.*
Rüger, Hans Peter: Die Weisheitsschrift aus der Kairoer Geniza. 1991. *Volume 53.*
Sänger, Dieter: Antikes Judentum und die Mysterien. 1980. *Volume II/5.*
– Die Verkündigung des Gekreuzigten und Israel. 1994. *Volume 75.*
Salzmann, Jorg Christian: Lehren und Ermahnen. 1994. *Volume II/59.*

Sandnes, Karl Olav: Paul – One of the Prophets? 1991. *Volume II/43.*
Sato, Migaku: Q und Prophetie. 1988. *Volume II/29.*
Schaper, Joachim: Eschatology in the Greek Psalter. 1995. *Volume II/76.*
Schimanowski, Gottfried: Weisheit und Messias. 1985. *Volume II/17.*
Schlichting, Günter: Ein jüdisches Leben Jesu. 1982. *Volume 24.*
Schnabel, Eckhard J.: Law and Wisdom from Ben Sira to Paul. 1985. *Volume II/16.*
Schutter, William L.: Hermeneutic and Composition in 1 Peter. 1989. *Volume II/30.*
Schwartz, Daniel R.: Studies in the Jewish Background of Christianity. 1992. *Volume 60.*
Schwemer, Anna Maria: see *Hengel, Martin*
Scott, James M.: Adoption as Sons of God. 1992. *Volume II/48.*
– Paul and the Nations. 1995. *Volume 84.*
Siegert, Folker: Drei hellenistisch-jüdische Predigten. Teil I 1980. *Volume 20* – Teil II 1992. *Volume 61.*
– Nag-Hammadi-Register. 1982. *Volume 26.*
– Argumentation bei Paulus. 1985. *Volume 34.*
– Philon von Alexandrien. 1988. *Volume 46.*
Simon, Marcel: Le christianisme antique et son contexte religieux I/II. 1981. *Volume 23.*
Snodgrass, Klyne: The Parable of the Wicked Tenants. 1983. *Volume 27.*
Söding, Thomas: Das Wort vom Kreuz. 1997. *Volume 93.*
– see *Thüsing, Wilhelm.*
Sommer, Urs: Die Passionsgeschichte des Markusevangeliums. 1993. *Volume II/58.*
Souček, Josef B.: see *Pokorný, Petr.*
Spangenberg, Volker: Herrlichkeit des Neuen Bundes. 1993. *Volume II/55.*
Speyer, Wolfgang: Frühes Christentum im antiken Strahlungsfeld. 1989. *Volume 50.*
Stadelmann, Helge: Ben Sira als Schriftgelehrter. 1980. *Volume II/6.*
Strobel, August: Die Stunde der Wahrheit. 1980. *Volume 21.*
Stuckenbruck, Loren T.: Angel Veneration and Christology. 1995. *Volume II/70.*
Stuhlmacher, Peter (Ed.): Das Evangelium und die Evangelien. 1983. *Volume 28.*
Sung, Chong-Hyon: Vergebung der Sünden. 1993. *Volume II/57.*
Tajra, Harry W.: The Trial of St. Paul. 1989. *Volume II/35.*
– The Martyrdom of St.Paul. 1994. *Volume II/67.*
Theißen, Gerd: Studien zur Soziologie des Urchristentums. 1979, [3]1989. *Volume 19.*
Thornton, Claus-Jürgen: Der Zeuge des Zeugen. 1991. *Volume 56.*
Thüsing, Wilhelm: Studien zur neutestamentlichen Theologie. Ed. by Thomas Söding. 1995. *Volume 82.*
Tsuji, Manabu: Glaube zwischen Vollkommenheit und Verweltlichung. 1997. *Volume II/93*
Twelftree, Graham H.: Jesus the Exorcist. 1993. *Volume II/54.*
Visotzky, Burton L.: Fathers of the World. 1995. *Volume 80.*
Wagener, Ulrike: Die Ordnung des „Hauses Gottes". 1994. *Volume II/65.*
Walter, Nikolaus: Praeparatio Evangelica. Ed. by Wolfgang Kraus and Florian Wilk. 1997. *Volume 98.*
Watts, Rikki: Isaiah's New Exodus and Mark. 1997. *Volume II/88.*
Wedderburn, A.J.M.: Baptism and Resurrection. 1987. *Volume 44.*
Wegner, Uwe: Der Hauptmann von Kafarnaum. 1985. *Volume II/14.*
Welck, Christian: Erzählte 'Zeichen'. 1994. *Volume II/69.*
Wilk, Florian: see *Walter, Nikolaus.*
Wilson, Walter T.: Love without Pretense. 1991. *Volume II/46.*
Zimmermann, Alfred E.: Die urchristlichen Lehrer. 1984, [2]1988. *Volume II/12.*

For a complete catalogue please write to the publisher
Mohr Siebeck, P.O. Box 2040, D–72010 Tübingen.